# Why Assembly Language?   Why Master Class?

Modern day PCs come laden with additional hardware and utilise many cache devices just to keep reasonable performance. PC application developers will need to lean on assembly language to optimise their projects; they will also need to conquer the language simply to compete at the hardware interface.

Master Classes address programmers who need 'edge' in their real world solutions. Why bother chasing all those White papers and specialist manuals, when the essential information on technique is distilled within a Wrox Master Class? Master Class is multi-author - it's the easiest way to have a dozen expert friends at your side.

# What is Wrox Press?

Wrox Press is a computer book publisher which promotes a brand new concept - clear, jargon-free programming and database titles that fulfill your real demands. We publish for everyone, from the novice through to the experienced programmer. To ensure our books meet your needs, we carry out continuous research on all our titles. Through our dialog with you we can craft the book you really need.

We welcome suggestions and take all of them to heart - your input is paramount in creating the next great Wrox title. Use the reply card inside this book or mail us at:

**feedback@wrox.demon.co.uk**
or
**Compuserve 100063, 2152**

**Wrox Press Ltd.**      **Tel:**   **(312) 465 3559**
**2710 W. Touhy**      **Fax:**   **(312) 465 4063**
**Chicago**
**IL 60645**
**USA**

# Assembly Language Master Class

Wrox Press Ltd ®

# Assembly Language Master Class

Chapter 1, 3 - © 1995 Sergei Shkredov.

Chapter 2 - © 1995 Dan Wronksi.

Chapter 4, 13, 15 - © 1995 Yuri Kiselev, Peter Kalatchin.

Chapter 5, 6, 7 - © 1995 Yuri Petrenko.

Chapter 8 - © 1995 Peter Kalatchin.

Chapter 9 - © 1995 Kiril Malakhov, Peter Kalatchin.

Chapter 10 - © 1995 Kiril Malakhov, Igor Chebotko.

Chapter 11, 12 - © 1995 Yuri Kiselev, Igor Chebotko.

Chapter 14 - © 1995 Yuri Kiselev, Peter Kalatchin, Efim Podvoisky.

Chapter 16, 18 - © 1995 Yuri Kiselev, Peter Kalatchin, Igor Chebotko.

Chapter 17 - © 1995 Gennady Soudlenkov.

Chapter 19, 20, 21 - © 1995 Mike Schmit

Published by Wrox Press Ltd. Unit 16, 20 James Road, Tyseley, Birmingham, B11 2BA   UK

Printed in Canada

Library of Congress Catalog No: 94-78396

ISBN   1-874416-34-6

# Trademark Acknowledgements

Wrox has endeavored to provide trademark information about all the companies and products mentioned in this book by the appropriate use of capitals. However, Wrox cannot guarantee the accuracy of this information.

# Credits

**Authors**
Igor Chebotko
Peter Kalatchin
Yuri Kiselev
Kiril Malakhov
Yuri Petrenko
Efim Podvoisky
Mike Schmit
Sergei Shkredov
Gennady Soudlenkov
Dan Wronski

**Technical Editors**
Dave Bolton
Sean Herd
Rosemary Lockie
Jim Mischel
Walter Oney
Ian Wells
Mike Schmit
Dan Wronski

**Series Editor**
Mark Holmes

**Managing Editor**
John Franklin

**Technical Reviewer**
Ian Wells

**CIS Project Co-ordinator**
Deb Somers

**Production Manager**
Gina Mance

**Book Layout**
Eddie Fisher
Greg Powell

**Proof Reader**
Pam Brand

**Cover Design**
Third Wave

**Cover Image supplied by**
Telegraph Colour Library

# About The Authors

## Igor Chebotko

Igor Chebotko graduated from the Physics faculty of Minsk University. He is a laboratory head in the Physical Technical Institute of the Byelorussian Academy of Science. He founded Control-Zed in 1989 and is the author of about 50 papers.

## Peter Kalatchin

Peter Kalatchin graduated from the Minsk Radio Engineering Institute. He worked as a programmer for Control-Zed for 4 years, specializing in user-interface design, before turning to computer-aided music.

## Yuri Kiselev

Yuri Kiselev graduated from the Minsk Radio Engineering Institute. For the last two years he has been working in Control-Zed as the main systems programmer.

## Efim Podvoisky

Efim works in the Physical Technical Institute of the Byelorussian Academy of Science, where he is involved in computer modelling in physics (cellular automata in particular), and for the last 5 years has also worked in Control-Zed. He is the author of over 10 papers.

## Control-Zed

**Control-Zed** is a software development company. Since its foundation the company has been writing and supporting, scientific and software projects, one of which was accepted by the Byelorussian Ministry of Energies as the industry standard database system. **Control-Zed** is the author of another Wrox title, **The Revolutionary Guide to Bitmapped Graphics**, which was first published in 1994.

### Kiril Malakhov

Kiril graduated from the Minsk Radioengineering Institute. He has worked in the Byelorussian Academy of Science, and is presently working for Dainova Co Ltd.

### Yuri Petrenko

Yuri Petrenko is the head of an operation systems department in a Moscow software development firm, where he specializes in drivers. He has over 20 years programming experience.

### Mike Schmit

Mike Schmit is President of Quantasm Corporation, a publisher of assembly language tools. He is the author of "Pentium Processor Optimization Tools." He has been programming for over 20 years, and began programming for the 80x86 in 1982 as the chief software architect for a Space Shuttle experiment-control computer.

### Sergei Shkredov

Sergei graduated from the Minsk Radioengineering Institute. He has worked in the Peleng Development Centre in Minsk.

### Gennady Soudlenkov

Gennady has his own software company in Minsk. He started programming in Pascal but now specializes in Assembly Language and C++.

### Daniel Wronski

Dan spent over 13 years with IBM developing software and hardware products. He has one European patent with others pending for microprocessor architectural design ideas for the IBM 386SLC and 486SLC. Currently Dan is a Senior Software Architect at PC Connection Inc. He can be reached via CompuServe at 70304,761.

# SUMMARY OF CONTENTS

## Contents

# CONTENTS

Contents

## Chapter 16: Practical Protected Mode Programming ......... 603

Contents

## Appendix C: DOS Protected Mode Interface (DPMI) Function Reference ........................ 917

Contents

# INTRODUCTION

# Assembly Language Master Class

## The Assembly Cornerstone

Assembly language programming is the cornerstone of PC development. As the one language which naturally reflects every element of a machine's hardware, and the basis of much software development, it is probably the fundamental requirement of all developers to at some stage master its power.

This naturally enough, brings with it a corollary which suggests that assembly language is a static discipline, a language waiting in the background like a solid uncle, never changing, standard and a little dull.

## The Master Class Approach

It was with an awareness of these two feelings that this book was commissioned and written. The Master Class concept is a simple one. It is to bring to a wider readership the most innovative, cutting edge information, the essentials of progress too often hidden to the programming world. It was our intention to find the experts not just in assembler as a whole, but also in specific areas of assembler, and offer them the chance to make more programmers into experts.

Assembly language gives the programmer the ultimate in control and speed, the two words he or she will most want to use in a professional environment. The language itself might have an excellent standard, but its implementation is a fascinating mixture of the solid and the innovative. Using hardware in an innovative way is a key ability of the language, and we have tried to expose this with the Master Class guide. We have also tried to be aware of the intermittent nature of assembler usage, that is, the need to place assembler use in its context as an insertion into high-level code.

## Assembly Language and Wrox Press

Permit us a brief resume of where we are, and where we have been. In 1993 Wrox went to Eastern Europe to find the leading-edge experts in Assembly language. The result was the best-selling book: *The Revolutionary Guide to Assembly Language.*

We didn't feel this was the last word by any means. We met a number of programmers who were surging ahead with practical use of the language, and who had much to contribute further to the study of assembly language at its highest levels. We then added more contributors, regarded as experts in the United States, and made a truly cosmopolitan and vanguard book which aims to reveal the full architecture of today's PCs.

## The 'Cutting Edge'

The book aims to reveal much that is at present undocumented. This is a difficult area to get right, as how does one judge the value and precise relevance of 'the cutting edge'? Our response in this book, as with all Wrox books, has been to elicit the assistance of the wide assembly community in order to measure where assembly language is going. If you look at the credits page you will see a wide range of assembler experts who, even if they haven't actually written a chapter, have had a big input into the direction of the book.

# The Range of the Book

The range of subjects was also something we spent some time debating. In the end we felt a wide ranging book best suited the needs of the fledgling expert. The author's varied backgrounds is, perhaps, one of the most useful features of their involvement in this title, in that they all come to assembly language from different angles, and so reveal the breadth of relevance of the language, both as a theoretical concern and as an engineering tool.

As we have already said, this book is a synthesis of the twin forces of range and detail. We have covered disk and memory management, protected mode programming and DOS extenders, compression techniques, how to most effectively optimize your code, how to program sound and screens, the development of efficient library routines, and effective protection against virus infection. We feel these are the major concerns of the assembler programmer, and each chapter will take you toward the standard of professionalism shown by the authors. This book is best used as a hands-on guide, where theory and practice are merged into practical example.

It is important to say at this point that if you are a beginner to the world of assembly language then you will probably need a grounding from elsewhere to fully appreciate this book. We have aimed fairly and squarely at the programmer who knows the basic application of assembly language.

# What You Need to Use This Book

A PC (probably)

A suitable ASM compiler.

Some of the chapters have reference to programming in C. This code can be successfully written and compiled with standard C++ compiler packages.

# Using the Disk

To install the contents of the disk:

Place the disk in your floppy drive and copy the file: MC_ASM.EXE
to some spare space on your hard drive. Go to your hard drive and type
mc_asm; the file will self-extract into a new directory called WROX_ASM, giving
the full contents of all source code. You will need approximately 3M of spare
space to hold all the expanded files.

We have also compacted a version of LHA compression software onto this disk,
which is also a self-extracting file. The compression of all the source code on
the disk was made using LHA.

# CHAPTER ONE

# Review of Assembly Language

## Introduction

Assembly language is the native tongue of any computer system. In fact, it makes direct use of processor instructions. So, you are in charge of the most efficient instructions without the mediation of high-level language compilers. As you can access system resources directly, your assembly language programs are small and fast. They take up less memory and use all the features of hardware.

Don't get excited. This chapter can't help you if you have no knowledge of an assembler. It's only purpose is to give you a quick overview of basic knowledge.

# PC Memory Addressing and Register Usage

Some things are forever. And it's absolutely true when we talk about Intel's architecture. The most remarkable feature about the 80x86 family is compatibility. Even considering the Pentium, we should take into account that this superscalar, 32-bit processor is oriented on the least-common denominator. This concerns the set of registers, instruction sets and so on.

Here's some explanation of the notation used below. The symbol 'E' means that a register is 32-bits long (in the 80386 or higher processors), as the least common denominator is 16-bit registers of the 8086 and 8088. To take advantage of 'double' registers, you have to use them with prefix 'E'. So, if the instruction MOV AX, BX manipulates 16-bit data, then MOV EAX, EBX deals with 32-bit operands. A phrase like 'AX (AL/AH)' shows that the register AX consists of two parts. Each part is an 8-bit register. The assembler allows you to use register halves independently. We can group the processor registers by functions.

General purpose registers can hold data and can be used in data addressing, program flow control and so on.

- [E]AX (AH/AL): the Accumulator register is used for I/O, arithmetic, calling DOS services and so on.

- [E]BX (BH/BL): the Base register is normally used as a pointer to the base address of some currently useful data.

- [E]CX (CH/CL): the Count register is for organizing shifts and loops.

- [E]DX (DH/DL): the Data register is used in arithmetic and I/O operations.

- [E]SI: index pointer and pointer to the source string in string operations.

- [E]DI: index pointer and pointer to the destination string in string operations.

- [E]BP: normally used as a base address to access the stack.

- [E]SP: pointer to the top of the stack.

The next group is the Segment Registers. Usually a program consists of a code segment, containing the sequence of instructions implementing the algorithm, and a data segment, containing the information being processed: variables, strings, symbols, arrays and so on. A program also needs a stack segment to work with dynamically allocated data. Each program component can occupy its own segment, or they can be combined into one segment. We'll return to this topic later. The idea behind segment registers is that they determine the location of segments used by a program.

CS, DS and SS are registers which contain the addresses of the code segment, the data segment and the stack segment respectively. ES, FS and GS are segment registers which specify extra segments for a program (FS and GS exist only in the 80386 and higher processors). All segment registers are 16-bit, and hold addresses of corresponding segments (in paragraphs).

The Flags Register consists of single-bit flags which reflect the CPU state, the result of each instruction, control I/O, interrupts, switching over tasks (on 80386+) and so on. As with the general purpose registers described above, it was extended to 32 bits in 80386+ processors.

Together with CS, the Instruction Pointer (IP) determines the memory location of the next instruction. You can't access the Instruction Pointer directly, but you can watch its value using a debugger, such as CodeView or Turbo Debugger.

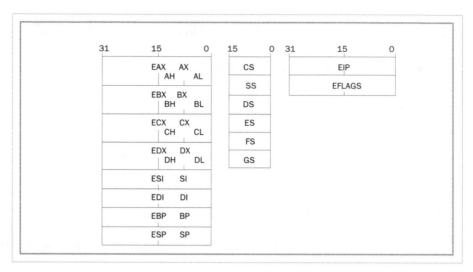

**Figure 1.1 The CPU Registers**

Now let's turn our attention to the numeric coprocessor or Floating Point Unit (FPU). Most programs work fine without a floating point unit. Of course, the coprocessor can't increase the speed of hard drive accesses or modem communications, but without an FPU, a program that performs a lot of floating point arithmetic may run extremely slow.

The 80x87 contains eight 80-bit registers as shown in Figure 1.2. Like the integer processor, the 80x87 has special registers that contain flags and control bits. The Control Word of the 80x87 has bits that control data flow between the CPU and coprocessor. The Status Word reflects the machine state (results of operations and the like). These words can be accessed by special assembly instructions.

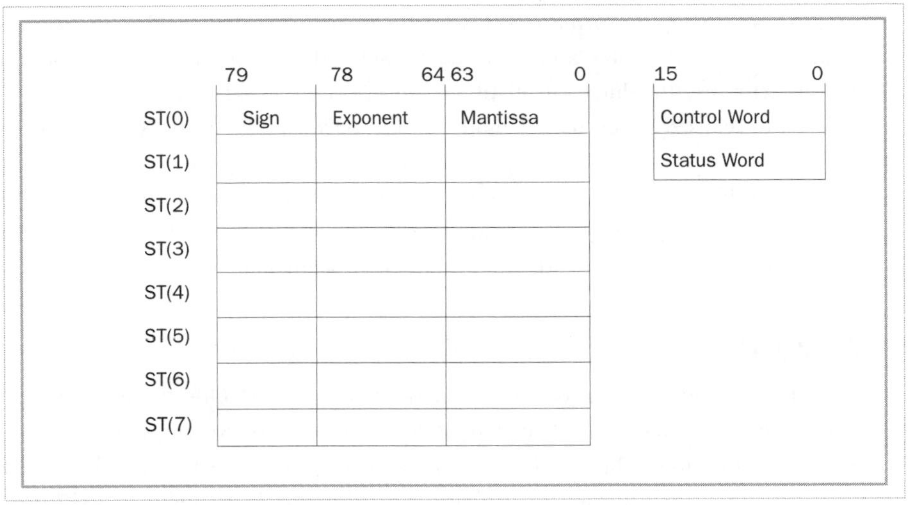

| | 79 | 78 | 64 63 | 0 | | 15 | 0 |
|-------|------|----------|----------|---|---|------------|---|
| ST(0) | Sign | Exponent | Mantissa | | | Control Word | |
| ST(1) | | | | | | Status Word | |
| ST(2) | | | | | | | |
| ST(3) | | | | | | | |
| ST(4) | | | | | | | |
| ST(5) | | | | | | | |
| ST(6) | | | | | | | |
| ST(7) | | | | | | | |

**Figure 1.2 The 80387 Registers**

## Addressing Memory

In this section we'll discuss memory addressing. We won't touch EMS, or such features of 286+ processors as protected mode, paging and cacheing, because they are covered in more detail in the following chapters. It is the basic principles of memory addressing that are considered here.

Computer memory is a sequence of bytes. As the CPU needs to distinguish between them, every byte in RAM has its own unique address. In any case, however the computer addresses the memory, it will ultimately use this reference, known as the physical address. The physical address is the absolute location of a byte in memory. The CPU does not need to use anything else.

Suppose we are going to address 1MB ($2^{20}$) of memory. We need 20-bit addresses to access any byte in this area. The 20-bit wide address bus is the least-common denominator for the Intel 80x86 processors. 24- and 32-bit wide physical addresses are used in protected mode by the 80286 and 80386DX+ respectively.

This seems like a problem when you think about the actual hardware. The 8086 only has 16-bit registers, so how can it make a 20-bit address? It has to combine values stored in them. This leads us to the topic of segmentation.

## Segmentation

Every physical address consists of two parts: Segment and Offset. They are both 16-bit. We can divide the calculation of the address into two steps. First, the segment is multiplied by 16. This operation is equivalent to shifting the segment by 4 bits (or by one hexadecimal digit). For example, if Segment = 0A12Bh, then Segment * 16 = A12B0h. Secondly, we add the offset to the shifted segment value:

Physical Address = Segment * 16 + Offset;
e.g.    Physical Address = A12Bh * 10h + B13Eh = AC3EEh.

Voilà, we've got a 20-bit physical address.

A segment can start at any address on the 16-byte paragraph boundary. This means that the location of a byte can be described in many ways, for example:

Segment:Offset = Physical Address
A12Bh:B13E  = AC3EEh is equivalent to
A12Ch:B12E  = AC3EEh

The offset part of the physical address is calculated from up to three components:

- Base (registers BX, BP)

- Index (registers SI, DI, SP)

- Displacement, which is included directly into the instruction.

A program works with data stored in RAM, and can address it in 7 possible ways. All these methods of addressing are described below. The examples use the assembler instruction - 'MOV DST, SRC'. This copies information from 'SRC' (source) to 'DST' (destination). Operand types can vary.

## Immediate Addressing: mov AX, 0122Bh

The number 0122Bh is a part of the instruction. This kind of addressing means that immediate data is used in the instruction.

## Direct Addressing: mov AX, NUMBER1

NUMBER1 is a variable. As NUMBER1 is defined by a special directive DW (we'll discuss this later), the assembler considers it as an address. So, the physical address is included into the instruction with this kind of addressing.

## Register Addressing: mov BX, AX

One or both operands are registers.

## Register Indirect Addressing: mov DX, [BX]

Square brackets ([BX]) mean that the operand is at the offset address stored in the register (in this case BX). Index registers DI, SI are also allowed for this kind of addressing. The segment address of the operand is by default DS. If you want another segment, you can specify it explicitly: mov DX, ES:[BX]

## Register Relative Addressing: mov AX, [BX+8]

According to this notation, the address of the second operand would be calculated as a sum of the address stored in register (BX) and offset (8 in our example). The offset can be 8-bit or 16-bit.

## Base Indexed Addressing: mov [BX+SI], AX

The base register (BX or BP) and the index register (DI or SI) determine the address. In the example above, the values of BX and SI are added to find the address where the value of AX will be copied to.

## Base Indexed Relative Addressing: mov AX, [BX+DI+2]

A base register, an index register, and an immediate offset (8-bit or 16-bit) are added.

It was mentioned above that the registers CS and IP determine the location of the current instruction. So, any control transfer in your program causes modification of IP and/or CS, even if the CPU simply fetches the next instruction. When you pass control to another memory location, you do this by specifying the new address.

There are two types of instruction that transfer control to a destination address and so break sequential execution of instructions:

- Unconditional or conditional jumps (instructions JMP, JC, JNC, JE etc.)

- Procedure calls (CALL) and returns (RET)

They can use the following kinds of addressing:

## Direct: jmp LABEL1

This instruction jumps to the address determined by the label LABEL1. To get the destination address, the processor adds the 8-bit (short) or 16-bit (near) offset LABEL1 (positive or negative) to IP. The value of CS (code segment) remains unchanged.

## Indirect: jmp BX or jmp [BX]

To calculate the offset of the destination instruction, the processor uses the value of the register (BX) or of the word addressed by the register ([BX]). The Code segment remains the same. In fact, these are two kinds of addressing for near jumps and calls: register indirect (i.e. jmp BX) and memory indirect (i.e. jmp [BX]).

## Direct Intersegment: jmp FAR LABEL

This kind of addressing allows transfer of control to another segment. Segment and Offset addresses of the destination instruction are placed directly into the command.

## Indirect Intersegment: jmp DWORD PTR [BX]

CS and IP are loaded with the contents of two words in memory, pointed to by BX. The internal type modifier DWORD PTR in this example commands the assembler to use double-word at the address stored in BX.

The instruction CALL can use all these addressing methods as well.

Some important notes:

- Intersegment jumps are specified as FAR.

- Intrasegment jumps are specified as NEAR or SHORT. This means that they are limited to the size of the segment.

- Conditional jumps such as JC, JE and JNB are always limited by an 8-bit(-128 to +127) offset and are always SHORT. As the offset is calculated from the start of the next instruction, the range is -126 to +129 from the instruction. 386+ allows 16-bit offsets for conditional jumps.

# Data Types in the Assembler

Instructions are executed by the processor at run time. Directives, another type of statement in the assembler, control the process of code generation, memory allocation and so on. Directives are the only way to define data in your programs.

Data of any kind included in a command is called an operand. Some assembler instructions don't include any data, but you can't have a real program without any operands at all.

As shown above, instructions use numbers, values stored in registers and data in memory pointed to by an operand.

By default, the assembler treats numbers as decimal. Often you may want to use hexadecimal or binary notation, and then you have to use Radix Specifiers after numbers to indicate the radix of a constant explicitly (see Table 1.1.):

**Table 1.1. Radix Specifiers**

| Radix | Specifier | Example |
|---|---|---|
| Binary | Y(y) or B(b) | 101b = 5 |
| Octal | Q(q) or O(o) | 33Q = 27 |
| Hexadecimal | H(h) | 12h = 18 |

As hexadecimal numbers use the symbols A to F, to allow the assembler to distinguish between variables and hex numbers, the latter must begin with a digit, e.g. 1FFFh or 0A2Eh.

The data types found in the assembler (MASM 6.0 and above) are shown in Table 1.2.

**Table 1.2. Data Types and Their Specifiers in Assembler**

| Type | Abbreviation | Size | Description |
|------|-------------|------|-------------|
| BYTE | db | 8 bits | Integer, character, string |
| WORD | dw | 16 bits | Integer, 16-bit near pointer |
| DWORD | dd | 32 bits | Integer, 32-bit far pointer |
| FWORD | df | 48 bits | 48-bit far pointer |
| QWORD | dq | 64 bits | Integer number |
| TBYTE | dt | 10 bytes | Decimal number in BCD code |
| REAL4 | dd | 4 bytes | Single precision real number |
| REAL8 | dq | 8 bytes | Double precision real number |
| REAL10 | dt | 10 bytes | 80-bit long real number |

The declaration format is the same for all types:

**1** The name of a variable (optional).

**2** The directive of declaration.

**3** If you want to initialize the variable with a value, you place the corresponding constant expression after the directive. Otherwise you can put '?' instead, which means that the data at that location is undefined until you write to it at run time.

These are examples of declaring variables:

```
LETTER1  BYTE 'A'        ; One byte is allocated, initialized
                         ; with the ASCII code of letter 'A'
                         ; addressable via the name LETTER1.
```

Example of addressing:

```
        mov al,LETTER1

LETTER2  BYTE 31h          ; Hexadecimal number 31h is placed
                           ; at the address LETTER2.

My_Num   REAL10 ?          ; 10 bytes allocated for
                           ; variable My_Num (undefined).
```

*You can use the old abbreviated directives (DB, DW, DD, etc.) as well as new ones.*

There is one important note for IBM-compatible computers. The following directive, Ex_Word WORD 0AA11h, will create in memory the sequence 11h AAh! This 'turned-over' notation (known as Intel, or little endian notation) always gives headaches to beginners. But it's easy to understand, if you know that the assembler places the higher byte in the higher memory location. The leftmost byte of this value is AAh, so it goes after the 11h.

You can write several values for one name. In this case, the name determines an array:

```
R_Numb REAL8 100.23, 1.123, 1200 ; R_Numb declares an array of 3 real numbers
```

The prefix DUP is often used for declaring a large array. It directs the assembler to repeat a declaration a specified number of times:

```
AR_zero  BYTE 100 DUP (0)     ; AR_zero is a 100-byte array
                              ; filled with 0.
```

Every new version MASM looks more and more like a high-level language. In some situations, such as in conditional expressions, the assembler should know if a value is signed or not. MASM 6.0 has the directives SBYTE, SWORD and SDWORD for declaring signed data:

```
S_Numb SBYTE  ?  ; S_Numb is a signed integer
                 ; variable with a range from -127 to 128
```

As for the 80x87, it has eight 80-bit registers. Any kind of data can be placed there in 80-bit floating-point format. The format has a 64-bit mantissa. So, a number of any type supported by the 80x86 can be converted to this format without loss of precision.

# Memory models

Your choice of memory model determines the way memory is allocated for a program's code and data. There are six different models to choose from.

## Tiny

If you choose the TINY model, your program will be limited to 64Kb. Programs of this kind cannot have relocatable addresses. Code and data segments are combined into one segment. Both code and data items are accessed via near addresses, so with all addressing methods only the offset part of the address is used.

Note that TINY model programs, as well as all other models, can have many segments if they are allocated at run time, but TINY model programs can have only one declared and loaded segment.

## Small

The SMALL memory model allows you to create a program that consists of two different segments (one for code and another for data). Code and data are limited to one 64Kb segment each. That is why near addressing is used for both code and data segments. Therefore the total size of your small-model program is limited to 128K.

## Compact

The COMPACT memory model is very much like SMALL but it allows multiple segments for program data. Compact-model programs are limited to one code segment but can have several data segments. That is why the default for COMPACT model programs is near code addressing and far data addressing.

## Medium

The MEDIUM memory model is commonly used for programs which consist of multiple code segments and a single data segment. This memory model assumes near data addressing, as it is limited to one segment of data, and far code addressing, because you deal with several code segments.

## Large And Huge

The LARGE and HUGE memory models are alike from the point of view of the assembler. They allow multiple segments for both code and data. Default addressing is naturally far for both program code and data. The assembler doesn't spawn data segments; when you need it, you have to do it by yourself. This function is supported by high-level languages (under the huge memory model), which is the only reason for using the huge model over the large model.

32-bit processors allow segments to be much bigger. The FLAT model in protected mode (which will be described in Chapter 15) assumes one segment for all programs, and the addresses are simply 32-bit offsets, so it can be regarded as a 32-bit version of the TINY model.

## .Model

The first step is to inform the assembler what particular memory model you want to use. There is a special directive .MODEL for this, e.g. .MODEL SMALL. In MASM 6.0 the .MODEL directive has some extra parameters. The first parameter commands the assembler to use naming, calling and returning conventions of a particular high-level language. With the second, you can select an operating system (os_dos or os_os2), while the third allows you to define the type of stack as either far or near. A near stack means that DS and SS will be filled with the same values. A far stack means the values will be different. All this fuss is connected with another new directive - .STARTUP. This directive initializes segment registers according to the parameters of .MODEL or by pre-defined defaults.

There are group directives like .186, .387 or .486 whose purpose is to declare the instruction set available for the program. The default for Intel processors is the 8086 instruction set. To take advantage of the features included with higher processors, you must declare the type of processor and/or coprocessor, which means that you can't declare a FLAT model if a 32-bit processor is not selected.

# Assembly Language Code Frameworks

We can create a program using directives and instructions. Instructions form the program body, processing data and controlling the program flow, or in other words, the implementation of the algorithm. Directives make it all possible.

First, the assembler has to know how it'll work. It needs to know the memory model, the number of segments and their types, etc. This means that there are some items to be defined. For example, Program 1.1 starts with the directive .DOSSEG. It is optional, as all it does is provide compatibility with older versions of the linker, but it forces the assembler to put the code segment first in the object file. As for the stack segment, it'll be at the very end. There are two more directives of this kind: .SEQ which puts segments as they appear in the source code and .ALPHA which puts segments in alphabetical order. The next step is to specify the memory model and some other parameters used with the directive .MODEL.

Second, we have to define each segment. As we only use one data segment in the program, by implementing the small memory model, we only need the directive .DATA to define the data segment; declarations of variables follow after this directive. The stack is defined by the .STACK directive. The number 100h shows the size of the stack reserved for the program (256 bytes, in this case).

A program normally begins with initialization of Segment Registers. For the small memory model, we can start with something like:

```
mov ax,@DATA
mov ds,ax              ;Load Data Segment register
```

Note that you don't have to load the stack pointer SS:SP 'manually'. The directive .STACK 400h will create a 400h byte stack, and DOS will initialize SS:SP at the beginning of the program. However, if you want to do it yourself, you do it this way:

```
cli
mov ss,ax
mov sp,OFFSET STACK    ; Load Stack Segment register
sti
```

The new directive .STARTUP makes segment register initialization even easier. Just write .STARTUP, and you don't have any problems with initialization. This directive even optimizes the starting sequence. This optimization means that instructions such as 'cli' and 'sti' will not be generated for 80286 or higher processors, as prohibition of interrupts during stack initialization is supported by the hardware.

At the end of the program, we have to put a sequence like:

```
mov ax,4C00h
int 21h                ; DOS function Terminate Program
```

Or, we can just write '.EXIT 0' instead. Both of these inform DOS that we have finished and that it can clean up.

Now, here is an example assembly program, Program 1.1:

```
//////////////////////////////////////////////////////////
Program 1.1.
//////////////////////////////////////////////////////////
; This program copies a string to video-RAM
; (in text-mode only). As a result, the string appears
; somewhere in the middle of your screen.
;
```

```
.DOSSEG
.MODEL small, c, os_dos, nearstack
                        ; SMALL memory model, DOS, DS=SS are selected.
.DATA                   ; Start of DATA segment.
    Str DB 'THIS STRING HAS BEEN PRINTED FROM video-RAM$'
.STACK 100h             ; Start of STACK segment.
.CODE                   ; Start of CODE segment.
.STARTUP                ; Initialize Segment Registers.

        mov ax,0b800h   ; Copy address of video-
        mov es,ax       ; -RAM to Segment Register ES.
        mov di,1620     ; Copy an offset DI.
        mov bx,OFFSET Str ; BX contains start address of the string Str now.
        call Out_Str    ; Call the procedure Out_Str.

.EXIT 0                 ; Generate the ending sequence.

Out_Str PROC NEAR       ; Start of NEAR procedure Out_Str.
Lab:    mov al,[bx]     ; Copy current byte of Str to AL.
        cmp al,'$'      ; Is it the end of the string?
        je Exit_p       ; Yes, exit.

        mov byte ptr es:[di],al ;Copy the current byte to video-RAM
        inc di          ; Change destination offset
        inc di          ; address (two bytes higher).
        inc bx          ; Change source offset address.
        jmp Lab         ; Unconditional jump
                        ;(to the loop start).

Exit_p:   ret           ; Return to caller
OUT_STR ENDP            ; End of procedure.

END                     ; End of program.
```

# MASM High-Level Constructs

The set of directives becomes wider with every new version of assembler. Above, we have discussed the directives to declare variables, define memory models and segment allocation, initialize Segment Registers and so on. It's sufficient to write a program, but MASM 6.0 provides some new possibilities.

One feature that may be very popular among high-level languages fans is the flow control directive. This generates loops and IF-structures of various types. The Notation used in MASM 6.0 is very similar to C or Pascal. Of course, it's not so difficult to write:

```
        cmp  ax, 0
        jne  Lab1
        mov  Var, 5
        jmp  Lab2
Lab1:   mov  Var, 1
Lab2:   mov  ax, bx
   ........
```

but the alternative source code:

```
   .IF  ax = 0
   mov  Var, 5
   .ELSE
   mov  Var, 1
   .ENDIF
   mov ax, bx
   ........
```

looks more readable. By the way, the assembler expands Control Flow directives into sequences of instructions quite similar to the first fragment. Labels generated this way are always unique (@c0010 or something like this).

## Conditional Directives

The greatest advantage of these directives is that we can use a complete set of conditional expressions. The relational operators are the same as operators used in C. They are listed in Table 1.3.

**Table 1.3 Relational Operators**

| Operator | Meaning |
|----------|---------|
| == | equal |
| != | not equal |
| > | greater than |
| < | less than |
| >= | greater than or equal to |
| <= | less than or equal to |
| & | bit test |

*Continued*

**Table 1.3 Relational Operators (Continued)**

| Operator | Meaning |
|---|---|
| ! | Logical NOT |
| && | Logical AND |
| \|\| | Logical OR |

Special operators reflect the state of flags: CARRY?, OVERFLOW?, PARITY?, SIGN?, ZERO?. Conditions can be more complicated:

```
.IF  (ax = 0)
mov Var1,0
.ELSEIF (bx = 2)
mov Var2,1
.ELSE
mov Var3,2
.ENDIF
mov ax, bx
```

## Loops

The assembler also supports while-loops (.WHILE, .ENDW) and until-loops (.REPEAT, .UNTIL). While the condition expression is true, the processor repeats the block of instructions placed between corresponding directives. .BREAK and .CONTINUE directives can be used to stop repetitions. Sequences like '.BREAK .IF <condition>' or 'CONTINUE .IF <condition>' are legible to the eye. Look at the example below:

```
.WHILE 1
mov  ah, 07h                              ; Read the key pressed.
int  21h
.BREAK  .IF al == 1Bh                     ; Terminate if Esc has been pressed.

.CONTINUE .IF (al < 30h) || (al > 39h)  ; don't print if the character is not a digit.
mov  dl, al
mov  ah, 02h                              ; Print character.
int  21h
.ENDW
```

The directive .WHILE 1 starts an unlimited loop, which analyzes keys pressed. The ASCII code of the pressed key is stored in register AL. The loop is terminated by pressing <Esc> (code 1Bh). The directive .CONTINUE skips the instructions that print the symbol if the symbol is not a digit (ASCII range 30h to 39h). So, the sequence above works until you press <Esc>. If you press a non-digit key then nothing will happen. If you press a digit key then the digit will be printed on the screen.

## New MASM Interface

Another enhanced feature in MASM 6.0 is a more convenient interface to high-level languages.

Some new parameters have been added to the PROC directive. This extended form of PROC can determine the stack frame, the registers to be pushed and popped, and the proper way of terminating the procedure after a RET instruction:

```
P_Proc PROC NEAR USES ax dx, Par1:BYTE, Par2:DWORD
```

Code corresponding to the selected option is generated automatically. This means that there are fewer problems with different memory models and calling conventions.

The new INVOKE directive can be used instead of pushing parameters onto the stack and using the CALL instruction. So INVOKE resembles PROC. The called procedure can be of a different memory model and convention:

```
INVOKE P_Proc, Par1, Par2
```

The directive PROTO solves an unpleasant problem. There was no way to identify the types of parameters used in the procedure. PROTO creates the procedure prototype for the assembler. The prototype informs the assembler about the number of arguments and their types. PROTO and PROC have the same syntax.

Program 1.2. shows the advantages of using the new directives. The program HI_LEVEL.ASM simply prints the string 'CLEAR!' on your screen:

```
//////////////////////////////////////////////////////////
Program 1.2. Demo Program with PROC, PROTO, INVOKE Directives.
//////////////////////////////////////////////////////////
; The program HI_LEVEL.ASM demonstrates the use of
; new directives PROTO, INVOKE and the extended form
; of the directive PROC.
;
.DOSSEG
.MODEL small, c
.STACK  100h
.DATA
  Number1  DW 5
  Number2  DD 0BB22AA11h
  String1  DB 'CLEAR!',10,13,'$'
; Prototype of procedure ROUTINE:
ROUTINE PROTO c Param1:word,Param2:dword
.CODE

.STARTUP
      mov dx,OFFSET String1    ; Prepare registers
      mov ah,09h               ; DX,AX to print String1.
   ; Call ROUTINE with Number1 and Number2:
      INVOKE ROUTINE, Number1,Number2
      int 21h                  ;Dos Function: Print a string.
.EXIT 0
   ; Declaration of ROUTINE (note that the procedure
   ; changes values stored in DX and AX):
ROUTINE PROC c USES ax dx, Param1:word,Param2:dword
      mov ax,Param1            ; AX=00005h
      mov dx,word ptr Param2+2 ; DX=0BB22h
      mov cx,word ptr Param2   ; CX=0AA11h
      ret
ROUTINE      ENDP

END
```

The sequence of instructions below shows how MASM 6.0 interprets the directive INVOKE (see Program 1.2.):

```
cs:002C FF360C00    push word ptr [000C]
cs:0030 FF360A00    push word ptr [000A]
cs:0034 FF360800    push word ptr [0008]
cs:0038 E80A00      call 0045
cs:003B 83C406      add  sp,0006
```

As you can see, parameters are pushed onto the stack according to C conventions because the C language was selected in the prototype (the directive

PROTO). We'll have a closer look at stack frame and parameters transfer later, but the following Turbo Debugger output shows a stack of maximum depth formed by Program 1.2:

```
ss:0120 0000 - Start position of stack pointer
ss:011E BB22
ss:011C AA11 - Parameter2 (this word and the previous one)
ss:011A 0005 - Parameter1
ss:0118 003B - Return address to main program.
ss:0116 0000 - BP
ss:0114 0900 - AX
ss:0112 000E - DX
```

The following example shows code generated by PROC. It shows how MASM 6.0 expands the code of the procedure ROUTINE:

```
cs:0045 55          push bp
cs:0046 8BEC        mov  bp,sp
cs:0048 50          push ax
cs:0049 52          push dx
cs:004A 8B4604      mov  ax,[bp+04]
cs:004D 8B5608      mov  dx,[bp+08]
cs:0050 8B4E06      mov  cx,[bp+06]
cs:0053 5A          pop  dx
cs:0054 58          pop  ax
cs:0055 5D          pop  bp
cs:0056 C3          ret
```

You can see that registers AX and DX (in Program 1.2) are preserved automatically. By the way, if the assembler didn't preserve these registers, the string 'String1' would not be printed and the program would print something from the address DS:BB22 (DX=0BB22h in procedure ROUTINE).

# Modules Interfacing with High-Level Languages

Mixed-language programming helps you use assembly language where it's most needed - in optimized low-level routines. The capability of combining the specific merits of different languages is very important because you can develop most of a large project, quickly and conveniently in C, Pascal, QuickBASIC or whatever high level language you prefer, while writing assembly routines where performance is critical.

Passing parameters to and from assembly language modules via a stack is widely used by high-level compilers. New 'high-level' type directives can hide this mechanism from the programmer. But, for you to understand the details, let's first discuss the older method, with which you have to implement parameter exchanges by yourself.

## Parameter Exchanges

The first thing you have to do is write an assembly procedure under a set of definite rules. Your procedure must start and terminate properly. It'll look like this:

```
push bp              ; Save BP
mov  bp,sp           ; Make SP the framepointer
sub  sp,<space>      ; Allocate local variables
push si              ; Preserve registers used
push di              ;  in the procedure
.........
pop  di              ; Restore registers'
pop  si              ;  original values
mov  sp,bp           ; Restore SP
pop  bp              ; Restore BP
ret <n>              ; Exit and free parameters
```

The first two instructions make BP the 'framepointer' (pointer to the parameters), because SP cannot be used to access parameters and local data on the stack. Decreasing SP reserves space on the stack for the local data, if any is required. This space must be released (SP must be restored) at the end of a procedure. A procedure called from any of the Microsoft high-level languages must also preserve the contents of SI, DI, SS, and DS (if the procedure changes their values), and pop the preserved registers before exit. If local data space was allocated at the beginning of the procedure, SP must be restored. Then you have to restore BP with 'POP BP'. The procedure must release parameters from the stack, if the called high-level language requires it. You can use the instruction 'RET <n>' to release n bytes of parameter from the stack. If the procedure is called by a C-module, then the calling module will do it by itself, which we'll discuss later.

> *Remember that SS must always be logically 'preserved' in any procedure that is called and then returns - unless the return address is jumped to, or some other strange operation is performed.*

The calling program pushes each of the parameters on to the stack (SP points to the last parameter pushed), and then executes a CALL instruction, which pushes the return address on to the stack. This address may be two (for NEAR calls) or four bytes long (for FAR calls). The first instruction of the procedure saves the old value of BP. SP now points to the copy of BP in the stack. So we can determine the address of each parameter. The offset of the parameter pushed first will be:

<size of return address (2 or 4)>
<space for all parameters>

When you have determined the displacement of each parameter, you may want to refer to it through a symbolic name in your assembly procedure. You can use the directive EQU to assign a name to a parameter:

```
PARAMn   EQU [bp+6]   ; PARAMn is the last parameter pushed onto stack for FAR calls.
```

Sometimes you want to return a value from your assembly function. If it's a value shorter than 4 bytes, it is returned in registers (see Table 1.4):

**Table 1.4  Returning Convention**

| Data size | Returned value |
|---|---|
| 2 bytes (1 byte) | in AX (AL) |
| 4 bytes | High-order word (e.g. segment address) in DX |
| | Low-order word (e.g. offset address) in AX |

When it is necessary to return a value larger than four bytes, a procedure called by BASIC or C must allocate space for the returned value and then load this address into DX:AX. The simplest way to do it is to declare this space in the data segment. Floating point results are returned on the top of the coprocessor's stack (if the coprocessor is present).

There are some differences for Pascal. Pascal modules allocate a space in the stack segment to hold the actual returned value. After a CALL instruction, an extra-parameter (last parameter pushed) is placed above the return address. This parameter (BP+6) contains the offset address of the return value. Of course, this extra quasi-parameter increases the displacement of the other parameters by two. The segment address of the returned value is in SS, as well as in DS. According to this convention, your assembly procedure must put the returned data at this address. The calling Pascal module expects DX:AX to point to the returned value. So, you must copy the offset from BP+6 to AX and the segment address from SS to DX before exiting from the procedure.

# And There's More ... Conventions

Different languages treat external modules and stacks in different ways. First, Pascal and BASIC demand that a called procedure restores the stack pointer. A C call cleans the stack by itself. So, Pascal and Basic procedures usually end with RET <n> ('n' depends on the number and size of parameters), and C ones simply with RET. Secondly, C and C++ compilers push parameters onto the stack in reverse order (the first parameter will be pushed last, which means that it'll be lowest in memory). This allows the caller to vary the number of parameters for each call. Thirdly, C and C++ compilers normally add a leading '_' to the name of every identifier in external modules.

## Assembler And C

Interfacing assembler to C-modules is demonstrated in Program 1.3. The C-module passes two parameters to the procedure C_to_ASM_add in the ASM-module. C_to_ASM adds the numbers and calls the procedure ASM_to_C in C-module to print the result. This means that Program 1.3 shows parameter exchange in two directions:

```
////////////////////////////////////////////////////////////
Program 1.3. Interface Between C and assembler
////////////////////////////////////////////////////////////
// C-module ARITHC_C.C calls ASM-module to sum two
// parameters. It includes a procedure which will be called
// from ASM-module and prints the result.
///
#include <stdio.h>        -
            //Definition of external procedure
            //(ASM-module C_to_ASM_add):
external void C_to_ASM_add (int Operand1,long Operand2);

void ASM_to_C (int i);  //The procedure ASM_to_C will be
            //called from ASM-module.

void main(void)
{
C_to_ASM_add(50,500); //Call ASM-module with parameters
            //50 and 500.
}

void ASM_to_C (int Res)
{
printf("RESULT = %d \n", Res);
            //To no surprise it prints that
            //500 + 50 = 550.
}


;-----------------------------------------------------------
;ASM-module ARITHA_C.ASM adds parameters
; Op1 and Op2 and calls procedure ASM_to_C
;   and prints the result.
; Demo program for ExpAsm Chapter1 "Review of Assembly
; Language".
;
.MODEL small
PUBLIC _C_to_ASM_add
EXTRN c ASM_to_C : PROC

.CODE
      ; Parameters from C-module
Op1     EQU word ptr [bp+6]
Op2     EQU word ptr [bp+4]
```

```
_C_to_ASM_add PROC NEAR
      push bp
      mov bp,sp

      mov ax,Op1    ; AX = Op1
      add ax,Op2    ; AX = Op1 + Op2

      push ax       ; Value to be passed
      call ASM_to_C; Call the printer!
      add sp,2      ; Clean up stack (deallocate the
                    ; parameter passed to ASM_to_C).
      pop bp
      ret
_C_to_ASM_add ENDP
END
```

## Assembler and Pascal

The example on interfacing between assembler and Pascal (Program 1.4.) is similar to the previous program. Parameters are also passed in both directions. There are only two differences: first, the ASM-module ARITHA_P.ASM uses the large memory model and second, one of the parameters passed to the ASM-module is a pointer to a variable. The procedure in the ASM-module does nothing useful or remarkable. In fact, its main purpose is to illustrate parameter transfer from Pascal to assembler:

```
//////////////////////////////////////////////////////////
Program 1.4. Demo Program on Pascal-assembler Interface.
//////////////////////////////////////////////////////////
{
 The program ARITHP_P.PAS calls the procedure from
 ASM-module ARITHA_P.ASM and includes the procedure
 used in ASM-module.
}

procedure ASM_to_PAS (j:word);
{The procedure prints a string and the parameter passed from the
Assembly module}
begin
  writeln('I''m Pascal! Called with parameter:', j);
end;

{$L aritha_p.obj}    {A note for linker}


{ Declare the external function PAS_to_ASM }
function PAS_to_ASM (i:integer;
          var ptr : integer) : word; external;
```

```
{ Program body }
var i : integer;
begin
PAS_to_ASM (10, i)              ; {Call ASM-module with parameter1 = 10 and
                                ; parameter2 = far pointer to i}
end.


;-----------------------------------------------------------
; ASM-module ARITHA_P.ASM gets parameters from PAS-module
; ARITHP_P.PAS and calls the procedure ASM_to_Pas in PAS-module.

;
.MODEL large,pascal
PUBLIC PAS_to_ASM
EXTRN ASM_to_PAS : PROC
.CODE
Par1    EQU word ptr [bp+10]
Par2    EQU dword ptr [bp+6]

PAS_to_ASM   PROC FAR
        push bp
        mov bp,sp

        mov ax,word ptr Par2+2
        mov ds,ax
        mov dx,word ptr Par2     ; DS:DX points to var i now.
        push Par1                ; Par1 is passed to PAS-
                                 ;module to be printed.
        call ASM_to_PAS          ; Call the procedure in PAS-module.
        pop bp
        ret 6
PAS_to_ASM   ENDP

END
```

# Managing Large Projects

The point of using assembler is to create small and fast procedures. But you can also develop large projects written entirely in assembly language.

Suppose that either program code or data exceeds 64K. It's not a big problem to divide data or code into several segments, but of course you have to use a suitable memory model (large, for instance) and declare all these segments.

You have to declare procedures that are accessed from other segments as FAR. Then the assembler will use FAR calls automatically. It's harder with data segments, as you have to reload DS by yourself:

```
mov ax,SEG Buffer
mov ds,ax
mov ax,Buffer
```

In this chapter we are considering just a simple multisegment program. Look at Program 1.5. As we have seen, .DOSSEG and .MODEL declare the amount of segments and their allocation in memory:

Each segment has a unique name and is framed by a pair of directives; SEGMENT and ENDS. Data segments Data1 and Data2 are filled with a number of short strings.

As we are demonstrating some possibilities of multi-segment programming, the code is simplified. Remember that when DS:DX points to a string ending with '$', the following sequence:

```
mov ah,09h
int 21h
```

prints that string, minus the '$' (via DOS function 9). The code segment Code1 includes the procedure Out_Exclamation which invokes this function. The procedure is declared as FAR. So we can call it from other segments. The program starts with this call and almost identical code is placed in the code segment Code2.

```
///////////////////////////////////////////////////////////
Program 1.5. Multisegment Program.
///////////////////////////////////////////////////////////

; Multisegment program. Procedures from two code segments
; print two exclamations from two data segments.
;
.DOSSEG
.MODEL large          ; Large model is used.
.STACK 1000h          ; Big stack.
```

```
.DATA                           ; Start of data segments.
Data1 SEGMENT                   ; Very big data segment.
    Exclamation1 DB 9000 DUP ('OOPS! $')
    Exclam   DB 7 DUP(?)
Data1 ENDS


Data2 SEGMENT                   ; One more big data segment.
    Exclamation2 DB 9000 DUP ('Aah! $')
Data2 ENDS


.CODE                           ; Start of code segments.
.STARTUP                        ; Initialization of Segment Registers.

      mov ax,SEG Exclamation1
      mov ds,ax
      mov si,offset Exclamation1
                                ; DS:SI points to Exclamation1 now.
      mov ax,SEG Exclam
      mov es,ax
      mov di,offset Exclam      ; ES:DI points to Exclam now.
      mov cx,7                  ; Using REP prefix,
      rep movsb                 ; Copy 6 bytes of Exclamation1
                                ; to Exclam.
      call Out_Exclamation      ; Print Exclamation2.

      jmp far ptr Entry_point   ; Jump to code segment Code2.

Code1 SEGMENT                   ; First code segment

Out_Exclamation PROC FAR
      push ds                   ; Preserve DS used in procedure.
      mov ax,SEG Exclam
      mov ds,ax
      mov dx,OFFSET Exclam      ; DS:DX points to Exclam now.
      mov ah,09h                ; Print Exclam using DOS service.
      int 21h
      pop ds
      ret
Out_Exclamation ENDP

Code1 ENDS                      ; End of code segment Code1.

Code2 SEGMENT                   ; Second code segment.
Entry_point:
      mov ax,SEG Exclamation2
      mov ds,ax
      mov si,OFFSET Exclamation2; DS:SI points to Exclamation1 now.
      mov ax,SEG Exclam
      mov es,ax
      mov di,OFFSET Exclam
                                ; ES:DI points to Exclam now.
      mov cx,7                  ; Equivalent to loop
      .REPEAT                   ; construction.
      movsb                     ; It copies 6 bytes
```

```
        .UNTILCXZ               ; from Exclamation2 to Exclam.
        call Out_Exclamation    ; Print Exclamation2.

.EXIT 0                         ; Exit the program with code 0.
Code2 ENDS                      ; End of code segment Code2.
END                             ; End of program.
```

To reload Segment Registers with the required address, use the operator SEG, which returns the segment address of a variable, just as OFFSET returns the offset. To copy characters to Exclam, use string operations (instruction MOVSB with prefix REP) before the first call to the Out_Exclamation. The same kind of thing is implemented via Control Flow directives before the second call.

Our next task is to build three assembly modules connected as shown in Figure 1.3. To simplify understanding, the small memory model is used:

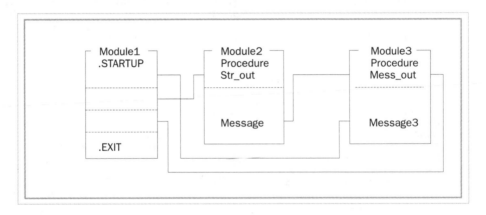

**Figure 1.3 Structure of Multimodule Program 1.6**

PUBLIC declaration of any variable or procedure allows use of the declared object in external modules. These variables or procedures from external modules must be declared with the directive EXTRN in other modules. This short explanation is all you need to understand the demo Program 1.6:

```
////////////////////////////////////////////////////////////
Program 1.6. Multimodule program.
////////////////////////////////////////////////////////////
; Module1 of multimodule program.
;
.DOSSEG
.MODEL small
.STACK 100h
EXTRN Message3: BYTE                 ; Message from Module3.
EXTRN Str_out : NEAR, Mess_out: NEAR ; Procedures Str_out (from Module2) and
                                     ; Mess_out (from Module3) are used in this
                                     ; module.
.DATA
    Data_for_nothing DB 20 DUP (90)  ; Unused data.
.CODE
.STARTUP                             ; Initialization of Segment Registers.

     mov dx,OFFSET Message3          ; Print string from Module3.
     call Str_out

     call Mess_out                   ; Print string from Module2 using
                                     ; procedure from Module3.

.EXIT 0                              ; Exit program with code 0.

END                                  ; End of program.
```

```
;-----------------------------------------------------------
;Module2 of multimodule program.
;
.DOSSEG
.MODEL small
PUBLIC Str_out                       ; Str_out can be used by other modules.
PUBLIC Message                       ; Message can be used by other modules.
.DATA
    Message DB 'Modules 2, 3 have already been used!';
        DB  10,13,'$'
.CODE

Str_out PROC NEAR
     mov ah,09h                      ; Function 09h.
     int 21h                         ; Call DOS service.
     ret
Str_out ENDP                         ; End of procedure.

END                                  ; End of Module2.
```

```
;-----------------------------------------------------------
; Module3 of multisegment program.
;
.DOSSEG
.MODEL small
PUBLIC Message3              ; String Message3 and procedure Mess_out
PUBLIC Mess_out             ; can be used by other modules.
EXTRN  Message: BYTE        ; Module3 uses string Message from Module2.
.DATA
    Message3  DB 'I am from Module 3! ',10,13,'$'
.CODE

Mess_out PROC NEAR          ; Start of the procedure.
     mov dx,OFFSET Message  ; Print string
     mov ah,09h             ; Message using
     int 21h                ; DOS function 09h.
     ret
Mess_out ENDP               ; End of procedure.

END                         ; End of Module3
```

Module 1 fills DX with the offset of string Message3 declared in Module3. Then it calls the procedure from Module2 to print this string on the screen. Next the procedure Mess_out prints another string. Module2 contains the procedure Str_out and the string Message to be used by other modules. Procedures Str_out (from Module1) and Mess_out (from Module3) are very much alike. But Mess_out prints the string Message (from Module2).

Now that you can write large projects, it's time to find out how MASM 6.0 treats these programs. Let's start from the moment when you have one or more .ASM files for your program.

The first way is to assemble it (or them) with command line utilities. You've probably done it with the help of MASM.EXE and LINK.EXE in MASM 5.1 and older. Even if you are not accustomed to assembling and linking your programs with the new utility ML.EXE, you don't have to change your habits, as well as .BAT files. MASM 6.0 provides converters MASM.EXE and LINK.EXE which translate 5.0-style command lines and runs ML.EXE with proper, new style command lines. So, if you wish, your working style will remain the same as before.

Alternatively use the PWB (Programmer's WorkBench). PWB looks and feels like a normal high-level language environment. You can edit source files, change link and compiler options, compile, link, debug, and run your programs. A full set of these standard functions propels MASM one step closer to high-level languages.

To create a single-module program, you usually have to take the following steps:

1   Edit source file.

2   Adjust build options.

3   Compile and link source file.

4   Fix bugs (using CodeView if necessary).

5   Rebuild and run the program.

The next sequence is to develop a program from multiple modules:

1   Edit source files.

2   Adjust compiler and linker options.

3   Create the program list for the project. You can set the paths for the libraries and include files. Source files can be included in the program list as well as object files. Using all this information NMAKE.EXE creates the makefile for your program.

4   Compile and link the project.

5   Fix the bugs. Apart from Code View, Source Browser is sometimes useful for tracing references.

6   Rebuild the project and run it.

# Summary

These are the basics of assembly language programming. We have discussed elementary system resources, data types, program sturcture, the main directives of the assembler, as well as interfacing with high-level languages and large projects.

Hopefully this chapter will have helped you to refresh your knowledge of assembly language. So far so good. Now you are ready to turn to more sophisticated and tricky issues.

# Programming Intel 80386/80486 Processors

## Introduction

This chapter assumes you know something about the Intel 8088/8086 microprocessors and now want to learn about the more advanced Intel 80286/80386/ 80486 and the new Pentium microprocessors. We will mostly limit our discussion to the programming aspects of these Intel microprocessors, and provide a way to tell them apart. We will conclude this chapter with a section on the Intel 'clone' microprocessors.

# Intel Microprocessor History

Let's first a take a few minutes to review the Intel family history. It actually started with the 4004 in 1971. It had 4-bit registers, consisted of 2300 transistors, and was designed to run at 108 KHz. It could address up to 640 bytes of memory. It was quickly followed by the 8008 in 1972 that had 8-bit registers and ran at 200 KHz. The 8008 could address up to 16K of memory. In 1974, Intel produced the 8080 that ran at 2 MHz and provided a superset of the 8008 commands that made it practical to use in a small computer. The 8080 could address 64K bytes and consisted of 6000 transistors.

In 1978, Intel produced the 8086 that ran at 5 MHz and had 29,000 transistors. The 8086 had 16-bit registers and a 16-bit data bus with a 20-bit address bus to access up to 1MB of memory. The 8086 may have been a bit ahead of its time. A year later, Intel provided the 8088, which still had the same 16-bit registers and 20-bit address bus, but its data bus was only 8-bit. IBM chose the 8088 over the 8086 in its first IBM PC because it was easier to build a system around the 8-bit data bus. IBM later used the 8086 in its low-end PS/2 line. In 1982, Intel produced the 80186, which was basically a 8086 with additional on-chip support functions such as a clock generator, interrupt controller, and bus controller. The 80188 was the 8088 version with on-chip support functions.

Intel's other 1982 microprocessor, the 80286, ran at 8 MHz and had 134,000 transistors. The 80286 became very popular when IBM used it in its PC AT computer in 1984. Not only was the 80286 faster than previous Intel microprocessors, it had a 24-bit address bus to access up to 16 MB of memory. The 80286 still had 16-bit registers and a 16-bit data bus, but provided some new instructions while remaining software compatible with the older microprocessors. The 80286 also introduced two new programming terms: Real Mode and Protected Mode. We will discuss these modes later, but we will mention here that the 80286 supported virtual memory for segments.

In 1985, Intel produced the 80386 which expanded its registers, data bus, and address bus to 32-bits. The 80386 could address up to 4 gigabytes of memory. It ran at 16 MHz and had 275,000 transistors. The 80386 still supported a 16-bit instruction set as well as providing 32-bit instructions. Segments could be larger than 64K. The 80386 provided virtual memory support using 4K memory pages and permitted programmers to write applications to run in a flat address space.

No more segments! The 80386 also added another programming mode called Virtual 8086 to better multitask DOS sessions. Later, the 80386 became known as the 386DX to distinguish it from the 386SX released in 1988. The 386SX went back to the 16-bit external data bus (hence SX, SiXteen) and 24-bit external address bus, but otherwise to the software it functioned the same as the 386DX. Intel used the 386SX to compete against the faster versions of the Intel 80286 made by other companies that second sourced the design from Intel. It was a major expense to build systems using a 32-bit data bus instead of the 16-bit data bus. At that time, just about all PC software was written for 16-bit operations, so the expansion to 32-bit did not offer much performance improvement. Performance was more affected by the clock speed of the processor than the size of the data bus.

In 1989, Intel produced the 80486. It offered an 8K on-chip cache and an on-chip numeric coprocessor. It had 1.2 million transistors and ran at 25MHz. Aside from the clock speed improvement, it also executed faster because some instructions only needed one processor cycle. The 80386 required a minimum of two cycles to execute an instruction. Like the 80386, the 80486 became the 486DX when Intel released the 486SX in 1991, but the 486SX still had a 32-bit data bus. So what did having the SX ending mean? In Intel's reasoning, SX may simply mean less than the DX. For the 486SX, what's missing is the numeric coprocessor so that Intel could sell a cheaper 80846 to compete against the 386 clones. Many PC applications did not use a lot of floating point operations, so having an on-chip numeric coprocessor was not much of a performance advantage.

In 1992, Intel produced the 486DX2. It was functionally the same as the 486DX, but its internal logic ran at twice the speed of the clock input. This allowed the 486DX2 to be used in a system designed for 33 MHz while the processor doubled its internal clock to 66 MHz.

In 1993, Intel produced its newest microprocessor, the Pentium. Everyone expected it to be called the 586, but Intel lost its legal effort to restrict the use of the 386 name to Intel products. The federal court ruled that the 386 number could not be trademarked, so Intel switched to something else to name its microprocessors. The Pentium has a 64-bit data bus and a 16K internal cache. It is capable of executing more than one instruction in a cycle, but depends on optimizing compilers to properly schedule instruction execution for peak performance. Amazingly, the Pentium remains compatible with PC software produced over ten years ago! The original Pentium ran at 60 MHz but required five volts. With 3.1 million transistors, the Pentium generated a lot of heat at five volts. The newer 90 MHz Pentium at 3.3 volts generates far less heat. At first, because the Pentium required a 64-bit data bus, there was some resistance to building new systems to use it.

In 1994, Intel produced the 486DX4, which used triple clocking instead of double clocking along with a 16K internal cache. This improved the performance of a 33MHz system still using a 32-bit data bus. However, Intel has been lowering its Pentium prices such that Pentium 64-bit data bus systems are becoming more popular.

While we omitted the Intel 8085, 386SL, 486SL, and a few other lesser known members of the Intel 80x86 family, hopefully you now have a better understanding of the great strides Intel has made in its microprocessor designs.

# Programming Modes

Intel has defined three programming modes: 8086 Real Address Mode, 80286 Protected Mode, and Virtual 8086 Mode. Depending on which Intel Programmer's Reference Manual you read, the names may slightly change but the concepts remain the same.

## Real Mode

All Intel 80x86 microprocessors start up in Real Mode. This is to ensure compatibility with software written for all the older microprocessors back to the 8086. So even if the microprocessor is a Pentium, upon starting up it can only address the first megabyte of memory. You might think you cannot use 32-bit registers in Real Mode, but you can if your instruction has an operand-size override prefix and the microprocessor supports 32-bit. Let's quickly review how memory is referenced in a 8086 microprocessor.

Because all registers are limited to 16 bits, the most bytes that a register can directly address is 64K or 65536. However, even back in 1978, 64K was too limiting to run software. So Intel provided four segment registers:

| | |
|---|---|
| CS | Code Segment |
| DS | Data Segment |
| ES | Extra (data) Segment |
| SS | Stack Segment |

Each segment register pointed to a 16-byte region of memory called a paragraph. To reference a memory location, the contents of a segment register was shifted left four bits and a 16-bit displacement was added. So, because of the 16-bit displacement value, the memory space became addressable in 64K memory segments. For example, suppose we wanted to execute

```
mov ax,[si]
```

and DS=1234h and SI=5678h. The MOV instruction would transfer the contents of memory location 179B8h into AX.

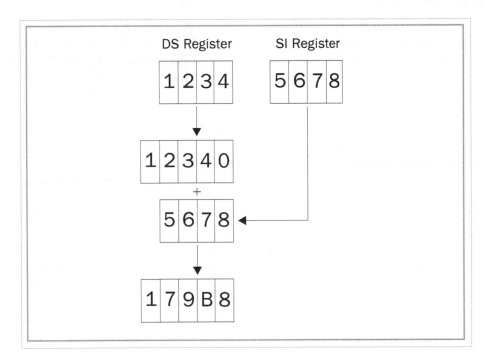

**Figure 2.1 Real Mode Segment Address Translation**

So normally in Real Mode we can only address memory locations 00000h to FFFFFh. On a 8088/8088 microprocessor with only 20 address lines, that would be correct. If a programmer loaded DS=FFFFh and SI=FFFFh, the new memory address would be 10FFEFh; however, it is truncated to 0FFEFh on the 20-bit address bus. But a 80286 has 24 address lines, so 10FFEFh would go out on the address bus. We don't know if Intel intended to provide almost an extra 64K bytes of address space in Real Mode, but they were in for a surprise when they discovered that some PC software stopped working on the 80286. For some reason, these programs expected the address to wrap around. So computer systems using the 80286 and higher microprocessors needed extra logic to mask off the 21st address line (A20) when requested by system software in order to keep the old programs working. Later, Microsoft in DOS 5.0 took advantage of the A20 logic to load DOS above 1 megabyte as part of the High Memory Area.

## Protected Mode

It didn't take Intel long to figure out that even one megabyte of memory was not going to be enough for new PC software. So in the 80286, Intel provided 16 MB of memory address space, but Intel still needed to support the old PC software. More importantly, Intel did not want to radically change the way PC programmers had to access the extra memory in their applications. So memory was still accessed in 64K segments. For the application to address beyond 1 megabytes, the operating system software has to switch to Protected Mode. All registers remain 16-bits, but the contents of the segment registers have a different meaning in Protected Mode. The segment registers now basically contain an index (selector) for the microprocessor to retrieve more information on how to build the linear address from the logical address (segment selector and displacement) provided by the programmer. The PC programmer still thinks in terms of 64K segments, but depends upon the operating system to correctly set the values in the segment registers. What exactly is in the segment register? Well, it has three fields. The first field is the index and it selects one of 8192 descriptors in a descriptor table. We will explain what a descriptor is later. The next field is the Table Indicator which tells the microprocessor which one of two tables (GDT and LDT) in memory this selector is to index. The last field is the Requester Privilege Level which limits what the current software can do without causing a protection exception.

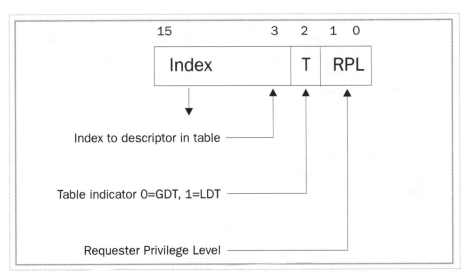

**Figure 2.2 Selector Format**

Let's explain the two tables before explaining what a descriptor is. The GDT is the Global Descriptor Table. It defines all the memory areas currently in use throughout the system. The LDT is the Local Descriptor Table and defines the memory areas in use by the current task. Different LDTs are used to prevent two different applications from harming each other. With one task's LDT properly loaded, the currently active task has no way to access the other task's memory. LDTs are used by multi-tasking operating systems. Only the operating system should update the LDT and GDT. How does the microprocessor find the GDT and LDT? Intel added the LGDT, LLDT, and LIDT instructions to load the address of the GDT, LDT, and IDT. We haven't mentioned the IDT yet. When an interrupt occurs while the processor is in Protected Mode, the Interrupt Descriptor Table is used to load the descriptor for the interrupt handler. Like the Interrupt Vector Table in Real Mode, the interrupt number is used to index into the IDT, so the IDT is limited to 256 entries.

A descriptor occupies eight bytes of memory and it provides the microprocessor with information about the segment size and location. The descriptor also provided control and status information. Before we get buried in the descriptor details, let's show how the descriptor is used to determine the linear address. Suppose we are running on a 80286 in Protected Mode and we execute

```
mov ax, [si]
```

again with DS=1234h, SI=5678h, and the descriptor's base address field has 012345h. The MOV instruction would transfer the contents of memory location 0179B8h into AX.

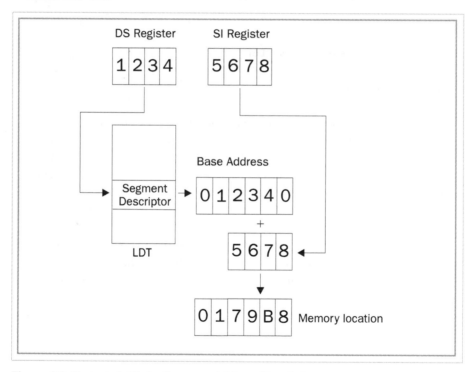

**Figure 2.3 Protected Mode Segment Address Translation**

On a 80386 and higher microprocessors, the base address in the descriptor is 32 bits instead of 24 bits, and the displacement can be 32 bits instead of 16 bits. Now you might be thinking that if the microprocessor has to load the descriptor from memory every time a memory reference is made, then the microprocessor is going to run very slowly. Well, Intel realized the same thing, so the microprocessor keeps a copy of each segment register's descriptor in an internal register. As long as the segment register remains the same, the internal copy can be used, but whenever the segment register is changed, then a new copy of the descriptor is loaded from memory - even if the segment register is updated with the same value. In the 80386 and higher microprocessors, Intel also added two more segment registers: FS and GS.

Now let's look at what is inside a descriptor. There's basically two kinds of descriptor: system and application. They both have the same format except for some system descriptors like the call gate descriptor:

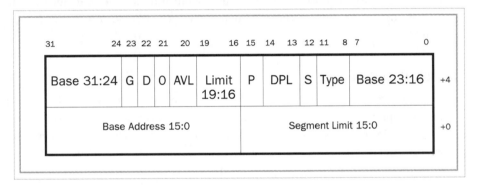

**Figure 2.4 Segment Descriptor**

You may notice from the above figure that the base address has been split into three fields. Well actually Base 23:16 and Base 15:0 are one 24 bit field, but Base 31:24 has eight more bits that are not directly connected to the other base address bits. When Intel originally designed the 80286 descriptor data structure, they only needed 24 bits for the base address. They may not have thought ahead to the 80386 someday needing 32-bits. Still, they managed to reserve enough bits so a 32-bit base address could be added later without breaking the 80286 system software. The same line of thought applies to the Limit 19:16 being combined with Segment Limit 15:0 to provide a 20-bit segment limit for the 80386 while the 80286 only used the Segment Limit 15:0 field.

## Base Address

This is either 24 bits for the 80286 or 32 bits for the 80386 and higher microprocessors. It defines the location of the segment within the entire addressable memory space.

## G - Granularity

1 bit, not used by the 80286. If off (0), then the segment limit is in bytes. If on (1), then the segment limit is in 4K pages. Up to now you might be wondering how a 80386 could have a segment greater than 1 megabyte if the segment limit only had 20 bits. Now you know. With the Granularity bit Intel did not need to expand the size of the descriptor beyond eight bytes to hold a 32-bit segment limit.

## D - Default Operation Size

1 bit, not used by the 80286 and only valid for a code segment. If off (0), then the microprocessor assumes all operands and addressing modes are 16-bit. If on (1), then the operands and addressing modes are 32-bit. The programmer can use the operand-size and address-size override prefixes on an instruction to temporarily switch from 16 or 32-bit mode.

## 0 - Reserved

1 bit left in the descriptor for some future use by Intel. It should be set to zero.

## AVL - Available

1 bit for use by system software.

## Segment Limit

Either 16 bits for the 80286 or 20 bits for the 80386 and higher microprocessors. Defines the maximum acceptable displacement for this segment. However, a value of zero either means a segment size of 1 byte (Granularity bit off) or 4K bytes (Granularity bit on). Normally the displacement has to be equal or less than the Segment Limit, unless it is an expand-down segment. Expand-down segments are used for stacks, and their displacements are valid if they are *not* 0 to the limit value. This allows the system software to keep expanding a stack from high to low memory without affecting the existing contents of the stack.

## P - Present

1 bit. If off (0), then the segment is not present in memory. If an attempt is made to use this segment with the Present bit off, a Not Present exception will be generated. This allows the operating system to read the segment from disk and set the Present bit on. If the Present bit is on (1), then the microprocessor will access the segment in memory. The Present bit helps the operating system support virtual memory on the 80286. An entire segment can be saved and restored from disk in order to make memory available for other segments in use by the active task. This bit and the remaining descriptor fields below exist in the 80286 and higher microprocessors.

## DPL - Descriptor Privilege Level

A 2-bit field that defines the privilege level of this segment. The DPL values range from 0 (most privileged, for system software) to 3 (least privileged, for application software).

## S - Segment Format

1 bit. If off (0), then this is a system segment, otherwise it is an application segment. System segments provide information about system tables, tasks, and gates.

## Type

A 4-bit field to further define the type of segment. The meaning of this field depends on the setting of the S bit. If the S bit is on (1), then the meanings of the Type field can be further divided into whether it is a code or data segment. If the high order bit in Type is off (0), then it is a data segment, otherwise it is a code segment. In a data segment the three lower bits in Type are E (expand-down), W (writeable), and A (accessed). In a code segment the three lower bits are C (conforming), R (readable), and A (accessed).

Table 2.1 Type Definitions for Code and Data Segments

| Type | Segment | E | W | A | Description |
|------|---------|---|---|---|-------------|
| 0000b | Data | 0 | 0 | 0 | Read-Only |
| 0001b | Data | 0 | 0 | 1 | Read-Only, Accessed |
| 0010b | Data | 0 | 1 | 0 | Read/Write |
| 0011b | Data | 0 | 1 | 1 | Read/Write, Accessed |
| 0100b | Data | 1 | 0 | 0 | Expand-down, Read-Only |
| 0101b | Data | 1 | 0 | 1 | Expand-down, Read-Only, Accessed |
| 0110b | Data | 1 | 1 | 0 | Expand-down, Read/Write |
| 0111b | Data | 1 | 1 | 1 | Expand-down, Read/Write, Accessed |
| 1000b | Code | 0 | 0 | 0 | Execute-Only |
| 1001b | Code | 0 | 0 | 1 | Execute-Only, Accessed |
| 1010b | Code | 0 | 1 | 0 | Execute/Read |
| 1011b | Code | 0 | 1 | 1 | Execute/Read, Accessed |
| 1100b | Code | 1 | 0 | 0 | Conforming, Execute-Only |
| 1101b | Code | 1 | 0 | 1 | Conforming, Execute-Only, Accessed |
| 1110b | Code | 1 | 1 | 0 | Conforming, Execute/Read |
| 1111b | Code | 1 | 1 | 1 | Conforming, Execute/Read, Accessed |

The displacement for an expand-down segment is checked differently against the segment limit as explained earlier. Should a program attempt to write a read-only data segment or read an execute-only code segment, a general protection exception is generated. The Accessed bit indicates whether the segment has been accessed, so the operating system can use this bit to determine whether the segment has been recently used, before attempting to write it to disk to make room in memory for another segment. When a transfer occurs into a more privileged code segment, a conforming segment uses the current privilege level. If the same transfer occurs to a non-conforming code segment, a general protection exception occurs unless a task gate is used.

If the S bit is off (0) then the Type field is defined as follows for a system segment:

**Table 2.2 Type Definitions for a System Segment**

| Type | Description |
|------|-------------|
| 0000b | Reserved |
| 0001b | Available 80286 TSS |
| 0010b | LDT |
| 0011b | Busy 80286 TSS |
| 0100b | Call Gate |
| 0101b | Task Gate |
| 0110b | 80286 Interrupt Gate |
| 0111b | 80286 Trap Gate |
| 1000b | Reserved |
| 1001b | Available 386+ CPU TSS |
| 1010b | Reserved |
| 1011b | Busy 386+ CPU TSS |
| 1100b | 386+ CPU Call Gate |
| 1101b | Reserved |
| 1110b | 386+ CPU Interrupt Gate |
| 1111b | 386+ CPU Task Gate |

Normally, only operating system programmers need to know about system segments. By now you might be getting tired of segment descriptors. Let's move on to paging.

## Paging

With the 80386 and higher microprocessors, Intel added support for further dividing memory into 4K pages. This made it far easier for the operating system to only keep in memory what was really needed. With segment swapping the entire segment had to be written and read back from disk. Pages are always fixed in size at 4K bytes. Without paging the linear address generated by the segment selector and displacement is the physical address in memory. Therefore a segment of 64K bytes require 64K bytes of continuous physical memory with paging off. With paging active, the same 64K segment can be mapped by the operating system into non-continuous 4K memory pages without affecting the application, and the entire application does not even have to be loaded into memory to run.

Paging is enabled by setting the PG bit in the CR0 register. To translate the linear address to a physical address, the top 20 bits of the linear address are used to index into a page table in memory. More specifically, the top ten bits index into a page directory pointed to by the content of the CR3 register. The page directory consists of 1K 32-bit entries. Each page directory entry may point to a page table in memory, or not point to anything if its Present bit is off (0). The page table also consists of 1K 32-bit entries. Actually the entries for the page directory and page table have the same format. Each page table entry may point to a 4K page frame in physical memory. The lower 12 bits in the linear address are used to select a specific memory location within the 4K page frame.

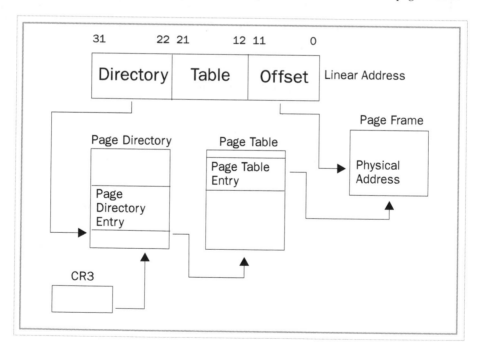

**Figure 2.5 Linear to Physical Address Translation via Paging**

The following figure shows the format of each entry in the page directory or page table. Both the page directory and page table are aligned on a 4K page physical memory boundary, therefore a page directory entry only needs the 22-bit page frame address to locate a specific page table. The remaining 10 bits in the entry are used to control access to the page. If the Present bit is off (0), the remaining 31 bits can be freely used by the operating system. If the R/W bit is on (1), the page is writeable, otherwise the page is read-only. While the segment descriptor provides four levels of privileges, paging only provides two levels: Supervisor (U/S bit = 0) and User (U/S bit = 1). If the microprocessor is running at segment descriptor privilege level 0, 1, or 2, then Supervisor level is in effect for paging, otherwise at privilege level 3 the microprocessor is running at the paging User level. When the microprocessor is running at Supervisor level, all pages are accessible. When the microprocessor is running at User level, then only pages marked with U/S bit = 1 are accessible. The 80486 defines two new bits for each page directory/table entry: PWT and PCD.

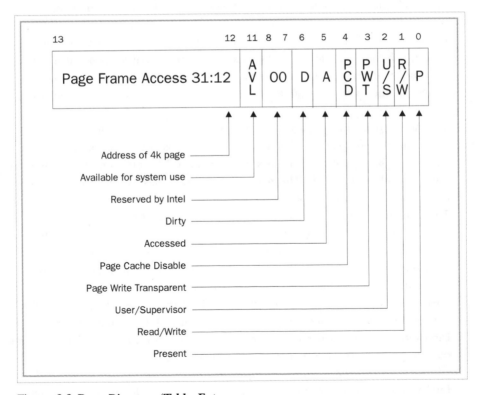

**Figure 2.6 Page Directory/Table Entry**

The 80486 has an 8K internal write-through cache, and is not affected by the value of the PWT bit. Intel provided the PWT bit for system designers who wanted to implement an external write-back cache. When a cache is write-through, any update to memory locations currently loaded in the cache is also written to the physical memory so that memory always matches the contents of the cache. The cache can then be safely flushed without losing valuable information. When a cache has a write-back policy, the updates to memory are delayed while the processor continues to execute instructions until it is convenient to write the new information to memory. Should the cache be flushed before the data is written back to memory, then the updated information would be lost. When there are a lot of memory updates a write-back cache can offer a significant performance improvement because multiple updates to the cache (fast) may result in only one update to the physical memory (slow). If the PWT bit is on (1), the updated contents of the 4K memory page should always be immediately written to memory. If the PWT bit is off (0), then the external write-back cache controller can delay writing back the updated contents.

If the PCD bit is on (1), then none of the locations within the 4K memory page will be loaded into the 80486 internal cache. There are some memory addresses that must always be directly accessed, such as memory mapped I/O devices. If the PCD bit is off (0), then the 4K memory page is cacheable.

The Accessed bit in the page directory/table entry has the same meaning as in the segment descriptor. It is on (1), if the page has been read or written. The Dirty bit is set (1), if the page has been updated. The operating system software must reset these bits to 0. The microprocessor only sets the bits to 1, with one exception: the microprocessor will not set the Dirty bit in a page directory entry. The operating system software uses the Accessed and Dirty bits to free up physical memory for use by other active tasks. The operating system will first free pages that do not have the Accessed bit on (1), because they have not been used since the last time the operating system checked. If all pages have the Accessed bit on (1), the operating system then checks the Dirty bits. If the operating system must free a page that has the Dirty bit on (1), the operating system knows it must save a copy of the page on disk to be reloaded later. If the Dirty bit is off (0), then the memory page doesn't have to be saved because the operating system can reload it from the original file.

Intel reserved two bits in the page directory/table entry for future use. Intel provided 3 bits in the AVAIL field for use by the operating system software.

Like the segment descriptors, the Intel microprocessors cannot access memory to look up the physical memory address for every memory reference without a severe impact on performance. To hold paging information, the microprocessors have a special on-chip cache called the translation lookaside buffer (TLB). The TLB is only updated when a new page is used or the operating system flushes the TLB by reloading CR3 or using the INVLPG instruction.

## Flat Address Space

For all PC programmers tired of dealing with segments, the best benefit the 80386 and higher microprocessors provide may be support for a flat 32-bit address space. There is no control bit to turn off segmentation, but by mapping the code, data, and stack spaces into the same very large segment, the 32-bit memory displacements can address all available memory and thereby eliminate the need to ever change the segment registers. If the segment registers remain unmodified the software will run faster in Protected Mode because the microprocessor will not be wasting cycles to reload the eight byte descriptors from memory. Memory protection can still be achieved using paging.

# Virtual 8086 Mode

This mode was introduced in the 80386 to help multitask DOS sessions. Real Mode offers no protection to keep applications from interfering with each other. Protected Mode offers some protection but the segment registers no longer work the same as in Real Mode. An old DOS program cannot simply take the contents of a segment register and increment it to point to the next 16 bytes of memory in Protected Mode. When Intel introduced the 80286, it may have thought that Real Mode applications would be quickly replaced by Protected Mode applications. Once the 80286 entered Protected Mode, it could not go back into Real Mode unless the microprocessor was reset. However, few users were willing to give up their old DOS applications! So to run these DOS programs, a Protected Mode operating system such as OS/2 running on a 80286 had to have a way to get back to Real Mode. The system designers provided special circuits to reset the microprocessor to go from Protected Mode to Real Mode that was different from the normal reset or power-on switch. Because the microprocessor goes through an internal self check every time it is reset, many cycles were wasted switching to Real Mode. Intel learned its lesson and provided a way to go between Real Mode and Protected Mode in the 80386 by simply changing a control register. But Virtual 8086 Mode goes one step beyond that.

The main purpose of Virtual 8086 Mode is to enable the operating system to create virtual machines. Each virtual machine has its own one megabyte of memory space separate from the other virtual machines. A program running in Virtual 8086 Mode can use segment registers as it did in Real Mode. Virtual 8086 Mode also allows the operating system to control the external interfaces of the virtual machines such as I/O and interrupts. The operating system can manage the I/O ports such that each application thinks it has exclusive use of a port. While a program in a virtual machine can only address memory up to 10FFEFh, the operating system can use paging to map these memory locations to anywhere within a 32-bit address space. The background multitasking DOS sessions in Windows Enhanced Mode would not be possible without Virtual 8086 Mode.

# Application Register Set

We want to make a distinction between the set of registers that an application would normally use versus the set of registers the system software must manage. In this section we will start with the original set of application registers defined for the 8086.

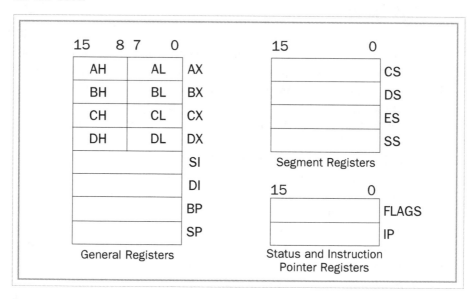

**Figure 2.7 8086 Application Register Set**

This same register set is used for writing applications to run on the 8088, 80186, 80188, and 80286. If you are familiar with the 8086, then we don't need to waste your time listing what each register does. You may be a bit unsure as to whether the IP or Instruction Pointer register should be included in this group. Since it is automatically updated whenever an instruction is executed we elected to place it here. As you can see in the following figure, Intel was able to expand to 32-bit registers in the 80386 without impacting the old 16-bit software.

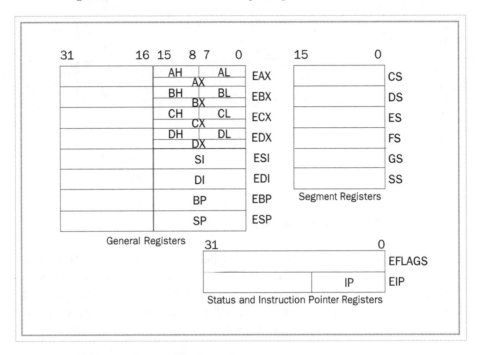

**Figure 2.8 80386 Application Register Set**

When running on a 32-bit Intel microprocessor, the 16-bit software only uses the lower 16 bits of the 32-bit registers while the upper 16 bits remain unchanged. Newer 32-bit software can use the entire 32 bits. If Intel decides to build a 64-bit microprocessor, they may use the same technique to expand out to 64 bits. Let's take a closer look at the FLAGS/EFLAGS register. As you will see later, it's going to become very useful in a way you may not expect.

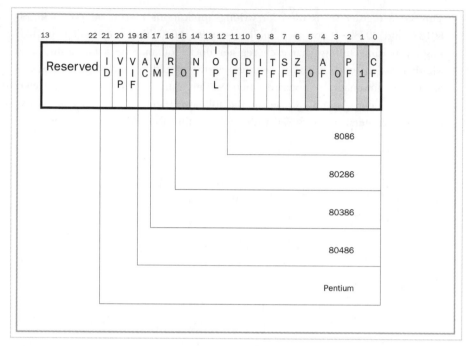

**Figure 2.9 FLAGS/EFLAGS Register**

As you can see, Intel still has room to define new bits in the EFLAGS register. Intel recommends not setting or resetting the reserved bits, but leaving the bits with the same values previously read from the EFLAGS register. Here's a table for a brief description of each bit. We will provide a more detailed explanation of what each bit does in a later chapter.

**Table 2.3 FLAGS/EFLAGS Definitions**

| Bit | Label | Description |
| --- | --- | --- |
| 0 | CF | Carry Flag |
| 1 | 1 | Reserved by Intel |
| 2 | PF | Parity Flag |
| 3 | 0 | Reserved by Intel |

*Continued*

Table 2.3 FLAGS/EFLAGS Definitions (Continued)

| Bit | Label | Description |
|-----|-------|-------------|
| 4 | AF | Auxiliary Carry Flag |
| 5 | 0 | Reserved by Intel |
| 6 | ZF | Zero Flag |
| 7 | SF | Sign Flag |
| 8 | TF | Trap Flag |
| 9 | IF | Interrupt Enable Flag |
| 10 | DF | Direction Flag |
| 11 | OF | Overflow Flag |
| 12-13 | IOPL | I/O Privilege Level |
| 14 | NT | Nested Task Flag |
| 15 | 0 | Reserved by Intel |
| 16 | RF | Resume Flag |
| 17 | VM | Virtual 8086 Mode Flag |
| 18 | AC | Alignment Check Flag |
| 19 | VIF | Virtual Interrupt Flag |
| 20 | VIP | Virtual Interrupt Pending Flag |
| 21 | ID | ID Flag |
| 22-31 | Reserved | Reserved by Intel |

In this chapter we will be using the NT, AC, and ID flag bits to help use solve a problem.

# System Register Set

Many application programmers don't know much about the system registers. It may just as well be that way, because the system registers are ones most likely to change when Intel develops a new microprocessor. System programmers working on operating systems, debuggers, and complex device drivers need to know about the system registers and how they differ from one Intel microprocessor to the next. What are the system registers? They consists of control registers (CR0, CR1,

CR2, CR3, CR4), debug registers (DR0, DR1, DR2, DR3, DR4, DR5, DR6, DR7), test registers (TR3, TR4, TR5, TR6, TR7), special segmentation registers (GDTR, IDTR, LDTR and TR) and machine specific registers. Now some of you might be tempted to say "But there are no CR1, DR4, and DR5 registers!" Well, yes and no. These registers exist as part of Intel 80x86 architecture but are not implemented in any Intel designed microprocessor today. Intel declared that they existed but reserved them for some future purpose. To help keep other companies that build Intel compatible microprocessors from using reserved registers, Intel introduced the concept of model-specific registers in the Pentium.

Prior to the 80286, you didn't have to worry about the system registers because there weren't any. The 80286 introduced the Machine Status Word register that later became the lower part of CR0 in the 80386. Because of Protected Mode, the 80286 also had the special segmentation registers. The 80386 introduced the control registers, debug registers and test registers. The 80486 provided some more test registers. The Pentium added one more control register but took away all the test registers. Well, we guess Intel never intended to make the system programmer's job easy. We will go into more details about these system registers in a later chapter.

# Instruction Set

Over all, Intel has done a remarkable job maintaining software compatibility with each new microprocessor it produces as part of its 80x86 family. It is quite a challenge to improve a processor architecture without forcing users to give up old applications. The most significant change was going from 16-bit registers and operands to 32-bit in the 80386. 32-bit operations and a 32-bit flat address space will help enable programmers to develop PC applications that previously required a super-mini or mainframe computer.

To make it easier for you to keep track of which instructions are supported by which microprocessors, we put together the following list:

## Non-floating Point Intel Microprocessor Instructions

**8086+**

| | | | | | | | |
|---|---|---|---|---|---|---|---|
| AAA | AAD | AAM | AAS | ADC | ADD | AND | CALL |
| CBW | CLC | CLD | CLI | CMC | CMP | CMPSB | CMPSW |
| CWD | DAA | DAS | DEC | DIV | ESC | HLT | IDIV |
| IMUL | IN | INC | INT | INTO | IRET | JA | JAE |
| JB | JBE | JC | JCXZ | JE | JG | JGE | JL |
| JLE | JMP | JNA | JNAE | JNB | JNBE | JNC | JNE |
| JNG | JNGE | JNL | JNLE | JNO | JNP | JNS | JNZ |
| JO | JP | JPE | JPO | JS | JZ | LHAF | LDS |
| LEA | LES | LOCK | LODSB | LODSW | LOOP | LOOPE | LOOPNE |
| LOOPNZ | LOOPZ | MOV | MOVSB | MOVSW | MUL | NEG | NOP |
| NOT | OR | OUT | POP | POPF | PUSH | PUSHF | RCL |
| RCR | REP | REPE | REPNE | REPNZ | REPZ | RET | ROL |
| ROR | SAHF | SAL | SAR | SBB | SCASB | SCASW | SHL |
| SHR | STC | STD | STOSB | STOSW | SUB | TEST | WAIT |
| XCHG | XLAT | XOR | | | | | |

**80186+**

| | | | | | | | |
|---|---|---|---|---|---|---|---|
| BOUND | ENTER | INS | INSB | INSW | LEAVE | OUTS | OUTSB |
| OUTSW | POPA | PUSHA | | | | | |

**80286+**

| | | | | | | | |
|---|---|---|---|---|---|---|---|
| ARPL | CLTS | LAR | LGDT | LIDT | LLDT | LMSW | LSL LTR |
| SGDT | SIDT | SLDT | SMSW | STR | VERR | VERW | |

**80386+**

| | | | | | | | |
|---|---|---|---|---|---|---|---|
| BSF | BSR | BT | BTC | BTR | BTS | CDQ | CMPSD |
| CWDE | INSD | JECXZ | LFS | LGS | LODSD | LSS | MOVSD |
| MOVSX | MOVZX | OUTSD | POPAD | POPFD | PUSHAD | PUSHFD | SCASD |
| SETA | SETAE | SETB | SETBE | SETC | SETE | SETG | SETGE |
| SETL | SETLE | SETNA | SETNAE | SETNB | SETNBE | SETNC | SETNE |
| SETNG | SETNGE | SETNL | SETNLE | SETNO | SETNP | SETNS | SETNZ |
| SETO | SETP | SETPE | SETPO | SETS | SETZ | SHLD | SHRD |
| STOSD | | | | | | | |

**80486+**

BSWAP   CMP   XCHG   INVD   INVLPG  WBINVD  XADD

**Pentium**

CMPX   CHG8B  CPUID  RDMSR  RDTSC  RSM   WRMSR

Intel also added new versions of the MOV instructions in the 80386 for reading and writing control registers (CR0, CR2, CR3), debug registers (DR0, DR1, DR2, DR3, DR6, DR7), and test registers (TR6, TR7). In the 80486, Intel expanded the MOV instruction to read and write the additional test registers (TR3, TR4, TR5). In the Pentium, Intel added a new version of the MOV instructions to read and write a new control register (CR4). However, Intel removed support in the Pentium for the MOV instruction to read and write all test registers. The RDMSR and WRMSR instructions must be used instead, otherwise an invalid opcode exception will occur.

# Processor Type

Wouldn't it be great if the microprocessor could tell the software what it is? Well starting with the 80386 it could. After a reset, the microprocessor loads a Device ID in DH and a Stepping ID in DL. For an 80386, DH would be 3, while for a 80486, DH would be 4 and for a Pentium, DH would be 5. The only problem is the BIOS code that handled the reset didn't bother to save the information for other software to use! Intel added the new CPUID instruction in the Pentium so software could ask the microprocessor any time it wanted, but that instruction is not supported on the older microprocessors. Fortunately, there are some subtle differences that we can exploit to determine which microprocessor is in the system. By performing a series of tests, we can narrow down the list of microprocessors so only one is left. We want our tests to be harmless to the system so we are not going to force a reset to check DH ourselves. Besides we want to identify the microprocessors going all the way back to the 8086. We also want the tests to work even if someone runs the utility in a Windows DOS session. So no privilege instructions aside from CLI and STI will be used. We will call the utility TEST_CPU.

TEST_CPU uses a series of subroutine calls to help determine the type of Intel microprocessor. We are only going to test for Intel microprocessors. However, if a system does not have an Intel microprocessor, TEST_CPU may indicate the Intel microprocessor that most likely matches it. The complete listing for TEST_CPU.ASM is provided on diskette. We will cover the important parts in this chapter. Each subroutine in TEST_CPU must be executed in the following sequence:

```
        call    Check_8086
        jnz     Print_Old           ; Print if 8088/8086/80188/80186

        call    Check_80286
        jnz     Print_Old           ; Print if 80286

        call    Check_80386
        jnz     Print_Old           ; Print if 386DX or 386SX

        call    Check_80486
        jnz     Print_Old           ; Print if 486DX or 486SX

        call    Check_Pentium
        jnz     Print_New           ; Print if we know what it is
```

Each of these subroutines have the same output:

```
;----------------------------------------------------------------------------
; Check_XXXXX - Determine if the CPU type is a specific microprocessor.
;               If a match is found then load SI with the CPU text string,
;               otherwise load zero into SI. ZF matches SI contents.
;   Inputs
;     None
;
;   Outputs
;     AX = Undefined
;     SI = Address of CPU text string or zero (ZF matches results)
;----------------------------------------------------------------------------
FLAG_ID_MASK    equ 200000h
FLAG_AC_MASK    equ 40000h
FLAG_NT_MASK    equ 4000h
```

The easiest way to start identifying the type of Intel microprocessor in your system is by setting and resetting bits in the FLAGS/EFLAGS register. Each of these subroutines uses this register in some way to help determine the microprocessor type. Let's start with the first subroutine.

```
Check_8086    proc
              push    di                      ; Save registers
              push    cx
              xor     si,si                   ; Assume no match
;
; First test is whether we can reset the NT flag
;
              pushf                           ; Save original flags
              cli                             ; Disable interrupts
              pushf                           ; Get current flags
              pop     ax
              or      ax,FLAG_NT_MASK         ; Clear only NT flag
              xor     ax,FLAG_NT_MASK
              push    ax
              popf                            ; Update flags
              pushf
              pop     ax                      ; Get "updated" flags
              popf                            ; Restore original flags
                                              ; (and restore interrupts)
              test    ax,FLAG_NT_MASK         ; Changed NT flag?
              jz      Finish_8086             ; Yes, not 8088/8086/80188/80186
              lea     si,Text_8088            ; No, assume we have an 8088
              lea     di,Text_8086            ; Second choice would be 8086
;
; Test whether it's an 8088/8086 or 80188/80186. The later will mask shift
; counts with 1Fh before shifting.
;
              mov     cl,21h                  ; Can't use 20h or ZF may
              mov     al,1                    ; not get set correctly
              shl     al,cl                   ; Is it an 8088/8086?
              jz      Check_8_Bit_Bus         ; Yes
              lea     si,Text_80188           ; No, assume we have an 80188
              lea     di,Text_80186           ; Second choice would be 80186
;
; Now we need to determine whether it's 8088/80188 (8-bit data bus) or
; 8086/80186 (16-bit data bus). Test whether the microprocessor has the
; 8-bit or 16-bit prefetcher unit by modifying an instruction after a jump.
;
Check_8_Bit_Bus:
              mov     ax,3                    ; Modify displacement 3
              call    Check_Prefetch          ; Did we modify instruction?
              jnz     Finish_8086             ; Yes, use first choice (8-bit)
              mov     si,di                   ; No,  use second choice (16-bit)
Finish_8086:
              pop     cx                      ; Restore registers
              pop     di
              or      si,si                   ; Set ZF to match results
              ret
Check_8086    endp
```

The NT flag was not defined for the Intel 8088, 8086, 80188, and 80186 microprocessors. These microprocessors always had this flag bit set to 1 and software can not reset it. Future Intel microprocessors allowed the NT flag to be set and cleared by software. So if we cannot reset the NT flag it has to be a pre-80286 Intel microprocessor. For any of our tests with the FLAGS/EFLAGS register we disabled interrupts to ensure the system timer or a device driver didn't interrupt us. If you decide to modify the TEST_CPU code to run under Windows as an 80286 protected mode application, please be warned that you may get different results. More importantly you may hang the system as the POPF instruction will not enable interrupts again. You will have to add a STI instruction after the POPF instruction. However, you can safely run TEST_CPU in a Windows DOS session.

The next test divides the pre-80286 Intel microprocessors into two groups: 8088/8086 and 80188/80186. The 80188/80186 added some new instructions, but we don't want to generate an invalid opcode exception to test which group a microprocessor belongs to. Fortunately, Intel also decided to change a few instructions to avoid wasting microprocessor cycles. Normally a programmer would not attempt to shift out more bits than a register held so Intel thought it could limit shifts to 31 bits by masking off the shift count. Most programs were unaffected by this change, but we can use this difference as a test. If we load register CL with a shift count such as 21h to left shift, the AX register then after 16 shifts the AX register is always cleared out on the 8088/8086. But because 80188/80186 masks the shift count, only one bit in the AX register is shifted out. We noticed that when we used a shift count of 20h, the ZF flag was not updated to match the AX register contents on a post-8088/8086 Intel microprocessor. This may have been a design oversight on Intel part, so we used 21h.

After we determine whether the microprocessor is a 8088/8086 or 80188/80186, we need to perform one more test in this subroutine. If the microprocessor is in the first group, is it a 8088 or 8086? If in the second group, is it a 80188 or 80186? For both groups the first choice has an 8-bit data bus and the second choice has a 16-bit data bus. Normally your software would not care about the size of the data bus because it gets the same results on either bus. In case you are not aware, the Intel microprocessor attempts to prefetch instructions while executing an instruction to improve performance. While one instruction is executing, the microprocessor is loading and preparing to execute the next instruction. Some instructions take a long time to execute so this time can be used to load an new instruction from memory. To hold these future instructions the microprocessor has a prefetch queue. The microprocessor will prefetch instructions until the prefetch queue is full or a jump occurs. If a jump occurs, the microprocessor has to discard the contents of the prefetch queue and start loading the instruction at the new address. Where are we going with all this? Hang on and we will get there. If a program attempts to modify an instruction in memory, the previous version of the instruction may already be loaded in the prefetch queue. In that case, the unmodified instruction will get executed unless a jump occurs before it. This is why if you use self-modifying code you should always perform an unconditional jump after making the modifications. On a Pentium, a jump does not always flush the prefetch queue, so the Pentium will look at the linear address of a memory location being modified to see if that linear address matches what is in the prefetch queue. However, even this does not work if the linear addresses are different, but paging maps the two linear addresses to the same physical memory page. Right now, though, we are just concerned with how to determine whether the microprocessor has a 8-bit or 16-bit data bus.

OK, we know if the instruction is in the prefetch queue it does not get modified. How does this help us determine the size of the data bus? The next piece of information we need is whether the microprocessor prefetches instructions in 8-bit units (for an 8-bit data bus) or 16-bit units (for a 16-bit data bus). On a 16-bit data bus, the microprocessor gets the entire 16-bit unit or none of it. On an 8-bit data bus, the microprocessor has to make two separate memory reads to fetch 16 bits. What if we have a code sequence that will modify an instruction at some displacement after a jump such that on an 8-bit bus the instruction is always modified but on the 16-bit data bus is not? Furthermore, how do we determine the correct displacement? Nice of you to ask. We can get the answer using the following routine:

```
;-------------------------------------------------------------------------
; Check_Prefetch  - Check to see if we can modify an instruction at a specific
;                   displacement after a jump. We can not modify displacement 0
;                   and we assume we can always modify after displacement 64.
;   Inputs
;     AX = instruction displacement (limited to 0 - 64)
;
;   Outputs
;     AX = 0 if could not modify instruction else undefined (ZF matches results)
;-------------------------------------------------------------------------
```

```
Check_Prefetch proc
                push    es                      ; Save registers
                push    si
                push    di
                push    dx
                push    cx
                push    bx

                mov     dx,ax                   ; Save displacement
                or      ax,ax                   ; Zero displacement?
                jz      Finish_Test             ; Yes, no need to test
                cmp     ax,64                   ; Displacement too big?
                ja      Finish_Test             ; Yes, no need to test
;
; We need to align the jump target address on a 16-byte boundary
;
                mov     ax,cs
                mov     es,ax                   ; Load ES with code segment
                lea     bx,cs:Test_Code         ; Get initial target address
                mov     di,bx
                mov     cx,80
                mov     al,90h                  ; Keep code reusable by filling
                rep     stosb                   ;    target area with nop's
                add     bx,15                   ;    Also ensure 4K page is loaded
                and     bx,0FFF0h               ; Align target to 16-byte
                mov     di,bx
                mov     al,0AAh                 ; Get "stosb" instruction
                stosb                           ; Place it at 0 displacement
                dec     di                      ; Restore 0 displacement offset
                add     di,dx                   ; Point to desired displacement
                mov     al,40h                  ; Get "inc ax" op-code to store
                cli                             ; Disable interrupts
                jmp     bx                      ; Flush prefetch queue
Test_Code:
                db      80 dup (90h)            ; string of "nop" instructions
                sti                             ; Restore interrupts
                cmp     al,40h                  ; Modified instruction?
                jne     Finish_Test             ; Yes
                xor     ax,ax                   ; No
Finish_Test:
                pop     bx                      ; Restore registers
                pop     cx
                pop     dx
                pop     di
                pop     si
                pop     es
                or      ax,ax                   ; Set SF to match results
                ret
Check_Prefetch endp
```

At first you might think this routine is overkill. Well, it is, but we also used it to help determine the difference between the Intel 386DX and 386SX microprocessors. We will discuss those microprocessors later. After we determined the special displacement values through testing, we could have rewritten Check_Prefetch for use in TEST_CPU, but we saved it intact for your benefit. You might be wondering why we disabled interrupts here. We did not want the system interrupting us and flushing the prefetch queue at the wrong moment. Regarding the comment about the 4K memory page, we also wanted to be sure that there was not a page miss while executing the critical part of Check_Prefetch. We successfully ran this code on both plain DOS and in a Windows DOS session.

Testing for an Intel 80286 was a bit easier. Once we knew the microprocessor was not a 8088, 8086, 80188 or 80186, we just needed to see if we could set the NT flag bit to 1. If we cannot, then it has to be an Intel 80286. However, this test is limited to running in Real Mode or Virtual 8086 Mode.

```
Check_80286    proc
               xor     si,si                   ; Assume no match
;
; Test whether we can set the NT flag (always zero in Real Mode on 80286)
;
               pushf                           ; Save original flags
               cli                             ; Disable interrupts
               pushf                           ; Get current flags
               pop     ax
               or      ax,FLAG_NT_MASK         ; Set NT flag
               push    ax
               popf                            ; Update flags
               pushf
               pop     ax                      ; Get "updated" flags
               popf                            ; Restore original flags
                                               ; (and restore interrupts)
               test    ax,FLAG_NT_MASK         ; Changed NT flag?
               jnz     Finish_80286            ; Yes, not 80286
               lea     si,Text_80286           ; No,  must be 80286
Finish_80286:
               or      si,si                   ; Set ZF to match results
               ret
Check_80286    endp
```

Once we know it's not an Intel 80286 or older microprocessor, then we know the microprocessor can handle 32-bit registers. Previously we used the .8086 assembler directive after .STACK 100h to ensure we generated only 8086 instructions. Now we use the .386 directive to allow us to safely use 32-bit operands and registers in our code.  We are still using 16-bit segments, but the assembler will provide operand-size override prefixes where we need them for 32-bit operations. You may notice in the following code that we added short on all the jumps. It ensures the assembler uses the minimum size of opcode to get us where we want to go. The first test for the 80386 is simply to see if we can set the AC flag bit in the 32-bit EFLAGS register. The AC flag is new for the 80486 and on the 80386 the AC flag is always zero. Here we have to be especially careful to avoid an alignment check exception occurring should the stack not be properly aligned while running on a 80486 or higher microprocessor.

```
;**********************************************************************
; From here to the end of this module is mixed 16-bit and 32-bit code
;**********************************************************************

                .386
Check_80386     proc
                xor     si,si                   ; Assume no match
;
; Test whether we can set the AC flag (always zero on 80386), but we need
; to make sure the stack is properly aligned to avoid an exception on
; 80486 or higher microprocessor.
;
                push    bp                      ; Save register
                mov     bp,sp                   ; Save current stack pointer
                and     sp,0FFFCh               ; Align stack to 32-bit
                push    eax                     ; Save 32-bit register

                pushfd                          ; Save original 32-bit flags
                cli                             ; Disable interrupts
                pushfd                          ; Get current flags
                pop     eax
                or      eax,FLAG_AC_MASK        ; Set AC flag
                push    eax
                popfd                           ; Update flags
                pushfd
                pop     eax                     ; Get "updated" flags
                popfd                           ; Restore original 32-bit flags
                                                ; (and restore interrupts)
                test    eax,FLAG_AC_MASK        ; AC flag still set?
                jnz     short Finish_80386      ; Yes, not an 80386
;
; Now we need to determine whether it's 386SX (16-bit data bus) or
; 386DX (32-bit data bus). It is possible the system could have a
; 16-bit data bus and still have an 386DX (it supports a 16-bit data bus)
; but it's very unlikely because the system performance would be slightly
; worse than having a 386SX. So test whether the microprocessor has the
; 16-bit or 32-bit prefetcher unit by modifying an instruction after a jump.
;
```

```
            lea     si,Text_386DX          ; Assume 386DX
            mov     ax,11                  ; Modify displacment 11
            call    Check_Prefetch         ; Did we modify instruction?
            jz      short Finish_80386     ; No,  must have 32-bit bus
            lea     si,Text_386SX          ; Yes, has to be 386SX
                                           ; (or might as well be)
Finish_80386:
            pop     eax                    ; Restore 32-bit register
            mov     sp,bp                  ; Restore stack pointer
            pop     bp                     ; Restore register
            or      si,si                  ; Set ZF to match results
            ret
Check_80386 endp
```

The second part of the Check_80386 subroutine identifies whether the
microprocessor is a 386DX and 386SX. Now some people might say you cannot
tell them apart. Both the Microsoft's MSD.EXE and Symantec's SYSINFO.EXE
utilities do not. Maybe you don't need to know. Our first approach at
determining the difference did not work out well. We will discuss why in a
moment. Then we decided to use the same approach we used for the Intel 8088
and 8086. The 386DX has a 32-bit data bus while the 386SX has a 16-bit data
bus. Our second approach using the Check_Prefetch subroutine worked well
once we came up with the right displacement. Will it work 100% of the time?
Only testing and time will tell. Let's look at our first approach as a lesson in
problem determination. We wanted to use the ET flag bit in the CR0 control
register. The 80386 can support either a 80287 or a 80387 numeric coprocessor.
The ET flag determines which coprocessor. But on the 386SX, this flag is always
set to 1 as the 386SX only supports the 387SX coprocessor.

```
FLAG_ET_MASK    equ 0010h
FLAG_PE_MASK    equ 0001h

            pushfd                         ; Save original 32-bit flags
            cli                            ; Disable interrupts
;
; To determine whether it's a 386DX or 386SX we can first check the ET
; flag in CR0. We can look at the lower 16-bit of CR0 using SMSW without
; worrying about getting a privilege instruction exception.
;
            lea     si,Text_386DX          ; Assume 386DX
            smsw    ax                     ; Get lower part of CR0
            test    ax,FLAG_ET_MASK        ; ET bit is off?
            jz      short Finish_80386     ; Yes, has to be 386DX
;
```

```
; Now it gets a bit harder since having ET on doesn't mean it's an 386SX.
; If a numeric coprocessor is not present then it has to be a 386SX.
;
                lea     si,Text_386SX           ; Assume 386SX
                call    Check_Coprocessor       ; Coprocessor in system?
                jnz     short Finish_80386       ; No, has to be 386SX
;
; So now it's either a 386DX with 387DX or 386SX with 387SX. To determine
; which we need to see if we can make the system think it has a 80287 by
; resetting the ET bit. But we can only do this as an application when we
; are in Real Mode (not Virtual 8086 mode).
;
                lea     si,Text_386             ; Assume can't tell
                smsw    ax                      ; Get lower part of CR0
                test    ax,FLAG_PE_MASK         ; Are we in protected mode?
                jnz     Finish_80386            ; Yes, bail out
                lea     si,Text_386DX           ; No,  assume it's a 386DX
                mov     eax,CR0                 ; Can't do this in Virtual 8086
                or      eax,FLAG_ET_MASK        ; Try resetting ET flag
                xor     eax,FLAG_ET_MASK
                mov     CR0,eax
                mov     eax,CR0
                test    eax,FLAG_ET_MASK        ; ET flag now off?
                jz      Restore_CR0             ; Yes, has to be 386DX
                lea     si,Text_386SX           ; No,  has to be 386SX
                jmp     Finish_80386
Restore_CR0:
                or      eax,FLAG_ET_MASK
                mov     CR0,eax
Finish_80306:
                popfd                           ; Restore original 32-bit flags
                                                ; (and restore interrupts)
```

Nice try, but testing showed it did not always work. Besides it took us away from our goal of not using privilege instructions. We found one 386DX system that had no coprocessor but the ET bit was still set. Then if you have EMM386.EXE active and you run this routine outside of Windows you will still be in Virtual 8086 mode, so the PE flag will always be set. Seems a shame to keep ending up with just plain 386 like the other utilities. It just goes to show how important is testing. You can read all the reference books you want including this one, but you never really know until you test it. There's also something to say about keeping trying since Check_Prefetch worked for us.

Check_80486 is next. Seems straight forward enough. If it is higher than a 80386 and it doesn't support the new CPUID instruction then it must be a 486. Right? Not quite, as we will explain later. Here's the subroutine.

```
Check_80486    proc
               xor     si,si                   ; Assume no match
;
; Make sure the stack is aligned to a 32-bit boundary
;
               push    bp                      ; Save register
               mov     bp,sp                   ; Save current stack pointer
               and     sp,0FFFCh               ; Align stack to 32-bit
               push    ebx                     ; Save 32-bit registers
               push    eax
;
; Test whether the CPUID instruction is supported on this microprocessor by
; toggling the ID flag.
;
               pushfd                          ; Save original 32-bit flags
               cli                             ; Disable interrupts
               pushfd                          ; Get current flags
               pop     eax
               mov     ebx,eax
               and     ebx,FLAG_ID_MASK        ; Save ID flag
               xor     eax,FLAG_ID_MASK        ; Toggle ID flag
               push    eax
               popfd                           ; Update flags
               pushfd
               pop     eax                     ; Get "updated" flags
               popfd                           ; Restore original 32-bit flags
                                               ; (and restore interrupts)
               and     eax,FLAG_ID_MASK        ; Only want ID flag
               cmp     eax,ebx                 ; ID flag changed?
               jne     short Finish_80486      ; Yes, not an 80486
;
; The only difference between a 486DX and 486SX is whether the numeric
; coprocessor unit is present inside the chip. (The 486SX doesn't have one.)
; So if there is no coprocessor present it has to be a 486SX. But if one
; is present then it could be a 486SX with 487SX or a 486DX. Since installing
; a 487SX disables the 486SX, for all practical purposes a 487SX is a
; 486DX and will therefore be reported as a 486DX.
;
               lea     si,Text_486SX           ; Assume 486SX
               call    Check_Coprocessor       ; Coprocessor in system?
               jnz     short Finish_80486      ; No,  has to be 486SX
               lea     si,Text_486DX           ; Yes, treat as a 486DX
Finish_80486:
               pop     eax                     ; Restore 32-bit registers
               pop     ebx
               mov     sp,bp                   ; Restore stack pointer
               pop     bp                      ; Restore register
               or      si,si                   ; Set ZF to match results
               ret
Check_80486    endp
```

We didn't check to see if the ID flag in the EFLAGS register was always on or off for a 486. Intel said the ability to change the ID flag indicates whether the microprocessors supports the CPUID instruction introduced in the Pentium. Unlike the 386DX/386SX effort, we did not waste much energy trying to tell whether a microprocessor was a 486DX or 486SX. If there is no numeric coprocessor then it is a 486SX. If a coprocessor exists then we consider it a 486DX even though the label on the machine may say otherwise. It should be hard for anyone to think the 487SX is as just a numeric coprocessor when once it's installed, it disables the 486SX chip. While Intel may not like the idea, it's possible to build a system with only the 487SX chip present.

How do we know if there is a numeric coprocessor present? Well we try to get it to report status to us. Here's a subroutine that works for all Intel 80x86 microprocessors including the Pentium.

```
                .DATA
FPU_Status      dw      0
                .CODE
;-------------------------------------------------------------------------
; Check_Coprocessor - Determine if a numeric coprocessor is in the system
;                     by trying to retrieve the hardware status.
;   Inputs
;     None
;
;   Outputs
;     AX = 0 if coprocessor exists else undefined (ZF matches results)
;-------------------------------------------------------------------------
Check_Coprocessor proc
                mov     FPU_Status,0FFFFh    ; Reset floating point status
                fninit                       ; Reset floating point hardware
                fnstsw  FPU_Status           ; Get floating point h/w status
                mov     ax,FPU_Status        ; FPU_Status = 0 if h/w exists
                or      ax,ax                ; Set ZF to match results
                ret
Check_Coprocessor endp
```

Last stop for determining Intel microprocessor type is the new Pentium. Well, sort of, but we will get back to the 486 question soon. Up to now we only dealt with microprocessors that did not know about the CPUID instruction. Remember the information that Intel provided after a reset in the DX register? Well, now you don't need a reset. Now you can get the microprocessor family, model and stepping level without being a system programmer. In fact, assuming the other microprocessor vendors don't dare copy Intel's signature ID of "GenuineIntel", with the CPUID instruction you will know for sure if the microprocessor was made by Intel. In case your assembler doesn't generate the CPUID instruction opcode yet, we also provided a CPU_ID macro. Check_Pentium is a bit different from the other processor type subroutines because it knows where to stick the information for family, model and stepping level. What Check_Pentium returns is a string pointer for just whether the part is genuine Intel or not.

```
CPU_ID          MACRO
                db      0Fh                     ; New Pentium CPUID instruction
                db      0A2h
                ENDM

Check_Pentium   proc
                xor     si,si                   ; Assume no match
;
; Make sure the stack is aligned to a 32-bit boundary
;
                push    bp                      ; Save register
                mov     bp,sp                   ; Save current stack pointer
                and     sp,0FFFCh               ; Align stack to 32-bit
                push    edx                     ; Save 32-bit registers
                push    ecx
                push    ebx
                push    eax
;
; First determine whether we can get the family, model, and stepping level ID
;
                xor     eax,eax                 ; Get ID string
                CPU_ID
                cmp     eax,1                   ; Can we get the ID?
                jb      short Finish_Pentium    ; No, treat as unknown
;
; Check whether this is a "genuine" Intel microprocessor.
;
                lea     si,Text_Clone           ; Assume not genuine Intel
                cmp     ebx,756E6547h           ; 1st part match Intel ID?
                jne     short Check_Family      ; No
                cmp     edx,49656E69h           ; 2nd part match Intel ID?
                jne     short Check_Family      ; No
                cmp     ecx,6C65746Eh           ; 3rd part match Intel ID?
                jne     short Check_Family      ; No
                lea     si,Text_Intel           ; Yes, have the genuine part
;
; Get microprocessor family, model, and stepping level ID
;
Check_Family:
                mov     eax,1                   ; Get family, model, stepping ID
                CPU_ID
```

```
            mov     bx,ax              ; Save family, model, stepping ID
            Convert_Hex                ; Make stepping ID printable
            mov     Text_Stepping,al   ; Place it in text
            mov     al,bl
            shr     al,4               ; Get model ID
            Convert_Hex                ; Make it printable
            mov     Text_Model,al      ; Place it in text
            mov     al,bh              ; Get family ID
            Convert_Hex                ; Make it printable
            mov     Text_Family,al     ; Place it in text

            mov     Text_Pentium,' '   ; Make code reuseable
            cmp     al,'5'             ; Is it a Pentium?
            je      short Finish_Pentium ; Yes, we are finish
            mov     Text_Pentium,0     ; No, leave out Pentium text
Finish_Pentium:
            pop     eax                ; Restore 32-bit registers
            pop     ebx
            pop     ecx
            pop     edx
            mov     sp,bp              ; Restore stack pointer
            pop     bp                 ; Restore register
            or      si,si              ; Set ZF to match results
            ret
Check_Pentium endp
```

We left out the Convert_Hex macro in the chapter, but it is in the TEST_CPU.ASM source file. The macro converts the lower 4-bits (nibble) of the AL register into a printable character. Well, maybe it would have been less trouble to stick on this page, but then again maybe it will get you to look at the rest of the program on diskette. Anyway, back to the 486 question. Intel did not provide the CPUID instruction until it brought out the Pentium. It seemed a safe bet if the microprocessor supported the new instruction it had to be a Pentium or higher. Imagine our surprise when we found one 486DX2/66 MHz system that failed the 486 test. However, it knew about the CPUID instruction and gave us a family ID of 4. Yet a different 486DX2/50 MHz passed the 486 test because it did not support the CPUID instruction. Now we are sure Intel thinks a Pentium is more advanced than a 486DX2, but apparently they couldn't resist slipping the CPUID instruction into some 486DX2 chips. Goes to show that once you think you got everything figured out, Intel changes the rules of the game again.

# Numeric Coprocessor History

Well it's time to discuss the Intel numeric coprocessors. The numeric coprocessor can process floating point calculations far faster than the Intel microprocessors using integer operations. The numeric coprocessor unit is either off-chip for the 8088, 8086, 80188, 80186, 80286, 386DX and 386SX microprocessors, or the coprocessor unit is on-chip for the 486DX, 487SX and Pentium microprocessors. In 1980, Intel produced the 8087, its first 80x86 family numeric coprocessor. The 8087 worked with the 8088, 8086, 80188 and 80186 microprocessors. In 1985, Intel produced the 80287 coprocessor to work with the 80286. In 1987, Intel produced the 80387 coprocessor to work with the 80386. Since the 80386 was produced two years earlier, the 80386 also worked with the 80287. Like the 80386, the 80387 was renamed to 387DX when the 387SX came out to support the 386SX microprocessor in 1990.

As a programmer, the coprocessor appears to simply extend the instruction set of the microprocessor to include new floating point operations and data types. You code your floating point instructions in the same stream as your other microprocessor instructions. What happens at the hardware level depends on the type of microprocessor and coprocessor you have. All floating point instructions have the same five first bits which are decoded by the microprocessor as ESC instructions. Basically, the microprocessor ignores the floating point instructions and permits the coprocessor to handle them. When the microprocessor encounters a WAIT instruction, it suspends itself until the coprocessor becomes inactive after finishing any prior floating point operation.

That's the simple explanation. Let's look at a system with a 8086 microprocessor and 8087 coprocessor. On the system board, the 8087 is wired directly to the 8086. The 8087 will watch for floating point instructions on the data bus being fetched by the microprocessor. The 8087 ignores any instruction that does not start with the ESC prefix. When the microprocessor processes the ESC instruction, it either treats it as a NOP or calculates the memory address and performs a dummy read to that location. The microprocessor ignores the data returned by the dummy read. The 8087 meanwhile has decoded the same instruction and will latch the memory address generated by the microprocessor. The 8087 will use the latched memory address to either load or store floating point data. The 8087 can tell the microprocessor to stay off the data and address buses so the 8087 can use them. The microprocessor continues to execute instructions until it gets a WAIT instruction, which suspends the microprocessor until the 8087 completes its floating point operation and signals the microprocessor to continue. To ensure the numeric coprocessor is always ready to process the next floating point instruction, some programmers always place a WAIT instruction before each floating point instruction.

On a system with a 80286 microprocessor and 80287 coprocessor, the hardware interaction is different, although the floating point software remains the same. The microprocessor uses I/O ports 00F8h, 00FAh and 00FCh to communicate with the coprocessor. The coprocessor no longer watches the data bus for floating point instructions being fetched by the microprocessor. Instead, the microprocessor decodes the ESC instructions to pass the floating point operation and data to the coprocessor and retrieves the floating point results from the coprocessor over the I/O ports. The programmer is not aware of these ports and Intel has reserved port addresses 00F8h to 00FFh for the 80286/80287 interface. Unlike the 8086/8087 system, the 80286/80287 system does not need WAIT instructions to synchronize all floating point operations. The WAIT instruction is only needed when loading or storing floating point data to memory. However, using an unnecessary WAIT instruction doesn't hurt and some programmers continue to use the WAIT instruction even when not needed.

On a system with a 80386 microprocessor and 80387 coprocessor, the hardware interaction is similar to the 80286 and 80287 with two exceptions. The data bus is now 32-bits and the reserved port addresses are 800000F8h through 800000FFh. On a system with a 386SX microprocessor and 387SX coprocessor, the data bus is back to 16-bit but the port address range is 8000F8h through 8000FFh. For a 486DX, 487SX and Pentium there are no off-chip connections to access the numeric coprocessor units. A WAIT instruction is no longer required to ensure synchronization of floating point operations with the Intel 387DX/SX coprocessor, 486DX and Pentium.

## Numeric Coprocessor Type

Maybe you were wondering why, in TEST_CPU, we omitted to identify which numeric coprocessor was used in a system. There's not much to do, so we left it to you. Once you know what type of microprocessor is used and whether a coprocessor is present then the answer is easy. See the following table. The only microprocessor requiring a bit more work on your part is the 386DX. You can use the ET bit in the Machine Status Word register to detect whether the coprocessor is a 80287 or 387DX.

Table 2.4 Intel Numeric Coprocessors

| Microprocessor | Coprocessor |
| --- | --- |
| 8088 | 8087 |
| 8086 | |
| 80188 | |
| 80186 | |
| 80286 | 80287 |
| 386DX | 80286 |
| | 387DX |
| 386SX | 387SX |

## Intel Compatible Microprocessors

Maybe "clone" is too harsh of a term for the other companies trying to build microprocessors that will accurately execute your DOS and Windows programs. After all, it's people like you that have put Intel where it is today because of the millions of PC systems sold. Many PC users probably couldn't care less how the Intel microprocessors work because all they see is the applications on the machines. But if you are going to write Intel assembly programs, you are going to care, and maybe by now you are starting to realize just how complex the Intel microprocessors can be. It's quite an amazing feat of engineering for any company to come up with new microprocessors that are compatible with Intel. How compatible are they? Well, as you have seen, even Intel can't build new microprocessors that are 100% compatible with the old ones. Otherwise the TEST_CPU program would be a total waste of time. That's not to say that other companies' microprocessors are not accurate enough. For the most part they are very accurate or they would not last very long in this business.

Do you have to worry about which company's microprocessor your assembly code runs on? For most programmers the answer is no. All the burden is on these companies to ensure your code will run. However, if you write BIOS code or system code out of the norm, then you may need to get the programming reference material from these companies. Let's use IBM as an example. If the IBM 386SLC was 100% compatible with the Intel 386SX, there would be no way to enable its on-chip 8K cache and run faster, because the Intel 386SX did not have an on-chip cache. So obviously, the IBM 386SLC is a superset of the Intel 386SX and some system programmer needed to write code that only worked on the IBM 386SLC.

Who are these companies that make Intel compatible microprocessors? Well, we've listed them in Table 2.6. We omitted the companies that manufactured Intel designs as second sources, which is why the 286 column is empty. Please forgive us if we overlooked anything.

**Table 2.6   Intel Compatible Microprocessors**

| Intel | 8086 | 286 | 386 | 486 | Pentium |
|---|---|---|---|---|---|
| Advanced Micro Devices (AMD) | | | 386SX<br>386DX<br>386DXLV | 486SX<br>486SXLV<br>486DX<br>486DXLV | K5* |
| Chips and Technologies | F8680 | | 38600SX<br>38605SX<br>38600DX<br>38605DX | | |
| Cyrix | | | | 486SLC<br>486DLC | M1* |
| IBM | | | 386SLC | 486SLC2<br>Blue Lightning | |
| NextGen | | | | | Nx586 |
| NEC | V20<br>V30 | | | | |
| Texas Instruments (TI) | | | | TI486SLC/E<br>TI486DLC/E | |

* Announced, but not available as of 12/94

# Summary

Well, we touched on the more advanced features of the Intel 80286/80386/80486 and Pentium microprocessors. We went over a program to tell the Intel microprocessors apart and we looked at floating point operations. Now you may have a better idea why programming Intel microprocessors in assembly language can be so complicated. A high level language like C can really hide you from what goes on "down below". You probably learned more about Intel microprocessors and coprocessors in this chapter than you may ever want to know. You didn't? Well, have we got more for you!

# CHAPTER THREE

# Fundamental System Programming Techniques

## Introduction

System programming is probably the most difficult (as well as the most interesting) part of programming. Programs of this kind directly control the system and hardware environment and give you access to all the hardware facilities. Of course, writing them demands extensive knowledge of both PC hardware and assembly language.

In this chapter we will discuss basic principles of system programming and some hardware features connected with it. We'll describe the interrupt system of the PC family and you'll see how to write your own interrupt handlers and TSR programs. Finally we'll include an overview of the BIOS and CMOS memory.

# Interrupts and the Interrupt Vector Table

Every now and then, all hardware components generate interrupts: the timer and disks drive, printers and modems, etc. The BIOS, device drivers and the operating system recognize and handle these inerrupts, so we don't normally notice this background work. Still, they are an essential part of the computer architecture.

Some interrupts occur at certain moments, e.g. the system clock generates interrupts every 55 miliseconds. Other interrupts occur only on specific events - when you press a key, the keyboard controller generates an interrupt.

80x86 systems handle 256 different interrupts. A number of them are used by the hardware and operating system. Some are used by the processor. Others are available for application programs.

When an interrupt occurs, the processor passes control to a special procedure called an interrupt service routine (ISR). Its location is determined by a pointer (vector) in the Interrupt Vector Table. Every interrupt has a number from 0 to 255, so the Interrupt Vector Table is an array of 256 pointers, which resides at the address 0000:0000.

At power-up time, the BIOS and the operating system initialize the required vectors. Later (if necessary) DOS, BIOS, a driver, or an application program can set a new vector in the Interrupt Vector Table.

When an interrupt occurs, the processor performs the following steps:

- It saves the current program's state on the stack so it can return to it when the interrupt has been handled.

- It fetches the interrupt vector.

- It transfers control to the routine pointed to by the vector.

- When the routine is finished, it returns to the interrupted program.

What must be saved, and when? The processor only saves three things when an interrupt happens: CS, IP, and the flags. CS and IP make the instruction pointer. The machine flags contain information about the current state of the program being executed. These three registers allow resumption of the interrupted execution.

The CPU saves the registers by pushing them on to the stack: first, the Flags Register, then CS and IP. Next, it loads CS:IP with the segment and offset from the interrupt vector table and the execution of the ISR begins.

Now we'll take a closer look at the 80x86 interrupt system. Interrupts can be generated by the CPU, hardware, or a program. They change the normal sequence of program execution. Their purpose is to process external asynchronous events (hardware interrupts) or synchronous events (generated by programs via the INT instruction).

There's a feature in the 8086+ processors that allows you to disable (mask) all interrupts except the Non-Maskable Interrupt (NMI), which uses vector 2. NMI has its own special pin on the CPU chip and normally reports catastrophic hardware failures. There are also two internal processor interrupts which can't be suppressed. All other interrupts are maskable. The Interrupt Flag (IF) indicates whether interrupts are disabled. When IF is clear, all maskable interrupts will be ignored by the CPU. You can control it by the instructions STI (enable interrupts) and CLI (disable interrupts). When an interrupt occurs, the CPU clears the IF to prevent all other interrupts from interfering with the invoked ISR.

## Exceptions

The 80286 and higher processors have a new feature called exceptions. Exceptions are akin to interrupts (both are processed in a similar way), but their purpose is different.

Interrupts deal with various system resources of the PC, whereas exceptions are for error handling and recovering protection faults. They are considered a separate topic and are explained in more detail in Chapter 15 'Protected Mode'.

# Programmable Interrupt Controller

The idea of hardware interrupt mechanisms revolutionized computer science. It's clear why this was a breakthrough - they mean that peripheral devices occupy the processor only when there's really something for them to do. Most of the time the CPU doesn't have to worry about them.

You normally install several interrupt capable devices in your PC. Because Intel processors only have one interrupt pin, there's a special chip (8259 Programmable Interrupt Controller or simply PIC), which allows several devices to share it. Its three main purposes are:

- To inform the processor which device is interrupting. Each PIC can manage up to 8 peripheral devices.

- To mask interrupts specified by the programmer. Masked interrupts will not be processed by the CPU.

- To handle several interrupts which occur simultaneously using a system of priorities.

Starting with the IBM PC/AT machines, two PICs are installed on the motherboard. There are 16 interrupt lines. These lines are numbered IRQ0 to IRQ15. The two Interrupt Controllers make a cascade system. This means that one line (IRQ2) is used to connect the slave PIC to the master one. IRQ2 is, of course, prevented from being used, but 8 new inputs are added. The output of this cascade system is connected to the processor's INTR pin.

Figure 3.1. shows possible interrupt inputs with standard peripheral devices (interrupt sources) connected to each pin. The figure also reflects standard priorities. According to the standard PIC initialization, the system timer (IRQ0) has the greatest privilege level.

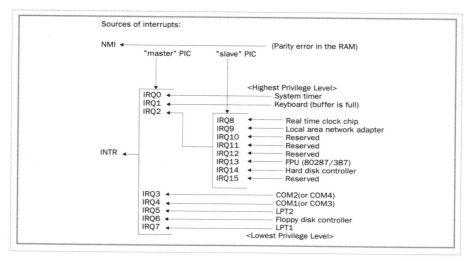

**Figure 3.1 Hardware Interrupt Sources**

The IRQ numbers are considered the identifiers of the inputs of this two-PIC cascade system. They represent the names of the signals passing through the chips. Vector numbers should not be confused with IRQ numbers - IRQ numbers don't correspond to interrupt vectors. IRQ0 uses vector 8 (not 0), IRQ1 uses vector 9, and so on.

An I8259 PIC consists of the units shown in Figure 3.2:

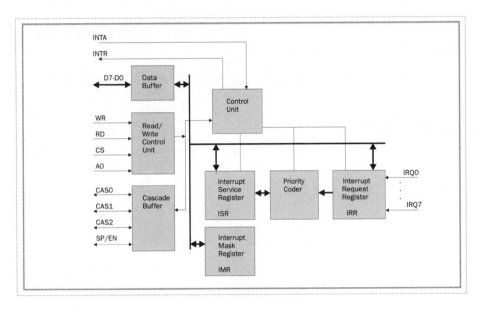

**Figure 3.2 The Structure of the PIC I8259**

Here are some points to note:

- The Data Buffer is used to connect the PIC to the computer system bus.

- The Read/Write Control Unit is responsible for initialization of the chip and operations with internal registers. The I8259 has 7 accessible registers: Operation Control Word 1, 2, 3 and Initialization Command Word 1, 2, 3, 4.

- The Interrupt Service Register (ISR) consists of 8 bits. When a PIC receives an interrupt request, it sets the corresponding bit in the ISR. A bit set in the ISR prohibits all the bits corresponding to interrupt requests with lower priority.

- The Interrupt Request Register (IRR) and the Priority Coder are used to access and manage interrupt requests from pins IRQ0 to IRQ7. The IRR is a bit vector that indicates which IRQ hardware events are waiting to be processed. The highest level interrupt is reset when the CPU acknowledges the interrupt.

- The Interrupt Mask Register allows some interrupt requests to be masked out.

- The Control Unit generates the INTR signal (Interrupt Request) and accepts INTA (Interrupt Allowed).

- The Cascade Buffer determines the slave PIC using pins CAS0 to CAS2.

## Processing Interrupts

Now that you are familiar with the interrupt hardware, here is the complete sequence of events that occur when an interrupt is processed from a peripheral device.

1   A device connected to a certain IRQ pin sends an interrupt request. The corresponding bit in the IRR is set.

2   The I8259 chip processes the request taking into account the mask and priorities. It then generates the INT signal for the CPU.

3   When the processor receives this signal, it finishes the current instruction and sends two pulses on the INTA line. The first pulse informs the PIC that the processor is ready to accept an interrupt. The PIC sets the corresponding bit in the ISR and clears a bit in the IRR. The second pulse causes the PIC to output the vector number to the data bus.

4   The processor pushes the values of the Flags Register, CS and IP on to the stack, as shown in Figure 3.3.

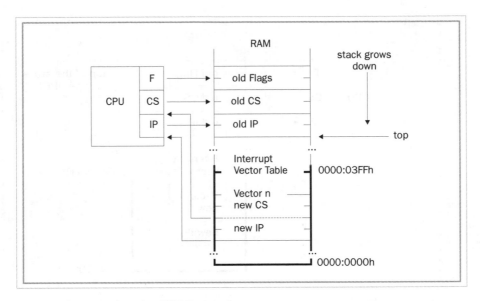

**Figure 3.3 Processing the INT Instruction**

**5**   The processor clears the TF and IF flags.

**6**   CS and IP are loaded with the new values from the Interrupt Vector Table.

**7**   Control is transferred to the corresponding Interrupt Service Routine.

**8**   The IRET instruction at the end of the Interrupt Service Routine restores the old values of CS, IP, and the Flags Register, as shown in Figure 3.4. The processor then continues execution of the interrupted program.

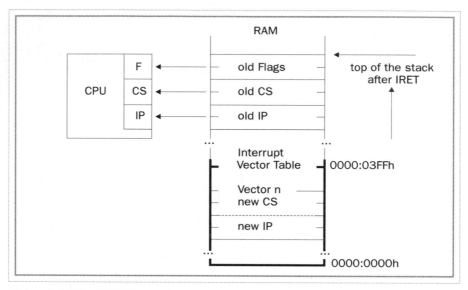

**Figure 3.4 The IRET Instruction**

# Initialization Command and Operation Control Words

Now back to the chips. The PIC accepts seven 8-bit commands. They are named ICW1 to ICW4 (Initialization Command Words) and OCW1 to OCW3 (Operation Control Words). There are two ports for each PIC. On the PC/AT architecture, the master PIC is accessed through ports 20h and 21h, the slave PIC through ports A0h and A1h. The I8259 differentiates among OCW1, 2, 3 and ICW1, 2, 3, 4 by the port addresses, special constant bits for each word, and the sending sequence (ICW1 must be always followed by ICW2, then ICW3, and then ICW4). You can send OCWs (Operation Control Words) to switch the I8259 into various interrupt modes at any point after initialization. To demonstrate possible ways of initialization and interrupt processing, below is an explanation of the meaning of the bits in each word:

## ICW1 (Port 20h or A0h)

Bit 0    If this is set, the PIC will expect ICW4 during initialization.

Bit 1    This must be clear if there's a slave PIC. If there's only one PIC, this bit must be set.

Bit 2    This must be clear if interrupt vectors are 4 bytes long (it is set in the case of 8-byte vectors).

Bit 3          If this bit is clear, it forces the edge triggered mode (80x86 systems), if it is set, it forces the level triggered mode (PS/2 systems).

Bit 4          Constant bit. When this bit is set, the PIC recognizes a command as ICW1.

Bits 5,6,7     These must be clear.

For example, command 11h (00010001b) sent to port 20h is interpreted by the master PIC as ICW1, demanding a cascade system of PICs, edge triggered mode, 4-byte vectors. The PIC will expect ICW4 in the initialization sequence.

## ICW2 (Port 21h or A1h)

This command must be the next command sent to PIC after ICW1.

Bits 0 - 2     Undefined.

Bits 3 - 7     These specify the five highest bits of the interrupt vector number for IRQ0 to IRQ7. These five bits and the IRQ number make the vector number for each IRQ.

## ICW3 (Port 21h or A1h)

This command must be the next command sent to the PIC after ICW2. It must correspond to the IRQ line which connects the slave PIC to the master, which in AT architecture is always IRQ2. For the master PIC, this command must be 04h (00000100b). For the slave PIC, this command must be 02h. For some strange reason the master recognizes the bit position, whereas the slave recognizes the actual value!

## ICW4 (Port 21h or A1h)

Bit 0          This must be 1.

Bit 1          This selects End Of Interrupt (EOI) mode. 1 corresponds to auto EOI and 0 corresponds to normal EOI. In auto EOI mode, the PIC automatically clears the bit that corresponds to the interrupt being processed, after the second pulse on the INTA line. In normal mode, the processor has to write OCW2 into the PIC at the end of every interrupt service routine.

Bits 2,3       These determine the buffered mode.

Bit 4          1 turns on Special Fully Nested Mode (SFNM) and 0 turns on Sequential Mode.

Bits 5,6,7     These are not used (they must be zero).

Once it has received the last initialization word, a PIC interprets all other commands sent to its ports as Operation Control Words unless it recognizes another ICW1. Then initialization begins anew.

## OCW1

You can directly modify the IMR (Interrupt Mask Register) writing to port 21h or A1h (OCW1). Each of the eight bits in OCW1 masks or enables one of the eight IRQ interrupt signals. Bit 0 controls IRQ0, bit 1 controls IRQ1, and so on. When a bit in the IMR is set, the corresponding interrupt is disabled. When you need to change this setting for a particular IRQ line, the proper way is to read the whole byte from the IMR (via OCW3 described below), modify the required bit and then write the new value back as OCW1.

## OCW2

OCW2 is sent to port 20h or A0h to inform a PIC that the CPU has finished processing the current interrupt. This word determines how the PIC will change priorities and what bit to clear in the Interrupt Service Register. You can influence the order of priorities in three ways: leave them as they are, rotate them by one (0 becomes 7, 1 becomes 0, etc.), or rotate them so that a line with a particular priority becomes the least privileged. An example is shown in Table 3.1, where numbers are the IRQ lines. The last column shows the rotation when priority 2 (IRQ3) is made the least privileged.

**Table 3.1. Rotation of IRQ Priorities**

| Privilege | Before | After rotation by one | After priority is decreased |
|-----------|--------|-----------------------|-----------------------------|
| most | 0 | 1 | 4 |
| | 1 | 2 | 5 |
| | 2 | 3 | 6 |
| | 3 | 4 | 7 |
| | 4 | 5 | 0 |
| | 5 | 6 | 1 |
| | 6 | 7 | 2 |
| least | 7 | 0 | 3 |

Bits 0 - 2      These determine the interrupt priority level to act upon. The level selected will be used to clear a bit in the Interrupt Service Register or to set a priority.

Bits 3, 4      These must be 0 (constant bits for OCW2).

Bit 5      If this is set it means End Of Interrupt.

Bit 6      This specifies how IRQ priorities are to be rotated. If this bit is clear, it means "rotate by one"; if set, then the line with the priority specified by bits 0, 1, and 2 becomes the least privileged.

Bit 7      If this is clear, the priorities remain the same; if set, they are rotated as specified in bit 6.

## OCW3

OCW3 is sent to port 20h or A0h is used for reading ISR and IRR registers and masking hardware interrupts.

Bit 1      If this is set, then bit 0 specifies the register to read (set for ISR, clear for IRR).

Bit 2      If set, the PIC enters polling mode (after that you can read the number of the IRQ line which caused the interrupt from this port). The Poll command is used if one program services several devices.

Bits 3, 4      These must be 1 and 0 respectively (constant bits for OCW3).

Bit 6      If set, then bit 5 controls special mask mode (1 turns it on, 0 - off). When this mode is on, all requests are processed with no privileges in order of appearance. This mode is used when you don't want to disable interrupts from devices with a lower privilege level.

Bit 7      Not used.

The initialization procedure for the PIC consists of the following steps:

**1**      Write ICW1.

**2**      Write ICW2.

**3**      If two PICs are cascaded (as on ATs), write ICW3.

**4**      Write an optional ICW4 (this must be demanded in ICW1).

Initialization starts from the master PIC in the cascade system. The following sequence of instructions performs a standard initialization of PICs.

## Master PIC

```
mov al,11h
out 20h,al    ;ICW1, level triggered mode, cascade mode,
              ;vectors are 4-byte wide, ICW4 present.
mov al,8
out 21h,al    ;ICW2, vector addresses are in the range from
              ;8h - 0Fh.
mov al,4
out 21h,al    ;ICW3, slave PIC is connected to IRQ2.

mov al,1
out 21h,al    ;ICW4, sequential mode.
```

## Slave PIC

```
mov al,11h
out A0h,al    ;ICW1, level triggered mode, cascade mode,
              ;ICW4 present.
mov al,70h
out A1h,al    ;ICW2, vector addresses are in the range from
              ;70h - 77h
mov al,2
out A1h,al    ;ICW3, slave PIC is connected to IRQ2.

mov al,1
out A1h,al    ;ICW4, sequential mode.
```

The PICs provide great possibilities for programming. You can make your own interrupt system in any way you want. An interesting use of these advantages is demonstrated in Program 3.1 (PIC_REPR), which re-initializes the PICs in a non-standard fashion.

```
;////////////////////////////////
;Program 3.1.
;////////////////////////////////
; PIC_REPR.
; This program changes the standard initialization
; set for both PICs (I8259). IRQ0-7 will be serviced through
; vectors 50-57h.
;
.DOSSEG
.MODEL small
.DATA
.STACK 100h
.CODE
.STARTUP
```

```
            cli             ;Interrupts are forbidden

            call Move8to50 ;Send vectors to the new area

            mov bx,5070h    ;BH:IRQ0-7, BL:IRQ8-15

            call Setdef     ;Re-initialise PICs

            sti
.EXIT 0

Move8to50   PROC near
            mov cx,32
            xor ax,ax
            mov es,ax
            mov ds,ax
            mov si,8*4      ;SI points to the first
                            ;byte of vectors 08-0Fh in the
                            ;Interrupt Vector Table.
            mov di,50h*4    ;DI points to the first
                            ;byte of vectors 50h-57h in
                            ;Interrupt Vector Table.

Lab1:       mov bl, BYTE ptr es:[si]
            mov BYTE ptr ds:[di],bl
            mov BYTE ptr es:[si],0
            inc di
            inc si
            loop Lab1

            ret
Move8to50   ENDP

Setdef      PROC  near
            mov al,11h       ;---+
            out 0A0h,al      ;   | Set ICW1 00010001b
            jmp short $+2    ;   |
            jmp short $+2    ;   |
            out 20h,al       ;---+
            jmp short $+2
            jmp short $+2
            mov al,bl        ;---+
            out 0A1h,al      ;   |01110xxx (BIOS 70-77h)
            jmp short $+2    ;   | Set ICW2
            jmp short $+2    ;   |
            mov al,bh        ;   |
            out 21h,al       ;---+00001xxx (BIOS 8-0Fh)
            jmp short $+2
            jmp short $+2
            mov al,2         ;---+
            out 0A1h,al      ;   |
            jmp short $+2    ;   | Set ICW3
            jmp short $+2    ;   |
            mov al,4         ;   |
            out 21h,al       ;---+
```

```
                jmp short $+2
                jmp short $+2
                mov al,1        ;---+
                out 0A1h,al     ;   |
                jmp short $+2    ;   | Set ICW4
                jmp short $+2    ;   |
                out 21h,al      ;---+
                jmp short $+2
                jmp short $+2
                mov al,0        ;---+
                out 0A1h,al     ;   | Set OCW1 (IMR(Mask))
                jmp short $+2    ;   |
                jmp short $+2    ;   |
                out 21h,al      ;---+
                ret
Setdef          ENDP
END
```

For example, our Interrupt Vector Table is as shown in Table 3.2 (note that the ISR address will vary from setup to setup):

**Table 3.2 Interrupt Vectors Before Running PIC_REPR**

| Vector | IRQ | ISR address | Usual Purpose |
|--------|--------|-------------|----------------|
| 08h | IRQ 00 | B780:003C | Timer Output 0 |
| 09h | IRQ 01 | 04A6:0565 | Mouse |
| 0Ah | IRQ 02 | B780:0057 | [Cascade] |
| 0Bh | IRQ 03 | B780:006F | COM2 |
| 0Ch | IRQ 04 | B48F:112D | COM1 |
| 0Dh | IRQ 05 | B780:009F | LPT2 |
| 0Eh | IRQ 06 | B780:00B7 | Floppy Disk |
| 0Fh | IRQ 07 | 0070:06F4 | LPT1 |

Run Program 3.1. It copies vectors 08h-0Fh to another part of the Interrupt Vector Table (to reserved vectors 50h-57h) and zeroes the vectors 08h-0Fh. Then it re-initializes the PICs. Finally, the hardware interrupts are redirected to new vectors (as shown in Table 3.3):

Table 3.3 Interrupt Vectors After Running PIC_REPR

| Vector | IRQ | ISR address | Usual Purpose |
|--------|--------|-------------|---------------|
| 08h | | 0000:0000 | Timer Output 0 |
| 09h | | 0000:0000 | Mouse |
| 0Ah | | 0000:0000 | [Cascade] |
| 0Bh | | 0000:0000 | COM2 |
| 0Ch | | 0000:0000 | COM1 |
| 0Dh | | 0000:0000 | LPT2 |
| 0Eh | | 0000:0000 | Floppy Disk |
| 0Fh | | 0000:0000 | LPT1 |
| . . . | | | |
| 50h | IRQ 00 | B780:003C | Reserved |
| 51h | IRQ 01 | 04A6:0565 | Reserved |
| T52h | IRQ 02 | B780:0057 | Reserved |
| 53h | IRQ 03 | B780:006F | Reserved |
| 54h | IRQ 04 | B48F:112D | Reserved |
| 55h | IRQ 05 | B780:009F | Reserved |
| 56h | IRQ 06 | B780:00B7 | Reserved |
| 57h | IRQ 07 | 0070:06F4 | Reserved |

After running the program, your computer will work efficiently, apart from the fact that system information software may report the absence of several important interrupt service routines.

# Writing Your Own Interrupt Service Routine

Writing ISRs is one of the more interesting parts of DOS programming. DOS is an open operating system. It provides good opportunities for writing and using procedures that expand its functionality. It has no priorities and no protection - programmers can control all system resources and write their own interrupt service routines (ISRs). Generally, ISRs are used in TSR (Terminate and Stay

Resident) programs (BIOSes have them too). Interrupt service programming is not a well documented area, but there are some basic principles and ways of writing procedures of this kind. The installation and execution of an ISR is divided into four phases:

**1**    Initialization phase.

**2**    Activation phase.

**3**    Execution of the interrupt service procedure.

**4**    Exit.

The purpose of the initialization phase is to load the ISR properly, to hook the required vectors and leave the resident part of the procedure in memory. This phase ends with calling DOS function 31h or interrupt 27h. Both are TSR functions of DOS. The traditional interrupt INT 27h limits your resident program to 64K, while function 31h doesn't have this limit.

However, before this, the initialization part of an ISR has a lot of work to do. First, DOS will not free the copy of the DOS environment when a program stays resident. To do this, you have to load the ES register with the environment segment (stored in the Program Segment Prefix (PSP) at offset 2Ch) and call DOS function 49h (Free Memory Block). You can obtain the address of the PSP by using function 62h. This function returns the address of the PSP of the currently active program in BX. The following code demonstrates the initialization part:

```
ASSUME cs:CODE,ds:CODE,es:CODE,ss:CODE

    mov ah,62h
    int 21h           ; Function 62h of DOS Service returns pointer
                      ; (ES:BX) to PSP
    mov PSP_Addr,WORD ptr es:[bx+2Ch]
    mov ah,49h
  mov es,WORD ptr PSP_Addr
int 21h               ; Free memory allocated for DOS environment.

. . . . . . . .

    mov dx,TSR_Size   ; DX = the size of TSR part in paragraphs.
    mov ax,3100h      ; Terminate and Stay Resident
    int 21h           ; DOS function.

code ENDS
```

To become the handler of a particular interrupt, an ISR hooks the interrupt vector via DOS functions 35h (Get Vector) and 25h (Set Vector). A user-installed ISR doesn't usually replace the original system interrupt service routine. Instead, on completion of its task, it passes control to the original routine. The value of the original vector must be saved, as it will be used later. The following example demonstrates the use of functions 35h and 25h:

```
        push es
        mov al,08h
        mov ah,35h
        int 21h                 ; Get vector 08h.
        mov VectOld,bx          ; Save Segment
        mov VectOld+2,es        ; Offset of the old vector.
        pop es
. . . . . .
        mov dx,WORD ptr NewOff  ; Load new values of
        mov ds,WORD ptr NewSeg  ; Segment and Offset.
        mov al,08h
        mov ah,25h
        int 21h                 ; Replace vector 08h
```

If your ISR uses any of the CPU registers, it must push their values onto the stack and restore them before exit. Having saved all the registers used, the ISR can function properly.

One more note: when the CPU passes control to an ISR, it clears the IF flag. This means that interrupts are disabled while the ISR is being executed, so you don't have to mask any unwanted requests. That is why some ISRs start with the STI instruction (Set Interrupt Flag).

When the ISR finishes its specific tasks, it must return control to the interrupted program. Of course, you have to pop all registers pushed on entry, or the system will most likely crash. The instruction IRET returns to the interrupted program.

Your ISRs can work on hardware interrupts. There's a special way of exiting from a hardware interrupt service routine: the ISR must notify the PIC (I8259) that the current request has been serviced. This is done by clearing the bit in the Interrupt Service Register.. So, the EOI command (End Of Interrupt code) is sent to the PIC. After this command the PIC clears the corresponding bit and is now prepared for other requests. You should keep in mind that hardware interrupts are shared between two controllers in PC AT architecture. The following sequence of instructions outputs the EOI command into both PICs and finishes an ISR:

```
        mov al,20h
        out 0Ah,al   ; EOI for slave PIC
        jmp $+2
        out 20h,al   ; EOI for master PIC
 . . . . . . .
        iret
```

Preliminary considerations over, let's discuss TSR programs.

# TSR-programming

First, it's not a bad idea to pay some attention to the DOS multiplex interrupt INT 2Fh. It's a standard way to establish communication with a TSR, although not followed properly by all third-party programs. The multiplex interrupt is used, for example, by such DOS utilities as ASSIGN, PRINT, SHARE and APPEND. Windows uses it a great deal, too.

It is used to find previously installed copies of a program and is widely used in TSR programming. A program fills register AH with a unique identification number, and then function 0 of INT 2Fh (AL=0) is used to check installation. A program calls INT 2Fh before installing its resident part in memory. If the corresponding TSR has not been installed, a zero value remains in AL. In other cases, the resident program with this identification number is already present in memory (AL=0FFh). Here is an example:

```
        mov ah,0E0h    ;Identification Number = 0E0h.
        mov al,0
        int 2Fh
        cmp al,0       ;If AL=0, then to label Cont.
        je  Cont
        mov Flag_C,1   ;The copy has been found.
 Cont:
     ...
```

You should note that ID numbers from 0h to 0BFh are reserved for DOS internal usage. For example, PRINT uses 01H, DOSKEY - 43H, and enhanced WINDOWS mode - 16H. Application programs struggle for the remaining 64 numbers. As several applications may use the same multiplex identification number, programs normally implement the more complicated mechanism of INT 2Fh processing. They place additional values in registers, or pass the address of a unique character string, or provide some technique for the dynamic change of identification numbers. A standard DOS ISR for INT 2Fh looks like the IRET instruction. You can write any service routine you want for this vector. Your resident program can return error codes and the minimum service sequence is as follows:

```
          cmp ah,0E0h       ; Is it my number?
          je Our_proc
          jmp DWORD ptr cs:OldInt2f
Our_proc: cmp al,0          ; If install check command
          jne Ex_int2f      ; then
          mov al,0FFh       ; set installation flag.
```

Good TSR programs should support features such as de-installation. Generally, special switches on the command line are used to request a program to de-install itself. A TSR program has to perform two main steps to remove itself from memory:

- Restore the contents of the Interrupt Vector Table. As every resident program normally saves the original vector, it's no problem to restore this value.

- Release the memory occupied by the TSR. Usually DOS function 49h - Free Memory Block (on INT 21h) is used for this. This function needs the PSP segment address of the program which occupies the block to be released. So, you have to somehow save the address of the resident program's PSP.

There are problems; for instance, suppose your resident hooks vector 09h. This means that the address in the Interrupt Vector Table is changed. Then you run another TSR program which hooks into the same vector. Again, the second resident program will save your vector and replace it with its own in the Interrupt Vector Table. These two TSR programs will form the chain of INT 09h processing. If you remove the resident program loaded first, it will break the chain. The second ISR will not be able to pass control further down the chain, because the first ISR will have been removed. To avoid problems of this kind, you have to check to see if your resident program is the last one in the chain of this vector's handlers before deinstalling it. The simplest way to do this is to compare the address of your service routine (saved during the installation) with the vector in the Interrupt Vector Table. If they are equal, then no other resident programs have hooked your vector:

```
mov cx,Segment_of_our_ISR
mov si,Offset_of_our_ISR

mov ax,3509h        ; Get current vector 09h
int 21h

mov ax,es
cmp cx,ax           ; Compare Segment Addresses.
jne Do_not_remove
cmp bx,si           ; Compare Offsets.
jz Release_memory
```

In case your TSR hooks several vectors, the described technique should be applied to all of them.

Use of all these techniques is demonstrated in the program PIANO9 on the disk. It controls vector 09h, detects its own presence in memory using INT 2Fh and can be de-installed.

Every time you run PIANO9, it looks for the switches /r or /R in the command line. It will inform the user if there aren't any, and in this case the program installs the ISR. The next step is to check the INT 2Fh service routine. PIANO9 uses the identification number 0E0h. If INT 2fH returns 0FFh, then PIANO9 has already been installed and it simply terminates. In other cases, the program installs interrupt service routines for INT 09h and 2Fh into memory.

On every interrupt 9, the ISR performs some additional actions. It checks the keyboard status byte in the BIOS Data Area. If it recognizes the <Ctrl> + <Right Shift> combination, it sets a special flag. After that there will be no normal keyboard input, but pressing a key will produce a sound (hence the name: PIANO9). The trick is to process all the keys at the low level so control is not passed to the standard ISR. This mode can be finished by pressing <Esc>. This key clears the "piano" flag and the keyboard can be used as normal.

# BIOS and CMOS

The BIOS (Basic Input/Output System) is the firmware part of the computer system. It can be considered as a collection of programs placed in a special area of memory. The BIOS supports the interface between the operating system, application software and hardware. The hardware specific programs of BIOS are written in assembly language and stored in the system ROM (Read Only Memory).

The BIOS includes programs which handle the base configuration of the PC hardware: the keyboard, display, hard drives, floppy drives, real time clock, parallel and serial ports etc. It consists of two parts.

# POST (Power-On Self Text)

The first part is the programs that perform the POST (Power-On Self Test) procedure. This code is the main part of the BIOS and is a powerful instrument for hardware error detection. The POST is normally combined with such hardware features as autotesting (about 85% of one-bit constant memory errors can be detected in the I80386 chips). First, the POST tests system components. It includes different tests in real and protected mode. There are several check points in the sequence of tests. If something is wrong with a test, the computer can inform you of the resource where an error has occurred. During the POST, test results are output to port 80h after each test. If a test fails, the last value sent to port 80h will indicate the problem. On some PS/2 computers, port 90h is used for this purpose. The POST also initializes each component with appropriate values.

What is tested and how? If you press the <Reset> button or simply turn the computer on, it'll start executing commands at address FFFF:0000. Then it makes an unconditional jump to the first command of the POST procedure. The first "victim" of the POST is the CPU. Flags, registers and the execution of conditional jumps are tested in Real Mode. The POST then gets to the Programmable Interrupt Controllers (I8259) and checks all Interrupt Control Words. The contents of ROM are tested by calculating a checksum. The POST tests and initializes the channel registers and all page registers of DMA controllers, after which it allows time for the keyboard controller (I8042) to perform an autotest and compares the returned result with a pre-defined constant. It then checks how this chip performs various commands. Checking the battery, the POST controls whether the data stored in CMOS is available for use during initialization. Then it tests memory. In protected mode it tests writing into system tables (LGDT, SGDT, LIDT, SIDT). The POST initializes the 6845 CRT controller. An error in this step may be reported by a sequence of beeps (since the display isn't working!). Then the BIOS fills up the Interrupt Vector Table by initializing all necessary vectors. The next task of the POST is loading the operation system. It switches over to a special loading procedure and then all hardware tests are over.

# BIOS Drivers

The second part of the BIOS is a set of programs controlling the hardware - sometimes called BIOS drivers. The main purpose of BIOS drivers is to provide an interface with certain devices for the operating system and application programs. This feature is implemented via a set of program interrupts. BIOS programs supporting low-level interfacing with hardware use Device Service Routines (DSR) (program interrupts). Every DSR has a vector in the Interrupt Vector Table. A DSR usually implements several functions. You can select a function by loading AH with the corresponding value.

```
mov ah,0    ; Select function "Print Symbol".
mov al,'#'  ; Symbol '#' will be printed.
mov dx,0    ; Select LPT1.
int 17h     ; Call BIOS service for printer.
```

There is a special BIOS in RAM intended for storing constants used by the BIOS. This area starts at address 0000:0400h. Table 3.4 briefly describes the BIOS Data Area.

**Table 3.4. BIOS Data Area**

| Offset | Contents |
|--------|----------|
| **RS232:** | |
| 0000h | Base address of COM1 port |
| 0002h | Base address of COM2 port |
| 0004h | Base address of COM3 port |
| 0006h | Base address of COM4 port |
| 007Ch | Timeout for COM1 |
| 007Dh | Timeout for COM2 |
| 007Eh | Timeout for COM3 |
| 007Fh | Timeout for COM4 |

*Continued*

**Table 3.4  BIOS Data Area (Continued)**

| Offset | Contents |
|--------|----------|
| **Printer:** | |
| 0008h | Base addresses of LPT1,2,3,4 ports |
| 0078h | Timeout time for LPT1 |
| 0079h | Timeout time for LPT2 |
| 007Ah | Timeout time for LPT3 |
| 007Bh | Timeout time for LPT4 |
| **Configuration:** | |
| 0010h | This word describes the current equipment set. |
| 0012h, | |
| 0015h, | |
| 0016h | These bytes are reserved (they contain POST error codes). |
| 0013h | This word contains the size of base memory (in Kbytes). |
| **Keyboard:** | |
| 0017h | First byte of the keyboard state. |
| 0018h | Second byte of the keyboard state. |
| 0019h | This byte is used for Alt-Numkey combinations. |
| 001Ah, | |
| 001Ch | The words point to the head and tail of the keyboard buffer (current values). If the two words are equal, the buffer is empty. |
| 001Eh | 16-words memory area for the keyboard buffer. |
| 0080h | Pointer to the start of keyboard buffer (absolute value). |

*Continued*

Table 3.4  BIOS Data Area (Continued)

Table 3.4  BIOS Data Area (Continued)

| Offset | Contents |
|--------|----------|
| 0082h | Pointer to the end of keyboard buffer (absolute value). |
| 0096h | Fourth byte of the keyboard state. |
| 0097h | Third byte of the keyboard state. |
| **Floppy disk:** | |
| 003Eh | Status byte of the floppy drives. |
| 003Fh | Status byte of the floppy disk motor. |
| 0040h | Timeout counter byte to turn the motor off. |
| 0041h | Status byte of the diskette controller. |
| 0042h | 7 bytes of disk controller status. |
| **Display:** | |
| 0049h | Current video mode. |
| 004Ah | Number of columns on the screen. |
| 004Ch | Size of regeneration buffer (in bytes). |
| 004Eh | Start address in regeneration buffer. |
| 0050h | 8 words: cursor position for eight video pages. |
| 0060h | Word, current cursor mode. |
| 0062h | The active display page. |
| 0063h | Base address of the display adapter. |
| 0065h | Current set of 3B8/3D8 register. |
| 0066h | Current set of 3B9/3D9 register. |
| **POST:** | |
| 0067h | Offset for jump if RESET. |
| 0069h | Segment for jump if RESET. |
| 006Bh | This byte indicates if an interrupt has occurred. |

*Continued*

Table 3.4  BIOS Data Area (Continued)

| Offset | Contents |
|--------|----------|
| **Timer:** | |
| 006Ch | Lowest word of timer counter. |
| 006Eh | Highest word of timer counter. |
| 0070h | The byte shows if the timer counter is full. |
| **Signs:** | |
| 0071h | Seventh bit of this byte indicates if <Ctrl-Break> is pressed. |
| 0072h | The word determines the kind of reset (1234h - keyboard request). |
| **Hard drive:** | |
| 0074h | Hard drive status. |
| 0075h | Number of hard drives. |
| 0076h | Reserved. |
| 0077h | Reserved. |
| **EGA/VGA area:** | |
| 0084h | Number of rows on active video page (byte). |
| 0085h | Word, number of pixels per symbol. |
| 0087h | Mode. |
| 0088h | Switches. |
| 0089h | Reserved. |
| 008Ah | Reserved. |
| **Additional drives information:** | |
| 008Bh | Current value of floppy disk drive data transfer speed. |
| 008Ch | State register of hard disk drive. |

*Continued*

Table 3.4   BIOS Data Area (Continued)

| Offset | Contents |
|--------|----------|
| 008Dh | Hard disk drive error register. |
| 008Eh | Interrupt flag of hard disk drive. |
| 008Fh | Type of floppy disk drive. |
| 0090h | Status byte of floppy disk drive 0. |
| 0091h | Status byte of floppy disk drive 1. |
| 0092h | Reserved. |
| 0093h | Reserved. |
| 0094h | Current cylinder of floppy disk drive 0. |
| 0095h | Current cylinder of floppy disk drive 1. |

**Real Time Clock:**

| Offset | Contents |
|--------|----------|
| 0098h | Offset of the user's timer flag. |
| 009Ah | Segment of the user's timer flag. |
| 009Ch | Lowest word of wait count. |
| 009Eh | Highest word of wait count. |
| 00A0h | Real Time Clock delay flag. |

**Net Adapter:**

| Offset | Contents |
|--------|----------|
| 00A1h | Seven bytes reserved for net adapter. |

**EGA/VGA parameters:**

| Offset | Contents |
|--------|----------|
| 00A8h | Pointer to video parameters control block. |

**Print Screen:**

| Offset | Contents |
|--------|----------|
| 0100 | Status byte for Print Screen operation. |

PC AT models have a special unit - power-independent CMOS memory - which uses very little power, and is kept running by a small rechargeable battery on the motherboard. The CMOS holds essential data like system configuration and special diagnostic flags, and supports the Real Time Clock system. CMOS memory consists of a minimum of 64 bytes. You can access the CMOS through ports 70h and 71h. You have to write the offset of the required byte to port 70h and then read the value from port 71h. The purpose of each CMOS byte is described in Table 3.5.

**Table 3.5 CMOS Information**

| Address | Purpose |
|---------|---------|
| 00h-0Dh | Real Time Clock information |
| 0Eh | Diagnostic state byte |
| 0Fh | Shutdown state byte |
| 10h | Type of the floppy disk drives |
| 11h | Reserved |
| 12h | Type of hard disk drive (less than 15). |
| 13h | Reserved |
| 14h | Equipment set byte |
| 15h-16h | Base memory size |
| 17h-18h | Extended memory size (above 1M) |
| 19h | Type of hard disk drive C (more than 15) |
| 1h | Type of hard disk drive D (more than 15) |
| 1Bh-20h | Reserved |
| 21h-2Dh | Reserved |
| 2h-2Fh | CMOS checksum |
| 30h-31h | Size of extended memory above 1M. |
| 32h | Current century (19x, for instance) |
| 33h | Additional information |
| 34h-3Fh | Reserved |

The BIOS allows IBM-compatible computers to be really compatible. BIOS routines are the basic routines for input/output operations. A program using BIOS services and the least common instruction set will run on a Pentium computer just as well as on an XT.

There are a lot of BIOS versions created by many different manufacturers. Normally, the computer displays the version, manufacturer's name, and date of production during the boot up process. From a programmer's point of view, the version doesn't matter. The biggest difference is in the POST codes used by the manufacturers. In AMI and Phoenix ISA/EISA BIOSes, the value 03h indicates ROM checksum error. The same value in the port 80h is used by IBM AT BIOSes to inform about CMOS read or write errors. AWARD BIOSes will interpret this value as an error during chips initialization. However, you never have to deal with this problem (unless you're diagnosing your PC by a special diagnostic board). In the best cases, the computer informs you that the test has failed with a beep or printed message.

In fact, different computer architectures cause differences in BIOSes. The architecture of a computer can be determined by the Model Byte stored at F000:FFFEh. Function INT 15h (AH=C0h) returns more detailed information: the Sub-model and Revision bytes. The date of the BIOS is stored at address F000:FFF5h.

You can use the BIOS date and the information returned by INT 15 Function 0C0h to identify the model of a computer.

# Summary

You are familiar with the interrupt system, TSR programming and the BIOS. You can write your own interrupt handlers and TSR programs. You can consider this chapter as a basis for further study of system programming. This chapter shows you how, and the following chapters will show you why.

# CHAPTER FOUR

# Disassembly

## Introduction

In the computer business, any knowledge quickly becomes out of date. Every two years a new style of programming emerges. It's up to you to stay ahead on what's new, and that means getting information from wherever you can. However, sometimes you don't have any source code - then you have to dive into the executable itself. If you look inside a program and open an .EXE file for text view, you often spot help-like text lines, that help you to understand how the program works. It's a great way to learn from other people's experience.

In this chapter we'll discuss different ways of reverse engineering, compare various ways to do it, and talk about some ways to protect your software from being cracked by a free-roaming hacker.

There's an atmosphere of crime about cracking, disassembling, and such like. We're not going to give an opinion on the moral values of these actions, nor are we going to discuss them in terms of the law. It's just another way to get programming experience.

There's no hack that can't be cracked...

# Why Do It?

You can of course be occupied in software development and never use reverse engineering. But often the most reliable source of information is to look at the actual program's code even if you have to get it via a disassembler.

Programming is a competitive business. Everyone is trying to stay ahead of the technology and the rest of the pack. Published documentation is both old, and freely available - it doesn't give you that all-important edge. To be really in front you've got to get the information yourself.

# How It Works

In theory reverse engineering looks quite simple. In the same way as command mnemonics in assembly language are directly translated into machine code, the reverse process is just backward translation. Of course, symbolic names of variables, labels, and procedures are lost during assembly, so the text generated by a disassembler isn't very legible to the eye (see Program 4.1), unless, of course, you are lucky enough to get an .EXE file with debug information left in it. In this case you still don't see the source lines, but you get the label and variable names which can be helpful.

```
;\\\\\\\\\\\\\\\\\\\\\\\\\\\\\\\\\\\\\\\\\\\\\\\\\\\\\\\\\\\\\\\\\\\\\\\\\
;Program 4.1 An Example of Disassembled Code
;\\\\\\\\\\\\\\\\\\\\\\\\\\\\\\\\\\\\\\\\\\\\\\\\\\\\\\\\\\\\\\\\\\\\\\\\\

sub_152     proc        far
            push        bp                  ; Save BP
            mov         bp,sp
            or          al,al
            jz          146345              ; Jump if zero
            . . .
  146345:
            mov         ah,9
            lea         dx,[data_2341]
            int         21h                 ; DOS Function 9 (output string)
            pop         bp                  ; Restore BP
            retf                            ; Return to caller
  sub_152   endp
```

If you're lucky you'll get something like this out of the process. The names are cryptic, but it's still a text in assembly. Sourcer, by V Communications, the disassembler we used, comments the output quite intelligently.

The following two listings are examples of the process failing to give you the right result. The essential part of the Program 4.2, the interrupt handler, is disassembled as data (see Program 4.3).

```
;\\\\\\\\\\\\\\\\\\\\\\\\\\\\\\\\\\\\\\\\\\\\\\\\\\\
;Program 4.2 A Resident Beeper
;\\\\\\\\\\\\\\\\\\\\\\\\\\\\\\\\\\\\\\\\\\\\\\\\\\\
    cseg            group cres,cinit
    cres            segment
    assume  cs:cseg
    oldint8 dw      2 dup (?)
    tik     dw      0
    int8    proc    far
            inc     tik
            cmp     tik,1092 ; one minute
            je      sound_on
            cmp     tik,18   ; one second
            je      sound_off
            jmp     dword ptr oldint8
sound_on:
            push    ax
            mov     tik,0

            in      al,61h   ; Get port setting
            or      al,3
            out     61h,al   : Turn speaker on
            mov     al,0b6h  ; control word 0B6h (10110110b)
                             ; switche channel 2 ofthe timer
                             ; into mode 3,
                             ; binary count,
                             ; load least significant byte first,
                             ; most significant byte next.

            out     43h,al
            mov     al,9     ; 1.19/1709h Mhz (frequency divisor)
            out     42h,al   ; load low part
            mov     al,17h
            out     42h,al   ; load high part
            pop     ax
            jmp     dword ptr oldint8
sound_off:
            push ax
            in      al,61h   ; Get port setting
            and     al,0fch
            out     61h,al   ; Turn speaker off
            pop     ax
            jmp     dword ptr oldint8
```

```
int8            endp
cres            ends

cinit           segment
start:
                push        ds
                mov         ax,3508h
                int         21h        ; Get old Int 8 vector
                mov         oldint8,bx
                mov         oldint8+2,es

                push        cs
                pop         ds
                lea         dx,int8
                mov         ax,2508h
                int         21h        ; Set new Int 8 vector

                pop         dx
                sub         dx,cinit
                neg         dx         ; Get # of paragraphs to keep
                mov         ax,3100h
                int         21h        ; Keep program in memory
cinit           ends
                end         start
```

```
;\\\\\\\\\\\\\\\\\\\\\\\\\\\\\\\\\\\\\\\\\\\\\\\\\\\\\\\\\\\\\\\\\\\\\\\\\\
;Program 4.3 The Resident Beeper Disassembled
;\\\\\\\\\\\\\\\\\\\\\\\\\\\\\\\\\\\\\\\\\\\\\\\\\\\\\\\\\\\\\\\\\\\\\\\\\\

seg_a           segment     byte public
        assume cs:seg_a ,   ds:seg_a

data_1          dd          00000h
data_2          dw          0
                db          2 Eh,0FFh, 06h, 04h, 00h, 2Eh
                db          81h, 3Eh, 04h, 00h, 44h, 04h
                db          74h, 0Dh, 2Eh, 83h, 3Eh, 04h
                db          00h, 12h, 74h, 22h, 2Eh,0FFh
                db          2Eh, 00h,
                db          50h, 2Eh,0C7h, 06h, 04h, 00h
                db          00h, 00h,0E4h, 61h, 0Ch, 03h
                db          0E6h, 61h,0B0h,0B6h,0E6h, 43h
                db          0B0h, 09h,0E6h, 42h,0B0h, 17h
                db          0E6h, 42h, 58h,0EBh, 06h
                db          50h,0B0h,0FCh,0E6h, 61h, 58h
loc_3:
                jmp         cs:data_1
                nop                    ;*ASM fixup - sign extn byte
                iret                   ; Interrupt return
                db          0, 0, 0, 0, 0, 0
```

```
;                       Program Entry Point

blam            proc    far

start:
                push    ds
                mov     ax,3508h

blam            endp

seg_a           ends

;---------------------------------------- seg_b ----

seg_b           segment byte public
        assume cs:seg_b ,  ds:seg_b

data_3          dw      0B81Eh
data_4          dw      3508h
                db      0CDh, 21h

;                       External Entry Point

int_08h_entry   proc    far
                mov     cs:data_3,bx
                nop                  ;*ASM fixup - sign extn byte
                mov     cs:data_4,es
                push    cs
                pop     ds
                mov     dx,offset int_08h_entry
                mov     ax,2508h
                int     21h      ; DOS Services  ah=function 25h
                                 ; set intrpt vector al to ds:dx

                pop     dx
                sub     dx,seg_b
                neg     dx
                mov     ax,3100h
                int 21h                  ; DOS Services  ah=function 31h
                                         ; terminate & stay resident
                                         ; al=return code,dx=paragraphs
int_08h_entry   endp

seg_b           ends

    end         start
```

But don't blame the disassembler here. In fact, it's hard to distinguish code from data, especially if the program is organized in a weird way. This is often done deliberately, which we'll discuss in this chapter under 'Cracking and Protection'. The variable instruction lengths make writing a disassembler harder, but on the other hand, fixed instruction lengths still wouldn't allow you to distinguish code from data. However some PC debuggers will allow you to tell them where to start disassembly.

# Disassemblers

Now, in the age of Windows and OS/2, programs are made up in accordance with strict templates. Every .EXE file contains a table of segments, so the disassembler will never mix them up. In DOS however, nothing's forbidden. There's no standard way of organizing programs. Data can be inside code and vice versa; code, data, and stack can be in one segment.

However, disassemblers are intelligent enough to analyze machine code and guess where to interpret it as data and where as code. To do this, the disassembler checks through an executable file several times. If there are control transfer instructions like jump or call, then the address they refer to is obviously code. On the next pass, the disassembler looks through the area it considers code for other jumps and calls. The process goes on until no more control transfers are revealed. All the areas to which control never passes are assumed to be data. That's why the interrupt service routine in Program 4.2 dropped out of code.

# Using Debuggers

Debugging is a more reliable way to get to the assembly code level. The processor is switched into debug mode, in which it invokes INT 01 (Single Step Interrupt) after executing each instruction. All the activity of the debugger is run inside an INT 01 handler. The debugger shows the contents of CPU registers, flags, the current block of disassembled code and the instruction to be executed next, the data and stack segment, etc. It's very convenient (and many pro programmers do so) to have two displays installed in the system (the IBM PS/2 Model 80 with an 8514 adapter is an exception)- one for program output (normally that's a big color monitor) and another for debugger's desktop (small monochrome monitor). If you have just one display installed, then on executing each instruction the debugger has to swap the display around. It stores the user screen and maintains its own display, allowing you to swap back to the program output when necessary.

## Display Swapping

There are three ways to swap - always, smart, and never.

- Always means that displays are swapped before and after execution of each instruction. This is likely to flash your head off in graphics mode, but is fine in text modes.

- Never is straight forward, and is useful when the program under debug does purely non-visual things like mathematics. However, if the program deals with video adapter ports in graphics modes, your system may crash.

- When swapping smartly, the debugger analyzes the current executing code and swaps only if it concerns the video system, or when the debugger loses control of running code for a while, e.g. when stepping over a function instead of tracing into it.

Tracing living code command by command is a great technique, but a debugger provides a more powerful means to walk through the code. You can browse through it, find the place you are interested in, and run the whole program up to there. This is done via INT 03 (Break Point Interrupt): the debugger remembers the byte of code and temporarily substitutes it with an INT 03 instruction, which is 1 byte long. Then it turns tracing mode off and starts executing the program. When the processor issues INT 03, it is trapped by the debugger. It restores the original code byte, and shows its normal screen with debug information.

INT 03 is also used for stepping over a call to a function or procedure. An INT 03 is inserted after the call instruction, and execution starts. On return from the call the debugger captures control again. The alternative is to trace the called procedure, when you and the debugger enter its code and have to trace in it until exit. If you're only interested in the result of the procedure, step over it and see.

A similar technique is used for setting breakpoints in the code. The program execution pauses at every INT 03 allowing you to view the output screen, the state of registers and data, and trace or run the program until the next breakpoint.

The 386 processor brought new facilities for debugging. It allows the debugger to do without inserting breakpoint instructions into the code. The processor has debug registers which hold memory addresses of breakpoints. Every time the processor notices a read or write to these addresses (the particular form is specified for each breakpoint), it generates an exception. As there's no need to insert instructions, breakpoints can be set in code, data, and even the ROM area.

Now that you understand the principles of disassembling and debugging, we can look at their practical application.

# Reverse Engineering in Action

As a simple example of reverse engineering and borrowing of both code and data, here's how to crack the .FLI format (Autodesk animation file). For your convenience we'll use imaginary symbolic names for procedures, although in reality we had to put down on paper only meaningless addresses like 53DC:00F2.

We had a copy of AAPLAY.EXE, the utility that shows animation in .FLI format, and several .FLI files. The aim was to decode the file format and write our own routines that would show .FLI files. Looking at the files in hex dump view, you'll recognize color palettes, RLE-like compressed pictures (see Chapter 12 for .PCX and TARGA graphics files formats and Chapter 10 'Data Compression Techniques'), and a distinct file header.

Trace AAPLAY under Turbo Debugger v2.0. Step over all calls until you find the procedure which shows the whole movie on the screen, call it ShowMovie. The next step is to find a procedure that would show individual frames, ShowFrame. Trace into ShowMovie and start to step over call by call. In fact, the process is repeated 6 times, every time giving you the address of yet another SubShowMovie. Eventually, when you trace SubShowMovie6, you'll see a procedure that shows the first frame but not the whole movie. Assume that SubShowMovie6 contained a loop, inside of which it called ShowFrame.

Soon after that call you'll notice a group of commands that look like a loop end condition:

```
inc [bp-06]
mov ax,[bp-06]
cmp ax,[8A4E]
ja 171
```

The jump was to be made to a point before ShowFrame. The debugger showed the value at ds:[8A4E] as 3Dh. You will have seen this already in the file header printed out at the start. The value at the address was 3Dh, so assume that this field must be the number of frames in the file. Set a breakpoint on entry to SubShowMovie6 and run the program again from the start. Trace it and you'll find:

- A procedure that returned 5 in AX. This is OpenFile, returning a file handle, because 5 is normally the first handle available. Run the program again and you'll see that OpenFile was given a pointer on the stack that pointed to the .FLI file name.

- A procedure which was given the constant 80h and a pointer. Set the data window to look at the pointer's destination, and find out that, after the call to this procedure, this buffer holds the first 80h bytes of the TEST.FLI file. This procedure was obviously ReadFile, and now you know the header size - 80h.

Having read the file header, the program wants to compare the word at offset 4 in the buffer with 0AF11h. This constant looks like a signature. Change JE after the check for JNE, and the program reveals: 'TEST.FLI isn't a .FLI file. Sorry!'

Restart the program and trace on, now entering a deeper level, into ShowFrame. The program reads 10h bytes more via ReadFile, and checks offset 4 for the word 0F1FAh. NOP the jump after the check and the message is: 'Bad magic! Not a .FLI frame'.

Then the program reads the rest of the frame. The frame size, which includes the size of the header, is the dword at offset 0 in the frame header. It analyzes a byte at offset 4 after the frame header and jumps elsewhere, using this value as the index in an address table. Follow, and you will find procedures that set the palette using data read from the file.

This gives you the general idea, so we'll skip every minute detail. A frame turned out to be divided into chunks (which you know by another forced error message "Unknown chunk type"). The size of a chunk header is 6 bytes long: offset 0 - dword size, offset 4 - word chunk type.

The chunk types shown in Table 4.1 were found.

**Table 4.1  .FLI Chunk Types**

| Tag | Type |
| --- | --- |
| 0Bh | Palette |
| 0Ch | Next picture |
| 0Dh | Clear screen |
| 0Fh | New picture |

You can find the authentic .FLI format described by its creator, Jim Kent, in Dr. Dobb's Journal, March '93.

When it comes to showing a picture, borrow the original code from the program. Analyzing PUSHes before the call to the procedure, you will find that they are: a pointer to a chunk of data after the header, the video buffer address, and the number of lines in the picture, read from the file header. Capture the debugger's screen with the procedure code, and put it in your own program.

Borrowing just the relevant section of code is evidently much easier than disassembling the whole program.

# Cracking and Protection

There are several reasons for protecting your programs from reverse engineering: to reinforce your copy protection, or to hide your intellectual property and algorithms. To defend your programs efficiently, you need to understand both locks and lockpicks.

One way to protect your code from disassembly is to encrypt it, e.g. XOR a certain part of it with another and at run time repeat the same operation. The encrypted part will be disassembled as either meaningless rubbish, or data which is no more readable than the .EXE file itself.

Another solution is a self-extracting program, which decompresses the main code into memory and starts the program. In this case the disassembler will give out the code of the decompressing routine, and a long listing of data.

## Confusing Calls

Sometimes, using an implicit calling construction can mislead the disassembler. For example, instead of just writing

```
call SubProc
```

you can create the following reference:

```
SubRef      DW      offset SubProc
            . . .
            call    SubRef
```

Now the disassembler won't see the procedure SubProc. So, by creating massive tables with procedure addresses, or by using object-oriented programming techniques, you can protect your code from the disassembler more efficiently.

## Self-Modifying Code

A good way to cheat a disassembler is to use self-modifying code. You can dynamically change call and jump addresses in the running code. But take care that the code that you modify can't be pre-fetched by the processor, in which case the modification doesn't take effect: the processor will execute the old instruction. To avoid this, you have to precede the modified command by a jump or call instruction to refresh the instruction pre-fetcher. For example:

```
Fixing mock jump:
    mov word ptr cs:MockJump[1], RealAddr
    jmp $+2             ; Refresh prefetcher
    mov bl,ah
    mov bl,ah
    mov bl,ah
```

```
MockJump:
    jmp MockAddr          ; Will jump to RealAddr!

Fixing mock far call:
    mov word ptr cs:MockCall[1], ProcOfs
    mov word ptr cs:MockCall[3], ProcSeg
    mov bl,ah
    mov bl,ah
    mov bl,ah
    jmp $+2               ; Refresh prefetcher

MockCall:
    call MockAddr         ; Will call ProcSeg:ProcOfs !

<.......... self-modifying commands ....>
```

## Fooling Debuggers

Protection from debugging is different. You'll never deceive the debugger by an implicit call. But there are some cruel tricks you can play on a debugger.

You can declare the stack segment on the code segment, as it's done in Program 4.4. The stack is rather small, but it's adequate for the purposes of the program. When the program is run under DOS, it says "My name is Prince" and terminates happily. But when the debugger loads and starts the program, it uses the program's stack, and 10 bytes of stack are not enough for a hefty monster like the debugger, so the stack overflows and the code that comes before it is overwritten. The program says nothing and dies.

```
;//////////////////////////////////////////////////
;Program 4.4 Crashing the Debugger by Stack Segment Overlap
;//////////////////////////////////////////////////
  dosseg
  .model large
  .data
      mess db 'My name is Prince',10,13,'$'
  .code
          mov ax,@data
          mov ds,ax
          mov ax,cs

          cli
          mov ss,ax
          mov sp,offset stck
          sti

          call tell
          mov ah,4ch
```

```
        int 21h         ; Terminate

        db 10 dup (?)   ; Reserve space for stack
stck:                   ; Initial stack pointer

tell    proc near
        lea dx,mess
        mov ah,9
        int 21h         ; Output string
        ret
tell    endp
end
```

Program 4.5 treats the debugger with more tolerance, but it can detect whether
trace mode is active. The instruction at the label Modify zeroes the jump
distance in the instruction that follows right after it. But when tracing mode is
off, by the time the modifying command is being executed, the jump command
is already sucked up into the processor's command pipeline. The code in
memory becomes modified, but the bird has already flown! So the program
jumps to the normal exit, and says "We are free". But when a hacker is tracing
the program, commands are fed to the pipeline one by one. Modification takes
effect, and the program reloads the string with "We are being traced"...

```
;/////////////////////////////////////////////////
;Program 4.5 Detecting Tracing by Means of Command Pipeline
;/////////////////////////////////////////////////
 dosseg
 .model small
 .data
   mess db 'We are free',10,13,'$'
   trace db 'We are being traced',10,13,'$'
 .code
        mov ax,@data
        mov ds,ax

        lea dx,mess
Modify: mov byte ptr cs:m+1,0   ; Zero jump distance at m
m:
        jmp short norm_ex
        lea dx,trace
norm_ex:
        mov ah,9
        int 21h                 ; Output string

        mov ah,4ch
        int 21h                 ; Terminate
 end
```

Of course, you can make the hacker work much harder. The purpose of this example was only to demonstrate the possibility of branching.

A nasty way to kill the debugger is to tarnish interrupt vectors 1 and 3. If you zero the vectors, the debugger (and the system) will crash.

```
xor ax,ax
mov es,ax
mov es:[4],ax
mov es:[6],ax
```

If you install your own INT 01 handler, the processor will stay in trace mode, but the debugger will lose control over your code. The program will run without stopping, only slower, maybe very much slower, depending on what you do in your handler. You can make the handler perform some essential part of your program's action, which won't cause any problem under DOS, but it will get hackers out of your special code. They can easily find the point where you set your own interrupt vector and NOP these commands out, but then the program will begin to function improperly if at all.

Even if you set all the above mentioned traps, it's better to retain control permanently. You can check some parts of your code for a control sum to detect a breakpoint and/or any other modification in your code.

Below, shown in Table 4.2, is the original code substituted by the Debugger.

**Table 4.2 Code Substituted by the Debugger**

| Original code | | | Code with a breakpoint |
|---|---|---|---|
| 8CC8 | | mov ax,cs | 8CC8 |
| 8EC0 | m: | mov es,ax | 8EC0 |
| 33C0 | | xor ax,ax | 33C0 |
| BF1900 | | mov di,offset m | BF1900 |
| B90F00 | | mov cx,000F | CC0F00 int 3 |
| 260205 | labl: | add al,es:[di] | 260205 |
| 80D400 | | adc ah,00 | 80D400 |

*Continued*

Table 4.2 Code Substituted by the Debugger (Continued)

| Original code | | Code with a breakpoint |
|---|---|---|
| 47 | inc di | 47 |
| E2F7 | loop labl | E2F7 |
| ——— | | ——— |
| 0562h | AX = Control sum | 0575h |

However, the checksum technique won't work if the 386 hardware debug registers are used (see Chapter 15 for details).

# Reverse Engineering of Data

Data files are often better guides to their format than any explicit written specification. There are several reasons for this:

- The number of subformats may be so enormous, that the author of the specification doesn't feel like going into detail on all of them.

- Everybody can make a mistake. The slightest error in the Offset field in a table can give you hours of pain and puzzlement.

- The data may be hidden or the format may be closed for publication.

Just as in espionage, there can hardly be any definite guidelines for cracking cranky data formats. It's entirely a matter of experience and luck. Some formats give their secrets away, other won't. However, if you do it again and again, you'll notice some common themes and develop an eye for picking them out. So here's some assorted pieces of practical knowledge to help you along the way.

## Analyzing File Formats

As an example of file format analysis, when we can compare different forms of the same test data, we're going to take a look at the process of exploring the .WAV file format.

Use a conversion utility to generate three different .WAV files from one raw sound file. Declare it to be 8-bit stereo (which it actually was), then 16-bit mono, and finally 16-bit stereo. Have a look at what is in a data dump program. All the dumps are reduced to the first 80 bytes:

### The Dump of the Raw 8-bit Stereo Sound File

```
Offset    Data

00        89 8A 91 85 8C 8B 7F 8E 7B 8A 83 89 8E 8C 8F 8F    ëèæàîï_Ä{èâëÄîÅÅ

10        83 8F 7A 8A 7E 87 86 8D 8A 91 8C 88 85 7D 78 7D    âÅzè~çàìèæîêà}x}

20        7A 84 85 83 87 84 7F 8B 7D 8C 88 85 8B 7B 80 80    zäàâçä_ï}îêàï{ÇÇ

30        79 8D 7C 8E 84 86 87 81 7C 84 75 84 7C 81 87 85    yì|Ääâçü|äuä|üçà

40        87 85 81 7D 7E 79 78 7E 76 86 80 87 86 81 80 7E    çàü}~yx~vâÇçâüÇ~
```

### The Dump of the 8-bit Stereo .WAV

```
Offset    Data

00        52 49 46 46 5B 53 07 00 57 41 56 45 66 6D 74 20    RIFF[S_.WAVEfmt

10        10 00 00 00 01 00 02 00 22 56 00 00 44 AC 00 00    ........"V..D¼..

20        02 00 08 00 64 61 74 61 3B 53 07 00 89 8A 91 85    ....data;S_.ëèæà

30        8C 8B 7F 8E 7B 8A 83 89 8E 8C 8F 8F 83 8F 7A 8A    îï_Ä{èâëÄîÅÅâÅzè

40        7E 87 86 8D 8A 91 8C 88 85 7D 78 7D 7A 84 85 83    ~çàìèæîêà}x}zäàâ
```

### The Dump of the 16-bit Mono .WAV

```
Offset    Data

00        52 49 46 46 5B 53 07 00 57 41 56 45 66 6D 74 20    RIFF[S_.WAVEfmt

10        10 00 00 00 01 00 01 00 22 56 00 00 44 AC 00 00    ........"V..D¼..

20        02 00 10 00 64 61 74 61 3B 53 07 00 89 8A 91 85    ....data;S_.ëèæà

30        8C 8B 7F 8E 7B 8A 83 89 8E 8C 8F 8F 83 8F 7A 8A    îï_Ä{èâëÄîÅÅâÅzè

40        7E 87 86 8D 8A 91 8C 88 85 7D 78 7D 7A 84 85 83    ~çàìèæîêà}x}zäàâ
```

### The Dump of the 16-bit Stereo .WAV

```
Offset    Data

00        52 49 46 46 5B 53 07 00 57 41 56 45 66 6D 74 20    RIFF[S_.WAVEfmt

10        10 00 00 00 01 00 02 00 22 56 00 00 88 58 01 00    ........"V..êX..

20        04 00 10 00 64 61 74 61 3B 53 07 00 89 8A 91 85    ....data;S_.ëèæà

30        8C 8B 7F 8E 7B 8A 83 89 8E 8C 8F 8F 83 8F 7A 8A    îï_Ä{èâëÄîÅÅâÅzè

40        7E 87 86 8D 8A 91 8C 88 85 7D 78 7D 7A 84 85 83    ~çàìèæîêà}x}zääâ
```

Well, this looks quite encouraging. A superficial look tells us that the word RIFF at the very beginning of the files is most probably the signature. Similarly, WAVEfmt a little later should mean that these files contain wave audio data. The English word "data" simply marks the place where the data itself starts from. The garbage that goes after the mark looks quite like normal sound data - irregular fluctuations around the level 80h. If you compare the raw file dump and a .WAV file dump, you'll see that the raw data in its original form goes into wave files right after the header from offset 44, hex 2C.

This is also proved by comparing file lengths:

| | |
|---|---|
| LSD~WIND.WAV | 480,103 |
| LSD~WIND.SND | (480,059) |
| | 44 |

# The File Headers

Now it's time to decode non-ASCII components of the header.

We know the length of the raw data (480059, hex 7533B). So we can search for the string 3B 53 07 in our dump, remembering that in Intel notation the less significant bytes go first, and find it at offset 40, straight after the word data. The conclusion is obvious: the DWORD at offset 40 is the raw data length. And the DWORD after the word RIFF (offset 4) is 32 more than the data length.

There should certainly be a field for sampling rate somewhere in the header. It was specified as 22050 Hz, hex 5622. Searching for 22 56, we find it at offset 24 in all of the files. The field may be a WORD or DWORD, because the next word is zero. This we don't know, so we'll assume it's a DWORD.

The value next to the sampling rate DWORD is twice greater, AC44h (dec 44100) in 8-bit stereo and 16-bit mono, and four times greater (15888h, dec 88200) in 16-bit stereo. This implies the bytes per second ratio.

The byte or word at offset 22 is 2 in stereo files and 1 in the mono one, so what could it be if not the number of channels? Again, the word at offset 32 is 2 in 8-bit stereo and 16-bit mono, but 4 in 16-bit stereo. This should mean bytes per sample. At offset 34 we see 8 in the 8-bit file and 10h (dec 16) in 16-bit files. We can call this bits per channel.

There are two bytes: 10h at offset 16 and 1 at offset 20 that never change. If they follow one another immediately perhaps they are the version number. But they don't, and so ignore them.

Now we can summarize what we know in Table 4.3:

**Table 4.3  The Decoded .WAV File Format**

| Offset | Size | Contents |
|--------|------|----------|
| 0 | 4 | ASCII "RIFF" |
| 4 | 4 | DWORD Data length + 32 |
| 8 | 8 | ASCII "WAVEfmt " |
| 16 | 4 | 10h (mystery) |
| 20 | 2 | 01 (mystery) |
| 22 | 2 | Number of channels |
| 24 | 4 | Samples per second (sampling rate) |
| 28 | 4 | Bytes per second |
| 32 | 2 | Bytes per sample |
| 34 | 2 | Bits per channel |
| 36 | 4 | ASCII "data" |
| 40 | 4 | DWORD data length |
| 44 | ? | Audio data |

In fact, the .WAV file format is a specimen of the more general RIFF (Resource Interchange File Format), used in Microsoft Windows for storing various multimedia data. RIFF files are organized in nested chunks, the whole file is itself a chunk, too. Generally, each RIFF chunk's structure is as follows:

```
<tag> <size> <data>
```

where tag is a four-character, space-padded ASCII identifier (e.g. "RIFF", "fmt ", or "data"), size is a 4-byte integer size of the chunk (without tag and size fields), and data is type dependent.

The ASCII string "WAVE" indicates a wave form chunk, which consists of two subchunks: a format subchunk, describing the parameters of a sample, and a data subchunk, containing the audio data.

So, the mysterious fields in Table 4.3 are:

Offset 4        RIFF chunk size
Offset 16       format subchunk size, 10h bytes
Offset 20       PCM audio data type

And strings "fmt " and "data" are subchunks' ID's. The meanings of other fields correspond to Microsoft's specification.

# The Experienced Eye

Theory is great, but usually reverse engineering of data consists of peering hopefully into data dumps. Often you need to recognize some kind of data in a file and determine its location. It's much easier to spot data blocks visually, prior to any sort of logical analysis. Fortunately, dumps of various kinds of data, such as sound, picture, bitmaps, palettes, bitmap fonts, etc., have their own characteristic patterns. They aren't signatures to search for in files, but their style of layout is quite distinguishable.

## Sound Data

The following dumps show sound data in the most popular 8-bit unsigned format. You can recognize it by the frequent occurrence of the letter "Ç" (hex 80h), which is the level of silence. Bytes go in increasing and decreasing sequences, and are often repeated.

**ASCII View of 8-bit Sound Data**

```
ÇÇÇÇÇÇÇÇÇÇÇÇÇÇÇÇÇÇÇÇÇÇÇÇÇÇÇÇÇÇÇÇÇÇÇÇÇÇÇÇÇÇ
ÇÇÇÇÇÇ_Ç__Ç_Ç__ÇÇÇÇÇÇÇÇÇÇÇÇÇÇÇÇüäÇxw|üäüéà
é~éé{x}|yÇàéâëäÇéézv{}z~âéäèëâéé|xzyx}äâ
äèèäâä|x{zv{ééâëèàää~yzyvzüüéêèàää_yzzvz
Çüéêèàää~yzzwzÇüéêèàää~yyywzÇéâêèâäâ~xxy
wzÇéâêèâää~yyywzÇéâêèâää_yyyvx_üâçèçààÇz
yyvw}Çéâèçàäü{yyvw|_üàëçâäé|zzww|_Çäêçàâ
```

```
â}{{xw|__äêçàáâ}{{xw|__âêçàáâ}{{xx|__âçá
äàâ~||yx|__éáâäáâ_||zy|__éàâäáâ_}}{y|__ü
àáâäâ_}}{y|~_üàáâäâÇ}}{y|~_üàáâäâÇ~}{z|~
_üàáâäâÇ~}|z{~_Çàáâäâç~}|z|~_Çâàâäâç~~|z
|~_Çâàâäâü~~|z|~_Çâàâäâü~~}{{~_Çâàâäâü~~
```

### Hex-ASCII View of 8-bit Sound Data

```
80 80 80 80 80 80 80 80 80 80 7F 80 7F 7F 80 7F   ÇÇÇÇÇÇÇÇÇÇ_Ç__Ç_
80 7F 7F 80 80 80 80 80 80 80 80 80 80 80 80 80   Ç__ÇÇÇÇÇÇÇÇÇÇÇÇ
80 81 84 80 78 77 7C 81 84 81 82 85 82 7E 82 82   ÇüäÇxw|üäüéàé~éé
7B 78 7D 7C 79 80 85 82 83 89 86 80 82 82 7A 76   {x}|yÇàéâëäÇééèzv
7B 7D 7A 7E 83 82 84 8A 89 83 82 82 7C 78 7A 79   {}z~âéäèëâéé|xzy
78 7D 84 83 84 8A 8A 84 83 83 7C 78 7B 7A 76 7B   x}äâäèèäââ|x{zv{
82 82 83 89 8A 85 84 84 7E 79 7A 79 76 7A 81 81   ééâëèàää~yzyvzüü
82 88 8A 85 84 84 7F 79 7A 7A 76 7A 80 81 82 88   éêèàää_yzzvzÇüéê
```

# Bitmaps

Picture bitmaps are harder to recognize. However, you can't expect color values to fluctuate a hundred percent stochastically. They should change more or less gradually. In hand-drawn 16-colored pictures there should be repetitive sequences of equal bytes, or words in areas of two-colored dithering. The following dump shows the hex view of a 256-colored .BMP file.

### A Fragment of 256-colored .BMP File

```
A3 AA AE B0 B2 B5 B7 B4 BA C0 BD BD BE BE C8 CA   úØ«º²m•´ºÀ½¾¼ÈÊ
CA BB B8 C3 B6 B1 B0 B1 B6 B6 BB B7 B8 B3 B4   B7_Ê»_Ã¶±º±¶¶»»•_³´•
BA C5 BA BF C4 C9 CD CA CA CC CC C8 CF D4 D8   DB_Åª¿ÄÉÍÊÊÌÌÈÏÔØÛ
DD DD E0 E1 E4 E5 E7 E8 EB EC ED EE EF F1 F1   F2_ÝÝaßSstFd¥feÇ±±³
F3 F4 F4 F5 F5 F4 F6 F4 F6 F6 F7 F6 F6 F6 F5   F7_£óôõõ_ó__»___õ»
F8 F7 F7 F7 F6 F7 F7 F6 F7 F7 F7 F7 F4 F6 F4   F6_º»»»_»»_»»»»ó_ó_
F7 F6 F6 F5 F6 F6 F6 F8 F7 F5 F6 F6 F8 F7 F6   F6_»__õ___º»õ__º»__
```

A palette is an easy case. You can notice groups of 3-byte RGB color settings. When a palette is in shades of gray, the values in a group are equal (like ??? @@@ AAA BBB) in the next example.

### A Fragment of a Palette in a .BMP File

```
24  20  25  25  25  20  26  26  26  20  27  27  27  20  28  28  $  %%%  &&&  `''  ((
28  20  29  29  29  20  2A  2A  2A  20  2B  2B  2B  20  2C  2C  (  )))  ***  +++  ,,
2C  20  2D  2D  2D  20  2E  2E  2E  20  2F  2F  2F  20  30  30  ,  ---  ...  ///  00
30  20  31  31  31  20  32  32  32  20  33  33  33  20  34  34  0  111  222  333  44
34  0D  0A  35  35  35  20  36  36  36  20  37  37  37  20  38  4  555  666  777  8
38  38  20  39  39  39  20  3A  3A  3A  20  3B  3B  3B  20  3C  88  999  :::  ;;;  <
3C  3C  20  3D  3D  3D  20  3E  3E  3E  20  3F  3F  3F  20  40  <<  ===  >>>  ???  @
40  40  20  41  41  41  20  42  42  42  20  43  43  43  20  44  @@  AAA  BBB  CCC  D
```

# Fonts

Bitmap fonts are probably the easiest prey. Especially when you're armed with a special viewing-editing utility. The following screen-shot shows a binary editor screen with a driver loaded:

### A Bitmap Font in a Bit Editor

| Bits       | Char | Dec | Hex  |         |         |
|------------|------|-----|------|---------|---------|
| ........   | 0    | 000 | 00h  | Offset: | 0000575 |
| 00..00..   | I    | 204 | CCh  | Offset: | 0000576 |
| 00..00..   | I    | 204 | CCh  | Offset: | 0000577 |
| 00..00..   | I    | 204 | CCh  | Offset: | 0000578 |
| 000000..   | _    | 252 | FCh  | Offset: | 0000579 |
| 00..00..   | I    | 204 | CCh  | Offset: | 0000580 |
| 00..00..   | I    | 204 | CCh  | Offset: | 0000581 |
| 00..00..   | I    | 204 | CCh  | Offset: | 0000582 |
| ........   | 0    | 000 | 00h  | Offset: | 0000583 |
| .0000...   | x    | 120 | 78h  | Offset: | 0000584 |
| ..00....   | 0    | 048 | 30h  | Offset: | 0000585 |
| ..00....   | 0    | 048 | 30h  | Offset: | 0000586 |
| ..00....   | 0    | 048 | 30h  | Offset: | 0000587 |
| ..00....   | 0    | 048 | 30h  | Offset: | 0000588 |
| ..00....   | 0    | 048 | 30h  | Offset: | 0000589 |
| .0000...   | x    | 120 | 78h  | Offset: | 0000590 |

If you don't have such a utility, you can still recognize a font in a file: there will be repetitive bytes (groups of 3 or 4), surrounded by zeroes, as shown below:

## Bitmap Fonts

**An 8-bit font (8 rows per character):**

```
00  00  CC  CC  CC  CC  CC  CC  CC  CC  CC  FE  06  06  00  00    ...........Û....
```

**A 16-bit font (16 rows per character):**

```
00  00  C6  C6  C6  C6  C6  7E  06  06  06  06  00  00  00  00    .......~........
00  00  DB  DB  DB  DB  DB  DB  DB  DB  DB  FF  00  00  00  00    ..ÛÛÛÛÛÛÛÛÛ....
00  00  DB  DB  DB  DB  DB  DB  DB  DB  DB  FF  03  03  00  00    ..ÛÛÛÛÛÛÛÛÛ....
00  00  F8  B0  30  30  3C  36  36  36  36  7C  00  00  00  00    ..°.00<6666|....
00  00  C3  C3  C3  C3  F3  DB  DB  DB  DB  F3  00  00  00  00    ......£ÛÛÛÛ£....
00  00  F0  60  60  60  7C  66  66  66  66  FC  00  00  00  00    ..ª```|ffff_....
00  00  7C  C6  06  26  3E  26  06  06  C6  7C  00  00  00  00    ..|..&>&...|....
00  00  CE  DB  DB  DB  FB  DB  DB  DB  DB  CE  00  00  00  00    ...ÛÛÛÛÛÛÛÛ.....
00  00  3F  66  66  66  3E  3E  66  66  66  E7  00  00  00  00    ..?fff>>ffft....
```

As an aside, the byte after the word "MISL" in most games' save-files holds the number of missiles on your aircraft.....

# Summary

You could easily write a complete book on reverse engineering, or a book of hackers' lore. Being limited to one chapter, we have left out the less relevant and efficient cracking and protection tricks. Reverse engineering tools become more and more impressive each year.

Also, you always have to have a stopping point. Borrowing code is illegal. You can use it for studying, but even this is a restricted area. However there is really nothing wrong with reverse engineering if that is the only way you can get the information you need to write your own code.

Frankly speaking, if you have to work as a system programmer, if you want to learn assembler as your mother tongue, or if you're going to develop large projects in assembly language, then you have to do some reverse engineering. Being able to read other people's code like a pro musician reads a sheet of music is the most powerful way to learn.

## CHAPTER FIVE

# Writing Device Drivers

## Introduction

If you want to create or adapt device drivers on the PC, then you have to know assembly language. Device drivers have to be as small and as fast as possible, making assembler almost mandatory. In this chapter, we will explain the structure, format, functions and commands of DOS device drivers. We'll develop some generic code templates and look at how to adapt these to control your own devices.

In this chapter you will learn what device drivers are and how they are installed, what their common structure is, and the functions that they are expected to provide. You will also learn how to create your own device driver template and how to add functions to that template.

# Device Driver Fundamentals

A device driver can be defined as a program specially developed to maintain an interface with system resources. These resources are typically peripheral devices, which require your driver to support various kinds of input-output operations.

# Installing Device Drivers

There are four ways to create a device driver:

1  A driver can be included in your application program and executed as a subroutine. You can see examples in most popup TSRs for keyboard drivers.

2  A driver can be implemented as a separate resident program, which is called either through an external interrupt or by passing control directly to designated driver entry points. These entry points are passed to the driver when it is initialized, and are then preserved in specially allocated areas of memory. A good example of such a driver is a mouse device driver, which hooks Interrupt 33h.

3  A driver can be included in the operating system. The user then has a simpler interface with the peripheral device, because the operating system executes the majority of common functions automatically. The most simple examples are DOS keyboard and console drivers, which are loaded and installed when DOS starts up. Another example is a joystick driver, which resides in BIOS.

4  You can create your own device driver and install it in the operating system. This is called an installable device driver. DOS allowed installable device drivers from v2.0. Installable device drivers are the core subject of this chapter.

DOS resident drivers are contained in BIOS. They support devices which are part of the standard PC configuration: keyboard, display, serial port, parallel port, real time clock and disk drives.

Installable device drivers are specially prepared programs which are loaded into DOS memory at start-up, using the DEVICE and DEVICEHIGH commands in your CONFIG.SYS file. These drivers provide a standard interface between DOS and non-standard equipment such as printers, plotters and co-ordinate devices. They enhance resident DOS driver functions or replace them completely. For example, the driver ANSI.SYS expands the functions of resident display drivers by controlling the cursor, as well as the color and form of symbols on the screen.

## Character and Block Drivers

DOS supports two types of device driver: character and block. Character devices input and output one character at a time. They support devices like the keyboard, display, and the parallel and serial ports. The most common examples of character drivers are the DOS drivers ANSY.SYS and PRINTER.SYS. Block device drivers input and output blocks of information with a predetermined structure. Block devices include all disk drives, as well as memory.

# The Structure of a Device Driver

Device drivers support a great variety of devices. Moreover, some device drivers must support a wide scope of functions. However, all of them interact with DOS according to defined rules and have a fairly defined structure. Each driver consists of three parts:

- The driver header

- Strategy routine

- Interrupt routines

All of these are united in one file, which contains the driver's binary image in memory. The name of this file can be almost anything, but it usually has the extension .SYS. The .SYS is really only the external sign of an installable driver, which helps you distinguish it from other types of program. As you will see, installable drivers must have a .COM structure that enables them to be installed. Some driver files have an executable file structure and the extension .EXE.

However, these .EXE files may not be installable drivers and should not be loaded by the DEVICE and DEVICEHIGH commands of the CONFIG.SYS file, because they are not binary image files and may contain relocation addresses. Moreover, at the driver loading time, the file COMMAND.COM is not yet loaded in the system memory itself. As a rule, drivers, implemented as .EXE files, are not loaded simultaneously with DOS, but later, as TSR programs. (Loading drivers and their memory allocation will be considered in more detail later.)

## The Driver Header

An installable device driver file doesn't usually contain more than one driver, but DOS does allow you to place several installable drivers in one file in order to load them simultaneously. However, each driver should still have a separate driver header.

The header tells DOS about the availability of the driver and its location in the system, gives pointers to the strategy and interrupt routine entry points, and defines the attributes of the device supported by that driver. The structure of a driver header is shown below. Later on we'll take a closer look at what its contents mean.

**Table 5.1 The Structure of a Driver Header**

| Offset | Size (bytes) | Name (bit) |
|--------|--------------|------------|
| 00h | 4 | Link: Pointer to next driver |
| 04h | 2 | |
| | | Character device attributes: |
| | | bit 0 = standard input device |
| | | bit 1 = standard output device |
| | | bit 2 = NUL character device |
| | | bit 3 = clock device |
| | | bit 4 = fast character output device |
| | | bit 5 = Always 0, reserved |
| | | bit 6 = device supports generic IOCTL functions |

*Continued*

**Table 5.1 The Structure of a Driver Header (Continued)**

| Offset | Size (bytes) | Name (bit) |
|--------|--------------|------------|
| | | bit 7 = device supports IOCTL queries |
| | | bit 8 = Always 0, reserved |
| | | bit 9 = Always 0, reserved |
| | | bit 10 = Always 0, reserved |
| | | bit 11 = device supports Open Device, Close Device |
| | | bit 12 = Always 0, reserved |
| | | bit 13 = device supports Output Until Busy |
| | | bit 14 = device supports IOCTL Read and IOCTL Write functions |
| | | bit 15 = character device driver |
| | | |
| | | Block device attributes: |
| | | bit 0 = Always 0, reserved |
| | | bit 1 = driver supports 32-bit sector address |
| | | bit 2 = Always 0, reserved |
| | | bit 3 = Always 0, reserved |
| | | bit 4 = Always 0, reserved |
| | | bit 5 = Always 0, reserved |
| | | bit 6 = device supports logical drives or generic IOCTL functions, or both |
| | | bit 7 = device supports IOCTL queries |
| | | bit 8 = Always 0, reserved |
| | | bit 9 = Always 0, reserved |
| | | bit 10 = Always 0, reserved |

*Continued*

Table 5.1 The Structure of a Driver Header (Continued)

| Offset | Size (bytes) | Name (bit) |
|--------|--------------|------------|
| | | bit 11 = device supports Open Device, Close Device, Removable Media functions |
| | | bit 12 = Always 0, reserved |
| | | bit 13 = driver not request from DOS first sector of FAT, for Device Driver Function 02h |
| | | bit 14 = driver supports IOCTL Read and IOCTL Write functions |
| | | bit 15 = Always 0 for block device |
| 06h | 2 | Strategy offset of a strategy routine |
| 08h | 2 | Interrupt offset of a interrupt routine |
| 0Ah | 8 | NameOrUnits: logical device name (for character device) or number of units (for block device) |
| 12h | | END: end of Device Driver Header |

In this chapter we use little-endian (15-0) bit ordering, because it is accepted in the Intel microprocessors. Do not forget that everywhere in the following text the most significant bit (MSB) is bit 15, and the least significant bit (LSB) is bit 0.

## The Link Field

The Link field is 4 bytes long. On loading the driver, its upper 16 bits are set to 0, and in the lower 16 is placed the distance in bytes from the beginning of the loaded image to the start of the following driver header, assuming there are several drivers in one file. This parameter obviously limits driver size to 64K. DOS places the address of the following driver header into this field as a far pointer, or if the driver is the last in the chain, DOS puts the value -1 there (0FFFFFFFFh).

## The Attribute Field

In the 15 bit Attribute field, the device driver informs DOS about its type and properties, as well as the characterisitics of the device it supports. DOS uses this information to format device driver requests. The format of this driver request and the meaning of its separate fields will be considered later.

For now, let's look at the Attribute field contents in more detail, at the level of its separate bits. Bit 15 is set to 1 for character devices and 0 for block ones.

For a character device, bits 0-3 determine the type of device. Bit 0, if set to 1, determines a standard input device, bit 1 has the same setting for a standard output device, bit 2 for a NUL device and bit 3 for a Clock device. For devices of other types, these bits must always be set to 0.

The very first DOS device driver is the NUL device. This is a 'bit bucket' device, that discards all output and provides no input. You can request this device for character input or output, when you must do nothing, or when you must formally open or close a driver, but do not wish to do it with any real device. DOS always places it at the very beginning of the driver chain. Bit 2 is used to identify the NUL device, so that this bit must always be set to 0 in your drivers, as you can't replace the NUL driver.

The real time device driver CLOCK$, which sets its own bit 3 of the Attribute field, also relates to character device drivers.

The last attribute unique to character devices is bit 4. If a device driver sets this bit to 1, it means that it supports what is known as fast output (INT 29h). This means that during initialization, the driver should set the interrupt 29h handler accordingly.

For block devices all these bits should equal 0, except perhaps for bit 1. If this bit equals 1, it means that the block device driver supports 32-bit sector addressing (Huge Sectors).

If bit 6 is set to 1, it indicates that the device supports either disk logical devices (functions 17h and 18h of the device driver) or generic IOCTL functions (function 13h of the device driver), or both, irrespective of device driver type. Device driver functions will be considered in more detail later on, when we come to the description of device driver commands.

Bit 7, if set to 1, indicates that the driver supports IOCTL queries (device driver function 19h).

If bit 11 is set to 1, it means that the device driver supports the Open Device, Close Device and Removable Media functions (device driver functions 0Dh, 0Eh and 0Fh respectively). Function 0Fh, however, is only supported by block device drivers.

Bit 13, when set to 1 for character device drivers, indicates that the driver supports the device driver function 10h - Output Until Busy. If bit 13 is set by the block device driver, it indicates that during the call of the device driver function 02h, Build BPB, DOS should report the address of the buffer which contains the first sector file allocation table (FAT) to the device driver.

Lastly, if the device driver sets bit 14 to 1, it means that the driver supports device driver functions 03h and 0Ch - IOCTL Read and IOCTL Write.

When the value of any bit of the Attribute field for the driver is not explicitly defined as equal to 1, this bit should be cleared (set to 0). The contents of the reserved (at least, reserved for DOS 6.0) bits 5, 8-10 and 12 must also always be cleared.

## Other Fields

The Strategy and Interrupt fields are each 2 bytes long. For .SYS type device drivers they contain near pointers to the strategy and interrupt routines. For .EXE type drivers these fields indicate the distance, in bytes, from the beginning of a loaded binary image file to the first executed command of the routine.

The 8 bytes long NameOrUnits field in the character device driver header contains the left-aligned logical device name, complemented by blank spaces if necessary. The device name field should not contain the colon character (:).

In block device drivers, the device name is not indicated. Instead, the first byte of the NameOrUnits field contains the total number of devices (logical or physical) which the driver supports. When a block device driver works, it does not distinguish between physical and logical devices. When the driver is being loaded, it may not report this number, because at device driver initialization (device driver function 00h), the driver must send the value to DOS which, in turn, puts it in the mentioned field of the driver header. The other 7 bytes of the NameOrUnits field in block device drivers are reserved by DOS and must not be touched by any driver.

## The Strategy Program

Each installable device driver has two 16-bit pointers within the code segment of the driver. They indicate the entry points of the strategy and interrupt routines. Inherited from large computers, these names puzzle many programmers. In fact, the strategy routine does not choose a strategy, and the interrupt routine is never called, because of an external interrupt.

Each time the driver is requested, DOS first issues the far call to the strategy program, and passes the address of a request block in the ES:BX registers. The block contains information that the driver needs to perform the operation. The strategy program stores this 32-bit address in fixed memory words and returns control to DOS through a far return. After that, DOS immediately passes control to the interrupt routine to perform the requested task.

There are very serious reasons for this two-step operation. It enables implementation of the two modes of driver operation.

The first mode is synchronous operation. In this mode, the strategy routine executes a minimum amount of work. It may only store the request parameters, and return control to DOS. DOS immediately passes control to the interrupt routine, which performs all the actual work expected from the driver. When the device driver returns control to DOS from the interrupt routine, the driver considers the request completed.

The second mode is asynchronous operation. It will probably be of wider application if future versions of DOS are multi-tasking, but it can be used by confident programmers even now. In this mode, the strategy begins its processing routine after receiving the current request. First of all, the routine places the request in a queue and checks the current conditions. Depending on the priority of the current request and on the status of the queue, the device and the system conditions, the strategy routine may or may not pass control to the driver's interrupt routine immediately. If not, the strategy routine returns control to the operating system. Subsequently, DOS may call the interrupt program to perform the request when convenient.

Let's take a look at how the interrupt routine actually functions.

# The Interrupt Program

After receiving the DOS call, the interrupt has to first find out what it is supposed to do. Its instructions are contained in the information block whose address was preserved by the strategy routine in a memory location accessible to the interrupt routine. The driver request block contains two types of structure - fixed and variable. The first one does not depend on a driver executed function and is referred to as the request header. The second one is defined as dependent on the command to be executed and, together with the first one, is simply referred to as the driver request. When you call the driver from your program, you must pass some relational information about your request to the driver in the driver request block and, maybe, receive some information from the driver when the request has been serviced. You can create the driver request block before calling the driver in your own program. For that, you must find sufficient spare space in your driver for placing the request block and fill it with the necessary data (the driver request format will be considered in detail later). Alternatively, you can use DOS input-and-output-control (IOCTL) functions, DOS Interrupt 21h, function 44h, choosing the appropriate subfunction. The latter may be much easier, because this function not only creates the driver request for you, but also executes it.

We'll look at the functions of these blocks shortly, but first let's take a look at their format.

## The Driver Request Header

**Table 5.2 The Driver Request Header**

| Offset | Size | Name | Brief Description |
|--------|------|------|-------------------|
| 00h | 1 | Length | Request length |
| 01h | 1 | Unit | Unit number (block device only) |
| 02h | 1 | Function | Function number |
| 03h | 2 | Status | Status word |
| 05h | 8 | Reserved | 8 bytes reserved |
| 0Dh | | END | End of Request Header |

The request header contains 5 fields. The first field, Length, is 1 byte long and contains the byte length of the request. Obviously, this byte length is not longer than 255 bytes.

The byte with offset 1, called the Unit, contains a value which means nothing for character devices. For block devices, this value corresponds to the number of the requested device. If you create driver request headers yourself, this is the place to really try and avoid errors. The fact is that no separate driver, even a block one that supports several devices at once, knows anything about the configuration of the whole system. Therefore, when you call it, you must set the serial number of the device in the Unit field out of the devices which the drive supports. The numbering of drivers should begin with 0. So for example, if the driver supports disks C, D, E and F, then, if you send a request for dealing with disk C, you should set device number 0 in the Unit field, and for disk F you would use device number 3.

The Function field, also 1 byte long, contains the number of the command which the driver should execute.

## Character Device Driver Functions

**Table 5.3 Character Device Driver Functions**

| Function | Name |
|----------|------|
| 00h | Init |
| 03h | IOCTL Read |
| 04h | Read |
| 05h | Nondestructive Read |
| 06h | Input Status |
| 07h | Input Flush |
| 08h | Write |
| 09h | Write with Verify |
| 0Ah | Output Status |
| 0Bh | Output Flush |
| 0Ch | IOCTL Write |
| 0Dh | Open Device |

*Continued*

**Table 5.3 Character Device Driver Functions (Continued)**

| Function | Name |
|----------|------|
| 0Eh | Close Device |
| 10h | Output Until Busy |
| 13h | Generic IOCTL |
| 19h | IOCTL Query |

## Block Device Driver Functions

**Table 5.4 Block Device Driver Functions**

| Function | Name |
|----------|------|
| 00h | Init |
| 01h | Media Check |
| 02h | Build BPB |
| 03h | IOCTL Read |
| 04h | Read |
| 08h | Write |
| 09h | Write with Verify |
| 0Ch | IOCTL Write |
| 0Dh | Open Device |
| 0Eh | Close Device |
| 0Fh | Removable Media |
| 13h | Generic IOCTL |
| 17h | Get Logical Device |
| 18h | Set Logical Device |
| 19h | IOCTL Query |

Comparing these two lists of functions, you can see that the command sets for character and block drivers are different. We'll look at each of the functions in detail later on.

Now let's see how to request the driver. We do it in three ways: explicitly, by hand or by the appropriate DOS function.

Suppose, you have somewhere in a code segment a data structure:

```
;ReadWriteRequest Structure:
ReqLength       DB   30
Unit            DB   ?
Function        DB   ?
Status          DW   ?
Reserved        DB   8 DUP(?)
MediaID         DB   ?
Buffer          DD   ?
BytesSec        DW   ?
StartSec        DW   ?
VolumeID        DD   ?
HugeStartSec    DD   ?
;
MyBuffer        DB            'There is data to write',0Dh,0Ah
BuffLength      DW   $ - OFFSET MyBuffer
Strategy        DW   9d2h        ; Segment
                DW   0A2h        ; Offset
Interrupt       DW   9D2h        ; Segment
                DW   0ADh        ; Offset
DevHandle       DW   ?           ; Device Handle
FileAccess      DB   1           ; Write only access
FileName        DB   'CON    ',0
```

which is sufficient for both purposes. We put real addresses, obtained by PRG5_1.COM, into the Strategy and Interrupt fields. You must fill in these fields (by hand) with your own CON driver addresses. When you do so, you can request the CON driver at low-level as follows:

```
    mov ax,cs
    mov ds,ax

;Filling the Request packet fields for character driver:

    mov Function,8                 ;Write operation Code
    mov ax,BuffLength
    mov BytesSec,ax                ;Byte number to Write
    mov ax,cs
    mov word ptr Buffer+2,ax
    mov ax,offset MyBuffer
    mov word ptr Buffer,ax         ;Data Buffer address
```

```
    mov ax,cs                    ;In es:bx = Request Packet Address
    mov es,ax
    mov bx,offset ReqLength

;Now you can call the CON driver

    call far ptr Strategy

    call far ptr Interrupt       ;All Done
```

The alternative is to use the DOS function. Nevertheless, you must first get the necessary information as follows:

```
;Get the device handle by means of Interrupt 21h
;Function 3Dh
   mov dx,offset FileName
   mov al,FileAccess
   mov ah,3dh
   int 21h
   mov DevHandle,ax          ;Write it to memory now
   mov bx,DevHandle          ;Handle of the CON Device
   mov cx,BuffLength         ;Number of bytes to write
   mov dx,offset MyBuffer     ;ds:dx points to MyBuffer
   mov ah,40h
   int 21h                    ;Interrupt 21h Function 40h -
                              ;Write File or Device
```

The Interrupt 21h Function 40h forms a Request packet and requests the CON driver automatically.

Executing both codes gives the same result - the contents of MyBuffer are displayed on the screen.

## The Call Status Word

The fourth field of the request header contains the status word. While calling the device driver, the content of this field has no meaning. The field is filled by the driver only after the request is completed. It's important to understand that the phrase 'completed request' here doesn't neccessarily mean the successful execution of that request, but the completion of an attempt to execute it. The interrupt routine regards any outcome of this attempt as the completion of the request. The status word tells the caller the outcome of the attempted call.

Let's look at the bits that make up the status word more closely.

Bit 8 is the Done bit, and is set to 1 if the operation is completed. If bit 15 of the status word (Error bit) is 0, then no errors occured during completion of the interrupt. If the Error bit is set to 1 then an error did occur and the code for it is placed in the low byte of the status word (bits 0-7). A list of possible errors is shown in the following table, where the format of the status word is given in full:

**Table 5.5 List of Possible Errors**

| Status Word | Meanings |
|---|---|
| Bits | |
| 0 - 7 | If bit 15 is set, they specify an error value: |
| | Error    Meaning |
| | 00h    Write protect violation |
| | 01h    Unknown unit |
| | 02h    Drive not ready |
| | 03h    Unknown command |
| | 04h    CRC error |
| | 05h    Incorrect drive request length |
| | 06h    Seek error |
| | 07h    Unknown media |
| | 08h    Sector not found |
| | 09h    Printer out of paper |
| | 0Ah    Write fault |
| | 0Bh    Read fault |
| | 0Ch    General failure |
| | 0Dh    Reserved |
| | 0Eh    Reserved |
| | 0Fh    Invalid disk change |
| | 27h    Disk full (on write request to compressed drive) |
| 8 | Operation Completed |
| 9 | Device is Busy |
| 15 | Error Occurred |

If the driver supports the functions 06h, 0Ah, 0Fh (Input Status, Output Status and Removable Area), there is one more possible outcome: the device is busy. In this case, the driver sets bit 9 (the busy bit) of the status word to 1.

# Device Driver Functions

So far we have only considered the static features of installed device drivers, namely the main driver components and their position in the driver location in RAM. It's time to look at the commands and functions that those drivers can implement. In terms of executable functions, installable device drivers are really no different to DOS resident drivers.

There are no common standards for device driver functions, but there are some definite rules and restrictions. There are differences between character and block device functions. If you compare the tables of functions we saw earlier, the following differences are apparent:

- Character and block device drivers execute different sets of functions.

- Only 3 functions, 00h, 04h and 08h, are obligatory for all drivers.

- Functions 01h and 02h are obligatory for all block device drivers.

- Functions 05h, 06h, 07h, 0Ah and 0Bh are obligatory for all character device drivers.

- Function 09h is obligatory for all block device drivers, but is optional for character device drivers. This is understandable in the case of the CON driver for example, where verification is impossible, because this driver writes on the display, but reads from the keyboard.

- Execution of about half the device driver functions is optional and depends on the bit settings of the Attributes word.

We'll discuss the more detailed features later, when we turn to separate device driver functions.

## Names

Character device drivers each support only one input device and one output device. Each driver has a logical device name. This name is used by other programs to open the logical device and to pass requests for functions to it. If an installable driver has the same name as a resident driver, it replaces this resident driver. We'll learn more about this when we consider driver allocation in RAM.

Block device drivers can support one or more devices, for example floppy, hard or virtual disks. These multiple devices can also be logical devices, such as hard disk partitions. It is important that you don't replace one of these drivers with one of your own. The block device driver alone knows how many devices it supports and it distinguishes its own devices in order of their allocation in a given driver. During initialization the driver reports the quantity of supported devices to DOS, and DOS in turn assigns each a unique number to distinguish them from other devices in the system.

One general point to note is that all types of installable drivers must preserve all registers and flags.

# Initialization (Device Driver Function 00h - Init)

Driver installation in DOS begins with the allocation of drivers in memory. This takes place in the same order as the appropriate DEVICE or DEVICEHIGH commands in the CONFIG.SYS file. After allocation of each driver, DOS calls the driver, issuing it with a request for driver initialization.

### Init (Device Driver Function 00h) Request Format

**Table 5.6 Init Request Format**

| Offset | Size | Name | Brief Description |
|--------|------|------|-------------------|
| 00h | 13 | | Request Header |
| 0Dh | 1 | Units | OUTPUT : number of units |
| 0Eh | 4 | EndAddress | INPUT : end available memory address |
| | | | OUTPUT : end resident code |
| 12h | 4 | ParamAddress | INPUT : addr CONFIG.SYS string |
| | | | OUTPUT : BPB pointer |
| 16h | 1 | DriveNumber | INPUT : first drive number |
| 17h | 2 | ErMessFlag | OUTPUT : error message flag |
| 19h | | | End of the Request Format |

*Continued*

The driver begins processing the initialization request by looking at the information supplied by DOS along with the request which the 32-bit address driver receives in ES:BX registers with every driver call. The strategy program saves this address and immediately returns to the caller. DOS then calls the interrupt routine, which performs the necessary request processing.

The first part of initialization information can be transferred to DOS in the CONFIG.SYS file as DEVICE or DEVICEHIGH command arguments. DOS places the far address of the string containing these parameters in the ParamAddress field of the device driver request.

The driver may read the second portion of request information in the Function field of the request header. There, you can check if initialization is really necessary. DOS performs driver initialization only once, so if the driver is already in place you may wish to prevent any subsequent attempts to repeat the process in your driver. Then your driver should determine the flag variable, which may be equal to 0 before initialization, and set this flag to a nonzero value when it receives the first initialization request. The driver then checks that flag on future requests.

The next stage of initialization is for the driver to check if there is enough accessible memory space for the driver. It does this by comparing the value in the EndAddress field of the request header with the last required memory address. This field is only supplied by DOS 5.0 upwards, therefore if the driver uses this information, it should first check the DOS version.

In the request header DriveNumber field, DOS passes the first disk device number to a driver. Adding that value to the quantity of driver supported devices gives you the number of the last device. DOS supports no more than 26 devices. To successfully initialize the driver, the total number of devices should not exceed this value.

After performing all the necessary actions for initialization, the driver in turn sends the necessary information back to DOS.

First, your driver should fill in the Status field in the request header that we looked at earlier. After successful initialization you must set bit 8, the Done bit, to 1, and in case of failure you set bit 15, the error bit, as well. In this case you place the appropriate error code in the low-order byte of the status word.

In the Units field the block device driver should indicate the quantity of driver supported devices. The character device driver should clear the Units field.

The EndAddress field is used by the driver to reserve memory. This field points to the nearest free byte of memory after driver initialization. As DOS only intializes drivers once, you can save the required RAM by excluding that part of the driver code which performs the initialization task from the reserved memory area by placing this code part at the end of the driver, beyond the address being pointed to by the EndAddress.

During initialization, only a few DOS system functions are available (Interrupt 21h functions 01h through 0Ch, 25h, 30h and 35h). You can display messages at the standard output device, but cannot open files or allocate additional memory. If you want to do something else, you can enable multiple driver initialization from your own program, by leaving the initialized part of the driver in memory. DOS does not explicitly prohibit you from doing this.

If initialization fails, the driver should write the initial address of the driver into the EndAddress field, thus releasing all earlier allocated memory. When allocating driver memory, the driver's own stack must be taken into account. When DOS calls the driver, it grants not more than 40-50 bytes of free memory to the stack. If you think more memory may be required for the driver, you should set your own stack.

After a character device driver has been initialized, you should write 0 in the ParamAddress field. For block devices you should put the far address of the BPB (BIOS Parameter Block) there. The BPB structure contains the information that defines the disk or other storage medium format which is necessary for DOS to support these devices. The BPBformat will be discussed later and is shown in Table 5.10.

If DOS returns an initialization failure message, the driver must set the ErrMessFlag field to 1 and place the error code in the status word.

It is generally not recommended to use DOS functions in the initialization part of a device driver, except for input/output functions like INT 21h, Fn 01h - 0Ch and functions Fn 25h - Set Interrupt Vector, Fn 35h - Get Interrupt Vector and Fn 30h - Get Version Number. Driver initialization takes place at boot up time, when DOS is not yet fully loaded, so calling other functions can have unpredictable results.

## Media Check (Device Driver Function 01h)

The Media Check function is used by block devices only to determine whether the floppy disk in the disk drive has changed. DOS issues this request if it needs disk access to open, close or rename files. This function is essential for the correct functioning of the file system. If it fails you may miss or destroy the data waiting to be written in the files at the previous request or write command.

The Media ID is the DOS abbreviation for the media descriptor. The media descriptor is a one-byte number which specifies the physical features and logical organization of the disk. The floppy disk media descriptors accepted for DOS 6.0 are shown in Table 5.7.

**Table 5.7 The Floppy Disk Media Descriptors**

| Value | Type of Medium |
|-------|----------------|
| 0F0h | 3.5-inch, 2 sides, 18 sector/track (1.44MB), |
|      | 3.5-inch, 2 sides, 36 sector/track(2.88MB), |
|      | 5.25 inch, 2 sides, 15 sector/track (1.2 MB). |
|      | This value also used for other media types. |
| 0F8h | Hard disk, any capacity. |
| 0F9h | 3.5-inch, 2 sides, 9 sector/track (720K), |
|      | 5.25 inch, 2 sides, 18 sector/track (1.2 MB) |
| 0FAh | 5.25 inch, 1 side, 8 sector/track (320K) |
| 0FBh | 3.5 inch, 2 sides, 8 sector/track (640K) |
| 0FCh | 5.25 inch, 1 side, 9 sector/track (180K) |
| 0FDh | 5.25 inch, 2 sides, 9 sector/track (360K). |
|      | The value also used for 8-inch disks. |
| 0FEh | 5.25 inch, 1 side, 8 sector/track (160K). |
|      | The value also used for 8-inch disks. |
| 0FFh | 5.25 inch, 2 sides, 8 sector/track (320K) |

The format of the Media Check function request is shown in Table 5.8.

**Table 5.8 Media Check Request Format**

| Offset | Size | Name | Brief Description |
|--------|------|------|------------------|
| 00h | 13 | | Request Header |
| 0Dh | 1 | MediaID | INPUT : current media ID |
| 0Eh | 1 | Return | OUTPUT : return value |
| 0Fh | 4 | VolumeID | OUTPUT : address of previous volume identifier |
| 13h | | | End of the Request Format |

When DOS calls the driver, it sets the device number on which the operation is to be performed in the Unit field of the request header. While fulfilling this request, DOS sets in the Media ID field, the current (old) disk identifier value from the Media ID field in the BPB, which DOS assumes hasn't changed. In turn, the driver must verify this and set the return code in the Return field and the pointer to the previous volume identifier. If the disk has not been replaced, you must set the Return code to 1. If you put in the 0FFh code, it means that the disk was changed. If you return 0 in this field, it means that the driver cannot determine whether the disk was changed or not (in which case DOS can check if the volume identifier was changed). The possible outcomes are:

If the disk was not changed, DOS continues the operation with the device.

If the driver reports that the disk has changed, DOS cancels everything connected with the device buffers and calls the device driver function 02h - Build BPB. If write information has remained in some buffers, it will be lost. If you set bit 11 of the driver Attribute word, the driver should return a 32-bit pointer to the ASCIIZ-string which contains the volume label of the current device. If the given device has not got a volume label, the driver should return a pointer to the string " NO NAME ". From then on, if volume labels coincide, DOS believes that the carrier was not changed and returns the error code 0Fh "Invalid disk change".

If the driver cannot determine whether the disk was changed and returns the code 0, DOS checks whether information remains in the internal buffers. If it does, DOS tries to write the data. If the record data is not present, DOS acts as if the disk was changed.

# Build BPB (Device Driver Function 02h)

The BIOS Parameter Block is the structure that contains the data which defines a disk or other storage format. It includes bytes per sector, sectors per cluster, sectors per track and other data which determines data storage organization. Without this information it is impossible to control storage, i.e. perform read and write operations.

The Build BPB function is requested by DOS whenever it finds out that the Media Check specifies that the medium (usually diskette) has changed.

This function is required only for block device drivers. DOS issues this function after the function Media Check (Device Driver Function 01h) has reported any real or potential change in the media and that all write operations on that disk have been completed.

The format of the request is shown in Table 5.9.

**Table 5.9 The Build BPB Request Format**

| Offset | Size | Name | Brief Description |
|--------|------|------|-------------------|
| 00h | 13 | | Request Header |
| 0Dh | 1 | MediaID | INPUT:  media descriptor |
| 0Eh | 4 | FATSector | INPUT:  pointer to first FAT |
| | | | Sector buffer |
| 12h | 4 | BPBAddress | OUTPUT: address of BPB |
| 16h | | | End of the Request Format |

When requesting a driver, DOS puts into the Unit field of the request header the unit number (usually number of drive) for which it is necessary to build a BPB, and in the Media ID field it puts the media descriptor of the disk that DOS assumes is in the drive.

In addition, DOS passes two far addresses to the driver. In the field FATSector, there is a pointer to a 1-sector long buffer. If you set bit 13 to 1 in the Attributes field of the driver header, this buffer contains the first sector of the first FAT table on the disk. The first byte of this buffer is used as the media ID of the disk. If you set the Attribute bit to 0, the contents of the buffer have no meaning and you can use this buffer in the driver as additional memory for your program. This can be very useful, because this buffer is located in the system memory region and cannot be destroyed, so you can, for example, place in it some parameters or addresses for communicating with several programs.

After completing the request, the driver should place the far pointer to the BIOS Parameter Block (BPB) in the BPBAddress field.

The structure of the BIOS Parameter Block is shown in Table 5.10.

**Table 5.10 The Structure of the BIOS Parameter Block**

| Offset | Size | Name | Brief Description |
|--------|------|------|-------------------|
| 00h | 2 | BytesPerSec | Bytes per Sector |
| 02h | 1 | SecPerClust | Sectors per Cluster |
| 03h | 2 | ResSectors | Number of Reserved Sectors |
| 05h | 1 | FATs | Number of File Allocation Tables |
| 06h | 2 | RootDirEnts | Number of Root Directory Entries |
| 08h | 2 | Sectors | Total Number of Sectors |
| | | | (if disk less then 32 Mb, else 0) |
| 0Ah | 1 | Media | Media Descriptor |
| 0Bh | 2 | SecPerFAT | Number of Sectors per FAT |
| 0Dh | 2 | SecPerTrack | Sectors per Track |
| 0Fh | 2 | Heads | Number of Heads |
| 11h | 4 | HiddenSecs | Number of Hidden Sectors |
| | | | (only 2 bytes if prior to DOS 4.0) |
| 15h | 4 | HugeSecs | Number of Sectors if Sectors field = 0, |
| | | | else 0 (DOS 4.0+) |
| 19h | | | End of BPB Format |

This BPB format is valid for DOS version 6.0.

This function causes the driver to fill in the BPB for various media. DOS doesn't actually define the order in which the driver completes each part of the job. A typical sequence of events would be:

First the driver compares byte Media ID, which it reads out from the first sector of the first FAT table, with the Media ID field of the request header. This checks whether this byte coincides with the correct DOS version. The driver then needs to check again to confirm that the media didn't change. If the driver supports Removable Media, it should read the volume label from the disk and save it. Before storing the label, it may be worth comparing it with the current one. If the volume labels coincide, the driver thinks that the media was not changed. Finally, if the driver still believes that the media has not been changed, it can check the Media ID byte in the current BPB structure. If it coincides with the first byte of the first sector of the first FAT table, and this byte value unequivocally defines the existing BPB structure, the driver can put the address of the current BPB into the BPB Address field. Otherwise, the driver should build a new BPB, using, for example, the floppy disk loading sector.

*Despite all that has been said above, if the driver supports removable media, and you want to control media change, you must read the disk volume label and save it! Otherwise, you cannot support removable media. You may write on a changed disk and lose your data, or destroy existing information. In either case you have to save it before completing the request.*

## IOCTL Read (Device Driver Function 03h)

This device driver function reads data from either character or block devices. DOS only issues this function if you set bit 14 of the driver Attributes field to 1; otherwise the driver will not implement this function.

The main purpose of this function is to execute IOCTL driver requests for Read operation from:

- Interrupt 21h Function 4402h - Receive Control Data from Character Device.

- Interrupt 21h Function 4404h - Receive Control Data from Block Device.

The Control Data may be of any length and format. The format of the information is device-specific and does not follow any standard. Strangely enough, among IOCTL functions, there are no functions for usual Read and Write operations. These are supported by Interrupt 21h Functions 3Dh through 40h (see below).

The format of the request is shown in Table 5.11.

**Table 5.11 The IOCTL Read Request Format**

| Offset | Size | Name | Brief Description |
|--------|------|----------|-------------------|
| 00h | 13 | | Request Header |
| 0Dh | 1 | Not used | |
| 0Eh | 4 | Buffer | INPUT : buffer Address |
| 12h | 2 | Bytes | INPUT : number of bytes to read |
| | | | OUTPUT : number of bytes read |
| 14h | | | End of the Request Format |

When DOS sends the request, the Unit field of the block device request header contains the block device number for which the control data exchange is intended. For character devices this field is meaningless.

The Buffer Address field contains a far pointer to the buffer that holds data that has been read from the device. When DOS calls the driver, it guarantees that the buffer volume is sufficient to hold all the necessary data that the driver should read. This allows the driver to read all the data during one exchange session, without stopping to transmit part of the received data.

When DOS calls the driver, the Number of Bytes field contains the number of bytes to exchange, which are contained in register CX when you call the Interrupt 21h, function 4402h or 4404h. After completing the request the driver should write the actual amount of data read or written here. This value should not exceed the number of bytes originally requested: if it does, then an error 0Bh, Read fault occurs.

After successfully completing the request, you should set the Done bit (bit 8) to 1 in the Status word of the request header.

If an error occurred, the driver should set both the Error and the Done bits (15 and 8) to 1 and copy the error value to the low-order byte of the Status word.

# Read (Device Driver Function 04h)

This device driver function is for reading data from either character or block devices. The data must be written into the specified buffer.

DOS usually requests this function from the DOS Interrupt 21h Function 3Fh - Read File or Device. The format of the request is shown in Table 5.12.

**Table 5.12 The Read Request Format**

| Offset | Size | Name | Brief Description |
|--------|------|------|-------------------|
| 00h | 13 | | Request Header |
| 0Dh | 1 | MediaID | INPUT : media descriptor |
| 0Eh | 4 | Buffer | INPUT : buffer address |
| 12h | 2 | BytesSec | INPUT : number of bytes/sectors to read |
| | | | OUTPUT : number of bytes/sectors read |
| 14h | 2 | StartSec | INPUT : starting sector number |
| 16h | 4 | VolumeAdd | OUTPUT : volume identifier address |
| 1Ah | 4 | HugeStartSec | INPUT : 32-bit starting sector number |
| | | | if StartSec=0FFFFh |
| 1Eh | | | End of the Request Format |

For block devices, the Unit field of the request header contains the logical unit number of the block device from which to read the data. The Buffer Address field contains a far pointer to the buffer where you must write the data.

When DOS calls the driver, it ensures that the buffer volume is sufficient for all data to be read. If the buffer is larger than required, no special action is required. If not, it may call the driver several times, requesting the data read quantity which is equal to or less than the buffer size. If you request the operation yourself, you must do the same.

At the time the driver request is made, the BytesSec field contains the number of bytes to read in the case of a character device, or the number of sectors for a block device. After completing the request, the driver should copy field the actual quantity of data read into the field. This value should not exceed that stated in the request, in which case no error is reported. You should always update this field. If an error does occur, you should indicate the actual number of bytes that were read before the error occurred.

The following fields are only valid for block device drivers.

The Media ID field indicates which media descriptor DOS assumes is in the drive. The allowable values for this field should correspond to the ones listed for the driver device function 01h (Media Check).

The Starting Sector Number field (2 bytes long) determines the first logical sector number from which to read. If this number exceeds 65534, then DOS places the value 0FFFFh in this field. In this case, you can find the right number of the first sector in the HugeStartSec field of 32-bit length. If the driver supports this field, you must set bit 1 of the Attributes word of the driver header to 1. The driver should translate the received number into the appropriate head, path and sector numbers. After successfully completing the request, you should set the Done bit (bit 8) in the Status word of the request header to 1.

If an error occurred, the driver should set both the Error and Done bits (15 and 8) to 1 and copy the error value to the low-order byte of the Status word.

If the driver returns the error code 0Fh (non-authorized media change), it should return a long pointer to the ASCII-string with the volume label for the most recently accessed disk to the Volume Identifier Address field.

To detect a situation for error 0Fh, the driver can count opened and closed files (see device driver functions 0Dh and 0Eh). Really, if there are no opened files and the disk was not changed, it is possible to assume that the intended exchange will be successful. If the disk was changed and there are opened files, then error 0Fh is possible.

# Nondestructive Read (Device Driver Function 05h)

This function is supported for character devices only. You can use it if you want to find out whether or not there is a character in the input buffer. If the buffer is not empty, you can do some filtering of the first character, without removing it from the buffer. This can be very useful when you want to pass the character to another routine for subsequent reading and processing. In this case, the next read operation must return the same character. Normal read operations must then restore the input buffer.

The format of the request is shown in Table 5.13.

**Table 5.13 The Nondestructive Read Request Format**

| Offset | Size | Name | Brief Description |
| --- | --- | --- | --- |
| 00h | 13 | | Request Header |
| 0Dh | 1 | CharOutput | Character |
| 0Eh | | | End of the Request Format |

When DOS requests this function from the driver, it reads the character from the device input buffer without removing it from the buffer. The driver then places the received character (i.e. the next character which DOS will read from the buffer by the normal read operation) in the Char field of the request header. This enables DOS to get the same character from the input buffer. A subsequent read operation will return the same character, because the nondestructive read function does not remove it from the input buffer.

After successfully completing the operation, you should set the Done bit (bit 8) in the Status word of the request header to 1. If the input buffer contains at least one character, the Busy bit (bit 9) in the Status word should be cleared, indicating that DOS should not wait to read the symbol. If the input buffer is empty, the driver should set the Busy bit in the Status word to 1.

If an error occurs, the driver should set both the Error and the Done bits (15 and 8) to 1 and copy the error value to the low-order byte of the Status word.

## Input Status (Device Driver Function 06h)

This function is supported for character devices only. The request for this function only contains the request header (13 bytes) that we have seen before.

After executing this function, the driver returns the Status word which indicates whether the input or output buffer contains any symbols. If there is no input buffer, or the buffer contains one or more character, the driver should clear the Busy bit (bit 9) in the Status word. If the input buffer is empty, the driver should set this bit to 1.

After successfully completing the request, you should set the Done bit (bit 8) in the Status word of the request header to 1. If an error occurred, the driver should set both the Error and the Done bits (15 and 8) to 1 and copy the error value to the low-order byte of the Status word.

## Input Flush (Device Driver Function 07h)

This function is only supported for character devices. If DOS calls the driver to execute the device driver function 07h, the driver interrupts the current read operation and resets the input buffer.

After successfully completing the request, you should set the Done bit (bit 8) in the Status word of the request header to 1. If an error occurred, the driver should set both the Error and Done bits (15 and 8) to 1 and copy the error value to the low-order byte of the Status word.

## Write/Write with Verify (Device Driver Function 08h and 09h)

These device driver functions are for exchanges with either character or block devices. Their main purpose is input/output support. DOS may request this function from DOS Interrupt 21h Function 3Fh - Read File or Device.

The format of the request is shown in Table 5.14.

**Table 5.14 The Write/Write with Verify Request Format**

| Offset | Size | Name | Brief Description |
|--------|------|------|-------------------|
| 00h | 13 | | Request Header |
| 0Dh | 1 | MediaID | INPUT : media descriptor |
| 0Eh | 4 | Buffer | INPUT : buffer Address |
| 12h | 2 | BytesSec | INPUT : number of bytes/sectors to write |
| | | | OUTPUT : number of bytes/sectors written |
| 14h | 2 | StartSec | INPUT : starting sector number |
| 16h | 4 | VolumeAdd | OUTPUT : volume identifier address |
| 1Ah | 4 | HugeStartSec | INPUT : 32-bit starting sector number |
| 1Eh | | | End of the Request Format |

For block devices the Unit field of the request header contains the logical unit number of the block device to write. The Buffer Address field contains a far pointer to the buffer into which the data is to be written.

This contains the number of bytes for the character device, or the number of sectors for the block device. After completing the request, the driver should copy the actual quantity of data written in that field. The driver should always fill in this field. If an error has occurred, you should return the actual byte or sector number written before the error occurred.

The following fields are only valid for block device drivers.

The Media ID field indicates which media descriptor DOS assumes is in the drive. The allowable values for this field should correspond to the ones listed for the driver device function 01h (Media Check).

The Starting Sector Number field (2 bytes) determines the first logical sector number to write. If this number exceeds 65534, then DOS places the value 0FFFFh in this field. In this case, you can find the right number of the first sector in the HugeStartSec field of 32-bit length. If the driver supports this field, you must set bit 1 of the Attributes word of the driver header to 1. The driver should translate the received number into the appropriate head, path and sector numbers.

After successfully completing the request, you should set the Done bit (bit 8) in the Status word of the request header to 1. If an error occurred, the driver should set both the Error and Done bits (15 and 8) to 1 and copy the error value to the low-order byte of the Status word.

If the driver returns the error code 0Fh (non-authorized media change), it should return a 32 bit pointer to the zero terminated ASCII-string, which contains the volume label for the most recently accessed disk in the Volume Identifier Address field.

To detect a situation for error 0Fh the driver can count opened and closed files (see device driver functions 0Dh and 0Eh below). Really, if there are no opened files and the disk was not changed, it is safe to assume that the proposed exchange will be successful. If the disk was changed and there are opened files, then error 0Fh may occur.

After writing data using the function Write with Verify (09h), the driver should read the data back from the device and check its accuracy.

# Output Status (Device Driver Function 0Ah)

This function is only supported for character devices. The request for this function just contains the Request Header we looked at earlier.

After executing this function, the driver returns the Status word which indicates whether the device output buffer contains any characters. If the buffer contains one or more characters, the driver should set the Busy bit (bit 9) in the Status word. If the input buffer is empty, the driver should clear the Busy bit.

After successfully completing the request, you should set the Done bit (bit 8) in the Status word of the request header to 1. If an error occurred, the driver should set both the Error and Done bits (15 and 8) to 1 and copy the error value to the low-order byte of the Status word.

## Output Flush (Device Driver Function 0Bh)

This function is only supported for character devices. It is useful if you want to stop the current write operation and reset the output buffer. The request for this function only contains the Request Header we looked at earlier.

If DOS calls the driver to execute the function 0Bh, the driver must stop the current write operation and reset the output buffer. After successfully completing the request, you should set the Done bit (bit 8) in the Status word of the request header to 1.

If an error occurred, the driver should set both the Error and Done bits (15 and 8) to 1 and copy the error value to the low-order byte of the Status word.

## IOCTL Write (Device Driver Function 0Ch)

This function writes data to either character or block devices. DOS only requests this function if you set bit 14 of the driver Attributes word to 1. The main purpose of the function is to support output IOCTL control sequences for:

- Interrupt 21h function 4403h - Send Control Data to Character Device.

- Interrupt 21h function 4405h - Send Control Data to Block Device.

The format of the request is shown in Table 5.15.

**Table 5.15 The IOCTL Write Request Format**

| Offset | Size | Name | Brief Description |
|--------|------|------|-------------------|
| 00h | 13 | | Request Header |
| 0Dh | 1 | Not used | |
| 0Eh | 4 | Buffer | INPUT : buffer Address |
| 12h | 2 | Bytes | INPUT : number of bytes to write |
| | | | OUTPUT : number of bytes written |
| 14h | | | End of the Request Format |

The Unit field of the block device request header contains the block device number we want to write. The Buffer field contains a far pointer to a buffer containing data to write to the device. When DOS calls the driver to read, it guarantees that the buffer volume is sufficient for all the required data the driver ought to write. This allows the driver to write all the data during one exchange session, without stopping to receive the next portion of data to write. The data format depends on the device type and does not adhere to any standard.

The bytes field contains the number of bytes to write. After completing the request you should update the Bytes field with the actual amount of data written. This value should not exceed the requested amount of data.

After successfully completing the request, you should set the Done bit (bit 8) in the Status word of the Request Header to 1.

If an error occurred, the driver should set both the Error and Done bits (15 and 8) to 1 and copy the error value to the low-order byte of the Status word.

## Open Device (Device Driver Function 0Dh)

This function informs the device driver that a character or block device is open or created. The function is available for either character or block devices. The request for this function only contains the Request Header.

For block devices, DOS copies the number of the device which contains the opened or closed file into the Unit field of the Request Header. DOS cooperates with the program SHARE in order to inform the device driver when a device is open. DOS requests the Open Device function only if you set bit 11 of the Attributes field of your driver device header to 1.

DOS requests this function on a number of different occasions, such as when an application program opens or creates a file or the device. The driver can use this function along with function 0Eh (Close Device) to control the internal buffers and the device initialization process.

For block devices the Open Device function increases the quantity of opened files on the disk, while the Close Device function reduces this quantity and resets the internal buffers once all open files have been closed.

For character device drivers, this function can be used before writing to a device to send a sequence of control characters to it. In such a case, the driver should also support the functions 03h and 0Ch (IOCTL Read and IOCTL Write) so that the driver can send and receive the control sequences.

After successfully completing the request, you should set the Done bit (bit 8) to 1 in the Status word of the Request Header. If an error occurred, the driver should set both the Error and the Done bits (15 and 8) to 1 and copy the error value to the low-order byte of the Status word.

## Close Device (Device Driver Function 0Eh)

This function tells the driver if a block or character device is closed. The request for this function contains only the Request Header.

For block devices, DOS places the device number in the Unit field of the Request Header. Again, DOS uses SHARE to determine which files are open. DOS only requests this function if bit 11 of the Attributes field of the device header is set to 1.

DOS requests this function whenever an application program closes a file or device. The driver can use this function along with function 0Dh (Open Device) for internal buffer control and device initialization.

After successfully completing the request, you should set the Done bit (bit 8) to 1 in the Status word of the Request Header.

If an error occurred, the driver should set both the Error and Done bits (15 and 8) to 1 and copy the error value to the low-order byte of the Status word.

## Removable Media (Device Driver Function 0Fh)

The Removable Media function determines whether the disk contains removable media. This function is only valid for block devices. To use it, you need to set bit 11 in the Attributes word of your driver header to 1. The request for this function contains only the Request Header.

DOS places the number of devices to be checked in the Unit field.

After successfully executing the request, the driver should set the Done bit (bit 8) to 1 in Status word of the Request Header. If the disk in the requested drive is removable, the driver should clear the Busy bit (bit 9) in the Status word. If it isn't removable, then set it to 1. DOS assumes that this function is always successful and ignores any error value.

## Output Until Busy (Device Driver Function 10h)

This function causes the driver to output data from the buffer until it can no longer accept data. The function is only applicable for character devices.

The format of the request is shown in Table 5.16.

**Table 5.16 The Output Until Busy Request Format**

| Offset | Size | Name | Brief Description |
|--------|------|------|-------------------|
| 00h | 13 | | Request Header |
| 0Dh | 1 | Not used | |
| 0Eh | 4 | Buffer | INPUT : buffer Address |
| 12h | 2 | Bytes | INPUT : number of bytes to write |
| | | | OUTPUT : number of bytes written |
| 14h | | | End of the Request Format |

When DOS requests the driver, the Buffer Address field contains the far address of the buffer that contains the data to be written. DOS puts the number of bytes to write in the Number of Bytes field. After the request has been completed, the driver writes into this field the number of bytes actually transferred, which shouldn't exceed the requested quantity.

This device driver function is intended to support slower devices which have an input buffer for increased efficiency. The driver usually writes as much data as possible to the device input buffer, and stops when the buffer is full. Thereafter, the driver updates the Bytes field with the number of bytes that were actually transferred and returns control to DOS. The requesting program releases the empty part of the buffer and is then free to execute other procedures. The program can then call the driver again later to write out the rest of the buffer.

After successfully completing the request, you should set the Done bit (bit 8) to 1 in the Status word of the Request Header. If an error occurs, the driver should set both the Error and Done bits (15 and 8) to 1 and copy the error value to the low-order byte of the Status word.

## Generic IOCTL (Device Driver Function 13h)

This function provides extended control over input and output. Now, for the first time, we meet the Category and the Minor Code terms. The device category specifies the type of device. This parameter may be one of the values shown in Table 5.17:

**Table 5.17 Device Categories**

| Value | Device |
|-------|--------|
| 1h | Serial device |
| 3h | Console (screen) |
| 5h | Parallel Printer |
| 8h | Drive |

If the driver supports a device other that those listed, you must give the device a unique name in the form of a one-byte number. You have to place this number into the Category field when requesting the driver, and the driver itself must check this value.

DOS calls the serial, console and parallel printer drivers via Interrupt 21h function 440Ch (Generic IOCTL for the Character Device Drivers), and the disk drivers via the Interrupt 21h function 440Dh (Generic IOCTL for the Block Device Drivers). When DOS calls the driver, it places a far pointer to a structure associated with that function in the IOCTL Data Address field. The type and contents of this structure depend on the Minor Code Function. The driver must interpret this data, carry out the request and, if necessary, return any applicable information in the same structure.

DOS only calls this function if you set bit 6 to 1 in the driver Attributes field. After successfully completing a request, you should set the Done bit (bit 8) to 1 in the Status word of the Request Header.

If an error occurs, the driver should set both the Error and Done bits (15 and 8) to 1 and copy the error value to the low-order byte of the Status word.

## The Minor Code DOS Function Subset

Minor Code is passed in the CL register when you call the Interrupt. For this request, the Category and Minor Code fields shown in the Request Header below determine whether the function refers to input or output. The function is applicable to both character and block devices. If your driver supports this function, you should set bit 6 to 1 in the Attributes word of your driver's device header.

The format of the request is shown in Table 5.18.

**Table 5.18 The Generic IOCTL Request Format**

| Offset | Size | Name |
|--------|------|------|
| 00h | 13 | Request Header |
| 0Dh | 1 | Device Category |
| 0Eh | 1 | Minor Code Function: |
| | | |
| | | For Character Device Drivers: |
| | |     45h - Set Iteration Count |
| | |     4Ah - Select Code Page |
| | |     4Ch - Start Code Page Prepare |
| | |     4Dh - End Code Page Prepare |
| | |     65h - Get Iteration Count |
| | |     6Ah - Query Selected Code Page |
| | |     6Bh - Query Code Page Prepare List |
| | | |
| | | For Block Device Drivers: |
| | |     40h - Set Device Parameters |
| | |     41h - Write Track on Logical Drive |
| | |     42h - Format Track on Logical Drive |

*Continued*

Table 5.18 The Generic IOCTL Request Format (Continued)

| Offset | Size | Name |
|--------|------|------|
| | | 46h - Set Media ID |
| | | 60h - Get Device Parameters |
| | | 62h - Read Track on Logical Drive |
| | | 66h - Get Media ID |
| | | 68h - Sense Media Type |
| 0Fh | 4 | Reserved |
| 13h | 4 | IOCTL Data Address |
| 17h | | End of Request Format |

DOS sets the Unit field in the request header to the number of the device.

# Get Logical Device (Device Driver Function 17h)

This function is for block devices. To use it, you have to set bit 6 in the Attribute word of the device header to 1. A request for this function contains only the Request Header.

When DOS requests this function, it passes the physical device (drive) number to the driver in the Unit field of the Request Header. The driver should return the name of the logical device referenced by the last Set Logical Device Command (1=A, 2=B, 3=C and so on). If the drive has no other logical drive numbers, then the function returns a zero.

After successfully completing the request, you should set the Done bit (bit 8) in the Status word of the request header to 1.

If an error occurs, the driver should set both the Error and Done bits (15 and 8) to 1 and copy the error value to the low-order byte of the Status word.

## Set Logical Device (Device Driver Function 18h)

This function is only for block devices. To use it, you have to set bit 6 of the Attribute word in the device header to 1. A request for this function contains only the Request Header.

For this function, DOS places the zero based (i.e. their numbers are in range 0 through the total unit number) logical drive number of the device to be made active in the Unit field of the request header.

After successfully completing the request, you should set the Done bit (bit 8) in the Status word of the Request Header to 1.

If an error occurs, the driver should set both the Error and Done bits (15 and 8) to 1, and copy the error value to the low-order byte of the Status word.

## IOCTL Query (Device Driver Function 19h)

The IOCTL Query Function detects whether the driver supports a generic IOCTL Function identified by a given minor code. The function is applicable both for character and block devices.

DOS only calls this function if you set bit 7 in the Attributes field of your driver to 1.

The format of the request is shown in Table 5.19.

**Table 5.19 The IOCTL Query Request Format**

| Offset | Size | Name | Brief Description |
|--------|------|------|-------------------|
| 00h | 13 | | Request Header |
| 0Dh | 1 | Category | INPUT : Device Category |
| 0Eh | 1 | MinorCode | INPUT : Minor Code |
| 0Fh | 4 | Reserved | |
| 13h | 4 | IOCTLData | INPUT : IOCTL Data Address |
| 17h | | | End of the Request Format |

DOS specifies the block device the request is for in the Unit field of the Request Header.

The Minor Code and Category fields specify the category and the minor code of the generic IOCTL function to be checked.

The driver receives the status of the query in the Status field.

If the driver does not support the given generic IOCTL function, it should set both the Error and Done bits (15 and 8) to 1 and copy the error value 03h (Unknown Function) to the low-order byte of the Status word before returning. Otherwise, you should set the Done bit in the Status word of the request header to 1 and return control to the requesting program.

# Allocation of DOS Device Drivers in RAM

Now you know what device drivers do and how they work, it's time to look at their implementation in detail.

You can work with device drivers at a number of different levels. You can simply call someone else's driver from your own application program, or examine that driver to see how it implements various functions. You may want to expand the functions of an exisiting driver, or to write a new one from scratch. Irrespective of which choice you make, there are some fundamental things you need to know about all device drivers.

First of all you need to know where drivers are placed in RAM. We already know that DOS allocates them in a kind of linked list. This list is uni-directional, which means that each element of the list contains a pointer to the last element containing an end marker. To work with a list like this you only need to know the address of the first element, and where to find each pointer within it.

## Finding the NUL Driver

The very first DOS device driver supports the NUL device. You can find the NUL driver using the DOS function INT 52h.

To return the address of the beginning of the list of lists in registers ES:BX, all you need to do is to execute the following commands through a debugger.

```
mov ah,52h
int 21h
```

On my machine this gives the result : ES=0283h, BX=0026h.

The Interrupt 21h function 52h is undocumented. It is used in a recent Microsoft program MSD.EXE in DOS version 6.2.

This list of lists, sometimes also referred to as a DOS system table, contains a lot of useful information. The first driver header is at the end of the list, at offset 22h (DOS 3.0+). On our machine this displacement is 26h + 22h=48h. So the address of the very first driver on our machine, the NUL driver, is 0283h:0048h.

## Examining Resident Drivers

Every DOS device driver begins with a device header, the first four bytes of which are a far pointer to the next driver. The layout of the header is the same as in Table 5.1, with the following functions added at the end.

**Table 5.20 The Device Driver Header Layout**

| Offset | Size (bytes) | Name (bit) | Brief Description |
|---|---|---|---|
| 0h | 8 | NameOrUnits | Logical device name (for character device) or number of units (for block device) |
| 12h | | END | End of Device Driver Header |

At offset 0Ah there is a logical device name for character device drivers.

Thus, after making the dump of memory, you can find out the name and addresses of the device driver, and the pointer to the next driver.

Repeating this procedure, you can trace the whole list of drivers in the chain. DOS marks the last driver in the chain by placing an offset value of 0FFFFh in the Link field of the driver.

We can now look up each of the drivers in the chain manually. However, it's not hard to write a program which will do this automatically. This is exactly what PRG5_1.ASM on the disk does. In fact, it goes a little further than this and displays all the information from each driver header.

As usual, you must translate this program to a .COM file. For example, you can create a .BAT file which contains the next three strings:

```
masm %1, , , ,
link %1, , , ,
exe2bin %1.exe %1.com
```

Then name this file as ASM_COM.BAT.

Type the string:

```
ASM_COM PRG5_1
```

and press the <Enter> key. It results in the file PRG5_1.COM.

So what's the result of this program? Well, some of the drivers that are loaded into our machine in our CONFIG.SYS file are as follows:

```
DEVICE=C:\DOS\ANSI.SYS
DEVICE=C:\DOS\RAMDRIVE.SYS 200 256 16 /e
```

After executing the program, we get the output shown in Figure 5.1.

```
RESIDENT DRIVERS CHAIN :

                                              Attributes
Memory        Driver      Strategy  Interrupt  FEDCBA9876543210

0283:0048     NUL         1599      159F       F                  2
0A35:0000     ..Q.....    00B0      00BB          B
09D2:0000     CON         00A2      00AD       F              4   10
0070:016E     CON         05DC      05E7       F              4   10
0070:0180     AUX         05DC      05ED       F
0070:0192     PRN         05DC      060A       F D        6
0070:01A4     CLOCK$      05DC      0630       F                3
0070:01B6     ........    05DC      0636          B     6
0070:01CA     COM1        05DC      05ED       F
0070:01DC     LPT1        05DC      0610       F D        6
0070:01EE     LPT2        05DC      0618       F D        6
0070:0200     LPT3        05DC      0620       F D        6
0070:0212     COM2        05DC      05F3       F
0070:0224     COM3        05DC      05F9       F
0070:0236     COM4        05DC      05FF       F

$C:\>
```

**Figure 5.1 Driver Listing**

That's a lot of different drivers! Their addresses show the order in which they were loaded into memory, and the names tell us what some of them are for. The device driver header addresses, along with the Strategy and Interrupt routine offsets, allow you to find the headers and programs of these drivers, and even to execute some of the driver commands using your debugger.

# Driver Allocation Principles

Our main concern at this point is how DOS allocates the drivers in RAM. In the current example, we can observe the following:

The first driver in the list is for the NUL device. It is followed by a driver with an unpronounceable name because it is a block device. After them comes a driver with the name CON. In our case that is the ANSI.SYS driver. This is then followed by the second CON driver, then by other drivers for standard DOS devices. The order in which RAMDRIVE.SYS and ANSI.SYS appear depends entirely on the order in which they are placed in the CONFIG.SYS file.

Driver names are stored only for character device drivers. DOS does not support names for block device drivers.

All drivers from the second CON driver in the chain, which has the offset 016Eh, have the same strategy routines as for many of its drivers. DOS uses the same strategy routine for all drivers.

The small amount of space that some of the character drivers occupy suggests that they are not active. You can check this by comparing Strategy and Interrupt addresses. If not active, several drivers may have the same addresses.

# Practical Driver Design

It's about time we had a go at creating our own driver from the ground up. This isn't a small job, so instead of trying to create a system disk device driver, which would require a chapter of its own, we will try to design a simple console driver. Despite its simplicity, it will be able to perform all the functions you would expect.

The main difficulties of driver construction arise not during writing but during driver debugging. These programs have an unpleasant tendency to destroy your system whenever an error occurs. So you must debug it as a whole, not step by step. This introduces the idea of driver hooking. The main idea is that in most cases you do not need to create a whole new driver. You will probably want to improve it or expand its functions. If there is already a driver in the system with the same destination, you cannot write the whole driver, however, you can hook it and add or modify some of its functions.

We'll create the driver in three steps.

## Step 1 - Creating a Driver Template

PRG5_2.ASM on the disk is a driver template which doesn't do anything. You can easily recognize the three main parts of a real driver: the device header, the strategy routine and an interrupt routine.

You can assemble and link this program using any assembler, only don't execute the resulting .EXE file. Instead, convert it into a .BIN or .COM file using the EXE2BIN program. Rename the extension of the resulting file .SYS to mark it out as a driver. Having done that, add into your CONFIG.SYS file a line like this:

```
DEVICE = C:\MY_DRIVERS\PRG5_2.SYS
```

Make sure you have a spare system floppy disk with editor on it to allow you to remove this line from your CONFIG.SYS file and reset your machine. Don't try to name the driver CON and set its attributes to 0 or 1. If you do, DOS will accept your driver in place of the existing driver. Such a misunderstanding will produce disappointing results.

If your program is correct, DOS will place it in RAM and send the newcomer a request for initialization. This is the only function the driver will perform. Any further requests, and the driver simply executes the strategy program.

This program is for developing character device drivers, but you can easily transform it into a block device driver template by changing a few commands. This applies to all the programs in this section.

## Step 2 - Adding Functions to Your Driver Template

You can now write all the commands your driver has to support directly into this template. You could add the appropriate code to the Read, NndRead and InpStatus labels. Having done that, you then have to debug the whole driver and test it on all your target systems. This is not a trivial task. So let's try and make it easier for ourselves by adapting our template bit by bit.

This next iteration of the program is much like the previous one. All we've done is to add a few commands to the shell to create probably the shortest possible working console driver.

What is the secret? This program is similar to the original up to initialization. But when DOS sends the driver the very first request, this driver goes off to explore the driver chain. The mechanics of the search are very similar to

Program 5.1. The aim of the search is to check for a duplicate driver to ours with exactly the same name, and then make that driver do the work of executing the functions. In our case, we've set up a CON driver, so the program identifies the location of the resident CON driver in the chain and makes that do the work. It's basically a lazy device driver.

When calling the existing driver, our lazy driver first of all calls the strategy routine, and then the requested interrupt routine. When it's finished, the driver sends DOS the return code appropriate to the outcome.

PRG5_3.ASM has a big advantage over the previous one. You can add commands to this template one by one, leaving the uncovered functions to be handled by the existing driver. The command that passes control on to the exisiting driver, JMP MakeIt is placed as a default into each of the function despatch lines of the new driver.

Having written the code to implement the function you want to replace, load it into your system and execute it through a debugger. You can send requests to your driver via the debugger. After debugging you need only add a semicolon ';' to comment out the jump:

```
; JMP MakeIt
```

or type the 90h (NOP) codes instead of the JMP command in your translated and, perhaps, loaded program and you switch this command in your driver. You can either do it in the .COM file on the disk and after that load the corrected code, or first, load the driver in system memory and then switch on the driver command before debugging it.

## Step 3 -  Add More Commands to Make a Real Driver

We can now take this a little further using the the techniques from Step 2. PRG5_4.ASM is a functioning, if not complete, device driver. It implements three keyboard commands that are just sufficient to control a basic keyboard system. You can add commands to this driver to implement a complete keyboard driver.

# Summary

In this chapter we've taken a look at what a device driver is, and how it fits into your system.

A device driver, in today's terms, is a program that extends your operating system to incorporate the functions provided by a new device. Device drivers are expected to provide a standard set of functions, and we looked at those functions in some detail. We then went on to look at the fundamental structure of a device driver, and created a generic template for writing our own drivers. After that, we added this template to our system in parallel with an existing driver, thus allowing us to add functions one by one, while still having a working driver to experiment with.

# CHAPTER SIX

# Interfacing to Other Devices

## Introduction

In this chapter we will look at how you use the parallel and serial interfaces to interact with other devices. You will learn about the common structure and exchange protocols in these interfaces and learn how to create your own programs and drivers for interface devices. We'll look at how to interface with the printer, mouse and joystick.

# Parallel and Serial Interfaces

Most modern personal computers interact with peripheral devices. A peripheral device is one that is not attached directly to internal buses of the central processor. These devices are connected by a channel with a transmitter and a receiver at each end. If the information in the channel only goes in one direction, then the channel is unidirectional and just requires one of the devices to be a transmitter, and the other a receiver. In more complicated bidirectional channels, each device can be either a transmitter or a receiver. If a bidirectional communication channel can only transmit information in one direction at a time, it is referred to as a simplex channel. A duplex channel allows information to be exchanged in both directions simultaneously.

A channel can be either serial or parallel. In a serial channel, the information is transmitted on one physical line, sequentially, bit by bit. A parallel channel can contain eight or more physical lines, and therefore can simultaneously transmit a byte (8 bits) of information, or even more.

The transmission speed of parallel channels can, of course, be far superior; however it is much more complex to organize and therefore more expensive. Consequently, parallel channels are usually used to transmit data quickly over comparatively short distances (several meters) and mostly for unidirectional data transmission. A serial communication channel is usually used for slower data exchange over comparatively long distances (300 meters and more), and is used for bidirectional and duplex communication.

A programmer who wants to write a program for managing a peripheral device interface needs to be aware of both the physical and logical organization of the device and also of the data exchange conditions and sequences, known as exchange protocols.

In this chapter, we'll consider some issues of interface programming for parallel and serial interface printers, as well as some other device interfaces.

# Parallel Interfaces

To understand parallel interfaces, let's look at the signal lines of a typical IBM/ EPSON printer with a 'Centronics' type parallel interface. The principal signals of the printer are in Table 6.1, viewed from the printer end of the connection.

**Table 6. The Main Printer Signalsr**

| Pin No. | Signal | Direction |
|---------|--------|-----------|
| 1 | NotStrobe | Input |
| 2-9 | Data_1_8 | Inputs |
| 10 | NotAcknlg | Output |
| 11 | Busy | Output |
| 12 | PaperOut | Output |
| 13 | Selected | Output |
| 14 | NotAutoFeed | Input |
| 31 | NotInit | Input |
| 32 | NotError | Output |
| 36 | NotInputSelect | Input |

*Some lines (not shown) are used for auxiliary signal transmission and ground.*

As you can see from this table, all the signals referring to exchange participants are divided between input and output signals. The input signals go from the computer to the printer. The output signals are generated by the printer itself.

Let's consider the signal assignment and description in detail. The printer is only capable of receiving data via lines 2 - 9. The data is input to the printer as Data_1_8 signals. During initialization, the printer generates the signal NotInit via line 31. The prefix Not in the signal's name indicates that the active (causing the initialization action) level is at the LOW, or 0 level. The absence of a Not prefix in the signal's name indicates that the active level is HIGH or 1. Under normal printer operations, the signal NotError is set at the high level, but when an error occurs, the printer sets this to condition 0.

The signal NotInputSelect selects a printer. Data entry to the printer is only possible when the level of this signal is LOW. When it receives this signal, the printer should set the selected signal to the HIGH condition. This signal indicates that the printer is in the selected state and ready to receive data.

The signal PaperOut indicates that only a small quantity of paper is left in the printer. The signal is normally low and goes high during a 'Paper Out' condition.

If the signal NotAutoFeed is LOW, this tells the printer that on the instruction to line feed, LF (printer commands will be discussed later), the printer must automatically add a carriage return command, CR. When this signal level is High, the action CR + LF does not arise.

## Parallel Interface Timing Requirements

Finally, let's consider the timing diagram for information exchange. The majority of peripheral devices and communication channels have established timing rules and logic sequences for the various signals that are necessary for sending and receiving information. This set of restrictions and rules, with reference to interfaces, is usually called an exchange protocol. The various sequences for sending data to the printer is shown in Figure 6.1.

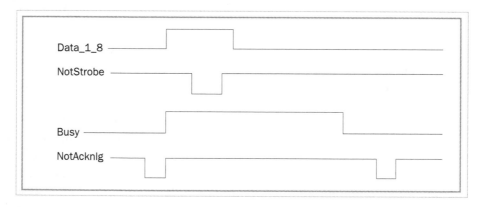

**Figure 6.1 The Various Signal Timing for Sending Data to the Printer**

The printer begins an exchange by sending the signal NotAcknlg at LOW level to the computer. This could occur as a response to an initialization signal from the computer, once it is in the ready condition. Alternatively, it may happen after a BUSY signal drops from high to low when a printer switches to ON

LINE. Therefore, the signal NotAcknlg at LOW level is assumed to be a data request pulse. You can see from Figure 6.1, that after receipt of the data request, the computer issues the data signal Data_1_8. After some time it confirms the send pulse by establishing the NotStrobe signal on LOW level and preserving the data on the lines Data_1_8 for some time after termination of the signal NotStrobe.

During this time interval, the printer accepts the data byte and changes to a busy condition. The printer informs the computer about the condition by establishing the signal Busy at the high level. This output signal indicates the status of the printer. The signal is high when a printer is busy and cannot receive data. The signal should be high under the following conditions:

- The receive buffer is full.

- The printer is processing data.

- The printer is OFF LINE.

- The printer is in an error condition.

Under normal working conditions, the printer would be busy for about 1ms or less if the buffer is not full and approximately 1 second if the buffer is full. You can see that when it is not busy, the printer sends the next pulse for data request, which begins the next data exchange cycle.

Thus, for printer management, the application program should send the data and control signals in the appropriate sequence to establish the channel lines which are connected to the printer. The computer executes this task using devices called controllers. The structure of controller registers depends on the device type and controller manufacturer. If you need full information you must obtain the particular controller description.

## Control Device Registers

The controller registers have various levels of operation. They can be allowed read-only access, read and write access, or neither. Access by reference is also possible when the reading from, or writing to, registers causes the controller to make a definite action which may be unconnected with the register's contents and destination.

Access to the controller registers is by the processor commands IN and OUT, which read information from, and write it to addresses within the range 0 to 64K. The elements relevant to these addresses and commands are called ports. DOS can support up to three parallel printer ports (LPT1- LPT3), and allows the connection of a fourth one. During the POST, the BIOS determines the availability of these port adapters in the following order:

- Port 3BCh of monochrome display and printer adapter.

- Port 378h of printer port adapter No 1.

- Port 278h of printer port adapter No 2.

If these adapters exist, the BIOS assigns them as LPT1-LPT3 and saves these base addresses in the BIOS data area, starting at 0:408h. To add a fourth printer, you can place its base address into the BIOS data word at 0:40Eh.

BIOS Interrupt 17h can provide full printer support for all four printer ports.

The printer LPT1 is used by DOS as the standard printer device (PRN), which has the prescribed handle number 4. You can re-assign the other printers as the standard printer by swapping the base port addresses, as follows:

```
; swapping printers No 1 and No 3
  xor  AX, AX
  mov  DS, AX
  mov  BX, 0408h          ; base address of standard printer
                          ; device LPT1
  mov  AX, [BX]           ; moving it to AX
  XCHG AX, [BX+4]         ; now old LPT1 became LPT3
  XCHG AX, [BX]           ; and old LPT3 became LPT1
```

Each of the parallel interface adapters contains three 'programmer accessible' registers with adjacent addresses, which are used for exchange management. Their description for a parallel interface port with the base address of 378h is shown in Table 6.2.

**Table 6.2 The Structure and Destination of Program Accessible Registers of the Parallel Interface Port Adapter**

| Address | Name | Structure and Destination |
|---------|------|---------------------------|
| 378h | Data Register | Write. Byte to be sent to the printer |
| | | Read. Last byte sent |
| 379h | Status Register | Read only |
| | | Bit meanings: |
| | | 0 - Time out |
| | | 1-2 - Must be zeros |
| | | 3 - Error bit |
| | |         0 = Printer in error state |
| | | 4 - Selected. |
| | |         1 = Printer is selected |
| | | 5 - PaperOut |
| | |         1 = Out of paper |
| | | 6 - NotAcknlg. |
| | |         0 = Printer ready for next character |
| | | 7 - NotBusy |
| | |         0 = Printer is busy or offline or error |
| 37Ah | Control Register | Read/Write. Bit meanings |
| | | 0 - Strobe |
| | |         1 = byte is sending |
| | | 1 - Auto Line Feed |
| | |         1 causes LF after CR |
| | | 2 - INIT |
| | |         0 resets the printer |
| | | 3 - Select input |
| | |         1 = select the printer |
| | | 4 - IRQ. Enables hardware interrupts, when NotAcknlg became LOW |
| | |         LPT2 => IRQ5 (Int 0Dh) |
| | | 5-7 - must be zeroes |

You can see that there are various commands which the application program may send to the control register. Using them, you can develop adapter initialization and data management, as well as printer interrupt masking and clearing. You can do it at a time and in an order that's convenient for printer control. The information about the condition of the printer is supplied by the status register. Some programs constantly interrogate this register to see when they can send new data to the printer. The same register contains the printer error codes.

Let's consider some standard procedures for printer management. First of all, we need a procedure for printer adapter initialization. The program should perform this controller initialization before the first printer access and after clearing each printer error condition. The initialization is performed as follows:

```
; LPT1 controller initialization
 mov    AX, 40h
 mov    ES, AX
 mov    DX, ES: [8]
 add    DX, 2
 mov    AL, 0Ch   ; 0000 1100 = printer selected + init
 out    DX, AL
 mov    CX, 800h ; delay interval
DELAY:
 jmp    $ + 2
 LOOP DELAY
 ;
 ;the required delay interval is defined by printer type. It is determined by the CX
 ;register value, but highly depends on processor speed. For practical application
 ;the delay can be adjusted during the printer driver or application program
 ;initialisation. You can produce the processor-independent delay using the timer.
 ;
 mov    AL, 8h    ; 0000 1000 = printer selected
 out    DX, AL
```

# The Printer and BIOS

When you write a program that interacts with the printer, and especially if you write a printer driver, you must take account of the printer interface not only on a hardware level, but also at a program level. Low-level interface with a printer is organized at the BIOS level. We'll consider it next.

## Interrupt 5h - Print Screen

INT 05h is automatically called by keyboard INT 09h, when the key <PrtScr> or <Print Screen> (or <Shift> + <Print Screen>) is pressed, as it is customized in DOS. You can hook this interrupt if you want to write your own screen-dump routine, or request it from your own program to use it as a standard handler.

In the BIOS data area at the address 0:500h, there is a status byte for the dump-screen utility (Print-Screen). This uses the following codes:

> 00 - no error.
> 01 - screen print in progress.
> FFh - error of screen print.

*Note that a program using the INT 05h service cannot be guaranteed to run correctly on all IBM-compatible computers.*

Interrupt 5 causes the screen to be output to the printer one display image per call. The Control character <Control + P> causes terminal output to be sent to the printer. After that, the output is echoed to the printer until the next input of the same control character.

Interrupt 5 usually only provides screen output in text mode. The DOS external command 'GRAPHICS' would replace the routine with a TSR program, which allows printing of graphic images from the screen to an IBM-compatible graphics printer.

Graphic image output to the printer from the screen is possible using INT 10h function 1220h.

## Interrupt 10h, Function 12h, Minor Code 20h - Print Screen

Some video cards (for example, EGA, VGA, MCGA) support the special function of Interrupt 10h for alternative screen print. This installs a PrintScreen routine from the video card's BIOS, rather than the INT 05h handler from ROM BIOS.

ROM BIOS doesn't usually understand screen heights other than 25 lines. You can request this function from your program using the following code:

```
mov         AH, 12h        ; function number
mov         BL, 20h        ; subfunction: print screen in graphic mode
int         10h            ; video service
```

Note that most printers do not take into acccount image distortion (or aspect ratio) of the display screen. The scale factor for displaying images on screen (the relationship between the number of pixels per inch for horizontal and vertical lines) for many graphic modes is not 1:1. In fact, when you want to display a circle on the screen in these modes, you must actually display an ellipse. On some printers you can change the scale factor when screen images are sent to the printer in graphics mode.

## Interrupt 0Fh (IRQ7 - Printer Interrupt)

This interrupt is generated by the printer adapter of LPT1, when the printer becomes ready.

## Interrupt 17h - Printer Support

The functions of this interrupt provide access to parallel ports. The addresses of these ports are stored in the data BIOS area at addresses 0:408h, 0:409h and 0:40Ah for LPT1, LPT2 and LPT3 respectively. Printer timeout values for these devices are stored in bytes at addresses 0:478h, 0:479h and 0:47Ah.

The function 00h - Print a Character - is intended for byte output to the printer. With this function you can output the given data from the buffer to the printer. For example, if you want to print a short message, you have to include the following code in your program:

```
Message              DB      'Printer output test',0Dh, 0Ah
Max_Bytes    EQU     $-Message
.................................
    mov          CX, Max_Bytes        ; number of bytes to write
    mov          BX, offset Message
                                      ; DS:DX points to buffer with data
    mov          DX, 0                ; DX = printer number (0,1 or 2)
PrintMessage:
    mov          AH, 0                ; AH = 0 - print a character
```

```
mov        AL,[BX]              ; character to print
int 17h                         ; this interrupt returns status byte in AH
test    AH, 8h                  ; error?
JNZ        Error_handler
INC        BX                   ; print next character
LOOP    PrintMessage
```

Interrupt 17h function 01h initializes a printer port and returns its status. To apply this function, it is necessary to put the port number in DX and call the interrupt:

```
mov    AH, 1                    ; Fn 01h - printer initialization
mov    DX, 0                    ; PRN = LPT1
int    17h
```

The printer status byte is returned in AH (see below).

Interrupt 17h function 02h - Get Printer Status - returns the printer status in the AH register. The printer number must be provided in DX:

```
mov    AH, 2                    ; Fn 02h - get printer status
mov    DX, 0                    ; PRN = LPT1
int    17h
```

The status byte is formed from the contents of the printer status register. It is modified to have the following format:

Bit 0 - Timeout

Bits 1-2 - Not used

Bit 3 - I / O error

Bit 4 - Selected (00h means OFFLINE)

Bit 5 - Out of paper

Bit 6 - Acknowledge (1 = printer attached)

Bit 7 - 1 = not busy; 0 = busy

*These values can differ for different computers and printers. For example, bit number 3 (I/O error) is sometimes not provided. Instead bit number 5 (out of paper) includes all I/O errors. Therefore, when writing a printer error handler, you must check this for each printer.*

# Printers and DOS

DOS interacts with printers in different ways at the interrupt and function level. Some features of this interface are considered below.

## Interrupt 21h Function 05h - Print Character

This function sends a character (ASCII value) from the DL register to a standard printer device. To call this function it is necessary to insert code in your program:

```
mov    DL, OutChar          ; character to standard printer device
mov    AH, 05h              ; Print Character
int    21h
```

The drawback of this function is that if the printer is busy, it waits until the device is ready.

## Standard Printer

The standard printer (STDPRN) corresponds to the PRN device. At the start of the program, by default, DOS opens some file handles, including standard printer handle 4. The PRN driver is loaded at DOS startup.

The program can use this handle in a system function such as Write File or Device (INT 21h function 40h) to write to the standard printer.

The user program can redirect the standard printer for the child program, connect it with another symbolic device or file by means of DOS function 45h - Duplicate File Handle, and function 46h - Force Duplicate File Handle. For example, you can redirect the whole print output to a given file. The problem is that DOS does not inform the program about where it redirects the output, so lack of disk space can cause problems. The Write File or Device function fails when the disk becomes full. To determine whether a standard device handle deals with a file or character device, you can use DOS function 4400h, Get Device Data.

If you want to deal with a non-standard printer, you have to open it by means of function 3Dh, as shown opposite.

## Interrupt 21h Function 3Dh - Open File with Handle

To open the printer device, it is necessary to insert the following code in your program:

```
        PDN_String    DB        'PRN',00h       ; zero-terminated string of device name
    .......................
        mov     DX, offset PDN_String           ; DS:DX - printer driver name pointer
        mov     AH, 3Dh                         ; Open File with Handle
        mov     AL, 01h                         ; write only attribute int 21h
        jc      Error_Handler                   ; carry set means error
        mov     Handle, AX                      ; handle of printer
```

If the Share program is loaded, you can also indicate the attribute 41h to enable write access to other programs. In addition, you can set the high bit (80h) if you want to prevent a child program created with DOS function 4B00h - Load and Execute Program - from inheriting the printer handle.

If the device PRN is not opened, DOS can return the error code 04h - Too many open files, or 05h - Access denied.

## Interrupt 21h Function 40h - Write File or Device

This function outputs the data from the buffer to the device specified by a handle. The following code is an example:

```
    Message           DB        'Printer output test', 0Dh, 0Ah
    Max_Bytes   EQU     $-Message
    ................................
        mov     BX, 4                           ; printer handle
        mov     CX, Max_Bytes                   ; number of bytes to write
        mov     DS, seg Message
        mov     DX, offset Message              ; DS: DX points to buffer with data
        mov     AH, 40h
        int     21h
        jc      Error_handler
        mov     Actual_Bytes, AX                ; number of bytes written
```

This function can be a problem if the printer is busy, since it waits until the device is ready.

If completed successfully, the carry flag is clear and the AX register contains the actual byte count sent. If the carry flag is set, AX contains the error code: 0005h - Access Denied, or 0006h - Invalid Handle. The handle can be 0004h - StdPrn = PRN (by default), or one created by using a function such as DOS function 3Dh (see previous page).

After finishing work with the device, don't forget to close it. The DOS function 3Eh does this.

## Interrupt 21h Function 3Eh - Close File with Handle

It is good practice to close the file or device after you finish using it. In this case, DOS performs any pending writes and frees all the resources: buffers, internal structures and memory blocks. If you want to close the PRN device using this function, use the following code:

```
mov     BX, Handle      ; PRN handle
mov     AH, 3Eh; Close File with Handle
int     21h
jc      Error_Handler  ; carry set means error
```

If the carry flag is set, the function has failed, and the AX register will contain an error value, which is often 0006h (Invalid Handle).

## Interrupt 21h Function 44h, Subfunction 03h - Send Control Data to Character Device

Using this function, you can send control information of any length to the printer. The call for this function is made as follows.

```
Cntrl_Info  DB                      '??????????'
Max_Bytes   EQU                     $-Cntr_Info
..............................
    mov     BX, 4                   ; printer handle
    mov     CX, Max_Bytes           ; number of bytes to write
    mov     DS, seg Cntrl_Info
    mov     DX, offset Cntrl_Info ; DS:DX points to buffer with data
    mov     AX, 4403h
    int     21h
    jc              Error_Handler ; carry set if error
    mov     ActualBytes, AX         ; actual quontity of bytes sent
```

If the carry flag is set, the AX register contains an error value, which may be as shown in Table 6.3.

**Table 6.3 AX Error Value**

| Error Value | Meaning |
| --- | --- |
| 0001h | Invalid function |
| 0005h | Access denied |
| 0006h | Invalid handle |
| 000Dh | Invalid data |

Otherwise the AX register contains the actual number of bytes sent. Printer drivers are not required to support this function, unless bit 14 in the driver Attribute field is set. This is also true for function 440Ch, which is considered later.

# Function Generic IOCTL for Character Devices (Interrupt 21h, Function 440Ch)

The standard printer (PRN) DOS driver supports Interrupt 21h function 440Ch for character devices. Together with the installed DOS driver PRINTER.SYS, these functions permit the various fonts to be loaded into the printer or the font to be changed while printing. These functions are listed in Table 6.4.

**Table 6.4 Printer Functions**

| Minor Code | Function |
| --- | --- |
| 45h | Set Iteration Count |
| 4Ah | Select Code Page |
| 4Ch | Start Code-Page Prepare |
| 4Dh | End Code-Page Prepare |
| 65h | Get Iteration Count |
| 6Ah | Query Selected Code Page |
| 6Bh | Query Code-Page Prepare List |

The same functions may also be executed by the external DOS command - MODE. A detailed description of this command and its applications can be obtained from the MS-DOS User Reference.

# Interrupt 2Fh, Function 01h - PRINT Command

The DOS interrupt 2Fh (Multiplex Interrupt) is a common entry point for TSR programs that support services to other programs. This interrupt is intended to be accessed by several processes that execute simultaneously. The functions 00h - 7Fh are reserved for DOS, and functions C0h - FFh - for application programs. Programs can use this interrupt to request services from and to check the status of the processes. The process 01h for this interrupt is defined for DOS version 3.0+ and serves as an identifier of the external DOS command Print (for background printing). To call this process, you must first execute the program PRINT. After completing this process, it loads its resident part and includes itself in the chain of interrupts hooked by INT 2Fh. Whenever you call this interrupt, the PRINT process, as well as all other processes, should test AH against their own multiplex process number 01h. If AH does not contain a matching value, control should be passed to initial the previous vector INT 2Fh (the address found at 0000:00BCh before installation). If AH=01h, the PRINT process has checked the AL register subfunction number to execute.

## AL=00 - Get PRINT Installed State

This function determines whether the resident portion of the print command has been loaded. The function has no parameters and can be executed by the following code:

```
mov AX, 0100h        ; Get PRINT.EXE installed state.
int 2Fh              ; Multiplex Interrupt
```

If PRINT has not been loaded, it returns 00h in AL. In this case you can install it. If AL = 0FFh, the printer has been installed.

## AL=01 - Add File to Queue

This function adds the file to the print queue. You can execute it as follows:

```
mov    AX, seg Pointer
mov    DS, AX
```

```
        mov   DX, offset Pointer
        mov   AX, 0101h                    ; Add File to Queue
        int   2Fh                          ; Multiplex Interrupt
```

The pointer points to a parameter structure with the following form:

```
QueuePacket  STRUC
QpLevel            DB    0               ; level, must be zero
QpFileName  DD     ?                     ; long pointer to ASCIIZ path
QueuePacket  ENDS                        ;(zero-padded ASCII-string)
```

If, after return, the carry flag is clear, the function is successful. Otherwise the AX register contains one of the error values shown in Table 6.5.

**Table 6.5 AX Error Values**

| Value | Name |
|-------|------|
| 0001h | Invalid function |
| 0002h | File not found |
| 0003h | Path not found |
| 0004h | Too many open files |
| 0005h | Access denied |
| 0008h | Queue full |
| 000Ch | Invalid access |
| 000Fh | Invalid drive |

## AL = 02h. Remove File from Print Queue

This function removes a file or multiple files (if the filename contains wildcards) from the print queue. You can execute it as follows:

```
        mov           AX, seg Filename
        mov           DS, AX
        mov           DX, offset Filename    ; DS:DX points to ASCIIZ filename
        mov           AX, 0102h              ; Remove file from print queue
        int 2Fh                              ; Multiplex Interrupt
```

If the carry flag is clear, the function is successful. Otherwise the AX register contains the error value 0002h.

## AL = 03h - Remove All Files from Print Queue

This function removes all files from the print queue. It has no parameters and no return value. You can execute it as follows:

```
mov         AX, 0103h              ; Remove All Files from Print Queue
int         2Fh                    ; Multiplex Interrupt
```

## AL = 04h - Hold Print Jobs and Get Status

This function stops the current print job. It can be executed as follows:

```
mov         AX, 0104h              ; Hold Print Jobs and Get Status
int         2Fh                    ; Multiplex Interrupt
mov         ErrorCount, DX         ; Errors during printing
mov         [PrintQueue],SI        ; DS:SI points to print queue
push        DS
pop         Word PTR [PrintQueue+2]
```

This function returns an error count in the DX register and DS:SI contains the pointer to the print queue. It consists of a series of 64-byte zero-terminated strings specifying the paths of files in the queue. The first is currently being printed. The last entry consists of only a null (00h) character. Programs must not change the queue content explicitly, but use the corresponding INT 2Fh functions.

The current print job is held until INT 2Fh function 0105h is called.

## AL = 05h - Release Print Jobs

This function restarts the current print job. It has no parameters or return value. You can execute it as follows:

```
mov   AX, 0105h                    ; Release Print Jobs
int   2Fh                          ; Multiplex Interrupt
```

## AL = 06h - Get Printer Device

This function returns the address of the device header for the current printer. It has no parameters and can be executed as follows:

```
mov         AX, 0106h              ; Get Printer Device
int         2Fh                    ; Multiplex Interrupt
JNC         queue_empty            ; Clear carry means queue is empty
mov         [DevHeader],SI
```

```
push        DS
pop         Word PTR [DevHeader+2],DS    ;DS:SI points to the device header
```

If the queue is empty, the carry flag is clear and AX=0000h. Otherwise the carry flag is set, AX=08h (Queue Full) and DS:SI points to the device header structure.

## Using Third Party Printer Drivers in Your Own Program

We have considered the various types of interface with printers, from the lowest level, when you use direct control of parallel port controller registers, to using built-in drivers and external DOS commands. In practice, you often use printer drivers developed by a third party. With assembly language, you can not only use such programs for printer output, but also build them into your own program. You can do this using DOS functions 4B00h and 4B01h.

## Interrupt 21h Function 4B00h - Load and Execute Program

Using this function, you can load or execute any program. What is important is that the file can be executed under the control of DOS - e.g. .BAT, .COM or .EXE files. You can perform the call for the Load and Execute Program function using:

```
mov    DX, Seg Name
mov    DS, DX
mov    DX, offset Name            ; DS:DX points to program name
mov    BX, LoadExec
mov    ES, BX
mov    BX, offset LoadExec        ; ES: BX points to LoadExec structure
mov    AX, 4B00h                  ; Load and Exec Program function
int    21h
jc     ErrorHandler               ; Error, if carry flag is set
```

This function loads the program as a child program, creating for it a new PSP (Program Segment Prefix), and transfers control to the program. The Name pointer points to the zero-terminated ASCII string of a valid DOS filename of the loaded program.

The LoadExec pointer points to the LOADEXEC structure, with information relevant to the child program in the following form:

```
LOADEXEC        STRUC
Environment             dw      ?        ; segment of environment block
CommandTail             dd      ?        ; address of command tail
FCB_1                   dd      ?        ; address of default FCB No 1
FCB_2                   dd      ?        ; address of default FCB No 2
LOADEXEC        ENDS
```

If an error occurs, the carry flag is set and the AX register contains an error value. The possible errors are shown in Table 6.6.

**Table 6.6 AX Error Values**

| Value | Name |
|-------|------|
| 0001h | Invalid function |
| 0002h | File not found |
| 0003h | Path not found |
| 0004h | Too many open files |
| 0005h | Access denied |
| 0008h | Not enough memory |
| 000Ah | Bad environment |
| 000Bh | Bad format |

# Interrupt 21h Function 4B01h - Load Program

This function is almost identical to the previous one, except that the loaded program is not executed immediately. It remains resident and waits to be called. In this case, ES:BX points to another structure as follows:

```
LOAD  STRUC
Environment             dw      ?        ; segment of environment block
CommandTail             dd      ?        ; address of command tail
FCB_1                   dd      ?        ; address of default FCB No 1
FCB_2                   dd      ?        ; address of default FCB No 2
SSSP                    dd      ?        ; starting stack address
CSIP                    dd      ?        ; starting code address
LOAD  ENDS
```

The action of function 4401h is demonstrated by the program PROG8_1.ASM on the accompanying disk, which loads and executes the program PRT.EXE from WordPerfect. You can use similar code in your own programs to use this or any other printer driver.

# How the Printer Works

It is impossible to describe each and every printer. All you need to study is a simple system and the principles it uses. Complex devices will then be easier to understand. Further consideration should be given to the most widespread matrix printers. Dot matrix printers print characters as a series of dots. Each column of dots is coded, depending on the quantity of dots, by one or several bytes. Usually, 1 corresponds to dot printing, and 0 to an empty space. The size of the dot matrix defines the size of the font, the density of printed points affects the print quality. Filling the code matrix with zeros and ones defines the printed character form.

As a rule, printers used with personal computers work in at least two modes - Bit Image (Graphics) Mode and Text Mode.

In Graphics Mode, the computer sends codes of images in dot columns to the printer. In Text Mode, the computer transmits the codes of previously defined symbols, usually the ASCII character set.

By default, the printer usually works in text mode. It is switched to graphics mode by a special control code.

The principle purpose of control codes is that each code represents a combination of bytes which cannot, by definition, occur in usual text. The printer recognizes these codes in text mode and uses them as commands to change the printer's operation. Once the printer has received the specified byte quantity, it returns to Text Mode until a new control sequence occurs. Let's consider the control codes in further detail. You can translate the code, then load and execute it using assembler and a debugger.

```
ContrCode    DB      1Bh,'K'                   ; control sequence (bit image mode)
             DW      17h                       ; 17h columns = bit image code length
Image        DB      1Eh,28h,48h,88h,48h,28h,1Eh,00h
             DB      6Ch,6Ch,00h,80h,40h,20h,10h,08h
             DB      04h,02h,00h,82h,44h,28h,10h   ; bit image code
             DB      0Dh,0Ah                   ; LF(line feed)+CR(carriage return)
Bytes        EQU     $-ContrCode
...........................................................
             Mov     BX,4                      ; printer handle
             Mov     CX,Bytes                  ; number of bytes to write = 1Dh
             mov     DX,Seg ContrCode
             mov     DS,DX
             mov     DX,offset ContrCode
                                               ; DS:DX points to buffer with data
             mov     AH,40h
             Int     21h                       ; Printing of image
```

This code prints an image of four symbols (A:\>). Be careful when you write it, because if you make an error in the ContrCode or Bytes fields, the program can hang.

Figures 6.2 and 6.3 explain the principle of the coding for this example.

| Columns: | 0 0 0 0 0 0 0 0 0 0 0 0 0 0 0 1 1 1 1 1 1 1 1 | Weight | Code |
|---|---|---|---|
| | 1 2 3 4 5 6 7 8 9 A B C D E F 0 1 2 3 4 5 6 7 | | |
| Rows: 7 | o o o * o o o o o o * o o o o o o o * o o o | 128 | 80h |
| 6 | o o * o * o o o * * o o * o o o o o o o * o o | 64 | 40h |
| 5 | o * o o o * o o * * o o o * o o o o o o * o | 32 | 20h |
| 4 | * o o o o o * o o o o o o * o o o o o o o * | 16 | 10h |
| 3 | * * * * * * * o * * o o o o o * o o o o * o | 8 | 8h |
| 2 | * o o o o o * o * * o o o o o o * o o o * o o | 4 | 4h |
| 1 | * o o o o o * o o o o o o o o o o * o * o o o | 2 | 2h |
| 0 | o o o o o o o o o o o o o o o o o o o o o o o o | 1 | 1h |
| Total: | 1 2 4 8 4 2 1 0 6 6 0 8 4 2 1 0 0 0 8 4 2 1 | | Upper 4 rows |
| | E 8 8 8 8 8 E 0 C C 0 0 0 0 8 4 2 1 2 4 8 0 | | Lower 4 rows |

**Figure 6.2 Principle of Bit Image Encoding**

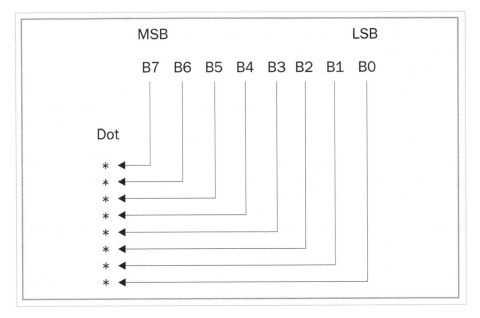

**Figure 6.3 Relationship Between Data Bits and Image Dots**

From Figure 6.2 you can see how to receive the separate codes of columns. Each of the 8 rows has an assigned binary weight. The top one has the largest weight - 128 (Most Significant Bit), the lowest - 1 (Least Significant Bit). If a dot is present, its weight is included; if not present, it has zero weight. All weights for separate image columns are summarized, giving the resulting byte.

Figure 6.3 shows the relationship between data bits and image dots. If you set a bit to 1, the printer produces the impact on the appropriate pin, resulting in a dot on the paper. After that, the printer head is moved a short distance. During this time the printer receives the next column code, and so on.

The printer does not actually print after receiving each separate byte, but accumulates codes in the buffer, until a whole line is received. Usually, for a 9 pin matrix impact printer, the distance between vertically positioned pins is 1/72". The horizontal replacement of the printing head in such printers usually varies from 60 to 140 steps per inch. In inkjet and laser printers, the distance between separate image dots is usually less, which increases print quality.

As we already know, the printer is in Text Mode by default after initialization, or is switched into it automatically after finishing a given task in Bit Image Mode. After receiving a code in Text Mode, the printer should print not one dot column, but one whole symbol from a previously given set of symbols, i.e. a font. Each symbol image represents the rectangular dot matrix. The size of the matrix is determined by the type of font and printer. The more columns and rows that are in each symbol image, the higher the print quality and the longer the text takes to print. For greater printing density, the size of the matrix can be altered for various symbols. The fonts can be stored in the printer's own memory or can be loaded into the printer immediately before printing, at printer initialization or during the print process.

The various operating modes of printers and font types are usually considered in detail in the technical manuals for each printer. From the programmer's point of view, the most important thing is that the printer is controlled by an alternating sequence of information bytes and command codes, which are only sent to the printer in Text Mode.

Besides mode switching, these commands are usually used when reloading fonts and for moving the printer head step-by-step horizontally (direct and return feed) and vertically (usually only direct feed).

We have already dealt with one control sequence, namely 1Bh, 'K',0017 h. The byte 1Bh, transmitted, for example, when the <Esc> key is pressed, represents the service code, i.e. the code which is not used for symbol display. The symbol 'K' is an expansion of the control code, and the value 17h (23 decimal) is a code parameter, which indicates how many bytes are necessary to print in Bit Image mode.

The control codes can be single-byte, selected from values which are never used for symbol representation, or extended (multi-byte) control codes, which always begin with the <Esc> character, and are therefore called escape–sequences. The code sets are defined by the printer manufacturer and can vary for different printers. The two most common are the IBM Proprinter and the EPSON Escape commands. They both have very similar codes.

To illustrate what control codes represent, and to show their benefit to a programmer, the printer control codes for IBM mode can be found on the disk in TABLE\TAB_COM.TXT. They can also be used to write printer driver routines, subject to slight alterations. This list of commands can be separated into groups, including:

- Print action codes, i.e. carriage return, form and line feed and vertical tabulation, backspace, printer initialization, selection and deselection of paper-end detector and so on.

- Paper formatting control codes, such as line spacing, set form length, form feed with and without print, set, execute and cancel horizontal and vertical tabulation, print spaces or line feeds, set left or right margin.

- Character designation codes and user-defined characters, such as enlarge, condense, double strike, near letter quality, italic, underlined, superscript or subscript modes.

- Access codes to Bit Image Mode (dot graphics) that select graphic densities and printer speed in that mode.

More detailed information is available in the manufacturers' manuals. Nevertheless, you now know enough for us to discuss how to write printer driver routines.

## The Printer Driver

Programmers usually write a printer driver for each adaptation of a new type of printer that is not supported by an available driver. In addition, a printer driver can be written to add new features, such as the ability to print a graphic image from the screen, to work in the background or to be integrated into a large system.

When you have decided what your printer should do, you should decide how it can be realized. First of all, you must decide on the form in which the driver program should be realized - as a built-in subroutine, as a .COM or .EXE file which is called from other programs, as a TSR program (more difficult to develop), or as a standard DOS device driver (even more difficult). We'll consider the last case, because it provides the most compatibility with other programs.

Having decided on a DOS device driver, you need to consider all possible forms of interaction with other programs. It is useful to consider the possible methods of printer interaction with DOS and the BIOS. If the majority of driver functions can be satisfactorily developed using DOS and the BIOS, you may not want to rewrite them in your own program. As a result, your driver is easier to write and maintain. If you have decided to design a function, it is worth looking at ways of how the printer/DOS and the BIOS relationship may interfere with your program. In such cases, you will have to hook the appropriate interrupts and sort their requests during operation. It is also important to select the correct printer interface. For example, if you access the printer using IOCTL functions, and the printer is not ready or an error has arisen, it can crash your system.

Once these problems are solved, you can begin the development of separate printer functions at the control level in text or graphics mode. You have to consider the printer command set and the features of the printer. Remember that it is very easy to create problems. In most cases you can find the relevant information in the printer technical manual. Note that some impact printers have no thermal protection and can be damaged as a result of working long periods in graphics mode.

All that remains is to write your program (see PROG6_2.ASM on the disk). Here we consider a simple printer driver which hooks printer requests and analyzes them. In text mode it prints the 'A' character as given by the user. To do so, the printer switches to graphics mode. The other tasks are left to the regular system driver.

The driver structure is explained in Chapter 5, which also shows how the driver framework is built, translated and run.

# Serial Port Interfaces

Serial interfaces have two main differences to parallel ones. First, the data is transmitted sequentially, one bit at a time. Each byte of data, transmitted through a serial port, is part of the following sequence of signal bits.

## One Starting Bit

When not transmitting data, the signal is permanently high, or equal to 1. The transmission of each data pack always begins from the starting bit. This bit value is always 0. It is used for synchronization, i.e. for warning the receiving device about a forthcoming data transmission (the signal is a constant 1, when 'idle', then a 0 is sent as the start bit, then the data bits, then the stop bit).

## 7 or 8 Data Bits

The first format was chosen because it contains all ASCII characters, the second because in this case the data pack corresponds exactly to the byte. In any case the bits are transmitted one after the other, from the least significant upwards.

## Optional Parity Bit

If the parity bit is present in the transmitted data pack, it is used for controlling data transmission and for error detection. For odd parity, the bit is set if there are an odd number of bits equal to 1, and for even parity the reverse is true.

## One or Two Stop Bits

The stop bits' value is always equal to 1 and they are used to separate two bytes transmitted one after the other. The number of stop bits doesn't usually make a significant difference - at the end of the data packet transmission, the stop bits are immediately transformed into intervals between two exchange cycles, during which the signal in line is always equal to 1. The serial port can operate with different transmission rates. The rate of 300 bits per second (baud) is considered the standard rate. There are slow devices, which have baud rates of 50, 100 or 150, and fast ones, for which 600, 1200, 2400, 4800, 9600 and 19,200 baud are allowed. The adapters for IBM serial interfaces can work up to 115,200 baud.

In fact, the operating speed of the BIOS routines restricts exchange rates to 19200 baud or less. The use of fast modern processors and drivers removes this restriction, but all the same, exchange speed can not exceed the channel capacity, which can be a few times less, particularly for long (or home-made) cables.

The second distinction between serial and parallel interfaces is that the serial port can be bi-directional.

One more complication is that serial interfaces allow two types of device. One of them played the role of information transmitting device - Data Communication Equipment (DCE) or modem. The set of terminals - Data Terminal Equipment (DTE), connected to the modem, can receive the information. The functions of these devices are complementary, and input signals from one of them are output signals for the other. To open a communication channel, all you have to do is connect different devices through lines with corresponding signals. But, obviously, there is one more possible combination - when devices of the same type (terminals) need to be connected.

This situation occurs when you want, for example, to connect one computer with another one or a computer with a printer. All of them are terminal types. If they are divided by a short distance, you need not use a modem - you can use a null modem cable, which means a connecting cable with crossed signal lines. The crossing means that a modem is not necessary as an intermediate device. The examples below use simplified null modems. All of the standard null modem connections are given at the end of this section.

If you want to know how to arrange information exchange for any possible case, let us first consider the various practical uses of serial interfaces. The serial ports used in IBM-compatible personal computers have the configuration standard RS-232C. The cable of this interface may consist of up to 25 lines. Here we shall consider the signal lines, exchange protocol and main types of interrelations for serial interfaces with 9 pins - sufficient for most purposes.

**Table 6.7 The Main Signals of Serial Interface (9 pins)**

| Pin No. | Signal | Direction |
|---------|--------|-----------|
| 1 | DCD (Data Carrier Detect) | IN |
| 2 | RxD (Received Data) | IN |
| 3 | TxD (Transmitted Data) | OUT |
| 4 | DTR (Data Terminal Ready) | OUT |
| 5 | GND (Ground) | - |
| 6 | DSR (Data Set Ready) | IN |
| 7 | RTS (Request to Send) | OUT |
| 8 | CTS (Clear to Send) | IN |
| 9 | RI (Ring Indicator) | IN |

Here are some further explanations:

| | |
|---|---|
| DCD (Data Carrier Detect) | The received signal contains information. |
| RxD (Received Data) | This line in the serial interface is used to receive data from the other device. |
| TxD (Transmitted Data) | The serial interface transmits the data using this line. |
| DTR (Data Terminal Ready) | The system and serial interface are ready for operation. |
| GND (Ground) | This line does not play an independent role, but is necessary for correct transmission of all other signals. |
| DSR (Data Set Ready) | Message to the system that the other device is ready for operation. |
| RTS (Request to Send) | The system informs that it is ready to transmit data and requests permission. |
| CTS (Clear to Send) | The device confirms that it is ready to receive data transmitted by the system. |
| RI (Ring Indicator) | This optional signal does not directly influence data exchange, but can be used for warning about forthcoming data exchange. |

There are numerous exchange protocols for serial interfaces and it is impossible to discuss them all here. However, we'll consider a few examples to let you get a feel for them.

The most simple is the DTR-protocol, which is used for uni-directional data exchange (for example, from computer to printer) using only two signal lines: TxD of computer and DTR of printer (and, of course, GND). The connection of the lines and signal transmission for such a protocol is shown below.

| Computer | | Device |
|---|---|---|
| TxD | ⟶ | RxD |
| DSR | ⟵ | DTR |
| GND | ⟷ | GND |

As you can see, the data is transmitted one way only - from the computer to the printer. The signal transmission timing for this type of exchange is shown in Figure 6.4 (a).

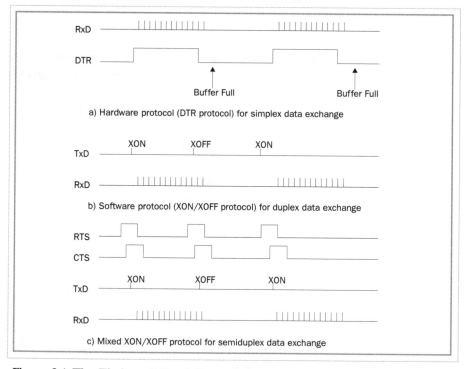

**Figure 6.4 The Timing of Signal Transmission for Various Exchange Protocols of Serial Interface**

After the printer (device) has switched to ON, and if it is ready to receive data, it sets the DTR signal to ON (1). The computer receives this signal from its input DSR and then transmits the data from its output TxD, checking the condition of the signal on the input DSR before transmission of each new byte. The printer receives the data from input RxD. If the printer cannot guarantee reception of the data, for example, when the printer buffer overflows, it switches the signal DTR to OFF (0). From the printer's DTR output, this signal arrives at the computer's DSR input and data transmission is terminated. When the buffer is empty, the printer reopens the DTR signal to ON (1), and data transmission is renewed. If the DTR signal does not change to ON, it means that the printer is OFFLINE. Possible reasons are operator interference, out of paper or printer failure. After eliminating all possibilities, switch the printer to ONLINE mode and the DTR signal is again switched to ON.

Data exchange in duplex mode is more difficult to implement. In this mode the computer and device (printer) can transmit data to and from each other simultaneously. While data is being exchanged, two signal lines are used, TxD and RxD, from both the computer and the printer. The line connection and transmission direction are shown below.

| Computer | | Device |
|---|---|---|
| TxD | ———————▶ | RxD |
| RxD | ◀——————— | TxD |
| GND | ◀——————▶ | GND |

The signal transmission timing is shown in Figure 6.4 (b).

After initialization and switching to ONLINE, the printer transmits the code ready to receive data, XON (usually 11h), to its TxD line.

In reply, the computer transmits the data on its TxD line. If the buffer is full, the printer transmits the code for not ready to receive data, XOFF (usually 13h). After receiving this code, the computer terminates data transmission. Everything else is similar to the previous exchange algorithm. This protocol is called the software protocol or XON/XOFF protocol.

Note that in Figure 6.4b, the unitary transmission for XON and XOFF signals is shown. Some printers use periodic transmission of these signals with a definite interval (for example, equal to 8 symbols transmission duration), to continually interrogate the printer condition.

Even more difficult from a development point of view is the half-duplex mode of exchange. In this mode, the computer or device can transmit the data in turn. The RTS and CTS lines are used for transmission direction control. Four signal lines are used: TxD, RxD, RTS and CTS. The line connection scheme and the signal transmission direction is shown below.

| Computer | Device |
|----------|--------|
| TxD ————————▶ | RxD |
| RxD ◀———————— | TxD |
| RTS ————————▶ | CTS |
| CTS ◀———————— | RTS |
| GND ◀———————▶ | GND |

The signal transmission timing is shown in Figure 6.4 (c).

After initialization and switching to ONLINE, the printer switches the RTS line to condition 1 (request for data transmission). As a result, the computer receives this signal on its CTS line and switches its own RTS line to condition 1 (acknowledging receipt of request to send from the printer). If the buffer is empty, the printer transmits the ready to receive data code to the TxD line. The computer, after receiving this code from its input RxD, begins data transmission. If the printer cannot ensure data reception, it again switches the RTS line to condition 0. After receiving the signal, the computer confirms by switching the CTS line to condition 0. Then the printer transmits the transmission termination code to the TxD line. This signal arrives at the computer's input RxD and it terminates transmission.

To conclude this section, we'll consider the standard null modem connection, which we mentioned before. For simplicity, both devices connected are presumed to be computers.

| First Terminal (Computer) | | Second Terminal (Computer) |
|---|---|---|
| TxD | ——————▶ | RxD |
| RxD | ◀—————— | TxD |
| RTS | ——————▶ | CTS |
| CTS | ◀—————— | RTS |
| DSR, DCD | ◀—————— | DTR |
| DTR | ——————▶ | DCD,DSR |
| GND | ◀—————▶ | GND |

As you can see, the null modem provides symmetrical connection of all signals required for two terminal devices to communicate.

# Serial Mouse Interface

Earlier, we discussed some properties of a serial interface. Now we will consider the serial mouse interface and the features of the mouse as an external sensing device.

From a hardware point of view, a mouse interfaces with the computer through a controller. It is possible to program the interface on low-level, accessing the appropriate port. Practically, however, when the user purchases the mouse, he also purchases the appropriate driver. After installation of the driver in DOS, it hooks INT 33h. Simultaneously, the user also gets the set of INT 33h functions. The number of mouse functions available depends on the version of your mouse driver. It ought be more then 35 and may be as many as 52. Here we are only interested in the coordinate functions of the mouse as an external sensing device.

## Mouse Coordinate Interface Functions of Interrupt 33h

We shall consider the Microsoft mouse functions, which have become the standard for such devices.

Unlike DOS functions, when you call INT 33h functions, you must set their numbers in the AL register and the AH register must be set to 0. Some of the mouse coordinate functions are considered next.

## Function 03h - Get Mouse Status

To call this function you can use the following code:

```
mov   AX,03h
      int     33h
      mov     X_Coord,CX
      mov     Y_Coord,DX
      CMP     BL,3
      JE      Both          ; Both buttons pressed
      test    BL,1
      JNZ     L_Pressed     ; Left button pressed
      test    BL,2
      JNZ     R_Pressed     ; Right button pressed
      NOP                   ; No button pressed
```

In return you have the valid horizontal and vertical cursor coordinates and the status of the buttons.

## Function 04h - Set Cursor Position

You can call this function using:

```
mov AX,04h
mov X_Coord,CX
mov Y_Coord,DX
int 33h
```

This function is the opposite to the previous one, and permits you to change the cursor position, if you display a mouse cursor.

## Function 07h - Set Horizontal Boundaries

This function restricts the horizontal boundaries of the mouse cursor within the valid range for the current screen mode. The CX and DX registers specify the lower and upper boundaries. If the CX value is greater than DX, the driver exchanges the values.

To call this function use the following code:

```
mov   AX,07h
mov   CX, LowerBnd    ; Lower Limit
mov   DX, UpperBnd    ; Upper Limit
int   33h
```

## Function 08h - Set Vertical Boundaries

This function restricts the vertical boundaries of the mouse cursor within the valid range for the current screen mode. This function is used exactly like the previous one, with one exception - set 08h in AX register.

## Function 0Bh - Read Motion Counters

You can call this function by using the code:

```
mov   AX,0Bh
int   33h
mov   ChangeX,CX          ; horizontal position change
mov   ChangeY,DX          ; vertical position change
```

This function returns the information about changes in the mouse position after the last call. Values in CX and DX registers are mickeys - the minimal steps of mouse motion in horizontal and vertical directions. The scales, i.e. the real length of one mickey, are determined by mouse resolution. When using this function, you must perform all global coodinate and boundary calculations yourself. If you do not want to do this, you can use those functions in the 33h interrupt which deal with virtual mouse coordinates (see below).

## Function 0Fh - Set Mickey-to-Pixel Ratio

This function changes the ratio of displacements of the mouse in mickeys to that of the cursor in pixels. So you can change the speed of the mouse on the screen. The default value is 8. If you want to halve the speed, use the following code:

```
mov AX,0Fh
mov CX,16          ; 16 mickey per pixel in a horizontal direction
mov DX,16          ; 16 mickey per pixel in a vertical direction
int 33h
```

## Function 13h - Set Double-Speed Threshold

If the mouse's speed exceeds the threshold, the cursor screen displacement is doubled. When you send a zero value, the default threshold (equal to 64 mickeys/sec) is set. If you want to set another threshold value, use the following code:

```
mov AX,13h
mov DX, DblThrshld        ; the DblThrshld parameter value determines
                          ; the threshold value in mickey per second
int 33h
```

## Function 1Ah - Set Mouse Sensitivity

This function does what the two previous functions can do together. You can call it by using the following code:

```
mov AX,1Ah
mov BX,HorMcPerPix        ; mickey per pixel horizontally
mov CX,VerMcPerPix        ; mickey per pixel vertically
mov DX, DblThrshld        ; threshold value in mickey per second
int 33h
```

## Function 1Bh - Get Mouse Sensitivity

This function is the reciprocal to function 1Ah and returns the sensitivity values.

```
mov AX,1Bh
int 33h
mov HorMcPerPix,BX        ; mickey per pixel in a horizontal direction
mov VerMcPerPix,CX        ; mickey per pixel in a vertical direction
mov DblThrshld, DX        ; threshold value in mickey per second
```

## Function 26h - Get Maximum Virtual Coordinates

This function returns the minimum and maximum coordinates allowed by the current video mode and, in addition, the mouse disabled flag.

```
mov AX,26h
int 33h
mov Disabled, BX          ; Mouse disabled flag
mov X_UpperBnd,CX         ; Upper Limit
mov Y_UpperBnd,DX         ; Upper Limit
```

## Function 31h - Get Current Virtual Coordinates

This function returns the minimum and maximum coordinates. You can call this function using the following code:

```
mov  AX,31h
int  33h
```

```
mov   X_LowerBnd,AX        ; Lower Limit
mov   Y_LowerBnd,BX        ; Lower Limit
mov   X_UpperBnd,CX        ; Upper Limit
mov   Y_UpperBnd,DX        ; Upper Limit
```

## A Simple Screen Pencil Program

As you can see from the description of mouse driver functions above, a programmer can create almost any program for coordinate device control. In the next program we shall use some of the mouse driver functions.

Usually, you will have to deal with two types of coordinate devices. The first type transmits the internal coordinates data directly to the control program, as it would for a joystick, for example. A mouse represents the other type of device, which only informs you about variations of the coordinates. In fact, these coordinates exist only as a parameter of the control program. The mouse driver not only informs you about coordinate changes, but also enables the application program to receive the coordinates and control them as virtual coordinates.

The Screen Pencil program (PROG6_3.ASM on disk) is intended to demonstrate mouse control. It deliberately does not use the virtual coordinate functions, because its main task is to show how you can manage the coordinates.

This program allows control of the mouse coordinates and their movement within a rectangle. Using the mouse buttons permits line drawing or erasing. Some keyboard buttons are also used for better functionality.

## The Mouse Driver Routine

You have learned about the I/O Port devices interface. We have also considered the high level Mouse interface via INT 33h. INT 33h shows that it is not supported by the BIOS and DOS. Usually after loading DOS, this interrupt vector address points to the IRET operator only. The real INT 33h handler is loaded in RAM by the Mouse device driver. We'll have a look at this driver's tasks, structure and functions now and write a simple program which has the same structure the Mouse driver and implements some of its functions.

The Mouse driver routine is a resident program that supports the INT 33h functions, some of which you are already acquainted with. To write a similar program, you should implement all INT 33h functions with all input parameters and output information for each function.

The Mouse driver should interface with the device on a low-level, through the Serial Port. To do this, the driver should hook all these port interrupts (INT 0Ch for COM1), filter them and execute the ones which come from the mouse. The driver should, of course, also initialize the port COM1. It is desirable (though not obligatory), to hook INT 14h to prevent COM1 from being interfered with by other programs.

The real driver should execute many other functions which ensure program reliability. However, our task here is to write a program that illustrates the mouse driver structure and performs the functions that relate to the interface between the mouse and the Screen Pencil program. To do this, we need some additional information about the low-level interface between the mouse and the Serial Port, as well as about the low and middle-level interface of user programs with the Serial Port.

# How a Mouse Interfaces with the Serial Port

The mouse interface with the serial port is very simple. The mouse checks its condition periodically and, if any change has occurred, it sends a message (packet) to the serial port. Each packet consists of 3 bytes for 2-button mice and 5 bytes for 3-button ones.

First let's consider the 2-button mouse exchange protocol. The mouse messages are transmitted at 1200 baud speed, without a parity check, 7 information bits per byte, 1 stop bit. The packet structure and separate bit destinations for a 3-button mouse are as follows:

### The First Byte

| | |
|---|---|
| Bit 0: | Bit 6 of X coordinate |
| Bit 1: | Bit 7 of X coordinate |
| Bit 2: | Bit 6 of Y coordinate |
| Bit 3: | Bit 7 of Y coordinate |
| Bit 4: | Right button: 1=ON,0=OFF |
| Bit 5: | Left-hand button: 1=ON,0=OFF |
| Bit 6: | Always = 1 |

## The Second Byte

|          |                          |
|----------|--------------------------|
| Bits 0-5: | 0-5 bits of X coordinate |
| Bit 6:   | Always 0                 |

## The Third Byte

|          |                                    |
|----------|------------------------------------|
| Bits 0-5: | 0-5 bits of Y coordinate increment |
| Bit 6:   | Always 0                           |

The mouse is designed so that when it is moving, the ball located on the bottom rotates. Its rotation is transmitted on two little wheels, relating to X and Y coordinates. Turning the wheels causes changes in the angle coordinate transmitter conditions. The angle coordinates are read approximately 40 times per second and are stored in the mouse memory. The mouse buttons have only 2 positions: 0 and 1, which are stored every duty cycle. Before they are stored, the value of each coordinate and the button positions are compared with preceding values. If they have changed, the mouse sends the 3-byte pack, in which the coordinate values and button positions are coded. Thus, if the mouse does not move, its conditions do not change and it does not send a message, so the interrupts from the serial port do not occur.

The 3-button mouse operates in much the same way. The difference is that each of the 5-byte packets contains the codes of the current and previous increments of the mouse coordinates. The packet structure and separate bit destination for a 3-button mouse is as follows:

## The First Byte

|          |                                  |
|----------|----------------------------------|
| Bits 0-4: | Always 00001                     |
| Bit 5:   | The left button: 0=ON,1=OFF      |
| Bit 6:   | The average button: 0=ON,1=OFF   |
| Bit 7:   | The right button: 0=ON,1=OFF     |

### The Second Byte

Bits 0-7:     Value of X coordinate after last packet transmission.

### The Third Byte

Bits 0-7     Value of Y coordinate after last packet transmission.

### The Forth Byte

Bits 0-7     Value of X coordinate relative to the position reported in byte 2.

### The Fifth Byte

Bits 0-7     Value of Y coordinate relative to the position reported in byte 3.

## How a Serial Port Transfers Mouse Byte Packets to DOS

Each byte received from the mouse device arrives in the serial port receive buffer. Having placed the byte in the buffer, the serial port controller issues an interrupt - IRQ4, or 0Ch (for COM1). If that interrupt is not masked either in the serial port or in the interrupt controller, it arrives at the processor and INT 0Ch results. The mouse driver should hook this interrupt and not permit it to do anything with the Mouse Byte packets. It is possible to do this by a low-level interface controlling the serial port controller, or by a middle-level one using the interrupt 14h - Serial Port I/O or by means of DOS function 03h - Auxiliary Input and 04h - Auxiliary Output. Next we will look at the middle-level interface. The tutorial Mouse Driver - PROG8_4ASM on the disk (see below) - illustrates support of the same functions on low-level.

## BIOS Interrupt 14h - Serial Port I/O

This interrupt supports access to the two serial ports. The BIOS only supports the first two of the four base serial port addresses, which are stored in 4 words, starting with address 040h:00. To support COM3 and COM4 ports, you must change their addresses from the previous ones.

## Function 00h: Initialize Communication Port

Expects:  DX = Port number (0-1)

      AH = 00h

      AL = Parameter bits (see below)

Returns:   AH = Serial Port Status (see Table 6.8)

The AL parameter bit meanings and destinations are as follows:

| Bits 0-1: | Word length | 10 = 7 bits |
|---|---|---|
| | | 11 = 8 bits |
| Bit 2: | Stop bits | 0 = 1, 1 = 2 |
| Bits 3-4: | Parity | 00,10 = none |
| | | 01 = odd |
| | | 10 = even |
| Bits 5-7: | Baud rate | 000 = 110 |
| | | 001 = 150 |
| | | 010 = 300 |
| | | 011 = 600 |
| | | 100 = 1200 |
| | | 101 = 2400 |
| | | 110 = 4800 |
| | | 111 = 9600 |

## Function 01h: Send a Character

Expects:  AH = 01h

      AL = Character to Sent

      DX = Port number (0-1)

Returns:   AL Preserved

You may use AL bits 0-6 only. Bit 7 must always be 0. If you set bit 7 = 1, an error occurs. In this case the function returns in AH the Serial Port communication line status (see Table 6.8).

## Function 02h: Receive a Character

Expects:  AH = 02h

      DX = Port number (0-1)

Returns:   AL = Character received

      AH = 0, if AH <> 0, it means that an error has occurred

### Function 03h: Get a Serial Port Status

Expects:     AH = 03h

DX = Port number (0-1)

Returns:     AX = Port Status

The Port Status word bits are described below:

**Table 6.8 AH = Line-control Status**

| Bit | Meaning |
| --- | --- |
| 0 | Data ready status |
| 1 | Overrun error |
| 2 | Parity error |
| 3 | Framing error |
| 4 | Break detect |
| 5 | Transmitter holding register empty |
| 6 | Transmitter shift register empty |
| 7 | Timeout |

# The Mouse Driver Imitation Program

This tutorial program illustrates a low-level mouse interface. It can replace the standard mouse driver. See PROG6_3.ASM on the accompanying disk. It has a common mouse driver structure, but only supports the functions which are required for that program. PROG6_4.ASM (on disk) hooks the 0Ch and 33h interrupts and checks if they have been loaded before. If not, it initializes the serial port and stays resident, waiting for the hooked interrupts.

If INT 0Ch occurs, the driver checks for a byte ready to be read and puts the byte in the buffer. The program recognizes and saves the first byte, because bit 6 is set to 1. The following two bytes are read and saved, then the group of 3 bytes is processed. When INT 33h occurs, the driver sends these parameters to the requesting program.

The driver recognizes PROG_6.3ASM because it passes 7373h in the SI register, which is not used for anything else. Without this flag, the driver answers requests as IRET, so it does not confuse other programs. Other programs request function 00h, but after this, other functions are not supported. You can use this program as a template for designing more sophisticated drivers.

# The Joystick

Games controllers can support 2 two-coordinate joysticks, each with two buttons. The joystick management supposes that the user's program:

- Monitors the buttons and coordinate conditions of each joystick.

- Responds to their static conditions and their dynamic changes in a predefined way.

It is clear that the last task is not specific to joystick control and we shall not consider it. The first task can be executed on low-level through port 201h or on a higher level by BIOS (INT 15h, function 84h).

## Joystick Management Via the Game Port

When you read the 201h port, it returns one byte of information about joystick conditions. The bit meanings are as follows:

**Table 6.9 Joystick Conditions**

| Bit | Meaning |
|-----|---------|
| 0 | Coordinate X of joystick A |
| 1 | Coordinate Y of joystick A |
| 2 | Coordinate X of joystick B |
| 3 | Coordinate Y of joystick B |
| 4 | Button #1 of joystick A |
| 5 | Button #2 of joystick A |
| 6 | Button #1 of joystick B |
| 7 | Button #2 of joystick B |

Thus, the values of bits 4-7 correspond to joystick button conditions (0 - button is released, 1 - button is pressed). The response of bits 0-3 to joystick coordinates will be considered later.

The joystick A button 1 condition, for example, is easy to check up on:

```
mov    DX, 201h
in     AL, DX              ; reading  joystick condition
test   AL, 10h             ; joystick A button 1 condition check
JNZ    Button1             ; the button is pressed, action required
```

If this code is included in the loop, the program will expect the relevant button to be pressed, but the processor will be busy. It is better to follow this button condition by hooking the user's interrupt 1Ch, which usually consists of only one command, IRET. IBM compatible machines issue interrupt 1Ch on each timer interrupt - approximately 18 times per second.

```
   Old_AL  DB 0
.................
   push  CS
   pop   DS
   mov   DX, offset Button1
   mov   AX, 251Ch               ; set interrupt 1Ch vector
   int 21h
Button1:
   mov   DX, 201h
   in    AL, DX                  ; get joystick condition
   and   AL,10h                  ; new condition of button 1,joystick A
   mov   DL, Old_AL
   and   DL, 10h                 ;old condition of button 1,joystick A
   CMP   AL, DL
   JZ    No_Change
   XOR   Old_AL,10h              ; change old condition
   CALL  Change1A                ; condition of button 1, joystick A has changed-call
                                 ; to reacting subroutine
 No_Change:                      ; no changes, return
   .........
    IRET
```

As we saw above, for each coordinate of a joystick the 201h port only grants one bit. But how is it possible to learn the exact values of coordinates? It appears that it is done by measuring time intervals. When you write any arbitrary value to the 201h port, the bits 0-3 are cleared. After that, each bit keeps a zero value during the time interval, the duration being proportional to the relative joystick position. The measurement of these intervals gives us the joystick coordinate values with great accuracy. We can do this, for example, as follows:

```
; Measurement of joystick coordinate

YA_Coord DB 0                           ; coordinate Y of joystick A
.....................
    mov   DX, 201h
    out   DX, AL                        ; clearing of bits 0-3
    jmp   $ + 2                         ; maybe, little delay is necessary
    mov   DI, 0
RPT:
    IN    AL, DX
    test  AL, 2
    JNZ   OK
    INC   DI
    LOOP  RPT                           ; wait until
OK:
    mov   YA_Coord, DI                  ; now Y-coordinate value in DI
```

## Joystick Control by Means of Interrupt 15h Function 84h

Joystick control is much easier if we use the BIOS. Interrupt 15h function 84h returns all joystick coordinates. You can call it by including the following code in your program:

```
; Getting joystick coordinates

XA_Coord    DB     0        ; Coordinate X for joystick A
YA_Coord    DB     0        ; Coordinate Y for joystick A
XB_Coord    DB     0        ; Coordinate X for joystick B
YB_Coord    DB     0        ; Coordinate Y for joystick B
..................
    mov     DX, 1           ; DX=1 for coordinate status
    mov     AH, 84h
    int 15h
    jc      No_Joystick     ; there are no joysticks in the system
    mov     XA_Coord, AX    ; Coordinate X for joystick A
    mov     YA_Coord, BX    ; Coordinate Y for joystick A
    mov     XB_Coord, CX    ; Coordinate X for joystick B
    mov     YB_Coord, CX    ; Coordinate Y for joystick B
```

Finding the button status is also very simple:

```
B_Status DB ?                         ; joystick button status
........................
mov         DX, 0                     ; DX=0 (get button status)
mov         AH, 84h
int         15h
jc          No_Joystick               ; there are no joysticks in the system
OR          AL, 0F0h                  ; mask for button status
mov         B_Status, AL
```

To monitor the status of the joystick button it is better to write the program using interrupt 1Ch, similar to what we have seen above.

# Summary

In this chapter you have been aquainted with parallel and serial port interfaces. We considered how to connect a computer with external devices via such interfaces and how DOS and BIOS manage them. You have learned how to create your own programs and drivers for these devices.

We have written a program for printers which uses external printer drivers. We used the driver templates from Chapter 5 for creating simple, but easily expandable printer and mouse drivers. We also used our own mouse driver in a screen pencil program. The chapter ends with a description of how to write a program which interfaces with a joystick.

In the next chapter we'll consider interfacing with ISA bus devices.

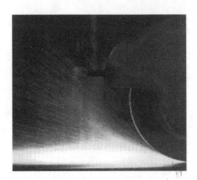

# Interfacing to ISA Bus Devices

## Introduction

This chapter is devoted to interfacing with ISA bus devices. There are many other bus architectures in use: EISA System Architecture, 80486 System Architecture, PCI System Architecture, Pentium Processor System Architecture, and MicroChannel System Architecture. In this chapter, we will look at ISA System Architecture, which is often considered as the platform upon which the others build. Once you know ISA, the other systems become more easily understood.

ISA stands for Industry Standard Architecture. Although it is difficult to give a strict definition of it, we mean, in this case, the ISA subsystem, which consists of the ISA bus itself (expansion bus) and auxiliary subsystems connected with the bus controller.

# Interrupt Programming

Microprocessor systems necessarily support many input-output devices (I/O devices). Using the polling mode can considerably reduce processor performance and restrict optimal use of the external device capabilities, unless you write single tasking communications programs and optimize the port throughput.

The alternative is the interrupt method, which considerably enlarges system capacity. In this case, the processor executes the main program, but interrupts it to serve the I/O device only when this device informs the processor about the need for I/O support and sends an interrupt request. After completing I/O support, the processor continues executing the main program from the exact location where it was interrupted by the interrupt request.

The main device of the interrupt service subsystem is the programmable interrupt controller or PIC. Usually, it is the 8259A interrupt controller or its equivalent VLSI component. The interrupt controller monitors multiple Interrupt Request (IRQ) lines for interrupt requests. Each IRQ line can pass one interrupt request signal. (The number of the IRQ line for the PIC chip, from 0 to 7, is sometimes called an interrupt level.) These device request signals are named according to the system IRQ line numbers, from IRQ0 to IRQ15. When an interrupt request is made, the PIC registers it, and checks its priority. If the priority level of the request is sufficiently high, the controller sends a message to the processor (an Interrupt Request signal, or INTR). This means that the interrupt of the currently executed program is needed for the I/O device interrupt service. If the priority level of the request is not sufficient, it is stored for possible subsequent execution. The ISA subsystem assumes that the system includes two interrupt controllers (we'll look at these later in the chapter). Besides the INTR, the Intel microprocessors also have an additional input for the Nonmaskable Interrupt Request. In addition to hardware interrupts, the processor can also be interrupted by software or by the processor itself, if an exception occurs.

Each I/O device uses one or more interrupts and is supported by the appropriate interrupt service programs. If such a program call is necessary, the interrupt controller passes one of the address indexes (interrupt vectors) to the processor. Each interrupt vector can point to the input of the interrupt supporting program.

## How the Interrupt Controller Works

The ISA subsystem usually assumes the presence of two identical PICs, each of which can support up to eight interrupt signal lines, also known as interrupt levels. In this case, one of the interrupt controllers is the main (or master) controller and the second is the slave. The initialization and support of the interrupt controller is controlled by the I/O ports. A choice of priority modes is available in the program and can be set or changed dynamically, that is, during program execution, depending on the equipment being installed and the peculiarities of the task.

The programmed interrupt controller contains the following main blocks and registers:

- The interrupt request register (IRR).

- The in-service interrupt register (ISR).

- The interrupt mask register (IMR).

- The priority resolver.

- The read/write and cascading control blocks.

The IRR register serves as a store for interrupt, and the ISR register stores the currently processed interrupt levels. The priority resolver acts as the priority definition for IRR bits, which are set to 1. The bit with the highest priority is the first candidate for action. The IMR contains the bits, which if set, prohibit processing of the appropriate IRR bits. This does not prohibit interrupt processing at a lower priority. The read/write control block is designed to receive processor commands and transmit the interrupt controller's status to the data bus. The 8259 PIC accepts two types of commands: Initialization Command Word (ICW) and Operational Command Word (OCW). In fact, these 'words' are bytes. The block contains the initialization command word (ICW) register and the operational command word (OCW) register, which in turn contains the necessary data for controller operation management. The cascading control block will be considered later, along with the slave interrupt controller.

## The Interrupt Request Processing Sequence

**1** On an ISA system, the external device interrupt request results in a negative pulse which is sent by the appropriate interrupt line, IRQ1-IRQ7. To be accepted, the request must be sustained until the second interrupt acknowledge (see below).

**2** Having received this pulse, the PIC sets the appropriate bit of the IRR register to 1.

**3** The controller analyzes this bit, using its priority level and masks. If required, it sends the INTR signal (set to 1) to the processor.

**4** When the next bus cycle is completed, the processor grabs the bus (provided the hardware interrupts do not prohibit it), and sends the first interrupt acknowledged by the -INTA signal to the interrupt controller.

**5** Having acknowledged the interrupt, the interrupt controller sets the current interrupt bit of the ISR register to 1, simultaneously zeroing the appropriate bit of the IRR register. The interrupt controller is not connected with the ISA bus during this process.

**6** The central processor sends a second -INTA pulse.

**7** The interrupt controller sends the index of the Interrupt Table Entry on one data byte to the data bus, representing the interrupt vector.

**8** The processor transforms this number into the real address of the given interrupt supporting program (Interrupt Handler) and calls it.

**9** The interrupt handler completes interrupt support.

**10** If the interrupt controller is in Automatic End of Interrupt mode (this is an infrequent occurrence), it resets the appropriate bit of the ISR register at the end of the second pulse of -INTA and terminates the interrupt process. More probably, the ISR register bit remains set to 1 until the arrival of the EOI command (End Of Interrupt, see below) which should be sent at the end of the interrupt handler routine.

**11** The EOI command ends the interrupt request processing sequence.

Until this command arrives, the installed ISR register bit prohibits processing of all interrupts with equal or lower priority. If, when the interrupt is first acknowledged, the level of IRQ signal ceases to be high (for example, in the case of an error pulse), the interrupt is considered false and the interrupt controller sends the interrupt request for level 7. As will become clearer later, for the master controller it will be IRQ7, and for the slave, IRQ15. Therefore, IRQ7 and IRQ15 routines should guard against the possibility of false interrupts. To enable this, read the contents of the appropriate interrupt controller's ISR register to be sure that bit 7 is set to 1. If it is not, the interrupt is false and the IRET command should be issued.

The purpose and formats of command words and registers of the interrupt controller is described below.

All interrupt controller registers are accessible through two I/O ports. For the master controller this port has the addresses 20h and 21h, and for the slave, the addresses 0A0h and 0A1h. Thus each of the 20h and 0A0h ports are associated with one of the interrupt controller inputs. In fact, they are used as the control bits. The processor can write the following two types of command words in the interrupt controller registers:

- Initialization Command Words, or ICW

- Operation Command Words, or OCW

See Chapter 3 for a detailed description of ICWs and OCWs.

Initialization Command Words, or ICWs, are used to set the interrupt controller to the starting position before working. Depending on the scenario, from 2 to 4 ICWs are required.

## The Interrupt Controller Operating Modes

To fully master controller programming there is a great deal of detail you need to understand to fully appreciate how it works. The PIC can work in several modes, in which the PIC commands and their operation may differ significantly. We shall consider the PIC modes in some detail. Some of them are rarely used, but it's useful to know they exist, especially when debugging programs.

## Fixed Priority Mode

This mode is set after controller initialization if another mode is not defined explicitly. All interrupt requests of the given controller have priority levels from 0 to 7 (0 being the highest one). After acknowledging the interrupt, the controller sets the bit of the highest priority interrupt to the ISR register, clears this bit in the IRR register, and puts its interrupt vector on the data bus. The interrupt bit in the ISR remains set until the PIC receives the EOI command, but can be cleared immediately after the second interrupt has been acknowledged if the automatic end of interrupt mode (see below) is set. As long as the given interrupt bit in the ISR register is not reset, all subsequent requests (whether with equal or lower priority) are not processed.

## End Of Interrupt Mode

This is used in 99% of cases. You can clear the bit in the ISR register using the command word OSW2, or automatically in Automatic End Of Interrupt mode (see below). If interrupt controller cascading is implemented in the system, then for the slave controller (that is, for IRQ8 - 15), you need to send the EOI command twice - firstly for the master, and then for the slave controller itself. There are two EOI command types: usual and special. In fixed priority mode the interrupt controller can always find out the bit that it ought to reset because it has the highest priority amongst those which have been set in the ISR register. Usually, the issued command is OSW2=20h, which must be written in port 20h or 0A0h.

If the controller does not preserve the fixed priority levels, in some cases it can't establish the acknowledged interrupt level. At this point the special EOI command may be used as follows: OSW2 = 0110 0YYY, where in the field YYY, the number of the ISR bit to be cleared is stated.

As for the ISR register bit, which is masked by the mask register bit, it should not be cleared by the normal EOI command if the interrupt controller operates in specific masking mode (see below).

## Automatic End Of Interrupt Mode

If bit 1 in ICW4 is set to 1, the controller operates in this mode until initialized by the ICW4. In this mode, the interrupt controller automatically executes the EOI command at each interrupt acknowledgment.

## Automatic Priority Rotation Mode

You can use this mode to operate several devices with the same priority. In this mode, the lowest priority is given to the device being serviced. The level of the following IRQ is given the highest priority, the next IRQ the next highest and so on. For example, if the level 3 device was served, the highest priority 0 will have the level 4 device, priority 1 will have level 5 device, and so on. If the given level 3 device requires the service again, it will wait until all other devices, which now possess higher priority, are served.

There are two ways of rotating priority. Firstly, you can use the EOI command for interrupt completion with bits 5-7 of the OCW2 word set to 101. Secondly, if the interrupt controller operates in automatic rotation priority mode, for priority rotation you need to set bits 5-7 to 100. You can switch off the automatic rotation priority mode by setting bits 5-7 of the OCW2 word to 000.

## Special Priority Rotation Mode

You can rotate all interrupt priorities however you want to if you set the lowest priority level number while developing the EOI by OSW2 as follows: OCW2 = 1110 0YYY, where the field YYY sets the lowest priority interrupt level.

## Masking Interrupts

Interrupt enabling and disabling is performed by masking with OCW1. The masking doesn't influence other functions for a given interrupt level and other level interrupts.

## The Specific Interrupt Masking Mode

If the interrupt request is already confirmed, but the EOI command has not yet reset the ISR bit, then the interrupt controller prohibits interrupts of current or lower priority, and the system may crash. One such situation is when your printer 'hangs' and disables the keyboard interrupt. At such a time, if the command of the interrupt handler clears the appropriate ISR bit, an interrupt of the same level can appear. This is inadmissible if the interrupt handler re-entering is not supported. If you want to allow lower level interrupts, you can use the specific interrupt masking mode. In this case, if the mask is set using OCW1, subsequent interrupts of the same level are prohibited, but interrupts with lower priority are allowed. You can switch the specific interrupt masking mode on and off if you set bit 6 in OCW3 to 1. If bit 4 of OCW3 is set to 1, this mode is enabled; if it is clear, the mode is disabled. If bit 6 of OCW3 is cleared, bit 4 is not valid.

## Polling Mode

If the PIC is operating in this mode, interrupts never occur, so the program must periodically check the PIC status and support interrupts if they occur. For IBM PC systems this mode does not apply.

## Fixed Priority Special Mode

The fixed priority special mode is implemented in systems with slave interrupt controllers if they wish to preserve the priority of the slave controllers. At this point the master controller works in the given mode. This mode is similar to the fixed priority mode except that when the interrupt request from the given slave controller is served, it is not masked by the master controller. The newly arrived request with the higher priority is passed into the master controller and can cause the processor to be interrupted. The slave controller is completely masked if it is in normal mode. Also, during the interrupt handler execution, it should check whether the serving interrupt from the given slave interrupt controller is unique. You can make the check by issuing the usual EOI command for the slave controller and afterwards reading its ISR register.

## Controller Cascading Mode

If the interrupt controller is a master one, it can be attached to 8 slave controllers. This gives up to 64 priority levels. The master and slave controllers are connected by the bi-directional internal three-line bus. During the first interrupt request acknowledgment, the master controller passes the current slave controller number through the bus and then permits the slave controller to set its interrupt vector.

If the interrupt controller operates in cascading mode, then any interrupt controller can be initialized independently and operate in its own mode, which differs from other controller modes. In this case the EOI commands are duplicated - one for the master, and one for the slave. Each controller has its own two I/O control ports.

## Interrupt Programming

The usual reason for interrupt programming is a desire to change or to improve an interrupt handler. You can do this by either completely, or partly, replacing the interrupt handler. In the first case, you write a TSR program, which is completely responsible for all given interrupt processing. However, this requires a great deal of effort, so more often than not, partial replacement or expansion of the standard handler functions is used. In such a case, you hook the interrupt, filter its functions, and then execute the ones that are needed. You pass the other functions to the old handler. You can replace the old interrupt 0Ch handler, as follows:

```
MOV AH,25h
MOV AL,0Ch
INT 21h                 ;get old interrupt vector
MOV OLD_0Ch_OFF,BX      ;store offset
MOV AX,ES
MOV OLD_0Ch_SEG,AX      ;store segment

MOV AX, SEG NEW_INT
MOV DS,AX
MOV DX,OFFSET Int_0Ch
MOV AL,0Ch
MOV AH,25h
INT 21h                 ;set as new Int 0Ch vector our own
```

Then, a handler may be as follows:

```
NEW_INT:                ;it is a new handler
PUSH AX                 ;save all registers which might be destroyed
PUSH BX
  ...
PUSH CS                 ;now you can do what you wish
POP DS
  ...
MOV AL,20h              ;and send the EOI command
OUT 20h,AL              ;to the Interrupt Controller
POP BX                  ;and then you must end the interrupt
POP AX                  ;restore registers
IRET
```

If you don't send the EOI command to the Interrupt controller after the hardware interrupt, it will refuse to service further interrupts, and the system will crash. For software interrupts you don't need to send the EOI command. At the end of your program you must restore the old interrupt vector as follows:

```
CLI                             ;clear interrupt flag
PUSH DS                         ;storing of current DS
MOV DX, OLD_0Ch_OFF             ;restore old interrupt
                                ;vector offset
MOV AX, OLD_0Ch_SEG             ;restore old interrupt
                                ;vector segment
MOV DS,AX                       ;put it in DS
MOV AH,25h                      ;DOS Fn 25h - Set Interrupt Vector
MOV AL,0Ch                      ;interrupt number
INT 21h
POP DS                          ;restoring of current DS
STI                             ;enable hardware interrupts
```

There are a number of other circumstances where the programmer needs some time interval to prohibit all or part of the hardware interrupts, and then to restore their execution. You can forbid all hardware interrupts using the CLI instruction, and re-enable them using the STI command. You must do this, because some hardware interrupts can delay your program action and interfere in the time critical sequence.

## How to Mask and Enable Interrupts

You can mask some (or all) interrupts by writing the appropriate mask in the IMR register. For example, if you wish to cancel the IRQ4, the COM1 interrupt, you must set bit 4. You can do this as follows:

```
IN AL,21h               ; read the IMR register
MOV OldIMR,AL           ; store its initial value

OR AL,10h               ; mask of COM1 interrupt - IRQ4
OUT 21h,AL              ; now it is masked
```

When you need to restore the interrupt function, you can write its old value in the IMR register (port 21h):

```
MOV AL,OldIMR           ; store its initial value
OUT 21h,AL              ; now it is restored
```

or clear the chosen bit:

```
IN AL,21h               ; read the IMR register
AND AL,0EFh             ; clearing the COM1 interrupt bit
OUT 21h,AL              ; now it works
```

Examples of most of these actions are contained in the simple tutorial interrupt 0Ch handler program PROG7-1.ASM.

# Direct Memory Access

The ISA subsystem of Direct Memory Access (DMA) is a peripheral interface system. It is designed to allow the exchange of information between external devices and system memory, bypassing the central processor. Direct Memory Access also permits the execution of data transfers between various areas of memory. The main purpose of DMA is the acceleration of exchange between the I/O device and RAM, as well as between different RAM domains. You can also achieve some other system improvements by using the processor to execute other tasks while DMA is being used. However, it must be done very carefully, because correct DMA programming often needs synchronization which is a complex and difficult process. To use DMA competently, we must first of all learn the main principles of the DMA controller.

## The DMA Controller

The ISA bus DMA subsystem contains two identical DMA controllers. Each of them contains memory, totaling 27 registers of 12 types, and the control system.

The control system consists of three blocks. The timing and control block produces the external control signals and defines the internal timing of the DMA controller. The command control block decodes the mode control word, determining the DMA-service type, as well as CPU commands.

The priority block distributes the execution sequence of simultaneously serviced requests. The DMA controller executes all operations during two main cycles - idle and working, each of which changes to various states. In total, the controller has 7 states, each one lasting a single clock period duration. The DMA controller can repeat some states several times. The first of them, SI (the Idle State), is a passive state. While in the idle state, the DMA controller polls all request channels, devices, and the CPU. In this state, the DMA controller is not active and allows programming by the processor. After receiving a request, the controller transits to S0 state. This is the first state of a DMA request service. In this state, the DMA controller sends the HOLD signal to the processor to request the use of the bus and waits for the HLDA signal from the bus. Until it has been received from the processor, you can continue programming the controller. After the bus hold (HLDA) has been confirmed, the processor is disconnected from the system bus, and the controller begins to transfer data using working states S1, S2, S3 and S4. If the data transfer can't be completed in the given number of steps, then one or more wait states, SW, can be inserted between states S3 and S4. The delay is executed on I/O device demand which sets the READY signal to low.

The DMA-controller is essentially an 8-bit device. Therefore, issuing 16-bit addresses, and then recording or reading 16-bit or 32-bit data, requires several working steps. If the DMA-controller needs to coordinate processor working speed with that of buses and external devices, it is done by the insertion of additional wait cycles. Fortunately, practically all necessary control is executed by the hardware. In the simplest cases for known I/O device types, the DMA-controller can be programmed to give the proper number of wait states. If the work rate of the device is unknown, or if it varies during the work, the ready signals are used to perform delays.

Let's look at the DMA-controller addresses, register structure and separate bits destination, as well as the controller and its channel operating modes. We shall also lookat examples of device programming.

## DMA Controller Modes

The controller as a whole can be in one of three modes: programming, active or passive.

Passive mode (S1) is the default mode for the controller. All its work consists of one cycle, in which it checks the state of inputs DREQ (the DMA-service requests) and HLDA (the signal of granting bus acknowledgment), as well as for processor access to DMA controller internal registers. In the first two cases, the DMA controller goes to active mode, and if the controller has addressed to the internal register, it goes to programming mode. If they occur simultaneously, the programming mode has a higher priority. Programming requires the reading from and writing to ports, whose addresses correspond to the given register (we'll look at address and destination of registers a little later). There are a lot of internal registers to reduce the number of I/O ports to the address register or to the counter to read or write. Thus, for regular work, the high and low bytes are alternated. This trigger can be set or reset for synchronization (that is, you always send the low byte first, then the high byte, but you can change this order). The DMA-controller also has a set of special commands which don't use the data bus. They only use the port addresses and transfer direction (read or write). These commands will be considered further when describing registers.

When the DMA-controller is programmed, the acknowledgment of the bus granting signal HLDA should be inactive for at least one clock period before, and up to, the end of programming. This means that for high-speed processors, programming the delay may be required. Therefore, any programming should begin with masking the appropriate channel or the DMA subsystem as a whole. If the DMA request occurs while the non-masked DMA channel is being programmed, it can cause an error in controller processing.

# DMA Channel Modes

## Single Transfer Mode

In single transfer mode, every time the DMA channel executes one cycle of data transfer, the controller releases the HOLD signal and releases the system bus. In response to this, the processor releases the HLDA signal and can then execute some work during one bus cycle. For example, the CPU can receive an interrupt or execute one or several instructions. If, after a while, the I/O device has not removed the request for the DMA-service (DREQ signal), on the following bus cycle, the DMA-controller again sends the HOLD request and executes the next data exchange (if a higher priority request has not been received (see below)). After each data transfer, the word counter decreases by 1, and the address counter decreases or increases by 1, depending on how the DMA controller is programmed.

When the contents of the word counter change from 0000h to 0FFFFh, the termination count bit (TC) in the status register is set and the count termination signal TC is produced. If auto-initialization is allowed, the channel loads the initial values into the word counter and the address counter and continues to work. Otherwise, the channel is masked and the further request service is terminated.

## Block Transfer Mode

The block transfer mode is similar to single transfer mode, but faster, because the DMA controller doesn't release the bus after each data transfer. The DMA-service request (DREQ) is active until transfer termination. Auto-initialization is also possible. You can use this mode for a short data exchange, but you should first guarantee that all transfers take a maximum of 15 microseconds, otherwise dynamic RAM refresh will be interrupted.

## Demand Transfer Mode

In demand transfer mode, the channel operation is actually controlled by the I/O device. The channel begins to work after receiving the DREQ signal and continues data transfer while this signal is active, or until the word counter reaches 0FFFFh. If the word counter has not yet reached this value, the DMA controller releases the bus and switches off the acknowledgment of the request service (DACKx signal) of the channel after each data transfer. During one bus cycle, the processor can again obtain control of the system bus, if necessary, and the I/O device can repeat the DREQ request, remove the request or keep the request. At this point the execution of the DMA request temporarily ceases, and is again renewed at the new request for the DMA service on this channel.

The demand transfer mode is a very convenient way of servicing external devices with small buffers. On breaks between such transfers, the processor is free to execute service work for this transfer, for example, using the current values of the address register and word counter.

## Cascade Mode

The cascade mode allows the use of more than 4 DMA channels in a system. The ISA standard supposes the use of two types of DMA controllers: the master and the slave. The master controller, namely the DMA2 controller, is connected, as usual, to the processor. Its maximum priority channel, channel 0, has now received the new number, channel 4, and the others, with numbers 1-3, receive numbers 5-7. The input DREQ4 and output DAC4 of the master controller are connected with output HOLD and input HLDA of the slave controller. The modes and programming of the slave controller remain as before, but programming the master controller is changed to channel 0.

The two DMA chips are connected together, with channel 4 of one chip being connected to the second, or 'cascaded' chip, thus creating channels 5, 6, 7, 8 from the 4 channels of the second chip. Therefore, channel 4 of the first isn't available to be used. The result is a larger number of DMA channels, and there are no conflicts between DMA controllers.

## DMA Transfer Types

The DMA subsystem supports four transfer types:

**Read type**. When programmed to perform read transfer, the DMA controller reads data from memory and writes it to the I/O device associated with the DMA channel.

**Write type**. In this case, data is read from the I/O device and is written to memory.

**Memory-to-memory transfer type**. This transfer type is used for moving data blocks from one memory location to another. For this transfer, the channels 0 and 1 are used, and bit 0 in command register DMA1 is set to 1. At the end of programming, the exchange can be started on program request, or after the arrival of the external request on channel 0. Note that the memory-to-memory transfer type is a unique operating mode, where the data passes through the DMA controller. In other modes, the controller only controls the exchange. During the first half of the exchange cycle, channel 0 generates the address for reading the byte, which is stored in a special register for temporary data storage, and in the second half of the exchange cycle, channel 1 produces an address to write to. Following on from this, data is transmitted to the data bus during the subsequent write operation. The specific address hold mode can be programmed in memory-to-memory transfer mode. Channel 0 can be programmed so that it doesn't change the source address at each cycle. It allows the filling of large data blocks to the same value. Data transfer continues until the channel 1 counter value reaches 0FFFFh.

**Verify transfer mode**. In this mode the DMA controller executes all the DMA transfer bus cycles, generates memory addresses, but doesn't activate Read or Write signals for bus control. Thus, the transfer isn't really executed. This transfer mode is used by channel 4 (zero) of the master DMA controller (DMA2) to implement dynamic RAM refreshing (undocumented).

## Channel Auto-initialization

As you can see, the mode register of each DMA channel contains a bit which controls the channel auto-initialization when its word counter reaches 0FFFFh. After writing initial values to the word counter and the current address register, these values are simultaneously written to the base word counter and the base address registers. The contents of these registers can only be changed using software - the channels don't influence it. If a channel is programmed for auto-initialization, it doesn't cease its operation at the end of transfer cycle. Instead, the contents of the appropriate base registers are rewritten to its base word counter and base address registers and the working cycle continues without processor interference. A necessary condition for correct auto-initialization, during the 'memory-to-memory' transfer, is the writing of identical values to word counters of channels 0 and 1.

## Priority Types for Service Requests

The DMA controller supports two types of service requests on DREQ inputs from I/O devices.

1 **Fixed Priorities**. The highest priority has channel 0 of the slave and the lowest has the channel 7 of the master controller.

2 **Rotating Priority.** The direction of priority increasing in dependence of a channel number is preserved, but the real value of priority of each channel varies. The last serviced channel receives the lowest priority. The channel with the next number receives the highest priority. The other channels receive priority, which decreases as the channel number increases.

If the same requests occur simultaneously (that is, in the same clock cycle or when the DMA controller is engaged and can't immediately begin its service), the controller activates the HOLD signal, but doesn't store the current priority order, until the HLDA signal is received. If new requests have arrived, they are included in the priority sequence on the same basis. As soon as the HLDA signal becomes active, the controller stores the current priority order and then sends the DACK signal to the device with the highest current priority. The priorities are not redistributed until the HLDA signal becomes inactive.

In demand transfer mode, the DMA controller should also take into account the DREQ signal condition when it distributes the request execution sequence.

## The Reduced DMA Working Cycle - Compressed Timing

When bit 3 of the command register is set to 1, it is possible to reduce the number of working cycles. The usual cycle (that is, for block or demand transfer mode) includes three states: S1, S2 and S3. 4 clock periods are required, as S3 is executed twice (as one wait state is inserted). The first part of the S3 cycle work can be executed in the S2 cycle, so it is possible to exclude one S3 state. Thus, the system only includes the S1 state when high bits of memory addresses are in the external address register.

The reduced DMA working cycle shouldn't be used for 'memory-to-memory' transfers because of the intensive change of all address components. Not all types of memory and I/O devices will tolerate the reduced read interval, so do take care.

# DMA Registers and Commands

## Current Address Register

Each DMA channel contains a 16-bit register. Each channel can be programmed so that the register increments, decrements or remains the same after each transfer cycle. The processor writes this value in two steps because it uses the 8-bit data bus XD0-XD7. During auto-initialization in this register, the initial value from the base address register is written. In the command register bit 1 is set to 1, and the contents of the zero channel current address register for memory-to-memory transfers don't vary.

## The Base Address Register

The base address register of the channel corresponds to each current address register. This register can only be accessed by software to write the initial value of the current address register. Each time this value is written into the current address register, it is simultaneously written into the base register. This value can only be changed by software, and is used for auto-initialization.

This register sets the starting RAM address from which the transfer begins. The register defines the address inside a page of 64k memory. You can program the page number by writing it to the page register.

## The Page Register

The internal address registers of the DMA controller only support addressing within a 64K page. The external page register is associated with the expansion of address space within each DMA channel. The page registers can be accessed by software. The addressing of these registers during transfer is executed by external logic using the DAKx signals from the DMA controllers. Such memory division doesn't allow transfer to a memory block in one step, if it is located on the intersection of two pages. Each page begins on an even 64K boundary.

## Current Word Counter

A 16-bit word counter register is present in each DMA channel. The word counter register must be programmed with the number of words to be moved, minus one. When the word counter contents reaches the 0FFFFh value, the controller produces the signal for count termination, TC. If auto-initialization is not programmed, channel masking occurs simultaneously and the counter stops. Otherwise, it writes the value of the word base counter into the current word counter, and the channel work continues.

## Base Word Counter

This register is intended for software initialization of each channel's current word counter. Each time a value is written to the current word counter, it is simultaneously written to the base word counter register. It is used at auto-initialization.

## Mode Register

Each channel has a corresponding software accessible mode register, which defines the channel operating mode. The structure and destination of the register fields is as follows:

**Table 7.3 Mode Register**

| Bits | Destination |
|------|-------------|
| 0-1  | Channel number: |
|      | 00 - 0 |
|      | 01 - 1 |
|      | 10 - 2 |
|      | 11 - 3 |
| 2    | Auto-initialization: |
|      | 1 - permitted |
|      | 0 - not permitted |

*Continued*

**Table 7.3 Mode Register (Continued)**

| Bits | Destination |
|------|-------------|
| 3 | Direction bit: |
| | 0 - increase of current address during transfer |
| | 1 - decrease of current address during transfer |
| 4-5 | Transfer type: |
| | 00 - demand transfer mode |
| | 01 - single transfer mode |
| | 10 - block transfer mode |
| | 11 - cascade mode |
| 6-7 | Mode: |
| | 00 - verify |
| | 01 - write (to memory) |
| | 10 - read (from memory) |
| | 11 - forbidden combination |

## Command Register

By now, you should be acquainted with the set of each channel registers. The command register and other registers, which we will look at later, are common for all channels and are present in each DMA controller.

The command register controls the operation of the controller. It can be programmed when the DMA controller is in the SI or S0 state. This register is cleared by the commands 'Reset' and 'Master clear'. Here is a description of these register bits:

**Table 7.4 Command Register**

| Bits | Destination |
|------|-------------|
| 0 | Transfers memory-to-memory: |
| | 0 - prohibited |
| | 1 - permitted |

*Continued*

Table 7.4 Command Register (Continued)

| Bits | Destination |
|------|-------------|
| 1 | Fixing of channel 0 address: |
|   | 0 - prohibited |
|   | 1 - permitted |
| 2 | 1 - block the controller |
|   | 0 - unblock it |
| 3 | Timing (this bit is ignored if bit 0 is set to 1): |
|   | 0 - normal |
|   | 1 - compressed timing |
| 4 | Priority Logic: |
|   | 0 - fixed priority mode |
|   | 1 - rotating priority mode |
| 5 | Extended Write mode (ignored if bit 3 is set to 1): |
|   | 1 - permitted |
|   | 0 - prohibited |
| 6 | DREQ active level: |
|   | 0 - high level |
|   | 1 - low level |
| 7 | DAC active level: |
|   | 1 - high level |
|   | 0 - low level |

## Status Register

This register reflects the current status of requests and transfers for all controller channels. If the auto-initialization mode is not set, bits 0 - 3 are set to 1 after the end of the transfer of channels 0 - 3 for the slave controller, or 4 - 7 for the master. Bits 0 - 3 are cleared by the Reset signal and after reading each status. Bits 4 - 7, set to 1, indicate the current active state of request signals DREQx of channels 0 - 3 for the slave controller, or 4 - 7 for the master. Bits 4 - 7 are set to 0 after the controller is reset, and if the I/O device removes its request. The condition of the mask register (see below) doesn't influence bits 4 - 7 of the status register.

## Mask Register

You can use this register to prohibit DMA service requests for any channel. When set to 1, bits 0 - 3 of this register prohibit the service on channels 0 - 3 for the slave controller, or 4 - 7 for the master. They are set to 1 after the controller is reset.

If the auto-initialization mode isn't set, the channel bit for counters which have reached the 0FFFFh value is set to 1. All bits of the mask register are cleared by the 'Reset mask register' command. This allows the external DMA requests service to work for all channels. You can write to the mask register in one of two ways.

Firstly, you can write a single bit. For this, you must write the byte to the 0Ah port for the slave DMA controller or 0D4h for the master DMA controller. Bit 2 sets or clears the mask bit of the channel, which is selected by bits 0-1, and its values are as follows:

00 - channel 4 selected
01 - channel 5 selected
10 - channel 6 selected
11 - channel 7 selected

The 1 in bit 2 position doesn't allow the hardware request's service.

Secondly, you can set or clear all 4 channel masks simultaneously, by writing the byte to 0Fh or 0DEh for the slave or master controller, respectively. Bits 0-3 correspond to the mask values for respective channels. Reading from the same ports returns the current mask register value in the same format.

## Request Register

Servicing the DMA channel request can start from a software or a hardware request. Bits 0 - 3 of these registers, if set to 1, cause a software request of the DMA channel service for channel 0 - 3 of the slave controller, or channel 4 - 7 for master controller. The processor can set and clear all the channel bits independently of each other. The service for software request can't be prohibited by the mask register. The high bits 4 - 7 always contain logic 1. Bits 0 - 3 are set to 0 by the 'Reset' command. You can start the channel work by a software request if you write the request byte to address 09h for the slave controller or 0D3h for the master. Bit 2, if set to 1, causes the software request of the channel, which is selected by bits 0-1 values as follows:

00 - 0 channel (4) selected
01 - 1 channel (5) selected
10 - 2 channel (6) selected
11 - 3 channel (7) selected

## Temporary Register

This register serves as a store for temporary data for 'memory-to-memory' transfers. The data from the last transfer remains in this register and can be read until the reset signal or the controller reset command is received.

## How to Write and Read the Data in Registers - Some DMA Commands

We will now teach you some more about the necessary addresses of DMA registers and some features of writing to and reading from them. Also, we will discuss some special commands which are connected with DMA register access.

As you already know, the DMA controller uses a special trigger which can be set by the software to reduce the quantity of registers. This trigger indicates that a low or high byte is read or written when the 16-bit register is accessed. It must be taken into account when you use the following table of port addresses of these registers. This table gives the channel numbers for the slave controller (or DMA2 controller). For the master controller channels (DMA1 controller), the numbers are greater by 4. Note that some of the commands, executed on access to the address from 08h (0D0h) and above, can't be executed in the old DMA controller models.

**Table 7.5 DMA Controller Register Addresses**

| Address of: | | Access | Destination |
| DMA1 | DMA2 | type | |
|------|------|--------|-------------|
| 000h | 0C0h | R/W | Channel 0 Memory Address Register: lower 16-bits of memory address accessed as 2 successive bytes. |
| 001h | 0C2h | R/W | Channel 0 Transfer Count Register: lower 16-bits of transfer count accessed as 2 successive bytes. |

Table 7.5 DMA Controller Register Addresses (Continued)

| Address of: DMA1 | DMA2 | Access type | Destination |
|---|---|---|---|
| 002h | 0C4h | R/W | Channel 1 Memory Address Register: lower 16-bits of memory address accessed as 2 successive bytes. |
| 003h | 0C6h | R/W | Channel 1 Transfer Count Register: lower 16-bits of transfer count accessed as 2 successive bytes. |
| 004h | 0C8h | R/W | Channel 2 Memory Address Register: lower 16-bits of memory address accessed as 2 successive bytes. |
| 005h | 0CAh | R/W | Channel 2 Transfer Count Register: lower 16-bits of transfer count accessed as 2 successive bytes. |
| 006h | 0CCh | R/W | Channel 3 Memory Address Register: lower 16-bits of memory address accessed as 2 successive bytes. |
| 007h | 0CEh | R/W | Channel 3 Transfer Count Register: lower 16-bits of transfer count accessed as 2 successive bytes. |
| 008h | 0D0h | Read | DMA Status Register. |
|  |  | Write | DMA Control Register. |
| 009h | 0D2h | Read | Request Register. |
|  |  | Write | Software DRQn Request. |
| 00Ah | 0D4h | Read | Read Control Register. |
|  |  | Write | Write 1 bit of DMA Mask Register. |
| 00Bh | 0D6h | R/W | DMA Mode Register. |
| 00Ch | 0D8h | Write | Reset DMA Byte Pointer Trigger to the low byte. |
| 00Dh | 0DAh | Read | Read the Temporary Register. |

*Continued*

**Table 7.5 DMA Controller Register Addresses (Continued)**

| Address of: DMA1 | DMA2 | Access type | Destination |
|---|---|---|---|
| | | Write | DMA Master Clear Command: writing to this address resets the DMA controller to the same state as a hardware reset. |
| 00Eh | 0DCh | Read | Resets the Mode Register Counter |
| | | Write | DMA Reset Mask Command: activates the four DMA channels. |
| 00Fh | 0DEh | R/W | DMA General Mask Register |

The page register addressing of the DMA subsystem is given below.

**Table 7.6 DMA Subsystem Page Register Addresses**

| Address | Register Destination |
|---|---|
| 080h | Not used |
| 081h | DMA1 (8-bit transfers) channel 2 (DACK2) |
| 082h | DMA1 (8-bit transfers) channel 3 (DACK3) |
| 083h | DMA1 (8-bit transfers) channel 1 (DACK1) |
| 084h | Not used |
| 085h | Not used |
| 086h | Not used |
| 087h | DMA1 (8-bit transfers) channel 0 (DACK0) |
| 088h | Not used |
| 089h | DMA2 (16-bit transfers) channel 6 (DACK6) |
| 08Ah | DMA2 (16-bit transfers) channel 7 (DACK7) |
| 08Bh | DMA2 (16-bit transfers) channel 5 (DACK5) |
| 08Ch | Not used |
| 08Dh | Not used |
| 08Eh | Not used |
| 08Fh | Memory Refresh |

*Continued*

## Special Commands

For easy DMA Subsystem programming, there are a set of special commands. They aren't executed after the command itself has been sent, but only after access to the port address, independent of the access type: read or write. If you write, the DMA controller ignores the current data bus condition. If you do read, it is necessary to ignore the data processor read outs.

Some of the commands listed in Table 7.5 are now considered below in more detail.

Reset DMA Byte Pointer Trigger to the low byte: This command is used to initialize the exchange with the address register or word counter from a low byte.

Set DMA Byte Pointer Trigger to the high byte: This command is used to initialize the exchange with the address register or word counter from a high byte.

Master Reset: This command acts in the same way as the signal 'Reset' at hardware reset. It sets the mask register bits and clears the command, status, request and temporary registers, the mode register counter and the byte pointer trigger. After execution, the DMA controller is idle.

Mask Register Reset: This command enables the DMA request service for all channels.

Mode Register Counter Reset: Some new machines use an additional counter to facilitate access to the four mode registers. You can reset this counter and then read all these registers successively, for channels 0 - 3 (4 - 7), using only one mode register address.

# DMA Programming

Now, having learnt the fundamentals of DMA, you can easily understand and write a DMA program. The common structure for DMA programming can be as follows:

1    Set the appropriate bit in the DMA mask register before channel programming.

2    Write the relevant data to set a given mode in the mode register.

3    Read or write any value in the clear byte pointer register to determine the low/high sequence.

4    Calculate the full address (page + offset) from the usual segment/offset address.

5    Write two bytes of the address offset into the memory address register.

6    Write the page number into the page register.

7    Write two bytes of transfer count to the transfer count register.

8    Clear the appropriate bit in the DMA mask register to start the DMA channel service.

This programming sequence is implemented in two programs on the accompanying disk, PROG7-2.ASM and PROG7-3.ASM, both of which read and write data to a floppy disk. Each step of both programs is supplied with comments so that you can more easily understand what they are doing.

# Timers

The PC architecture provides two independent timers for all PC-compatible computers (though some machines only have one). Each timer contains the data bus buffer, the I/O control circuit and three independent timer channels. From the programmer's point of view, all channels are functionally identical, but differ with regard to the degree of availability and their position within the system. (Note that one of the channels is completely inaccessible for software, and is not used.) Thus, the system uses 5 timers:

1    Timer 0, or System Timer

2    Timer 1, or Refresh Timer

3    Timer 2, or Speaker Timer

**4**   The Watchdog Timer

**5**   The Slowdown Timer

Each channel counter contains the mode register, status register and 16-bit subtract counter, two 8-bit input registers (CIL and CIH) for initial counter value storage, and two 8-bit output registers (COL and COH ) for reading current counter contents.

Each channel has several input and output signals:

**Clock frequency inputs**. The first three channels use a 1.19318 MHz Timer Clock as the input signal.

**Control input gate**. The gate inputs for timers 0 and 1 are not accessible. They are always connected to the high level line. However, you can control the timer 2 gate input from your program (see below).

**Output signal out**. The output counter 0 is always connected with input IRQ0 of the interrupt controller. In some high-speed machines, this signal initially arrives at the IRQ0 Latch, whose output can be switched off by software, through bit 7, system port B. Counter 1 output is used by the DRAM Refresh logic to become the bus master every 15 microseconds. Counter 2 output is connected with the speaker driver input through the AND gate.

You can set the second input of the gate by using bit 1 of system port B (see below). The output status of each counter can be determined by reading the status register.

Reading the status register determines the channel conditions to decide if you need to read the contents of the mode and counter registers.

The mode register contains the information about the channel's current mode. To write in it you must write the control byte in port 43h for counters 0-2, and in port 46h for counters 3-5. The control byte contains the channel number and the control information. Each timer has 6 operating modes:

**Table 7.7 Timer Operating Modes**

| Mode | Description |
|------|-------------|
| 0 | Count with interrupt |
| 1 | Delay flip-flop with external start |
| 2 | Rate generator |
| 3 | Square wave generator |
| 4 | Counter with software strobe |
| 5 | Counter with hardware strobe |

Each channel counter is a 16-bit decrementing counter. Writing in the counter happens on the negative front edge of Timer Clock signal. The maximum divider value is reached by loading a counter value of 0, which corresponds to a divider value of 65536 for binary mode count or 10000 for binary-coded decimal (BCD) mode. When zeroing, the counter doesn't stop. In all modes of operation, except for 2 and 3, it continues operation with the value 0FFFFh for binary mode or 9999 for BCD mode. When the counter operates in modes 2 or 3, after zeroing, the counter rewrites its initial value from the CIL and CHL registers.

The initial value is loaded into the counter from the input registers CIL and CIH. It only permits the reloading of one byte, high or low, while the old value remains in the other byte. You can also load the whole word with one step of the counter. To do so, firstly you must load the previously mentioned registers into the low byte, and then into the high byte. Direct reading of the initial value is impossible. You can read the current value of the counter indirectly through the contents of output registers COL and COH, and you can store the current value of the counter in these registers.

Let's now have a look at the formats and descriptions of the counter commands and the register contents.

After the power is switched ON, the counter status is not defined, therefore each counter must be programmed before use. You can program each counter channel by writing the control byte into the mode register of the channel which is write only. Having written the control byte, you can read to or write from other timer registers (see below).

The addresses of the timer's ports are given in Table 7.8.

**Table 7.8 Timer Port Addresses**

| I/O Port | Access | Destination |
|---|---|---|
| 40h | Read/Write | Counter 0, PIT #1 System Timer |
| 41h | Read/Write | Counter 1, PIT #1 Refresh Timer (not to be changed) |
| 42h | Read/Write | Counter 2, PIT #1 Speaker Timer |
| 43h | Write only | Mode Control Register |
| 48h | Read/Write | Counter 0, PIT #2 Watchdog Timer |
| 49h | Read/Write | Counter 1, PIT #2 not used |
| 4Ah | Read/Write | Counter 2, PIT #2 Slowdown Timer |
| 4Bh | Write only | Mode Control Register |

The timer control byte format is given below:

| Bytes: | 7 | 6 | 5 | 4 | 3 | 2 | 1 | 0 |
|---|---|---|---|---|---|---|---|---|
| Bit values: | F3 | F2 | F1 | F0 | M2 | M1 | M0 | BCD |

The field F0 - F3 determines the counter commands for counters 0 - 2 (as shown below). For counters 3 - 5, add the base value 3 to each counter number of the table.

**Table 7.9 Counter Commands**

| F0-F3 Value | Command |
|---|---|
| 0 | Store the counter 0 value |
| 1 | Read and write only the low byte in counter 0 |
| 2 | Read and write only the high byte in counter 0 |
| 3 | Read and write first the low and then the high byte in counter 0 |
| 4 | Store the counter 1 value |
| 5 | Read and write only the low byte in counter 1 |

*Continued*

Table 7.9 Counter Commands (Continued)

| F0-F3 Value | Command |
|---|---|
| 6 | Read and write only the high byte in counter 1 |
| 7 | Read and write first the low and then the high byte in counter 1 |
| 8 | Store the counter 2 value |
| 9 | Read and write only the low byte in counter 2 |
| 0Ah | Read and write only the high byte in counter 2 |
| 0Bh | Read and write first the low and then the high byte in counter 2 |
| 0Ch-0Fh | 'Counter status reading' Command |

The mode set commands, bits M0 - M2, determine the channel operating mode, and in read commands they determine the channel number.

The BCD bit determines the choice of binary or BCD operating mode of the counter. When 'Reading the counter status' this bit should be set to zero.

In commands for reading and writing counter values before the first writing, the command must be written in the mode register of the appropriate channel. The required value must be written in the format given by the aforementioned command (that is, to write low or high bytes, or at first low and then high byte). The mode installation command, bits M0 - M2, determine the channel operating mode, as shown below:

Table 7.10 Mode Installation Commands

| M0-M3 Value | Function |
|---|---|
| 0 | Mode 0 is chosen |
| 1 | Mode 1 is chosen |
| 2,6 | Mode 2 is chosen |

*Continued*

**Table 7.10 Mode Installation Commands (Continued)**

| M0-M3 Value | Function |
|---|---|
| 3,7 | Mode 3 is chosen |
| 4 | Mode 4 is chosen |
| 5 | Mode 5 is chosen |

The initial value of the channel counter can be rewritten at any time (also after programming the mode register) without rewriting the mode command.

Upon execution of a command like 'Store the counter value or status', the current counter value or status is stored in the COL and COH registers. It is stored there until it is read out, or until the next reprogramming. To synchronize and improve operating accuracy of the counters in a program, this command can be given in turn to several channel counters before the values are read. The next execution of the command doesn't affect the stored value. This means that having used this command you can only receive the new counter value after reading it. The same is true when reading the counter status value. The command 'Store the current counter value' stores the current counter value of the channel.

The format of the command is as follows:

| Bytes: | 7 | 6 | 5 | 4 | 3 | 2 | 1 | 0 |
|---|---|---|---|---|---|---|---|---|
| Values: | 1 | 1 | 0 | 1 | C2 | C1 | C0 | 0 |

The bits C0 - C2 determine the channel number. Setting 1 to the appropriate bit determines the channel number to which the given command relates. Bit C0 relates to channel 0. Bits C1 and C2 relate to channels 1 and 2 accordingly. 'Register current status' stores the current mode status register of the channel. The next reading of the counter will give the status byte. The values in bits C0 - C2 values are the same as in the previous command. The stored value doesn't change as long as it isn't read, and the channel isn't reprogrammed.

The 'Store the current counter value and status' command format is the same as above, except for bit 4, which is set to 0.

After this command has been executed, the counter reading returns the status byte. After that, subsequent reading operations return one or two bytes of the counter's stored value, depending on the programming of the counter. The stored value doesn't change as long as it isn't read and the channel isn't reprogrammed.

The format and bit meaning of the status byte is:

| Bytes: | 7 | 6 | 5 | 4 | 3 | 2 | 1 | 0 |
|--------|-----|----|----|----|----|----|----|-----|
| Values: | OUT | NC | F1 | F0 | M2 | M1 | M0 | BCD |

**OUT**. Gives the status of the channel output.

**NC**. This bit stores the condition of the reloading flag. Upon writing the initial value into the counter or mode register, the flag is set to 1. If during the counter operation, reloading of its initial value from input registers occurs, the flag is set to 0.

**F1-F0.** These bits store the value of the appropriate command bits, which were written into the mode register at initialization. Using them, you can find out how you must read and write the counter value - only low or only high byte, or in turn low and high bytes.

M0-M2 = counter operating mode.
BCD - 0 = binary-coded decimal.
1 = the binary count mode.

## The Timer Operating Modes

Each channel has two input signals - the counter input (Clock Input) and the control input (GATE) and one output - OUT. The first two channels have no inputs for external control signals, so should not be programmed for modes 1 and 5. Timer 2 has the input gate and can be programmed for operation in any of the six modes. We'll have a look at the other timers function a little later. The first three timers, timers 0, 1 and 2, use 1.19318 MHz (1,193,180 cycles per second) as the Clock Input. This is always provided as an input to timers 0 and 1. You can permit or prohibit the input pulses to timer 2 by means of the control signal GATE, which you can control, because it repeats with the value of bit 0 of the 61h port (or System Port B). If the bit is set to 1, it enables the Timer 2 speaker gate. You can also control the output signals of timer 2 by software. Bit 1 of port 61h enables the speaker.

Now let's consider the timer operating modes in detail. (Each timer has 6 operating modes.)

## Mode 0: The Count With Interrupt on Count Completion

Having written the control word into the counter mode register, the counter output is set to the low level of the OUT signal. Loading the counter value doesn't change this condition. After loading, the counter begins to decrement its contents by each input clock pulse with a frequency of 1.19318 MHz. When the counter is zeroed, its output OUT is set to the high level, which is preserved up to the next loading of a new initial counter value, or of the control word which is setting mode 0.

The count is only available at GATE = 1, that is, (for timer 2) when loading 1 in bit 0 of the 61h port. If you clear this bit it inhibits the clock pulses and interrupts the count. If you set this bit, the count is renewed. The condition of the input GATE doesn't influence the counter output OUT. Loading the initial value into the counter after loading the control word only happens on the following pulse of the signal Timer Clock. The first pulse doesn't decrement the counter, therefore if you load in the N value, output OUT is zeroed after N + 1 pulses. Reloading the operating counter by the two-byte loading mode gives the following results: loading the low byte suspends the current count, while loading the following high byte starts the new count cycle. The minimum allowable value of the counter is 2. If you load the initial value when GATE=0, loading occurs after the following clock pulse, and the count only begins after the transition of signal GATE in 1 and is terminated after N (instead of N + 1) clock pulses.

## Mode 1: The Flip-flop Delay

Initially, the output of the counter is set to the high level. The first clock pulse switches it to 0 and it starts the counter. For counter 2, the low level is set on the counter output at the following clock pulse after writing 1 into bit 0 of the 61h port. Completion of the count switches the Out signal to 1 (end of a delay pulse). This signal level is preserved up to the following start command. Thus, on OUT output, the low level pulse of N clock periods occurs, where N is the initial counter value. The condition of the input GATE doesn't influence the counter output OUT.

If you load a new value into the counter during the operational period, it doesn't influence the counter. The new counter value will be used only during the next start-up. The new counter 2 start-up is gained by writing 1 to port 61h, bit 0, after first resetting it to 0. However, if you load the new control word and the new initial value during the counter operating period, the counter immediately begins the new working cycle after the first clock pulse, even if the previous pulse is not completed. The minimum allowable counter value of N = 1.

## Mode 2: Rate Generator

In this mode, the counter operates as the frequency divider. Originally, the counter output is set to the high level of the OUT signal. Each time the counter value decreases to 1, the output signal is low (0) for one clock period. If GATE = 1 (that is, bit 0 of 61h port contains 0 in the case of counter 2), and after zeroing, the counter is automatically reloaded and the count is renewed. If GATE = 0 (in bit 0 of 61h port, the 1 having been loaded) the count is instantaneously interrupted and the high level immediately appears at the counter output OUT, not even waiting for the clock period to end. Counter reloading doesn't influence its work and is taken into account only after the restart or completion of the current working cycle. Having written the new control word and the new initial value, the counter is loaded by the first clock pulse.

## Mode 3: The Square Wave Generator

In this mode, the counter output alternates between low and high levels. When N is even, the durations are equal to N/2 of the clock generator periods. If N is odd, the high level signal has a duration of (N+1)/2 and low level, (N-1)/2. In this mode, the N=3 value is prohibited. For counter 2, setting 1 in port 61h, bit 0 enables the count, and clearing the bit causes start-up of the counter from the initial condition.

GATE = 1 allows counting. If GATE transits to 0 (loading 0 in bit 0 of port 61h), it interrupts the count instantaneously and, if it has occurred during a low level of output OUT, this signal transits to the high level immediately, not even waiting for the end of the clock period.

Having written the control word and initial value, the counter is loaded by the new clock pulse. The initial high signal OUT is preserved for the first half of the clock period, after which it reverts to zero, and the counter is loaded by the initial value. An even initial value is loaded without change, while an odd value is decreased by 1. The contents of counter are decreased by 2 for each clock period.

## Mode 4: Counter With Software Strobe

Initially, the level of the output signal OUT is high. In this mode, the counter counts the number of clock pulses. After zeroing the counter, its output is a low level pulse lasting one clock period.

GATE = 1 permits the count, and at GATE = 0 (loading 1 in 0 bit of port 61h) the count ceases, and the output signal preserves its value. Afterwards, high level GATE is renewed, and the count proceeds. The pulses of the GATE control input don't reload the counter. Writing the low byte during the count period doesn't influence the counter, but writing the high byte restarts the counter on the next step. For counter 2, setting 1 in port 61h, bit 0 prohibits the count. Clearing the bit permits the count. The minimum allowable counter value is equal to 1.

## Mode 5: Counter With Hardware Strobe

Having written the control word, the counter output OUT is set to the high level. The start-up signal is the leading edge of the control signal GATE. On its arrival, the counter begins working. Firstly, it loads the new counter value, and then the counter begins decrementing. After N+1 steps the counter output is a low-level pulse for one clock period. When the counter restarts, during the operating period, the old value of the counter is loaded from the internal registers. Therefore, in this case, the output counter pulse occurs after N clock pulses. Reloading the counter during operation doesn't influence it until the new start pulse arrives, that is, up to the positive front of GATE signal. For counter 2, this signal occurs when you clear bit 0 of the port 61h to 0.

## The System Timer (Timer 0)

The system timer, or timer 0, is used by the programmed frequency generator. During POST (Power-On Self-Test) this timer channel, namely, the counter register which is located at port 40h, is loaded with the initial counter value 0h. It results in division factor 0FFFFh+1, or 65536 decimal. You can write a program in this way:

```
; Setup Timer 0 to mode 3
  MOV AL, 0FFFFh          ; Disable all device interrupts
  OUT 21h, AL
  MOV AL, 36h             ; Select Timer 0, Least Significant Byte,
                          ; Most Significant Byte, mode 3
  OUT 43h,AL              ; Write Timer mode Register
  MOV AL,0
  OUT TIMER, AL           ; Write low byte to Timer 0
  OUT TIMER, AL           ; Write high byte to Timer 0
```

These values are also written in the counter buffer. Each time the Clock Input Pulse reaches the Counter Input, the counter value is decreased by 1. When the counter is zeroed, its output is set to 1, and its initial value is reloaded from the buffer. Thus, a division of the input frequency occurs. The division factor is equal to the initial counter value, therefore this factor is also known as the divider. For this standard value of the timer divider, the counter outputs pulses with a frequency of 18.2 per second (or every 54.9 msec), also known as ticks.

The output signal of the system timer arrives on the IRQ0 line of the PICs. Each pulse causes an interrupt which corresponds to IRQ0, namely INT 8h. You can prohibit the ticks by masking the IRQ0 Latch if you set bit 7 of the 61h port to 1. You can also restore IRQ0 ticks if you clear the bit. This operation can be dangerous for the operating system. If you really do go ahead and try to do it, the system quickly reprograms the Timer 0, so if you do it in the debugger, you may not notice any effect. You can change the system counter divider to set a new tick frequency value, for example 100 per second, as follows:

```
; reloading system counter divider
  MOV AL, 00110110b           ; the installation of 0 channel command
                              ; writing in buffer
  OUT 43h, AL                 ; the port number for the control
register
  MOV AX, 2E9Ch               ; 2E9Ch = 11932 divider for 100 Hz
  OUT 40h, AL                 ; lower byte of the divider
  XCHG AL, AH
  OUT 40h, AL                 ; high byte of the divider
```

If you have changed the Timer 0 Divider, you have simultaneously changed the system clock (the given example is 5.4 times). Don't worry - you can reset the system clock. An even worse scenario would be if you simultaneously changed the system delay factor (for example, there are reduced delays at access to parallel and serial ports, as well as to floppy disks). Therefore, as soon as you have changed the system timer in a program, you must restore it using code such as this:

```
; restoring system counter divider
    MOV AL, 00110110b       ; the installation of 0 channel command,
                            ; writing in buffer
    OUT 43h, AL             ; the port number for control register
    XOR AL,AL               ; standard divider for ticks
    OUT 40h,AL              ; lower byte of divider
    OUT 40h,AL              ; high byte of divider
```

## Memory Refresh Timer (Timer 1)

This timer is also used in the system as a frequency divider. This timer divider, which is equal to 18 decimal, as well as a system timer divider, is loaded into the port 41h during the POST. The input pulse frequency 1.19318 MHz results in an output timer frequency of about 66 kHz, that is, the output pulses are repeated every 15 microseconds. These pulses are used to start the memory refresh, which is necessary for the RAM to function correctly. This timer doesn't differ considerably from the other timers in the system, except for one feature - you must never reprogram it. If you change its parameters, you can cause a memory loss. Worse, this failure can be a random one. It can have no effect on RAM under normal conditions, but can show up when you least expect it, and cause data loss, or a crash.

## Speaker Data Timer (Timer 2)

This timer, which can be addressed at port 42h, is really a user timer, because it gives the programmer maximum scope. For this reason, let's consider it in detail.

From the programmer's point of view, this timer has nothing different from timers 0 and 1. The only difference is in its purpose and means of access. Therefore, all that we have said here about operating modes programming relates equally to all timers. Programming the timer (channel) is preceded by writing a control word to its mode register (as previously described). You have already seen how to program the tick frequency. There will be times when you'll need to program a software delay. You can count a number of timer ticks to do this. Sometimes it is best to hook the 1Ch interrupt and count the requests. However, a simpler way is to read the ticks from the BIOS data, as follows:

```
; this subroutine returns after a time interval, which
; is set by tick quantity in the AX register
Delay_Value DW ?
 Delay:
 MOV Delay_Value,AX
 PUSH ES
 MOV AX,40h
 MOV ES,AX
 MOV AX,ES:[6Ch]            ; counter value which is set by the  1Ch interrupt
 XOR CX,CX
D1:
 MOV BX,ES:[6Ch]
 CMP BX,AX
 JZ D1
 MOV AX,BX
 INC CX                     ; CX increases each time, when the counter value changes
 CMP CX,DELAY_Value
 JNZ D1                     ; not enough
 POP ES
 RET
```

Timer 2 allows you to generate sound and reproduce it through your speaker. There are many ways to do this, but we'll just look at the simplest. You can set the Timer 2 frequency as follows:

```
MOV AX,1193               ; 1000hz
PUSH AX                   ; store timer counter (divider) value
MOV AL, 0Bh               ; channel 2, mode 3, binary word
OUT 43h,AL
POP AX                    ; restore divider value
OUT 42h,AL                ; low byte first
XCHG AL,AH
OUT 42h,AL                ; then high byte
```

Now you can switch the speaker ON, as follows:

```
IN AL,61h
MOV Old_AL,AL
OR AL,3
OUT 61h,AL                ; now the speaker sounds
```

Then, after some delay, switch it OFF:

```
Sound_OFF:
MOV AL,Old_AL
OUT 61h,AL                    ; now it stops!
RET
```

## The Watchdog Timer

The Watchdog Timer is used for time restriction in a multitasking operating system. Usually, the operating time for each task in such systems is limited by a task algorithm. Problems may arise when interrupts are disabled or masked for a long period of time. Similar problems can also arise when running DOS. For example, if the printer fails, the high level of the printer interrupt priority frequently makes it impossible for the keyboard to function, and forces the user to restart the system. Sometimes information may be lost.

Similar problems can arise for other types of devices, resulting in a long delay in the interrupt service request. The Watchdog Timer detects long periods of disabling of IRQ0, the timer tick interrupt.

## Timer Programming

You have already met the fundamentals of timer programming. The program PROG7-4.ASM on the disk illustrates some programming tricks of the trade. This program reprograms the tick frequency of counter 0; it also has a subroutine, which produces the ticks count to obtain a given delay. Furthermore, you will learn how to switch the speaker sound on and off using the Timer 2 control, as well as how to set the sound frequency, generated by timers. Also in the program, you will see two examples of using tabulation methods of programming. In the first one, the processor itself creates a working table of decoding letters in the appropriate working codes for your own use. It frees you from the routine work of table creation, and eliminates the possibility of errors.

The second trick is confined to the use of tables for imitating the action of complex digital devices. Together, these allows the program to imitate the action of a radio operator which transforms a given text into a sequence of Morse Code, and then transmits it.

# Real Time Clock and Configuration RAM

This subsystem includes:

- Real Time Clock with Alarm

- 100 year calendar

- Periodic interrupt block

- CMOS memory

This system can be powered from an external battery to preserve the time, date and contents of the CMOS memory when the power is switched off.

Let's consider the contents and destination of the real time system registers. The first 14 addresses are allocated for storing the data of the real time clock, alarm and their status. The others are used for other system functions.

**Table 7.11 Real Time Clock Bytes**

| Address | Destination |
| --- | --- |
| 0 | Seconds |
| 1 | Seconds Alarm |
| 2 | Minutes |
| 3 | Minutes Alarm |
| 4 | Hours |
| 5 | Hours Alarm |
| 6 | Day of Week |
| 7 | Date of Month |
| 8 | Month |
| 9 | Year |

When the contents of bytes 1,3 and 5 coincide with the appropriate contents of bytes 0,2 and 4, the alarm event occurs (interrupt IRQ8 will be invoked). For real time clock control, the status registers A - D are used. The description of their content and file destination is shown below.

## Status Register A

Table 7.12 Status Register A

| Bits | Destination |
|------|-------------|
| 0 - 3 | Rate Selection. If set to 0110 b, select output frequency 1.024 kHz and 976.6 μs periodic interrupt |
| 6 - 4 | 22-stage divider control: |
| | 000 - 4.194304 MHz work |
| | 001 - 1.048576 MHz work |
| | 010 - 32.768 KHz work |
| | 11X - divider reset |
| 7 | If 1, indicates updating the time and date is in progress. Read only bit |

The 4 low bits control the periodic interrupt rate. The divider for the periodic interrupt frequency is controlled by the preliminary frequency divider, and doesn't depend on timer interrupts. However, both periodic interrupts and the alarm use the same interrupt request line of the interrupt controller (IRQ8). The maximum frequency of the timer interrupt in periodic mode is 1 sec. The periodic interrupts may be caused more often, as you can see from the following table.

Table 7.13 Periodic Interrupts

| Bits 0 - 3 Value | Periodic Interrupts Period Value |
|------------------|----------------------------------|
| 0h | No interrupts |
| 1h | 3.905 μs |
| 2h | 7.812 μs |
| 3h | 122.1 μs |
| 4h | 244.1 μs |
| 5h | 488.3 μs |
| 6h | 976.6 μs |
| 7h | 1.95 ms |

*Continued*

**277**

**Table 7.13 Periodic Interrupts (Continued)**

| Bits 0 - 3 Value | Periodic Interrupts Period Value |
|---|---|
| 8h | 3.9 ms |
| 9h | 7.81 ms |
| 0Ah | 15.6 ms |
| 0Bh | 31.2 ms |
| 0Ch | 62.5 ms |
| 0Dh | 125 ms |
| 0Eh | 250 ms |
| 0Fh | 500 ms |

# Status Register B

| Bits: | 7 | 6 | 5 | 4 | 3 | 2 | 1 | 0 |
|---|---|---|---|---|---|---|---|---|
| Names: | SET | PIE | AIE | UIE | SWE | DMD | 24/12 | DSE |

The bit meanings:

**SET**   If set to 1, it prohibits the work of the real time clock. The hardware is reset by the signal RESET and doesn't change this bit condition.

**PIE**   Periodic Interrupt Enable. 1 in this bit position permits the generation of periodic interrupts. Their frequency is controlled by 0-3 bits of the A register.

**AIE**   Alarm Interrupt Enable. 1 enables the alarm to work. It is cleared by the RESET signal.

**UIE**   Update-Ended Interrupt Enable. When set to 1, it causes the IRQ8 interrupt after each updating of date or time is completed. This bit is usually set to 0.

**SWE** Square Wave Enabled. When set in 1, enables square wave generation. Frequency is controlled by 0-3 bits of the A register.

**DMD** Data mode. 1 selects binary mode. This bit is usually set to 0.

**24/12** If set to 1, selects 24 hour mode.

**DSE** 1 enables Daylight-Savings Time mode. This bit is usually set to 0.

## Status Register C

| Bits: | 7 | 6 | 5 | 4 | 3 | 2 | 1 | 0 |
|-------|------|----|----|----|---|---|---|---|
| Names: | IRQF | PF | AF | UF | 0 | 0 | 0 | 0 |

The bit meanings:

**IRQF** Interrupt Request Flag. This bit is set to 1 when IRQ8 has been generated. The cause of the interrupt can be determined from bits 4 - 6. This bit is reset when the C register is read.

**PF** Periodic Interrupt Flag. If 1, the interrupt occurs.

**AF** Alarm Interrupt Flag. If 1, the interrupt occurs.

**UF** Update-Ended Interrupt Flag. If 1, the interrupt occurs.

The Status Register C is read only. Writing to this register doesn't influence its contents.

## Status Register D

In this register, only bit 7 is used. When set to 1, it means that the Configuration RAM chip was updated after reset. If set to 0, it indicates a dead battery and RAM data has been lost.

## Configuration RAM

The following table shows the contents of the Configuration RAM locations.

Table 7.14 RAM Contents

| Location | Destination |
|----------|-------------|
| 0Eh | Diagnostic Status Byte |
| 0Fh | Reset Code Byte |
| 10h | Diskette Drive Type Byte |
| 11h | Reserved |
| 12h | Fixed Disk Drive Type Byte |
| 13h | Reserved |
| 14h | Equipment Installed Byte |
| 15h-16h | Low and High Base Memory Bytes |
| 17h-18h | Low and High Extended Memory Bytes |
| 19h-2Ch | Reserved |
| 2Dh | Additional Flags |
| 2Eh-2Fh | Checksum Value |
| 30h-31h | Memory Above 1Mb |
| 32h | Century part of time and date function |
| 33h | System Information |
| 34h-3Fh | Reserved |

## The Real Time Clock and Configuration RAM Subsystem Register Byte Access

To access the contents of memory or registers in the system, you should first write the appropriate address to port 70h, and then read or write port 71h. To avoid the problems of an unreliable system, it isn't advisable to make the access in port 70h without subsequent access in port 71h. You can write in any memory byte except for registers C, D and bit 7 of register A, but the seventh bit of bytes with 00h and 01h addresses should always contain 0. For initialization of the real time clock, you need to write the appropriate value in the time and date registers. But before doing so, you need to set the SET bit (80h) of register B to 1 to prevent the clock updating.

After the end of initialization the SET bit must be cleared to 0. Choose 12 or 24 hours format by setting bit 12/24 of the B register. This bit value can be changed only after new initialization. The same applies to the alarm. For 12 hour format, the information about hours is stored as 0 - 12 till mid-day and 81 - 92 after mid-day; for 24 hour format, as 0-23. Thus, it is clear that the high byte value for 12 hour format is set to 1 in the afternoon.

The real time clock updates its contents once per second during a 2 msec period for 244 μs after bit SET is set to 1. If the program develops the data exchange with the real time clock for a period less than 244 μs, the program can read the clock safely, if the bit 7 of A register is set to 0. The other method consists of repeating the cycle of the UF bit of register C. This bit is set immediately after the end of the next update. After it is set, the data exchange begins. In this case, the access time of the real time clock is not a limiting factor.

You can use the alarm for causing the interrupt at a given time of day or for periodic interrupts. In the first case, the coincidence of the appropriate alarm and real clock registers are checked. To generate periodic interrupts, you need to set two high bits in one (or several) alarm registers to 1. Then, at checks, these registers are ignored. The writing of value C0h in all three alarm registers causes periodic interrupt generation with a frequency of one time per second. The clock operation docs not influence the other bytes of CMOS memory.

# Summary

This chapter was devoted to interfacing with such ISA bus devices as Interrupt and DMA Controllers, Timers, Real Time Clock and Configuration RAM. Controlling the system is never easy, because of the complexity of the devices being programmed, and the necessity of applying knowledge to two different domains: programming and electronics. These devices are used as widespread blocks in many other systems, so you can use the principles and methods seen here for developing new and more sophisticated systems.

# Programming Sound

## Introduction

Can you imagine a modern computer game without music and sound effects? If you're writing up-to-date software, you can't carry on in silence, no matter how artistic your graphics are. It's time to reach for a sound card.

In this chapter we'll discuss sound generation theory and some practical techniques for incorporating sound in your software, recording and playing digitized sound in popular formats (WAV and VOC files), and playing MIDI music. The examples presented here are for the Sound Blaster line of sound boards, as they're the most widely used and emulated. If you write for the Sound Blaster and compatibles, you're sure to reach a major chunk of the market.

# Sound Generation Theory

## The Straight-Forward Approach: Additive Synthesis

Mathematicians and physicists have known for a long time that a sound wave can be broken down into a sum of harmonics, or sine waves. This made it naturally tempting to try to work backwards: generate a sound using simple oscillators. This is called *additive synthesis*. To generate sound using additive synthesis, you simply choose volume levels for the first, second, third, etc. harmonics. The results, though, are less than satisfactory, as the sounds produced by these synthesizers are all of a similar character and don't sound like real instruments. The most commercially successful of this type of synthesizer was the venerable Hammond organ.

## The Subtractive Method

The next attempt to solve the problem came from the opposite direction: the subtractive method, where tunable filters chopped unwanted harmonics of the wave form with a rich spectrum (square, saw-tooth, etc.) The results of this method were no more impressive.

## FM Synthesis

More flexibility together with a wider range of timbres became possible with the invention of what is commonly known as FM (frequency modulation) synthesis in the mid 1970's. The essence of this technique is that one or more oscillators modulate the frequency of another, thus producing a complex spectrum in the resulting sound. Engineers manipulate different parameters such as the waveforms of the carrier and modulator (called operators), their wave shapes and frequency sets, to approximate the sound of the desired instrument. FM was found to be quite efficient for PC entertainment purposes, and was implemented in many popular sound cards, such as AdLib, Sound Blaster, Thunder Board, and others. Sound Blaster's synthesizer uses two operators, and some cards from the Sound Blaster Pro series use up to four. The more operators there are, the richer the sound is.

## Wave Form Synthesis

Despite these advances the result was still artificial. The desire to reproduce more natural music on synthesizers led to wave form (or wavetable) synthesis. The main difference between this and earlier methods is that the controlled wave is not generated, but is instead a digitally pre-recorded real sound. The accuracy of modern digital recording equipment allows a digitized sound to be played back as clearly as if it were mastered on an audio CD. Wave form synthesis, sometimes in combination with the FM method, is now used in all professional synthesizers. Just as music is recorded on an audio CD, the sound of each instrument is recorded and stored in a WF synth, so if you read 'CD quality music on our 16-bit sound card', it's not just hype. Check out cards like Gravis Ultrasound, and Sound Blaster 16 with add-in Wave Blaster daughter boards, and you'll hear for yourself.

# Sampling

Digital recording (sampling) and playback are now standard features of every sound card on the market, even if its music synthesizer is based on the FM method. Using the recording capabilities of your sound board is a very easy and effective way to add speech to your presentations or, of course, sound effects for games programming.

## So What is Sampling?

To record an analog electric signal from an audio input source, the computer has to sample input every few microseconds, measure the signal's voltage value, and store it in digital form. Such measurements are repeated at a frequency called the sampling rate. The higher the sampling rate, the more accurate the recording. Figure 8.1 shows how sampling at a low rate fails to capture high-frequency components of sound. In this figure, only the frequencies in the shaded areas are recorded. The frequencies outside of this range are clipped, making for a poor recording.

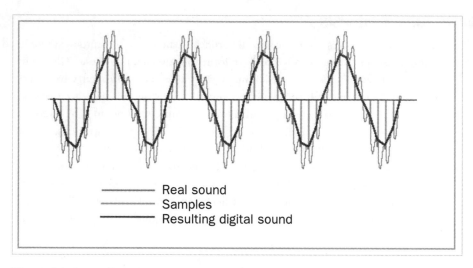

**Figure 8.1 Recording at a Low Sampling Rate**

A sampling rate of 44100 Hz (used in compact discs) allows you to record the whole audible frequency range (up to 20000 Hz). However, choosing a higher sampling rate increases the amount of data to be stored, so you must always find a compromise between sound quality and storage capability. For most recording purposes, a sampling rate of 20kHz will be more than sufficient.

Another aspect of accuracy is quantization, or the number of bits used to store each sample. 8-bit samplers use 1 byte per sample, so the actual value of the sound wave at any instant is rounded to one of 256 possible values. 16-bit samplers, which are the CD standard, are much more precise, with each sample taking on one of 65536 values, but of course it takes twice as much media space to store your recordings. Most applications settle for 8 bits, as it's a reasonable compromise between quality and storage/speed.

For optimal sampling, you should adjust the level of the recorded signal so that it oscillates over the sampler's full range. If amplitudes are too high, the sampler will clip them, and the sound will be distorted, as when you shout too loud into a microphone or overdrive an amplifier. If the sound input is too quiet, only a small subrange of possible sampling values will be used, and the result will sound like 5-bit sampling or even worse. I usually pass a tape or CD player's output through an equalizer to filter noises out and fit the sound wave fully into the sampler's dynamic range.

## Playback

When playing back a digitized sound, samples are converted into a series of short pulses of corresponding amplitude, at the frequency at which they were recorded. This process is called Pulse Code Modulation (PCM). A filter softens the square pulses, and the sound is given back to you.

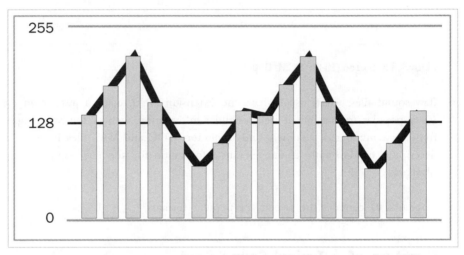

**Figure 8.2 A Sample Playback**

## How is it Stored on My Disk?

There are lots of formats to store digital sound. They depend mainly on the resolution of sampling (8, 12, 16, 24, or 32 bits), the number of audio channels, and the data compression type. Usually, PCM data is stored in the most natural way: uncompressed, sample by sample, in signed or unsigned integer numbers. VOC files, recorded via the Sound Blaster, or Microsoft Windows WAV files, store unsigned PCM data (for 8-bit monaural samples) as a simple series of bytes in the file. For stereo sound, samples are normally stored with the left and right channels alternating so that the file will contain the left channel of the first sample, then the right channel of the first sample, then the second sample, etc. Figure 8.3 shows a byte sequence for 16-bit stereo PCM data (LSB - least significant, MSB - most significant byte of 2-byte integer values).

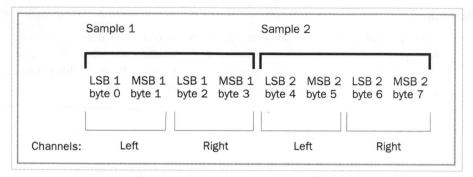

**Figure 8.3 Stereo 16-bit PCM Data**

Raw sound files, which usually have the extension .SND, contain just sound data. It's a popular format, but it lacks essential information such as the sampling frequency, number of channels, and resolution. VOC and WAV files have descriptive headers with all the relevant information for adequate sample playback.

Appendix D contains the layouts for popular formats.

## The Structure of a Typical Sound Card

A typical sound card contains quite a few different parts. Some of the most important are:

- A digital-to-analog converter (DAC) to play back digitized sound.

- An analog-to-digital converter (ADC) to sample from various input sources.

- MIDI synthesizer to play music.

- Microphone and line-in connectors.

- Line-out and/or amplified out connector for speakers or headphones.

- MIDI port to connect an external MIDI keyboard and/or synthesizer.

- Mixer to control levels of all input and output signals.

- Filter.

- Joystick port.

Figure 8.4 shows the logical connections between these and other (optional) components of a sound card.

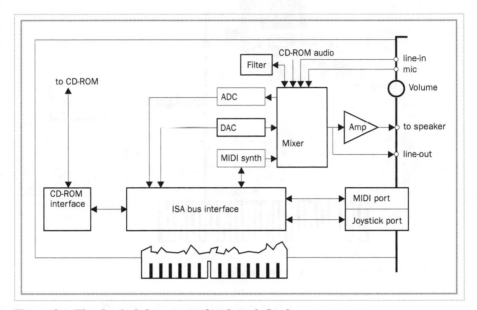

**Figure 8.4 The Logical Structure of a Sound Card**

## Understanding MIDI

Musical Instrument Digital Interface (MIDI) is a standard introduced in 1983 by Roland, which allows you to connect different MIDI-equipped hardware for simultaneous cooperative use. All modules such as keyboards, drum machines, reverbs, mixers, and computers are connected by simple 5-pin DIN cables. These transfer digital data that control the musical performance. The sound itself is not transmitted. This data consists of messages, such as note struck, pitch bender moved, stereo pan position changed, note released, etc. This unified system of commands allows you to play an external synthesizer on your MIDI keyboard and at the same time record what you play on a computer or a sequencer, as shown in Figure 8.5.

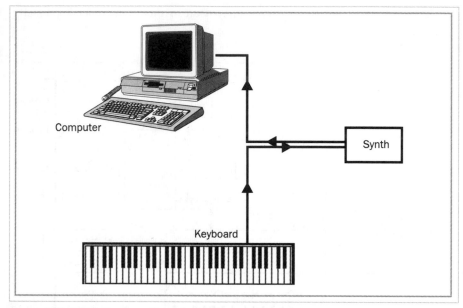

**Figure 8.5 MIDI Devices Communication**

Alternatively you can write a complete composition on your PC, and then play it on your sound card's synthesizer. For each of 16 MIDI channels you can specify a program number, representing an instrument sound, or 'patch', the volume level, panning position, and various other parameters, but you don't have to stack a rack of sixteen synthesizers on the desktop to sound like an orchestra. Sound cards support all of the channels inside, thereby functioning as a multiprogram synthesizer.

An important advantage of the MIDI standard is that a composition can be saved on disk in a MIDI file format and later transferred to any sequencer or computer which supports MIDI. So if your friend and you both have a compatible sound card and/or the same set of synthesizers, you can e-mail your songs to each other as compact MIDI files, instead of posting tapes. Computer networks throughout the world are stuffed with shareware MIDI music that you can download and examine.

# Programming Sound

In addition to the drivers and required setup files, most sound cards come with general programs that allow you to play and record sounds from DOS or Windows. While these programs are quite useful and fun to play with, they don't help us programmers when we need to add sound to our latest creation. For that, we need access to the sound board's drivers or hardware.

There are two methods of programming most sound boards. You can load a standard driver and communicate with it, telling it what sounds to play or what input sources to control. Standard drivers are easier to use, but don't give you as much control over the sound board as does programming the hardware directly. In this section, we'll look at examples of both types of sound board programming.

## Using Standard Drivers

Working with drivers provided by the sound board manufacturer gives you easy access to most of the major functions of the hardware. These easy-to-use functions provide you with the following advantages:

- Your program will work on different standards of hardware and on a wider range of sound cards.

- You can forget about tedious technical details and save time.

- You don't have to get down to port-level programming, such as controlling the DMA chip, processing interrupts, etc.

## CT-VOICE - Working with Digitized Sound in Memory

The CT-VOICE driver provided by Creative Labs allows other programs to interface a Sound Blaster's sampling and digital playback functions. This is a loadable driver, not a memory-resident, interrupt-driven one. To use it, your program must:

1    Find the file containing the driver. This can be done by examining the SOUND variable in the DOS environment. For example, if the SOUND environment variable is set to C:\SBPRO, then the pathname of the driver is C:\SBPRO\DRV\CT-VOICE.DRV.

2    Allocate a block of memory for the driver. As the driver must be loaded at a paragraph boundary, you either have to allocate a block that is 16 bytes longer than the file's size and then find the first paragraph boundary, or you must use the DOS memory allocation function (which automatically allocates the block on a paragraph boundary) to obtain the memory.

3    Read the CT-VOICE.DRV into memory starting at the found address. This address is the driver's entry point.

4    Once the driver is loaded, you can access the driver's functions by filling certain registers and making a FAR CALL to the driver's entry point.

CT-VOICE has functions to set up the driver's parameters, and to play and record sounds from and to memory. The individual functions are selected by placing the corresponding function number in the BX register. Here are descriptions of the functions supported by CT-VOICE.

## Function 00h - Get Version Number

Registers on entry:                    On return:
BX = 0                                 AH = major version number
                                       AL = minor version number

## Function 01h - Set Base I/O Address

Registers on entry:                    On return:
BX = 1                                 AX = 0 if successful
                                             error value otherwise

AX = I/O Address

Requirements:  Legal values for the base I/O address vary depending on the card's version. Generic values are 220h and 240h.

## Function 02h - Set DMA IRQ Number

Registers on entry:                          On return:
BX = 2                                        AX = 0 if successful,
                                                      error value otherwise

AX = IRQ Number

Requirements: Legal values for the Interrupt Request Line vary depending on the card's version. Generic values are 2, 3, 5 or 7.

## Function 3h - Initialize Driver

This function must be called prior to all subsequent functions, except for function 13h Set DMA Channel.

Registers on entry:                          On return:
BX = 3                                        AX = 0 - successful
                                                   1 - general failure
                                                   2 - I/O error
                                                   3 - DMA error

Requirements: Functions 1, 2, and 19 must be called prior to this one.

## Function 4h - Turn Speaker On/Off

When the speaker is off, the DAC is disconnected from the output and playback of digitized voice will not be heard. You can use this function to mute a voice while it plays on. You must turn the speaker off before you can record (see function 7). On initialization of the driver, the speaker is ON.

Registers on entry:                          On return:
BX = 4                                        none
AX = 0 (off) or 1 (on)

### Function 05h - Set Up Status Word

The driver will set the specified word to FFFFh while the driver is BUSY performing digitized input or output, and reset it to 0000h when READY for a new I/O operation.

Registers on entry:                    On return:
BX = 5                                         none
ES = Segment of status word
DI = Offset of status word

### Function 06h - Play VOC File from Conventional Memory

Sound output is performed in the background via DMA. Control is immediately returned to your program which can perform other functions while the sound plays.

Registers on entry:                    On return:
BX = 6                                         AX = 0 (successful), or 1 (error)
ES = Segment of VOC file image
DI = Offset of VOC file image

Requirements: ES:DI points to a VOC file image that has been loaded into conventional memory. The size of VOC file that can be played using this function is limited by the amount of free contiguous conventional memory. All types of block (Sound, Silence, Repeat, etc.) are properly handled by the driver. When the driver encounters a marker block during playback, it stores the marker's value into a status word, allowing your application to synchronize other activities with the sound playback.

### Function 07h - Record to Conventional Memory

Record a sound block into the pre-allocated buffer specified by ES:DI. Recording continues until the buffer is filled, or until function 8 (Stop Playing or Recording) is called. Recording is performed in the background via DMA, allowing your program to perform other tasks while recording continues.

Registers on entry:                 On return:
BX = 7                               AX = 0 (successful), or 1 (error)
AX = Sampling Rate
BX =  7
ES =  Seg
DI = Ofs
DX = Length (high word)
CX = Length (low word)

Requirements: Prior to recording, the DAC speaker must be turned off via function 4. Some sources claim this has no effect on Sound Blaster Pro or later, but my experience indicates that you simply can't record with DAC output enabled. When saving a VOC file, you must add a file header, but you can play back the buffer just after recording.

## Function 08h - Stop Playing or Recording

This function terminates any play or record functions that the driver has in progress. The status word is set to 0.

Registers on entry:                 On return:
BX =  8                              none

## Function 09h - Deinitialize Driver

Halts any pending operations, and closes down the driver. If your program initializes the driver, it must call this function before exiting to DOS.

Registers on entry:                 On return:
BX =  9                              none

## Function 0Ah - Pause Playing

This function pauses any playback that the driver is currently performing. The status word is unchanged.

Registers on entry:                 On return:
BX = 10                              AX =  0 (successful), or 1 (not playing)

## Function 0Bh - Continue Playing

This function continues playing after a pause.

Registers on entry:           On return:

BX = 11           AX = 0 (successful), or 1 (not paused)

## Function 0Ch - Cancel Loop

This function cancels a playback loop.

Registers on entry:           On return:

BX = 12           AX = 0 (successful), or 1 (no loop is active)

AX = 0 - finish current loop

     1- cancel immediately

## Function 0Eh - Play VOC File from Extended Memory

This function is the same as function 6 (Play VOC File from Conventional Memory) except that it plays from extended, rather than conventional, memory.

Registers on entry:           On return:

BX = 14           AX = 0 (successful), or 1 (error)

DX = Extended memory handle

DI:SI = Segment:offset of extended

     memory block

## Function 0Fh - Record to Extended Memory

This function is the same as function 7 (Record VOC File to Conventional Memory) except that it plays from extended, rather than conventional, memory.

Registers on entry:           On return:

BX = 15           AX = 0 (successful), or 1 (error)

AX = Sampling rate in Hz

CX = Length of buffer in Kb

DX = Extended memory handle

DI:SI = Segment:Offset of extended

     memory block

### Function 10h - Set Recording Mode (Sound Blaster Pro only)

Registers on entry:                          On return:
BX = 16                                      AX = previous mode
AX = 0 (mono), or 1 (stereo)

### Function 11h - Set Recording Source (Sound Blaster Pro only)

Registers on entry:                          On return:
BX = 17                                      AX = previous source
AX =
   0 : mic (default)
   1 : CD
   2 : mic
   3 : line-in

### Function 12h - Set Recording Filter (Sound Blaster Pro only)

Select the cut-off frequency for the low-pass filter used during sampling.

Registers on entry:                          On return:
BX = 18                                      AX = previous filter setting
AX = 0 (low), or 1(high)

### Function 13h - Set DMA Channel (Sound Blaster Pro only)

Registers on entry:                          On return:
BX = 19                                      none
AX = Channel   (0,1, or 3)

This function must be called after functions 1 and 2 and before function 3.

### Function 20 - Get Card Type

Registers on entry:                          On return:
BX = 20                                      AX =
                                                1 :- Sound Blaster 1.5
                                              2 -  Sound Blaster Pro

## Function 22 - Filter On/Off (Sound Blaster Pro only)

This function enables or disables the filter on the Sound Blaster Pro.

Registers on entry:                     On return:

BX = 22                                 AX = previous filter state

AX = 0 (off), or 1 (on)

# Playing and Recording WAV Files

Playing and recording WAV files in memory is a fairly straightforward task. First, load and initialize the CT-VOICE driver. Then, to play just load the WAV file into memory, construct a sound block from the WAV file, and call the driver. To record, set up the parameters and call the driver. When recording is finished, construct a WAV file header and then write the header and sound data to disk. Program 9.1, SBWAV.C, contains a C program that will play or record WAV files using the CT-VOICE driver:

```
Program 9.1 -- SBWAV.C - Play and record WAV files using CT-VOICE.DRV
/*
    SBWAV.C
    This program plays and records WAV files, using driver
    CT-VOICE.DRV by Creative Labs. When loading a file, the
    program substitutes file header with VOC sound block header.
    Backward conversion is done when saving recorded sample.

    Compiled and tested in large model with Borland C++ 3.1
*/
#include <stdio.h>
#include <conio.h>
#include <ctype.h>

#include "sbenv.h"
#include "wav.h"

WORD double_buffer_size = 2;  /* 128Kb */

BYTE play_wav = 0;
BYTE record_wav = 0;

int wav_handle;

int _argc;
char **argum;

WORD wav_status;
void far *driver;
char *wav_file = NULL;
```

```
/* Load CT-VOICE.DRV, open WAV file */
void prepare_wav(void) {
  int i;
  char driver_name[80];
  WORD drv_error;
  BYTE version_major, version_minor;

  /* Find WAV file name in command line */
  for (i = 1; i < _argc; i++) {
    if (strstr(argum[i], ".WAV") != NULL) {
      wav_file = argum[i];
      break;
    }
  }

  /* No file! */
  if (wav_file == NULL) return;

  /* Shall we record? */
  for (i = 1; i < _argc; i++) {
    if (strcmp(argum[i], "/R") == 0) {
      record_wav = 1;
      break;
    }
  }

  /* Query Sound Blaster settings */
  get_sb_env();

  strcpy(driver_name, sb_dir);
  strcat(driver_name, "\\DRV\\CT-VOICE.DRV");
  driver = load_driver(driver_name);
  if (driver == NULL) {
    printf("Can't load driver %s\n", driver_name);
    exit(8);
  }

  asm {
    xor bx,bx   /* Get driver version */
    call driver
    mov version_major,ah
    mov version_minor,al
  }

  printf("Driver version %d.%d.\n", version_major, version_minor);

  asm {
    mov bx,1    /* Set base address */
    mov ax,base_port
    call driver

    mov bx,2    /* Set IRQ line */
    mov ax,IRQ_line
    call driver
```

```
    mov bx,19   /* Set DMA channel */
    mov ax,DMA_channel
    call driver

    mov bx, 3   /* Initialize */
    call driver
    mov drv_error,ax
  }

  if (drv_error != 0) {
    printf(
      "Error %d initializing Sound Blaster!\n", drv_error);
    exit(drv_error);
  }

  asm {
    push es
    push di
    mov bx,5    /* Set up status word */
    mov di, seg wav_status
    mov es, di
    lea di, wav_status
    call driver
    pop di
    pop es
  }

  if (record_wav)
    wav_handle = open(wav_file, O_WRONLY | O_CREAT | O_BINARY);
  else
    wav_handle = open(wav_file, O_RDONLY | O_BINARY);

  if (wav_handle == -1) {
    printf("Error opening %s !\n", wav_file );
    record_wav = 0;
    return;
  }

  play_wav = !record_wav;
}  /* prepare_wav */

/* Load and convert WAV file */
void load_wav(void){
  int res;
  BYTE huge *cur_pos;
  BYTE huge *data_pos;

  read( wav_handle, &wav_head, sizeof( WAV_HEADER ) );

  if ((strncmp(wav_head.WAVEfmt_txt, "WAVEfmt", 7) )) {
    printf("%s is not a WAV file!", wav_file);
    exit(1);
  }
```

```c
    if (wav_head.data_size + 20 > double_buffer_size*0x10000){
      printf("%s is too big to fit in memory !", wav_file);
      exit(2);
    }

    cur_pos = double_buffer;

    if ( (wav_head.channels > 1) || (wav_head.sample_rate > 22050) ){
      /* Create additional prefix -
         "override" block before sound block */
      *cur_pos = 8; /* block tag */
      cur_pos += 3;
      *cur_pos++ = 4; /* block size */
      /* time constant*/
      *((WORD*) cur_pos) = (0x10000UL - 256000000UL /
         (wav_head.channels * wav_head.sample_rate) );
      cur_pos += 2;
      *cur_pos++ = 0;
      *cur_pos++ = wav_head.channels - 1;
    }
    /* Create sound block prefix */
    cur_pos++;
    *((DWORD*) cur_pos) = wav_head.data_size + 2; /* Sound data length*/
    *--cur_pos = 1; /* Sound block tag */
    cur_pos += 4;
    /* Time constant*/
    *cur_pos++ = 256 - 1000000/wav_head.sample_rate;
    *cur_pos++ = 0; /* no compression */
    data_pos = cur_pos;
    /* Read digitized sound data */
    while ( (cur_pos - data_pos) < wav_head.data_size )
      cur_pos += read(wav_handle, cur_pos, 32000);
    *cur_pos++ = 0; /* Terminator, too */
    close( wav_handle );
} /* load_wav */

void save_wav(void){
  BYTE huge *cur_pos;
  BYTE huge *data_pos;
  WORD channels, rate;
  DWORD data_length;

  cur_pos = double_buffer;
  if (*cur_pos == 8) {
    /* Parse override block's info */
    channels = cur_pos[7] + 1;
    cur_pos += 4;
    rate = *((WORD*) cur_pos);
    rate = 256000000 / (0x10000 - rate) /channels;
    cur_pos += 8;
    data_pos = cur_pos + 6;
    data_length = *(DWORD *)cur_pos & 0x00FFFFFFu - 2;
  }
```

```
    else if (*cur_pos == 9) {
      channels = cur_pos[9];
      rate = *(DWORD *)&cur_pos[4];
      data_pos = cur_pos + 16;
      data_length = *( (DWORD*) &cur_pos[1]) & 0x00FFFFFFu - 12;
    }
    else {  /* There's only sound block */
      channels = 1;
      rate = 1000000 /(256 - cur_pos[4]);
      data_pos = cur_pos + 6;
      data_length = *(DWORD *)cur_pos & 0x00FFFFFFu - 2;
    }
    /* Calculate all excessive data in WAV header */
    calc_wav_header( &wav_head, channels, 8, rate, data_length );
    /* Write WAV header */
    write(wav_handle, &wav_head, sizeof(WAV_HEADER) );

    cur_pos = data_pos;
    /* Write sound data */
    while ( (cur_pos - data_pos) < wav_head.data_size )
      cur_pos += write(wav_handle, cur_pos, 32000);
    close( wav_handle );
} /* save_wav */

void main(int argc, char **argv) {
  int i;
  char key;
  WORD rec_source;
  WORD sampling_rate;

  printf("SBWAV Plays/records WAV files.\n");
  if (argc == 1) {
    printf("Syntax : SBWAV myvoice.wav [/r]\n"
      "/r is optional command to record a WAV,"
      " default is to play.\n");
    exit(1);
  }

  for(i = 0; i < argc; i++)
    strupr(argv[i]);

  _argc = argc;
  argum = argv;

  alloc_common_buffer(double_buffer_size);
  if (common_buffer == NULL) {
    printf ("No memory for buffer.\n");
    exit (1);
  }

  prepare_wav();
  if (play_wav)
    load_wav();
```

```
if (!(play_wav | record_wav ))
  exit(0);  // Nothing to do

if (record_wav) {
  printf(
     "To select recording source on Sound Blaster Pro, press:\n"
     "[M] - microphone (default), [C] - CD, [L] - line-in\n");

  switch (toupper(getch())) {
    case '\0' : getch();

    default :
    case 'M' : rec_source = 0; break;

    case 'C' : rec_source = 1; break;

    case 'L' : rec_source = 3; break;

    case '\x1b' :
asm {
  mov bx,9 /* Terminate driver */
  call driver
      };
  exit(0);
  }

  asm {
    // Set recording source
    mov bx,17
    mov ax, rec_source
    call driver
    // Set recording mode
    mov bx,16
    mov ax,0  // mono
    call driver
  }

  printf("Enter sampling rate in Hz: ");
  scanf("%d", &sampling_rate);
}

printf("Hit any key to start...\r");
if (getch() == 0) getch();

if (record_wav) {
  asm {
    push di
    push es

    mov bx,4    /* DAC speaker off */
    mov al, 0
    call driver
```

```
        mov bx,7  /* Record */
        les di, double_buffer
        mov ax,sampling_rate
        /* double_buffer_size is in 64Kb blocks */
        mov dx, double_buffer_size
        xor cx,cx
        call driver
        pop es
        pop di
    }
}

if (play_wav) {
    asm {
        push di
        push es

        mov bx,4  /* DAC speaker on */
        mov al, 1
        call driver

        mov bx,6  /* Play */
        les di, double_buffer
        call driver
        pop es
        pop di
    }
}

printf("Hit any key to stop...   ");
if (getch() == 0) getch();

if (record_wav | play_wav)
    asm {
        mov bx,8  /* Stop VOC I/O */
        call driver

        mov bx,4  /* DAC speaker off */
        mov al, 0
        call driver

        mov bx,9  /* Terminate driver */
        call driver
    }

if (record_wav)
    save_wav();
}
```

# CTVDSK: Working with Digitized Sound on Disk

CTVDSK.DRV, another loadable driver from Creative Labs, is CT_VOICE's twin brother. Its functions are identical except that it plays and records files from and to disk, rather than memory. This approach has two major advantages over memory-based playing and recording.

Samples can be as big as the room on your hard disk. Your program can allocate a relatively small buffer and leave the rest of system memory for other purposes.

Data transfer from disk to the sound card (and vice versa) is performed using a double-buffering technique, which requires a memory buffer split into two equal parts. The driver reads data from disk to the first half of the buffer and starts playing it via DMA. It immediately reads data into the second half of the buffer, and then stands by until the first half has been played. When the DMA controller issues an interrupt indicating that it has completed transferring data from the first half of the block to the sound card, the driver instructs the DMA controller to begin playing from the second half of the buffer, while it fills the first half of the buffer with the next block of data.

Because hard disks, particularly with disk caching, normally provide a high data transfer rate and the whole process is interrupt driven, the CPU has enough time to pay attention to your application, which can do graphics and calculations while sound is playing in the background.

You can find and load CTVDSK just like CT-VOICE. Furthermore, most of the functions of these drivers are identical. The following information shows those functions that differ between the two drivers.

## Function 03h - Initialize Driver

This function must be called prior to any other except 0, 1, 2, 15, and 19 (all those that configure the driver). It allocates a DMA buffer of specified size (unless you've called function 15 before). See function 15, Set Double Buffer Address.

| Registers on entry | On return: |
|---|---|
| BX = 3 | AX = |
| AX = Size of double buffer in | 0 - successful |
| 2KB blocks | 1 - general failure |
| | 2 - I/O error |
| | 3 - DMA error |

For example, if you want a buffer of two 16Kb blocks, the value in AX is 16/2 = 8.

Requirements: functions 1,2, and 19 must be invoked prior to this one.

## Function 06h - Play VOC File

This function plays a VOC file from a file. The file handle passed in AX must be a valid file handle, and the file must be open for reading.

| Registers on entry: | On return: |
|---|---|
| BX = 6 | AX = 0 (successful), or non-zero (error) |
| AX = File handle | |

## Function 07h - Record VOC File

Writes a VOC file header and starts recording sound data to a file.

| Registers on entry: | On return: |
|---|---|
| BX = 7 | AX = 0 (successful), or non-zero (error) |
| DX = Sampling Rate in Hz | |

Requirements: File must be opened for write. Prior to recording, the DAC speaker MUST be turned off via function 4.

### Function 0Fh - Set Double Buffer Address

Sometimes you may want to create your own custom buffer, rather than ask the driver to allocate it (see function 3, Initialize Driver). In this case, you must call function 15 before initialization. After the driver is initialized, you may use this function to relocate the buffer or change its size.

Registers on entry:

BX = 15

DX:AX = Buffer address

CX = Size of double buffer

in 2Kb per block

On return:

# SBMIDI: Playing MIDI Music

SBMIDI.EXE is a resident driver provided by Creative Labs to give programs an easy-to-use method of playing MIDI files. Since this is a memory-resident driver, it must be installed before your program starts. Unlike voice drivers, it requires no initialization or configuring. You access functions by placing parameters in registers and invoking software interrupt number 80h. Functions are selected via the BX register. You may be able to procure a full specification for the SBMIDI Driver, but the basic essentials are explained below:

### Function 00h - Get Version Number

Registers on entry:

BX = 0

On return:

AH = major version number

AL = minor version number

### Function 03h - Set Status Word

On entry:

BX = 3

DX = Status Word Segment

On return:

noneAX = Status Word Offset

As for digitized voice I/O, the status word is set to FFFFh while music is playing, and reset to 0000h when it stops (either at the end of a song or if requested by function 4).

### Function 04h - Prepare/Stop MIDI File

Registers on entry:                    On return:

BX = 4                                 none

AX = MIDI File Offset

DX = MIDI File Segment

This function must be called to specify a buffer that contains an image of the MIDI file in memory. After this, you can start playing it. Call function 4 again to stop playing (status word will be reset to 0000h).

### Function 05h - Play

On entry:                              On return:

BX = 5                                 none

This function starts the background playing of a MIDI song from the buffer specified by function 4, and immediately returns control to your program. The status word is set to FFFFh.

### Function 07h - Pause Playing

On entry:                              On return:

BX = 7                                 AX = 0 - music paused

                                            1 - not playing

### Function 08h - Continue Playing

On entry:                              On return:

BX = 8                                 AX = 0 - music resumed

                                            1 - not paused

## Playing VOC and MIDI Voices Together

By combining the functions of the loadable CTVDSK driver and the resident SBMIDI driver, it's possible to play MIDI music while at the same time recording or playing a VOC file. VOCNMID.C, shown in Program 9.2, illustrates how this is done.

```
Program 9.2 -- VOCNMID.C - Playing MIDI music while playing or recording VOC files

/*
   VOCMID.C
   Demonstrates usage of CTVDSK.DRV, a driver by
   Creative Labs for digital sound I/O, and SBMIDI.EXE, a
   resident driver by Creative Labs for MIDI music.

   The program is a simple solution for synchronizing
   digital voice with MIDI, because it plays MID and VOC
   files together.

   Compiled and tested under large model with Borland C++ 3.1.
*/
#include <stdio.h>
#include <conio.h>
#include <ctype.h>

#include "sbenv.h"

/* How many physical memory pages to use for double buffer */
WORD double_buffer_size = 1; /* 64Kb */

BYTE play_voc = 0;
BYTE record_voc = 0;
BYTE play_mid = 0;
int voc_handle;
int argcnt;
char **argum;
WORD voc_status, mid_status;
void *driver;

/* Open VOC file for read or write. Load and initialize driver. */
void prepare_voc(void) {
  int i;
  char *voc_file = NULL;
  char driver_name[80];
  WORD drv_error;
  BYTE version_major, version_minor;

  /* Find VOC file name */
  for (i = 1; i < argcnt; i++) {
    if (strstr(argum[i], ".VOC") != NULL) {
      voc_file = argum[i];
      break;
    }
  }

  /* No VOCs! */
  if (voc_file == NULL) return;

  /* Shall we record? */
  for (i = 1; i < argcnt; i++) {
    if (strcmp(argum[i], "/R") == 0) {
      record_voc = 1;
```

```
    break;
  }
}

/* Query Sound Blaster settings */
get_sb_env();

strcpy(driver_name, sb_dir);
strcat(driver_name, "\\DRV\\CTVDSK.DRV");
driver = load_driver(driver_name);

if (driver == NULL) {
  printf("Can't load driver %s\n", driver_name);
  exit(8);
}

asm {
  xor bx,bx   /* Ask version number */
  call driver
  mov version_major,ah
  mov version_minor,al
}

printf("Driver version %d.%d.\n", version_major, version_minor);

asm {
  mov bx,1    /* Set base address */
  mov ax,base_port
  call driver

  mov bx,2    /* Set IRQ line */
  mov ax,IRQ_line
  call driver

  mov bx,19   /* Set DMA channel */
  mov ax,DMA_channel
  call driver

  mov bx,15              /* Set up double buffer*/
  mov ax, WORD PTR double_buffer
  mov dx, WORD PTR double_buffer+2
  /* Half-size of double buffer in 2Kb units */
  mov cx, double_buffer_size
  shl cx,1
  shl cx,1
  shl cx,1
  shl cx,1
  call driver

  mov bx, 3   /* Initialize */
  mov ax, 8
  call driver
  mov drv_error,ax
}
```

```
  if (drv_error != 0) {
    printf("Error %d initializing Sound Blaster!\n", drv_error);
    exit(drv_error);
  }

  asm {
    push es
    push di
    mov bx,5    /* Set up status word */
    mov di, seg voc_status
    mov es, di
    lea di, voc_status
    call driver
    pop di
    pop es
  }

  if (record_voc)
    voc_handle = open(voc_file, O_TRUNC |
      O_CREAT | O_BINARY, S_IWRITE);
  else
    voc_handle = open(voc_file, O_RDONLY | O_BINARY);

  if (voc_handle == -1) {
    printf("Error opening %s !\n", voc_file );
    record_voc = 0;
    return;
  }
  play_voc = !record_voc;
}  /* prepare_voc */

/* Load MIDI file and prepare driver. */
void prepare_mid(void) {
  int i;
  char *mid_file = NULL;
  int mid_handle;
  void *int80h;

  /* Find MID file name in command line */
  for (i = 1; i < argcnt; i++) {
    if (strstr(argum[i], ".MID") != NULL) {
      mid_file = argum[i];
      break;
    }
  }

  /* No MIDs! */
  if (mid_file == NULL) return;


  /* Is SBMIDI installed! */
  int80h = MK_FP( peek(0, 0x80*4 + 2), peek(0, 0x80*4 ) );
  if (int80h == NULL) {
    printf("SBMIDI not installed.\n");
```

```
    return;
  }

  mid_handle = open(mid_file, O_RDONLY | O_BINARY);

  if (mid_handle == -1) {
    printf("Error opening %s !\n", mid_file );
    return;
  }

  if (filelength(mid_handle) > midi_size) {
    printf("%s is too long!\n", mid_file );
    close(mid_handle);
    return;
  }

  read(mid_handle, midi_buffer, filelength(mid_handle));
  close(mid_handle);

  asm{
    mov bx,3    /* Set up status word */
    mov dx, seg mid_status
    lea ax, mid_status
    int 80h     /* Call MIDI driver */

    mov bx,4    /* Set up MIDI buffer */
    mov dx, WORD PTR midi_buffer + 2
    mov ax, WORD PTR midi_buffer
    int 80h
  }

  play_mid = 1;
} /* prepare_mid */


void main(int argc, char **argv) {
  int i;
  char key;
  WORD rec_source;
  WORD sampling_rate;

  printf("VOC'n'MID\n"
    "Plays/records VOC file while MIDI file is being played.\n");
  if (argc == 1) {
    printf("Syntax : VOCMID mysong.mid myvoice.voc [/r]\n"
    "/r is optional command to record a VOC, default is to play.\n");
    exit(1);
  }

  for(i = 0; i < argc; i++)
    strupr(argv[i]);

  argcnt = argc;
  argum = argv;
```

```
/* Allocate all buffers */
alloc_common_buffer(double_buffer_size);

if (common_buffer == NULL) {
  printf("No memory for buffer.\n");
  exit(1);
}

prepare_mid();
prepare_voc();

if (!(play_mid | play_voc | record_voc ))
  exit(0); /* Nothing to do! */

if (record_voc) {
  printf(
    "To select recording source on Sound Blaster Pro, press:\n"
    "[M] - microphone (default), [C] - CD, [L] - line-in\n");
  switch (toupper(getch())) {
    case '\0' : getch();

    default :
    case 'M' : rec_source = 0; break;

    case 'C' : rec_source = 1; break;

    case 'L' : rec_source = 3; break;

    case '\x1b' :
      asm {
  mov bx,9 /* Terminate */
  call driver
};
exit(0);
  }

  asm {
    mov bx,17 /* Set recording source */
    mov ax, rec_source
    call driver
  }

  printf("Enter sampling rate in Hz: ");
  scanf("%d", &sampling_rate);
}

printf("Hit any key to start...\r");
if (getch() == 0) getch();

if (record_voc) {
  asm {
    mov bx,4  /* DAC speaker off*/
    mov al, 0
    call driver
```

```
        mov bx,7 /* Record... */
        mov ax,voc_handle /* ... to file... */
        mov dx,sampling_rate /* ... at rate */
        call driver
    }
}

if (play_voc) {
  asm {
    mov bx,4  /* DAC speaker on */
    mov al, 1
    call driver
    mov bx,6
    mov ax,voc_handle
    call driver
  }
}

if (play_mid) {
  asm {
    mov bx,5  /* Play song */
    int 80h
  }
}

printf("Hit any key to stop...   ");
if (getch() == 0) getch();

if (record_voc | play_voc)
  asm {
    mov bx,8    /* Stop VOC I/O */
    call driver

    mov bx,4    /* DAC speaker off */
    mov al, 0
    call driver

    mov bx,9    /* Terminate driver */
    call driver
  }

if (play_mid)
  asm {
    mov bx,4 /* Stop MIDI */
    int 80h
  }
} /* The end. */
```

# Programming the Hardware

As handy as the supplied drivers are, there are times when they simply aren't enough. Generating complex sounds or synchronizing sound and visual activity are just two examples of functions that can't be accomplished using the supplied drivers. When the supplied drivers won't do it, it's time to get down to bits and ports, and control the hardware directly.

If you're going to be supporting more than just Sound Blaster and compatible cards, your first task will be to determine which sound card is present in the computer. We're not going to cover identifying the different sound cards here, but instead will concentrate on programming the Sound Blaster Digital Signal Processor (DSP), and the Sound Blaster Pro's mixer chip at the hardware level.

Although there are many different versions of Sound Blaster on the market now, there is some general compatibility throughout nearly all versions. This means that in some cases you can write a program that deals with the card's ports and registers without having to distribute a bundle of hardware-specific drivers with it.

## DSP Programming Basics

The Sound Blaster is controlled via several hardware ports. These ports may be configured at different locations to avoid possible conflicts with other add-in cards. The base I/O port address is jumper-selectable, depending on the Sound Blaster version, to at least 2 options: 220h and 240h. The following table shows addresses of functional ports as offsets from the base port address.

**Table 8.1 Sound Blaster DSP I/O Address Map**

| Port Address | Function | Attributes |
|---|---|---|
| Base + 06h | Reset | Write only |
| Base + 0Ah | Read Data | Read only |
| Base + 0Ch | Write Command/Data | Write |
|  | Write-Buffer Status | Read, bit 7 |
|  |  | (clear if ready) |
| Base + 0Eh | Read-Buffer Status | Read only, bit 7 |
|  |  | (set if ready) |

# Resetting the DSP

Before you can start programming the DSP, it must be initialized. This is also the way to return the chip to its power-on default state. To reset the DSP, perform the following steps:

- Write 1 to the Reset port and wait for 10 microseconds.

- Write 0 to the Reset port.

- Wait until bit 7 in the Read-Buffer Status port is set (this means "Data Ready"), and read a byte the from Read Data port. If this byte is AAh, then the DSP is successfully initialized. If not, Sound Blaster is not installed at the specified base I/O address.

Program 9.3, RESET.INC, shows how to reset the DSP in assembly language.

```
Program 9.3 - RESET.INC - Initializing the DSP in assembly language

   mov dx,BasePort
   add dl,6            ; Reset port, Base + 6
   mov al,1
   out dx,al           ; Send 1 to reset port

   sub al,al           ; Wait a little...
WaitLoop:
   dec al
   jnz WaitLoop

   out dx,al           ; Send 0 to reset port

   xor cx,cx           ; Try up to 10000h times
   add dl,8            ; Read Buffer Status port
                       ; Base + Eh
NoData:
   in  al,dx           ; Read Data Ready status
   or  al,al           ; Is bit 7 set?
   jns TryAgain        ; Bit 7 clear, no data

   sub dl,4            ; Read Data port, Base + Ah
   in  al,dx           ; Read DSP data
   cmp al,0AAh         ; Is it AAh?
   je  Success         ; Yes, O.K.
TryAgain:
   loop NoData         ; Try again...
   ;
   ; Sound Blaster not found...

Success:
   ;
   ; Sound Blaster initialized successfully!
```

## Reading and Writing the DSP

Writing to the DSP requires that you read the DSP's Write Status port until bit 7 is clear, indicating that the DSP is ready to accept a command. Once the DSP is ready to accept a command, output the command byte and return. Reading is similar: simply loop reading the Read Status port until the bit is set, and then read the data. The assembly source code of Program 9.4, READWRIT.INC, shows how to read and write to the DSP. Two procedures, WriteDSP and ReadDSP, assume that the correct value of the base I/O address is stored in the variable BasePort.

```
Program 9.4 -- READWRIT.INC - Reading and Writing the DSP

WriteDSP PROC
;
; Send byte in AH to DSP Write port
;
   push dx
   mov  dx,BasePort
   add  dx,0Ch          ; Write status port, Base + 0Ch
WriteBusy:
   in   al,dx           ; Get status
   or   al,al
   js   WriteBusy       ; Bit 7 set, wait...

   mov  al,ah           ; Get command or data into AL
   out  dx,al           ; Send it to DSP
   pop  dx
   ret
WriteDSP ENDP


ReadDSP    PROC
;
; Reads byte from DSP into AL
;
   push dx
   mov  dx,BasePort
   add  dx,0Eh          ; Write status port, Base + 0Eh
ReadBusy:
   in   al,dx           ; Get status
   or   al,al
   jns  ReadBusy        ; Bit 7 clear, wait...

   sub  dx, 4           ; Read Data port, Base + 0Ah
   in   al,dx           ; Read byte from DSP
   pop  dx
   ret
ReadDSP    ENDP
```

## Programming the Mixer Chip

A mixing facility has been available in the family since the Sound Blaster 2.0 (CD Interface with a CT 1335 mixer chip on board). When the Sound Blaster Pro was introduced, it had an improved mixer chip: the CT 1345, which is completely incompatible with the CT 1335, as registers changed or had different meanings. The Sound Blaster 16 is descended from the Sound Blaster Pro, and its chip, the CT 1745, retains some compatibility concerning volume control with the Sound Blaster Pro's, but has a wider range of functions and is normally programmed in a different way.

Despite the incompatibilities, the basics of programming all three chips are the same. A mixer chip has several internal registers whose bits hold settings like volume level for all sources (microphone, CD, etc.), ADC source, and input/output filtering. You can access each register by writing its index to the mixer's address port, and then simply reading from or writing to the mixer's data port. The mixer chip's ports are shown in Table 8.2.

**Table 8.2 Mixer I/O ports**

| Address | Function |
| --- | --- |
| Base + 4 | Address port (write only).  Activates a register. |
| Base + 5 | Data port (read and write). Is a "window" on the current active register. |

In contrast to the DSP, you don't have to poll for a 'data ready' bit. The mixer is always ready. Program 9.5, MIXER.INC, shows how to change and retrieve mixer settings.

```
Program 9.5 -- MIXER.INC - Reading and writing the mixer ports

WriteMixer PROC
;
; Write a byte in BL into a mixer register specified in BH
;
    push dx
    mov  dx,BasePort
    add  dx,4                    ; Mixer's address port,
                                 ; Base + 4
    mov  al,bh                   ; Index of a Mixer's register
```

```
        out dx,al              ; Select the register

        inc dx                 ; Mixer's address port,
                               ; Base + 5
        mov al,bl              ; Byte to write into the register
        out dx,al
        pop dx
        ret
WriteMixer ENDP


ReadMixer   PROC
;
; Reads into AL settings of a mixer register specified in BH
;
        push dx
        mov dx,BasePort
        add dx,4               ; Mixer's address port,
                               ; Base + 4
        mov al,bh              ; Index of a Mixer's register
        out dx,al              ; Select the register

        inc dx                 ; Mixer's address port,
                               ; Base + 5
        in  al,dx              ; Read the register's setting
        pop dx
        ret
ReadMixer   ENDP
```

The mixer registers and their meanings are shown below.

## Register 00h - Reset Mixer

This is a write-only register. You may write any 8-bit value here to return the
mixer to its default state. The mixer's default is a bit strange: all filters on, all
volume levels zeroed. "Enjoy the silence!"

## Register 04h - Voice Volume

This is the volume of digitized sound playback. The high-order nibble is for the
left channel, and the low-order nibble for the right channel. Thus writing FFh to
this register plays sound at maximum volume.  Writing 0Fh mutes the left
channel, etc.

## Register 0Ah - Microphone Volume (mono)

Only the 3 low-order bits are used, providing 8 volume levels.  Value 7 runs the
mic at full blast.

### Register 0Ch - Input Options

This is a bit-mapped register. The bit meanings are:

Bit 5            - Input through low-pass filter (0 = on, 1 = off).

Bit 3            - Low-pass filters cut-off frequency (0 = low, 1 = high).

Bits 1 and 2 - select input source (0 or 2 = microphone, 1 = CD,
                       3 = line-in).

Example: Value 2Eh (binary 00101110) turns the input filter off and enables recording from the line-in jack.

### Register 0Eh - Voice Output Options

This is a bit-mapped register. The bit meanings are:

Bit 5            - Output through low-pass filter (0 = on, 1 = off).

Bit 2            - Output mode (0 = mono, 1 = stereo).

Registers 22h, 26h, 28h, and 2Eh are Master, FM synthesizer, CD, and line-in volumes respectively. They are treated just like register 4, Voice Volume.

*Note that some features of the mixer chip can be accessed through CT-VOICE or CTVDSK drivers (input selection, filter switching), but not the volume controls.*

# Writing Your Own Driver

As an example of programming the Sound Blaster at the hardware level, Program 9.6, MYDRIVER.ASM, is a sample sound driver that works directly with the sound card ports. The driver is effectively one big far procedure, with entry point at offset 0. It checks the function selector in AL and jumps to the corresponding function. After executing, the function issues a far return to the calling program.

To build the driver, assemble and link it to an EXE file, and then use the EXE2BIN utility to convert it into a binary image. The binary image can be loaded and called just like CT-VOICE.DRV was loaded in the previous section. Remember, of course, that this is just a sample driver, and it has very few functions.

```
Program 9.6 - MYDRIVER.ASM - Programming the Sound Blaster hardware

;
; MYDRIVER.ASM -- Sample Sound Blaster driver.
;
; Assemble and link, then:
;    EXE2BIN MYDRIVER,MYDRIVER.DRV
;
CODE    SEGMENT 'CODE'
        ASSUME CS:CODE

        ORG 0

        ; Function select
        cmp     al,0
        je      InitDSP
        cmp     al,1
        je      Version
        cmp     al,2
        je      Input
        cmp     al,3
        je      MixerReset
        cmp     al,4
        je      MixerVolume
        cmp     al,5
        je      SetSource
        cmp     al,6
        je      Function6
        retf    ; Unknown function


BasePort        dw      220h            ; Sound Blaster's Base I/O
                                        ; port

; Function 0. Set Base I/O address, passed in BX and initialize DSP.
; Must be called before any other function

InitDSP:
        mov     BasePort,bx
        mov     dx,BasePort
        add     dx,6            ; Reset port, Base + 6
        mov     al,1
        out     dx,al           ; Send 1 to reset port

        mov     cx,500          ; Wait a little...
WaitLoop:
        loop    WaitLoop

        xor     al,al
        out     dx,al           ; Send 0 to reset port

        xor     cx,cx           ; Try up to 10000h times
        add     dx,8            ; Read-Buffer Status port
                                ; Base + Eh
```

```
NoData:
        in      al,dx           ; Read Data-Ready status
        or      al,al           ; Is bit 7 set?
        jns     TryAgain        ; No, data not ready

        sub     dx,4            ; Read Data port, Base + Ah
        in      al,dx           ; Read DSP data
        cmp     al,0AAh         ; Is it AAh?
        je      Success         ; Yes, O.K.
TryAgain:
        loop    NoData          ; Try more...

        mov     ax,1            ; Sound Blaster not found...
        retf

Success:
        mov     ax,0            ; Sound Blaster initialized successfully!
        retf


; Function 1. Get DSP Version. Returns AH = major, AL = minor
; version numbers.

Version:
        mov     ah,0E1h         ; Command : Get DSP Version
        call    WriteDSP        ; Send the command
        call    ReadDSP         ; Read version's major byte
        mov     ah,al           ; Major into AH
        call    ReadDSP         ; Read version's minor byte
        retf

; Function 2. 8-bit direct mode digitized sound input.
; Returns sample in AL.

Input:
        mov     ah,20h          ; Command : direct input
        call    WriteDSP        ; Send the command
        call    ReadDSP         ; Read one sample
        retf


; Function 3. Reset mixer to its default state.
; Sound Blaster Pro only.

MixerReset:
        push    bx
        xor     bx,bx           ; Reset register, index 0.
        call    WriteMixer
        pop     bx
        retf

; Function 4. Set volume of the source specified in AH.
; Sound Blaster Pro only.
```

```
; AH =   04  - Voice
;        0Ah - Microphone
;        22h - Master
;        26h - FM synthesizer
;        28h - CD
;        2Eh - Line-in

; For microphone: DH = volume level (0 - 7).
; For stereo sources:
; DL - volume for left channel, DH - right.
; Available levels are 0 - 15.

MixerVolume:
        push    bx
        mov     bl,dl           ; Form high-order nibble
        shl     bl,1            ; of register value
        shl     bl,1
        shl     bl,1
        shl     bl,1

        and     dh,0Fh          ; Form low-order nibble
        or      bl,dh

        mov     bh,ah           ; Index of register for
                                ; the specified source
        call    WriteMixer
        pop     bx
        retf

Function6:
        jmp     SpeakerOn       ; Too far to jump directly

; Function 5. Set ADC Input Source.
; Sound Blaster Pro only.

; AH =   0 or 2 - Microphone
;        1 - CD
;        3 - Line-in
;

SetSource:
        push    bx
        mov     bh,0Ch          ; Input Options register 0Ch
        call    ReadMixer       ; Read Input Options

        shl     ah,1            ; Make mask for input source
        and     ah,6

        mov     bl,al           ; Input Options read from mixer
        and     bl,not 6        ; Clear input source bits
        or      bl,ah           ; Set new input source bits
        call    WriteMixer
        pop     bx
        retf
```

```
; Function 6. Turn DAC Speaker On.
; AH =  0 - off
;       1 - on

SpeakerOn:
        and     ah,ah
        jz      Off
        mov     ah,0D1h          ; Command : DAC speaker on
        call    WriteDSP         ; Send the command
        retf
Off:
        mov     ah,0D3h          ; Command : DAC speaker off
        call    WriteDSP         ; Send the command
        retf


INCLUDE READWRIT.INC
INCLUDE MIXER.INC


CODE            ENDS
END
```

## Using the Custom Driver

Using the custom driver is as simple as using any of the drivers that were
supplied with your Sound Blaster.  A test program, TESTDRV.C, is shown in
Listing 9.7. This program samples 2,000 bytes from the input source that you
select, and then draws a simple volume indicator that shows the peak input level
read during the sampling period. In order to run TESTDRV, you must first
assemble, link, and convert MYDRIVER.ASM as described in the previous section.

```
Listing 9.7 - TESTDRV.C - Testing the custom sound driver

/*
   TESTDRV.C
   This program demonstrates cooperation with
   demo driver MYDRIVER.ASM.
   It performs digitized sound input and displays volume level.
*/

/* Large memory model */
#pragma -ml
#include <stdio.h>
#include <conio.h>
#include <ctype.h>

#include "sbenv.h"

void *driver;
```

```
/* Show volume level of sampled sound */
void indicate(void) {
  char s[18];
  int level, i;
  BYTE sample;
  BYTE max_level = 0;
  s[16] = '\xc3';
  s[17] = '\0';

  /* Sample 2000 bytes to find out peak level */
  for (i = 0; i < 2000; i++) {
    asm {
      mov al,2          /* Sample one byte */
      call driver
      mov sample,al
    }
    level = ((sample > 128) ? sample - 128 : 127 - sample) / 8;
    if (level > max_level) max_level = max_level;
  }

  for(i = 0; i <= level; i++) s[i] = 'þ';
  for(i = level + 1; i < 16; i++) s[i] = '-';
  printf("\r%s", s);
}

/* To make SBDEMO.BIN, MYDRIVER.ASM be compiled with MASM,
linked with LINK, and converted with EXE2BIN */
char driver_name[] = "MYDRIVER.DRV";

void main(void) {
  WORD drv_error;
  BYTE version_major, version_minor;
  signed char source = -1; /* ADC source */

  get_sb_env(); /* Query Sound Blaster settings */
  driver = load_driver(driver_name); /* Load driver */
  if (driver == NULL) {
    printf("Can't load driver %s\n", driver_name);
    exit(8);
  }

  asm {
    xor al,al          /* Function 0 :
                            Set Base Address */
    mov bx,base_port
    call driver
    mov drv_error,ax
  }

  if (drv_error != 0) {
    printf("Error initializing Sound Blaster\n");
    exit(8);
  }
```

```
asm {
  mov al,1            /* Get DSP version */
  call driver
  mov version_major,ah
  mov version_minor,al
}

printf("DSP version %d.%d\n", version_major, version_minor);

asm {
  mov al,6            /* Turn speaker... */
  mov ah,0            /*      ... off */
  call driver
}

printf("This is sample volume indicator.\n");
printf("SB Pro users: to test input from a source press :\n");
printf("[M] - mic, [C] - CD, [L] - Line-in\n");

while(1) {
  indicate();

  if (kbhit()) {
    switch (toupper(getch())) {
      case '\0': getch(); break;

      case '\x1b': exit(0);

      case 'M' :
        source = 2;
        printf("\r\t\t\tMicrophone");
        break;

      case 'C' :
        source = 1;
        printf("\r\t\t\tCD player ");
        break;

      case 'L' :
        source = 3;
        printf("\r\t\t\tLine-in   ");
        break;
    }

    if (source != -1) {
      asm {
        mov al,5  /* Set ADC source */
        mov ah,source
        call driver
      }
      source = -1;
    }
  }
}
}
/* The end. */
```

# DMA Programming Guidelines

If you need to perform input or output of raw digitized sound data without any headers, you should use the Sound Blaster's DSP commands for DMA operations. The DSP will transfer data between DAC or ADC and system memory via DMA and issue a hardware interrupt at the end of every transfer. Your program must set up a routine to service these interrupts.

To set up the DMA and sound board to begin playing or recording, perform these steps:

1   Install the interrupt service routine.

2   Enable the interrupt.

3   Turn the DAC speaker on for output (DSP command D1h), off for input (DSP command D3h).

4   Program the DMA controller for 8-bit single-cycle mode, specifying memory page, offset and length of the buffer holding sound data. The buffer must not cross a physical 64KB page.

5   Tell the DSP the sampling rate (command 40h, followed by time constant = 256 - 1,000,000/channels*sampling rate).

6   Send the DSP a command to begin transfer (14h - 8-bit PCM output, 24h - 8-bit PCM input), followed by two bytes: low and high bytes of the buffer length. This length is one less than the size of the buffer in bytes.

Once you've performed those steps, playing or recording begins. When completed, turn the DAC speaker off, disable the interrupt, and restore the original interrupt vector. Using this method, the DSP transfers the buffer and performs a hardware interrupt. To play or record a sound longer than 64KB, you must separate it into several blocks, each within a physical page, and the ISR (interrupt service routine) will feed the DSP with subsequent blocks as they are to be played or recorded. The ISR should handle interrupts in the following way:

1    On entry: save all CPU registers.

2    Program DMA for the next block.

3    Send the DSP the same command as for the start (see above), with the new block length.

4    Acknowledge the DSP interrupt (read from Read Buffer Status port once).

5    Issue EOI (End of Interrupt) command to the interrupt controller.

6    Restore CPU registers.

7    Execute IRET.

*Note that if there are no more blocks to transfer, steps 2 and 3 in the ISR must be skipped.*

These are generic guidelines, which will perform 8-bit mono PCM output at sampling rates up to 22050 Hz on Sound Blaster 1.5 and later versions.

# Customizing Sounds

A sound card is a great addition to any computer. In addition to providing CD-playback while you're working, and cool sound effects to those after-hours games, you can use it to create some very interesting sounds. Here are a few lighthearted suggestions.

## House/Disco and Other Mixes

Find a record with a steady rhythm and sample a bar or two. Add some effects, like turning it backwards, which is my favorite, or add echo, panning, fading in or out, etc. Then play it in a loop and glue several loops into a single VOC file. Sometimes just a half-second of somebody else's music can turn into something completely different: trance, dance, techno, rap, thrash metal, or whatever, blasting out of your stereo. The hodge-podge compilation DISCO.VOC is just a modest demo. I believe you can go much farther if you give it a try. Also, don't forget - you can speak or sing through the mike, or play other input sources along with the samples that you've recorded.

Maybe you can imagine yourself as an editor at a weird radio station, and, just by cutting and pasting samples, you can compile sentences or even long stories out of different persons' speech. Wicked claims, unanswerable questions, dubious and bizarre insinuations.

It's my duty to remind you, though, that sampling, like copying by any other means, may be done only at home and for personal use. Any public reproduction of recorded material, unpaid or commercial, unchanged or in any way modified, is strictly prohibited by international copyright laws.

## Actual Music

During the last decade, sampling has become so widely used in music that it has even given birth to a sort of esthetical movement. Some musicians include in their arrangements recorded natural or technical sounds, such as rain, trains, animal screeches or hammers. Others create their own custom-made instruments. It can be a straight-forward process, as when a musician records an exotic drum in Africa and then plays it in his studio in Los Angeles. You can sample from any source: the crackles and hisses of interference on a radio receiver, a tape recorder rewinding a tape, or the clunk of opening gates. You can find either a sharp piece to use as percussion, or a slice of a waveform to loop and create a continuously playing melodic instrument.

My best find of that sort came when I got hold of a record of Mexican grasshoppers. They make a sound like "grssss", "grssssssss", very softly. Then, on the advice of a friend (who is anything but a programming expert), I cut a short piece of that sample, FADED it sharply IN at the start and slowly OUT at the end, and we eventually got an eerie instrument that sounded like bright tinkling percussion at high pitches, and like a complex keyboard chord sequence at low ones.

It was impossible to recognize the good old grasshoppers, or to identify the nature of these sounds. Metallic? Wooden? Glass? Something in between? No! Something new and different. Waveform synthesis opens the door into the hidden world of abstract sound. This is why I often use the Gravis UltraSound card, not a Sound Blaster. The Sound Blaster Pro samples quite well, but the Gravis turns samples into musical instruments, limitlessly expanding its tone bank.

### The Best Alarm Clock Ever

The regular buzz or beep of alarm clocks doesn't wake me up. I need a sound booster - a little audio dynamite - to meet the new day properly. Not having a timer, I just let my PC count hours through the night, and at the dreaded time, play a specially designed WAV or VOC through my stereo until I jump out of bed.

# Summary

Putting sound into your programs will not add too much code and data, certainly when compared to the additional impression on the user. Even if you aren't a multimedia producer or game wizard, sound might find a place in your applications. It might be considerate of you to play a song while, say, defragmenting a hard disk, and with the last chord inform the user: 'Successfully accomplished!'

We have looked mainly at sound and music for the PC. It is then nothing more than a byte of fun? Not at all! Sound cards are getting better and better, and 16-bit stereo is becoming a standard. 'CD-quality card for the price of old whisky' is heard on every corner. Now PCs will set the standards for sound and music. PCs with fast and large hard disks are already serving as digital recording platforms.

## CHAPTER NINE

# Low-Level Disk Techniques

## Introduction

Back in the 80's, a young gentleman called Peter Norton surprised his friends by recovering lost files on their disks. The small utility UNERASE, in his own words, started his famous career in the programming business. Although we don't suppose that you can walk in his footsteps quite as easily in the mid-90's, this chapter may still prove interesting to you.

We'll discuss the structure of floppy and hard disks at physical and logical levels. We'll show how the DOS file system is organized, including disk partitions, file allocation tables, directories, files and clusters. You'll find some techniques for managing disk information via DOS and BIOS interrupts. You will also be able to unerase data, or alternatively, erase it for good, defragment files, or retrieve every bit of disk information.

# Low-Level Disk Structure

## Floppy Disks

Information is recorded on disk bit by bit, and, unlike CD or vinyl audio disks, the records on magnetic disks don't go in a continuous sequence. Their tracks are closed concentric circles. There are usually 40 or 80 tracks on a floppy, depending on the density. There are single and double-sided disks, where the sides are numbered 0 and 1. Tracks on a floppy are numbered from zero, from the edge to the center.

Tracks are divided into sectors, which are the smallest chunks of information a disk drive can read or write. Each sector contains an equal amount of data, the standard for DOS being 512 bytes. The number of sectors per track also depends on the format density - it is normally 9 for double and 15 for high density, and, unlike tracks, sectors are numbered starting with 1.

When you buy a disk, its surface is absolutely clean - both from dirt and, more importantly, from magnetic records. Format it and it will be ready to use.

Although no files are recorded on the disk, it does contain some information. On the top level, this includes the root directory, file allocation table and boot record - structures that occupy the first cylinders. The rest of the tracks also have something on them - low-level service information describing each track format. These invisible records are used for track synchronization, error checking, etc, and take about 30% of the total disk capacity. After each write operation, the CRC is increased by two bytes and the data is written to the disk.

During any read operation, the internal disk controller calculates the CRC using the same algorithm and compares it with the value read from the sector. If they aren't equal, the controller reports an error.

## Disk Capacity

There are several ways to increase the capacity of a disk:

1    Increase the number of the tracks. This is limited by the capabilities of the drive.

**2**    Enlarge the sector capacity. This is limited by the density of the disk.

**3**    Increase the number of sectors, depending on the quality of the disk material.

# Hard Disks

A hard disk unit usually consists of several double-sided disks in a stack on a single axis. Track numbering starts from the outmost one, numbered 0. There can be 256, 512, or 1024 bytes per sector - the actual number depends on the hard disk type and is defined during the format process. The usual numbers of sectors per track is 9, 17, or 34. The number of disks, tracks, sectors per track, etc. defines the parameters of the particular hard disk drive.

Sectors consist of two parts: the ID and the data area. The ID contains the service information neccesary to access the data.

# Physical Disk Structure

Each logical drive or a hard disk partition has the layout shown in Table 9.1:

**Table 9.1 Hard Disk Layout**

| Part | Location |
|------|----------|
| Boot sector | First sector |
| FAT 1 | Variable |
| FAT 2 | Variable |
| Root directory | Variable |
| Data | Remaining space |

This sequence only shows how different parts follow each other - the FAT (file allocation table) and root directory sizes vary widely depending on the disk size.

We'll now describe each part of the disk structure in more detail.

## The Boot Sector

The boot sector contains several disk parameters, such as the size of various structures on the disk and so on. It's located in the first sector of a disk, and the sector itself begins with the BOOT structure.

The BPB (BIOS Parameters Block) is the part of the boot sector record which is used by drivers. Here is an example boot record:

```
BOOT      STRUC
                          bsJMP         db       3 dup(?)
                          bsOEM         db       8 dup(?)
          ; Start of BPB
                          bsSECTSIZE    dw       ?
                          bsCLUSTSIZE   db       ?
                          bsRESSECT     dw       ?
                          bsFATCNT      db       ?
                          bsROOTSIZE    dw       ?
                          bsTOTALSECT   dw       ?
                          bsMEDIA       db       ?
                          bsFATSIZE     dw       ?
                          bsTRACKSECT   dw       ?
                          bsHEADCNT     dw       ?
                          bsHIDENSECT   dd       ?
                          bsHUGESECT    dd       ?
          ; End of BPB
                          bsDRIVENUM    db       ?
                          bsRESERV      db       ?
                          bsBOOTSIGN    db       ?
                          bsVOLID       dd       ?
                          bsVOLABEL     db       11 dup(?)
                          bsFILESTYPE   db       8 dup(?)
          BOOT      ENDS
```

### Boot Sector Fields

bsJMP:              Contains a jmp instruction to the boot code which loads the operating system from disk. Usually the value here is 0E9h,XX,XX or 0EBh,XX,90h (XX - offset of jump).

bsOEM:              This is the OEM (original equipment manufacturer) company name and version. Not used by DOS.

bsSECTSIZE:     Bytes per sector.

bsCLUSTSIZE:    Sectors per cluster.

bsRESSECT:     The number of reserved sectors, beginning with sector 0. This value (usually 1) defines the number of sectors preceeding the first copy of the FAT.

bsFATCNT:     The number of File Allocation Tables (normally 2). DOS uses the first FAT to hold the information about    files and the second FAT is simply a duplicate of the first one, used to restore the FAT in case it's corrupt.

bsROOTSIZE:     The maximum number of directory entries (32 bytes each).

bsTOTALSECT:     The total number of sectors on the drive or partition. If the size of a partition is greater than 32 Mb, this value is 0 and the number of sectors is specified in bsHUGESECT.

bsMEDIA:     Media Descriptor, defined by DOS, can be used to identify the type of media being used in a drive. DOS passes the Media Descriptor to the drivers so that they can check the media type. You can also use the Media Descriptor to check whether the disk in the drive is changed. The Media Descriptor is usually (but not always) the first byte of the FAT. You can find the Media Descriptor:

- In the boot sector, offset +15h

- In the BPB, offset +0ah

- In the first byte of the FAT

- As the value returned from DOS Functions 1bh, 1ch, and 31h.

The meanings of Media Descriptor codes are shown in Table 9.2.

**Table 9.2 Media Descriptor Codes**

| Value | Media Type |
|-------|------------|
| 0F0h | 5.25", 2 sides, 15 sectors per track (1.2MB) |
| | 3.5", 2 sides, 18 sectors per track (1.44MB) |
| | 3.5", 2 sides, 36 sectors per track (2.88MB) |
| | CD-ROM |
| | Other unlisted types of the media |
| 0F8h | Hard disk |
| 0F9h | 3.5", 2 sides, 9 sectors per track (720K) |
| | 5.25", 2 sides, 15 sectors per track (1.2MB) |
| 0FAh | 5.25", 1 side, 8 sectors per track (320K) |
| 0FBh | 3.5", 2 sides, 8 sectors per track (640K) |
| 0FCh | 5.25", 1 side, 9 sectors per track (180K) |
| 0FDh | 5.25", 2 sides, 9 sectors per track (360K) |
| | 8" (IBM 3740) |
| 0FEh | 5.25", 1 side, 8 sectors per track (160K) |
| | 8" (IBM 3740) |
| 0FFh | 5.25", 2 sides, 8 sectors per track (320K) |

You should rely on the boot record and not on the Media Descriptor when analyzing disk format.

bsFATSIZE:          The number of sectors in one FAT.

bsTRACKSECT:        The number of sectors per track.

bsHEADCNT:          The number of read-write heads.

bsHIDENSECT:        The number of hidden sectors.

bsHUGESECT:         If bsTOTALSECT is zero, then this value specifies the number of sectors.

| | |
|---|---|
| bsDRIVENUM: | 80h if it's the boot drive, otherwise 0. Used by DOS. |
| bsRESERV: | It's still not used. |
| bsBOOTSIGN: | Extended boot signature = 29h. |
| bsVOLID: | Volume serial number. |
| bsVOLABEL: | Volume label (up to 11 characters). |
| bsFILESTYPE: | File system type, can be either 'FAT12' (for a 12-bit FAT), or 'FAT16' (for a 16-bit FAT). This string is padded with spaces. |

This structure is followed by the main boot code which looks for the files IO.SYS and MSDOS.SYS and loads them. (These names may vary in different versions of DOS.) The Boot sector ends with the signature 0AA55h.

## Reading the Boot Sector

The following program reads the boot sector of disk A:

```
btbuff     db       512 dup(?)   ; buffer to receive the data
i25startsec  dd       ?          ; int 25h packet
i25countsec  dw       ?
i25off     dw       ?
i25seg     dw       ?


           mov     al,0          ; DRIVE NUMBER A:-0,B:-1,...
           mov     cx,1          ; number of sectors to read
           xor     dx,dx         ; DOS logical sector 0
           lds     bx,btbuff     ; address of the buffer in
                                 ; ds:[bx]
           int     25h           ; Read sector
           pop     dx            ; discard the extra word on
                                 ; the stack (DOS bug!)
           jc      next          ; error during disk reading
                                 ; (AX - error code)
                                 ; or disk is larger than 32Mb

next:
; Try to read with parameters for disk larger than
;32Mb.
```

```
        mov     word ptr i25startsec,0
                            ; DOS logical sector 0
        mov     word ptr i25startsec+2,0
        mov     i25countsec,1
                            ; number of sectors to read
        lds     bx,btbuff
        mov     i25off,bx       ; buffer address
        mov     i25seg,ds
        mov     al,drive        ; drive number

; A: - 0, B: - 1,...
        mov     cx,0ffffh       ; Disk is > 32Mb
        lds     bx,i25startsec  ; Address of Int25h
                            ; packet
        int     25h             ; Read sector
        pop     dx
        jc      @@error         ; error code in AX
```

# Logical Drives on a Hard Disk

Hard disks can be divided into several logical drives or partitions. One of the partitions is used for booting and is marked as active. Each partition has a boot record, FATs, and a root directory as mentioned previously.

The information about how the disk is divided is stored in a special structure called the Partition Table, which is recorded in sector 1, head 0, cylinder 0 (i.e. the first physical sector) of a fixed disk, in the area called the Master Boot Record.

The Partition Table layout is shown in Table 9.3:

**Table 9.3 The Partition Table Layout**

| Offset | Size | Contents |
|--------|------|----------|
| +0 | 1BEh | Code that detects the active partition and boots DOS from it. |
| +1BEh | 10h | Partition 1 entry |
| +1CEh | 10h | Partition 2 entry |
| +1DEh | 10h | Partition 3 entry |
| +1EEh | 10h | Partition 4 entry |
| +1FEh | 2 | Partition signature (0AA55h). |

Each entry specifies the size, starting and ending sectors, and other parameters of the corresponding partition. The following assembly language structure illustrates the format of a Partition Table entry.

```
PARTITION       STRUC
                pnBOOT      db      ?
                pnBEGHEAD   db      ?
                pnBEGSECYL  dw      ?
                pnSYSCODE   db      ?
                pnENDHEAD   db      ?
                pnENDSECYL  dw      ?
                pnSTARTSEC  dd      ?
                pnSIZE      dd      ?
        PARTITION       ENDS
```

Let's look in detail at what these fields contain:

pnBOOT:     This is the boot flag - it shows whether a partition is bootable. A bootable partition has 80h in this field, non-active ones have zeroes. The flag is used by the Master Boot Record to determine which partition to boot from.

pnBEGHEAD:  The head number (number of physical disk side) of the first track in the partition.

pnBEGSECYL: The sector and cylinder of the boot sector in the partition. The sector is in 6 low-order bits, the cylinder is in 10 high-order bits - as shown below:

| 15 | 14 | 13 | 12 | 11 | 10 | 9 | 8 | 7 | 6 | 5 | 4 | 3 | 2 | 1 | 0 |
|----|----|----|----|----|----|---|---|---|---|---|---|---|---|---|---|
| C  | C  | C  | C  | C  | C  | C | C | C | C | S | S | S | S | S | S |

C = cylinder, S = sector.

pnSYSCODE:  This represents the system type, according to the codes shown in Table 9.4:

**Table 9.4 System Type Codes**

| Code | Meaning |
| --- | --- |
| 00h | Unknown |
| 01h | 12-bit FAT, partition smaller than 32MB |
| 04h | 16-bit FAT, partition smaller than 32MB |
| 05h | Extended DOS partition |
| 06h | 16-bit FAT, partition equal to or larger than 32MB |

If the value is 5, then the partition is an extended DOS partition and is treated as if it's another physical drive. You may find some other values in this field, but DOS will only recognize the above.

pnENDHEAD:     The head of the last track in the partition.

pnENDSECYL:    The last sector and cylinder of the partition. The structure of this field is the same as of pnBEGSECYL. The sector number is relative to the first track of the partition.

pnSTARTSEC:    The number of the first sector of the partition relative to the beginning of the disk.

Relative sector 0 is cylinder 0, head 0, sector 1 of the disk. This value is calculated by the following formula:

RelativeSector = Cylinder * SectorsPerTrack * Heads
+ Head * SectorsPerTrack + Sector -1

pnSIZE:    The total number of sectors in the partition.

During the boot, the Master Boot Record is loaded into memory at the address 0:7C00h and executed. This code determines the active partition, loads the boot sector with DOS boot code from that partition and executes it.

The following program is an example of a disassembled Master Boot Record:

```
d_0000_0600_e    equ    600h
d_0000_068B_e    equ    68Bh
d_0000_7C00_e    equ    7C00h
d_0000_7DFE_e    equ    7DFEh

                 cli
                 xor     ax,ax
                 mov     ss,ax
                 mov     sp,7C00h
                 mov     si,sp
                 push    ax
                 pop     es
                 push    ax
                 pop     ds
                 sti
                 cld
                 mov     di,d_0000_0600_e
                 mov     cx,100h
                 repne   movsw
                 jmp     far ptr 1_0000_061D
                           ; db 0EAh,61Dh,0
                 mov     si,07BEh
                 mov     bl,4
1_0122::
                 cmp     byte ptr [si],80h
                 je      1_0135
                 cmp     byte ptr [si],0
                 jne     1_0148
                 add     si,10h
                 dec     bl
                 jnz     1_0122
                 int     18h
1_0135::
                 mov     dx,[si]
                 mov     cx,[si+2]
                 mov     bp,si
1_013C::
                 add     si,10h
                 dec     bl
                 jz      1_015D
                 cmp     byte ptr [si],0
                 je      1_013C
1_0148::
                 mov     si,d_0000_068B_e
1_014B::
                 lodsb
                 cmp     al,0
                 je      1_015B
                 push    si
```

```
                        mov     bx,7
                        mov     ah,0Eh
                        int     10h
                        pop     si
                        jmp     short 1_014B
        1_015B::
                        jmp     short 1_015B
        1_015D::
                        mov     di,5
        1_0160::
                        mov     bx,d_0000_7C00_e
                        mov     ax,201h
                        push    di
                        int     13h
                        pop     di
                        jnc     1_0178
                        xor     ax,ax
                        int     13h
                        dec     di
                        jnz     1_0160
                        mov     si,6A3h
                        jmp     short 1_014B
        1_0178::
                        mov     si,6C2h
                        mov     di,d_0000_7DFE_e
                        cmp     word ptr [di],0AA55h
                        jne     1_014B
                        mov     si,bp
                        jmp     far ptr 1_0000_7C00
                                  ;db 0EAh,7C00h,0
                        db      'Invalid partition table', 0
                        db      'Error loading operating
                                  system', 0
                        db      'Missing operating system'
```

# Extended DOS Partitions

DOS provides you with a way to divide one physical disk into several smaller volumes, which DOS treats as separate disks. If the field pnSYSCODE in a Partition Table entry contains code 5, then this partition entry defines the location and size of a secondary Master Boot Sector which contains its own partition table called the Logical Drive Table. This table defines the size and location of other DOS partitions (logical drives). Each partition table may contain code 5 in pnSYSCODE and so point to another Logical Drive Table, and so on, in chains.

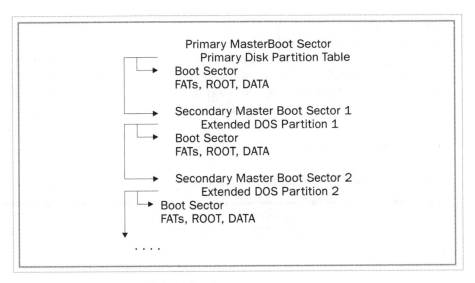

**Figure 9.1 Extended DOS Partitions**

Extended DOS partitions differ from primary ones. They aren't bootable, and a secondary Master Boot sector can't contain the boot code.

When pnSYSCODE contains value 5 (marking the extended DOS partition), then pnBEGHEAD, pnBEGSECYL, pnENDHEAD and pnENDSECYL values are relative to the begining of the physical disk - otherwise they are relative to the secondary Master Boot sector.

## The FAT Structure

DOS maps the space on disk using clusters, not sectors. Each cluster consists of a certain number of consecutive sectors - the number depends on the capacity and type of the disk, but it is always a power of 2. When you create a new file or modify an old one, the system allocates a chain of clusters to the file, writes data to those clusters and stores the information about each cluster location in the File Allocation Table (FAT).

DOS uses the FAT to find a file on disk and allocate or free clusters. A disk usually has two copies of the FAT - the first is used during disk operations, the second is just a backup, in case the first gets corrupted.

The FAT is an array of 12-bit or 16-bit entries. The entry size depends on the number of clusters on the disk. When there are no more than 4096 clusters on a disk, it has a 12-bit FAT; if there are more, then the FAT is of the 16-bit type. Each entry in the FAT corresponds to one cluster on disk. The first 3 bytes for the 12-bit FAT or 4 bytes for the 16-bit FAT are reserved. Usually the first byte of a FAT contains a media descriptor (see bsMEDIA in BOOT), and the rest of the reserved bytes are filled with 0FFh. Table 9.5 shows possible FAT entry values and their meanings (hexadecimal digits in brackets apply to 16-bit FATs).

**Table 9.5 FAT Entry Values and Their Meanings**

| Value | Meaning |
|---|---|
| (0)000h | Free cluster |
| (F)FF0h-(F)FF6h | Reserved cluster |
| (F)FF7h | Bad cluster |
| (0)002h-(F)FEFh | Allocated cluster, the number is the next cluster in the chain. |
| (F)FF8h-(F)FFFh | The last cluster in a chain. |

Whenever DOS creates a new file or directory, it stores the index of the first cluster in the chain in the destination directory, at the offset 1Ah of a directory entry. At the same time, this is the index of the first FAT entry for this file. The value in this FAT entry shows the next cluster occupied by the file and, correspondingly, the next entry in the FAT. And so the chain goes on until an entry contains a value in the range (F)FF8h-(F)FFFh, which means this cluster is the last in the chain.

## Mapping Files in the FAT

Figure 9.2 shows how a file is mapped in the FAT.

The directory entry for the file \FILE1.EXE in the root directory contains the index 04 of the first cluster occupied by this file. The entry 04 in the FAT contains the index of the next entry in the chain. So we can determine that the file resides in clusters 4, 5, 6, 8, 1Ah, and 1Bh. The entry 1Bh contains the value FFFh which shows that this cluster is the last cluster in the file. Clusters 2, 3, 7, 1Ch are free and the cluster 9 is bad.

Root Directory:

· · · ·

File1.EXE......04...

· · · ·

FAT:

| Index: | 00 | 01 | 02 | 03 | 04 | 05 | 06 | 07 | 08 | 09 | 0a | 0b | 0c |
|--------|----|----|----|----|----|----|----|----|----|----|----|----|----|
| | | | | | ... | | | | | | | | |
| Value: | ID | FFF | 000 | 000 | **005** | **006** | **008** | 000 | **00a** | FF7 | **00b** | **FFF** | 000 |

**Figure 9.2 A File Mapped in the FAT**

When allocating a new cluster, DOS chooses the first free cluster available (in our example this would be cluster 2) and concatenates it to the chain. If the clusters in a chain go contiguously, then access to the file will be faster because the controller doesn't need to reposition read/write heads. When you delete a file from disk, DOS fills the corresponding entries in the FAT with zeroes, and a hole appears. Then, when DOS allocates clusters for a new file, the hole may not be enough for the file and its clusters will be scattered, sometimes throughout the whole partition. However small a file or directory is, it occupies at least one cluster. So it's not reasonable to keep a lot of tiny files and a large directory tree.

## Working with the FAT

When accessing the FAT you should remember the following rules:

1   To find the FAT, use the value from the field bsRESSEC (boot record, offset 0Eh).

2   To find out the FAT size in sectors, use the value from the field bsFATSIZE (boot record, offset 16h). To convert this to bytes, you have to multiply the value by the sector size found in the field bsSECTSIZE in boot record, offset 0Bh. The result may be quite huge. Sometimes you won't be able to read the full FAT into memory, so you have to take care to read and work with parts of the FAT.

3   To find out the number of FATs, use the field bsFATCNT (boot record, offset 10h).

To access the entries of a 12-bit FAT:

**1**   Round the cluster number down to the nearest even number, then multiply this by 3.

**2**   Read 3 bytes from the resulting offset.

**3**   If the cluster index is even, take the lower 12 bits of this value, else take the higher 12 bits.

16-bit FATs are easier:

**1**   Multiply the cluster index by 2.

**2**   Read 2 bytes from that offset.

To convert the cluster index to a logical sector:

**1**   Subtract 2 from the cluster index.

**2**   Multiply the result by the number of sectors per cluster (which can be found in the boot record, offset 0Dh).

## Scanning the FAT

This next program explores the contents of the FAT:

```
ftbuff          db      1024 dup(?)            ; FAT buffer
        btSTRUC         BOOT    <>            ; BOOT structure

                        . . .

; Find and read the FAT

            mov     al,0           ; drive number A:-0,...
            mov     cx,2           ; sector count = 2
            mov     dx,btSTRUC.bsRESSECT        ; beginning sector
            lds     bx,ftbuff      ; address of FAT buffer
            int     25h            ; read 2 sectors of FAT
            pop     dx             ; discard the extra word
                                   ; from the stack
```

```
                    jc      @@error             ; error during disk
                                                ; reading (AX = error code)
                            . . .

; Example for a 12-bit FAT

                    mov     ax,3                ; the first file's cluster
                                                ;from the root directory
                    mov     si,ax               ; SI = AX * 1.5
                    shr     si,1
                    add     si,ax
                    mov     dx,word ptr ds:[bx+si]
                                                ; read a word from  FAT
                    test    ax,1                ; is the cluster index even
                    jnz     @@neven_cluster     ; not even
                    and     dx,0000111111111111b ; even
                    jmp     @@continue

@@neven_cluster:
                    mov     cl,4        ; not even
                    shr     dx,cl
                    jmp     @@continue

; Example for a 16-bit FAT

                    mov     si,3                ; the first file's cluster
                                                ;from the root directory
                    shl     si,1
                    mov     dx,word ptr ds:[bx+si]
                                                ; read a word from FAT


@@continue:                                     ; DX - FAT entry
                                                    . . .

@@error:             . . .
```

*Do not forget to change the INT 25h call for partitions larger than 32Mb, as we described when we explained the boot record structure.*

# Root Directory Structure

Every disk has one root directory and may have other directories, either in the root one or hierarchically in any directory. Each directory is an array of records called directory entries. The number of files and directories in the root directory is defined in the boot record and can't be changed. Unlike the root directory, which has a fixed size and location on disk - after the last copy of the FAT -

subdirectories are stored as files with a Directory attribute, and can be anywhere in the data area on disk, so their sizes are limited only by the disk capacity.

The following structure in assembly language shows directory entry layout:

```
DIRENTRY        STRUC
                deFILENAME      db      8 dup(?)
                deFILEEXT       db      3 dup(?)
                deATRIB         db      ?
                deRESERV        db      0Ah dup(?)
                deTIME          dw      ?
                deDATE          dw      ?
                deCLUSTNUM      dw      ?
                deFILESIZE      dd      ?
DIRENTRY        ENDS

        ; Total size: 32 bytes
```

# Fields

deFILENAME:     Left-justified, blank-padded file name. The first byte of this field may have a special meaning, as shown in Table 9.6.

**Table 9.6 The First Byte of a Filename in a Directory Entry**

| Contents | Meaning |
|---|---|
| 0 | The entry has never been used. |
| 05h | This value means that the first character in the file name is ASCII 0E5h (see below). |
| 02Eh | If the rest of the bytes in this field are spaces (20h), then the field deCLUSTNUM contains the starting cluster of this directory. If the second byte is also 02Eh and the others are spaces, then the field deCLUSTNUM contains the starting cluster of the parent directory, or 0 if the parent directory is the root. |
| 0E5h | This file or directory is deleted. The rest of the name is kept unchanged. |

deFILEEXT:      Left-justified blank-padded file extention.

deATRIB:     File Attribute Byte. The two high order bits are reserved. A normal file (without any special attributes) has 0 in this field. You can see the meanings of individual bits in Figure 9.3:

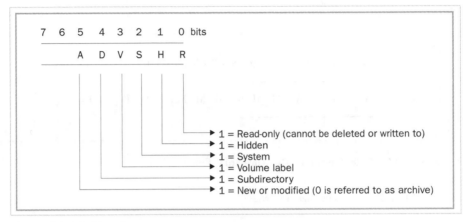

**Figure 9.3 Bit Meanings**

deRESERV:    Reserved.

deTIME:      The time when this directory or file was created or last updated. The bit layout of this two-byte field is as follows:

```
15 14 13 12 11 10 09 08 07 06 05 04 03 02 01 00 Bits

 H  H  H  H  H  M  M  M  M  M  M  S  S  S  S  S
```

**Figure 9.4 Time Layout in the Directory Entry**

Here D is day (1 - 31), M is month (1 - 12), and Y is year relative to 1980.

deCLUSTNUM:  The starting cluster of the directory or file.

Here S are seconds in two-second units (0 - 29), M are minutes (0 - 59), and H are hours (0 - 23).

deDATE:    The date when this directory or file was created or last updated.

```
15 14 13 12 11 10 09 08 07 06 05 04 03 02 01 00 Bits
────────────────
Y Y  Y  Y  Y  M  M  M  M  M  D  D  D  D  D
────────────────
```

**Figure 9.5   Date Layout in the Directory Entry**

deFILESIZE:    File size in bytes.

To access the root directory you should observe the following rules:

1    To find the root directory use the values from the boot record fields bsRESSEC (offset 0Eh), bsFATSIZE (offset 16h) and bsFATCNT (offset 10h). The first sector of the root is bsRESSEC + bsFATSIZE * bsFATCNT.

2    To find the maximum number of root entries, read the value from boot record field bsROOTSIZE (offset 11h). To get the size of the root in bytes, multiply this value by 32, the size of a directory entry. To get the size of the root in sectors, divide the size in bytes by the value in the bootrecord field bsSECTSIZE (offset 0Bh).

Here's an example of reading the root directory:

```
rtbuff          db      16384 dup(?)          ; ROOT buffer
btSTRUC         BOOT    <>                    ; BOOT structure

                    . . .

; Find and read the ROOT

        mov     ax,btSTRUC.bsFATSIZE
        mov     cl,btSTRUC.bsFATCNT
        xor     ch,ch
        mul     cx
        mov     bx,btSTRUC.bsRESSEC
        add     bx,ax                    ; bx = 1st sector
        mov     ax,btSTRUC.bsROOTSIZE
        mov     cx,32
        mul     cx
        mov     cx,btSTRUC.bsSECTSIZE
        div     cx
        mov     cx,ax                    ; cx = ROOT length
                                         ;in sectors
        mov     dx,bx                    ; dx = 1st sector
        mov     al,0                     ; drive number A: - 0,...
        lds     bx,rtbuff                ; address of the
                                         ;ROOT buffer
        int     25h                      ; read sectors of the ROOT
        pop     dx                       ; discard the extra word
                                         ;from the stack
        jc      @@error  n               ; read error
                                         ; (AX - error code)

                    . . .

@@error:
```

*Do not forget to change the INT 25h call for partitions larger than 32Mb. We've shown how when we explained the boot record structure.*

# Unerasing Files

In the previous section, we looked at loads of highly technical low-level information. It's not exactly fun. It's more interesting when you try modifying those vital areas of the file system.

Having carefully read all the instructions given above, you're ready for surgical operations on the disk. More often than not, it's possible to recover an erased file, and now we'll show you how.

## How DOS Deletes Files

First of all, we'll explain what DOS actually does when it says it deletes files. In fact, executing a command like:

```
del MYBUDGET.123 ,
```

DOS performs the following operations:

1   It finds the file name in the directory and replaces the first letter with ASCII value 0E5h;

2   It zeroes all FAT entries that have been used by the file.

So, if we then write some data to the disk, it can fall into some of the empty clusters which used to belong to our file. Fortunately, DOS tries to preserve directory entries of deleted files as long as possible, using virgin entries if they are available. Only in the root directory will it treat free and deleted entries without priority.

As we've already said, DOS changes some records about a file, but doesn't erase the data itself. This gives us a chance to unerase the deleted file. The information about the file is still written in the root or a subdirectory entry, which we can find using the name. Only the first character will be ASCII 0E5h. So in our example it'll be:

```
YBUDGET.123
```

But this is not the end of it yet. We should find out what our chances are of recovering the file. There can be three possible situations:

1   Lucky: all the data from our file still lies complete on disk and the file hasn't been fragmented.

2   Maybe: as above, but the file has been fragmented.

3   No way: the data is overwritten - the file's gone.

# Finding the Erased File

To locate the file we use the field deCLUSTNUM in the directory entry. Then we begin scanning the FAT. Find the starting cluster entry (index deCLUSTNUM) of the file and see if the value there is 0. If not, then the data is overwritten and the file can't be recovered. If the value is 0 and the first cluster is still unoccupied, we can try.

The next step is to calculate the file length in clusters by dividing the value in the field deFILESIZE in the directory entry by the boot record values bsSECTSIZE and bsCLUSTSIZE:

$$Length_{cl} = \frac{FILESIZE_{byte}}{(Bytes\ per\ sector) * (Sectors\ per\ cluster)}$$

and rounding this up to the nearest integer value. Then we scan the FAT from the starting cluster of the file through the amount we've just calculated. If free FAT entries directly follow one another, then our file will most probably unerase well. If the sequence is split into several parts, then our chances are so-so. Below is an example of the three situations:

Directory Entry: YBUDGET.123, ..., deCLUSTNUM=04, deFILESIZE=2080.
FAT index:
00   01   02   03   04   05   06   07   08   0a   0b

FAT contents (three versions):

**Lucky:**

ID   FFF   003   FFF   **000   000   000**   008   00A   FF7   00B   FFF
[————————————]

**Maybe:**

ID   FFF   003   FFF   **000   000**   008   **000**   00A   FF7   00B   FFF
[————————] +   [———]

**No way:**

ID   FFF   003   FFF   FFF   000   000   008   00A   FF7   00B   FFF

In the 'Lucky' example, the file MYBUDGET.123 had occupied clusters 4, 5, 6. The sector size is 512 bytes (bsSECTSIZE=512) and the cluster size is two sectors (bsCLUSTSIZE=2). The file size is 2080 bytes. Calculate the file size in clusters and it equals 3. Then examine the first cluster of the file (index deCLUSTNUM) and see that the value here is 0, so we can try to unerase the file. We find the next free entry (number 5) and write its index (5) into entry 4, and so on until we complete the chain of 3 clusters. In the last entry, we write code 0(F)FFFh. The result is a recovered cluster chain something like this:

FAT index:

```
00   01   02   03   04   05   06   07   08   09   0a   0b
```

FAT contents (recovered):

```
ID   FFF   003   FFF   005   006   FFF   008   00A   FF7   00B   FFF
```

In the 'Maybe' example the file had been split into two parts. FAT entry 6 is used by another file so we skip it and find the next free one. It's entry 7. The result is:

FAT index:
```
00   01   02   03   04   05   06   07   08   09   0a   0b
```

FAT contents (recovered):

```
ID   FFF   003   FFF   005   007   008   FFF   00A   FF7   00B   FFF   000
```

In the 'No way' example, the first cluster of our file had already been used by some other file, so our BUDGET file is gone for ever.

## UNERASE.ASM

A full scale implementation of these unerasing techniques is on the disk in the file UNERASE.ASM.

## Rebuilding Files

There is still a way to rescue the file contents, even if we can't recover the whole file. We can scan all the free clusters on the disk starting with the first cluster of the deleted file, find the required data and save it to a file. This file can damage the data you recover, so it's better to save it to another disk. Of course, this method works mostly with text files, but sometimes it's the only way to get back at least some of your day's work.

There's a special case with files of 0 length. No clusters are allocated for them and, naturally, no FAT entries. So they're the easiest to unerase, since all you have to do is to correct the first letter of the file name in the directory entry.

Another special case is unerasing directories. The problem is that DOS doesn't store the subdirectory size in the corresponding directory entry. If you read the field deFILESIZE, it's always 0. So, we can find the starting cluster of a subdirectory, but never find out how long it was. We can unerase only the first cluster of the subdirectory. And, of course, like Norton Unerase, you may try to scan the information in free clusters to locate the continuation of the subdirectory.

# Defragmenting Files

We've already said a file on disk can become fragmented, i.e. occupy a non-continuous group of clusters. When we read a file from disk, the controller has to seek the track and then read the data. If a file is fragmented, then the controller needs to perform more seek operations which slows down access to the disk.

Fragmentation is very crucial from the point of view of performance when you deal with vast amounts of data. Databases are processed much slower, digitized sound plays clicky and jagged, animation goes jerkily, and so on. Luckily, there are utilities that take care of this and defragment both files and free space, like DEFRAG in later versions of MS-DOS.

Defragmentation is an inherently risky process. One cluster out of place will destroy your data. For that reason we aren't going to show you a full implementation of a defrag program. What we will do is to cover the principles involved, so if you're feeling brave you can go ahead on your own.

## How It Works

During defragmentation, we first get rid of the holes in the data space. We analyze the FAT, and move some files to shut the holes. The particular way to do this is up to you. The simplest way is to find the first hole, shift all the data following the hole, and repeat these two steps until the free space becomes unfragmented.

For example, suppose that the initial situation on the disk is like this:

Root directory:

                    FILE1.EXE......deCLUSTNUM=04

                    TEST.TXT.......deCLUSTNUM=08

      FAT

Index:

| 03 | 04 | 05 | 06 | 07 | 08 | 09 | 0a | 0b | 0c |
|----|----|----|----|----|----|----|----|----|----|

Contents:

| 000 | **005** | **007** | 000 | **009** | FFF | **00B** | FF7 | **FFF** | 000 |
|-----|---------|---------|-----|---------|-----|---------|-----|---------|-----|

Here:  FILE1.EXE lies in clusters 4, 5, 7, 9, and 01Bh.

        TEST.TXT - in cluster 8.

        Cluster 01Ah is marked as bad.

        Clusters 3, 6, 01Ch are free.

During defragmentation, we move the data from cluster to cluster as follows:

| | | |
|------|-----|---|
| 4 | -> | 3 |
| 5 | -> | 4 |
| 7 | -> | 5 |
| 9 | -> | 6 |
| 00bh | -> | 7 |

We then zero the freed cluster entries (9 and 01Bh), and write new indexes of starting clusters to directory entries in the field deCLUSTNUM. The FAT will look like this:

Root directory:      File1.EXE......deCLUSTNUM=03

                          TEST.TXT.......deCLUSTNUM=08

FAT
Index:

| 03 | 04 | 05 | 06 | 07 | 08 | 09 | 0a | 0b | 0c |
|----|----|----|----|----|----|----|----|----|----|

Contents:

| **004** | **005** | **006** | **007** | **FFF** | FFF | 000 | FF7 | 000 | 000 |
|---------|---------|---------|---------|---------|-----|-----|-----|-----|-----|

In this example, the length of the file FILE1.EXE allowed us to move the whole file into the hole. Should it happen that the size of the hole is smaller than the file length, we would have first moved some clusters to the free area at the end of the disk to extend the hole giving room for the file (like Norton Speedisk does).

In practice, you'll encounter much more tortuous fragmentation, and the optimization resembles the operations at a big railway yard.

In the following example the file FILE1.EXE can't be defragmented without moving the files FILE2.EXE and FILE3.EXE. The initial FAT is

Root directory:      FILE1.EXE......deCLUSTNUM=04
                     File2.EXE......deCLUSTNUM=06
                     FILE3.EXE......deATTRIB= H & S......deCLUSTNUM=08

FAT
Index:

| 04 | 05 | 06 | 07 | 08 | 09 | 0a | 0b | 0c |
|----|----|----|----|----|----|----|----|----|

Contents:

| **005** | **007** | FFF | **009** | FFF | **00B** | FF7 | **FFF** | 000 |
|---------|---------|-----|---------|-----|---------|-----|---------|-----|
|         |         |     |         | [—] |         | [—] |         |     |

Unmovable clusters: System Bad

We temporarily move FILE2.EXE to the end of the disk but we can't move the file FILE3.EXE because it has attributes System and Hidden, which indicate that this file is probably used by the operating system and must remain in its place. Also, there's a bad cluster in our example, cluster 0Ah, to which nothing can be written. In these rather complicated circumstances, there are two ways to continue our defragmentation.

The first is to split the file FILE1.EXE, moving the clusters like this:

| Cluster | To cluster |
|---|---|
| 6 | The end of the disk |
| 7 | 6 |
| 9 | 7 |
| 0bh | 9 |
| The end of the disk | 0bh |

The defragmented FAT is:

Root directory:
        FILE1.EXE......deCLUSTNUM=04
        File2.EXE......deCLUSTNUM=01Bh
        FILE3.EXE......deATTRIB= H & S.....deCLUSTNUM=08

FAT
Index:

| 04 | 05 | 06 | 07 | 08 | 09 | 0a | 0b | 0c |
|---|---|---|---|---|---|---|---|---|

Contents:

| **005** | **006** | **007** | **009** | FFF | **FFF** | FF7 | FFF | 000 |
|---|---|---|---|---|---|---|---|---|

The second, and a better way, is to write the file to the free place, moving the clusters this way:

| Cluster | To cluster |
|---|---|
| 4,5,7,9,0bh | The end of the disk |
| 6 | 4 |
| The end of the disk | 0bh,0ch,0dh,0eh,0fh |

This way the defragmented FAT will look like this:

**Root directory:**
> FILE1.EXE......deCLUSTNUM=01Bh
> FILE2.EXE......deCLUSTNUM=04
> FILE3.EXE......deATTRIB= H & S......deCLUSTNUM=08

FAT
Index:

| 04 | 05 | 06 | 07 | 08 | 09 | 0a | 0b | 0c |
|----|----|----|----|----|----|----|----|----|

Contents:

| FFF | 000 | 000 | 000 | FFF | 000 | FF7 | **00C** | **00D** |
|-----|-----|-----|-----|-----|-----|-----|---------|---------|

It's better to move the file FILE1.EXE to the end of the disk to allow you to optimize small files like FILE2.EXE.

Whatever logic you choose, your defragmenting program needs a relatively low-level routine that moves a cluster N to a free space (cluster F). What it has to do is:

- Write data from cluster N to cluster F.

- Relink the FAT image in memory (the entry that pointed to N must now point to F, the entry F must point to where the entry N pointed, and the entry N must be nulled).

On the logical level, it's safer to move clusters of one file at a time. You copy data from the file's clusters to free clusters, and this leaves the FAT on disk valid (you just double the data).

When the operation on the file is finished, you write the modified FAT image from memory to disk. This moment is the only critical point in defragmenting where there's a risk to corrupt disk structure, say, due to unexpected power loss.

# Summary

These are some of the secrets of magnetic media. Under the black plastic cover, between the two soft layers, there hides boots, FATs and roots, no longer strange to you. Read them, write them, handle them with care and patience.

We didn't describe tricks like crashing down hard disk heads or scratching notches on the disk surface (though this has been done by some successful viruses). Injury wasn't the purpose here. Conversely, we hope that this chapter will help you avoid fatal errors.

# Data Compression Techniques

## Introduction

It usually happens like this: you collect programs, images, personal data and records, cramming more and more megabytes onto your disk. At last, flooded with data, you drown and your precious computer drowns with you. But then comes the rescue service with its zippy packing tools. In an instant, as your treasure trove is squeezed down to one floppy, you see how little real information there is in all that data.

However, the most amazing thing about these packing tools is that they're always ready to restore your data to its full glory, all in an instant.

# Compression, OK - But How?

We are led to believe that there is a solid mathematical bedrock for each and every compression method used today. However, it seems that it is largely a matter of luck. Someone looked at a piece of data, suddenly spotted a row of repeated symbols, and here we are with Run Length Encoding (RLE). Someone else unexpectedly ran into rather long chains of symbols frequently repeated in a document. Surely they could be coded more efficiently? They could, and another compression algorithm was born.

It was estimated long ago that the characters of the alphabet are used with different frequencies, so if the more frequently experienced characters had shorter codes it would result in considerable compression. In fact, although the implementation of almost every compression algorithm is complex, often as a result of the drive to squeeze extra speed and efficiency out of the method, the underlying algorithms are usually fairly simple.

## Basic Compression Techniques

### Code Table Optimization

First of all let's take a short look at the ways that various compression programs handle data.

Let's assume you only work with text and use the Latin alphabet, figures 0..9 and the set of usual punctuation signs. In this case, the total number of characters you need can be limited to 64 symbols. If so, then the byte-per-symbol coding scheme, usually used in the computer world, is too extravagant for your particular case. If your information contains only 64 different symbols you can code it with 6 bit-code and so compress the data by 25%, no problem.

This seems almost too simple to work. However, it does and it also gives us the opportunity to examine a typical coding/decoding data handling technique.

First, we'll define the coding table:

Table 10.1 Code Transalation Table

| Character | Code (8-bit) | New code (6-bit) |
|:---:|:---:|:---:|
| A | 65 | 000000 |
| B | 66 | 000001 |
| ... | | ... |
| Z | 90 | 011010 |
| ... | | ... |
| . | 46 | 111110 |

Let's assume that the 6-bit symbol codes are stored in the array TAB6bit (256 bytes long), so that the 6-bit code for the letter A (ASCII 65) is stored as the 65th element of the array. The rest is easy: we merely take every symbol from the incoming data stream, use its 8 bit code as the index and read the 6-bit code from our table.

To send the 6-bit codes to the outgoing data stream, we need a 16 bit buffer in which to construct the packed bytes. We also define the bit counter COUNTER which points to the last bit of the previous symbol. Initially the COUNTER is equal to 0.

## Encoding

Encoding works like this. We take a symbol and determine its 6-bit code. Then we use the COUNTER to calculate the shift and the mask to apply, to ensure it takes its correct place in the output stream. We will then add the 6-bit code to the contents of the BUFFER by using a logical OR, and update the COUNTER. When we have accumulated 8 bits in the BUFFER, we are ready to transfer our first byte to the output stream, after which we move the low byte of the BUFFER to the vacated high byte position, and update the COUNTER. And so on, again and again.

Consider the following code fragment, which explains what's going on.

```
          . . .
        mov  COUNTER,0                    ; Set bit COUNTER to 0
          . . .

@@loop_010:
        mov  bl,INPUT                     ; Get the next character or
                                          ; exit if empty
        xor  bh,bh
        mov  al,byte ptr TAB6bit[bx]    ;The code from the table
        xor  ah,ah
        mov  cl,10
        sub  cl,COUNTER                   ; Calculate the shift
        shl  ax,cl                        ; Shift the code
        or   BUFFER,ax                    ; Mask the code into BUFFER
        add  COUNTER,6                    ; Increase COUNTER by the size
                                          ; of the code
        cmp  COUNTER,8                    ; Check for 8 bit length
        jb   @@loop_010                     ; Byte not ready!
; Byte is ready
        mov  ax,BUFFER
        mov  OUTPUT,ah                    ; Send ready byte to OUTPUT
        mov  ah,al                        ; Move the low byte to the high
        xor  al,al
        mov  BUFFER,ax
        sub  COUNTER,8                    ; Decrease COUNTER by 8
        jmp  @@loop_010
```

You can modify the algorithm, or sometimes just the code table, to work with any alphabet. This technique will compress only if an alphabet is comprised of no more than 127 symbols.

# Decoding

Not surprisingly, when it comes to decoding, it works in reverse. We extract the necessary number of bits from the incoming coded data stream, process it with an AND mask, which we calculate with the help of the COUNTER. Then we shift the code to the beginning of the byte and use it as the index into the reverse decoding table of symbols TAB8bit. The symbol read from the table is then placed in the outgoing data stream.

```
          . . .
        mov  COUNTER,0                    ; Set COUNTER to 0
```

. . .

```
@@loop_010:
  mov  ax,INPUT              ; Get next code
  xchg al,ah                ; switch low byte and high
  mov  dx,ax                ; Store ax in dx
@@loop_020:
  mov  bx,0FFFFh            ; Prepare mask
  mov  cl,10               ; Word length (16 bit) -
                            ; code length (6 bit)  = 10 bit
  shr  bx,cl               ; BX - mask
  sub  cl,COUNTER          ; Calculate code shift
  shr  ax,cl               ; Shift code
  and  bx,ax               ; Mask code
  mov  al,byte ptr TAB8bit[bx] ; Get character
  mov  OUTPUT,al           ; Send character to OUTPUT
  add  COUNTER,6           ; Increase COUNTER by the
                            ; length of code

  cmp  COUNTER,8           ; Check byte overflow
  jae  @@loop_030          ; Overflow
  mov  ax,dx               ; No overflow. Restore AX from
                            ; DX.
  jmp  short @@loop_020    ; Repeat loop
@@loop_030:
  sub  COUNTER,8           ; Decrease COUNTER by 8 (byte length)
  jmp  @@loop_010          ; Repeat loop
```

This doesn't show you any real compression technique. However, we need to understand coding/decoding before we can get onto the real thing. In fact, more complicated techniques differ only in using variable code length (Huffman) and adaptive code tables (LZW).

# Huffman Compression

## Huffman Coding

Think about the code length we used just now. Does it have to be the same for all symbols in the alphabet? Certainly not. Moreover, if you associate the length of the code with how frequently a symbol is met, the compression will become much more efficient. This technique is usually referred to as Huffman coding.

There are two quite different questions to answer in each implementation of the Huffman method:

- How do you create the optimal code table for the given data stream to be compressed?

- How do you implement coding/decoding routines if the code length isn't fixed?

The first is optional, strictly speaking, as you can use a predefined code table. Doing this has the advantage of making it a one pass operation. However, for small files, as well as specific types of text (like assembler source code for example), an adaptive code table may provide a significantly better compression ratio. So that's where we'll start.

## Adaptive Code Table

Suppose, for example, that we have an innocuous phrase like 'better late than never'. It contains:

5 letters   'e',

4 letters   't',

2 letters   'r',

2 letters   'a',

2 letters   'n',

1 letter   'b',

1 letter   'l',

1 letter   'h',

1 letter   'v'.

_____

total   19

The total storage required is 19 bytes or 152 bits. Now we're going to build the code table for this information. We will use a binary tree structure for our table, although you can in fact choose any structure you like, and some of them are likely to look better than this one! Access to an item in such a table involves a series of comparisons and branches. The process starts at the root of the tree. The test item is compared with the root, or first item in the table. If it is less, we follow the path to the left of the root item, if greater - to the right. This process continues until a match is found, or it reaches a 'leaf' node - one where there are no more entries to the right or left to compare with.

For the above example, we'll define the element of comparison as the 'weight' of the symbol, or the number of times it occurs in the text. Then assume we have prepared the list of our symbols sorted in descending order by weight.

First of all we'll split our list into two parts with approximately the same total weights. If you can't select parts of the same weight, don't worry, make the upper part weightier. To those symbols which fall into the upper part of the list use a 1 as the first bit of their code and for those from the lower part the code start with a 0. This is equivalent to coding a 1 bit for the left hand branch of the tree and a 0 bit for the right.

Then each part of the list should be split in two again and the process repeated until all the sublists obtained contain only one symbol. When the process is finished we only have to trace the codes of the symbols along the tree.

| | v | h | l | b | n | a | r | t | e |
|---|---|---|---|---|---|---|---|---|---|
| symbols | v | h | l | b | n | a | r | t | e |
| frequency | 1 | 1 | 1 | 1 | 2 | 2 | 2 | 4 | 5 |
| | 0 | 0 | 0 | 0 | 0 | 0 | 0 | 1 | 1 |
| | 0 | 0 | 0 | 0 | 0 | 1 | 1 | 0 | 1 |
| codes | 0 | 0 | 0 | 1 | 1 | 0 | 1 | | |
| | 0 | 0 | 1 | 0 | 1 | | | | |
| | 0 | 1 | | | | | | | |

Figure 10.1 Binary Tree for Construction of Huffman Compression Code Table

The result is:

| Letter | Code |
|--------|-------|
| e | 11 |
| t | 10 |
| r | 011 |
| a | 010 |
| n | 0011 |
| b | 0010 |
| l | 00011 |
| h | 00001 |
| v | 00000 |

Clearly, the more frequently a symbol occurs the shorter its code, exactly as we planned. Once the process is complete the proverb looks like this:

001011101011011 000110101011 10000010100011 0011110000011011

*The spaces have been skipped in this example. They are usually coded too, just like the other symbols.*

The total length of the compressed information is 57 bits or 8 bytes. That makes a 42% compression ratio. Not bad.

## Coding the Huffman Algorithm

Having had a look at the general scheme of things, let's get into the details of the actual implementation. As we said above, Huffman coding can be implemented as a one or two pass operation. Using a one pass routine is simple. Your decoder just has to use an existing code table.

However if you really want your compression to shrink something in grand style then you have to use a two pass operation and build the code table yourself. The first pass calculates the frequencies of the symbols in order to create the tree and build the table. The actual coding occurs during the second pass.

If you build your own code table, you obviously have to save it within the compressed file. The alternative, and probably better way, is to save the table of frequencies, to enable reconstruction of the code table during the decoding process. This means we need some way to differentiate the table from the code. The easiest way is to start the compressed file with the code table - use a field specifying the table length and place the table directly after this field.

## Decompression

The decompression sequence remains the same:

- Extract the code from the coded data stream (compressed file).

- Find an appropriate symbol in the code table.

- Send the symbol found to the outgoing data stream (decompressed file).

Our particular implementation is a bit more complicated because the code length isn't fixed yet. The variant we look at here works reasonably quickly but you have to buy this speed in terms of memory. We need more of it in order to allocate the internal table. If the longest code is 16 bits long we need $2^{16}$ x $2^{16}$ = 65536 bytes for the table.

The table is filled specifically so that the code always addresses the appropriate symbol. For our example proverb, with a maximum code length of 5 bits, the table is as shown overleaf.

**Table 10.2 Decompression Table**

| Code | Table Contents | Code | Table Contents | Code | Table Contents |
|---|---|---|---|---|---|
| **00000** | 'v' | **00110** | 'n' | 10000 | |
| **00001** | 'h' | **00111** | 'n' | ..... | 't' |
| 00010 | – | | | **10111** | |
| **00011** | 'l' | 01000 | | | |
| | | ..... | 'a' | 11000 | |
| **00100** | 'b' | **01011** | | ..... | 'e' |
| **00101** | 'b' | | | **11111** | |
| | | 01100 | | | |
| | | ..... | 'r' | | |
| | | **01111** | | | |

*What we've marked is the actual coding 'gene' for each symbol; we have skipped the first three bits that are 0 for every entry. The 'code' column is merely the binary count, from 00000 to 11111.*

Let's have a go at decoding in practice. The first word is 001011101011011. We read the first byte (**00101110**). This is shifted, providing that it's not the first code to be processed - which is never shifted. We then impose a 5 bit mask to leave only the leftmost five bits (**00101**000) and shift it to the right end of the byte (000**00101**). We use this as the address and find the character in the table. Fortunately, it is 'b' for '**b**etter'.

This is placed in the outgoing stream and the next character is fetched. We know the code length for 'b' was only 4 bits, so we set the bit counter to shift the code that follows by that amount. The byte being processed is still the same, but now we shift it to the left by 4 bits corresponding to the length of previously processed code (**1110**—), impose the same 5 bit mask to leave only the leftmost 5 bits (**11100**000), shift it to the right end of the byte (000**11100**) and check the table. It fits! There is 'e' for 'b**e**tter'. And so on. Have a look at ARHH6.ASM for an implementation of Huffman encoding and ARHH7.ASM for decoding.

# Lempel-Ziv-Welch (LZW)

LZW is a compression technique based on the coding of repeated data chains.

Consider the following comparison. Suppose you are packing text files only and you have a vocabulary of 65536 of the most frequently used words. If so, you can code each word of text with two bytes, corresponding to its position within this limited vocabulary. Such a routine would compress your data by half or more. Unfortunately in practice the vocabulary you need is too large to use such a simple method. However the idea seems too elegant to be ignored.

The **LZ77** and **LZSS** versions of the **Lempel-Ziv** algorithm do work somewhat like we imagined above. The difference is that the vocabulary is built using a raw block of the text file to be compressed without any ordering or filtering. The **LZW** version removes the problem of needing a large predefined vocabulary in a rather more sophisticated way. Usually LZW implementations build their own adaptive code tables.

## Building the LZW Code Table

Let's see how this works. We'll compress the message 'acbcbacbcbd' and, as we do so, we'll form a table consisting of all the chains of letters we find in the message. Firstly it's obvious that the message contains only 4 different characters: **a,b,c,d.** So we can add all of them to the table of chains for future reference. Let's assume that in the table of chains they have the numbers **a - 0, b - 1, c - 2, d - 3.** The numbers from 4 and above are free, so we'll set them to -1 which we'll treat in future as an EOF symbol.

The chain table now looks like this:

| Number   | 0 | 1 | 2 | 3 | 4  | 5   |
|----------|---|---|---|---|----|-----|
| Contents | a | b | c | d | -1 | ... |

Now we take the first symbol from the input, - **a**, and look it up in the chain table. It's already there in field 0. Now, we'll work on pairs of symbols; take the first pair, **ac**, and look for it in the table of chains. It isn't in the table, so we place it there in the first free position, number 5. We will keep number 4 as the EOF symbol to indicate the end of the input alphabet table. We also have to output the number 0 to represent the first symbol which was read - **a**.

The contents of the table of chains now looks like this:

```
Number   0  1  2  3  4   5  6   7
Contents a  b  c  d  -1  ac -1  ...
```

Output: 0

The character **c** which we have just read is already in the table at number 2, so we read the next symbol **b** and try to find a pair **cb**. Such a pair isn't present in the table of chains, so we add it to the table as before, this time at position 6 and output the number 2 to represent the last letter read which was **c**.

Now the table of chains looks like this:

```
Number   0  1  2  3  4   5  6  7   8
Contents a  b  c  d  -1  ac cb -1  ...
```

Output: 0,2

The character **b** is also already in the table so we read the next symbol - **c** and search for the pair **bc**. There is no such pair so we again add it to the table at position 7 and output the number 1 to the output stream to represent **b**.

Current contents of the table of chains:

```
Number   0  1  2  3  4   5  6  7  8   9
Contents a  b  c  d  -1  ac cb bc -1  ...
```

Output: 0,2,1

The character **c** is present in the table and the next pair is **cb**, but when we search for this pair we find it at position 6 in the table. So we continue by reading the next symbol and try to find a three symbol fragment: **cba**. This isn't in the table so we add it to the table at position 8 and output number 6 to represent the chain **cb**.

Current contents of the table of chains:

| Number | 0 | 1 | 2 | 3 | 4 | 5 | 6 | 7 | 8 | 9 |
|---|---|---|---|---|---|---|---|---|---|---|
| Contents | a | b | c | d | -1 | ac | cb | bc | cba | ... |

Output: 0,2,1,6

The next symbol is **a**, which is in the table already, so we read the next one, **c**. The chain **ac** is already in the table at position 5. The chain **acb** isn't present in the table so we add it at position 9. The output code for **ac** is 5.

Current contents of the table of chains:

| Number | 0 | 1 | 2 | 3 | 4 | 5 | 6 | 7 | 8 | 9 | 10 |
|---|---|---|---|---|---|---|---|---|---|---|---|
| Contents | a | b | c | d | -1 | ac | cb | bc | cba | acb | ... |

Output: 0,2,1,6,5

The next chain **bcb** we add at position 10 and output code 7. The chain after that, **bd**, we put at position 11 and output code 1. Finally we output code 3 for d and add the reserved code 4 that signals the end of the file.

The final contents of the table of chains is:

| Number | 0 | 1 | 2 | 3 | 4 | 5 | 6 | 7 | 8 | 9 | 10 | 11 |
|---|---|---|---|---|---|---|---|---|---|---|---|---|
| Contents | a | b | c | d | -1 | ac | cb | bc | cba | acb | bcb | bd |

Output: 0,2,1,6,5,7,1,3,4.

Here's the algorithm in general form:

> [ 1 ]  Initialization of the table of chains;
> [ 2 ] [.c.] < - empty;
> [ 3 ] K < - next symbol in the input stream;
> [ 4 ] If [.c.]K is present in the table of chains?
> ( then: [.c.] < - [.c.]K;
>   Go to [ 3 ];
> )
> ( else: add [.c.]K to the table of chains;
>   Output the code for [.c.] to the output stream;
>   [.c.] < - K;
>   Go to [ 3 ];
> )

## Designing a Compression Algorithm

It's worth saying a few things about efficiency at this point. We recommend basing your implementation of a procedure to access the table of chains on a hashing algorithm. A hashing algorithm is a way of encoding table access parameters (for instance by calculating a checksum of their values) to form arithmetic indexes that can be used directly and therefore quickly without searching. Hence, for the fastest possible implementation, it's probably best not to search the table of chains for a substring and in this case we could improve the addressing process as follows:

Encode substrings as (segment, offset) pairs such that, with a substring **ac** in the example above, you use the letter **a** as the segment in the address and the letter **c** as the offset.

Use the table to retrieve the code for the letters **a** - 0, and **c** - 2. Add the two together to form a single arithmetic index by shifting the code for the letter **a** (0) to the left by 4 bits and adding to it the code for letter **c** (2). Do the same thing for strings such as **abc**. If we are searching for substring **acb**, it means that we must have already found the substring **ac**. So instead of using **ac** we use its corresponding code position in the table, calculated according to the usual rules.

Then the segment will be code 5 and the offset code 1, and the arithmetic index is the addition of the two defined above.

You can also use this method for storing the new substring in the table of chains. Instead of storing the complete substring, we need only store a code made up of the initial substring and the last symbol (acb - 5,1).

You need to be aware of the fact that direct LZW compression, as this method is known, runs the risk of exceeding the bounds of your table of chains. There is a simple way to solve this problem. You must control the number of bits in the code and the number of entries in the table of chains. If there's a risk of overflow, stop working at the current point in the input data stream, and output all the necessary codes. Then output a special reserved code - an EOF character - which informs the decompression program that it should interrupt the decoding process and re-initialize all tables and variables. It can then continue working as before.

In the most extreme case, we may have an input data stream of say 11 symbols which could contain 10 unique code sequences. With an input alphabet of 4 symbols this will produce a total of 14 symbols in the table of chains - more than the original data stream. If we have an input alphabet of 256 symbols (that means 8 bits of information to represent each symbol), the table of chains may contain more symbols than can be fitted into the 8 bit-code which is needed for addressing them. So the output code must be larger than 8 bits. For example GIF (Graphics Interchange Format) uses a 12-bit output code.

## Decompression

Decompression uses a somewhat more complex algorithm, but the implementation is actually easier. First of all, let's look at how the algorithm works.

First we initialize the table of chains using the input alphabet, as we did during compression. You can save the original table in the output file during compression, but this obviously increases the size of the compressed file. The other way is to use a fixed input alphabet for all cases. For example we could reserve the first 256 bytes of the table for ASCII characters and then make byte 257 the first control byte.

Remember that the compression was executed in such way that we never met a sequence of codes which we could not transform into a chain. At the beginning, the table of chains contains the following information:

Input chain:   0,2,1,6,5,7,1,3,4

Contents of the table of chains:

Number   0   1   2   3   4   5
Contents   a   b   c   d   -1   ...

We need two variables to contain the current and previous output strings. We read the first code 0 and take the corresponding symbol from the table. This is the letter **a**, which we then output. We then take the second code, 2, locate it in the table and output the letter **c**. Now we can link this with the previous string to make the original string sequence **ac**, which we then put in the first free position in the table. This is at position 5 because position 4 has been reserved for the EOF character.

Contents of the table of chains:

Number   0   1   2   3   4   5   6   7
Contents   a   b   c   d   -1   ac   -1   ...

Output:   ac

We read the next code, 1, find it in the table, output the corresponding symbol **b**, and again link the previous string **c** with first letter of string **b** - **cb** and put it into the table at position 6.

Contents of the table of chains:

Number   0   1   2   3   4   5   6   7   8
Contents   a   b   c   d   -1   ac   cb   -1   ...

Output:   acb

We read the next code, 6, and find it in the table of chains to produce output **cb**, link the previous string - **b** with the first letter of string **cb** - **c** to get a resulting string - **bc**, which we store at position 7.

Contents of the table of chains:

| Number | 0 | 1 | 2 | 3 | 4 | 5 | 6 | 7 | 8 | 9 |
|--------|---|---|---|---|----|----|----|----|----|---|
| Contents | a | b | c | d | -1 | ac | cb | bc | -1 | ... |

Output:  a,c,b,cb,

We read the next code, 5, find it in the table of chains, output string **ac**, concatenate the previous string **cb** with the first letter of string **ac** - **a**. The resulting string is cba which we store in the table at position 8 and so on.

Contents of the table of chains:

| Number | 0 | 1 | 2 | 3 | 4 | 5 | 6 | 7 | 8 | 9 | 10 | 11 |
|--------|---|---|---|---|----|----|----|----|-----|-----|-----|----|
| Contents | a | b | c | d | -1 | ac | cb | bc | cba | acb | bcb | bd |

Output:  a,c,b,cb,ac,bc,b,d

Finally we read code 4 (End Of File) which terminates the algorithm.

There are some special cases that you need to be aware of. One such problem is an input message consisting of a repeated single character such as aaa.... Assuming that we again have a 4 symbol input alphabet and the character a corresponds to code 0, the compression routine will generate the code sequence 0, 5 which corresponds to the code 0 for character a and the code 5 to represent the two following a's - aa. The decompression routine finds code 0 in the table, outputs it as character a, but then doesn't find code 5 because at that time the table contains only the 5 elements 0,1,2,3 and the special code for 4. In this special case the decompression routine must independently generate the codes that correspond to the previous chain - in our example one character a, plus the first character from the previous chain - in our example also character a. So the decompression routine generates a new string aa, stores it in the table at address 5 and outputs the right code - aa.

Here's a generic example of the decompression algorithm:

[ 1 ] Initialization of a string of chains;
  [ 2 ] take the first code: <code>;
  [ 3 ] output the chain for <code> to the output stream of symbols;
  [ 4 ] <old> = <code>;
  [ 5 ] <code> < - following code in a flow of codes;
  [ 6 ] if <code> exists in the table of chains?
  ( then: output a chain for <code> to the output stream of symbols;
    [...] < - compilation for <old>;
    K < - first symbol of compilation for <code>;
    Add [...]K to the table of chains;
    <old> < - <code>;
  )
  ( else: [...] < - compilation for <old>;
    K < - first symbol [...];
    Link [...]K to the output stream of symbols and add it
                          to the table of chains;
    <old> < - <code>
  )
  [ 7 ] go to [ 5 ];

See LZW1.ASM for an implementaion of LZW compression (routines lzw_encode and lzw_decode).

# Run Length Encoding

You may have noticed fragments of data that have repeating patterns like aaaaaaaaaabbbbbbb, and thought it's a terrible waste of memory. Why not transform such fragments into two pieces of information: a single symbol and a number of recurrences of this symbol. Following the most intuitive schema, this would end up something like 9a7b.

However, consider fragments of data which are impossible to compress in this way because each successive byte is unique. To deal with these, let us define an attribute which will indicate that the data following it is compressed. Let this attribute be such that the two high order bits of a byte of data are both set to 1. Then when the two high bits of a byte are set to 1, it defines the attribute to indicate that the byte of data following it is repeated. The remaining 6 bits in the byte can be used for recording the number of recurrences of a byte of data. You will see that, under this schema, the maximum number of any repeated byte is $2^6$-1 i.e. 63 symbols. However, the problem arises of what to do with input data which already has the two high order bits of a byte set to 1. Let us, prior to such a byte being output, write a special byte with the number of recurrences equal to 1 (in other words, 0C1h). Also it's fairly obvious that coding should begin with a minimum of three repeated symbols - with fewer than that the encoding process results in as many or more bytes than in the input stream.

Example:

The input data is (in HEX):

08h, 08h, 3Ah, 3Ah, 3Ah, 3Ah, 0D4h, 0D4h, 0D4h, 0F7h...

The compressed date is (in HEX):

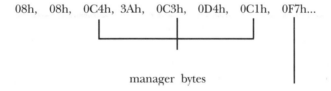

08h, 08h, 0C4h, 3Ah, 0C3h, 0D4h, 0C1h, 0F7h...

manager bytes

This byte has the two high order bits set to 1.

This method of compression is used in the PCX format. There is one major defect in the method. It results in a poor compression ratio if the file to be compressed contains a large number of bytes, for which the two high order bits are equal to 1. In the worst case, where the whole file consists of bytes of value greater than 0BFh, the file size will be doubled. There is at least one way to improve the compression ratio in these circumstances. Instead of using the two high order bits at the start of a byte, we could use just one bit to represent the compression attribute. Then the remaining 7 bits can be used to determine the number of recurrences, with a maximum of 127 bytes. Thus, if the high order bit is set to 1, the following control byte will be repeated the specified number of times. If the high order bit is 0, then the number in the 7 bit field will contain the quantity of uncompressed bytes following the control byte.

Of course we could equally well switch the meaning of the high order bit - that is, by setting it to 0 to determine the number of repeats of the following byte, and to 1 to indicate that the 7-bit field contains the number of uncompressed bytes following; in fact it is this latter method that we have implemented in the source code RLE.ASM on the accompanying disk.

# Arithmetic Compression

The arithmetic coding method is based on the idea of transforming a source file into a single floating point number which will always lie between 0 and 1. Given the resulting number, it is possible to reconstruct the original sequence of symbols in the source file. Let's take a look at how an arithmetic compressor works on a simple example, in this case the message 'ASSEMBLER.' The method is based on the probability of a particular symbol occurring in the message, or in other words, the number of times the symbol occurs divided by the total number of symbols.

**Table 10.3 The Probability of Symbols in 'ASSEMBLER.'**

| Symbol | Probability |
|--------|-------------|
| A | 1/10 |
| B | 1/10 |
| E | 2/10 |
| L | 1/10 |
| M | 1/10 |
| R | 1/10 |
| S | 2/10 |
| .(blank) | 1/10 |

The next step is to define an interval of probability for each symbol ranging from 0 to 1. The size of this interval for each symbol is equal to the probability of it occurring in the message. The actual position of the interval of probability for each symbol is not significant. What's important is that both the coder and decoder use the same rules.

Table 10.4 Spread of Probabilities for Symbols in the Message

| Symbol | Probability | Interval |
|--------|-------------|----------|
| A | 1/10 | 0.00-0.10 |
| B | 1/10 | 0.10-0.20 |
| E | 2/10 | 0.20-0.40 |
| L | 1/10 | 0.40-0.50 |
| M | 1/10 | 0.50-0.60 |
| R | 1/10 | 0.60-0.70 |
| S | 2/10 | 0.70-0.90 |
| . (blank) | 1/10 | 0.90-1.00 |

## The Compression Algorithm

We begin by taking the first symbol from the source file, which is a blank character. At this point in the algorithm, the current interval of probability is equal to 1 - with an upper limit of 1 and a lower limit of 0. The algorithm involves the calculation, at each symbol in the source file, of new upper and lower limits on the interval of probability. The new upper limit is defined as the old lower limit, which is 0, plus the upper limit of the interval of probability for the current symbol, A, which is 0.10, multiplied by the size of the interval, which is 1 at this point. The resulting new upper limit is thus 0.10. The new lower limit is defined similarly - as the old lower limit of the interval, 0, plus the lower limit of the interval of probability of the current symbol, A, which is 0.00, multiplied by the size of the interval which is still 1 at this point. The resulting new lower limit is 0.00. We repeat these steps for each symbol in the source file until there are no more symbols left, at which time we output the final lower limit as the floating point number representing the coded form of the input file.

Let's take a look at an example compression algorithm.

```
LowLimit = 0.0
HighLimit = 1.0
while (( NextChar = GetNextChar()) <> END)
begin
 Interval = HighLimit - LowLimit
 HighLimit = LowLimit + Interval * HighLimitChar ( NextChar )
 LowLimit = LowLimit + Interval * LowLimitChar ( NextChar )
end
Output ( LowLimit )
```

As an example, the values LowLimitChar and HighLimitChar for the letter A are 0.0 and 0.10 (see Table 10.4).

For our example the algorithm will produce the following iterations:

**Table 10.5 The Steps of Arithmetic Compression**

| Char | LowLimit | HighLimit |
|------|----------|-----------|
|  | 0.0 | 1.0 |
| A | 0.0 | 0.1 |
| S | 0.07 | 0.09 |
| S | 0.084 | 0.088 |
| E | 0.0848 | 0.0856 |
| M | 0.0852 | 0.08528 |
| B | 0.085208 | 0.085216 |
| L | 0.0852112 | 0.085212 |
| E | 0.08521136 | 0.085211152 |
| R | 0.085211456 | 0.0852111472 |
| . | 0.0852114704 | 0.0852111472 |

So the compressed form of the source file is the floating point number 0.0852114704

Now let's decompress our compressed source file. In order to do this, we need more information to allow the decompression routine to construct tables similar to those used by the compression routine. The information we need to construct the tables is therefore preserved in the compressed file, and the decompression routine builds a table similar to Table 10.4 used by the compression routine.

The process is as follows. We read the floating point number from the compressed output file and determine the interval within which it fits. Given the interval, we can output the symbol corresponding to that interval, and calculate a new current value of the number on which to repeat the process. In this case the first value is 0.0852114704 which lies within the interval 0.00-0.10, corresponding to the letter A, which can be output. The new interval is then calculated as the upper limit of the interval of probability for the symbol A, 0.10, minus the lower one, 0.00, giving a result of 0.10. The new value of the number is calculated as the old value, 0.0852114704, minus the lower limit of the interval of probability for the symbol, 0.00, divided by the interval, 0.10. The result in this case is 0.0852114704/0.10 or 0.852114704, which lies within the interval 0.7-0.9, and corresponds to the letter S, and so on.

The usual method to terminate both the compression and decompression algorithms is to assume a special EOF symbol at the end of the source file to indicate end of file. The decompression algorithm stops processing when it outputs an EOF symbol.

A sample decompression algorithm would appear as follows:

```
Number = ReadNumber ()
[ 1 ]
 Char = FindCharWhichIntervalContainsNumber (Number)
 Output (Char)
 Interval = HighLimitChar (Char) - LowLimitChar (Char)
 Number = Number - LowLimitChar (Char)
 Number = Number / Interval
Goto [ 1 ]
```

*In this example there is no exit. A suitable exit method would use the special character EOF (end of file) in the data.*

Let's take a quick look at how we might actually implement the algorithm in reality. To be really fast it should use integer arithmetic rather than floating point. It's possible to use 16-bit or 32-bit registers to represent the limits. If we use 16-bit registers we can make the limits significant to an interval of 0 and 1, represented respectively by 00000h and 0FFFFh. In accordance with our scheme, during our calculations we will maintain significance on the left - in other words, results of calculations will be left-justified. To take the simplification one stage further, let's work to base 10, with decimal values. Then 0 and 1 will be represented by 00000 and 99999 instead of 00000h and 0FFFFh. In addition, we will take the first symbol to be A. The upper limit of probability for A, equal to 0.1 will be represented by a value 09999 (because 1 is represented by 99999). The lower limit is equal to 0.0, and under our decimal system we record this as 00000.

        LowLimit = 00000
        HighLimit = 09999

We see that the high order digits of the numbers are equal. The feature of this version of the algorithm is that when they do not change, they can be output. This can be achieved by a shift of the registers left by one digit. Calculating the new high limit is done by shifting the digit 9 into the right of the current high limit, and similarly for the new low limit shifting the digit 0.

        LowLimit = 00000
        HighLimit = 99999

During the calculation, the low and high limits become closer until the high order digits become equal. When that happens, the high order digit is output. When all symbols are processed, the last two digits should be output.

Table 10.6 Integer Implementation of Arithmetic Coding

| NextChar | LowLimit | HighLimit | Interval | Output Code |
|----------|----------|-----------|----------|-------------|
|          | 00000    | 9999      | 100000   |             |
| A        | 00000    | 09999     |          |             |
| Shift 0  | 00000    | 99999     | 100000   | .0          |
| S        | 70000    | 89999     | 20000    |             |
| S        | 84000    | 87999     |          |             |
| Shift 8  | 40000    | 79999     | 40000    | .08         |
| E        | 48000    | 55999     | 8000     |             |
| M        | 52000    | 52799     |          |             |
| Shift 5  | 20000    | 27999     | 8000     | .085        |
| B        | 20800    | 21599     |          |             |
| Shift 2  | 08000    | 15999     | 8000     | .0852       |
| L        | 11200    | 11999     |          |             |
| Shift 1  | 12000    | 19999     | 8000     | .08521      |
| E        | 13600    | 15199     |          |             |
| Shift 1  | 36000    | 51999     | 16000    | .085211     |
| R        | 45600    | 47199     |          |             |
| Shift 4  | 56000    | 71999     | 16000    | .0852114    |
| .        | 70400    | 71999     |          |             |
| Shift 7  | 04000    | —         |          | .08521147   |
| Shift 0  | 40000    | —         |          | .085211470  |
| Shift 4  | 00000    | —         |          | .0852114704 |

There is, however, a problem with this method which has to be overcome.
During the execution of this method of implementing the algorithm, a situation
can arise when, for example, the high limit will become equal to 50000, and the

low to 49999. All subsequent steps will not change these limits and the algorithm will not produce a final result. One of the possible solutions might be to decide that if the high order digits do not coincide, we check successive significant digits. If, for the low limit, the digit is equal to 9, and the upper limit digit is 0, we discard the second digits (0 and 9), and other digits of the limits are shifted to the left in accordance with the rules described above.

If during execution, we flag the fact that we have discarded digits (for example in a special variable), we can continue the actions described above until the high order digits of our limits do coincide. We then output the concurrent high order digit and after it a sequence of 9s or 0s, depending on which limit (high or low) the high order digits became equal to.

# Summary

Data compression is a complicated subject. It's also an essential everyday tool.

Don't rush off to write your own compression utility right after you've finished this chapter. There are quite enough utilities written already. If you really do have something which needs compressing within your application, try one of the utilities which are already available to do the compression for you (look at Appendix A for details of one) or, at least, use the subroutines we supply on the accompanying disk.

You would also be well advised to steer clear of the complications of direct access to stacked or double spaced disks. Indeed, if you are already using DOS 6.x DoubleSpace to conserve space on your disk, you should be aware that you may not gain much in the way of space-saving by compressing your files again. This is because most compressed files tend not to have any of the characteristics which make them susceptible again to the compression techniques we've described - for example, no repeated strings, and apart from RLE encoded files, flat (uniform) frequency counts. Indeed, as you may deduce from what you have learnt in this chapter - for instance taking the example described in the section on LZW coding, where you have 4 unique elements in an input stream of 11 characters which in the worst possible case generate 10 unique combinations, plus the 4 elements generating 14 'compressed' elements - compressing data without such features may even result in a larger file than you started with!

Sometimes, however, a real time compression is badly needed, usually to decompress something previously compressed. This is essential when trying to read some of the 'standard' graphic files formats, such as PCX, GIF, TIFF and so on, each with its own unique version of a compression technique.

## CHAPTER ELEVEN

# PC Video Architecture

## Introduction

Writing about graphics today is quite a challenge. Anyone who has spent the last
few years working with a PC will remember the golden days of text mode. All
applications looked the same. All you had to do was keep choosing from
numerous pulldown menus.

Graphics mode was strictly for graphics editors, and as for high resolution and
256-color graphics modes, these were only used by bearded and barefoot I(mage)
A(nalysis) gurus. About the trickiest thing to be done was to push your VGA
into mode 13h and show an array of bytes in 256 (well, at least 64) shades of
gray.

This was a time when smooth image scrolling or panning was something quite
exciting. There were lots of SVGA adapters around, but SVGA programming was
a mysterious and dangerous field.

We're not going to be able to completely demystify video hardware programming
or cover the entire subject inside out in this one chapter. What we will try to do
is describe the different approaches to graphics programming up to and
including TrueColor mode. We'll look at the classification of memory models
rather than at the details of circuit design. We'll provide tested and optimized
examples of the basic techniques, which together with the examples from the
next chapter will form the foundation for your own graphics library.

# From EGA to TrueColor Adapters

Although there is no point in dwelling on ancient history, it is instructive to first run briefly through the genealogy of the modern video adapter. Unless you understand the evolution of these beasts, you'll find it hard to relate to some of the inherited design features.

## The IBM Enhanced Graphics Adapter (EGA)

The IBM Enhanced Graphics Adapter was released in early 1985. It is called 'Enhanced' because, unlike its predecessors, it can display 16-color text, graphics images with up to 640-by-350 resolution and more colors (16 from 64). Although the resolution and color capabilities of the EGA are no longer anything to write home about, at the time they were considered to be a breakthrough. The availability of inexpensive EGAs and color software based on the adapter's capabilities quickly made the EGA standard a defacto.

## The Multi-Color Graphics Array (MCGA)

The Multi-Color Graphics Array, introduced in 1987, is the video subsystem used in the junior models (25 and 30) of the PS/2 series. A key difference between the MCGA and EGA is that the MCGA generates analog RGB video signals, so that with its 18 bit Digital to Analog Converter (DAC), the MCGA can display as many as 256 different colors simultaneously from a palette of 262,144 ($2^{18}$) colors.

## The Video Graphics Array (VGA)

The Video Graphics Array, which was introduced in April 1987, was strictly speaking a chip in the video subsystem of the PS/2 models 50, 60, and 80. Nevertheless, the abbreviation VGA is now used to refer to the video standard which was the standard in PC graphics programming. The VGA interface is almost identical to that of the EGA, however the VGA supports a higher display resolution (640 by 480 in 16 color mode) and a 256 color mode with a resolution of 320 by 200. Like the MCGA, the VGA uses a DAC to generate up to 256 colors at a time from a possible 262,144. It also includes a larger percentage of readable video registers, hardware detection by means of BIOS (VGA BIOS Extension), as well as more space for fonts.

Table 11.1 The VGA 'Standard' Display Modes

| Mode# | Number of Colors | Resolution | Display Type |
|-------|------------------|------------|--------------|
| 0/1 | 16/256K | 40x25 | Text |
| 2/3 | 16/256K | 80x25 | Text |
| 4/5 | 4/256K | 320x200 | Graphics |
| 6 | 2/256K | 640x200 | B/W Graphics |
| 7 | mono | 80x25 | Text |
| 0D | 16/256K | 320x200 | Graphics |
| 0E | 16/256K | 640x200 | Graphics |
| 0F | mono | 640x350 | Graphics |
| 10 | 16/256K | 640x350 | Enhanced Graphics |
| 11 | 2/256K | 640x480 | Graphics |
| 12 | 16/256K | 640x480 | Graphics |
| 13 | 256/256K | 320x200 | Graphics |

Text mode resolutions are expressed as 'TextCharacters x TextRows' and the graphics mode resolutions as 'Pixels x PixelsRows'.

# The Super VGA

The Super VGA appeared around the end of 1987. You could say that NEC Home Electronics created the first SVGA with its adapter that supported a 800x600 resolution in 256-color mode. IBM replied with the 8514/A which offered an even higher, though interlaced, resolution of up to 1024x768, together with an onboard graphics co-processor.

Unfortunately, IBM didn't publish the hardware specification for the 8514/A, but instead offered programmers a set of software hooks called The Application Interface. This started a wave of reverse engineering. Could this have been one of the reasons why the 8514/A failed as an industry standard? Whatever the reason, it did and other manufacturers were ready with their own SVGA cards.

There was no standardization whatsoever in the jungle of SVGAs. Take a look at the following list of SVGA video mode numbers from different manufacturers:

**Table 11.2 1024x768 16 Color Video Mode Numbers for Different SVGAs**

| Firm | Video mode # |
|------|--------------|
| ATI Technologies, Inc. | 55h (planar) or 65h (packed) |
| Chips & Technologies | 72h |
| Oak Technology | 56h |
| Realtek Semiconductors Co.Ltd. | 27h |
| Trident Microsystems | 5Fh |
| Western Digital | 5Dh |

Everyone was waiting for IBM to put an end to the chaos with its XGA standard, but unfortunately for IBM, this also failed to be a success.

# The Video Electronics Standards Association (VESA)

The Video Electronics Standards Association was given the task of setting the SVGA standard. The VESA standard versions 1.0 and 1.1 (1989-1990) defined 8 calls at INT 10h function 4Fh, which are now referred to as the VESA BIOS Extension. The main advantages of these are as follows:

- The information service provided by the extended BIOS almost completely cut out the problem of hardware detection.

- Using the VESA BIOS extensions, you can obtain and set all accessible video modes, including vendor-specific ones, and also get all the information you need for programming.

- Bank switching: you can do this either with a special call or you can get the address of a vendor-specific function and do it yourself (this is probably the faster way). We'll discuss this later.

We'll look at the VESA BIOS Extension in greater detail later in this chapter. Since almost all modern SVGAs now support VESA, either in video BIOS or a vendor-provided software driver, it is worth devoting a few pages to this subject. Most of the older non VESA SVGA cards can be made VESA compatible by obtaining a small TSR, usually available in the public domain.

## Programming SVGAs without VESA Support

We still have a gap in our coverage of adapters because there are some old SVGA adapters which have neither VESA extensions in ROM BIOS nor have an accessible VESA driver. However, these boards have the capability to display more colors in higher resolution. Programming them to do this is no easy task.

It is however worth a try. The key issue is to master the vendor-specific functions for bank switching, while gleaning the somewhat mystical knowledge you need about the numbers of the available video modes. There are three different scenarios for this:

**1**   You have your own SVGA card and you want to use its SVGA modes in your own code. To do it, you'll have to look through your SVGA card manual to find the information below. Once you've found it it's not actually that hard. You require:

●   A list of screen mode values for the card's SVGA modes

●   A list of register port addresses and how those registers work, e.g. TSENG and Trident cards have different addresses and registers for memory mapping. This information is very hard to get (i.e. write to card manufacturer)

●   Also, any information on the special features such as zoom windows, 32 x 32 pixel characters, etc.

**2**   You are developing an application for resale and you'd like it to support such SVGAs. This is a lot harder. However, there is a way around it. First of all you need to compile information on all the possible SVGA adapters your application needs. Don't bore your users with questions like 'Pick your SVGA from the list below', when you can easily find this out for yourself (although, unfortunately, some SVGA cards are hard to recognize). There are as many cryptic ways to recognize one particular SVGA card as there are SVGA cards. As soon as you find out which SVGA you've got, tune the application up for it and let it fly.

3   Buy a professional toolkit such as MetaWindow or Genus, which supports virtually every SVGA around. Although defeating the purpose of learning to program SVGAs, it offers total compatibility. You are unlikely to obtain every SVGA card and be able to test your program out on it.

## Video Accelerators

Whether you like it or not, MS Windows is the de facto standard in PC operating systems today. However, because of its universality, the GDI (Graphic Driver Interface, the 'video heart' of MS Windows) is rather slow. In response to this, a large number of video accelerators have appeared to improve its performance.

Sophisticated graphics co-processors have a long history, but they were always deemed to be a special class of video device for image processing, animation and so on. Almost all of them support graphics primitives ranging from the simple to the complex, such as line and circle drawing, polygon filling, zooming and so on. IBM's 8514/A, mentioned earlier, was one of the first intended for common use. Texas Instruments with their TMS34010 and TMS34020 chips, and Hitachi's HD 63484 were also popular.

Most graphics operations can be reduced to a few simple operations. Line drawing is only pixel plotting. Drawing rectangular graphic images is 'blitting', or in other words, rapidly copying data on to the screen. These very low level operations (pixel plotting, blitting) are called primitives. The operations are very simple (i.e. primitive), but everything depends on them. The faster the primitive, the quicker the operation, which is why some primitives are done through hardware accelerator cards instead of software. Line drawing, for example, requires simple (for straight lines) and not so simple (for curves) arithmetic. An accelerator chip can do the maths far faster than the PCs processor chip.

Since the arrival of MS Windows 3, the number of video adapters of this kind has doubled each year. The most popular chips are the S3 86C928 and CL-GD5426, and the most powerful systems are probably Diamond Stealth Pro and Genoa Windows VGA24, both supporting the TrueColor mode.

# An Outline of PC Video Architecture

## The Anatomy of a Video System

Here's a simple schematic of a modern video system:

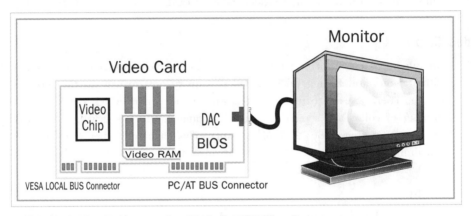

**Figure 11.1 The Structure of a Modern PC Video System**

Now a brief description of all the elements of this diagram.

## Video RAM

This is RAM on the Video card which holds the graphical images, plus additional information such as RAM character sets. It is not a part of the PC's main RAM, but is seen by the PC at addresses 0A000h-0BFFFh.

### DAC - Digital to Analog Converter

This converts color signals in digital format to analog (i.e. continuous varying) voltages used by the video monitor.

### BIOS

This is a set of low-level routines that control all the standard devices in the PC such as the keyboard, disk and video subsystem. These routines are built into the ROM BIOS chips. In theory, the BIOS is written so there is a standard interface to different brands of devices. The part of BIOS that controls the video subsystem is mounted onto the video adapter card.

### Video Chip

An integrated circuit or two (on the video card) which connects video memory with the monitor. Placing values in video memory puts images on the monitor screen. There are also control registers on the video chip which control the number of colors and screen size, etc. It is quite hard work driving a video card, but the BIOS does about 95% of the work. This chapter teaches you the remaining 5%.

### Raster Scan

The video chip scans sequentially through video memory between 50-70 times per second (depending on screen resolution), creating a stream of electronic signals which are output to the monitor. This stream is referred to as the raster scan, and can be imagined as a very fast pen which redraws the screen at a very fast rate. It starts at the top left, then draws each line left to right. When it gets to the bottom, it moves to the top of the screen again. The movement time from bottom to top is called the vertical retrace and is useful for synchronizing displays with the raster. If an image is placed in screen memory without regard to raster scan and the raster scan catches it while drawing the image then flickering will occur.

## Video Memory

The video RAM or Video Memory (VM) is a part of the video subsystem where data to be displayed is stored.

The logical structure of VM, or in other words, the way in which a VM's bytes translate into the pixels of a raster display, varies for different video modes. If you want to use direct memory techniques, you need a good understanding of the memory organization of VM. It's a bit like using a hard disk. To work with files in DOS, you don't need to know the details of the FAT, root directory and so on. However, as soon as you need to write special bytes directly to special sectors (for example for copy protection), you have to master these more sophisticated techniques.

We shall take a detailed look at how VM is used by different display modes later on in the chapter. Whatever display mode we use however, the video memory can be categorized under two headings - namely 'Planar' and 'Non-Planar'.

## Planar Display Memory

Planar display memory is made up of two or more areas of memory addressed in parallel - these are usually called planes or bit planes.

With 16 color display modes the VM is arranged as four bit planes All four planes share the same address space in memory, starting at A000h:0000h. In other words, it's as if there were four areas of memory superimposed on top of each other. Writing a byte of data to memory location A000:1234h for example, would therefore fill not just one byte, but rather the four bytes - one in each plane - that share that particular address. It is up to the programmer to select which planes are written to. Writing a byte of data will place that byte in those planes the programmer has pre-selected. This could be one, two, three or all four planes.

Each of the four bit planes used for 16 color display modes is used to contain one bit of a 4 bit pixel color code, so you have $2^4$ = 16 colors. Adapters decode a particular color code by referring to color palette tables.

## Non-Planar Display Memory (Packed Pixel)

With non-planar display modes, there is only one plane of memory. One or more bytes of VM is used to store the color code for each pixel displayed on the screen. The number of bytes used per pixel differs between display modes. On standard VGA, there is only one byte per pixel. On HighColor and TrueColor cards, there are two or three bytes per pixel modes.

## Addressing Video Memory

The area of system memory reserved for VM lies between memory locations A000:0000h and B000:FFFFh. Area A000:AFFFh is used for graphic modes, while B000-BFFFh is used for text modes. Although memory from C000:0000h onwards is available in the system memory map, it is usually used by disk drive controllers. This 128K byte area of memory - consisting of two 64K banks of memory - used to be considered by IBM as enough space for the video, 64K for each adapter of a possible two-monitor system.

The VM of modern adapters, however, often needs to be 2Mb or more. A quick calculation will tell you why it needs to be so big. Suppose you want a TrueColor mode, a non-planar VM where 3 bytes of video memory are used to store the data for each pixel on the screen, at a resolution of 1024x768. Such a screen would require a total of 1024*768*3, or about 2.3 Mb of video memory in total. TrueColor is a mode which offers 16 or so million shades of color, using three bytes per pixel to present photographic quality images.

## Bank Switching

There is a special window in the address space of the CPU which is used to access the video buffer. The segment address of the upper left hand corner of the window is A000h and the size of the window is 64K. Therefore, if you want to read from or write to a VM 2Mb or more in size, you have to use a more sophisticated addressing method called bank switching. Talking of which, the idea of bank switching is much older than LIM 4.0. The first implementation of PC memory bank switching was the LIM (Lotus Intel Microsoft) introduced in 1985, which allowed extra banks of memory to be added to the memory map. This is what underpins Expanded Memory (EMS), but the LIM name is now forgotten, and everyone calls it EMS. The final version was LIM 4.0, released in 1987, marking a milestone in bank switching's 30-40 year history.

Bank switching is very important, because the video card has from 512Kb to 3Mb (maybe more depending on the card) of video RAM. Unfortunately, the PC can only see 64Kb (at its own addresses A000h-AFFFh) at a time. So for a 1024 x 768 in 256 color mode (occupying 768x1024 bytes), there are 12 banks (0-11). To read or write from the entire screen image, the PC must select each bank (which maps it into the A000h-AFFFh area) in turn, then read or write bytes there.

This bank switching is also known as windowing, or in other words, moving a 64Kb window through the entire video RAM area.

## Vesa Memory Windowing

If you're working in SVGA mode, you'll be using bank switching a lot. As different adapters are incompatible, you can't use SVGA modes without understanding bank switching. Each adapter has an almost unique bank switching method. The VESA SVGA standard specifies the most common approaches.

VESA calls mapped-in video memory banks 'windows', and there are two possible configurations, Single or Dual windows.

If your SVGA has a single window organization, you can write from and read to one bank which is usually 64K in size. If your hardware supports a Dual window configuration, you can read from and write to two memory banks. This is useful for moving data blocks in the video memory.

With a dual window, one window is for reading bytes, the other is for writing. For example, reading memory in the PC's address space (A000h-AFFFh) reads from whichever bank in video memory the read window has been mapped to. The write window might even be over a different bank. All this means that the following code doesn't do quite what it appears to do:

```
mov  ax,0a000h
mov  es,ax    ; Both segments refer to a000
mov  ds,ax

mov  cx,32000
xor  di,di
mov  si,di
rep  movsw
```

What it appears to do is copy 64000 bytes (32000 words) back over itself. What it actually does is copy 64000 bytes from the read window to the write window. With a single window, copying bytes in the SVGA memory is a slower task, because you have to copy first from video RAM to system RAM, and then back to another location in video memory.

We've used the term bank switching dozens of times without really giving you a full explanation. Now's the time to take a closer look at what it means, particularly for pixel addressing. The main idea is that you have less address space than accessible memory. You therefore have to shift the beginning of the addressing window to access the parts of the memory you want at any one particular time.

For pixel addressing, this means that all you need is the bank number and offset within the bank. The actual calculation depends on the size of the bank and its granularity.

## Window Granularity

This refers to the smallest step you can take to change the offset of the upper left hand corner of the window in the video memory. It's like reading a book - the window is your eyes looking at the paragraph that you are reading. As you shift to the next paragraph, the window is moved. The window in the PC is the area of memory at A000h which is moved to (i.e. mapped onto) a new area in VM in exactly the same way as reading the book.

If the granularity is equal to the window size, then all you can do is switch from one window position to another. If it is smaller you can move the window smoothly. For example, the Paradise SVGA has a window granularity of 4K, therefore its windows offsets can be 0, 4K, 8K and so on.

## Color Palettes and Colors

A color palette is a special table used to translate pixel color codes stored in video memory into the actual color of a pixel displayed on the CRT. Palette tables allow you to display more colors than your pixel encoding technique permits (providing of course that your hardware permits it).

There are really two different color palette tables used by the VGA. First, there is the EGA Color Palette table consisting of 16 8 bit color palette registers (only 6 bits of each register are used) and second, there are the DAC Color registers of which there are 256 18 bit registers.

With 16 color modes, each pixel color code is defined in video memory as a 4 bit code - this allows a possible 16 different colors ($2^4$) to be displayed simultaneously on the screen at any one time. The color code stored in video memory is not used to define the pixel color itself however, but rather to index to one of the registers in the EGA Color Palette table.

With EGA machines, it is the 6 bit color code stored in each EGA color palette register that defines the actual pixel color sent to the monitor. Note that whilst the 'Enhanced' EGA uses all 6 bits of this code - thus allowing 16 simultaneously displayed colors to be chosen from a palette of 64 colors ($2^6$) - the 'Standard' EGA only uses 4 of these bits allowing us to select from a palette of only 16 colors ($2^4$).

With VGA machines operating in 16 color modes, the setup is slightly different. The 4 bit code stored in video memory is still used as an index to an EGA Color Palette register, only this time the 6 bit color code stored in this register is not sent straight to the monitor but is used instead as an index to one of the VGA's 256 DAC Color registers. Once selected, it is the 18 bit code in the indexed DAC color register that is used to define the pixel color displayed on the screen. Note, that because the code used to index the DAC color register consists of only 6 bits, we can only use the first 64 DAC color registers when using 16 color modes. The net result of all this is that we can display 16 colors simultaneously from a palette of 64 colors and each of the colors in the 64 color palette can be selected from a possible 256K ($2^{18}$) different colors.

With 256 color VGA modes, the color code stored in video memory is an 8 bit code. Because this 8 bit code allows numbers in the range from 0 to 255 ($2^8$) this code is used to directly index a DAC Color register without having to go via the EGA Palette Color registers. We can therefore simultaneously display 256 colors from a palette of 256K possible colors.

With HighColor and TrueColor modes, the color codes stored in video memory are themselves used to define the pixel colors to be displayed on the screen. Palette or DAC Color registers are therefore not used as there is no need to translate the stored codes into color codes. In theory, you could have a palette for a HighColor mode that would choose 64K from a possible 16M, but it would have to be a rather large table.

You can perform some pretty good tricks using palettes. You can 'draw' lots of pixels at once by changing their palette entry from the background to a foreground color. With VGA/SVGA cards, a palette change is like running a magic brush over a painting. Rub this brush over the painting and every dot drawn in one color will be changed to another. Suppose there is a picture on the screen. By changing all colors in the palette to black, the screen will clear. Another picture could then be drawn (while the palette colors are all black), then voilà, change back to the correct palette, and the new picture magically appears. This is how screen fades are done.

# BIOS Video Programming - An Overview

Although it's hard to believe, there was once a time when programmers relied on video BIOS to perform most graphics hardware programming. Today, BIOS is mostly used to return hardware information and to control adapter settings such as modes. It's rarely used to actually draw anything on the screen. It's not only slow, but even with all the BIOS extensions you can't really use it to PutPixel in HighColor and TrueColor modes.

An actual call to the Video BIOS is done by executing an interrupt 10h with the desired function number placed in the AH register and with other registers set, if necessary - we shall see how to do this in a little while.

When you program using BIOS functions, you are using a set of sub-routines or functions. These routines may be part of a particular ROM BIOS or any of its extensions, or they may belong to a higher level set of functions like the Borland Graphics Interface (BGI) driver or the Graphic Driver Interface (GDI) of MS Windows. What unites them is trust. You trust something or someone - IBM, Microsoft or whoever else - to do your graphics programming for you, as opposed to using homemade graphics routines which may not work on all adapters, but are as fast and as imaginative as you want to make them. BIOS routines are slow because they have to work in every screen mode. This adds a lot of baggage to the code. So drawing a dot is a slowish process. By contrast, drawing routines (user programmed) are usually done for one screen mode, and therefore can be optimized for that mode.

Obviously, if you are designing commercial applications to sell, you have to consider compatibility with different hardware configurations, future upgrades and so on. From the very beginning, IBM suggested BIOS style programming as the easiest solution to these problems. However, this idea has become less useful with the introduction of a new generation of hardware and software. An alternative to using the BIOS is to use the BGI driver, Windows GDI or a professional toolkit to draw for you. This insulates you from the underlying hardware and makes life much easier.

However, problems may still arise. Try testing the performance ratio of some SVGA adapters and the results differ drastically under MS Windows when compared to writing directly into memory. Moreover, there often isn't any correlation between functions. There were gaps for almost every card on the mode scale or operation scale (polygons, text scrolling, patterns, etc.) in which operation speed vanishes. If you want maximum performance and control, you can't always rely on drivers written by someone else. To really do the job well, you may have to roll up your sleeves and write your own.

## VGA BIOS

The VGA 'Video' BIOS provides 23 basic functions that work with the display. Twenty are inherited from the EGA (0-13h), and the VGA itself added 1Ah-1Ch. But the video BIOS does none of the primitives, such as line, circle or bar. The only primitive it has is PutPixel, but it's too slow to be used.

In addition to these common functions, each manufacturer supplies a unique BIOS extension. There is also a VESA BIOS extension for Super VGA adapters, including 8 sub-function calls via function 4Fh.

## Setting the Video mode using BIOS calls

The video mode can be set by using function 00h of the Video BIOS interrupt 10h. To do this, we simply place the function call number into AH (i.e. 0), the mode number into AL and then execute an interrupt 10h, like this:

```
Mov ax,0013h    ; Setting video mode 13h
int 10h         ; 320x200, 256 colors.
```

## Modifying the Color Registers Using BIOS Calls

There are several BIOS calls that you can use to read to or write from the VGA DAC color registers. You can set or read a single DAC color register, a group of DAC color registers, or select or read the DAC color page. Below is a list of the BIOS calls relating to the DAC color registers:

**Table 11.3 Function 10h**

| Sub-function | Description |
| --- | --- |
| 10h | Set individual DAC color register |
| 12h | Set block of DAC color registers |
| 13h | Set DAC color subset |
| 15h | Get individual DAC color register |
| 17h | Get block of DAC color registers |
| 1Ah | Read DAC color page state |
| 1Bh | Sum DAC color registers to gray shades |

The following example shows how you can set DAC color registers using BIOS:

```
mov ax,1012h   ;AH = Function 10h
               ;AL = Subfunction 12h (Set block of Color registers)
mov bx,First   ;BX = start DAC Color Register (0 to 255)
mov cx,Count   ;CX = number of DAC Color Registers to set (1 to 256)
les dx,Palette ;ES:DX point to Palette table (R,G,B value)
int 10h        ;do it
```

# VESA BIOS Extensions

The VESA extensions provide a common solution to the problem of adapter incompatibility and thus greatly simplifies the task of programming a range of SVGA systems. The main advantages VESA provides are:

- A standard way to get information on the SVGA modes supported by a particular adapter.

- A standard table of SVGA modes, including the manufacturer's unique modes.

- A standard procedure for bank switching.

The VESA BIOS extensions (v1.0, 1.1) define 8 sub-function calls via INT 10h, function 4Fh. At the time of writing, most manufacturers have incorporated the VESA Extensions into their cards, either as part of the ROM BIOS or as an additional VESA compatible driver.

Each function, when called, will return a status in AX. The meaning of each of the possible values reported in AX is:

| | |
|---|---|
| AL = 4Fh | Function supported |
| AL != 4Fh | Function not supported |
| AH = 00h | OK |
| AH = 01h | The call failed |

The eight VESA calls consist of information service functions and action service functions and are as follows:

## Function 00h Return SVGA Information

Used to confirm VESA compatibility for the adapter and get vendor-specific information about the hardware. A 256 byte buffer should be reserved to hold the return information.

Input:
    AX:    Set to 4F00h
    ES:DI far pointer to the 256 byte buffer.

Output:
    AX:    Status

Table 11.4 Table Located at ES:DI

| Name | Offset | Size(bytes) | Description |
|------|--------|-------------|-------------|
| VESASignature | 0 | 4 | Signature (usually 'VESA') |
| VESAVersion | 4 | 2 | VESA version number |
| OEMStringPtr | 6 | 4 | Far pointer to OEM string |
| Capabilities | 10 | 4 | Capabilities (currently undefined) |
| VideoModePtr | 14 | 4 | Far pointer to the mode table |
| MemoryAmount | 18 | 2 | 64K memory blocks installed (version 1.1) |

The higher byte of the VESA version field specifies the major version number and the lower one the minor version number. Version 1.2 is the latest.

The OEMStringPtr field is a far pointer to a null terminated OEM-defined string, which may be used to identify the video chip, adapter and configuration. There are no standards as to what you will find here, but you will probably find the manufacturer's name and adapter type.

The Capabilities field is currently reserved. In a future version, it may specify general features of the adapter.

The mode table is simply a list of the supported mode numbers, terminated by 0FFFFh. Each mode number is a 16 bit word defining either VESA standard SVGA or a manufacturer-specific mode. Standard VESA modes begin with 100h. Vendor specific modes cover the range 14h-7Fh, with the exception of 6Ah which is the original VESA mode.

The MemoryAmount field contains the size of video memory in 64K blocks. For example, an adapter with 1M would return 10h.

## Function 01h Return SVGA Mode Information

Used to get information about a particular SVGA mode. Again, a 256-byte buffer should be reserved to hold the return information.

Input:

     AX:    Set to 4F01h

     ES:DI  far pointer to the 256 byte buffer.

Output:

     AX:    Status

**Table 11.5 Structure of the ES:DI Table**

| Name | Offset | Size(bytes) | Description |
| --- | --- | --- | --- |
| ModeAttributes | 0 | 2 | Mode attributes |
| WinAAttributes | 2 | 1 | Window A attributes |
| WinBAttributes | 3 | 1 | Window B attributes |
| WinGranularity | 4 | 2 | Window granularity |
| WinSize | 6 | 2 | Window size |
| WinASegment | 8 | 2 | Segment address of Window A |
| WinBSegment | 10 | 2 | Segment address of Window B |
| WinFuncPtr | 12 | 4 | Address of the Window Function Call |
| BytesPerScnLine | 16 | 2 | Bytes per scan line |
| XResolution | 18 | 2 | Horizontal resolution |
| YResolution | 20 | 2 | Vertical resolution |
| XCharSize | 22 | 1 | Character cell width |
| YCharSize | 23 | 1 | Character cell height |
| NumberOfPlanes | 24 | 1 | Number of bit planes |
| BitsPerPixel | 25 | 1 | Total number of bits per pixel |
| NumberOfBanks | 26 | 1 | Number of memory banks |
| MemoryModel | 27 | 1 | Memory model type |
| BankSize | 28 | 1 | Size of memory bank in Kb |
| NumberOfPages | 29 | 1 | Number of display pages available |
| . | 30 | 1 | Reserved |

For version 1.2, the SVGA Mode information block contains 6-7 more fields.

Fields with offsets 0 - 16 are obligatory, from 18 onwards are optional. The optional part of the Mode Information Block is mostly used for manufacturer-specific modes. If this information is available, bit 1 of the Mode attributes will be set.

**Table 11.6 Mode Attributes Bit Meanings**

| Bit | Description |
|-----|-------------|
| 0 | Set to 1 if the hardware configuration supports this mode |
| 1 | Set to 1 if the optional mode information is available |
| 2 | Set to 1 if the BIOS functions (PutPixel,..) support this mode |
| 3 | Set to 1 if the mode is color (register and memory configuration not the monitor type) |
| 4 | Set to 1 if the mode is graphics |
| 5-15 | Reserved |

When programming in both VESA standard and vendor-specific SVGA modes using BIOS functions, you should remember that some functions are not supported. Sometimes only the most useful functions, such as PutPixel or write string, are present. You determine which calls are supported through this function call using bit 2.

The 01h function also returns information on the windowing method that particular mode uses. You can get it by reading the status bits of the WinA(B)Attributes field.

**Table 11.7 Status Bits for the Win_Attributes Field**

| Bit | Description |
|-----|-------------|
| 0 | Set to 1 if particular window exists |
| 1 | Set to 1 if the window is readable |
| 2 | Set to 1 if the window is writeable |
| 3-7 | Reserved |

You will, of course, remember what the Window Granularity is from earlier on. It's the smallest step allowed when the addressing Window is moved (switched) within video memory.

The WinSize usually is 64K or 32K. The WinA(B)Segment is simply the CPU segment address for the window. The WinFuncPtr is the address of the routine that changes the starting offset of a Window, or in other words, executes a bank switch. A far call to this address is much faster than using the BIOS call 4F05h. Unlike the BIOS call, the registers are not preserved by a direct call, and AX will not contain any return information.

The optional X and Y resolution information will be in either character cell units (for text modes) or pixel units (for graphics modes). The XCharSize and YCharSize are character cell sizes in pixel units. NumberOfPlanes is usually 4 for 16 color modes and 1 for 256 and higher modes. The BitsPerPixel field determines the number of colors available. The Memory Model is defined below:

**Table 11.8 Memory Model**

| Value | Memory Model |
|-------|-------------|
| 0 | Text Mode |
| 1 | CGA Graphics |
| 2 | Hercules Graphics |
| 3 | 4-plane planar |
| 4 | Packed pixel |
| 5 | Non-chain 4, 256-color |
| 6 | HighColor & TrueColor modes (Version 1.2) |
| 7-0Fh | Reserved by VESA |
| 10h-0FFh | Vendor defined |

Version 1.1 added a new field, The NumberOfPages, which returns the maximum number of screen buffers available for page switching, like the standard BIOS display pages.

On the accompanying disk is a useful program called VESATEST.EXE, which shows what modes and capabilities are available on your machine. It provides a practical example of how function 01h can be used to extract information.

## Function 02h Set SVGA Mode

Sets an SVGA mode and is used instead of a call to the standard Video BIOS function 00h (Set Mode). Bit 15 works like bit 7 of the standard VGA Set Mode, or, in other words, if the call fails, the mode doesn't change and the old environment remains.

Not all VESA adapters will support every mode. You should use functions 4F00h and 4F01h to determine which modes are available. A manufacturer's specific modes may also be set by this function call.

Input:

      AX:    Set to 4F02h

      BX:    SVGA mode number (See Table 11.9 below)

Output:

      AX:    Status

The following table shows a list of SVGA modes along with the appropriate VESA mode number:

**Table 11.9 SVGA Modes**

| VESA Mode # | Number of Colors | Resolution Type | Display |
|---|---|---|---|
| 100 | 256/256K | 640x400 | Graphics |
| 101 | 256/256K | 640x480 | Graphics |
| 102(6A) | 16/256K | 800x600 | Graphics |
| 103 | 256/256K | 800x600 | Graphics |
| 104 | 16/256K | 1024x768 | Graphics |
| 105 | 256/256K | 1024x768 | Graphics |
| 106 | 16/256K | 1280x1024 | Graphics |

*Continued*

Table 11.9 SVGA Modes (Continued)

| VESA Mode # | Number of Colors | Resolution Type | Display |
|---|---|---|---|
| 107 | 256/256K | 1280x1024 | Graphics |
| 109 | 16/256K | 132x25 | Text |
| 10A | 16/256K | 132x43 | Text |
| 10B | 16/256k | 132x50 | Text |
| 10C | 16/256k | 132x60 | Text |
| 10D | 32K/32K | 320x200 | Graphics |
| 10E | 64K/64K | 320x200 | Graphics |
| 10F | 16M/16M | 320x200 | Graphics |
| 110 | 32K/32K | 640x480 | Graphics |
| 111 | 64K/64K | 640x480 | Graphics |
| 112 | 16M/16M | 640x480 | Graphics |
| 113 | 32K/32K | 800x600 | Graphics |
| 114 | 64K/64K | 800x600 | Graphics |
| 117 | 64K/64K | 1024/768 | Graphics |
| 170 | 32K/32K | 512/480 | Graphics |
| 171 | 64K/64K | 512/480 | Graphics |

## Function 03h Return SVGA Mode

Gets the current SVGA Mode. This call should be used instead of call 0Fh, the standard video BIOS Current VideoState function. All modes - standard VGA, VESA, and vendor specific - can be determined through this call.

Input:

AX:     set to 4F03h

Output:

AX:     Status
BX:     Mode Number

## Function 04h Save/Restore SVGA Video State

This function contains three subfunctions which save and restore SVGA state information and report the buffer size required to do so in 64 byte blocks. This function is analogous to the standard BIOS function 1Ch, Save/Restore Video State. Unlike the standard function, the structure of the memory blocks is a unique and contains additional SVGA information.

Input:

AX: set to 4F04h
CX: Selected States
ES:BX: points to buffer

Four possible states may be saved in various combinations depending on the value of CX, as shown in the table below:

**Table 11.10 CX States**

| Bit | Description |
|-----|-------------|
| 0 | Video Hardware state (registers) |
| 1 | BIOS Data state |
| 2 | DAC state |
| 3 | SVGA state |

Which particular subfunction will be called depends on the value of the DL register.

Subfunction DL = 0 Get Buffer Size
Output:

AX: Status
BX: Buffer Size Required (in 64 byte blocks)

Subfunction DL = 1 Save state
Output:

AX: Status

Subfunction DL = 2 Restore state
Output:

AX: Status

## Function 05h Video Memory Window Control

This function contains two subfunctions which are used to set or get the position of a specified window in the video memory. You can control both windows A and B. Function 05h is used to perform bank switching via the VESA BIOS extensions.

The offset is specified in the units of Window Granularity (see function 4F01h field WinGranularity). The Window Granularity value may differ for different adapters. For example, the Paradise SVGA from Western Digital has a granularity of 4K, so possible offsets from the beginning of Video memory are 0, 4K, 8K and so on. As in the previous example, you could use a far call to improve performance, to the address given in call 4F01h field WinFuncPtr.

Input:

    AX:         set to 4F05h

Which particular subfunction will be called depends on the value of the BH register.

Subfunction 0 - Set Window Position
Input:

    BH = 0
    BL:         Window Number (0 = Window A, 1 = Window B)
    DX:         Offset in video memory (in granularity units)

Output:

    AX:         Status

Subfunction 1 - Get Window Position:
Input:

    BL:         Window Number (0 = Window A, 1 = Window B)

Output:

    AX:         Status
    DX:         Offset in video memory (in granularity units)

Here are two examples of how to switch banks - one using the VESA BIOS extension function 05h, the other a direct far call. We have assumed that the granularity is 64K in both cases:

```
; These procedures expect one parameter, bank number
; in granularity units in DX register.
SwitchBank    proc    near
  push bx
  xor    bx,bx                ;BH = 0 (Set Window Position)
                              ;BL = 0 (Window A)
  mov    ax,4f05h             ;Video Memory Control function
  int    10h                  ;switch bank
  pop bx
  ret
SwitchBank    endp

SwitchBank    proc    near    ;DX = bank number
  push bx
  xor    bx,bx                ;BH = 0 (Set Window Position)
                              ;BL = 0 (Window A)
  call dword ptr WinFuncPtr   ;switch bank
  pop bx
  ret
SwitchBank    endp
```

## Function 06h Get/Set Logical Scan Line Length

This function contains two subfunctions which set and report on the BytesPerLine value. It is most useful when you want to display an object that's larger than the physical display size, meaning that only a proportion of the complete image will be displayed. This is useful for neat little tricks like smooth horizontal scrolling and panning (also see function 4F07h). You can also use it to pad scan line lengths to prevent a scan line from splitting across 64K segments.

The line length is set in pixels. You can request any value you like, but it's hard to predict whether it will be valid for your particular VESA hardware. You should try different settings to see how your adapter responds. Some of them will round up the value to make it 16 (or 8) pixels aligned, some will set only already aligned values. The function may or may not work in the True and HighColor modes. The actual value you've set may be checked using the output of Subfunction 1:

Input:

      AX:    set to 4F06h

Which particular subfunction is called depends on the value of the BL register.

Subfunction BL = 0 Set Scan Line Length

      CX:    New scan line length in pixels

Output:

      AX:    Status
      BX:    Number of bytes in one scan line
      CX:    Number of pixels in one scan line
      DX:    Maximum number of scan lines (virtual vertical resolution)

Subfunction BL = 1 Get Scan Line Length

Output:

      AX:    Status
      BX:    Number of bytes in one scan line
      CX:    Number of pixels in one scan line
      DX:    Maximum number of scan lines (virtual vertical resolution)

## Function 07h Get/Set Start of Display

This function contains two subfunctions which set or get the starting address (upper left corner) of the physical CRT image within the virtual one. Subfunction 6 could be used to set up a virtual screen that is larger than the physical screen. This function allows the physical screen to move around within the virtual screen. This makes smooth scrolling possible (see function 4F06h), or switching of the display page in multiple page mode.

The offsets are specified in terms of horizontal and vertical pixels. Again, try this function before relying on it for anything serious:

Input:

      AX:    set to 4F07h

Which subfunction will be called depends on value in the BL register.

Subfunction BL = 0 Set Position

        BH:    0 (Reserved, must be 0)
        CX:    Horizontal Pixel Offset
        DX:    Vertical Pixel Offset

Output:
        AX:    Status

Subfunction BL = 1 Get Position

Output:
        AX:    Status
        BH:    0 (Reserved, always 0)
        CX:    Horizontal Pixel Offset
        DX:    Vertical Pixel Offset

# Advanced Video Programming

## The VGA Register Set and Video Register Programming

Each graphics adapter has several registers which organize its internal functions. The registers which are common to all VGAs fall into six major groups:

- External registers, which provide miscellaneous functions such as specifying screen size and status information for vertical retrace, which is important for processor independent timing.

- Graphics Controller registers which support graphics mode functions and assist in the modification of data being read from and written to planar display memory.

- Sequencer registers, which control memory access, timing and data flow among the other registers.

- CRT (Cathode Ray Tube) Controller (or CRTC) registers, which deal with timing related to the display.

- Attribute Controller registers which handle the color palette selections.

- DAC (Digital to Analog Converter) registers which convert the color codes to a voltage for your analog monitor.

# Programming Using Registers

Most programmers think that register programming is the basis for each and every sophisticated or tricky technique in graphics. And they're not wrong - however, there are registers and REGISTERS.

You can make your programs really attractive by juggling colors. If you really know how to work with your DAC and Attribute Controller, fading, glimmering, transparency and a whole host of fairground effects are awaiting you. If you use direct memory techniques for planar display modes, it usually means you'll be working with the Graphics Controller and possibly the Sequencer's Map Mask Register in order to access the video memory both quickly and efficiently enough to write graphics programs that use these modes. For hardware assisted screen effects such as splitting and panning, you will need to use some of the more helpful registers of the CRTC.

## Ground Rules to Addressing Video Registers

Before we dive into more detail there are some important points to note:

- All VGA registers are read/writeable, except for the Attribute address register, and the Input Status registers. This is one advantage VGA has over EGA.

- Some VGA registers must be read and written at different port addresses, such as 3C2h, which is read from 3CCh.

- A simple, but useful, rule to remember when changing register states that is essential for tricky programming, is that the port should be read, only the desired bits modified, and the result written back to the port.

Some changes can have the monitor trying to show more lines than is possible and upsetting the display. Leaving it in this state is not considered a good idea. However, unlike the old Commodore Pet, there is no software command that can do physical damage.

## Accessing the Video Registers

Video registers are accessed via ports. Some registers, such as the external registers and the DAC registers, have their own unique ports and can therefore be accessed directly.

**Table 11.11 External and DAC Registers**

| Register | Port |
|----------|------|
| Miscellaneous Output register | 03C2h (to write), 3CCh (to read VGA only) |
| Feature Control register (EGA only) | 3BAh (mono), 3DAh(color) |
| Input Status register 0 (read only) | 3C2h (to read) |
| Input Status register 1 (read only) | 3BAh (mono), 3DAh (Color) |
| VGA Enable register | 3C3h |
| Registers that access the DAC | 3C6h, 3C7h, 3C8h and 3C9h |

Other registers, however, belong to one of the major register groups and have to be accessed indirectly via the parent group.

**Table 11.12 Parent Group Access**

| Parent Register Group | Mono Modes | | Color Modes | |
|-----------------------|------------|----------|-------------|----------|
| | Index Port | Data Port | Index Port | Data Port |
| Graphics Controller | 03CEh | 03CFh | 03CEh | 03CFh |
| Sequencer | 03C4h | 03C5h | 03C4h | 03C5h |
| Attribute Controller | 03C0h | 03C0h | 03C0h | 03C0h |
| CRTC | 03B4h | 03B5h | 03D4h | 03D5h |

External registers and the Color Select Registers block in the Attribute Controller are accessed directly, each of them having its unique host port. All others are accessed indirectly.

There is special address register for each group and it's used to select the register to be modified. All of the indirectly addressed registers have their unique index within the associated group. This index is written into the address register of the corresponding group, and then the desired register is accessed through the data port of that group.

**Table 11.13 Address and Data Ports**

| Registers Group | Direct I/O Port | Address Port | Data Port |
|---|---|---|---|
| Sequencer | — | 3C4h | 3C5h |
| CRTC | — | 3?4h | 3?5h |
| External | 3?Ah, 3CAh 3C2h, 3CCh | — | — |
| Graphics Controller | — | 3CEh | 3CFh |
| Attribute Controller | — | 3C0h | 3C1h |
| DAC | 3c6h, 3c7h 3c8h, 3c9h | — | — |

For External and CRTC registers, the host port address has B instead of ? if the VGA adapter is in monochrome emulation mode (3B4h, 3B5h, 3BAh), and D if in color mode (3D4h, 3D5h, 3DAh).

Each register within a register group has its own unique index number. To access the register, this index number is sent to the index port of the group that the register belongs to. As an example, let's look at how we can address the Bitmask register (index number 8), which is one of the registers belonging to the Graphics Controller:

```
mov  dx,3CEh      ;Graphics Controller addressing register
mov  al,8         ;Index of bit mask register
out  dx,al        ;select this register
inc  dx           ;Graphics Controller data register
mov  al,0EFh      ;AL = data (the mask)
out  dx,al        ;set bit mask
```

The following alternative method is a little bit shorter and faster:

```
mov  dx,3CEh        ;Graphics Controller addressing register
mov  ax,0EF08h      ;AH = value, AL = index
out  dx,ax          ;set bit mask
```

Once the index of the address register has been set, it will remain in effect until it is changed (except in the case of the Attribute Register - see below).

Therefore, if you are changing the same register repeatedly, you can create faster code by setting the index outside the loop - something like this:

```
    mov  dx,3CEh        ;Graphics Controller Addressing register
    mov  al,8           ;Index of Bit Mask register
    out  dx,al          ;select this register
    inc  dx             ;Graphics Controller data register
    mov  cx,100h        ;CX = counter

next:
    ...
    mov  al,[di]        ;AL = mask
    out  dx,al          ;set bit mask
    ...
    inc  di
    loop next           ;load next mask
```

# The Graphics Controller

The Graphics Controller (GC) assists in data transfer operations in 16 color modes. It has 9 registers. These are addressed indirectly by passing an index number of the required register through port 3CEh, and data to the selected register through port 3CFh. These registers are as follows:

**Table 11.14 Graphics Controller Registers**

| Index | Register |
|-------|----------|
| 0 | Set/Reset register |
| 1 | Enable Set/Reset register |
| 2 | Color Compare register |
| 3 | Data Rotate/Function Select register |
| 4 | Read Map Select register |

*Continued*

Table 11.14 Graphics Controller Registers (Continued)

| Index | Register |
|-------|----------|
| 5 | Mode register |
| 6 | Miscellaneous register |
| 7 | Color Don't Care register |
| 8 | Bit Mask register |

All of the registers, apart from the miscellaneous one, are designed to be used exclusively in 16 color modes.

The purpose of the graphic controller registers is to determine how data is transferred to and from planar video memory. The exact way this happens depends on which READ and WRITE modes are currently set, which is achieved via the Mode register. VGA has two READ modes and four WRITE modes, but before we examine these read and write modes in detail, we should first discuss the four on-board data latches that are key to understanding all write and read operations in planar video memory.

# Data Latches

The latches are a speed up device built into the VGA chip for use in planar modes. A read of a memory location causes all four latches to be updated. The value returned is one of these four latch values, according to which plane was selected. It is possible to copy a byte from all four planes to elsewhere in VM, using the Write Mode 1 method of operation. This is four times faster than the plane-by-plane method.

## Read Mode 0

In this mode, the CPU reads the contents of one of the 4 data latches. The number of the latch read is taken from bits 0 and 1 of the Read Map Select register (index 4).

*To obtain the color of a pixel, you have to execute four CPU read operations.*

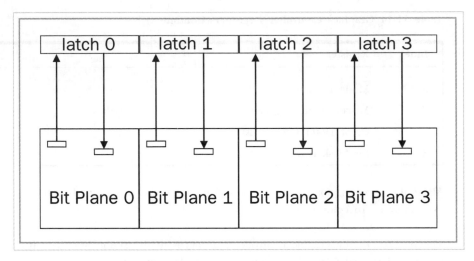

**Figure 11.2 VGA in Read Mode 0**

This example shows how to read a pixel in Read Mode 0:

```
;DS:SI points to byte for read in video memory
;ES:DI points to bytes array

    mov dx,3ceh        ;Graphics Controller addressing register
    mov al,4           ;AL = Read Map Select register index
    out dx,al
    inc dx             ;Graphics Controller data register
    mov cx,4           ;bit plane counter
    xor al,al          ;first read from 0 bit plane

next_bit_plane:
    out dx,al          ;select bit plane for read
    mov ah,si          ;read byte from bit plane
    mov es:di,ah       ;save byte somewhere
    inc di
    inc al             ;read next bit plane
    loop next_bit_plane
```

## Read Mode 1

In this mode, the CPU gets the result of comparing the color in the Color Compare register (index 2, bits 0..3) with the pixel colors stored in the data latches. If the colors are the same, the corresponding bit of the CPU byte is set

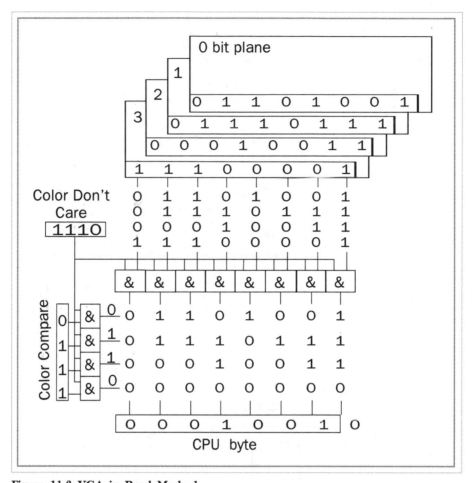

**Figure 11.3 VGA in Read Mode 1**

to 1, otherwise to it stays as 0. The Color Don't Care register can be used to exclude some bits of the color code, or in other words, some of the bit planes, from the comparison - if any bit of Color Don't Care is 0, then the corresponding bit of the pixel's color is ignored. Thus, if the Color Don't Care register is 0000, all colors are considered the same and the CPU always gets OFFh. In the example below, the color in row 10 is changed for another:

```
mov ax,0a000h
mov es,ax      ;ES = video memory segment
mov di,800
mov si,di      ;SI = DI = offset 10 row
```

```
mov dx,3ceh              ;Graphics Controller addressing register
mov ax,0b05h             ;AL = Mode register index
                         ;AH = 1011h (write mode 3, read mode 1)
out dx,ax                ;set write and read mode 1

mov ah,OldColor          ;AH = old color
mov al,2                 ;AL = Color Compare Register
out dx,ax

mov al,0                 ;AL = Set/Reset register index
mov ah,NewColor          ;AH = new color
out dx,ax

mov ax,0ff08h            ;AH = 0ffh (bit mask)
                         ;AL = Bit Mask register index
out dx,ax
mov cx,80                ;bytes per row
rep movsb                ;fire!
```

## Write Mode 0

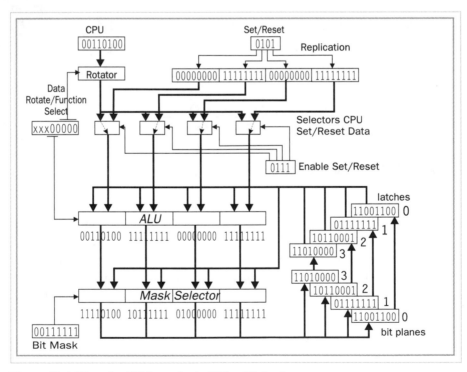

**Figure 11.4 How the VGA works in Write Mode 0**

This is the most difficult Write mode to understand as you can see from the diagram.

The rotator rotates the CPU byte to the right by the number of bits set in the Data Rotate/Function Select register (index 3 bits 0..2). This is almost never used, so don't worry too much about it.

The Selector selects data flow from either the CPU or Set/Reset register (index 0, bits 0..3) depending on the Enable Set/Reset register setting (index 1, bits 0..3). If any bit in the Enable Set/Reset register is 0, then the data for the corresponding plane is taken from the CPU, otherwise the data source is the Set/Reset register.

The ALU performs logical operations with the data from the CPU or the Set/Reset register and from the latches. The ALU is controlled by bits 3 and 4 of the Data Rotate/Function Select register. The bits work like this:

    00 - Replace, CPU or Set/Reset data pass unchanged
    01 - AND
    02 - OR
    03 - XOR

The Mask Selector makes sure that data bits prohibited by the Bit Mask register (index 8) are not placed in the video memory. More precisely, if any bit of the register is 1, the corresponding bit is taken from the ALU for each bit plane, and if any bit is 0, then the corresponding bit is taken from the latches. Therefore, as the latches normally contain the same data as the video memory when you address 8 pixels, the Mask Selector enables you to modify just those pixels you want to change.

There are two methods of working in Write Mode 0: color oriented and byte oriented.

## Writing to the Screen in Mode 0 - Color Oriented Method

This method can be used to draw a pixel or color in any area of the screen. To do so you will need to set all the bits of the Enable Set/Reset register to 1. The color code from the Set/Reset register is the data source. Each bit of this register expands into 8 bits: 0 into 00000000 and 1 into 11111111. As a result, you have 32 bits which then go into the ALU. The mask selector then selects bits from either the ALU or latches in the normal way and the bits are placed into the video memory.

The following example writes a pixel in Write Mode 0, color logic - XOR:

```
mov  dx,3ceh              ;Graphics Controller Addressing register

mov  ah,BitMask           ;AH = bit mask - Select pixel(s) within byte being
                          ;written to
mov  al,8                 ;AL = Bit Mask register index
out  dx,ax                ;set bit mask

mov  ah,PixelColor        ;AH = pixel color (0 - 15)
mov  al,0                 ;AL = Set/Register register index
out  dx,ax                ;set draw color

mov  ah,0fh               ;AH = 0fh - this set bits 0 to 3 of Enable Set/Reset
                          ;register which will enable a color oriented
                          ;Write Mode 0.
mov  al,1                 ;AL = Enable Set/Reset register index
out  dx,ax

mov  ah,18h               ;Select logic function XOR - i.e. set bits 3 and 4
mov  AL,3                 ;AL = Data Rotate/Function Select register index
out  dx,ax

;Point ES:BX to the address of the byte in video memory containing the pixel
;to be updated and then execute the following line

xchg es:[bx],al           ;use the advantages of xchg instruction to
                          ;update bit planes (i.e. one instruction
                          ;performs both read & write of data)
```

## Writing to the Screen in Mode 0 - Byte Oriented Method

If you want to use the byte oriented method, you need to set all the bits of the Enable Set/Reset register to 0. In this case, the byte from the CPU first passes through the Rotator and then goes to the ALU, where the necessary logical operation is performed. The result is then masked and written to the bit planes as normal. This method is particularly suitable for sending images that were previously saved in the conventional memory to the screen.

You are not limited to writing 0000 or 1111 in the Enable Set/Reset register. If you want to write something more sophisticated, you needn't worry about scaring the Graphics Controller; it will carefully send the data from the CPU to the necessary bit planes and the data from the Set/Reset register to the others.

Resetting latches before a write operation doesn't constitute the eleventh commandment, it's just a common technique. If you want to update all 8 pixels that correspond to a byte and don't need logical combining, you don't need a read operation. However, if you want to mask some of the bits (pixels), or if you are going to use any type of color logic, you have to perform a read operation first.

## Write Mode 1

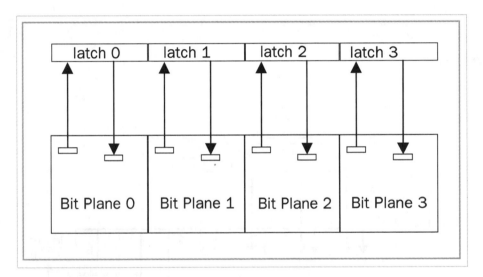

**Figure 11.5 VGA in Write Mode 1**

This mode is extremely useful for fast copying within the video memory. When the CPU reads, information is moved to the latches and when it writes, data is transferred from the latches into video memory. The settings of the Set/Reset register, the Bit Mask register and the value of the CPU data have no effect. Write Mode 1 allows you to perform 32-bit transfers 4 times faster than in Write mode 0.

The following example shows how to copy the contents of row 0 to row 10:

```
mov  dx,3ceh          ;Graphics Controller addressing register
mov  ax,0105h         ;AH = 1 (write mode 1)
                      ;AL = 5 (Mode register index)
out  dx,ax            ;set write mode 1

mov  ax,0a000h
mov  es,ax
mov  ds,ax            ;ES = DS = video memory segment

xor  si,si            ;source offset = 0 (beginning of row 0)
mov  di,800           ;target offset = BytesPerRow x Row = 10 x 80
                      ;(beginning of row 10)
mov  cx,80            ;counter moved bytes

rep  movsb            ;move data from DS:SI to ES:DI
```

## Write Mode 2

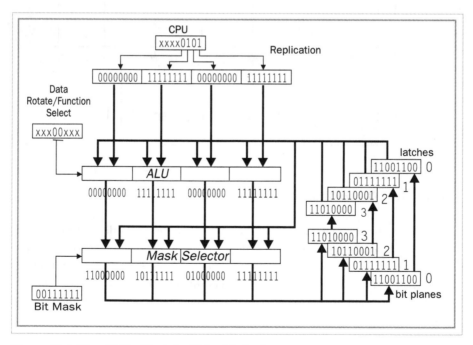

**Figure 11.6 How VGAs Work in Write Mode 2**

This mode is usually used in much the same way as the color oriented method in write mode 0. The main difference being that, instead of the Set/Reset register, you use the 4 low bits of the CPU byte. The ALU and the Bit Mask register perform the same actions as in write mode 0. However, the data Rotator and the Enable Set/Reset registers are not used.

The next example writes a pixel in write mode 2, color logic - AND:

```
mov  dx,3ceh          ;Graphics Controller addressing register

mov  ah,BitMask       ;AH = bit mask - Select pixel(s) within byte
                      ;being written to
mov  al,8             ;AL = Bit Mask register index
out  dx,ax            ;set bit mask

mov  ax,0205h         ;AL = 5 (Mode register index)
                      ;AH = 2(write mode 2)
out  dx,ax            ;set write mode 2

mov  ax,0803h         ;AL = 3 (Data Rotate/Function Select register index)
                      ;AH = 08h (Select logic function AND - i.e. set
                      ;bit 3 only)
out  dx,ax            ;set AND operation

;Point ES:BX to the address of the byte in video memory containing the pixel to
;be updated and then execute the following line

mov  al,PixelColor    ;AL = pixel color
xchg es:bx,al         ;update bit planes
```

## Write Mode 3

This mode is only accessible for VGAs. The color code is taken from the Set/Reset register. The Enable Set/Reset register can have any settings. The ALU still works as it does in mode 0. The CPU byte passes through the Rotator and is ANDed bit by bit with the value in the Bit Mask register. This has the same result as the mask in write mode 0. Therefore, it's possible to save one OUT instruction without updating the Bit Mask register.

This mode allows us to use the CPU as a bit mask, instead of the Bit Mask register itself. However, to do this without interference from the Bit Mask register, we have to make sure that the Bit Mask register is set to 0ffh (which it is usually by default).

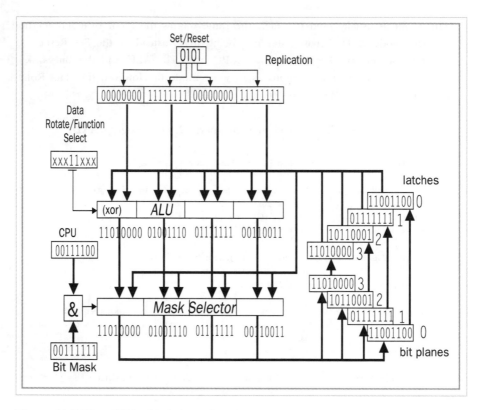

**Figure 11.7 How VGAs Work in Write Mode 3**

The following example writes a pixel in write mode 3:

```
mov  dx,3ceh          ;Graphics Controller addressing register

mov  ax,0305h         ;AL = 5 (Mode register index)
                      ;AH = 3 (write mode 3)
out  dx,ax            ;set write mode 3

mov  ah,PixelColor    ;AH = pixel color
mov  al,0             ;AL = Set/Reset register index
out  dx,ax            ;set draw color

mov  al,BitMask       ;AL = bit mask

;Point ES:BX to the address of the byte in video memory containing the pixel to be
;updated and then execute the following line

xchg es:bx,al         ;update bit planes
```

## The Sequencer Map Mask Register

The Sequencer's primary task is to control data flow. Anyway, it's best not to touch most of these registers, unless you like creating video modes of your own.

One particularly useful register worth mentioning here is the Map Mask register. This register is one of a group of registers belonging to the Sequencer (Index number 02h). Its purpose is to enable or disable bitplanes from being written to. Placing a 1 in bits 0 to 3 of this register will enable the corresponding bit plane to be written to, whereas a 0 disables the bit plane from being updated. It should be said that this register is active (works) in ALL write modes, so don't forget about it, especially when using write mode 1.

In the following example, we'll copy planes 0 and 1 of a byte from one area of display memory to another by using the Sequencer Map Mask register to prevent the bytes in planes 2 and 3 being written to:

```
mov  dl,03c4h          ;Sequencer addressing register
mov  ah,00000011b      ;AH = 3 (i.e. set bits 0 and 1 only to enable planes 0
                       ;and 1 only
mov  al,2              ;AL = Map Mask register index
out  dx,ax             ;set map mask

mov  dx,3ceh           ;Graphics Controller addressing register

mov  ax,0105h          ;AH = 1 (write mode 1)
                       ;AL = 5 (Mode register index)
out  dx,ax             ;set write mode 1

mov  ax,0a000h
mov  es,ax
mov  ds,ax             ;ES = DS = video memory segment

mov  cx,8000h
mov  si,start
mov  di,dest

rep  movsb             ;move data from DS:SI to ES:DI
```

## CRT Controller

The CRTC is used for low-level control of the CRT, as you may have guessed. It can be used for a lot of things, but the registers that most people work with are the Start Address, the index (0Ch for low bytes and 0Dh for high), the Offset (index 13h) and the Line Compare index (for smooth scrolling and splitting).

# The Attribute Controller and DAC

The DAC (Digital to Analog Converter) is used to convert the digital pixel color codes stored in the DAC color registers into analog signals for the CRT. The DAC contains 256 color registers, each of which defines one color. Each color register consists of 3 parts which correspond to the red, green, and blue components. Each of the 3 parts are six bits wide, so the components can have a maximum of 64 levels of saturation. You can get any of the 262,144 ($2^{18}$) available colors by mixing the RGB components for a particular level.

The DAC has five registers for managing color registers - two of which share the same port address:

**Table 11.15 DAC Registers for Managing Color Registers**

| Address | Read/Write | Function |
|---------|------------|----------|
| 3C6h | Read/Write | PEL Mask Register |
| 3C7h | Read | DAC State Register |
| 3C7h | Write | PEL Address Register for reading |
| 3C8h | Read/Write | PEL Address Register for writing |
| 3C9h | Read/Write | PEL Data Register |

The PEL Address Register is used to select the particular Color Register you want to work with and to choose a read or write operation. A rather strange technique is used to select the operation; irrespective of whether you going to read or write, you must send the Color Register's address to port 3C7h or 3C8h. Data is read or written through the PEL Data Register. What's more, every read or write procedure consists of three sequential operations, one for each of the RGB components. After a complete read or write operation, or in other words, one that contains the three sequential operations for R, G and B, the PEL Address Register is automatically incremented to address the next PEL Data Register.

It is generally believed that a delay of 240 nanoseconds is needed between successive read or write operations. Experience shows that this delay can be omitted.

When the Color Registers are modified, snow may appear on the screen. To avoid this complication, you should only change Color Registers when the display is in the vertical retrace period. Have a look at the following examples that set the Color Register. The first example is with a delay (of about 240ns):

```
        mov cx,Count          ;CX = amount of Color Registers to be set
        mov dx,3dah           ;DX = Input Status Register #1
                              ;3bah - for monochrome displays, 3dah for color

@ActWait:                     ;wait for vertical retrace
   in al,dx                   ;AL = status
   test al,8                  ;test bit 3
   jz @ActWait                ;loop while not in vertical retrace

   mov dl,0c8h                ;PEL Address register
   mov al,First               ;AL = first Color Register to be set
   out dx,al
   inc dx                     ;PEL Data Register
   lds si,Palette             ;Palette points to array of R,G,B values
   cld                        ;clear direction flag
   cli                        ;disable interrupts

next_col_reg:
   outsb                      ;set Red component
   jmp $+2
   jmp $+2                    ;short delay
   outsb                      ;set Green component
   jmp $+2
   jmp $+2                    ;short delay
   outsb                      ;set Blue component
   loop next_col_reg          ;set next Color Register
   sti                        ;enable interrupts
```

The next example is without a delay:

```
        mov cx,Count          ;CX = amount of Color Registers to be
        shl cx,1              ;CX = CX*2
        add cx,Count          ;CX = CX*3
        mov dx,3dah           ;DX = Input Status Register #1

@BefActWait:                  ;wait for vertical retrace
   in al,dx                   ;AL = status
   test al,8                  ;test bit 3
   jnz @BefActWait            ;loop while not in vertical retrace

   mov dl,0c8h                ;PEL Address register
   mov al,First               ;AL = First Color Register
```

```
out dx,al
inc dx                  ;PEL Data Register
lds si,Palette          ;Palette point to array of R,G,B values
cld                     ;clear direction flag
cli                     ;disable interrupts
rep outsb               ;to make it shorter
sti                     ;enable interrupts
```

The DAC State Register is used to determine whether the DAC is in read or write mode. If first two bits (0,1) of the DAC State Register are both set to 1, then the DAC is in read mode. If they are both set to 0 then the DAC is in write mode.

The PEL Mask Register is set to FFh by BIOS, and you're advised not to touch it.

The Attribute Controller includes a second group of registers that deal with colors in 16 color modes. These are the 16 EGA Palette registers (index 0 - 0Fh), a Color Select register (index 14h) and the seventh bit of Mode Control register (index 10h). The latter determines which of the two methods of color decoding will be used.

With the first method, the seventh bit of the Mode Control register is set to 0, so a pixel's 4 bit color code points to one of the 16 Palette registers, which in turn, contains the 6 lower bits of the Color register's address. The 2 upper bits of this address are taken from the Color Select Register bits 2 and 3.

The second method is a bit different. Only the 4 lower bits of the Color register's address are taken from the Palette register, while the 4 upper bits are taken from the Color Select Register bits 0-3.

Access to the Attribute Controller registers is like a Chinese puzzle. The best way to understand it is to look at an example. To write to the Attribute Controller, the register 03C0h is used, for both register index and data. How does the AC know which value you are writing? It has a flip-flop circuit inside (just like a light switch). When the switch is in position 1, the value written selects the register. In position 2, the value goes to the register previously selected. How is the switch changed? Simple. Just read Input Status Register #1. This puts the switch into position 1, so the byte written to 03c0h selects the register and also flicks the switch into position 2. The next byte then written goes to the register.

The following code sets the Attribute Controller register:

```
mov dx,3dah              ;DX = Input Status Register #1
in al,dx                 ;IN from Input Status Register #1
                         ;will always set the port 3c0h to the Address mode
mov al,RegNumber         ;AL = register index
mov dx,3c0h              ;DX = Attribute Address Register
out dx,al                ;set register index
                         ;and now port 3c0h set to the Data mode
mov al,Value             ;AL = new value of register
out dx,al                ;set register

mov al,20h               ;set bit 5
out dx,al                ;enable display
```

# Video Memory and Programming Techniques - VRAM

This is the most important section of the chapter where we will demonstrate how to Put and Get pixels in various graphics modes up to and including TrueColor. The techniques we will examine will provide a basis for understanding the real bones of graphics programming.

This section is arranged according to video modes and memory models rather than the types of adapters. This is because we are discussing direct memory techniques and different video modes have different methods of addressing memory.

## Addressing Pixels

In any mode, before you draw a pixel you have to calculate which address is to be written to in the video memory. A pixel on the screen is usually addressed using X and Y coordinates, where Y is the number of the row and X is the pixel's position in that row. Both X and Y start from 0 and the pixel with coordinates (0,0) is in the upper left corner of the screen.

In all modes and for all adapters described in this chapter, pixels are stored in the video memory in the order in which they appear on the screen, or in other words, from left to right within a row, starting from the top row and working down. Therefore, to determine the address of a pixel all you have to do is add the offset of the row in the video memory calculated using Y, together with the offset of the pixel from the beginning of the row calculated using X.

The crucial thing to know when calculating a pixel's address is how many bytes of video memory are required for each row of the screen (call this BytesPerLine) and how many bytes are used for each pixel displayed on the screen (call this BytesPerPixel). We can then use the following formula to calculate the address of the pixel:

addr = Y*BytesPerLine + X*BytesPerPixel

Remember, that because BytesPerLine is calculated by multiplying the X_Resolution by the number of BytesPerPixel, we can transpose this into the above formula and then use the following alternative calculation:

addr = (Y*X_Resolution + X)*BytesPerPixel

## 16 Color Modes

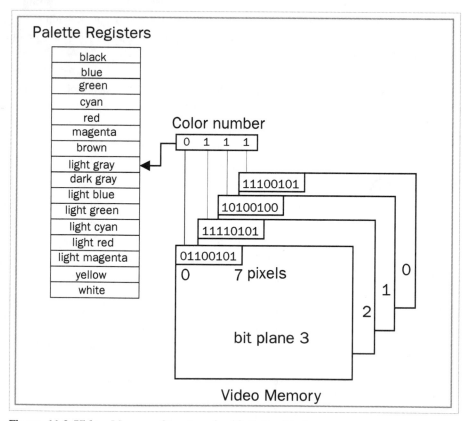

**Figure 11.8 Video Memory Structure in 16 Color Mode**

With 16 color modes, the VM is treated as four superimposed bit planes. Although you might think that this means that you need four read/write operations to get/put a pixel, this is not necessarily true if you make use of some of the Graphic Controller registers.

To calculate the address of a pixel when using 16 color modes, we need to remember that each byte of the video memory, i.e. each address, corresponds to 8 pixels. BytesPerLine is therefore 8 times less than the number of pixels in a line. For example, in 640x480 mode, BytesPerLine = 640/8 = 80 bytes.

The quotient of the integer division X by 8 gives the offset of the byte from the beginning of the row, and the remainder gives the number of the bit in the byte. So the expression to calculate a pixel's address is as follows:

$$addr = Y*BytesPerLine + X / 8.$$

The nearer a pixel is to the left of the screen, the higher the bit of the byte used. To extract a particular pixel from this byte, you'll need a special mask in which the corresponding bit is set to 1 and the others are set to 0. The following example shows how a pixel's address can be calculated:

```
PixelAddress      macro   Y,X
    mov  ax,Y                    ;AX = Y Coordinate
    mov  bx,X                    ;BX = X Coordinate
    mov  cl,bl                   ;Save in CL low byte of BX
    mul  BytesPerLine            ;AX = row offset in video memory (Y*BytesPerLine)
    shr  bx,3                    ;BX = byte offset in row X / 8
    add  bx,ax                   ;BX = byte offset in video memory
    and  cl,7                    ;CL = CL & 7
    xor  cl,7                    ;CL = number of bits to shift left
    mov  ax,0a000h
    mov  es,ax                   ;ES = video memory segment
    mov  al,1                    ;AL = unshifted bit mask
    shl  al,cl                   ;AL = bit mask
                                 ;ES:BX pointer to byte in video memory
    endm
```

The fact of the matter is that there is no direct memory technique that's useable in this mode. The technique of getting a picture on the screen is not really a memory technique at all.

## 16 Color SVGA 800x600 and Above

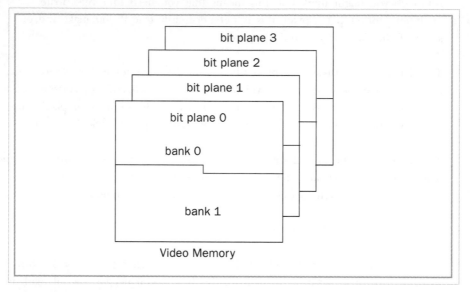

**Figure 11.9 Video Memory for 16 Color SVGA**

For the high resolution 16 color modes of the SVGA, the programming techniques remain the same as for lower resolution 16 color modes, although pixel addressing is somewhat more complicated. This is because you should take into account bank switching. Real programmers will enjoy creative programming in this mode.

Here's an example of the pixel's address calculation for SVGA 16 color modes above 800x600 (bank size = 64K, and Granularity = 64K):

```
PixelAddress macro Y,X
    mov ax,Y                ;AX = Y coordinate
    mov bx,X                ;BX = X coordinate
    mov cl,bl               ;Save in CL low byte of BX
    mul BytesPerLine        ;AX = row offset in video memory from
                            ;the beginning of the bank Lo(Y*BytesPerLine)
                            ;DX = bank number Hi(Y*BytesPerLine)
    shr bx,3                ;BX = byte offset in row X / 8
    add bx,ax               ;BX = byte offset in video memory from
```

```
                             ;the beginning of the bank
   adc dx,0                  ;catching bank-split-row occasion
   and cl,7                  ;CL = CL & 7
   xor cl,7                  ;CL = number of bits to shift left
   mov ax,0a000h
   mov es,ax                 ;ES = video memory segment
   mov al,1                  ;AL = unshifted bit mask
   shl al,cl                 ;AL = bit mask
                             ;ES:BX pointer to byte in video memory from the
                             ;beginning of the bank DX = bank number
endm
```

## 256 Color VGA 320x200

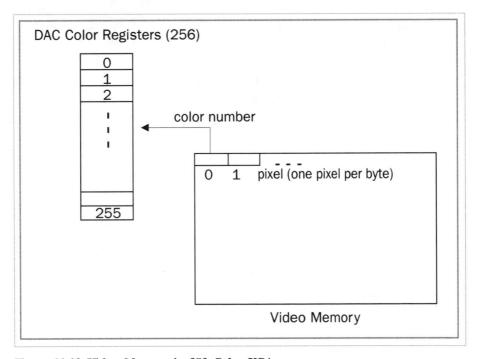

**Figure 11.10 Video Memory in 256 Color VGA**

This mode uses one whole byte for each pixel color code, which means that you have 256 ($2^8$) accessible colors. Therefore, the adapter uses all 256 entries of the DAC register table. The starting address remains the same - A000:0h, and all pixels are stored consecutively as they appear on the screen. The calculation of the memory address of each pixel is considerably simplified by having one byte per pixel and a continuous memory map. In a continuous memory map there are 320 pixels on each line. The first is at byte 0, the second at byte 1 (offset from 0a000h), the 400th at byte 399, the 50000th at byte 49999. This is because, in this mode, screen memory is completely continuous. In comparison with 16 color modes, programming 256 color mode is easy.

The VGA 256 color 320x200 video memory may be thought of as an array of bytes with dimensions [200][320]. You address each pixel the same way you would a certain element of any array. You can calculate each pixel address like this:

addr = Y*BytesPerLine + X
For this mode BytesPerLine = 320

For any 256 color mode the BytesPerLine is equal to the X resolution (one byte per pixel). The following sample of code shows how to read and write a pixel in 320x200 256 color mode:

```
;Calculate Pixel Address
  mov ax,Y                  ;AX = Y coordinate (0-199)
  mov bx,X                  ;BX = X coordinate (0-319)
  xchg al,ah                ;AX = Y*256
  add bx,ax                 ;BX = X + Y*256
  shr ax,2                  ;AX = Y*64
  add bx,ax                 ;BX = byte offset in video memory (Y*256 + Y*64 +
                            ;X) = (Y*320 + X)
  mov ax,0a000h
  mov es,ax                 ;ES = video memory segment

;To Get a Pixel
  mov al,es:[bx]             ;read pixel

;To Put a pixel
  mov al,Color              ;AL = pixel color
  mov es:[bx],al             ;set pixel
```

You may be upset to hear it, but no color logic is supported by your hardware in this mode. To provide it, the MOV instruction should be changed with XOR, OR or AND.

Unlike 16 color modes, where there are hardware registers to do the ANDing and so on, in 320x 200 x 256 colors, there is no hardware support. If an object is to be moved round the screen (like a sprite) over a colored background, the programmer must write code to handle non-rectangular sprites, or sprites with holes in them (through which the background can be seen). Sprites are rarely solid rectangles, but it is usual to store them as rectangular objects with a blank surround, like the cow below:

```
. . . . . . . . . . . . . .
. ++ . . . . . . . . . . .
. . . . ++++++ . . . .
. . . . . + . . . . + . . .
. . . . . . . . . . . . . .
```

One way of doing this is creating a 'mask', which is a rectangular object that completely surrounds the sprite. Every byte (or pixel) in the mask is either a 1 or a 0. If it is 1, the corresponding byte in the sprite is placed into the screen. If it is a 0, the screen data is left unchanged.

## 256 Color SVGA above 320x200

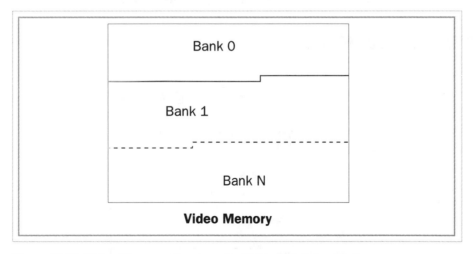

**Figure 11.11 Video Memory Structure in SVGA 256 Color Modes**

This diagram illustrates memory organization for 256-color SVGA modes exceeding 320x200 (640x400, 640x480, 800x600 and so on). The addressing technique remains the same as for 320x200, but bank switching is also used (as it is in all the following modes).

For example, to read and write a pixel in 256 color SVGA mode:

```
;Calculate Pixel Address
  mov ax,Y              ;AX = Y coordinate
  mov bx,X              ;BX = X coordinate
  mul BytesPerLine      ;AX = row offset in video memory from
                        ;the beginning of the bank Lo(Y*BytesPerLine)
                        ;DX = bank number Hi(Y*BytesPerLine)
  add bx,ax             ;BX = byte offset in video memory from
                        ;the beginning of the bank
  adc dx,0              ;bank-split-row catching
  mov ax,0a000h
  mov es,ax             ;ES = video memory segment
  call  SwitchBank      ; look*Note

;To Get a Pixel
  mov al,es:[bx]        ;read pixel

;To Put a pixel
  mov al,Color          ;AL = pixel color
  mov es:[bx],al         ;set pixel
```

*This procedure uses bank switching to look through particular code. For more detail on this, see the section on VESA BIOS Extensions (function 5h).*

## SVGA HighColor Modes

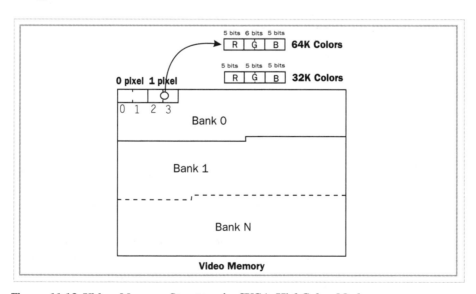

**Figure 11.12 Video Memory Structure in SVGA HighColor Modes**

HighColor moves into yet another new level of mysterious coding, with a word (2 bytes, 16 bits) for each pixel. There is no palette. The two-byte pixel code simply contains different intensities of the Red, Green and Blue components of the color. However, it's not quite that simple. For 32K color modes (meaning 32K different colors!), it is 5 bits per RGB component, and the sixteenth bit isn't used. For 64K color modes, the Green component occupies 6 bits, with Red and Blue at 5 bits each.

You can think of video memory as an array of words for HighColor modes. The way to address pixcls in this mode looks like this:

addr = Y*BytesPerLine + X*2.
where BytesPerLine = X_Resolution*2.

The value of BytesPerLine is taken from the VESA SVGA information service (Function 4f01h: Return SVGA Mode Information, Offset 16h).

The following example writes a pixel in HighColor mode:

```
mov  ax,Y              ;AX = Y coordinate
mov  bx,X              ;BX = X coordinate
mul  BytesPerLine      ;AX = row offset in video memory from the beginning of
                       ;the bank Lo(Y*BytesPerLine)
                       ;DX = bank number Hi(Y*BytesPerLine)
shl  bx,1              ;BX = X*2 (word per pixel)
add  bx,ax             ;BX = word offset in video memory from
                       ;the beginning of the bank
adc  dx,0              ;bank-split-row catching
mov  ax,0a000h
mov  es,ax             ;ES = video memory segment
call SwitchBank
mov  al,Blue           ;AL = blue component of pixel color
mov  ah,Red            ;AH = red component of pixel color
shl  ah,3              ;shift by 2 if 32K colors, by 3 if 64K
xor  bx,bx
mov  bl,Green          ;BX = green component of pixel color
shl  bx,5
or   ax,bx
mov  es:[bx],ax        ;do it
```

## SVGA TrueColor Modes

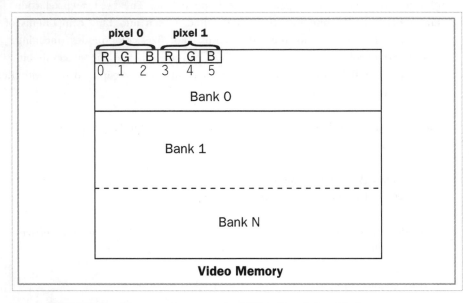

**Figure 11.13 Video Memory Structure in SVGA TrueColor Modes**

TrueColor modes are very similar to HighColor modes, except that this time there are 3 bytes or 24 bits for each pixel, 8 bits per RGB component. If you have 24 bits per pixel this is called twenty four bit graphics and you can use $2^{24}$ = 16,777,216 colors simultaneously, or at least you could do if you had that many pixels on the screen!

To address pixels in TrueColor modes you can use the following formula:

addr = Y*BytesPerLine + X*3.
where BytesPerLine = X_Resolution*3.

In screen modes like 1024 x 768 (768 rows of 1024 pixels), there are 64 rows per bank (12 banks in all). Each bank starts at the beginning of the row. In 640 x 480, there are some five banks of rows. Each bank has 65536/640 = 102.4 rows. What this means is that a bank doesn't start at the beginning of a row, but somewhere along it. When writing pixels to a row, you must first check that the pixel doesn't cross a bank. In the middle of a sprite this is quite likely!

This example writes a pixel in TrueColor mode:

```
mov ax,Y              ;AX = Y coordinate
mov bx,X              ;BX = X coordinate
mul BytesPerLine      ;AX = row offset in video memory from
                      ;the beginning of the bank
                      ;Lo(Y*BytesPerLine)
                      ;DX = bank number Hi(Y*BytesPerLine)
shl bx,1              ;BX = X*2
add bx,X              ;BX = X*3 (tree bytes per pixel)
add bx,ax             ;BX = word offset in video memory from
                      ;the beginning of the bank
adc dx,0                 ;bank-split-row catching
mov ax,0a000h
mov es,ax             ;ES = video memory segment
call SwitchBank
mov ah,Green          ;AH = green component of pixel color
mov al,Blue           ;AL = blue component of pixel color
mov es:[bx],ax           ;putting blue and green bytes
mov al,Red            ;AL = red component of pixel color
mov es:[bx+2],al         ;now red byte
```

# Summary

The story of the SVGA is almost fully written now. The VGA is already a matter for history. In this constantly evolving world of graphics programming, what remains the same is the need for tenacious programmers to unravel the secrets of each new system.

The VESA standards have gone a long way to making programming SVGA cards an activity fit for human beings. However, these standards are not perfectly implemented and there are signs that not everyone may adhere to them in the future. If that's not enough then there's always accelerators to worry about.

In this chapter, we've had a lightning tour of the PC video system. We've covered a lot of ground and we haven't had time to look at much real code. All of that will be put right in the next chapter, when we look at how to program the SVGA to maximum effect.

# Advanced Video Techniques

## Introduction

Years ago, when the term dialog was associated with text screens rather than a resource workshop, and when your mouse didn't keep turning into a pouring sand-glass the whole time, a graphics library was a separate, but essential, part of each and every compiler package on the market. Whether your favourite compiler was Turbo Prolog or Quick Pascal, it had to provide access to graphics via its own graphics library.

On the disk accompanying this book (directory GRAPH\) you will find an optimized custom graphics library GRAPH.LIB, along with all the source code it took to write this library. The library contains many useful graphics routines and can be used by your own graphics programs, or can provide a basis on which to develop your own library of routines. This chapter will therefore begin by discussing the design principles involved in creating your own optimized graphics library and then go on to examine some of the coding techniques used by some of the routines in the GRAPH.LIB library itself. Finally, we will finish off by taking a look at some other graphics programming topics that might also prove useful.

# Graphics Library Design

Graphical applications used to be specialised software. Nowadays, a simple notepad program can look more like 3D-Studio. Despite this, the internal structure of any graphical application remains broadly the same. Every graphics library tries to be both complete and universal. Its components are designed to match the widest possible spectrum of user demands. The inevitable result of this is a certain commonality in the scope and design of all libraries. The list of primitives (routines) that a library supports, as well as its logical structure, has become a kind of established tradition. Almost all libraries have the same two tier structure:

- **The Kernel** - This is the code that forms the heart of the library. It contains hardware and/or video mode independent code for primitives as well as data structures and set/get style procedures.

- **Drivers** - These contain hardware and/or video mode dependent low-level code for fundamental primitives, such as pixel plotting and line drawing.

**Table 12.1 Routines for a Typical Graphics Library**

| Operation | Library Examples |
|---|---|
| Mode switching | Init Graph, SwitchMode |
| System setting, color | Set/Get Palette, |
| Manipulation, etc. | ViewPort, FillStyle |
| Raster primitives | Get/Put Pixel, Image |
| Vector primitives | Draw/Fill Line, Bar, |
| | Polygon, Ellipse |
| Raster and vector fonts | OutText |

Applications use the library routines as building blocks to develop applications for morphing and ray tracing, etc. These are beyond the scope of this particular book. Here, we'll focus on the level of the graphics driver and the graphics kernel, the two of which together we'll call the graphics system.

## Library Compatibility

The graphics library we've included with this book supports a wide range of video modes including SVGA. However, the system provides access to SVGA modes only if it finds a VESA compatible adapter installed or a VESA driver loaded. We have also added shareware drivers for some popular video cards (see VESA directory on the disk).

Historically low-level or hardware dependent graphic drivers were written to handle the differences in the way that different video adapters used and organised video memory (for example the Borland graphics library used external files: HERC.BGI for Hercules adapters, CGI.BGI for CGA, etc.). More modern adapters however, such as the SVGA, are able to handle far too many different video modes and memory mapping schemes to sensibly combine them all into one driver. Instead, a more detailed grading system is required.

For instance, it would be a real mistake to combine 16 and 256 color modes in the same driver, because the actual implementation of low-level primitives for these modes varies drastically. It also makes sense to separate video modes that work without bank switching from high resolution modes to save the time taken to check for the bank border crossing.

**Table 12.2 A Possible Grouping of VGA and SVGA Drivers by Video Mode**

| Name | Description | Bank switching |
|------|-------------|----------------|
| VGA16 | All 16 colors modes up to 800x600 | No |
| VGA256 | VGA 256 colors mode 320x200 | No |
| SVGA | 256 Byte-per-pixel modes except 320x200 | Yes |
| HighColor | All word-per-pixel modes | Yes |
| TrueColor | All 24-bits-per-pixel modes | Yes |

We've left out 16-color SVGA modes exceeding 800x600 from the above list. These use bit planes and bank switching, which cause a lot of hassle for not a lot of speed. If you need a resolution beyond 800x600, you'll have to work with 256 colors. Also, in our library, we didn't implement High and True Color modes. If you need them, you can give yourself a little training and rework the

SVGA 256-color driver. See Chapter 11 for video memory structure for High and True Color Modes, and you'll find it pretty similar to that of 256-color mode, with the exception that you have to write 2 or 3 bytes per pixel.

# Selecting Library Routines

Before we look in detail at some of the routines that make up our graphics system, we need to decide which routines actually belong in the driver and which belong in the kernel. Speed and mode dependence are the keys to making this selection.

## The Driver

Without a doubt, the right place for a routine such as a pixel plotting primitive is in the driver, just because it's hardware and video mode dependent. But what about Line or Polygon routines? We could just draw them both via a pixel primitive, which would be a more general approach, but it would be far too slow. Here, as everywhere, you have to make a trade-off between speed and universality.

The following drivers are supplied on disk:

- GRAPH\EGAVGA16.ASM for EGA/VGA 16-color modes up to 800x600

- GRAPH\VGA256.ASM for VGA 256-colors 320x200 (mode 13h)

- GRAPH\SVGA256.ASM for SVGA 256-colors all resolutions

We decided to include the following primitives in the drivers:

- Get/Put Pixel

- Put Row (of pixels)

- Draw Line (with all special cases monitored)

- Bar

- Get/Put Image (rectangular area on the screen)

- Fill Polygon (without a border)

- ClipRectArea (EGAVGA16 driver only)

### The Kernel

When we say 'include' in the driver, we mean that only the hardware dependent part of each primitive's code is implanted into the driver. Clipping, rasterizing or the like shouldn't be included in the driver - these routines are generalized and should reside in the kernel.

The kernel part of our library will contain:

- Some general procedures like Init Graph.

- The high level part of all primitives.

- The block of system settings.

Below we'll explain the kernel routines in detail. The kernel consists of the following source files:

- GRAPH\GRAPH.H       Declares all variables, structures, and procedures in the kernel

- GRAPH\GRAPH.CPP    Implements high-level routines of the kernel

- GRAPH\GRAPHC.ASM   Implements low-level routines of the kernel

## The Library Structure

The following lists show the internal structure of the graphics library GRAPH.LIB, which is included with this book.

### Library System Settings - Tables and Variables

**Table 12.3 Tables and Variables**

| Table/ Variable | Description |
| --- | --- |
| proctable16 | The table of driver procedures' entry points for 16-color modes |
| proctable256 | The table of driver procedures' entry points for 256-color modes |

*Continued*

Table 12.3 Tables and Variables (Continued)

| Table/ Variable | Description |
|---|---|
| proctables256 | The table of driver procedures' entry points for SVGA 256-color modes |
| viewport | Current view port settings |
| viewport32767 | |
| videoselector | The segment address of the video buffer (0A000h) |
| bytesperline | The number of bytes in one display scan line |
| linepattern | The current pattern for lines |
| fillpatternptr | The current pattern for filling |
| patterntypetrflag | |
| drawcolor | The current color for lines |
| fillcolor | The current foreground color for filling |
| backcolor | The current background color for filling |
| writemode | The current bit-logic operation (AND,XOR, etc) |
| wasy | |
| sizeonerow | |
| ArrayScanLinesPtr | The pointer to the array of scanlines (used in the procedure fillpoly ) |
| grshift | |
| callVESAswbnkptr | The pointer to the VESA switch-bank procedure |

## Library Kernel - C Routines

The following routines are called the same way as in the Borland Graphics Interface, with minor difference in parameters (see GRAPH\GRAPH.H on disk).

| | | | |
|---|---|---|---|
| bar | circle | closegraph | ellipse |
| getcolor | getimage | getmaxx | getmaxy |
| getpixel | imagesize | linerel | lineto |
| moverel | moveto | putimage | putpixel |
| rectangle | setbkcolor | setcolor | setfillpattern |

setfillstyle  setlinestyle  setviewport  setwritemode

widthline

The rest of the C routines are proprietary to our library:

**Table 12.4 Proprietary C Routines**

| Routine | Description |
|---------|-------------|
| graphinit | Initializes all the variables and drivers and turns on the default 16-color mode |
| switchmode | Switches to a particular video mode (as available). |
| setglassflag | Toggles 'glass background' mode: when on, it suppresses drawing the background component of fill patterns. Default is off. |
| putrow | Displays a row of pixels (useful for displaying images). |

## Library Kernel - Assembly Code Routines

**Table 12.5 Assembly Code Routines**

| Routine | Description |
|---------|-------------|
| _testadapter | Detects the video adapter type |
| _normalline | Clips a line and calls the procedure DrawLine from a driver |
| _VESAcallswitchbank | Switches banks via a call to VESA procedure |
| _VESAintswitchbank | Switches banks via a call to VESA interrupt |
| _getDACblock | Reads a block of DAC registers |
| _setDACblock | Writes a block of DAC registers |
| _setVGApalette | Writes the VGA palette in 16-color mode |
| _clippixel | Clips a pixel to the current view port |
| _fillpoly | Rasterizes a polygon and calls the driver's procedure DrawPolygon |
| _drawpoly | Draws a polygon with lines |
| ClipRectArea | Calculates the intersection of a rectangular area and the current view port |

### Library Driver Routines

The library driver routines are as follows:

PutPixel    GetPixel    DrawLine    PutRow    Bar    ImageSize

GetImage    PutImage    DrawPolygon

The term driver, which we use here to refer to the low-level part of the system, doesn't presuppose a particular implementation, for example a set of drivers in separate files. As a matter of fact, we prefer to link drivers into the body of the application. This reduces the number of files for distribution and makes your intellectual property a little more secure.

# Some GRAPH.LIB Routines Explored

The graphics library accompanying this book was designed to support a wide range of video modes, from EGA 640x350 16-color up to SVGA 256-color modes of high resolution, and contains a large number of routines. Rather than give you a blow by blow account of how to create each and every routine, which is not in itself difficult, we'll concentrate on exploring some of the background and technical know-how behind some of these routines.

## Mode Switching

Before we can use any of the graphic routines in the library, first we have to select the appropriate graphics mode we wish to use. To do this, we need to call the GRAPHINIT routine, which tests your hardware and chooses the appropriate system settings. It also fills the table of supported video modes used by the SwitchMode routine. This table contains a text label for the mode name and useful information about the resolution and the amount of colors available. Having called GRAPHINIT, we can then call the SwitchMode routine to actually change modes.

## Line Drawing

One way of drawing lines on to the video screen is by simply drawing them pixel by pixel using the line equation:

$$Y = Mx + C$$

M is the gradient and C is the intercept of the Y axis. For each X co-ordinate you simply calculate the corresponding Y co-ordinate. However, this can cause problems. For instance, the equation is, in effect, a vector primitive and therefore is not totally suitable for lines that are raster represented. In addition, using the equation in programs, though easy to implement, is too cumbersome to be fast, especially as it requires some floating point calculations. For arbitrary curves we'll have to apply this kind of technique. However, there is a much faster way for straight lines. The line is the most frequently used graphic primitive, so it's got to be fast.

When you think about it, calculating the Y co-ordinate of each pixel in the line independently is a bit odd. It would seem that in a straight line there should be a kind of order that could be described by a simple iterative rule that could be used to calculate the Y co-ordinates of the line. Such a method is bound to be more efficient. There are several approaches to this problem, but here we'll just describe Bresenham's algorithm which we have actually utilised in the code for the driver routine (DRAWLINE).

## Bresenham's Line-drawing Algorithm

This algorithm was devised by J. E. Bresenham in 1965. The central idea is elegant, simple and powerful. Generally speaking, any method of rasterizing means there's the issue of error. Suppose you are choosing the right place for some pixel to plot. You should compare the errors of all possible positions and chose the one with the smallest error. It is actually the estimation of that error that is the basis for Bresenham's algorithm.

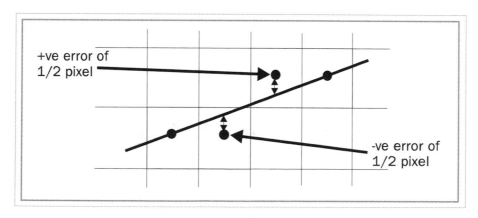

**Figure 12.1   Error Estimation for Bresenham's Algorithm**

To visualise how Bresenham's algorithm works, consider the portion of the line shown in the above diagram. After plotting a pixel, the algorithm determines whether the next pixel should be plotted at the same Y scan line or at the next one. The algorithm compares the errors that occur in both cases. The case with the smaller error will be chosen, and so on. While pixels are put on one scan line (one Y coordinate), the error is accumulated, and is compensated when the algorithm gets to the next scan line. The error is usually initialized by 1/2 in order to compare the sign of the error rather than the number (see the pseudocode fragment below).

The following pseudocode fragment illustrates the algorithm. It draws the set of pixels that lie closest to the line between two given pixels (X1,Y1) and (X2,Y2), assuming that X1 is less than X2 and that the slope of the line is between 0 and 1.

```
X  = X1; Y  = Y1; DX = X2 - X1; DY = Y2 - Y1;
Er=1/2 // Er = 2 * DY - DX; for integer variant

for X = X1 to X2 do
begin
PutPixel(X,Y)
if Er >= 0 then
        begin
        Y = Y + 1;
        Er = Er - 1; // Er = Er - 2 * DX for integer the variant
        end;
X = X + 1;
Er = Er + DY/DX; // Er = Er + 2 * DY for integer the variant
end;
```

You should avoid floating-point arithmetic wherever possible, so the program comments indicate the integer variant of the algorithm. For other octants and ABS(DY/DX) > 1 you should exchange X for Y or increment for decrement. Look through the actual code on disk for more details.

The resulting algorithm is efficient, because it doesn't use complicated floating-point calculations. However, there is still room for improvement.

## Optimization

After implementing such a clever algorithm for line approximation, it'd be absurd to throw away its efficiency in a tedious pixel address calculation. So the first stage of optimization should be to create a more efficient method of pixel addressing.

Certainly the pixel addresses calculation could itself be iterative. After calculating the address of the first pixel in the line, you can easily find its neighbours in the video buffer. Calculating pixel addresses incrementally is significantly faster than performing the computation from scratch for each (X,Y) pair on the line. Actual implementation depends on your particular video memory organization. Look through the code of the procedure DRAWLINE on the disk to find the details.

## Special Cases

For further improvement, consider some special cases of line drawing. It is possible for a special-purpose routine to draw horizontal lines at least 10 times faster than a general-purpose line-drawing procedure. Horizontal lines are represented in the video memory by a continuous sequence of bytes. You can fill them with a single REP STOSB instruction, which runs much faster than the iterative loop of the general line-drawing routine.

For vertical lines, a special-purpose routine can be about 25 percent faster. In drawing vertical lines, no logic is required to determine pixel locations. You simply increment the pixel address. Again, the resulting code is simpler and faster.

A final trick is to exploit the fact that for lines with a slope (DX/DY) less than 1, i.e. DY > DX, the algorithm usually produces sections of horizontal lines. In 16 color mode, it's worth making the algorithm a bit more complicated to plot these sections as fast horizontal lines.

This situation with the special cases of line plotting isn't unique. Time spent considering the special cases of a process is never wasted. In many applications, these special cases account for a surprisingly large percentage of the actual calls to the primitive library.

## Line Attributes

Lines have some defining attributes:

- Color

- Pattern

- Width

**Color:** The color attribute is the simplest. You simply transfer the desired color to the pixel plotting routine. This routine arranges everything itself, even if you're after a dithered color.

**Pattern:** In some applications, you might want to draw dashed or multicolored lines with a varying pixel pattern. To do this, modify the inner loop of your line-drawing routine to select pixel values from a circular list of possible values. Rotate the list each time you set a pixel. You can refer to the source code of the procedure DRAWLINE in every driver to see how patterned lines are drawn.

**Width:** Diagonal lines that are one pixel wide appear less bright than horizontal or vertical lines. You can fatten diagonal lines by modifying the inner plotting loop of a Bresenham line drawing routine so that it always sets both pixels if the error is close to 0. The resulting line looks fatter, but of course, the routine runs more slowly. To draw lines that are 2 or 3 pixels wide, you can simply draw neighbouring parallel lines. You could also consider a wide line to be a polygon and use the FILLPOLY routine to draw it.

# Clipping

Sometimes, you'd like your graphics to only appear in a limited region of the screen (in a window). Preventing graphics primitives from drawing outside a window is called clipping. Clipping is used even if no actual window (Viewport) is set, just to prevent drawing 'outside' the screen. The implentation of clipping varies for different graphics primitives, but it's always done at the kernel level, not in the drivers. Line clipping is discussed below.

## Pixel Level Clipping

The simplest and most general way to clip your line is to include a clipping test into the updating routine for each pixel. Before plotting any pixels, your routine compares the current pixel address with the system's viewport limits. This seems like a tedious approach. However, for arbitrary clipping limits, it's the only way possible. For clipping a line in a rectangular window there are much more efficient algorithms.

In general, you should avoid including any condition-testing code in low-level routines, regardless of how efficient the code might be. You can do it only if you are absolutely sure that the particular routine will never limit overall performance.

## A More Line-specific Approach

Another way to clip a line is to use its equation to calculate where, if anywhere, the line intersects the edges of the clipping region. If the clipping window is rectangular such a calculation isn't too complex.

To calculate the co-ordinates where the line and the edge of the window intersect, you just have to successively substitute the co-ordinates of the window's edge (X for vertical and Y for horizontal) into the line equation, solve the equation and check the result to see whether the intersection point actually lies within the line segment to be drawn, as well as within the rectangle. Although, actually calculating the intersection point co-ordinates is relatively simple, such an approach is slow, primarily because the whole calculation cycle is performed four times for every line segment you clip. Furthermore, you have to handle special cases of horizontal and vertical lines.

## A More Case Sensitive Algorithm

An algorithm that works in the way mentioned above can be made more efficient by sorting the lines to be clipped beforehand. By simply comparing the line's endpoint co-ordinates with the boundaries of the rectangular region you can skip the lines that don't need clipping. The Sutherland-Cohen algorithm, which uses this approach, is widely known because of its simplicity and computational efficiency.

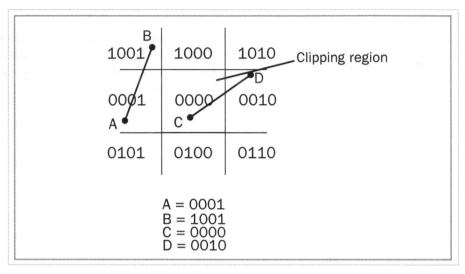

**Figure 12.2  Sutherland-Cohen Coding for Line Clipping in a Rectangular Window**

The first step of the algorithm is to code the endpoints of the line relative to the clipping window. Each endpoint of the line segment to be clipped falls into one of nine possible sub-regions. The algorithm uses a computational shortcut to mark the relative location of the line segment. Each of the nine sub-regions is marked with a 4-bit code. The endpoint is coded with the code of the sub-region it belongs to. Every line segment is identified by the codes of its endpoints. The location of the line segment relative to the rectangular clipping window can be quickly estimated by simple logical operations on the codes, so you can select the lines that really should be clipped.

**Table 12.6 Some Examples of the Endpoint Codes and Their Meanings**

| Endpoints | Codes | OR | AND | Meaning |
|-----------|-------|------|------|---------|
| 0000 | 0000 | 0000 | 0000 | No clipping |
| 0001 | 0001 | 0001 | 0001 | No clipping |
| 1001 | 0001 | 1001 | 0001 | No clipping |
| 1001 | 0100 | 1101 | 0000 | Partly visible, clipping required |

If the logical OR of two codes is 0, as in the first row of the table, both endpoints are within the window and no clipping is needed. If the logical AND of the codes is non-zero, both endpoints lie outside the boundaries of the window and again, no clipping is required. These tests can be performed rapidly by AND and OR instructions.

If it happens that the line segment is partly visible and so clipping is required, then the values of the endpoint codes determine which edge is crossed. The resulting intersection point becomes a new endpoint for the line segment. Line clipping is performed by the assembly language routine _NORMALLINE in the kernel.

# Filling Polygons

Filling the polygonal areas of the screen is the most complex of the primitives. We are going to look at an outline of the procedures involved, but skip all the details of the actual implementation as you can easily review these in the code itself, in the file GRAPH\GRAPHC.ASM, procedure _FILLPOLY.

The system has a preallocated data buffer which can be addressed through the ArrayScanLinePtr created by GRAPHINIT. This buffer is used for the scan conversion (rasterizing) of polygons, as well as by every other primitive that needs it. During scan conversion, a polygon is transformed into a set of scan lines. Each scan line is a pack of horizontal lines that fall on to the polygon at this scan line. So, the whole polygon becomes covered with these pieces of horizontal lines.

The scan line buffer structure is:

| first scan row | Num_of_points | Xin Xout | Xin Xout | ... |
| second scan row | Num_of_points | Xin Xout | Xin Xout | ... |
| : | | | | |
| Ymax-th scan row | Num_of_points | Xin Xout | Xin Xout | ... |

Num_of_points is the number of intersections of each scan line with the polygon, Xin and Xout are X co-ordinates of the entry and exit points of the intersection.

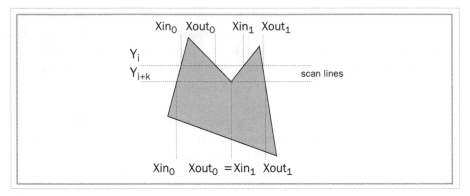

**Figure 12.5  Scan Conversion of the Polygonal Region**

The buffer is initially allocated to keep Ymax scan rows and up to 8 intersection pairs for every row, but the size of the buffer can be increased if necessary.

Each time you need a filled polygon, the system performs the scan conversion (rasterizing). It starts from the first vertex you specify and moves to the second one filling the scan line buffer.

From vertex to vertex it goes around the polygon writing its X co-ordinate into the corresponding Y row of the scan buffer for each point of the polygon's border. At the same time, it determines the maximum and minimum Y co-ordinates of the polygon, which we need to specify the boundaries of the filling cycle. Scanning is also the right time to perform Y co-ordinate clipping. Here you just stop writing to the scan line buffer if the current Y goes beyond the clipping window boundaries. After scanning, each row must contain an even number of intersection co-ordinates, which should then be sorted into ascending order.

There are some specific cases that must be checked for when scanning the polygon boundaries. The vertex which is the local minimum (has a smaller Y value than its neighbours), or the local maximum (has a greater Y value), must be written twice to the scan line buffer.

We now have to clip each row. It's easy because the X co-ordinates are already sorted. The algorithm scans each row from the beginning and exchanges X co-ordinates which appear to be clipped off with -1. If it finds a region of the scan line that is only partly visible, it updates Xin or Xout with the left or right X co-ordinate of the clipping window. Having prepared the scan line buffer by rasterizing the polygon, all that remains is for the low-level plotting routine to display all the scan lines.

Creating fills is a much larger subject than just filling polygons. For instance, there are algorithms that fill a region of arbitrary shape, starting with a single point inside the shape. This technique of rasterizing seems to be one of the most common and we'll use it again in this book. True Type fonts, sprite animation and many other techniques are based in part on this rasterizing method. The difference is in the condition to be tested while scanning the rows and how that scanning is organized.

# More Graphics Programming Topics

## Color Dithering

Dithering is a method of systematically or randomly combining pixels of basic colors to produce more shades of color or gray. It's a very popular technique which you can use when you need more colors and can put up with some loss of spatial resolution. It would not be necessary if all computers were equipped with True (or at least High) Color video subsystem, which have enough 'hardware' colors, but there are lots of VGAs on the market with poor color resolution. Dithering allows you to achieve reasonable results even on these.

### Pattern Dithering

First, let's look at simple pattern dithering to make things clear. A single pixel in most CRT color modes isn't made up of just one single RGB triad. For example, in 320x200 mode there are quite a lot of them in one single pixel. When using pattern dithering, it's best to think of each pixel as a dither cell, usually made up of either 8x8 or 4x4 hardware pixels. The color mix of the pixel is generated just like the RGB triad mosaic that generates the color of each hardware pixel.

Pattern dithering is in fashion now due to MS Windows. However, it was invented and perfected long ago as a way of producing halftones for black and white or color printing. For printing it's really crucial because it's very hard to provide a lot of shades of color or gray in a simple output device. The only way to do it is through dithering.

In this book we'll only describe the details of a pattern dithering implementation in 16 color mode. Dithering is a powerful technique. However, it isn't a magic wand, particularly when using only simple pattern dithering. You need to be clear about what you gain and what you lose. Pattern dithering is a compromise between resolution and color. It's most useful in GDI systems to implement hardware independent color processing.

## Implementing a 16 Color 8x8 Dither Cell

By combining 8x8=64 color dots in 16 color mode, you can theoretically provide a huge number of colors. In practice, creative combining is needed even to map 256K colors. There are a lot of different approaches to implementing a dithering program. However, our experience shows that, on the whole, the best palette map is an 8x8 dither cell like the one used by MS Windows.

There are two stages in implementing a dithering technique:

- Deciding the geometrical process you will use for creating the cell pattern.

- Deciding what method you will use to mix colors.

The first step is not hard, just time consuming. We strongly recommend that you use a ready made cell pattern. Even so, it's worth taking a brief look at the process of creating your own.

## The Dither Cell Pattern

Firstly, what do we mean by a dither cell pattern? Imagine a chessboard, the white tiles of which represent bright color dots and the black ones, dark color dots. We need a set of such chessboards with a smoothly increasing density of white (or decreasing of black) to use as cell patterns for dithering. The chessboard itself is a famous pattern usually referred to as 50% gray: i.e. halfway between dark and light.

Besides having smoothly increasing density, the pattern must also be uniformly distributed in such a way that two cells placed next door to each other don't generate lines on the border.

The dither cells in our implementation are 8x8 (see the code fragment below). This makes dithering faster, with the slight drawback that one light or one dark dot in an 8x8 matrix has an imperceptible effect in the overall appearance. We therefore increased the density in increments of two dots at a time. This means there are 32 sequential patterns. The following diagram represents the four first and four last patterns:

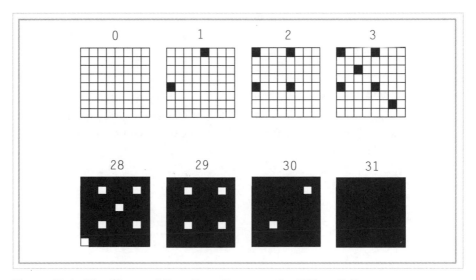

**Figure 12.4   The First and Last Four Patterns of a Dither Cell**

## Adding Colors

Having prepared the cell pattern, it's time to add the colors. There are various ways to mix color in a dither cell. We'll look at the simplest and most popular method.

In 16 color mode, we have two pairs of pixels for each RGB color, each of a different intensity. For instance, they could be black & dark blue or dark blue & bright blue. Each of the pairs can produce 32 shades of color. In total, that's 64 shades for each of red, green and blue. Then you just mix them in the same way you would RGB. For each colored dot of the dithering pattern, the corresponding RGB mixture is calculated and displayed.

So how many colors have we gained through dithering? Let's see. We have 32*2 shades for each of RGB, 6 bits per component: theoretically we should have 2 power 6*3 = 256K colors. However, some of them are identical so really about 160K are available. It's not TrueColor yet, but it's close.

Similar techniques may be applied to 256 color mode. Here your dither cell should be 4x4, so that each row of the cell fits into a double word. Four, or even five, pairs of pixels of differing intensity provide 4*8 = 32 shades of each pure color, giving 128K colors. We are still assuming that the pattern density is increased by two at a time.

## The Dithering Code

The following program is a routine _SETRGBCOL which generates a tiny bitmap (one dither cell 8x8) in accordance with the RGB representation of the particular color.

```
; base colors - number of "pure" colors in system palette
; (numbers of palette registers)
Red         EQU    4
LightRed    EQU    12
Green       EQU    2
LightGreen  EQU    10
Blue        EQU    1
LightBlue   EQU    9


RGBcolor struc                        ; 8x8 bitmap structure
     Plan0 db 8 dup (?)               ; 8 bytes per each bit plane
     Plan1 db 8 dup (?)
     Plan2 db 8 dup (?)
     Plan3 db 8 dup (?)
RGBcolor ends

.data

fillRGBcol   RGBcolor <0>   ; allocate memory for bitmap in data segment

.code

; R,G,B components [0..63]
B     EQU byte ptr [bp+10]
G     EQU byte ptr [bp+8]
R     EQU byte ptr [bp+6]

_setrgbcol           proc far
                     push bp
                     mov bp,sp
                     push di                  ; preserve caller registers
```

```
                mov ax,@data
                mov es,ax
                lea di,fillRGBcol.RGBcolor.Plan0     ; ES:DI point to bitmap

                cld                     ; clear direction flag
                mov cx,16               ; CX = word in bitmap
                xor ax,ax               ; AX = 0
                rep stosw               ; zero bitmap

                lea di,fillRGBcol.RGBcolor.Plan0
                add al,R                ; AL = Red component
                jz no_red               ; jamp if R = 0

                mov cl,0                ; CL = 0 (Black)
                mov ch,Red              ; CH = number of "Red" register
                cmp al,32               ; if R < 32 then will be mixed
                                        ; Black and Red colors
                jb BlackRed
                                        ; mixed Red and LightRed colors
                mov cl,ch               ; CL = number of "Red" register
                mov ch,LightRed         ; CH = number of "LightRed" register
                sub al,32               ; AL = 0..31
BlackRed:
                call CalcMaskColor      ; create mask for the first four
                                        ; rows of bitmap
                call CreatBitMap        ; create the first four rows
                                        ; of bitmap
no_red:
                mov al,G                ; AL = Green component
                or al,al
                jz no_green             ; jamp if R = 0
                lea di,fillRGBcol.RGBcolor.Plan0
                mov cl,0                ; CL = 0 (Black)
                mov ch,Green            ; CH = number of "Green" register
                cmp al,32               ; if G < 32 then will be mixed
                                        ; Black and Green colors
                jb BlackGreen
                                        ; mixed Green and LightGreen colors
                mov cl,ch               ; CL = number of "Green" register
                mov ch,LightGreen       ; CH = number of "LightGreen" register
                sub al,32               ; AL = 0..31
BlackGreen:
                call CalcMaskColor      ; create mask for the first four
                                        ; rows of bitmap
                call CreatBitMap        ; create the first four rows
                                        ; of bitmap
no_green:
                mov al,B                ; AL = Blue component
                or al,al
                jz no_blue              ; jump if B = 0
                lea di,fillRGBcol.RGBcolor.Plan0
                mov cl,0                ; CL = 0 (Black)
                mov ch,Blue             ; CH = number of "Blue" register
                cmp al,32               ; if B < 32 then will be mixed
                                        ; Black and Blue colors
```

```
                     jb BlackBlue
                                          ; mixed Blue and LightBlue colors
                     mov cl,ch            ; CL = number of "Blue" register
                     mov ch,LightBlue     ; CH = number of "LightBlue" register
                     sub al,32            ; AL = 0..31
BlackBlue:
                     call CalcMaskColor   ; create mask for the first four
                                          ; rows of bitmap
                     call CreatBitMap     ; create the first four rows
                                          ; of bitmap
no_blue:
                                          ; make last four rows of bitmap

                     lea di,fillRGBcol.RGBcolor.Plan0
                     mov dl,4             ; plan counter
                     mov cl,4             ; shift counter
shift_next_plan:
                     mov ch,4             ; row counter
shift_row:
                     mov al,es:[di]       ; AL = row from first half of bitmap
                     rol al,cl            ; shift AL at 4
                     mov es:[di+4],al     ; create row the second half of bitmap
                     inc di               ; DI point to next row
                     dec ch
                     jnz shift_row        ; shift next row

                     add di,4             ; DI point to next bit plane of bitmap
                     dec dl
                     jnz shift_next_plan  ; next bit plane
debug_exit:
                     pop di
                     pop bp               ; restore registers
                     ret                  ; and return
_setrgbcol    endp

; subroutine for creating the first four rows of bitmap
; input: DL,DH,BL,BH - masks for corresponding rows
CreatBitMap  proc near
                     call CalcBitMap      ;first row
                     mov bl,bh
                     inc di
                     call CalcBitMap      ;second row
                     mov bl,dl
                     inc di
                     call CalcBitMap      ;third row
                     mov bl,dh
                     inc di
                     call CalcBitMap      ;fourth row
                     ret
CreatBitMap  endp

; subroutine for creating one row of bitmap
; input: BL - mask for that row
;      CL,CH - base colors
```

```
CalcBitMap     proc near
               push dx
               mov dl,8                ; bit counter
               mov ah,1                ; unshifted bit mask
next_bit_mask:
               push di
               mov al,cl               ; AL = base color 1
               shr bl,1                ; shifted BL bit by bit we monitoring
               jnc color1              ; CF flag to arise in dependence with
                                       ; this choosing color for mix
               mov al,ch               ; AL = base color 2
color1:
               mov dh,4                ; plane counter
next_bit_plane:
               shr al,1                ; load AH to bit planes in
               jnc no_or               ; according with four lower
               or es:[di],ah           ; bits AL (base color)
no_or:
               add di,8                ; DI = points to next bit plane
               dec dh
               jnz next_bit_plane

               pop di
               shl ah,1                ; next bit
               dec dl
               jnz next_bit_mask
               pop dx
               ret
CalcBitMap     endp

; masks table (32 items)
DitherTable:
               db 08,0,0,0
               db 88h,0,0,0
               db 88h,0,20h,0
               db 88h,0,22h,0
               db 0a8h,0,22h,0
               db 0aah,0,22h,0
               db 0aah,0,0a2h,0
               db 0aah,0,0aah,0
               db 0aah,0,0aah,40h
               db 0aah,0,0aah,44h
               db 0aah,1,0aah,44h
               db 0aah,11h,0aah,44h
               db 0aah,11h,0aah,54h
               db 0aah,11h,0aah,55h
               db 0aah,51h,0aah,55h
               db 0aah,55h,0aah,55h
               db 0bah,55h,0aah,55h
               db 0bbh,55h,0aah,55h
               db 0bbh,55h,0eah,55h
               db 0bbh,55h,0eeh,55h
               db 0fbh,55h,0eeh,55h
               db 0ffh,55h,0eeh,55h
```

```
                db 0ffh,55h,0feh,55h
                db 0ffh,55h,0ffh,55h
                db 0ffh,55h,0ffh,75h
                db 0ffh,55h,0ffh,77h
                db 0ffh,0d5h,0ffh,77h
                db 0ffh,0ddh,0ffh,77h
                db 0ffh,0ddh,0ffh,0f7h
                db 0ffh,0ddh,0ffh,0ffh
                db 0ffh,0fdh,0ffh,0ffh
                db 0ffh,0ffh,0ffh,0ffh

; load to DX and BX masks for the first four rows of bitmap
; input: AL - mask number
CalcMaskColorproc near
                cbw                     ; AX = mask number
         mov bx,Offset DitherTable      ; CS:BX - point to masks table
                shl ax,2                ; AX = AX*4
                add bx,ax               ; BX = points to mask ???
                mov dx,cs:[bx+2]        ; DX = masks for first and second rows
                mov bx,cs:[bx]          ; DX = masks for 3rd and 4th rows
                ret
CalcMaskColor endp

end;
```

This dithering technique can be implemented for both 16 and 256 colors modes, making uniform color processing possible. You can display HighColor-like images even though that mode may not be supported by the hardware. You can see our implementation of 16-color dithering in the file COLORS\DITHER.ASM. The program DITHTEST.CPP demonstrates this technique.

# Text and Fonts

## What Are Fonts?

Whatever graphics software you write, you inevitably have to deal with text. Even with modern GUI style icons and buttons, and with extra means of expression like sound cards, the major part of your dialog with the user is still done via screen text. Some applications only need simple text to communicate with the user, while others, like publishing systems, require multiple typesets and font sizes.

In this section, we'll discuss various types of fonts used on the PC, and give you simple and fast bitmap fonts to incorporate in your programs.

## Font Fundamentals

A font is a complete set of characters that have common style. The design of a font includes its weight (light, normal, or bold), shape (round, oval, or straight), x-height (height of text body - i.e. lower case letters), posture (oblique and italic), and the presence or absence of serifs (the short crossline at the end of the main strokes).

There are three kinds of fonts used in the computer industry.

- Raster (sometimes referred as bitmap)

- Vector

- True type

Let's look at each of these in more detail.

## Raster Fonts

Historically, these are the first breed of fonts that appeared on computer displays. Simple and compact, they are built into devices like video adapters or printers to provide the fastest possible text output.

As you might have guessed by the name, raster font data represents the pixel layout of each character exactly as it should appear on display. Every pixel that will be put on the screen is represented with a bit in the bitmap. Let's build a demo raster for the letter 'I', working on the assumption that the font is 8 pixels wide and high.

**Table 12.7  A Raster Font Bitmap of the Letter 'I'**

| Offset | Hex value | Binary value |
|--------|-----------|--------------|
| 0 | 00h | 00000000 |
| 1 | 3Ch | 00111100 |
| 2 | 18h | 00011000 |
| 3 | 18h | 00011000 |

*Continued*

Table 12.7   A Raster Font Bitmap of the Letter 'I' (Continued)

| Offset | Hex value | Binary value |
|--------|-----------|--------------|
| 4 | 18h | 00011000 |
| 5 | 18h | 00011000 |
| 6 | 3Ch | 00111100 |
| 7 | 00h | 00000000 |

The characters in raster fonts are of fixed width and height. Bitmaps of each separate letter are stored in a font one by one, so the offset address of the first byte of a character from the start of the font data can be calculated as follows:

Offset = (ASCII code) * (Bytes per character)

Thus, letter 'A' (ASCII code = 65) in an 8x8 font starts from the offset address of 520.

Raster fonts have these obvious advantages:

- They are extremely small

- They can be displayed at top speed

- It's very easy to create and modify them

However, not everything about raster fonts is so great. As they are mosaically composed of individual pixels, you can't scale a character at an arbitrary rate. It will most probably turn out very distorted. It's possible, of course, to enlarge a character by substituting each pixel with two or three, but again, it will look all blocky. To solve this problem, vector fonts were invented.

## Vector Fonts

Vector fonts make much more use of computing power than raster ones. They are not simply coded shapes of letters, but rather coded information using a sort of language. This language consists of commands like "Line", "Curve", "Polygon" and other primitive figures which are used to draw the desired symbol. The primitives, naturally, have co-ordinates relative to a rectangular area occupied by the symbol. The routine that displays the text translates the primitives into symbols by reading and executing the commands that draw the lines and polygons on the screen.

As a vector font only works with relative co-ordinates and not pixels, letters can easily be scaled while retaining their original proportions, their shapes remaining as smooth as the screen resolution allows. All we have to do is to recalculate the relative position of each primitive component. With a little more code we can implement special effects like bending, curving, rotating, adding perspective, etc.

Some systems manage to combine the flexibility of vector fonts with the speed of raster fonts by rasterizing the vector font outlines. The rasterizer is a program module that creates a scaled bitmap image of the vector font. The prepared bitmap is then shown on screen similar to a raster font.

Drawn in sufficient space, the lines and curves of a rasterized vector font appear to run freely and smoothly. If crowded into a small space, they mix up and even drop out of the pixel grid. It's easy to lose the dot from the top of a 'i' with a very small font size. However, all is not lost.

## True Type Fonts

The True Type font (TTF) is a logical evolution of the vector concept. Letter outlines are made up of lines and quadratic splines (special kind of smooth curves), but in addition, TTFs are smart enough to give hints to the graphics system to compensate for low screen resolution. It's this unique hinting mechanism that provides convincing WYSIWYG fonts in Windows.

Each TrueType font remembers the ideal outline of a perfectly shaped symbol. A symbol outline consists of a series of connected contours and lines, which are defined by a series of points to be interpolated by quadratic B-splines. There are two types of points: those that are ON the curve and those that are OFF. These two types may be freely combined to make the desired curve shape. Straight lines are defined just by their endpoints.

Point positions are coded in font units, or FUnits. An FUnit is the smallest measurable unit in the 'em' square, which is an imaginary Cartesian co-ordinate square in some abstract high resolution space that is used to store, resize and align symbols. Why em? It's a term inherited from real world typography, where it means 'the space that contains a capital M'. The greater the dimension of this M-space (in FUnits per em), the more precise point addressing and outline scaling will be. Outline scaling will be faster if the units per em chosen is a power of 2 (usually 2048).

In order to bring TT fonts before our eyes, Windows has to do the following:

1    Load the font.

2    Transfer it to the rasterizer.

3    Scale the outline to the actual point size for the given resolution of the output device.

4    Apply the hints to the outline, transforming the contours to build what is known as a grid fitted (or hinted) outline.

5    Fill the grid fitted outline with pixels, creating a solid letter bitmap.

6    Scan for dropouts if required by the font.

7    Cache the raster bitmap.

8    Transfer the raster bitmap to the display.

## BIOS Support

The video BIOS provides some support for displaying text. Its software character generator allows you to set up a dynamic raster font which is used whenever INT 10h functions 09h (Write Character and Attribute at Cursor Position), 0Ah (Write Character Only at Cursor Position), 0Eh (Write Character and Advance Cursor), and 13h (Write Text String) are called in graphics modes.

Originally, in IBM PC and AT models, the software character generator only used the 8-by-8 characters defined in ROM at F000:FA6Eh (ASCII 0 through 127) and at the address pointed to by interrupt vector 1Fh (ASCII 128 through 255). After boot-up the upper half of the character set was undefined, and had to be installed by the DOS GRAFTABL utility.

The BIOS versions in EGA, VGA and PS/2 machines use a font table for the entire character set to which interrupt vector 43h points. The character height is stored in the BIOS variable POINTS (WORD) at 0040:0085. When you boot up your PC and initialize graphics mode, these BIOSes set vector 43h to point at a font in video ROM.

You can use the BIOS software character generator to display characters from any raster font table by modifying the appropriate interrupt vectors to point to the new table. The most convenient way to do this is to use the INT 10h character generator function 11h to do this.

When you've installed your custom font, you simply use BIOS interrupt 10h functions to display text. Using function 13h, available on the EGA and VGA was the old method:

Interrupt 10h (Video Service)
Function 13h (Display string)

On entry:    AH = 13h
ES:BP = address of string to display
CX = character count
DH, DL = row, column to start the string
BH = video page number
BL = color attributes
AL = 0

Alhough it's very convenient and code efficient, the BIOS route has a few disadvantages. It supports only 8-bit wide fonts and displays characters byte aligned, i.e. possible x-coordinates are 0, 8, 16, 24, etc. It's also not the fastest way to do the job and BIOS will not support text output in HighColor or TrueColor video modes.

So, if you're writing a small utility program in graphics mode which doesn't need a lot of text interaction, you can get along with BIOS alone. In more complex graphics and text environments you'll most probably need a more sophisticated technique as described below.

## Show Me Some Fonts!

Now it's time to write some code. Displaying raster fonts is no harder than displaying a bitmap picture. You simply replace the appropriate pixels in the video buffer according to bit patterns in a character table. In sending one byte from a character bitmap, you update eight pixels at once by selecting a corresponding mask.

As graphics modes allow arbitrary positioning of text on screen, your routines have to check whether a character falls into the video buffer within a single byte's boundary or crosses it. If one part of a character gets into one byte and the rest into another, you should transfer these two parts separately by properly shifting and masking bit patterns.

You should also check the output for clipping. Practically all output must be clipped if not to some square window, then at least to the entire screen area. For example, if in 640x480 mode you write an 8 bits wide letter at the position (636,200) near the right edge of display, then only 4 bits of the pattern can fit the screen. So you must output exactly 4 bits (i.e. update 4 pixels), or else the remaining 4 will wrap over to the left edge of the screen.

To clip characters horizontally, you should mask the unfitting part of a bit pattern, so that it doesn't update the video buffer. Vertical clipping, however, is easier. Just don't transfer those bytes which would get beyond the screen limits.

The code on the disk, in the file RASTFONT\PUTSTR.ASM, is not just a sample. It is used commercially, and naturally, we've optimized the routine for speed as much as we can.

## Getting More Out of Bitmap Fonts

## Bold Effects

You can apply a simple trick to embolden a raster font. Display a line of text once, increase its horizontal position by 1 and then display it again. Vertical stems of letters will swell, while horizontal ones will look nearly the same. This is a simple technique, but it does give quite consistent results with all fonts. Of course, it's half the speed of non bold output, but even so, it's still pretty fast.

```
DisplayString( 100, 200, "Get bolder!", black);
DisplayString( 101, 200, "Get bolder!", black);
```

If you're really after speed, you can modify the actual bitmaps without too much trouble. Every byte in the font's bitmap should be ORed with its right-shifted equivalent. The code of a simple boldifying routine might look something like this:

```
        mov cx,FontSize              ; initialize the counter
        xor di,di                    ; start from offset 0
  NextByte:
        mov al,[Font+di]             ; get a byte
        shr al,1                     ; shift it right one bit (i.e. one pixel)
        or [Font+di],al              ; store back to the font
        inc di                       ; next byte
        loop NextByte
```

As often happens, faster performance means retaining a larger amount of data. The choice is yours.

## Shadow Effects

Objects can cast shadows in lots of ways, depending on the position and structure of the light source, and the qualities of the surrounding surface. Again, there is a simple way to simulate shadow effects by displaying the same text in a bright color one pixel higher and to the left of your original darker text. The result looks as if the letters rise above the background shadow.

```
        DisplayString( 100, 200, "Just me and my shadow...", black);
        DisplayString( 99, 199, "Just me and my shadow...", yellow);
```

Alternatively, if you make the underlaid text brighter and the covering text darker, and display the latter one pixel lower and to the right, the letters appear engraved on the surface.

```
        DisplayString( 100, 200, "Sir Crouchback, Esq", light_red);
        DisplayString( 101, 201, "Sir Crouchback, Esq", black);
```

The program RASTFONT\DEMOFONT.CPP demonstrates using the procedure DisplayString and the effects mentioned above.

# Animation

## Is PC Animation Real?

Everyone's seen excellent PC animation. Computer animation is one of the most exciting parts of bitmap graphics programming. But what is animation? Certainly its appearance is of something living and moving. However, formally speaking, animation is based on a trick of human vision. If you view a series of specially created images in fast enough succession, your brain perceives them as smooth continuous motion.

What do we mean by fast enough? The number of pictures (frames) you need to show per second varies from one person to another, but it's usually at least 12 (though if page flipping techniques are used for flicker free screen updates, as low as five is acceptable). The higher the frame rate, the more perfect the illusion of motion. Increasing the frame rate beyond 30 frames per second (the NTSC standard) is usually considered useless, as it is faster than the persistence of the human eye.

As you might expect, implementing a realistic animation is not easy, and each stage of the process has its own issues to contend with, especially on a PC platform.

### Implementing Animation

Table 12.8 shows all the stages in a computer animation life cycle from creation to display, just to give you a feel for the problems of each.

**Table 12.8   Computer Animation Life Cycle**

| Animation Stage | Key Problem | Solution |
|---|---|---|
| Creation | Too many frames | Key framing, modelling |
| Storage | Huge media space | Compression (FLC, MPEG) |
| Show | Fast transmission | New generation of PC |

If you decide to animate something, the first problem is the huge amount of images you have to create. Each minute of animation requires from 720 (60*12 frames/per second) to 1800 frames (60*30), depending on the smoothness of the motion you'd like to achieve. Assembling this quantity of pre-prepared drawings is a big job; creating them on-the-fly is no simpler.

Suppose you've created the number of frames required for one minute of your animation by employing artists or purchasing Autodesk Animator, for instance, in 640x480 256 color graphics mode. If you estimate the amount of storage space you need for this minute, it'll be

640 * 480 * 1800 = 550 Megabytes.

Well, that's almost one complete CD's worth! Even if you decide to moderate your appetite and choose more 'reasonable' specifications, say a 256 color 320x200 resolution mode with 20 frames per second, you will still need 77M of animated bytes to be stored somewhere, all for just one minute of animation. Thus you need a huge amount of media space to work with real animation.

Imagine, at last, you have your animation ready and stored, and are about to show it. You need a high enough transfer rate to move successive frames to the video system of your computer. It's rather difficult to estimate the particular figures as they depend largely on your bus, processor and video adapter. So we decided to use a simple test.

## Testing Frame Transfer Speed

We used the simplest and fastest assembly routine we could write that only moved data blocks 64K in size from conventional memory to the video buffer. The overall time for 1000 transfers was measured. Why 64K? Because it's a whole screen frame in 320x200 256 color video mode, so we could measure transfer rate directly in frames per second. You can easily recalculate this frame size for any other video mode. We made two versions of the test routine, one for word and another for double word transfer. We've tested various computers, and the results of the test are given on the next page.

Table 12.9 Transfer Rates into Video Memory

| CPU Type | Frequency | Cache Size | Bus Type | Video Adapter | Frames per second 640x480, HighColor | |
| --- | --- | --- | --- | --- | --- | --- |
| | | | | | Word | DWord |
| 386SX | 33 | 0 | ISA | VGAArt 800 | 3.05 | 3.11 |
| 386DX | 20 | 0 | ISA | WD90C3X | 5.00 | 6.02 |
| 386DX | 40 | 128K | ISA | Realtec | 1.04 | 1.12 |
| 486DX | 33 | 128K | VLB | TGUI 9400 | 10.38 | 18.94 |
| 486DX | 33 | 128K | VLB | CVGA-5426VL | 15.5 | 15.5 |

The figures show the upper limit of the PC's performance applied to animation. Only 486 machines with VLB (VESA Local Bus) provide an adequate transfer rate. Moreover, if a hard disk is used as the data source, which is most likely the case, the results are much worse.

So what are we trying to prove? We simply want to show that, even if you could realistically create and store it, Real Time Video animation can't be shown on today's PCs without special equipment. If it could, then this whole section would consist of a couple of pages of program text. Instead, we need to look at what we can do to bridge the performance gap, both for the animation artist and the programmer.

## The Animation Artist

From the animation artist's point of view, the main problem is the number of frames to be drawn. There are two different ways to tackle this issue.

The first way is to increase the artist's productivity by computer aided generation of [be]tweens. This is called keyframing. Most of the frames in cartoons are routine incremental changes of figures in the picture - a bullet swishing across the screen or a stretching arm - or are simple background scrolling like running trees behind a car. Software exists that can interpolate handmade keyframes to produce all the necessary tweens. The artist still has to write a local scenario to specify each character's motion and action. The language that describes this is evolving rapidly. We can already describe complex effects using phrases such as precise perspective projection, stretching morph, biomechanically realistic motion, etc.

The second way is to use a kind of modelling. The artist defines an artificial nature, creates the rules, invents the characters and leaves his creations to act out their own existence. For we mortals creation is no easy job. However, for interactive animations such as games, tutorials and simulators, modelling is the only option.

## The Animation Programmer

From the programmer's point of view, the three main problems of computer animation (number of frames required, lack of storage space and transmission rates) can be solved in two different ways:

- **Windowing**, which means displaying a real video in a section of the screen. The alternative is to show a succession of frames compressed by a powerful algorithm like FLC, MPEG, or Fractal compression. Some of these use a compression ratio of up to 1:125 and so provide both decompression in real time and the ability to fit into the available media space on the PC.

- **Modelling**, which means a sophisticated Virtual Reality engine that calculates graphics fast enough to look like video.

Modelling is the oldest, and in the long term, the most promising avenue of development in computer animation. If you've played the game 'Doom', you'll remember the 'polygonal' robot-like characters. They are a good example of modelled animation.

It was polygonal constructions that came before all other models (certainly from CAD systems). And they brought the polygonal shadowing technique that's still very popular in games (due to its simplicity and speed). Polygonal landscapes or other objects are more or less detailed meshes (systems of connected polygons that define modelled surfaces), which are relatively easy to project and shadow. However, it's rather difficult to make a polygonal model of a human being look natural, no matter how smoothly it moves.

You need something more creative to generate surface texture. Maybe you'll choose B-splines applied to a polygonal framework, like the skin pulled over a mannequin. Splines themselves are rather complicated, and would require even more artful projecting and shadowing. It becomes unreal for real time animation even on present high-end graphics workstations. On top of all this, you need some inventive methods to manage objects structure and features. That's why, at present, these methods may only be used in keyframing to prepare tweens, but soon we'll play games with modelled animation and complex texture generation (some of the most recent games employ sophisticated techniques like 'voxels' to produce detailed terrain mapped worlds). Indy Car 500 has very detailed 3D cars with all the detail down to sponsors and the drivers name on the vehicle.

# Practical Animation Techniques

## Using the Palette

This is a tricky technique that only works in 256 color mode. Despite that, it's not that difficult and does produce impressive results. It's useful for simple jobs like a screen saver.

The underlying idea is very simple. By changing a single DAC register, you can affect a lot of pixels almost immediately. Changing the palette successively can create a good illusion of motion. In fact, nothing really moves in this case. As you play with the palette you successively expose and hide frozen frames. All you need is a picture prepared in a special way.

There's a simple palette trick we call ColorWheel. You display an image and then spin the palette, i.e. rotate the colors in it as if the palette was a big register. You'll see something moving, although we can't predict the character of motion.

Here is the routine ColorWheel, which provides a base for many palette tricks. All it does is to cyclically shift right the palette table values from first to first + count.

```
void ColorWheel(int first,int count,void *Pal)
{
asm {
      cld            // clear decrement flag
      push ds        // preserve registers
      push di
      push si
      les di,Pal     // ES:DI -> palette
      mov ax,es
      mov ds,ax
      mov ax,first
```

```
        add ax,ax
        add ax,first
        add di,ax               // ES:DI -> Pal[first]
        mov si,di
        add si,3                // DS:SI -> Pal[first+1]
        mov bx,[di]
        mov dl,[di+2]           // save Pal[first] in BX & DL
        mov cx,count
        add cx,cx
        add cx,count            // CX = byte counter
        rep movsb               // shift palette
        mov [di],bx
        mov [di+2],dl           // load Pal[first+count] from BX & DL
        pop si                  // restore registers
        pop di
        pop ds
    }
    }
```

The same technique can be applied to a real picture. The result is unpredictable but usually very exciting. Run the demo program EFFECTS\EFFECTS.EXE to see what happens. Note that impressive results can be obtained if you use fractals for palette animation.

## Picture Changing Effects

The previous section should have proved that animation can be produced by relatively simple means. Nothing really moves in the example program EFFECTS\EFFECTS.EXE. We will now look at some useful animation-like effects that can be used when changing one picture into another. A simple kind of keyframing is often used with this type of picture presentation. All you need is a set of pictures and a script to control the order and method by which each picture changes into the next one.

Included on the disk is a comprehensive collection of picture changing effects - from the simplest Slide to complicated effects such as those that go by the names of Jalousie, RandomFillArea and Gone_with_the_wind. It's not necessary to discuss here the particular C implementation of these effects. See the code in EFFECTS\SCREFF.CPP and EFFECTS\SCREFF.H.

All routines are designed to work in windows of any size, as well as on a full screen. They are designed for 320x200 256 color mode, VGA standard. Both the video memory and images in RAM appear as continuous arrays of bytes. Playing with the order in which lines of the image are displayed on the screen, we create various technically simple but wavy effects.

# Sprite Techniques

The most commonly used technique for simple animation is to use sprites. A sprite is an animated object, able to show a certain phase of its motion or projection in a certain place on the screen. 'Sprites' is also the group name for animation techniques usually applied to a separate figure distinguished from the background.

This sounds more promising. There are a lot of different ways to use sprites, but they all have one thing in common. The key thing is to preserve the background overlapped by the picture and to restore it after the picture is moved. Let's run through some of the available techniques.

## XOR Animation

This makes use of the fact that showing the picture twice, by using the XOR operator to set the relevant bits, automatically restores the background. This technique is excellent for cursors. Its usefulness is restricted by the rather ghostly appearance of the resulting image and by the absence of XOR hardware support for video modes above 16 colors. XOR animation is best just for two color. For more than this, the palette requires very special design to ensure that the correct color is produced. If 2 and 7 are XORed, the value 5 is obtained, i.e. color 2 and color 7 gives color 5, but palette colors usually have no significance, i.e. color 5 could be medium grey, red, pink or whatever has been defined for it, but it's unlikely to be related to colors 2 and 7.

## Successive Getting and Putting

The procedure is usually as follows:

- Copy background to a buffer.

- Put image onto the screen where the background was, perhaps masking (for non-rectangular shapes).

- To replace the sprite, just copy the background over it.

You just have to do this fast enough. The only restriction stems from the fact that the moving picture has to be rectangular, so you can't have bits of the background showing through the sprite. The Get-Put method is good for such things as moving icons (Drag&Drop) or cards in Solitaire, where the moving object itself is rectangular. With this method, care has to be taken if several sprites are moving over each other. If each sprite stores the background it sees before placement, then they have to be removed in reverse order.

There are ways to adapt this method to cope with large objects and higher speeds, for instance when your user drags the mouse very quickly. You can make the step depend on the speed (the higher the speed the larger the step). You can also show only a certain part of the image in the 'tween' phase of motion. Also, quite often the human brain thinks it sees the intermediate step, even if there isn't one!

## The Sprite or Masking Technique

Not all sprite 'images' are rectangular. To display such images, we need to display a rectangular sprite containing the non-rectangular 'sprite image', and make the background visible through the parts of the sprite rectangle not occupied by the image. This is called sprite masking. To do this, you must in some way control the output of the rectangular sprite onto the screen, so that only pixels of the sprite 'image' replace background pixels already on the screen.

There are two possible ways to do this:

- Prepare a mask for the sprite.

- Use interval coding to specify which pixels are to be changed.

*In a complex image, it may be faster to check each and every pixel instead.*

## Masks

A mask is a bit array of exactly the same size as the sprite, where the value 1 means output the corresponding pixel of the sprite, and a value 0 means do not output the pixel. It's like a silhouette of the sprite.

In 16 color mode, you can use the hardware mask register to mask the background. Before writing every 8 pixels of the sprite to the video buffer, you send a corresponding byte from the mask array to the mask register, which is only available in 16-color modes. Quicker by far though, is to take a pre-drawn sprite and generate a mask, and use this combined sprite+mask. A byte of the mask is created by ORing together all four bytes (one from each plane), then inverting each bit.

```
01011100
00110010
11101000
01010000
————————
11111110  = All 4 ORed together
00000001 =  Mask
```

There's a trick that makes transfer faster. With the EGA and VGA, there are normally unused parts of video memory which you can use as buffers to preserve the background and overlap a sprite on it. In this case, you should use Write Mode 1 to transfer data between buffers within video memory.

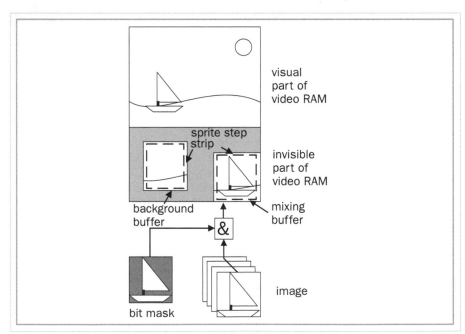

Figure 12.5   Using Masks for 16 Color Mode Sprite Animation

## Interval Coding

This technique should only be used in 256 color modes, where there's no hardware support for masking. The sprite area is divided into rows of pixels, and on every row we find continuous intervals of pixels that should replace the background.

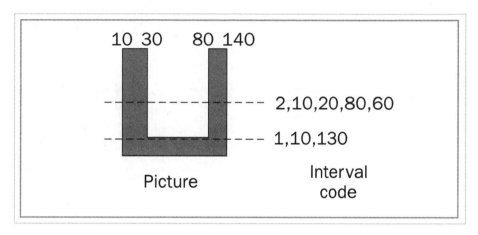

**Figure 12.6    Interval Coding**

When creating the sprite image, we assume one color to be transparent, allowing the background to be seen through it. Then we scan the 256-colored bitmap and code every interval between the transparent color blocks. Here is the code fragment, illustrating the encoding part of the technique:

```
// format of row coding looks like :
// N,(offset1, repeat count1,..., offsetN,repeat countN),
// where
// N - number of the intervals in row,
// offset - offset from the beginning of a row
// repeat count - bytes to be copied

void Createofmask(void *tmpp)
// tmpp - pointer to the intervals array
{
    void *maskp;
    unsigned char repcount,offset,counter,j,i,flag;
    unsigned int k,commonk;

    commonk = 0;
    maskp = malloc(65000);
    for(i=0;i<=SizeY-1;i++)
```

```
        {
            offset = counter = flag = 0;
            k = commonk+1;
            for(j=0;j<=SizeX-1;j++)
            {
            if ((*&bytesptr(DataPtr)[i*SizeX+j] != _BackColor) && (flag = 0))
                {
                        repcount = 0;
                        counter++;
                        *&bytesptr(maskp)[k] = offset;
                        flag = 1;
                        k++;
                }
                if ((*&bytesptr(DataPtr)[i*SizeX+j] = _BackColor) && (flag != 0))
                {
                        flag = 0;
                        *&bytesptr(maskp)[k] = repcount;
                        k++;
                }
            }
        repcount++;
        offset++;
        }
        if(flag == 1)
            {
            *&bytesptr(maskp)[k] = repcount;
            k++;
            }
        *&bytesptr(maskp)[commonk] = counter;
        commonk = k;
        }
        tmpp = malloc(commonk);
        memcpy(maskp,tmpp,commonk);
        free(maskp);
    }
```

The interval coding technique works faster than if we kept the raw sprite image in memory and compared every pixel of it with the transparent color. Moreover, interval coding allows you to save memory because you don't need to keep areas of transparent color.

It is possible to have two or three moving figures on the screen, with say one appearing closer to the users and the others further away. This effect can be achieved by using something like the painter's algorithm: all sprites ordered by depth. When you show them, you assemble them in a single buffer (where the background already lies), putting the remoter ones first and the closer ones later, so that this buffer becomes a single picture for this animation frame. Now all you have to do is copy it to the screen or use a flip screen technique.

## Further Discussion on Sprite Display Techniques

**Redraw backround:** Where the background display changes (perhaps panning or scrolling), it can be quicker to redraw the screen and display sprites on top without worrying about saving what is underneath.

**Flipscreen techniques:** In 640 x 350 (and the non standard 640 x 400) 16 color modes, each screen occupies 128Kb or less. The standard VGA card has 256Kb and it is possible to display the second screen by outputting the new screen address to the CRT controller registers 0Ch and 0Dh. If this is synchronized with the vertical retrace, the display changes very smoothly.

# Summary

Now you've got a fast, flexible graphics library and plenty of information about graphics programming techniques. Feel free to enhance and expand the library as much as you wish. Table 12.10 gives a few figures to highlight what needs enhancing. The table contains the results of some simple tests on the BGI graphics system versus GRAPH.LIB.

**Table 12.10 The Results of Performance Tests (486DX33, VLB) in Seconds**

| Primitive | Test Details | BGI in 16 colors | This system in 16 colors | 256 colors |
|---|---|---|---|---|
| 1000 bars: | 200x200 | | | |
| Solid | | 3 | 1.3 | 4 |
| Pattern | | 7 | 6 | 23 |
| | | | | |
| 1000 polygons: | | | | |
| Solid | | 21 | 10 | 16 |
| Pattern | | 27 | 17 | 50 |

*Continued*

**Table 12.10 The Results of Performance Tests (486DX33, VLB) in Seconds (Continued)**

| Primitive | Test Details | BGI in 16 colors | This system in 16 colors | This system in 256 colors |
|---|---|---|---|---|
| 20000 lines | 5000 steep +5000 gently sloping +5000 horizontal +5000 vertical | 5 | 3.5 | 2.5 |
| GetImage | 1000 times | 22 | 13 | 13 |
| PutImage | (500 same & 500 different position) | 51 | 43 | 5 |

## CHAPTER THIRTEEN

# Memory under 1Mb

## Introduction

Memory is probably the most critical resource in your PC. Its importance is exaggerated due to the design of the PC and XT series with their 640Kb limitation. Since then, the AT models have seen many different attempts to increase their capacity, such as EMM and XMS, and still the battle for 1Mb goes on. DOS gets bigger and bigger with every new version, and since version 5.0 it has tried to utilize any available gaps in the ROM address space, high memory and even the video buffer.

In this chapter you'll find real advice and detailed recipes to make use of all the memory available in a 1Mb address space. You'll become familiar with DOS's system of memory allocation, the functions it provides to allocate memory blocks in different areas of address space, and how to share memory when running child processes from your programs.

# Overview

The PC's memory is far from homogenous. Not only because part of it is read-only, but because what remains is reserved for different purposes and differently accessed. There are three major parts: conventional memory, upper memory, and extended memory (above 1Mb). These form a logical group in the way that the programmer deals with them. There is a small amount of memory above 1Mb that is usable in the same way, which we'll also cover here, but the great plains beyond 1Mb are a different story that we'll cover in the next chapter. The two types of memory we will cover here are:

- **Conventional** memory resides in address spaces under 640Kb. This limit is historically inherited from early PC models. Everyone was happy to have that much memory, and DOS makes you cram all your code into this area.

- **Upper** memory is above conventional memory and under 1Mb. It's basically used for video adapter buffers and ROM BIOS. But if there are holes (e.g. between video memory and ROM), DOS can map available RAM to them by using the 386+ paging system.

Figure 13.1 shows how PC memory is typically allocated.

## Conventional Memory (Under 640Kb)

This memory, from addresses 0000:0000 through 9FFF:0000, begins with the interrupt vector table (IVT), 0000:0000 - 0000:03FF. This is a table of 256 pointers which normally point to interrupt service routines, but are sometimes used to store addresses of public access data structures, such as fonts. Unused vectors are nulled or made to point to IRET.

Then comes the BIOS data area (0000:0400 - 0000:05FF), a collection of variables that reflect the modes and status of the hardware. It's followed by DOS's communication area. This area contains global variables used by ROM BIOS and DOS. You can use these variables directly, but although it's possible to modify some of them, it's not a good idea to do so directly. It's better to use DOS and BIOS functions where possible.

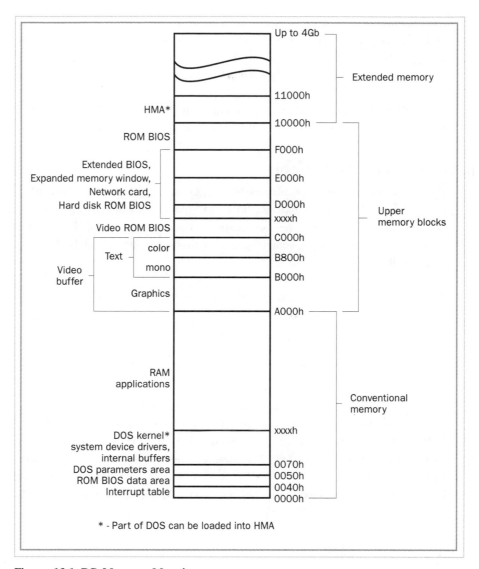

**Figure 13.1 PC Memory Mapping**

In the next area, DOS loads system drivers for disks, printer ports, COM ports, and so on. Then comes DOS data including file control blocks, disk buffers, stacks, the code of DOS itself, if it's not relocated into the High Memory Area (HMA), and the installable drivers listed in CONFIG.SYS. The order of these

**499**

components is, in fact, not strictly standardized. In different versions and brands of DOS, drivers and data can be mixed up in various ways. Memory managers like QEMM add their own bit of chaos too. Some of the components may go in upper memory when there are free blocks in it.

Above DOS the memory is free for programs. In the later sections we'll discuss how DOS controls this resource and how to use it in your programs.

## Upper Memory (Under 1Mb)

Upper memory lies in the addresses from A000:0000 through FFFF:0000. It's reserved for video adapter buffers, ROM BIOS, and other devices mapped in memory such as expanded memory boards. There are almost always holes in the address space, for example between video memory and ROM, and DOS can map available RAM to them.

RAM can be mapped to upper memory only under the following conditions:

1   The CPU is 386 or higher.

2   A memory manager such as EMM386.EXE is loaded.

Your programs can then allocate upper memory via calls to the memory manager functions. An easier and more universal way is to load the DOS driver HIMEM.SYS and put a command dos=umb into your CONFIG.SYS file. You can then allocate upper memory via DOS functions, and even load your program there using the DOS command loadhigh. Even when a program is loaded high, it can use both conventional and upper memory. We'll discuss this later in the section on Working with Memory.

## Memory Above 1Mb

Though MS-DOS doesn't provide access to extended memory, there's a small block of memory, about 64Kb, above 1Mb that can be used by DOS. Of course, this isn't available on an 8086 machine whose CPU addresses are limited to less than 1Mb. Processors from the 286 and higher have access to 16Mb or more. But to provide compatibility with 8086, manufacturers support an address wrap-around feature, which means that when an address goes above FFFF:000Fh, it wraps to address 0000:0000. This mode is the default for the real mode of the processor. Wrap-around can also be switched off. This is controlled by processor address line A20. When it's disabled, the processor works like an 8086. When it's enabled, the processor can access addresses up to FFFF:FFFFh, thus gaining an extra 64Kb.

Usage of this High Memory Area is limited. DOS can relocate a major part of its kernel to it if you specify dos=high in your CONFIG.SYS. However, DOS doesn't allow your programs to allocate any memory in HMA. You can try to address it directly, but it's not good practice if DOS is already sitting there. You can determine this by calling DOS function Get Version (Int 21h Function 3306h). Bit 4 in DH will be set if DOS is relocated to high memory.

# Working with Memory

## How DOS Keeps Account of Memory

DOS traces memory allocation by means of Memory Control Blocks (MCB), otherwise referred to as Memory Arenas. Arena is a better description, but historically MCB has been more widely used. An MCB is a 16-byte structure, which is placed at the beginning of every memory block, free or allocated. The only area that is not masked with MCBs is the area where DOS loads system drivers and data, which is natural because the area can't be allocated or disposed.

Each MCB holds information about the type of the block, the program that owns it, and the block size. Table 13.1 shows the structure of the MCB.

**Table 13.1 Memory Control Block Structure**

| Offset | Size | Description |
|--------|------|-------------|
| 0 | 1 | Block type: 'Z' (5Ah) if the last block, 'M' (4Dh) otherwise. |
| 1 | 2 | PSP segment of the owner (0 if the block is free, 8 if owned by DOS) |
| 3 | 2 | Block size in paragraphs (not including MCB) |
| 5 | 3 | Not used |

*Continued*

**Table 13.1 Memory Control Block Structure (Continued)**

| Offset | Size | Description |
|--------|------|-------------|
| 8 | 8 | Not used in DOS versions 2.x and 3.x<br>Since DOS 4.0:<br>Program filename (ASCII) if the block contains owner's PSP (ASCIIZ if less than 8 chars), otherwise undefined.<br>Since DOS 5.0:<br>If the block is owned by system data, this field contains ASCII "SD".<br>If the block is owned by system code, this field contains ASCII "SC". |

To illustrate memory allocation in reality and the structure of MCB, here's a partial memory dump under MS-DOS 6.2 with EMM386.EXE and HIMEM.SYS, dos=high,umb.

```
0266:0000 4D 08 00 13 03 00 DF 7F   M. . . . . . . System data
0266:0008 53 44 00 00 00 00 00 00   SD . . . . . .

057A:0000 4D 08 00 04 00 00 00 00   M. . . . . . . System code
057A:0008 53 43 00 00 00 00 00 00   SC . . . . . .

057F:0000 4D 00 00 07 00 D1 E9 74   M. . . . . . . Free block
057F:0008 06 03 04 46 46 E2 FA BE   . . . . . . . .

0587:0000 4D 88 05 B5 02 00 00 00   M. . . . . . Program(SMARTDRV)
0587:0008 53 4D 41 52 54 44 52 56   SMARTDRV(Owner field points
0588:0000 CD 20 3D 08 00 9A F0 FE   . . . . . . . . to the next paragraph,
                                                    where the PSP resides:
                                                    CD 20 is for INT 20)

083D:0000 4D 3E 08 26 01 00 00 00   M. . . . . . Program (1st
                                                    COMMAND)
083D:0008 43 4F 4D 4D 41 4E 44 00   COMMAND.
083E:0000 CD 20 FF 9F 00 9A F0 FE   . . . . . . . .
```

```
0964:0000 4D 3E 08 04 00 01 FE C0   M. . . . . . Block owned by the 1st
0964:0008 CD 21 BA 55 01 FE C0 CD   . . . . . . . COMMAND.COM

0969:0000 4D 3E 08 80 00 0A FC F3   M. . . . . . Block owned by the 1st
0969:0008 A4 58 59 5F 06 1F E8 A2   . . . . . . . . COMMAND.COM
096A:0000 43 4F 4D 53 50 45 43 3D   COMSPEC= (contains environment)
096A:0008 43 3A 5C 44 4F 53 5C 43   C:\DOS\C

09EA:0000 4D AD 0F 1A 00 8C 1E 16   M. . . . . . Block owned by the
09EA:0008 00 BA 3F 01 B8 2E 25 CD   . . . . . . . 2nd COMMAND.COM
09EB:0000 43 4F 4D 53 50 45 43 3D   COMSPEC= (see at 0FAC:0000)
                                                   Not environment!

0A05:0000 4D 06 0A D6 03 00 F3 A5   M. . . . . . Program MSCDEX
0A05:0008 4D 53 43 44 45 58 00 00   MSCDEX..
0A06:0000 CD 20 DC 0D 00 9A F0 FE   . . . . . . . .

0DDC:0000 4D AD 0F 19 00 21 E8 C0   M. . . . . . Environment of
0DDC:0008 43 4F 4D 4D 41 4E 44 00   COMMAND.the 2nd
0DDD:0000 43 4F 4D 53 50 45 43 3D   COMSPEC= COMMAND.COM

              . . . more MCBs . . .

0FAC:0000 4D AD 0F A5 00 1E D9 26   M. . . . . . Program (2nd
0FAC:0008 43 4F 4D 4D 41 4E 44 00   COMMAND. copy of
0FAC:0010 CD 20 FF 9F 00 9A F0 FE   . . . . . . . . COMMAND.COM)

              . . . more MCBs . . .

57ED:0000 4D 00 00 11 48 00 00 00   M. . . . . . Free block
57ED:0008 00 00 00 00 00 00 00 00   . . . . . . .

9FFF:0000 4D 08 00 4A 29 00 00 00   M. . . . . . Dummy block
9FFF:0008 53 43 00 00 00 00 00 00   SC . . . . . (video buffer)
A000:0000 FF FF FF FF FF FF FF FF   . . . . . . . used to link with UMB
```

Upper Memory

```
C94A:0000 4D 08 00 06 0D 00 00 00   M. . . . . . System data
C94A:0008 53 44 00 00 00 00 00 00   SD . . . . .
```

```
D651:0000 4D 88 05 00 04 48 49 54   M. . . . HIT   Block owned by
D651:0008 41 58 58 58 58 43 52 2D   AXXXXCR-      SMARTDRV

DA52:0000 4D 59 DA 05 00 00 00 00   M. . . . . . .   Block owned by
DA52:0008 00 00 00 00 00 00 00 00   . . . . . . . .   GMOUSE
DA53:0000 50 41 54 48 3D 43 3A 5C   PATH=C :\     (Environment)

DA58:0000 4D 59 DA 3F 02 00 00 00   M. . . . . . .   Program
                                                     (GMOUSE)
DA58:0008 47 4D 4F 55 53 45 00 00   GMOUSE. .
DA59:0000 CD 20 98 DC 00 9A C0 00   . . . . . . . .

                    . . .

DFEA:0000 5A 00 00 15 00 00 00 00   Z. . . . . . .   The last block
DFEA:0008 00 00 00 00 00 00 00 00   . . . . . . . .   (free).
```

## Viewing Memory

This dump was sceen-copied during a debug session of the program MEMVIEW.EXE (see disk). The program searches memory and prints out the listing of MCBs with their addresses, owner names, size, and type. If a block contains the environment block of a program, MEMVIEW mentions this, too. Typing MEMVIEW /D gives you a list of device drivers.

The address of the first MCB is acquired by DOS function 52h Get List Of Lists (certainly undocumented). This function returns a pointer to the very heart of the List-Of-Lists (ES:BX). The segment of the first MCB lies at the offset -2. Then, iteratively analyzing MCB sizes, MEMVIEW finds all MCBs in memory under 1Mb until it runs into the last block.

## Allocating Memory in Your Programs

DOS provides three functions to work with conventional memory:

- Function 48h Allocate Memory Block.

- Function 49h Free Memory Block.

- Function 4Ah Set Memory Block Size.

These are simple and convenient, the two qualities that so often stand for powerful.

## Allocate

On entry:    AH = 48h

BX = Block size in paragraphs

On return:   If there was an error, CF is set and AX contains the error code:

7 = Memory arena trashed

8 = Not enough memory

If everything's alright, CF is clear,  AX = Segment address of the created memory block

In the case of a not-enough-memory error, BX holds the size of the largest free block available (ask for FFFFh paragraphs to find this out).

## Free

On entry:    AH = 49h

ES = Segment address of the memory block to free

On return:   If there was an error, CF is set and AX contains the error code:

7 = Memory arena trashed

9 = Invalid block

If everything's alright CF is clear

However, when trying to corrupt an MCB and free the corresponding block of memory, the error appears (Invalid Block) only if the MCB.BlockType field is neither M nor Z, and the system crashes on leaving the program. Changes in the MCB.Owner have no effect, and leave the system perfectly stable. Change the MCB.Size and there is no error signal, but the system crashes.

## Set Size

On entry:    AH = 4Ah

BX = New size in paragraphs (greater or less than the current size)

ES = Segment address of the block to resize

On return:   If there was an error, CF is set and AX contains the error code:

7 = Memory arena trashed

8 = Not enough memory

9 = Invalid block

This set of functions is quite enough for most routine work, providing you do your own safety checks. If you REP MOVSB a string that's one byte longer than the destination block, you'll overwrite the M in the next MCB, which will crash the system.

That's the theory, now what about the practice? When loading your .COM file, DOS allocates the largest available block. That's why, if you try to allocate a paragraph or two, you normally get the hypocritical reply from DOS 'not enough memory', although your program may only be 200 bytes. The situation is different for .EXE files. There's a file called exMaxAlloc (offset 12) in the .EXE file header. This field tells DOS how much memory to allocate for the program's memory block. If a block of that size is not available, DOS allocates the largest possible one. Most linkers, however, set this field to 0FFFFh, and such .EXE files eat up the whole memory altogether. The normal practice is to resize the block allocated for the program to the size actually required to hold all its segments. Use the assembler directive DOSSEG which arranges the segments in strict order according to MS-DOS convention, as shown in the figure below. In this case, when your program loads, the stack pointer points to the end of the area required by the program. The distance between the PSP and this initial stack pointer should be the new size of the program memory block.

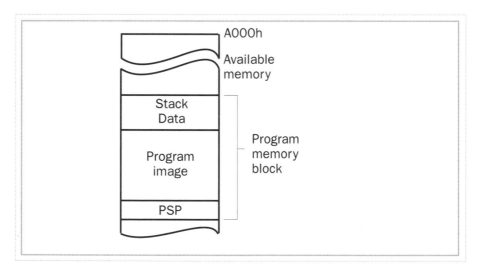

**Figure 13.2 Resizing Program Memory Block**

Program 13.1 demonstrates this technique, as well as using DOS memory functions.

```
;\\\\\\\\\\\\\\\\\\\\\\\\\\\\\\\\\\\\\\\\\\\\\\\\\\\\
;Program 13.1 Handling Conventional Memory via DOS
;\\\\\\\\\\\\\\\\\\\\\\\\\\\\\\\\\\\\\\\\\\\\\\\\\\\\

.286
dosseg
.model small
.stack 100h
.data
ptr1        dw ?
.code
; When a program starts DS and ES both point to PSP.
; Use unmodified ES as segment address of the beginning of
; the program space.

Start:
        mov ax,@data
        mov ds,ax           ; Load data segment

        mov bx,ss
        sub bx,ax
        shl bx,4
        cli
        mov ss,ax           ; Load stack pointer
        add sp,bx
        sti

        mov bx,sp
        add bx,15           ; Round up to next paragraph
        shr bx,4
        add ax,bx           ; AX = SS + SP / 16 = segment address
                            ; of the end of the program space
        mov bx,es
        sub ax,bx           ; AX = required amount of paragraphs
        mov bx,ax
        mov ah,4ah
        int 21h             ; Resize block
        jc  Resize_Error

        mov ah,48h          ; Allocate
        mov bx,1000         ; 16K
        int 21h
        jc  Alloc_Error
        mov ptr1,ax
;                    . . .
        mov ah,4Ah          ; Resize up to
        mov bx,2000         ; 32K
        mov es,ptr1
        int 21h
        jc  Resize_Error
;                    . . .
```

```
        mov ah,49h        ; Free block
        mov es,ptr1
        int 21h
        jc  Free_Error
        xor al,al         ; Successful
Resize_Error:
Alloc_Error:
Free_Error:
        mov ah,4ch
        int 21h
end Start
```

## Accessing Upper Memory

Since DOS version 5.0, you can use memory functions 48h, 49h, and 4Ah to access upper memory, too. To do this you have to link upper memory and set the appropriate memory allocation strategy. The Link flag enables DOS functions to allocate blocks in upper memory, while the strategy determines how and where DOS searches for available memory blocks when requested to allocate a new one. These can both be set with special DOS calls.

The dummy block, beginning at the video buffer, serves as the link to upper memory MCB's. If DOS is started with dos=umb specified in CONFIG.SYS, it creates this dummy block with the size field adjusted to link with the first MCB in upper memory. While the link flag is off, this block is not seen, because some other real MCB in conventional memory is marked as the last block and has the type 'Z'. When the link flag is set, DOS changes the type tag of the last MCB in conventional memory to 'M', and so all MCBs through 1Mb become linked. If the link flag is then turned off, the type field of the highest MCB in conventional memory is set to 'Z' again, and all MCBs above it are cut off.

You can get the current link state via DOS function 5802h:

On entry:     AX = 5802h

On exit:      CF is clear
              AL = Link flag: 1 if upper memory is linked, 0 if not.

You can set the current link state via DOS function 5803h:

On entry:     AX = 5803h
              BX = Link flag (1 = link, 0 = unlink).

On exit:    If there was an error, CF is set and AX contains the error code:

1 = Invalid function (when dos = umb is missing in CONFIG.SYS)

7 = Memory arena trashed.

If everything's alright, CF is clear.

You can retrieve and set the current strategy by using DOS functions 5800h (Get Allocation Strategy) and 5801h (Set Allocation Strategy).

## Function 5800h

On entry:    AX = 5800h

On exit:    CF is clear

AX = Current allocation strategy

There are 9 different strategies, which I think deserve a separate table:

**Table 13.2 Memory Allocation Strategy Codes**

| Code: | Explanation: |
|---|---|
| 0 | First-fit-low (default). Search conventional memory for the lowest fitting block. |
| 1 | Best-fit-low. Search conventional memory for the best fitting block. |
| 2 | Last-fit-low. Search conventional memory for the highest fitting block. |
| 80h | First-fit-high. Search upper memory for the lowest fitting block. If none found, continue in conventional memory. |
| 81h | Best-fit-high. Search upper memory for the best fitting block. If none found, continue in conventional memory. |
| 82h | Last-fit-high. Search upper memory for the highest fitting block. If none found, continue in conventional memory. |
| 40h | First-fit-high-only. Search upper memory for the lowest fitting block. |

*Continued*

Table 13.2 Memory Allocation Strategy Codes (Continued)

| Code: | Explanation: |
| --- | --- |
| 41h | Best-fit-high-only. Search upper memory for the best fitting block. |
| 42h | Last-fit-high-only. Search upper memory for the highest fitting block. |

### Function 5801h

On entry:    AX = 5801h

BX = allocation strategy (see above)

On exit:    If there was an error, CF is set and AX contains the error code 1. If everything's alright, CF is clear.

## Working with Upper Memory

Program 13.2 demonstrates working with upper memory. I haven't shown the complete program text - I've left out irrelevant fragments, like those for loading segment registers and resizing program memory blocks.

First the program saves the current setting of the allocation strategy and link flag, then it sets a new strategy (First-fit-high), and links upper memory. It then allocates 10,000 bytes, which can probably be found as a block in upper memory unless you've loaded DOS and a lot of programs high. Having played with the block, it deallocates it, restores the aforementioned settings and terminates.

```
;\\\\\\\\\\\\\\\\\\\\\\\\\\\\\\\\\\\\\\\\\\\\\\\\\\\
;Program 13.2. Allocating memory blocks in upper memory
;\\\\\\\\\\\\\\\\\\\\\\\\\\\\\\\\\\\\\\\\\\\\\\\\\\\

ptr1        dw 0
save_str    dw 0
link_flag   db 0

; . . .

mov ax,5800h              ; Get allocation strategy
int 21h
mov save_str,ax           ; Save it
```

```
mov ax,5802h              ; Get link flag
int 21h
mov link_flag,al          ; Save it


mov bx,80h                ; New strategy is First-fit-high
mov ax,5801h              ; Set allocation strategy
int 21h
jc bad_strategy

mov bx,1                  ; New link flag = on
mov ax,5803h              ; Set it
int 21h
jc link_error

mov bx,625                ; Allocate 625 paragraphs
mov ah,48h
int 21h
jc alloc_err
mov ptr1,ax               ; Store new segment address

; . . .                   ; Make use of it...

mov es,ptr1               ; Dispose of it
mov ah,49h
int 21h
jc free_error

mov bx,save_str           ; Restore strategy
mov ax,5801h
int 21h
jc bad_strategy

mov ax,5803h              ; Restore link flag
xor bx,bx
mov bl,link_flag
int 21h
jc link_error
```

# Reaching into the HMA

DOS doesn't offer any mechanism to access high memory area directly. There are no functions or strategies to allocate a memory block in the HMA. You can make use of the HMA only by placing DOS there and so freeing an extra 50K or so in conventional memory.

When DOS hides in the HMA, it actually leaves a small piece of its code in conventional memory. Until a program calls any DOS function, addressing line A20 is disabled, meaning addresses FFFF:0010 - FFFF:FFFF are inaccessible, and address wrap-around is active. On calling a function, DOS enables A20 and calls the actual code of the function in the HMA. On return, it disables A20 again.

Let's look at this in pseudo-assembly:

```
Int21  proc far
            EnableA20
            call dword ptr HighProc ; = FFFF:0345h
            DisableA20
            iret
Int21  endp
```

You can in fact do the same if you want. Don't load DOS high, then your program can:

- Enable A20,

- Copy its own body to FFFF:xxxx,

- Disable A20,

- Terminate and leave a tiny resident part, as DOS does, in conventional memory.

But what's the point? The high memory area is not huge. After all it's only 64K. Thrust DOS into it and forget the whole business.

Your PC is almost certainly equipped with much more memory than FFFF:FFFF. So it's more fun to work with all of it via BIOS Int 15h, XMS or EMM standards supported by HIMEM.SYS and EMM386.EXE, the drivers supplied with DOS. This subject will be covered in Chapter 15.

# Child Processes

There are many cases when you need to run a child program from your main one. If you write a DOS shell program like COMMAND.COM or Norton Commander, it has to deal with child processes all the time. Another example can be an installation program for an add-in card, which must copy the software and test the hardware. The testing utility, say HARDTEST.EXE, can then be a separate program called from the installation program as a child process.

You can organize large projects as a set of command line utilities with no user interface at all, which are run by the main program to perform their specific tasks only when needed. Both Norton Utilities and Norton Commander are designed in this way.

You run child processes via DOS function family 4Bh.

# Function 4B00h - Load and Execute Program

This function loads a program into memory, creates a new PSP and passes control to it. When the child process terminates, control returns to your program. This function is used a lot because it does all the dirty work for you, unlike function 4B01h.

On entry:    AX = 4B00h

              DS:DX points to program name (ASCIIZ string)

              ES:BX points to EXEC parameter block

On exit:     If there was an error, CF is set and AX contains the error code:

              1 = Invalid function

              2 = File not found

              3 = Path not found

              4 = Too many open files

              5 = Access denied

              8 = Not enough memory

              10= Bad environment

              11= Bad format

              If everything's alright CF is clear.

**Table 13.3 Structure of the EXEC Parameter**

| Offset | Size | Description |
|--------|------|-------------|
| 0 | 2 | Segment of environment block (if 0000, use caller's environment block) |
| 2 | 4 | Pointer to command tail |
| 6 | 4 | Pointer to first FCB |
| 0ah | 4 | Pointer to second FCB |

Program 13.3 demonstrates the usage of function 4B00h. It runs the program
D:\MEMVIEW.EXE with the command tail /d.

```
;\\\\\\\\\\\\\\\\\\\\\\\\\\\\\\\\\\\\\\\\\\\\\\\\\\\\\\\
;Program 13.3 Executing a Child Process via Function 4B00h
;\\\\\\\\\\\\\\\\\\\\\\\\\\\\\\\\\\\\\\\\\\\\\\\\\\\\\\\

.286
dosseg
.model small
.stack 100h
.data
comm_tail  db 3,' /d', 0Dh                 ; Command tail
prog_name  db 'memview.exe',0
;
; EXEC parameter block
           align 2
Env        dw 0                            ; parent's environment
comlin     dw offset comm_tail,0
FCB1       dw 5ch,0                         ; 5Ch is FCB1 offset in PSP
FCB2       dw 6ch,0                         ; 6Ch is FCB2 offset in PSP

ok_mess    db 'Alright!',10,13,'$'
ret_val    db 0
method     db 0
.code
Start:
           mov ax,@data
           mov ds,ax                        ; Load data segment

           mov bx,ss
           sub bx,ax
           shl bx,4
           cli
           mov ss,ax                        ; Load stack pointer
           add sp,bx
           sti

           mov bx,sp
           add bx,15                         ; Round up to next paragraph
           shr bx,4
           add ax,bx                         ; AX = SS + SP / 16 = segment address
                                             ; of the end of the program space
           mov bx,es
           sub ax,bx                         ; AX = required amount of paragraphs
           mov bx,ax
           mov ah,4ah
           int 21h                           ; Resize program
           jc  Exit                          ; Exit on error

           mov comlin+2,ds                   ; Load segment of command tail
           mov FCB1+2,es                     ; Copy FCBs from parent's PSP
           mov FCB2+2,es
```

```
                mov ax,es:[2ch]        ; Load environment segment
                mov Env,ax             ; from parent's PSP

                mov ax,4b00h
                mov dx,offset prog_name ; DS:DX points to child pathname
                mov cx,ds
                mov es,cx
                mov bx,offset Env      ; ES:BX points to EXEC parameter
                                       ; block
                int 21h                ; Run child
                jc  Exit               ; Exit on error

                mov ah,4dh
                int 21h                ; Get child-program return value
                mov ret_val,al         ; AL = return value
                mov method,ah          ; AH = termination method

                mov ah,9
                mov dx,offset ok_mess
                int 21h
                xor al,al              ; Successful
Exit:
                mov ah,4ch
                int 21h
end Start
```

## Function 4B01h - Load Program

The interface to this function is the same as to function 4B00h.

This function loads a program into memory and creates a new PSP. The child program is not run, and control returns to your program. Then you can run the loaded program when you like. The only difference from the previous function is that EXEC parameter block has two extra fields as shown in Table 13.4.

**Table 13.4 Extra Fields in the EXEC Parameter Block**

| Offset | Size | Description |
|--------|------|-------------|
| 0eh    | 4    | SS:SP       |
| 12h    | 4    | CS:IP       |

Having succesfully loaded a child function, 4B01h fills these fields with the initial stack pointer and the entry point. To run the child, you have to load the stack registers and far jump to the entry point. Program 13.4 demonstrates this technique. It loads the child program C:\WINDOWS\WIN.COM with the command tail " :" and runs it.

```
;\\\\\\\\\\\\\\\\\\\\\\\\\\\\\
; Program 13.4 Loading a Child
;\\\\\\\\\\\\\\\\\\\\\\\\\\\\\
.286
dosseg
.model small
.stack 100h
.data
comm_tail  db 3,' :',0Dh                ; Command tail
prog_name  db '\windows\win.com',0

; EXEC parameter block
           align 2
Env        dw 0                         ; parent's environment
comlin     dw offset comm_tail,0
FCB1       dw 5ch,0                     ; 5Ch is FCB1 offset in PSP
FCB2       dw 6ch,0                     ; 6Ch is FCB2 offset in PSP
SS_SP      dw 0,0                       ; Child's stack pointer
CS_IP      dw 0,0                       ; Child's entry point

ok_mess    db 'Alright!',10,13,'$'

ret_val    db 0
method     db 0

.code
; Use code segment to store variables for invoking child program
;
save_ds    dw 0                         ; Parent's DS
save_sp    dw 0                         ; Parent's SP
save_ss    dw 0                         ; Parent's SS
child_ptr  dw 0,0                       ; Child's starting address
Start:
           mov  ax,@data
           mov  ds,ax                   ; Load data segment
           call Init                    ; Resize program memory block
           jnc  Init_OK
           jmp  Exit                    ; Exit on error
Init_OK:
           mov  comlin+2,ds             ; Load segment of command tail
           mov  FCB1+2,es               ; Copy FCBs from parent's PSP
           mov  FCB2+2,es
           mov  ax,es:[2ch]             ; Load environment segment
           mov  Env,ax                  ; from parent's PSP

           mov  ax,4b01h
           mov  dx,offset prog_name     ; DS:DX points to child pathname
           mov  cx,ds
           mov  es,cx
           mov  bx,offset Env           ; ES:BX points to EXEC parameter
                                        ; block
           int 21h                      ; Load child
           jc  Exit                     ; CF set if error

           mov  cs:save_ds,ds           ; Save DS in code segment
           mov  cs:save_ss,ss           ; Save parent's stack pointer also
```

```
                mov cs:save_sp,sp

                mov ax,CS_IP             ; Copy child pointer to code segment
                mov child_ptr,ax         ; so can reference it after changing
                mov ax,CS_IP+2           ; DS, ES, SS
                mov child_ptr+2,ax

                mov ah,62h
                int 21h                  ; Get current PSP (child's) in BX

                cli
                mov ss,SS_SP+2           ; Load child's stack
                mov sp,SS_SP
                sti

                mov es,bx                ; ES and DS must point to the
                mov ds,bx                ; child PSP before invoking it

                ; put return address in child's PSP
                mov word ptr es:[10],offset cs:addr_back
                mov es:[12],cs

                jmp dword ptr cs:child_ptr   ; Run child program

addr_back:
                cli
                mov ss,cs:save_ss        ; Restore parent's stack
                mov sp,cs:save_sp
                sti
                mov ds,cs:save_ds        ; Restore parent's DS

                mov ah,4dh
                int 21h                  ; Get child-program return value
                mov ret_val,al           ; AL = return value
                mov method,ah            ; AH = termination method

                mov ah,9
                mov dx,offset ok_mess
                int 21h
                xor al,al                ; Successful
Exit:
                mov ah,4ch
                int 21h

Init            proc
; Input:  ax=ds, es=PSP segment, SS:SP as set by DOS
; Output: SS:SP adjusted, CF=0 if resize is successful
;
                mov bx,ss
                sub bx,ax
                shl bx,4
                cli
                mov ss,ax                ; Load stack pointer
                add sp,bx
                sti
```

```
            mov bx,sp
            add bx,15                   ; Round up to next paragraph
            shr bx,4
            add ax,bx                   ; AX = SS + SP / 16 = segment address
                                        ; of the end of the program space

            mov bx,es
            sub ax,bx                   ; AX = required amount of paragraphs
            mov bx,ax
            mov ah,4ah
            int 21h                     ; Resize program
            ret
Init        endp

end Start
```

## Function 4B03h Load Overlay

An overlay is an .EXE or .COM file which contains part of your program code that you don't need the whole time. You can load an overlay at run-time, let it do its work, and then dispose of it. You can separate functions that don't constitute the program kernel and put them into overlays. The kernel always resides in memory, overlays are loaded from disk only when they're needed. This allows you to save memory and write huge programs. This is the way most large commercial programs work.

The interface to this function is the same as to function 4B00h, but the structure of the EXEC parameter block for function 4B03h is shown in Table 13.5.

**Table 13.5 EXEC Parameter Block Structures:**

| Offset | Size | Description |
|--------|------|-------------|
| 0 | 2 | Segment address of overlay memory block |
| 2 | 2 | 0 if .COM file, else relocation factor if .EXE (most often the same as the previous field) |

The program OVLDEMO.ASM supplied on disk demonstrates using overlays.

There are various overlay managers, formats and loading conventions. The overlay concept is now a bit out-dated in the world of DLL's.

## Function 4Dh Get Child-Program Return Value

This function returns the value specified by the last child process run. Child processes pass this value to parents via DOS functions 4Ch (End Program) or 31h (Keep Program). Function 4Dh also returns information about the way the child program was terminated.

On entry:    AH = 4Dh

On exit:    AL = child-program return value
              AH = child-program termination method:
               0 = normal termination
               1 = terminated by <Ctrl-C>
               2 = critical device error
               3 = terminated by the Keep Program (function 31h)

The return value can be retrieved only once after a child program has terminated. Subsequent calls to function 4Dh will return meaningless values in AX. The same will happen if you call this function not having run any child programs.

# Summary

In this chapter you've seen how to use all memory available in the 1Mb address space. You now know how DOS controls memory and the functions and strategies it provides for memory allocation in different areas of address space.

What seemed a generous amount of memory in 1983 looks small now. What good is 1Mb if you have a TrueColor image of 1Mb? Read on and we'll find out about how to work beyond the confines of 1Mb.

## CHAPTER FOURTEEN

# Memory
# Above 1Mb

# Introduction

In Chapter 13 we looked at how to make the most of memory under 1Mb, including upper and high memory. Frankly, it's a nuisance to grope for odds and ends of memory behind the video buffer, especailly if your system has 4Mb or more RAM in it already, which is the norm for most PC's today.

In this chapter we'll cover using all PC memory via EMS, XMS, and other protocols. As an illustration of the techniques and functions described in this chapter, we'll develop our own memory manager based on EMS and XMS protocols in chapter 15.

This is intended to be a user-oriented chapter, containing programming guidelines rather than a detailed reference. We'll skip the less relevant functions, concentrating on those you'll use most often, and provide you with extended programming examples.

# Overview of Existing Protocols

The demand for more memory on the PC gave birth to expanded memory created by a Lotus-Intel-Microsoft (LIM) alliance in 1985. The user had to plug in a huge card with memory chips. It was really a memory device, because the processor couldn't address this memory directly. It could expand memory up to 32Mb and worked even on XT models, which had been originally doomed to 640Kb.

Then came PC AT models based on the 80286 processor which could address 16Mb installed on the motherboard, and though DOS still operated in 640Kb, programs appeared which worked with all memory above 1Mb (extended memory). DOS was shipped with RAMDRIVE.SYS, a driver which could organize a virtual drive in this space. The ROM BIOS in AT models provided two INT 15h functions for working with extended memory, a so-called "top-down" protocol.

Extended memory was much more convenient and pushed expanded memory cards off the market. But the same problem arose as ever: there'd been a lot of programs written to work with expanded memory. So since then every memory manager such as QEMM386, EMM386, 386MAX, etc., feels duty bound to emulate the LIM specification on expanded memory.

After the introduction of the 80386 processor, memory management protocols proliferated. One of them was the Virtual Control Program Interface (VCPI), introduced by Phar Lap Software and Quaterdeck Office Systems in 1987. It emulated LIM EMS and provided a simple API, comprising of 13 functions: allocate or free a number of 4Kb pages, read or write debug registers, switch to protected mode, and so on.

In 1988 Microsoft issued the eXtended Memory Specification (XMS) which standardized usage of extended, upper (UMB) and high (HMA) memories via 12 functions (see Chapter 13 for description of these areas). It also included 5 functions for A20-line control.

The DOS Protected Mode Interface (DPMI) appeared as a side product of Windows 3.0 development. It was Microsoft's official specification for DOS extenders. The main idea of a DOS extender is to make DOS and ROM BIOS functions transparent for application operation in protected mode. The API of a powerful DOS extender should include a full range of services: extended and DOS memory management, page management, interrupt management, etc.

# Top-down (Int 15h) Protocol

The Top-down protocol is the simplest API for extended memory management. There aren't many functions but they're enough to get by on. Top-down is implemented in ROM BIOS (since AT models) as a subset of the INT 15h functions.

Let's have a look at the functions it provides.

## Function 87h. Copy Extended Memory Block

Transfers a block of data from one memory location to another. It doesn't matter where these locations are (above 1Mb or in conventional memory) because the function operates with 24-bit linear addresses.

On entry:    AH = 87h

CX = number of words to copy

ES:SI points to Global Descriptor Table (GDT)

On exit:    CF is set if error

AH = status:

0 = no error

1 = parity error

2 = exception interrupt occurred

3 = address line 20 gating failed

The Format of the GDT for function 87h is shown in Table 14.5.

**Table 14.1 GDT Format for 87h**

| Offset | Size | Description |
|--------|------|-------------|
| 0 | DB 8 DUP(0) | Dummy descriptor |
| 8 | DB 8 DUP(0) | GDT alias |

*Continued*

Table 14.1 GDT Format fot 87h (Continued)

| Offset | Size | Description |
|--------|------|-------------|
| 10h | DW | Source block limit value |
| 12h | DW | Low part of 24-bit linear source address |
| 14h | DB | High part of 24-bit linear source address |
| 15h | DB | Source access right (93h) |
| 16h | DW 0 | Reserved |
| 18h | DW | Destination block limit value |
| 1Ah | DW | Low part of 24-bit linear destination address |
| 1Ch | DB | High part of 24-bit linear destination address |
| 1Dh | DB | Destination access right (93h) |
| 1Eh | DB 16 DUP(0) | Reserved |

If you're not familiar with descriptors and GDTs, it's best to avoid using this function. Please refer to Chapter 15, 'Programming in Protected Mode'

This function actually switches the processor to protected mode, moves the block from one address to another, and switches back to real mode.

## Function 88h. Get Extended Memory Size

Returns the total amount of memory above 1Mb (by reading the value from the CMOS).

On entry:     AH = 88h

On exit:      CF is set if error
              CF is clear and AX = number of continuous 1Kb
              blocks above 1Mb

The following code example demonstrates moving blocks using the Top-down protocol.

```
gd_tabl db 8 dup (0)     ; GDT
        db 8 dup (0)
        dw 0ffffh
```

```
src_lo   dw ?
src_hi   db ?
         db 93h
         dw 0
         dw 0ffffh
dest_lo  dw ?
dest_hi  db ?
         db 93h
         db 16 dup (0)

buff dw 3000 dup (0)

         .
         .

         mov eax,SEG buff      ; source = buff
         shl eax,4             ; calculate 24-bit address of buff
         add eax,offset buff
         mov src_lo,ax         ; AX = low part of 24-bit address
         shr eax,16
         mov src_hi,al         ; AL = hi part of 24-bit address

         mov dest_lo,0
         mov dest_hi,25h       ; destination address = 250000h

         mov ax,SEG gd_tabl
         mov es,ax
         lea si,gd_tabl        ; ES:SI points to GDT
         mov cx,3000           ; 3000 words
         mov ah,87h
         int 15h               ; move block
         jc error              ; CF = 1 if error
```

## Function 89h. Switch to Protected Mode

Switches to protected mode and transfers control to the address specified by the code segment descriptor and offset.

On entry:   ES:SI points to Global Descriptor Table, which in this case consists of 8 descriptors.
            BH = offset in IDT of IRQ0 - IRQ7
            BL = offset in IDT of IRQ8 - IRQ15
            CX = offset in CS (as it will be in protected mode) to jump to

On exit:    If an error occurs then CF is set.
            AH = FFh if error enabling line A20

All segment registers are changed.

80286 goes into protected mode with no direct exit to real mode.

The Format of GDT for function 89h is shown in Table 14.2.

**Table 14.2 GDT Format for 89h**

| Offset | Description |
|--------|-------------|
| 0 | dummy descriptor (zeroed) |
| 8 | GDT descriptor |
| 10h | IDT descriptor |
| 18h | DS descriptor |
| 20h | ES descriptor |
| 28h | SS descriptor |
| 30h | CS descriptor |
| 38h | undefined (used for BIOS CS) |

To be honest, this old top-down protocol isn't all that useful today, for obvious reasons: it provides absolutely nothing in the way of memory management. This is due to the fact that the BIOS can only perform the low-level part of the job: get-send, retrieve size, and that's about all it does. Full-featured memory management is up to your own software.

# Expanded Memory

When Lotus, Intel, and Microsoft originally introduced their Expanded Memory Specification (EMS), it was really aimed to provide an API to the Expanded Memory Manager, a driver that controls an expanded memory card. Since then, these cards have become less and less popular, but all existing memory managers still support the specification, emulating expanded memory.

Before we discuss programming under the LIM 4.0 Expanded Memory Specification, we need to understand what expanded memory is and how it works.

# A Tour of Expanded Memory

Because the 80286, in real mode and earlier processors could only access memory within a 1Mb limit, expanded memory, which could be up to 32Mb, was designed to be accessed by the processor through a physical window in the address space under 1Mb. This window is located in upper memory, somewhere between the video BIOS and the system ROM BIOS, typically E000h or D000h, and normally occupies 64Kb. The entire expanded memory is segmented into 16Kb logical pages, and each page can be mapped to this window, which is therefore called the page frame. So, if the page frame is 64Kb wide, then any four logical, but not necessarily continuous, frames can be mapped into it at a time. Each logical page maps into one physical page within the page frame.

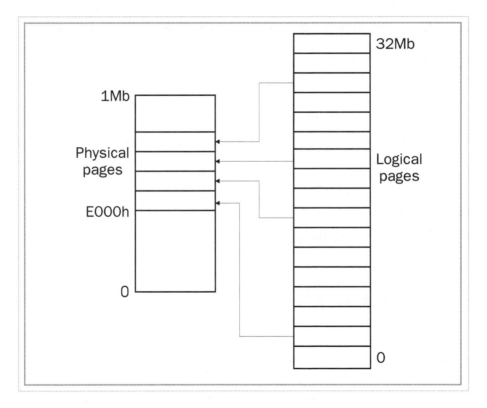

**Figure 14.1 Expanded Memory Mapping**

When a logical frame is mapped into the page frame, the processor can move data to and from it, and execute code in it, the same way it does in conventional memory. This sounds cumbersome, but it's just the same as editing a long document in a word processor. The whole document is there somewhere, either in memory or paged out to disk, but so long as the page you are working is on the screen, it doesn't matter.

## Working with Expanded Memory

To use expanded memory in your program you must take the following steps:

1   Detect whether EMM is installed.

2   Determine if enough free expanded memory pages are available.

3   Allocate pages.

4   Retrieve the base address of the page frame.

5   Map pages into the page frame.

6   Read and write your data or load and execute code in the page frame.

7   Since LIM 4.0, you can move around pages within expanded memory, or exchange pages in conventional and expanded memory without mapping logical pages into the frame page.

8   Before exiting the program you should free your expanded memory pages.

## The Expanded Memory Manager API

EMM provides 30 functions, many of them with several subfunctions, and this chapter simply can't cover them all. Anyway, unless you plan to write your own operating system, you need only a subset of the most basic ones.

However, it's worth having a look at the categories of functions that are available.

### Basic Functions

These are the functions we'll talk about in detail later. They check the hardware, find the page frame, allocate, resize, and deallocate blocks, etc.

## Save/Restore State

These functions are used by interrupt service routines, drivers, and resident programs to save the state of the mapping hardware in order to preserve other programs' data and context, then map in their own logical pages, work with them, and restore the EMM context before exiting.

## Handle/Page Count

For applications which need to know the current layout of expanded memory.

## Mapping Multiple Pages

You can often increase access to huge blocks in expanded memory by mapping several pages into the page frame at one time. You can also map a logical page to a specific memory segment, e.g. D400h.

## Aliases And Attributes

You can assign a symbolic name (e.g. "COMMON" or "DEBORAH") to a handle and search a handle by alias. This feature can be used to establish dynamic data sharing between two or more programs.

You can also set an attribute (volatile or non-volatile) to a handle. Non-volatile will retain its data after a hot reboot. Obviously, this feature can be implemented only on real expanded memory hardware, so if for any reason you need this, make sure that it's supported (Get Attribute Capability subfunction).

## Program Code In Expanded Memory

You can command the EMM to alter mapping and pass control to a specified entry point within 1Mb address space. This allows you to keep huge overlays in expanded memory.

## Moving And Exchanging Memory Blocks

This is a really powerful feature of the LIM 4.0 specification. With a single function call you can move a memory block of up to 1Mb between conventional and/or expanded memory. The mapping context remains intact, so you don't need to bother saving and restoring it.

### Getting Physical Layout Of The Page Frame

You may sometimes need to know the correspondence between the physical page number and its actual segment address. Different expanded memory cards often use different numbers and addresses for physical pages.

### Operating System Functions

These are reserved for use by operating systems and may sometimes be disabled. So don't rely on these functions or you'll end up with an application conflict or incompatibility with other software or operating environments.

# Programming Practice

The best way to learn programming is to do it by example. Here's a demo program which works with expanded memory.

The Expanded Memory Manager is accessed by Int 67h, with the function number in AH, the subfunction number in AL.

First, we check if the Expanded Memory Manager is installed. We get interrupt vector 67h, and check the string at offset 0Ah in the segment of the returned vector. This should contain the driver name, 'EMMXXXX0'. If so, then the EMM is installed. There's also an alternative technique for working with the EMM driver: instead of using INT 67h, you open a file "EMMXXXX0" and work with the EMM via this file handle. But you can't use this open-handle technique with device drivers or when interrupting DOS file operations. That's why INT 67h is usually a more convenient way to get hold of the EMM.

```
EMM_dev_name  db  'EMMXXXX0'

    mov ah,35h                  ; DOS Function 35h Get Interrupt
    mov al,67h                  ; Int 67h vector
    int 21h

    mov di,000Ah                ; ES:000A must point to the
                                ; device name
    mov si,offset EMM_dev_name
    mov cx,4
    rep cmpsw                   ; Compare strings
    jne prg_exit                ; If not 'EMMXXXX0', exit
```

Then we check if the EMM driver installed is version 4.0.

### Function 46h - Get Version

On entry:    AH = 46h

On exit:     AL =   EMM version (high nibble - major number, low
                      nibble - minor number, so for 4.0 it will be 40h)

                AH = status (see Table 14.5)

```
mov ah,46h
int 67h          ; Get version
cmp al,40h        ; Earlier than 4.0?
jb old_version
```

Then we check if there are enough pages available by calling EMM function 42h.

### Function 42h - Get Page Count

On entry:    AH = 42h

On exit:     BX = available pages
                DX = total pages
                AH = status (see Table 14.5)

In this example we want to allocate 4 pages (64Kb):

```
mov ah,42h
int 67h          ; Get Page Count
or ah,ah         ; AH = 0?
jnz error
cmp bx,4         ; Are there 4 pages available?
jb mem_full
```

If there's enough memory, we allocate a block of 4 pages via Function 43h.

### Function 43h. Allocate Block

On entry:    AH = 43h
                BX = number of pages

On exit:     DX = handle (valid numbers are 1 through 254)
                AH = status (see Table 14.5)

```
mov ah,43h
mov bx,4                        ; 4 pages
int 67h                         ; Allocate EMS block
or ah,ah                        ; AH = 0?
jnz error
mov handle,dx                   ; Store handle
```

Now we ask the driver where the physical address of the page frame is.

## Function 41h - Get Page Frame Address

On entry:    AH = 41h

On exit:     AH = status (see Table 14.5)
             BX = page frame segment address (only if AH = 0)

```
mov ah,41h
int 67h                         ; Get page frame address
or ah,ah                        ; Error?
jnz error
mov pageframe,bx                ; Store page frame segment
```

Now it's time to map in our logical pages.

## Function 44h - Map In / Unmap Logical Pages

On entry:    AH = 44h
             DX = handle
             BX = logical page index (0-based) in the block associated with this handle;
             If BX = FFFF this function unmaps the physical page specified in AL (makes the corresponding logical page inaccessible for reading writing).
             AL = physical page number (0-based) into which the logical page will be mapped.

On exit:
             AH = status (see Table 14.5)

```
mov ah,44h
mov dx,handle
mov bx,1                        ; Map logical page 1
```

```
mov al,1                        ; into physical page 1
int 67h                         ; Do map!
```

Now our logical page is mapped in, you can do what you like with it. Let's fill it up with zeroes for the hell of it.

```
cld
mov cx,2000h                    ; 2000h WORDs = 16Kb = 1 page
xor ax,ax                       ; Zero will be sent
mov es,pageframe                ; Page frame segment
mov di,4000h                    ; Page 1 offset
rep stosw                       ; Fill the page with zeroes!
```

There's a good alternative way of exchanging data:

## Function 57h. Move/Exchange Memory Block

This function moves or swaps memory blocks up to 1Mb between conventional and expanded memory without mapping in. Both the source or destination can be in either conventional or expanded memory.

On entry:     AH = 57h

AL = 0 if move, 1 if exchange (swap)

DS:SI points to Move Structure

On exit:

AH = status (see Table 14.5)

**Table 14.3 Move Structure**

| Offset | Size | Description |
|--------|------|-------------|
| 0 | 4 | Length of the block to move (in bytes) (1Mb maximum) |
| Source description: | | |
| 4 | 1 | Source memory type: 0 = conventional, 1 = expanded |
| 5 | 2 | Handle if in expanded memory, 0 if in conventional memory |

*Continued*

**Table 14.3 Move Structure (Continued)**

| Offset | Size | Description |
|---|---|---|
| 7 | 2 | Offset in the source block. If it's in conventional memory, then this field is the offset part of the address; if in expanded memory, then this is offset within a logical page. |
| 9 | 2 | If the source block is in conventional memory, then this field is the segment part of the address; if in expanded, then this is the logical page number. |
| Destination description: | | |
| 0Bh | 1 | Destination memory type: <br> 0 - conventional, 1 - expanded |
| 0Ch | 2 | Handle if in expanded memory, <br> 0 if in conventional memory |
| 0Eh | 2 | Offset in the destination block. If it's in conventional memory, then this field is the offset part of the address; if in expanded memory, then this is the offset within a logical page. |
| 11h | 2 | If the destination block is in conventional memory, then this field is the segment part of the address; if in expanded memory, then this is the   logical page number. |

The Move Structure is rather bulky, but this function saves a lot of programming: you can move everything with a single call. You don't have to save and restore the mapping context, map in pages, etc.

*If source and destination blocks overlap, the EMM chooses the right move direction to fill the destination area with the original copy of the source block. The overlap, however, is signalled in the returned status byte (AH).*

```
emm_move struc
        length dd 0
        source_mem_type db 0
        source_handle dw 0
        source_init_ofs dw 0
        source_init_seg_page dw 0
        dest_mem_type db 0
        dest_handle dw 0
        dest_init_ofs dw 0
        dest_init_seg_page dw 0
emm_move ends

my_EMM_move emm_move <>

        mov si,offset my_EMM_move
        mov word ptr [si].length,50000      ; Move 50000 bytes
        mov word ptr [si].length+2,0

        mov [si].source_mem_type,0          ; from conventional
        mov [si].source_handle,0
        les di,my_buffer                    ; ES:DI points to my buffer
        mov [si].source_init_ofs,di
        mov [si].source_init_seg_page,es

        mov [si].dest_mem_type,1            ; to expanded
        mov ax,handle
        mov [si].dest_handle,ax            ; my handle
        mov [si].dest_init_ofs,5000        ; offset 5000
        mov [si].dest_init_seg_page,0      ; in page 0
        mov ax,5700h                        ; AL = 0 (move, not swap)
        int 67h                             ; Move it!
        or  ah,ah                           ; Check status
        jnz move_error
```

Now we want to deallocate that expanded memory block and exit the program.

## Function 45h Deallocate Pages

On entry:    AH = 45h

DX = handle

On exit:    AH = status (see Table 14.5)

Learn to like this function, and call it before you exit from your programs:

```
        mov dx,handle
        mov ah,45h
        int 67h        ; Deallocate

        . . .


        mov ah,4Ch
        int 21h        ; Terminate
```

That's pretty much all you need to work with the EMM. There are some more advanced functions, which we'll run through briefly.

## Function 50h. Map in / Unmap Multiple Pages

This function maps (or unmaps) several logical pages to physical pages with a single call. The correspondence is specified by an array of pairs each consisting of a logical page and a matching physical page.

On entry:   AH = 50h

AL = 0 - physical pages are specified by indexes
      1 - by segment addresses

DX = handle

CX = number of entries in the page array

DS:SI points to the page array. Each array element is a simple structure:

```
log_to_phys    struc
               Log_page dw ?    ; logical page index,
                                ; FFFF means "unmap the
                                ; physical page"
               Phys_page dw ?   ; segment address or index
                                ; depending on AL
log_to_phys    ends
```

On exit:    AH = status (see Table 14.5)

## Function 4Eh. Save/Restore Mapping Context

This set of four subfunctions allows you to save the current correspondence between logical and physical pages (mapping context) and restore it. You need them to write TSR's which deal with expanded memory. When your TSR is invoked, you get the context, save it into your buffer, map in the pages that you need for your task, work with them, and set the saved context before exiting.

Function 4E00h. Get Mapping Context
Function 4E01h. Set Mapping Context
Function 4E02h. Get and Set Mapping Context
Function 4E03h. Retrieve Mapping Context Size

## Function 4E00h. Get Mapping Context

This reads the context into a buffer.

On entry:    AX = 4E00h

              ES:DI points to a buffer to accept the context

On exit:     AH = status (see Table 14.5)

*To use Functions 4E00h - 4E02h properly, you must call Function 4E03h first to know the required buffer size.*

## Function 4E01h. Set Mapping Context

This restores the context which has been saved before.

On entry:    AX = 4E01h

              DS:SI points to a buffer with the context

On exit:     AH = status (see Table 14.5)

## Function 4E02h. Get and Set Mapping Context

This reads the current context and sets the context which has been saved before.

On entry:    AX = 4E02h

              ES:DI points to the buffer to accept the context

              DS:SI points to the buffer with the context to set

On exit:     AH = status (see Table 14.5)

## Function 4E03h. Acquire Context Array Size

On entry:     AX = 4E03h

On exit:      AL = array size in bytes

              AH = status (see Table 14.5)

## Aliasing Functions

## Function 5301h. Assign Alias

Assign a symbolic name up to 8-characters long to a handle.

On entry:     AX = 5301h

              DX = handle

              DS:SI points to a 8-byte symbol array which contains the name.

                      This is in no way an ASCIIZ string! The name can be any 8 characters except all nulls (ASCII 0). Examples:

```
Alias1   db   'Deborah',0
Alias2   db   'Kevin',0,0,0
Alias3   db   'S',0,'Handle'
```

Padding names shorter than 8 characters with ASCII 0 to avoid confusion is a good idea.

On exit:      AH = status (see Table 14.5)

## Function 5300h. Get Alias

Get the name of a handle.

On entry:     AX = 5300h

              DX = handle

              ES:DI points to a symbol array to store the name

On exit:      AH = status (see Table 14.5)

## Function 5401h.

Find a handle by name.

On entry:     AX = 5401h

                     DS:SI points to the 8-character array with the name

On exit:     DX = handle

                     AH = status (see Table 14.5)

*If a handle hasn't been given an alias, its name is all zeroes. To identify a handle, you must give it a name with at least one non-zero character.*

## Function 56h. Alter Page Map And Call

This function actually does a lot of work for you:

**1**   Saves the current mapping context.

**2**   Maps in the new context.

**3**   Performs a FAR CALL to a specified address within a page frame.

**4**   Restores the original context and returns to caller.

On entry:     AH = 56h

                     AL = 0 - map to physical page numbers

                                    1 - map to segment addresses

                     DX =   handle

                     DS:SI points to map_and_call structure.

**Table 14.4 Map_and_call Structure**

| Offset | Size | Description |
|--------|------|-------------|
| 0 | 4 | Target entry point (Segment:Offset) |
| 4 | 1 | Number of entries in the new mapping context array |

*Continued*

**Table 14.4 Map_and_call Structure (Continued)**

| Offset | Size | Description |
|--------|------|-------------|
| 5 | 4 | Pointer to the new mapping context array |
| 9 | 1 | Number of entries in the old mapping context array |
| 0Ah | 4 | Pointer to the old mapping context array |
| 0Eh | 8 | Reserved |

An entry of the mapping context arrays consisting of a pair 'logical page - physical page' as in Function 50h (Map Multiple Pages) is described above.

On exit:    AH = status

This function provides the most powerful and convenient way to work with overlays loaded into expanded memory.

This function needs some stack space for internal use, approx 200 - 300 bytes. Make sure this is available when you use Map'n'Call. Function 56h provides subfunction 2 to determine how much stack space the function requires:

On entry:    AH = 56h
             AL = 2

On exit:    AH = status
            BX = stack size in bytes

The EMM provides a highly developed API. In fact, it contains more than you need for most jobs. Another advantage, depending on your point of view, is that you can still work in  real mode, the only difference being that you have to map in data or overlays before you can really access them. Table 14.5  shows codes returned by the operations mentioned in this section.

**Table 14.5 Status Codes**

| Code | Description |
|------|-------------|
| **EMM Operations** | |
| 00 | Successful |
| 80h | Internal error in memory manager software |
| 81h | Error in expanded memory hardware |
| 83h | Invalid handle |
| 84h | Undefined function code |
| 85h | No more handles available |
| 86h | Error in saving/restoring mapping context |
| 87h | More pages requested than physically exist |
| 88h | More pages requested than currently available |
| 89h | Zero pages requested |
| 8Ah | Invalid logical page number |
| 8Bh | Invalid physical page number |
| 8Fh | The subfunction parameters are invalid |
| A0h | No such handle name |
| A1h | A handle with this name already exists |
| **Status codes of move/exchange functions** | |
| 92h | Successful, but the source and destination memory regions have the same handle and overlap |
| 93h | The length of the source or destination expanded memory region specified exceeds the length of the expanded memory region allocated for either the source or destination handle |
| 94h | The conventional and expanded memory regions overlap |
| 95h | The offset within the logical page exceeds the length of the logical page |
| 96h | Region length exceeds 1Mb |
| 98h | The memory source and destination types are undefined |
| A2h | Attempted to wrap around 1Mb conventional address space |

# eXtended Memory Standard (XMS)

The eXtended Memory Specification (XMS) standardized the use of extended, upper (UMB) and high (HMA) memories. We'll look at XMS as implemented in HIMEM.SYS, a driver that comes with MS-DOS 5.x+.

To access the functions, fill the registers and FAR CALL the driver. I'll explain how to find the entry point later, in some program examples.

This a quick function reference grouped by the memory areas.

## General Purpose Functions

### Function 0. Get XMS Version Number

On entry:     AH = 0

On exit:      AX = XMS version (in BCD)
              BX = internal revision number
              DX = 1 if HMA exists, 0 if not

## HMA Control Functions

### Function 1. Request HMA

On entry:     AH = 1
              DX = memory needed (in bytes)

On exit:      if successful - AX = 1
              if failure - AX = 0
              BL = error code (see Table 14.7)

### Function 2. Release HMA

On entry:     AH = 2

On exit:      if successful - AX = 1
              if failure - AX = 0
              BL = error code (see Table 14.7)

# A20 Control Functions

## Function 3. Global Enable A20

On entry:    AH = 3

On exit:     if successful - AX = 1
             if failure - AX = 0
             BL = error code (see Table 14.7)

## Function 4. Global Disable A20

On entry:    AH = 4

On exit:     if successful - AX = 1
             if failure - AX = 0
             BL = error code (see Table 14.7)

## Function 5. Local Enable A20

On entry:    AH = 5

On exit:     if successful - AX = 1
             if failure - AX = 0
             BL = error code (see Table 14.7)

## Function 6. Local Disable A20

On entry:    AH = 6

On exit:     if successful - AX = 1
             if failure - AX = 0
             BL = error code (see Table 14.7)

## Function 7. Query A20 State

On entry:    AH = 7

On exit:     AX = 1 if A20 enabled, otherwise if disabled
             BL = 0 if successful, elsc error code (see Table 14.7)

# Extended Memory Block (EMB) Control Functions

### Function 8. Get Free Extended Memory (Without HMA)

On entry:     AH = 8

On exit:     AX = size of largest EMB (in Kb)
DX = total extended memory (in Kb)
BL = error code (see Table 14.7)

### Function 9. Allocate EMB

On entry:     AH = 9
DX = size of EMB (in Kb)

On exit:     DX = handle for EMB
if successful - AX = 1
if failure - AX = 0
BL = error code (see Table 14.7)

By default HIMEM.SYS sets its internal limits for 32 handles, so if you've allocated 32 blocks of 1 kilobyte each, you're out of extended memory. You can extend this limit by specifying, for instance:

```
device=HIMEM.SYS /numhandles=64
```

in your CONFIG.SYS. You can ask the driver for the amount of available handles before trying to allocate a block (see function 0Eh below).

### Function 0Ah. Free EMB

On entry:     AH = 0Ah
DX = handle of EMB to free

On exit:     if successful - AX = 1
if failure - AX = 0
BL = error code (see Table 14.7)

## Function 0Bh. Move EMB

On entry:       AH = 0Bh

               DS:SI points to Extended Memory Move structure

On exit:        If successful - AX = 1

               If failure - AX = 0

               BL = error code (see Table 14.7)

The format of extended memory move structure is shown in table 14.6.

**Table 14.6 Extended Memory Move Structure**

| Offset | Size | Description |
|--------|------|-------------|
| 0  | 4 | Number of bytes to move (must be even) |
| 4  | 2 | Source handle |
| 6  | 4 | Source address |
| 10 | 2 | Destination handle |
| 12 | 4 | Destination address |

If handle = 0, then source address is Seg:Ofs in conventional memory, else address is offset in EMB.

## Function 0Ch. Lock EMB

On entry:       AH = 0Ch

               DX = handle of EMB to lock

On exit:        DX:BX = 32-bit linear address of locked EMB

               if successful - AX = 1

               if failure - AX = 0

               BL = error code (see Table 14.7)

## Function 0Dh. Unlock EMB

On entry:       AH = 0Dh

               DX = handle of EMB to unlock

On exit:    if successful - AX = 1

if failure - AX = 0

BL = error code (see Table 14.7)

### Function 0Eh. Get Handle Information

On entry:   AH = 0Eh

DX = handle to get information for

On exit:    BH = block's lock count

BL = numbers of free handles left

DX = block size (in Kb)

if successful - AX = 1

if failure - AX = 0

BL = error code (see Table 14.7)

### Function 0Fh. Reallocate EMB

On entry:   AH = 0Fh

DX = handle of EMB

BX = new block size (in Kb)

On exit:    if successful - AX = 1

if failure - AX = 0

BL = error code (see Table 14.7)

# UMB Control Functions

### Function 10h. Request UMB

On entry:   AH = 10h

DX = size of block (in paragraphs)

On exit:    BX = segment address of block

DX = actual size of block

DX = largest available block

if successful - AX = 1

if failure - AX = 0

BL = error code (see Table 14.7)

## Function 11h. Release UMB

On entry:   AH = 11h

DX = segment address of UMB

On exit:   if successful - AX = 1

if failure - AX = 0

BL = error code (see Table 14.7)

**Table 14.7 HIMEM.SYS Error Codes for XMS**

| Error code | Description |
|------------|-------------|
| 80h | Function not implemented |
| 81h | Vdisk was detected |
| 82h | A20 error occurred |
| 8Eh | General driver error |
| 8Fh | Unrecoverable driver error |
| 90h | HMA does not exist |
| 91h | HMA is already in use |
| 92h | DX is less than the /HMAMIN= parameter |
| 93h | HMA is not allocated |
| 94h | A20 line still enabled |
| A0h | All extended memory is allocated |
| A1h | All available extended memory handles are allocated |
| A2h | Invalid handle |
| A3h | Source handle is invalid |
| A4h | Source offset is invalid |
| A5h | Destination handle is invalid |
| A6h | Destination offset is invalid |
| A7h | Length is invalid |
| A8h | Move has an invalid overlap |
| A9h | Parity error occurred |

*Continued*

**Table 14.7 HIMEM.SYS Error Codes for XMS (Continued)**

| Error code | Description |
|---|---|
| AAh | Block is not locked |
| ABh | Block is locked |
| ACh | Block lock count overflowed |
| ADh | Lock failed |
| B0h | Only a smaller UMB is available |
| B1h | No UMB's are available |
| B2h | UMB segment number is invalid |

Your program must first check if any XMS driver is present. You call Multiplex Interrupt 2Fh Function 43h Subfunction 0. On return AL will hold 80h if an XMS driver is present:

```
mov ax,  4300h     ; AX = 4300h
int 2fh            ; Installation check
cmp al,80h         ; AL = 80 if XMS drv is present
je xms_drv_inst
```

If the driver is installed then you can retrieve its entry point by Subfunction 10h (returned in ES:BX):

```
mov ax,4310h              ; AX = 4310h
int 2fh                   ; Get XMS driver address
mov word ptr xms_call,bx  ; the entry point ES:BX
mov word ptr xms_call+2,es
```

Now you can access the driver functions by storing a function number in AH and FAR CALLing the driver entry point. For example, to get the driver version:

```
mov ah,0
call xms_call
mov XMS_ver,ax            ; AX = version in BCD
```

In practice, you'll most often need a small subset of the XMS driver facilities: Enable/Disable A20 to access the HMA, Allocate/Free/Move extended memory block. The following code example shows how to allocate an EMB, move data from conventional memory to there, and free the EMB. These are the most common functions:

```
; Extended Memory Move structure (see Function 0Bh above)
ext_mem_move           struc
    counter dd 0
    source_handle dw 0
    ofs_into_source dd 0
    dest_handle dw 0
    ofs_into_dest dd 0
ext_mem_move           ends

my_buffer   db 8888h    dup(8)
handle                  dw 0
move_block              ext_mem_move <>

    . . .

    mov ah,9
    mov dx,35                       ; 35Kb block size
    call xms_call                   ; Allocate EMB
    dec ax                          ; AX = 1 if successful
    jnz alloc_error
    mov handle,dx                   ; DX = EMB handle

    mov move_block.counter,8888h    ; number of bytes to move
    mov move_block.source_handle,0  ; handle = 0, source is
                                    ; in conventional memory

    les si,my_buffer                ; source is my_buffer
    mov word ptr move_block.ofs_into_source,si
    mov word ptr move_block.ofs_into_source,es

    mov ax,handle                   ; EMB handle
    mov move_block.dest_handle,ax
    mov move_block.ofs_into_dest,100 ; offset in EMB

    mov ah,0Bh
    mov si,offset move_block        ; DS:SI points to
                                    ; Extended Memory
                                    ; Move structure
    call xms_call                   ; move block
    dec ax                          ; AX = 1 if successful
    jnz move_error

    mov ah,0Ah
    mov dx,handle                   ; DX = EMB handle
    call xms_call                   ; free EMB
    dec ax
    jnz free_error                  ; AX = 1 if successful
```

## Accessing HMA in Practice

Understanding how to allocate a block in the HMA via the XMS driver is difficult. In the interface of functions 1 and 2 (Request and Release HMA), we see no pointers, segment addresses or handles. It appears you can request memory, but from where?

Here are two undocumented functions of INT 2FH, Functions 4A01H and 4A02H.

### Function 4A01H. Get Free HMA Address

Returns the start address and size of the free block in HMA.

On entry:     AX = 4A01h

On exit:      ES:DI points to the beginning of the free HMA block
              BX = size of the block (in bytes).

If MS-DOS is not loaded high, BX = 0 and ES:DI = FFFF:FFFF. This seems quite logical, because these undocumented functions are reserved for DOS internal use. If DOS isn't high, they don't perform even this minimal HMA management.

### Function 4A02H. Allocates HMA Block.

On entry:     AX = 4A02H
              BX = block size (in bytes)

On exit:      ES:DI points to the allocated block if successful
              FFFF:FFFF if block of the specified size
              is not available or DOS is not loaded high.

There's no function to deallocate an HMA block. This is due to the poor allocation strategy. You can allocate several blocks, each subsequent block being higher than the previous one, and all DOS will do is increment the free pointer.

Now here's Program 14.1 which actually does all that's necessary to work in HMA (including enabling the A20 line):

```
;//////////////////////////////////////
;Program 14.1 Using High Memory Blocks
;//////////////////////////////////////
dosseg
.model small
.stack 100h
.data
    xms_call dd 0               ; XMS driver entry point
    my_buffer db 400h dup (90)
.code
.286
    mov ax,@data
    mov ds,ax                  ; load data segment

    mov ss,ax                  ; load stack pointer
    mov sp,offset stack

    mov ax,4300h               ; AX = 4300h
    int 2fh                    ; Installation check
    cmp al,80h                 ; AL = 80 if XMS drv is present
    jne exit

    mov ax,4310h               ; AX = 4310h
    int 2fh                    ; Get XMS driver address
    mov word ptr xms_call,bx   ; the entry point ES:BX
    mov word ptr xms_call+2,es

    mov ax,4A01h
    int 2Fh                    ; Get Free HMA Address
    or bx,bx                   ; BX = Free block size
    jz exit

    cmp bx,400h                ; Is there enough space?
    jb exit

    mov ax,4A02h
    mov bx,400h                ; Size = 1Kb
    int 2Fh                    ; Allocate 1Kb in the HMA
                               ; ES:DI points to our HMA block
    mov ah,05h
    call xms_call              ; Enable A20 line
    dec ax                     ; AX = 1 if successful
    jnz exit

    cld
    mov si,offset my_buffer    ; DS:SI points to my_buffer
    mov cx,200h                ; ES:DI points to our HMA block
    rep movsw                  ; move data block

    mov ah,06h
```

```
    call xms_call              ; Disable A20 line
exit:
    mov ax,4c00h
    int 21h                    ; Exit program
end
```

Of course you can't expect that DOS will leave too much of this 64Kb area free.

## Accessing UMBs via XMS

XMS provides Functions 10h and 11h (Allocate UMB and Free UMB) to work in upper memory. However, these functions are available only if DOS is not loaded in upper memory, ie. if your CONFIG.SYS doesn't contain dos=umb. In this case the XMS driver allocates blocks in upper memory with prefixes like DOS Memory Control Blocks (see Chapter 13), but DOS gives no access to UMBs.

If DOS is loaded in upper memory using dos=umb, the situation is reversed. You can use DOS functions to allocate blocks in upper memory by selecting an appropriate allocation strategy, but the XMS Function 10h (Allocate UMB) returns a 'No UMB is available' error.

Certainly, working with UMBs and HMA has no real advantage. With XMS it's much easier to organize your huge data buffers above 1Mb. However, you have to be very careful and dispose of all extended memory blocks that you've allocated in your program prior to terminating it. The XMS driver won't do it for you as DOS does.

## Summary

In this chapter we've described memory management above 1Mb, giving definite guidelines and function descriptions for expanded and extended memory. EMS and XMS specifications pertain to good old real mode programming, their APIs are merely to allocate-move-free.

Don't worry, we're not going to give up protected mode! There will be plenty of it in the next chapters.

However, there's still a market for real mode applications, and you can quickly get hold of memory above 1Mb by incorporating the memory manager (supplied on disk) into your programs.

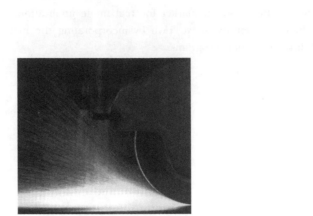

## CHAPTER FIFTEEN

# Programming in Protected Mode

## Introduction

With the development of the modern concept of the operating environment, it soon became obvious that the 8086 wasn't able to cope, and even the 80286 couldn't solve the problem. A more sophisticated hardware platform was urgently required, and the introduction of the Intel 80386 processor, together with its protected mode, opened a new stage in PC programming. The 386 protected mode differs so much from the real mode that this chapter is devoted to porting you over to this new programming ideology.

This chapter will introduce you to the new terms, structures and concepts of the protected mode. We will describe the features of 386 and 486 protected mode, such as memory management, privilege levels, I/O, multitasking and the interrupt and exception system. There won't be any code examples in this chapter, as this chapter is designed to act as a bedrock for the DOS Extenders chapter, where we'll describe the practical techniques of getting around in the protected mode.

# Memory Management - An Overview

The Intel 386 and higher processors have a hardware mechanism designed to simplify and standardize memory management and includes support for segmentation and paging. Segmentation is the method by which every program can have its own memory segments for code, data and stack, all the segments being protected from access by any other code. Paging allows the operating system to organize virtual memory using some disk storage. When the paging mode is turned off, linear addresses are equivalent to physical addresses in the address space up to 4Gb.

Of course, if you have 32Mb installed on your system, then you hardly need to add any virtual memory with the associated loss in performance. But if you only have 4Mb, then in order to run an operating System like MS Windows, you will need to add more RAM or use the 386+ processors paging mode to simulate addresses beyond the system's physical memory.

All memory is divided into 4Kb units or pages, and each logical page, which exists somewhere in the linear address space, can be mapped to a physical page. When the processor attempts to access a page which is not present in RAM, because it has been temporarily written out to disk, it generates an exception. This exception gives the operating system an opportunity to read the page back in, and thus probably write out another page. When the exception has been handled, the program can be restarted from the instruction which caused it, and it is in this way that virtual memory support can be hidden from an application.

Virtual memory can be organized on a segment by segment basis, but this will complicate the operating system. Segments are normally of different sizes, and the required disk operations may take longer. Small, fixed size pages are a more natural way to virtualize memory. This means that when the processor needs to access an element of a huge array or a particular procedure, it doesn't have to read in the whole segment, just one page.

Paging also allows physical memory to be mapped anywhere throughout the 4Gb linear address space. Figure 15.1 illustrates the idea:

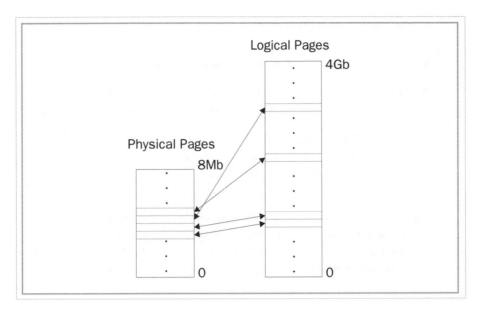

**Figure 15.1 Mapping Physical Pages into Logical Pages**

## Registers, Selectors, Tables

The contents of the segment registers have different meanings when the processor is in protected mode. These registers don't hold the paragraphs of segments, but segment selectors. A selector is an implicit reference to a memory location. The processor uses this reference to select, from the descriptor table, a descriptor, a structure that describes a segment (its base address, size etc.)

As shown in Figure 15.2, the segment selector consists of a descriptor index, a Table Indicator (TI), and a Request Privilege Level (RPL):

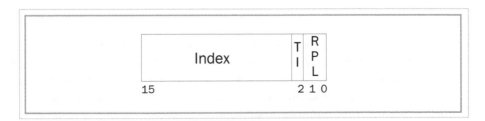

**Figure 15.2 Segment Selector**

Here is a detailed description of the elements of a selector:

- Index: specifies one of 8192 ($2^{13}$) descriptors in a descriptor table

- TI bit: indicates the table to use; either the Global Descriptor Table (GDT) which always exists or the Local Descriptor Table (LDT) which may exist

  RPL: this field is used to protect a more privileged segment against security
- violations from a less privileged segment. We'll explain the privilege control system in more detail later in the chapter

Descriptor tables can be anywhere in memory. Their locations are specified by the GDTR and LDTR system registers. The GDTR consists of the 32-bit base address (bits 16-47) and the 16-bit limit (bits 0-15) of the GDT. The limit is the offset of the last valid byte in the table. As descriptors are 8 bytes in size, the limit must always be:

    8*N - 1

if you allocate a table for up to N descriptors.

> *The processor never uses the first descriptor (with null index) in the GDT. You can load a segment register with 0, but any attempt to access memory via this register will generate an exception.*

The LDTR holds the segment selector of an LDT. You should always align these tables to a 16-byte boundary to improve performance, due to better cacheing.

Figure 15.3 shows how the descriptor is selected from the corresponding table.

Now we understand the descriptor selection process, let's look at a descriptor in more detail. It provides the processor with the location and size of a segment, as well as with control information. Basically, there are two types of descriptors: code and data segment descriptors and system descriptors. In this section we shall only cover code and data descriptors. Later in this chapter we'll explain the various kinds of system descriptors as they arise.

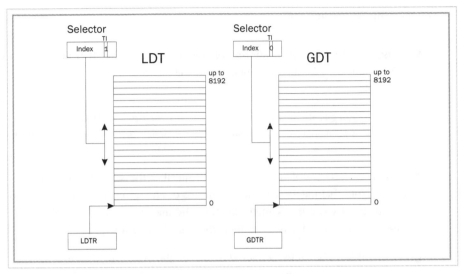

**Figure 15.3 Descriptor Tables**

Figure 15.4 shows the structure of code, data and system segment descriptors. Some system descriptors such as gate descriptors have a different format. These will be described where necessary.

**Data Segment Decriptor**

| | | | | | | | | | | | | | |
|---|---|---|---|---|---|---|---|---|---|---|---|---|---|
| Base (24-31) | G | D | 0 | A V L | Limit (16-19) | P | D P L | 1 0 | E W A | Base (16-23) | | | +4 |
| Base (0-15) | | | | | | Limit (0-15) | | | | | | | 0 |

**Code Segment Decriptor**

| | | | | | | | | | | | | | |
|---|---|---|---|---|---|---|---|---|---|---|---|---|---|
| Base (24-31) | G | D | 0 | A V L | Limit (16-19) | P | D P L | 1 1 | C R A | Base (16-23) | | | +4 |
| Base (0-15) | | | | | | Limit (0-15) | | | | | | | 0 |

**System Segment Decriptor**

| | | | | | | | | | | | |
|---|---|---|---|---|---|---|---|---|---|---|---|
| Base (24-31) | G | D | 0 | A V L | Limit (16-19) | P | D P L | 0 | Type | Base (16-23) | +4 |
| Base (0-15) | | | | | | Limit (0-15) | | | | | 0 |

**Figure 15.4 Segment Descriptors**

And now the fields in detail:

- Base address: the 32-bit address of the segment in the 4Gb address space. This value is split into two fields in a descriptor.

*Aligning code segments to 16-byte boundaries will increase the speed of instruction fetching on 486 processors. Data segments are recommended to be 4-byte aligned.*

- Granularity (G-bit): if set, the limit field specifies the segment limit in 4Kb units. Note that the 12 least significant bits of an address are not checked to see if they exceed the segment limit, so the maximum size is Limit*4Kb + 4095 bytes. If this bit is clear, then the limit is in bytes.

- Limit: this 20-bit field defines the size of the segment. If the processor encounters an attempt to access memory areas beyond the limit, it generates an exception. Below is a specific case of an expand-down segment.

- Accessed (A-bit): the processor sets this bit if the segment has been loaded into segment registers (no matter if there was no actual reading/ writing or instruction fetching).

- Big (B-bit): for data segments this bit affects stack operations; if the B-bit is set, the stack pointer (ESP) is 32-bit, if clear then 16-bit (SP); for expand-down segment, if the B-bit is set, then the upper bound is 0FFFFFFFFh, if clear, then 0FFFFh.

- Default (D-bit): for code segments, this is the default segment attribute. If the D-bit is clear then by default all instructions are assumed to use 16-bit addresses and 16-bit operand sizes, unless they have operand-size and/or address-size prefixes. If the D-bit is set, then the default mode is 32-bit and the prefixes mean 16-bit sizes. See Table 15.1.

**Table 15.1 Example D bit Opcodes.**

| D bit clear opcodes | Instructions | D bit set opcodes |
|---|---|---|
| 8B07 | mov ax,[bx] | 67668B07 |
| 668B07 | mov eax,[bx] | 678B07 |
| 678B03 | mov ax,[ebx] | 668B03 |
| 67668B03 | mov eax,[ebx] | 8B03 |

● Type field: indicates the purpose of a specific descriptor type; the different types are described throughout the rest of this chapter

● Expand-down (E-bit): a normal (expand-up) data segment is accessed with valid offsets from 0 to the limit. All other offsets will generate an exception. Alternatively, for an expand-down data segment, valid offsets are any outside the range from the top to the limit. For example, if the B-bit is clear, the valid offsets in an expand-down segment are from the limit to 0FFFFh, as shown in Figure 15.5. You can allocate new memory at the bottom of an existing expand-down segment by simply decreasing the limit. This option is useful for a stack segment you need to resize dynamically.

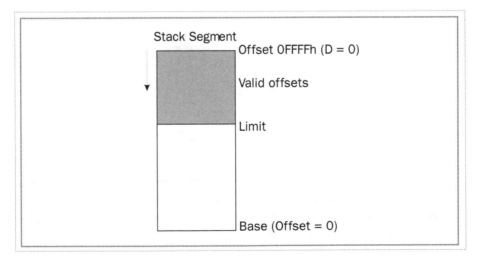

**Figure 15.5 An Expand-down Segment**

- Writable (W-bit): for a data segment, if this bit is clear, this segment can't be written to

- Conforming (C-bit): a code segment can be either conforming or non-conforming. If execution is passed from a less privileged segment to a more privileged conforming one, then the Current Privilege Level (CPL) remains unchanged. Control cannot be passed to a non-conforming segment whose Descriptor Privilege Level (DPL) is not equal to the current privilege level

- Readable (R-bit): for a code segment, if this bit is clear then this segment is only executable, or in other words you can't read from it

Now let's see how the processor accesses memory using these structures. Translation of a logical address (a combination of a selector and offset) to the linear address (in 4Gb space) is illustrated in Figure 15.6:

**Figure 15.6 Segment Address Translation**

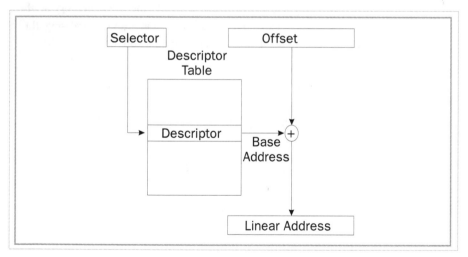

It may seem that each time the processor reads a byte from memory, it has to fetch a descriptor from a table and analyze the information held in it, but this would be far too slow. In fact, the processor has internal structures to keep some frequently used parameters handy (these structures are invisible to the programmer). Figure 15.7 shows the visible parts of the segment and system registers (which can be read and written by programs) and their invisible parts (used by the processor internally):

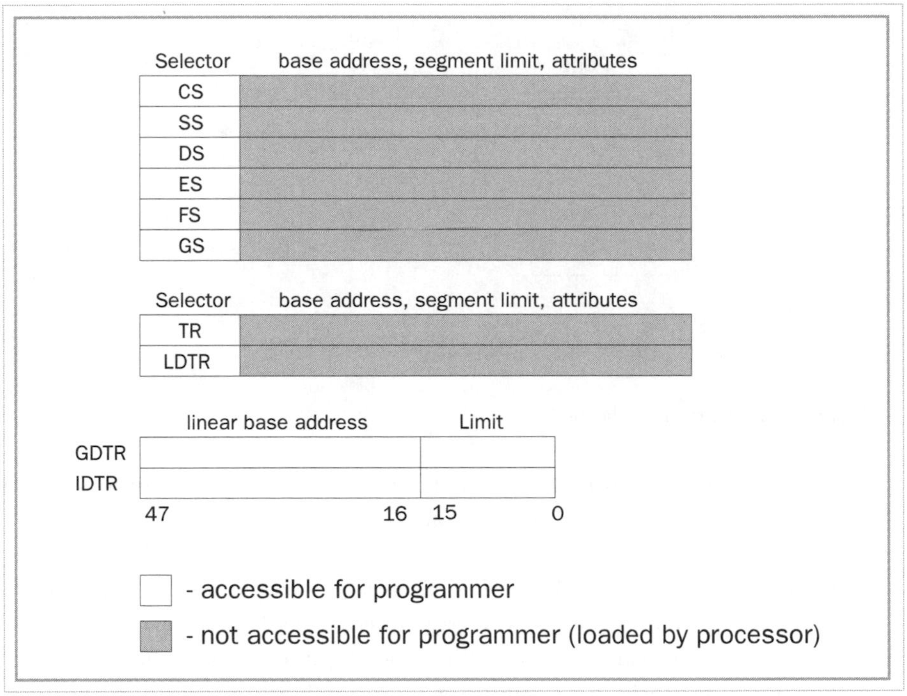

| | Selector | base address, segment limit, attributes |
|---|---|---|
| | CS | |
| | SS | |
| | DS | |
| | ES | |
| | FS | |
| | GS | |

| | Selector | base address, segment limit, attributes |
|---|---|---|
| | TR | |
| | LDTR | |

| | linear base address | Limit |
|---|---|---|
| GDTR | | |
| IDTR | | |
| | 47          16 | 15          0 |

☐ - accessible for programmer

▓ - not accessible for programmer (loaded by processor)

**Figure 15.7 Registers and Their Internals**

In Figure 15.7 you can see the TR (Task Register) and IDTR (Interrupt Descriptor Table Register), which we'll describe in the next sections.

# Pages

The page mapping information is held in data structures called page tables. They can be anywhere in memory (but must be page aligned), and there can be as many of them as is necessary for the operating system. When paging mode is on (bit 31 in the CR0 register is set), the linear address is a three-component structure, which is translated to the physical address as shown in Figure 15.8.

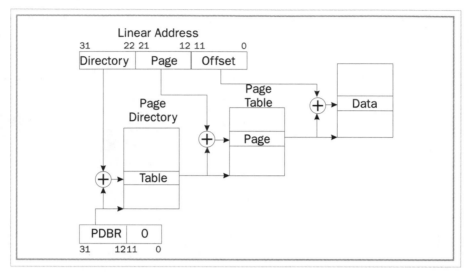

**Figure 15.8 Page Translation**

The linear address contains a 10-bit index in the current page directory, a 10-bit index in the page table, and a 12-bit offset within the page.

Page tables are arrays of 32-bit entries. Each table occupies exactly one page, so it can hold up to 1024 entries. The page directory itself is a page table whose entries point to second-level tables. Second-level entries contain the base addresses of pages. The base address of the page directory is held in the CR3 register, also known as the Page Directory Base Register (PDBR).

Let's take a close-up look at a page table entry (see Figure 15.9):

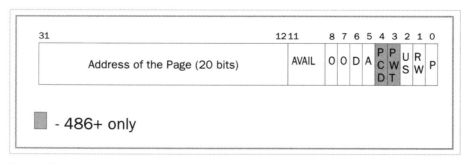

**Figure 15.9 Page Table Entry**

Now let's consider the details of the page table entry components:

- Base address: the 20-bit physical address of the page

- Available (AVAIL): 3 bits available for operating system. They can be used as extra page attributes (Free, Locked, Discardable) by a memory management algorithm

- Dirty (D-bit): set if the page has been written to. This bit is undefined in the page directory entries

- Accessed (A-bit): set if the page has been accessed. If you're writing an operating system, you have to implement an efficient page swapping algorithm. This allows you to check all the page tables entries at intervals to update the statistics of the page access. If a page has been accessed, you remember the time of the last update and clear the Accessed bit. Then, when time comes to write out a page, you can choose the least recently used one to keep the currently used pages in memory. Also, if the Dirty bit is clear, you don't have to update the page image on disk. Loading a page from disk, your operating system must clear the Dirty bit.

*It's up to the operating system to clear Dirty and Accessed bits. The processor only sets them (before read/write operations).*

- User/Supervisor (US bit): sets a sort of privilege level to protect some pages, such as page tables, from unauthorized access. 1 stands for 'user', while 0 stands for 'supervisor'

- Writable (RW bit): if clear then the page is read-only.

*We'll explain page-based protection in the section on 'Privileges'.*

- Present (P-bit): if this bit is set, then this page table entry refers to a page in the physical memory. If this bit is clear, the rest of the entry is undefined for the processor, and must be handled by the operating system. The processor generates an exception whenever it registers an attempt to access a non-present page (i.e. the Present bit is clear). The linear address at which access has been attempted is stored in the CR2 register. Your operating system must handle this exception to read the page from disk. We suggest the following routine:

1   Analyze the address in the CR2 register to find the corresponding page table entry

2   Find the page image on disk using the information in the page table entry (this can be the sector number, or the record index in the swap file, or whatever you decide this should be)

3   Free a page in the physical memory (by discarding a non-dirty least used page if available, or by writing out a dirty page)

4   Load the required page into the free physical page

5   Fill up the page table entry (set physical address, Present bit, clear Dirty, Accessed, and Available bits, etc.)

●   Restart the instruction that caused the exception

*With the 486 processor and later, two bits in a page table entry control the way the page is cached.*

●   Page Cache Disabled (PCD bit): if set, this bit prevents the page from being cached. This is useful for pages with memory-mapped I/O ports. Also, you can disable the caching of code which is seldom used, such as initialization routines, because in this case, caching gives no performance benefit

●   Page Write Through (PWT bit): specifies the cache policy for write operations. If this bit is set, the write-through is assumed for the page Clear means write-back. Although the 486 processor only has a write-through internal cache, an external cache can be controlled by this bit.

# Memory Models

There are two memory models usually mentioned in the literature on protected mode. From the processor's point of view, they are identical. For the programmer, they are two different ways to maintain memory management, the flat model and multi-segment models.

The flat model is the simpler of the two. All segments occupy the full 4Gb linear address space, by which we mean that their base addresses are 0 and their limits are 4Gb. If paging is off, then there's no protection at all, and therefore any program can read and write to any memory location. If paging is turned on, an operating system can be written that provides a 2-level protection mechanism (supervisor/user) on the page level. Supervisor code is then run on privilege levels 0 to 2, user code on level 3.

The multi-segment model allows you to implement a fully protected operating system. Each program is given its own separate segments, which other programs don't recognise, and therefore can't access. As protection is maintained by the hardware on the segment level, there can be 4 privilege levels. This can be combined with page level protection, if paging is turned on. This model is preferable for building complex, but stable, operating systems.

Of course, you don't have to follow either of the models strictly. It's up to you to decide how many segments and privilege levels you need. If writing an operating system is beyond your purposes (or ambitions), you can write a program that uses some advantages of protected mode, but without multitasking or protection.

## Control Registers and System Flags

In this section we'll consider the control registers in 386+ processors, which are essential for programming in protected mode. These registers are CR0 to CR3, normally only accessible to operating systems.

### CR0 Register

The CR0 register holds the system control flags which control the modes and indicate the states of the processor itself, rather than individual programs. Figure 15.10 shows the structure of the CR0 register:

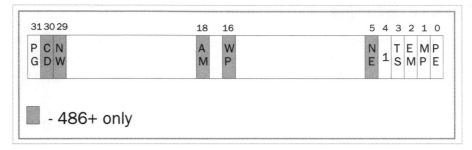

**Figure 15.10 The CR0 Register**

- Protection Enable (PE bit): setting this bit switches the processor to protected mode. Of course, this is not the only thing you have to do to enter protected mode, although you can experiment and see what happens.

- Math Present (MP bit): this bit is set if a numeric coprocessor is installed.

- Emulation (EM bit): when this bit is set, the processor generates a coprocessor-not-available exception (INT 7) on execution of a floating-point instruction. This allows emulation of the coprocessor by intercepting this exception.

- Task Switched (TS bit): the processor sets this bit each time it switches to another task and tests it while processing floating-point instructions. If it encounters a floating-point instruction and TS is set, it generates exception 7, which gives the operating system a chance to save and restore the coprocessor's state and clear this bit. So, if a task doesn't use floating-point arithmetic, the operating system doesn't have to swap the coprocessor's registers.

- Extension Type (ET bit): when this bit is set, it indicates that 387 instructions are supported.

- Numeric Error (NE bit): being set, this bit enables the standard mechanism for reporting the floating-point numeric errors.

- Write Protect (WP bit): in 486+, setting this bit protects the user-level pages from being written by the supervisor. When this bit is clear, the supervisor can always write to user pages.

- Alignment Mask (AM bit): in 486+, setting this bit turns on alignment checking. This bit works together with the AC flag (see subsection 'System Flags' for details).

- Not Write-through (NW bit): this bit controls the operation of the processor cache. When clear, it enables write-through and cache invalidation, and disables them when set.

- Cache Disable (CD bit): this bit disables the processor cache when set and enables it when clear. When the cache is disabled, cache misses don't update the cached data. However, when a cache hit happens, the processor uses data from the cache. To disable the cache completely, you have to flush it.

- Paging (PG bit): this bit turns paging on when set, and off when clear.

## CR1 Register

The CR1 register is reserved.

## CR2 Register

The CR2 register holds the 32-bit linear address of the instruction that has caused a page fault exception (see section on 'Interrupts and Exceptions' for details).

## CR3 Register

CR3 (the Page Directory Base Register, PDBR) holds the 20 high order bits of the Page Directory address, and two flags (see Figure 15.11):

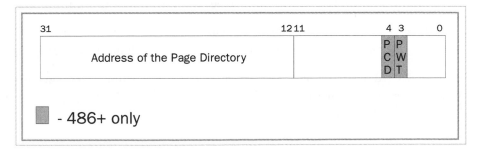

**Figure 15.11. CR3 Structure**

These two flags are Page-Level Writes Transparent (PWT bit) and Page-Level Cache Disable (PCD bit). They control whether pages are cached and how it is achieved. The same bits exist in Page Table entries. The bits in the CR3 control the corresponding processor pins (PCD and PWT) during operations when paging is not used for addressing (like accessing page directory entries). The bits in the Page Directory entries control the processor pins when accessing second-level Page Table entries. Bits in Page Table entries control the processor pins during access to data or instructions. Of course, when paging is turned off, these bits have no effect (the CPU assumes them to be clear).

## System Flags

There's a register called EFlags which holds system flags. They control I/O, maskable interrupts, debugging, multitasking and Virtual-86 mode. Figure 15.12 shows the contents of the EFlags register:

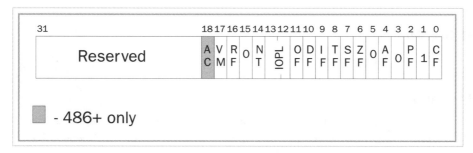

**Figure 15.12 System Flags (EFlags)**

- Trap Flag (TF bit): setting this flag switches the processor into single-step mode, when the processor issues INT 1 after each instruction. It is used for debugging.

- Interrupt-Enable Flag (IF bit): suppresses maskable interrupts when clear.

- I/O Privilege Level (IOPL bits): reflects privilege of the currently active program for accessing I/O ports (see section on 'Input/Output').

- Nested Task (NT bit): used by the processor to control nested tasks (see section on 'Multitasking').

- Resume Flag (RF bit): the processor clears this flag after any successful instruction execution, except for the following instructions: IRET, POPF, and JMP, CALL or INT, that cause a task switch. Setting this flag disables the debug exception INT 1 (see section on 'Debugging' for details).

- Virtual-86 Mode (VM bit): setting this flag switches the processor to Virtual-86 mode. However, you can't change the state of this flag other than during task-switching or via an IRET from privilege level 0.

- Alignment Check (AC bit): works together with AM-bit in the CR0 register. When both flags are set, the processor checks all the memory references for alignment. In this mode, any reference to an unaligned operand causes an alignment-check exception. Unaligned operands are, for example, a word at an odd byte address or a double word on an odd word address. These exceptions only occur on privilege level 3.

# Protection

## Privileges

Protection on the segment level guarantees that strict discipline will be kept during access to segments. This includes limit checking (no one can read or write beyond a segment) and type checking (no one can write to a read-only or code segment). Apart from these two kinds of restrictions, there's another based on the concept of privileges.

A segment can have the privilege level 0 to 3, 0 being the most privileged level and 3 the least. Privilege levels are stated in the following structures:

- In the two lowest bits of CS - this is the Current Privilege Level (CPL), the privilege level of the currently running code segment. Also, there's a copy of the CPL in SS.

- In the DPL (Descriptor Privilege Level) field of every segment descriptor.

- In the Requester Privilege Level (RPL) field of a selector. To access a segment, a program has to create the corresponding selector and specify the privilege level of access. Why this is needed is explained on the following page.

## How Protection Is Performed

Data is accessed via segment registers DS, ES, FS, GS and SS. When you load a segment register with a selector value, the protection check is performed. The processor compares the current privilege level, the requester privilege level and the privilege level of the descriptor specified by the selector. The segment register will be loaded successfully if:

```
DPL >= max(CPL,RPL)
```

otherwise an exception is generated. If you're running with privilege level 1, and request access with level 2, you can access data segments with DPL 2 and 3.

Access rules for code segments are more complicated. This section concerns CALL, JMP, and RET instructions, because INT and IRET cases will be covered in the section on 'Interrupts and Exceptions'. NEAR versions of CALL and JMP have nothing to do with privilege checking, because they work within a single segment.

There are two ways CALL and JMP instruction can be used for intersegment control transfer:

- When the instructions refer to a destination segment descriptor.

- When they refer to a call gate descriptor (see below).

Protection for CALLs and JMPs via a descriptor is regulated by either of the following rules:

```
DPL = CPL
```

or

```
DPL <= CPL
```

and the destination segment is a conforming one, by which we mean that it allows transfers from less privileged code segments. Conforming segments are used for service providers, such as general purpose libraries, which are accessed by both the operating system and applications. When control is passed to a conforming segment, the CPL doesn't change, even if it differs from the RPL in the selector used to access the segment.

To transfer control to a more privileged non-conforming code segment, you have to use a CALL instruction with a call gate (see Figure 15.13):

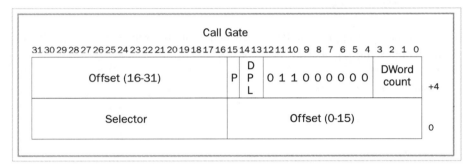

**Figure 15.13 Call Gate**

A call gate is a special type of descriptor, which specifies:

- The entry point to a procedure (the Offset field).

- The code segment containing this procedure (the Selector field).

- The privilege level from which the procedure can be accessed (the DPL field).

- The total size of parameters pushed onto the stack (the DWord Count field).

A call gate can be used by CALL and JMP instructions. However, unlike a normal CALL or JMP, the offset part of the operand is not used. The selector part points to a gate descriptor. The selector part in the gate descriptor points to a code segment which contains the called procedure. The offset part in the call gate specifies the entry point to the procedure.

*Call gates can be in the GDT or an LDT, but never in IDTs (Interrupt Descriptor Tables).*

A CALL instruction will be executed successfully if both of the following conditions are satisfied:

```
Gate DPL >= max(CPL,RPL)
```

and

```
destination DPL =< CPL
```

The same rules apply to a JMP instruction to a conforming segment. JMPs to a non-conforming segment are only possible if:

```
Gate DPL >= max(CPL,RPL)
```

and

```
destination DPL = CPL.
```

For example, you can:

- Call a procedure in a level 0 segment via a level 2 gate from segments with levels 0, 1, or 2.

- Call a procedure in a level 1 segment via a level 3 gate from segments with levels 1, 2, or 3.

On the other hand, you can't:

- Call a procedure in a level 3 segment via a level 3 gate from segments with levels 0, 1, or 2.

When a procedure call via a call gate changes the privilege level, the processor uses another stack segment. It checks the destination code segment DPL (which will become the new CPL) and reloads SS:ESP to point to the stack segment with the corresponding privilege level. The new values for the stack pointer are read from the TSS (Task State Segment) of the current task (the TSS will be described in the section on 'Multitasking').

If the caller pushes parameters on to the stack, they will be copied to the stack of the destination privilege level. The called procedure can access them via addresses relative to the stack pointer. The DWord Count field in the call gate specifies how many double words are to be copied to the new stack, with a set maximum of 31.

There is a set of instructions that can be executed only when CPL is 0, and they are shown below in Table 15.2. The execution of these instructions on any other level generates an exception:

**Table 15.2 Instructions Executable Only When CPL = 0.**

| Instruction | Description |
| --- | --- |
| CLTS | Clear task-switched flag |
| HLT | Halt the processor |
| INVD | Invalidate cache |
| INVLPG | Invalidate TLB entry |
| LGDT | Load the GDTR |
| LIDT | Load the IDTR |
| LLDT | Load the LDTR |
| LMSW | Load machine status word |
| LTR | Load the TR |
| MOV to/from CRx | Read/write control registers |
| MOV to/from DRx | Read/write debug registers |
| MOV to/from TRx | Read/write test registers |
| WBINVD | Write back and invalidate cache |

Protection on the page level prevents writing to read-only pages and accessing supervisor pages. If the CPL is less than 3, the running code is considered as the supervisor's and the processor allows access to both supervisor and user pages. If the CPL is 3, only user pages are allowed.

When the processor is running at the user level, an attempt to write to a read-only page generates an exception. The 486+ processors can also protect user read-only pages against being accessed by the supervisor. When the WP bit in CR0 is set, an attempt to write to user read-only page generates an exception.

It may happen that a page has different attributes in the page directory and the page table. If either of the entries has Supervisor attributes, it overrides the User attributes in the other. Supervisor pages are always writable. If either of the entries for a user page has read-only attributes, it overrides writable attributes in the other.

The segment level and the page level protection can be used at the same time. In this case, the processor first checks for the segment level protection and then for the page level. If an exception occurs on the segment level, the page level is not checked.

# Input/Output

There are two protection mechanisms for I/O via hardware ports; I/O privilege levels and I/O permission bit map.

## I/O Privilege Level

There's a two-bit field in the EFlags register called I/O Privilege Level (IOPL). This field determines whether a program can use I/O instructions, modify the IF flag, and change IOPL. Instructions IN, OUT, INS, OUTS, CLI and STI can only be executed if:

```
CPL <= IOPL.
```

If CPL > IOPL, then IN, OUT, INS, and OUTS generate a general protection fault if the bit in the I/O permission bitmap (see below) is set. This allows an operating system to control access to ports.

A program can't change its IOPL, unless it is at privilege level 0. If CPL > IOPL, then CLI and STI cause a general protection fault but POPF, POPFD, IRET or IRETD neither cause a general protection fault nor change IF or IOPL.

## I/O Permission Bit Map

In addition to privileges, individual tasks can be granted access to individual ports. This is controlled by the I/O Permission Bitmap, a structure in the TSS (see the section on 'Multitasking'). This bitmap is a bit array, in which every bit specifies whether access is allowed to the corresponding port address. This means that a program with CPL <= IOPL can access all ports, while all programs with CPL > IOPL have some ports masked in I/O permission bitmap (set bits), while other ports are transparent (clear bits).

# Interrupts and Exceptions

Interrupts are used to handle signals from hardware. At any time, when an interrupt occurs, the currently active program is suspended and control is passed to the interrupt service routine. When this routine, known as an interrupt handler, is finished, the control returns to the interrupted program. Interrupts, invisible for application software and hardware, are handled in the background.

Software interrupts are used by service providers (ROM BIOS, operating systems, etc.). These interrupts are invoked by programs explicitly by using the INT instruction.

Exceptions are generated by the processor itself. For example, on division by zero, the processor will force INT 0. They are normally processed by an operating system to protect its integrity.

There are three classes of exceptions:

- Traps: when an exception reports (pushes onto stack) the address of the next instruction after the one that caused it. A typical trap is Break Point (INT 3), used by debuggers.

- Faults: when the address of the 'faulty' instruction itself is reported. This allows recovery from the fault and restarts the troublesome instruction. A good example is page fault; a reference to a memory page which is presently rolled out to disk causing a page fault. The operating system suspends the running application, swaps pages to load the missing page, and restarts the interrupted program from the last executed command.

- Aborts: when it's not always possible to localize the command that caused the exception. These are normally caused by irrecoverable hardware errors, rubbish in system tables, etc.

# Processing Interrupts

This is much simpler in real mode, where the Interrupt Vector Table always lies at 0000:0000 and vectors are simply far pointers to handlers. Protected mode also has an interrupt table, the Interrupt Descriptor Table (IDT), which contains up to 256 8-byte descriptors. The IDT can be anywhere in memory, so you can create an individual IDT for every task. There's a special register IDTR, which contains the 32-bit base address (bits 16-47) and 16-bit limit (bits 0-15) of the IDT.

IDT entries can be of three types: task, interrupt or trap gates. Task gate will be explained in the section on 'Multitasking'. Interrupt and trap gates are shown in Figure 15.14:

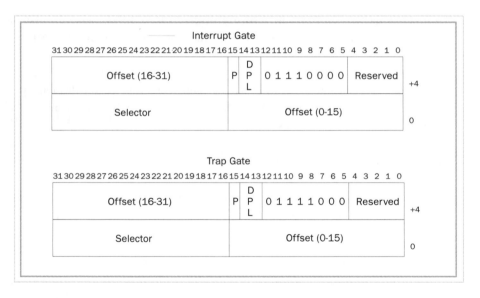

**Figure 15.14 Interrupt and Trap Gates**

Here are the meanings for the fields in Figure 15.14:

- DPL bits: descriptor privilege level

- P bit: present

- Selector: selects the code segment containing the handler

- Offset: offset of the handler in it's segment

As you can see, interrupt and trap gates are almost identical. The only difference between them is that when the processor invokes an interrupt handler through an interrupt gate, it clears the IF flag, while a trap gate doesn't.

Now look at how the processor reacts to an interrupt or exception:

**1** When an interrupt (or exception) N occurs, the processor reads gate N from the IDT. To find the handler's address, it takes the segment descriptor (specified in the gate's selector field) from the GDT or LDT (depending on the selector). The offset of the handler is taken directly from the gate's offset field.

**2** Then the processor saves its state on the stack.

**3** The processor clears the TF flag (to disable single step mode). Also, if the gate is an interrupt gate, the processor clears the IF flag to disable maskable interrupts.

**4** CS is loaded with the handlers segment selector, and EIP with its offset. Control passes to the handler.

**5** The handler returns control by executing the IRET instruction.

But what about the stack structure during an interrupt invocation? In the simplest situation, when the privilege level doesn't change, the processor pushes EFlags, CS and EIP before transferring control to the handler. Some exceptions push an error code onto the stack and when this occurs, it's pushed after EIP. If the handler has a different privilege level, then SS and ESP are pushed before EFlags. It's easier to see in Figure 15.15.

The privilege checking rule is similar to that for procedure calls (see section on 'Privileges'). Basically, control can't be passed to a less privileged handler (with DPL greater than CPL), because this will cause a general protection fault. As you can't predict when or in what code segment an interrupt will happen, there are two solutions for organizing interrupt handlers:

**1** Put interrupt handlers in conforming code segments.

**2** Put them in code segments with privilege level 0.

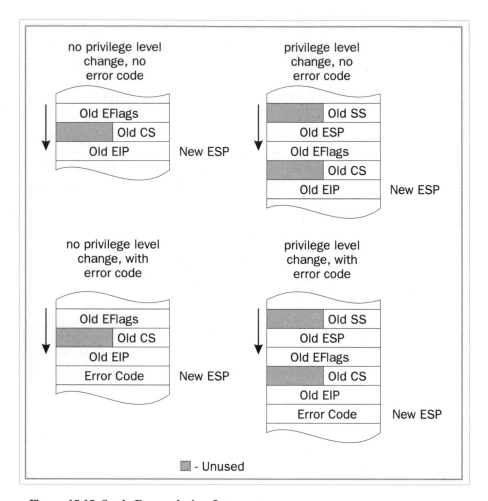

**Figure 15.15 Stack Frame during Interrupts**

# Exception Error Code

In a 32-bit exception error code, the higher word is not used. The lower word is similar to a segment selector (bits 3 to 15 contain a segment selector index). This does not necessarily indicate the segment where the error occurred; it can be a segment somehow referenced by the faulty instruction. The difference between the error code and selector is that instead of the RPL field (bits 0 and 1), the error code uses these two bits as:

- Bit 0 (External): set by the processor if the event which caused the exception is external to the current program.

- Bit 1 (IDT): set by the processor if the index portion of the error code refers to a gate descriptor in the IDT.

Some exceptions always produce a null error code.

## Details On The Exceptions

Table 15.3 describes the purpose of each exception:

**Table 15.3 Exceptions**

| Vector | Purpose |
|--------|---------|
| 0 | Divide Error |
| 1 | Debug Exception |
| 2 | NMI Interrupt |
| 3 | Breakpoint |
| 4 | INTO-detected overflow |
| 5 | BOUND range exceeded |
| 6 | Invalid opcode |
| 7 | Device not available |
| 8 | Double fault |
| 9 | Co-processor segment overrun |
| 10 | Invalid TSS |
| 11 | Segment not present |
| 12 | Stack fault |
| 13 | General protection fault |
| 14 | Page fault |
| 16 | Floating-point error |
| 17 | Alignment check (486+) |

## INT 0

INT 0, Division by Zero, happens when a divisor is zero (in DIV and IDIV instructions).

## INT 1

INT 1, Debug Exception, and INT 3, Breakpoint, will be described in the section on 'Debugging'.

## INT 2

INT 2, Nonmaskable Interrupt (NMI), signals a hardware disaster such as power drop-down or parity check error. In the XT, this interrupt was also generated by the numeric coprocessor in the event of an error. Since AT, numeric coprocessor reports errors by the IRQ 13 line (INT 75h). To retain compatibility with XT, the BIOS handler for INT 75h invokes INT 2. If you wish to handle FPU errors, then it's better to intercept INT 75h, to separate it from NMI.

## INT 4

INT 4, Overflow Exception, is generated when the INTO instruction is executed with the OF flag set. This can be used during program development to detect incorrect calculations. For example:

```
var1 db 255
var2 db 256

mov ax,var1
imul var2      ; The result is greater than integer
               ; OF becomes set
into           ; Check OF and invoke the error handler
```

## INT 5

INT 5, Bound Check, is generated when the BOUND instruction's operand is out of range.

## INT 6

INT 6, Invalid Opcode, is generated when an attempt to execute a command is not identified by the processor. This exception will also occur if an operand is illegal for this command, even if the opcode is recognized, e.g. lds esi, edi.

## INT 7

INT 7, Coprocessor Not Available, is generated on either of two conditions:

- The processor executes a floating-point instruction and the EM (emulation) bit in CR0 is set. This allows emulation of floating-point arithmetic on machines without a coprocessor.

- The processor executes a floating-point instruction and both the MP (math present) and TS (task switched) bits in CR0 are set. This preserves the coprocessor state in a multitasking systems (see section on 'Control Register and System Flags', TS bit).

## INT 8

INT 8, Double Fault, is generated when the processor detects an exception while calling a handler for a prior exception, and cannot handle them serially. The decision depends on the types of the two exceptions. In this respect, Intel classifies exceptions in three groups: benign (INT 1-7 and 16), contributory (INT 0 and 10-13), and page faults (INT 14). If one of the two instructions is benign, the processor can handle them. All other cases generate a double fault, except for when a page fault follows a contributory exception, which is allowed.

Double faults always push an error code onto the stack, but it's always 0.

## INT 9

INT 9, Coprocessor Segment Overrun (387 only), occurs when a part of a floating-point operand violates page or segment protection. 486+ machines generate INT 13 (general protection fault) instead.

## INT 10

INT 10, Invalid TSS, can occur during task switching. This fault pushes the error code onto the handler's stack. See section on 'Multitasking' for details.

## INT 11

INT 11, Segment Not Present, occurs when the processor tries to use a descriptor (segment descriptor or gate) with Present-bit clear. However, if it occurs while loading SS, a stack fault (INT 12) is generated; when loading the LDTR from a TSS, this situation generates an Invalid TSS exception (INT 10).

This exception is a means to organize segment-based virtual memory. If the handler manages to load the missing segment, the instruction which caused the exception is then restarted.

Problems arise when this exception occurs in the middle of task-switching. In this case, the handler cannot assume that all the segment registers are loaded with valid values. The handler must be intelligent enough to treat this situation properly.

For example, you can handle this exception as a separate task (via a task gate). Then the handler checks all the segment registers in the TSS being switched to, and reloads all the missing segments into memory. On exit from the handler task the processor switches 'back' to the new task, which now has all segments present.

Another solution is to check all segment descriptors in the new TSS before switching to a task. The Segment-Not-Present exception pushes the error code onto the stack.

## INT 12

INT 12, Stack Exception, is generated on either of the following two conditions:

- If any command referring to the stack via SS register, implicitly (PUSH, POP, ENTER, LEAVE) or explicitly (MOV EAX,[EBP+8] or MOV EAX,SS:[ESI+8]) results in a stack limit violation.

- On an attempt to load SS with a selector of a non-present segment.

This exception is restartable. It pushes the error code onto the stack of the handler. This allows the operating system to increase the stack size or swap in the missing stack segment and resume the interrupted program.

## INT 13

INT 13, General Protection Fault, is generated in a variety of situations. Examples are:

- Exceeding a segment limit.

- Writing to a read-only segment.

- Privilege violation.

- Instruction longer than 15 bytes.

- Reading from a fetch-only code segment.

- Accessing memory via a segment register with null selector.

This fault pushes an error code onto the handler's stack. If the fault is due to the loading of a selector into a segment register, the error code contains the selector, otherwise it is zero.

## INT 14

INT 14, Page Fault, is generated when a page is not present in memory or the running code has insufficient privilege to access a page. Naturally, if paging is turned off (PG-bit in CR0 is clear), page faults are not generated.

This fault pushes the error code onto the stack. The error code format is different from all other exceptions, as only three minor bits are used:

- bit 0; clear if the fault was caused by a non-present page, set if the fault occurred due to an access rights violation

- bit 1; clear if the access was read, set if write

- bit 2; clear if the processor was running at the supervisor level, set if at the user level

The processor places the linear address of the instruction that caused the fault into the CR2 register. If the handler can generate recursive page faults then it should be reentrant, and push CR2 onto the stack if another page fault occurs during execution of the handler. If all the structures that manage paging are always present in memory, then the handler doesn't need to be reentrant.

A troublesome situation is when a page fault happens while the stack pointer is being reloaded with a new value. For example:

```
mov ss,eax              ; Stack segment is just reloaded.
                        ; Bang! Page fault!
mov esp,NewTopOfStack   ; but ESP is still old
```

or the second instruction itself causes a page fault, if the variable NewTopOfStack is in a non-present page, for example. The stack pointer SS:ESP isn't valid, but if the handler is on the same privilege level as the code being run, you have no other choice than to use it! Nothing good will come out of it, and so to avoid this problem, you can:

- Use the LSS instruction to load the stack pointer; never a pair of commands like above. This would be okay, but can you make all third-party programmers toe the line?

- Grant the page fault handler with privilege level 0 and write your operating system kernel using exclusively LSS commands. Your operating system will run at level 0, and all applications at other levels. Then, if a page fault occurs at other levels, the handler uses its own stack (where it takes its own stack from you'll see in the section on 'Multitasking').

- Handle page faults with a task.

## INT 16

INT 16, Floating-Point Error, is generated on any error in a floating-point instruction. This fault is generated only if the NE-bit in CR0 is set.

## INT 17

INT 17, Alignment Check (486 only), is generated on a reference to an unaligned operand, such as a word at an odd byte address or a double word on an odd word address. Alignment check is performed when both the AC flag in EFlags and the AM-bit in CR0 register are set, and only at privilege level 3 (user level).

The error code pushed by this fault is always zero.

# Multitasking

Multitasking operating systems have been around for a long time. It was only natural for big mainframe computers to share their resources between many users in real time. The PC revolution changed the way programmers and users thought about computers, and set a new standard for the way computers should communicate with the end user. However, the ability to do several things at the same time was something the user really missed in the early years of the PC. Attempts were being made to bring multitasking to the PC; remember the DOS utility PRINT that printed files in the background, or the operating system Double-DOS that ran two DOS sessions at a time (even on XT). Finally, Intel began to design a processor with hardware support for multitasking. Now we have multitasking operating environments such as MS Windows or OS/2 where you can, in theory, play Solitaire while the terminal program is receiving files and your spreadsheets are recalculating.

It's no miracle that several programs (or tasks) can run simultaneously on a single-processor machine. In fact, as you may know, when a processor is multitasking, each program is given a short time with the CPU before its attention is moved on. This means that while one program is working, all the others are waiting for their turn.

We will discuss in more detail how to manage multitasking in your protected mode programs. In this section we'll only describe the hardware basis; all the data structures the processor uses for managing tasks.

These structures are:

- Task state segment (TSS)

- Task register

- Task state segment descriptor

- Task gate descriptor

# Task State Segment

The processor needs this structure to save the context of a task (the contents of registers and flags) before switching to another. To resume the other task, the processor restores its state from its own TSS. The structure of TSS is shown in Figure 15.16:

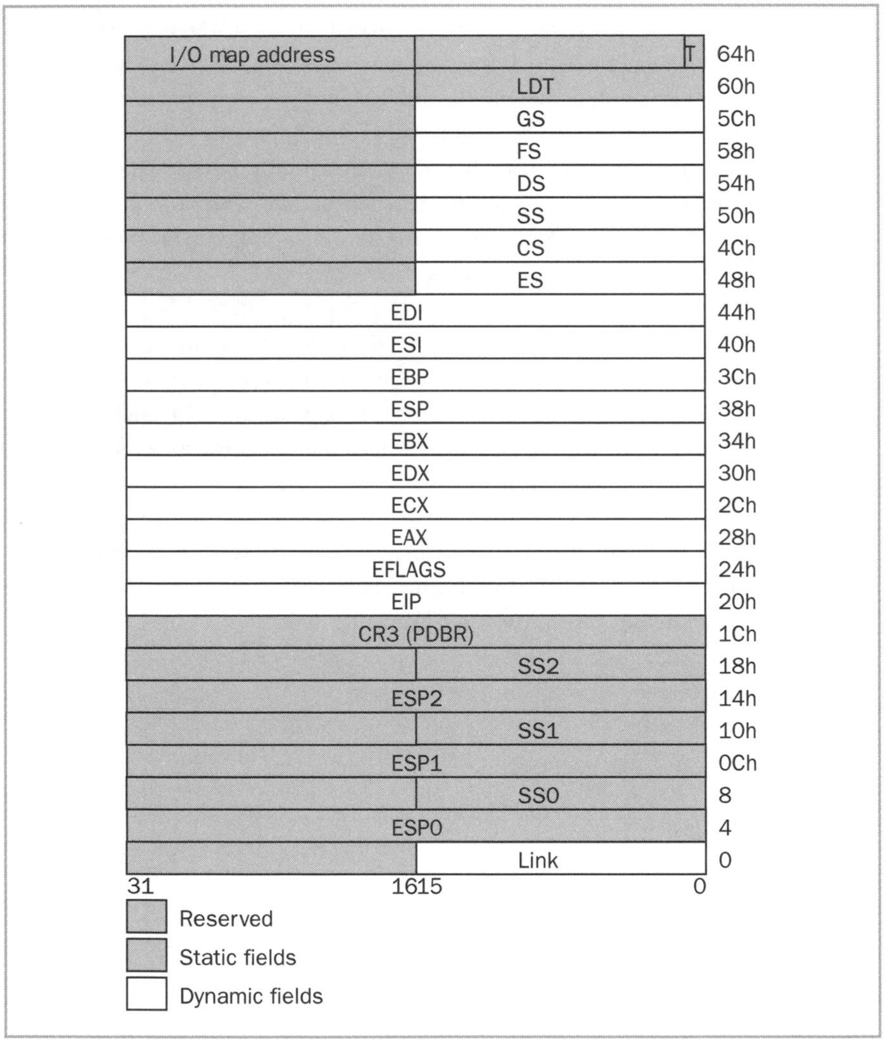

| | | |
|---|---|---|
| I/O map address | |T| 64h |
| | LDT | 60h |
| | GS | 5Ch |
| | FS | 58h |
| | DS | 54h |
| | SS | 50h |
| | CS | 4Ch |
| | ES | 48h |
| EDI | | 44h |
| ESI | | 40h |
| EBP | | 3Ch |
| ESP | | 38h |
| EBX | | 34h |
| EDX | | 30h |
| ECX | | 2Ch |
| EAX | | 28h |
| EFLAGS | | 24h |
| EIP | | 20h |
| CR3 (PDBR) | | 1Ch |
| | SS2 | 18h |
| ESP2 | | 14h |
| | SS1 | 10h |
| ESP1 | | 0Ch |
| | SS0 | 8 |
| ESP0 | | 4 |
| | Link | 0 |

31          1615          0

☐ Reserved
☐ Static fields
☐ Dynamic fields

**Figure 15.16 Task State Segment Structure**

The fields of the TSS can be divided into two categories: static and dynamic. The static fields are those which don't need to be updated during a task switch, such as the I/O permission bitmap, stacks for privilege level 0, 1, and 2, the LDT selector, CR3 register (PDBR) and T-bit. Dynamic fields are updated every time switching between tasks takes place, such as general purpose registers, segment registers, the EFlags register, EIP and the selector of the previous tasks's TSS.

The fields that need explanation are:

- Link: this is the selector of the previous task. When a task terminates (by using IRET), control passes to the task specified by link.

- Stacks (SS0,ESP0) - (SS2,ESP2): specify three stack segments, one for each of privilege levels 0, 1, 2. When an interrupt occurs with privilege level 1, the processor reloads the stack pointer with the values of SS1 and ESP1 from the current TSS, so that the interrupt handler uses its level's stack, not the application program's stack.

- CR3 (PDBR) and the Selector for the task's LDT: these fields are used for organizing a task's private address space. Each task can be given it's own page directory and tables as well as an LDT. This allows tasks to be isolated from each other, as well as setting up shared memory area, which is accessible by all task at any time.

- Debug Trap (T-bit): if set, it causes the processor to generate a debug exception (INT 1) when the task has received control (before the first instruction of the task).

- I/O permission bitmap base address: this field points to the task's I/O permission bitmap (if it exists, it begins after the TSS, at offset 68h).

# Task Register (TR)

This register holds the selector for the current TSS, so the processor always has TSS handy. The task register, complete with it's invisible part, was shown in Figure 15.7.

# TSS Descriptor

The structure of a TSS descriptor shown in Figure 15.17 is very similar to that of a data segment descriptor, except for one minor difference - the Busy bit (B-bit). This bit indicates that the task is running or waiting to run (or in other words, it hasn't finished). An attempt to switch to a busy task (with the B-bit set) causes a general protection fault (INT 13):

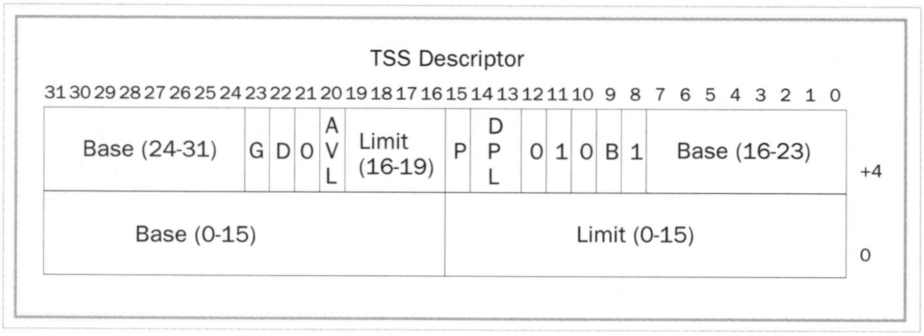

**Figure 15.17 TSS Descriptor**

Task switching will be performed if:

```
max(CPL,RPL) <= DPL
```

where CPL is the privilege level of the program that requested the switch, and where RPL is in the selector for a TSS descriptor and DPL, all contained in the TSS descriptor.

You can't access a TSS via its descriptor (an attempt to load it into a segment register will result in an exception). To read or modify a TSS, you have to create an alias data segment descriptor and work through that.

TSS descriptors can only be found in the GDT, never in local tables.

## Task Gate Descriptor

The task gate descriptor, or simply task gate, (see Figure 15.18) is used for indirect task switching in a protected fashion. For instance, your operating system can give a less privileged program (say, with CPL=2) the right to call a task with TSS DPL=0 by creating a task gate with privilege level 2 or 3:

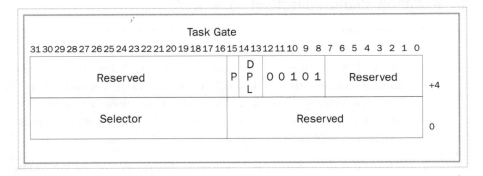

**Figure 15.18 Task Gate Descriptor**

Here the TSS segment selector points to the TSS descriptor of the task.

The general rule is:

```
max(CPL,RPL) <= task gate's DPL
```

where CPL is the level of the program that requires a task switch, RPL - in the selector for the task gate. DPL in the TSS descriptor is not used in this case, as well as RPL of the TSS segment selector in the task gate.

*If you want to handle an interrupt with a task, you have to put a task gate into the interrupt descriptor table.*

## How to Switch to a Task

You can switch to a task in one of the following ways:

- CALL or JMP to a TSS descriptor.

- CALL or JMP to a task gate.

- Invoke an interrupt handled via a task gate.

- Execute an IRET instruction while NT flag is set to finish a running task and return to the previous one.

## What Happens When Switching to a Task

The processor takes the following steps when switching to a task:

**1**  Checks if it can switch to the requested task. This takes account of the privilege rules for the CALL and JMP instructions as described above. Note that interrupts, exceptions, and IRET instructions are always allowed to switch tasks, no matter what the DPL. A TSS must be present and have a valid limit (no less than 67h).

**2**  Saves the state of the current task; general purpose, segment and EFlags registers to the TSS of the current task (which is always visible to the processor through the TR register).

**3**  Reloads the TR with the selector for the TSS of the new task, sets the Busy bit in the new task's TSS descriptor and TS-bit (Task Switched) in the CR0 register. In case of the CALL instruction or an interrupt, the processor copies the selector for the old TSS into the Link field of the new TSS.

**4**  Loads the state of the new task from its TSS as follows: first the LDTR, then if paging is turned on, the CR3 (PDBR), EFlags, general and then the segment registers. The new task then resumes execution.

When something goes wrong during task switching, it can result in various kinds of exceptions: segment not present, stack or general protection fault. There is another exception specially reserved for task switching: Invalid TSS fault (INT 10).

When the processor reaches out for the new TSS and finds that it's not present, it generates a 'segment not present' exception in the context of the old task. Once it is satisfied that the TSS is present, it reloads the TR register with the selector for the new TSS and considers the switching performed. After this, any error connected with the TSS will cause an exception in the context of the new task. The error code will hold the index of the segment which caused the exception. Here are some examples:

- If the TSS limit is less than 67h, the error code will hold the selector for the new TSS.

- If any segment doesn't correspond to the current privilege level, the error code will hold the selector for this segment.

- If the LDT selector is not valid, or LDT is not present in memory, the error code will hold the selector for the new TSS.

## Nested Tasks

The combination of the NT-flag (Nested Task) and the Link field in TSS allows the processor to return to the old task after the new task has terminated (via the IRET instruction). However, there are several mechanisms for entering and leaving tasks, and now let's consider them separately in more detail:

- JMP sets the Busy bit in the new TSS descriptor and clears the Busy bit in the old TSS descriptor. JMP doesn't suppose that control will be returned. That's why it doesn't affect NT flags and Link fields of both the old and new tasks.

- CALL or an interrupt sets the Busy bit in the new TSS descriptor, but leaves the Busy bit in the old TSS descriptor unchanged (it remains set, naturally). It then sets the NT flag in the new task and loads the Link field in the new task's state segment. NT flag and Link fields in the old task remain unchanged.

- IRET terminates a task. It doesn't change anything in the new task (because control returns to it). It clears the Busy bit and the NT flag in the old task. There are no particular changes in the Link field of the old task.

# Virtual 8086 Mode

The protected mode opens powerful perspectives for the programmer. The software market is full of good applications that run well even on 8086 models. To retain the possibility of using those programs in multitasking protected mode environments, Intel 386+ processors have a special Virtual-86 mode, which gives the processor the facility to emulate the real mode of 8086 machines.

Virtual-86 mode, supported by Intel 386+ hardware, allows applications written for 8086 to be run concurrently with programs that use all features of protected mode and multitasking. You create a virtual 8086 machine as a separate task, or even run several virtual machines at the same time, each with its own program environment. For a program running on a virtual machine, this environment appears the same as in real mode, with several minor restrictions.

# Entering Virtual-86 Mode

Virtual-86 mode is controlled by the VM flag in the EFlags register. However, you can't switch to Virtual-86 mode by simply setting this flag. There are two ways to enter Virtual-86 mode from protected mode:

- Create a TSS and set the VM-flag in the image of the EFlags register. Then, when you switch to this task, the processor loads the EFlags and enters Virtual-86 mode.

- Write a procedure that pushes the images of the segment registers, the address of a 8086 procedure and the EFlags register onto the stack. Then it sets the VM-flag in the EFlags image on the stack and executes the IRET instruction. The processor loads EFlags with the VM-flag set, and interprets the destination procedure as 8086 code. This technique requires that IRET must be executed at privilege level 0, otherwise the processor will ignore the VM-flag.

The TSS method appears more convenient, as you can initialize the registers in the TSS before switching to Virtual-86 mode. If you use the IRET method, you have to save and restore registers after you have switched to Virtual-86 mode. Anyway, as far as multitasking is concerned, the TSS method appears more suitable.

# Exiting Virtual-86 Mode

The processor exits Virtual-86 mode when an interrupt or exception occurs. If this interrupt or exception is handled via a task gate, then the processor loads EFlags from the handler's TSS. If it's handled via an interrupt or trap gate, then the processor will push the EFlags register onto the stack and then clear the VM-flag, thus exiting Virtual-86 mode. Interrupts and exceptions are processed via the Interrupt Descriptor Table; the Interrupt Vector Table in the virtual machine is ignored by the processor.

When handling Virtual-86 mode interrupts and exceptions without task switching (or in other words via interrupts or trap gates), the processor pushes the segment registers onto the stack before the standard return frame (see Figure 15.19):

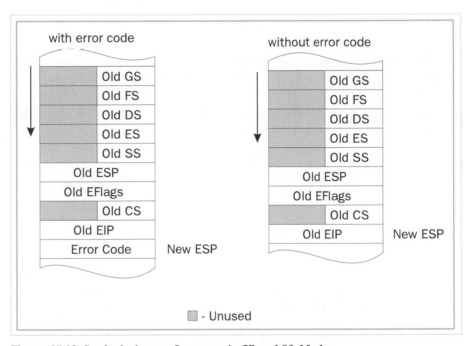

**Figure 15.19 Stack during an Interrupt in Virtual-86 Mode**

The processor then zeroes the segment registers. This is done to avoid the general protection fault when Virtual-86 mode values will pass to protected mode. So, if you write a protected mode interrupt handler, remember to load segment registers on entry to it, or else any attempt to address anything will generate an exception.

## More Virtualization

Because Virtual-86 mode is supposed to work in a multitasking environment, you can't allow a virtual machine to gain full control over interrupts and I/O. That's why these features are IOPL-dependent; as described in the section on 'Control

Registers and System Flags', IOPL is determined by two bits in the EFlags registers.

There's a set of IOPL-sensitive instructions: CLI, STI, PUSHF, POPF, IRET, INT. If IOPL is less than 3, any attempt to execute these instructions generates a general protection fault. Therefore a virtual machine has no direct access to the IF (Interrupt Enable) flag and so can't disable interrupts. This is really important for timer-driven multitasking systems. Also, IOPL-sensitive INTs allow the operating system to emulate interrupt calls.

Unlike protected mode, the instructions that access I/O ports work regardless of the CPL and IOPL combination. Only the I/O permission bitmap controls access to hardware ports; if a bit in the I/O map is set, then any attempt to access the corresponding port generates a general protection fault; a clear bit makes the corresponding port transparent to the system.

Paging is required to create several concurrent Virtual-86 machines. Each of them will have its own address space; they will see it as memory under 1Mb, with memory mapped I/O devices in this area.

Here are several differences between Virtual-86 mode and real mode:

- Performance drop-down: because the protected mode operating system has to emulate interrupt calls and even I/O, the same program will normally run slower in Virtual-86 mode than in real mode on the same machine.

- No wrap around 64Kb segment: in real mode, a memory access that exceeds 65535 bytes (e.g. reading a DWORD from offset 65535) will cause the offset to wrap around. In Virtual-86 mode, the same situation will result in a general protection fault.

- Some instructions are not available: in Virtual-86 mode, some instructions will generate a general protection fault, because the virtual machine always runs on CPL = 3. It's the same set of instructions that was listed in the section on 'Privileges', with the additional instruction ARPL.

# Debugging

The Intel 386+ processor provides powerful hardware support for debugging. This includes the following features:

- 6 debug registers to control debugging

- Debug exceptions

- Trap bit in TSS

- The Resume and Trap flags in the EFlags register

Now let's have a look at all these components in more detail.

## Debug Registers

These are 6 registers, DR0 to DR3, DR6 and DR7, accessible via the MOV instruction. DR0 to DR3 hold the linear addresses of breakpoints, DR6 reflects which condition triggered the exception and DR7 controls the conditions for these breakpoints. The structure of DR6 and DR7 is shown in Figure 15.20:

| | 31 30 | 29 28 | 27 26 | 25 24 | 23 22 | 21 20 | 19 18 | 17 16 | 15 14 | 13 | 12 11 10 | 9 | 8 | 7 | 6 | 5 | 4 | 3 | 2 | 1 | 0 |
|---|---|---|---|---|---|---|---|---|---|---|---|---|---|---|---|---|---|---|---|---|---|
| DR7 | LEN3 | RW3 | LEN2 | RW2 | LEN1 | RW1 | LEN0 | RW0 | 0 0 | GD | 0 0 1 | GE | LE | G3 | L3 | G2 | L2 | G1 | L1 | G0 | L0 |
| DR6 | 1 1 | 1 1 | 1 1 | 1 1 | 1 1 | 1 1 | 1 1 | 1 1 | BT BS | BD | 0 1 1 | 1 | 1 | 1 | 1 | 1 | 1 | B3 | B2 | B1 | B0 |

Figure 15.20 Debug Registers DR6 and DR7

### The Debug Control Register, DR7

The four pairs of bits (L0,G0) to (L3,G3) determine whether breakpoints DR0 to DR3 are enabled locally within a task and/or globally. Local bits, L0 to L3, are cleared by the processor during each task switch, while the global bits remain unchanged. Therefore by setting local bits you can turn debugging on for an individual task, and, by setting global bits, debug your operating system or whatever.

The LE and GE are the local and global exact data breakpoint match flags, respectively. When either of them are set, the processor analyzes data breakpoint conditions before executing an instruction, so it can stop on the very instruction that satisfies the break condition, not on the instruction after. This mode is slower than when LE and GE are off. However, the i486+ ignores these bits and always uses exact data breakpoint match.

The GD bit is available on i486+. Setting it enables a breakpoint on access to debug registers. The GD bit is cleared by the processor on entry to the debug exception handler. The four 2-bit entries RW0 to RW3 define the kind of access for each of the four breakpoint conditions, as shown in Table 15.4:

**Table 15.4 RWx Contents and Breakpoints Conditions**

| Value | Condition |
|-------|-----------|
| 00 | Instruction execution |
| 01 | Data writes |
| 10 | Undefined |
| 11 | Data reads/writes but doesn't instruction fetch |

The four 2-bit entries LEN0 to LEN3 define the length of operand for each of the four breakpoint conditions, as shown in Table 15.5:

**Table 15.5 LENx Contents and the Operand Length**

| Value | Condition |
|-------|-----------|
| 00 | Byte or instruction execution |
| 01 | Two bytes |
| 10 | Undefined |
| 11 | Four bytes |

*If you want to access an unaligned operand, such as word an odd address, you have to set up two breakpoint conditions in two registers, one for the lower byte and another for the higher byte.*

### The Debug Status Register, DR6

This register reflects the conditions that caused the breakpoint. Note that if several breakpoint conditions were satisfied at the exception time, they are all flagged in the DR6 register. Here are the following flag bits in DR6:

- The B0 to B3 for each of the DR0-DR3 registers.

- The BD - set if the next instruction will access any of the debug registers.

- The BS - set if the debug exception was caused by single step mode (controlled by the TF flag).

- The BT bit - set when a task with a set Trap bit (T-bit) in the TSS has been switched to.

## Debug Exceptions

There are two debug exceptions which trigger the specified procedure or task on the specified event. The simpler of the two is INT 3, the breakpoint instruction. It's used by debuggers to interrupt the program execution at a certain point. The debugger temporarily substitutes the first byte of the instruction opcode with the single-byte instruction INT 3 (0CCh). When the processor arrives at this instruction, the control is passed to the debugger, which restores the original opcode of the modified instruction. This technique is useful when you want to set more than four breakpoints; in other words, more than registers DR0 to DR3 allow.

Another debug exception is INT 1, caused by all debug events that the debug control register (DR6) flags. These are single-step traps (breakpoints defined by DR0-DR3) task switches with a set T-bit and access to debug registers when the GD bit in DR7 is set. Different conditions generate different types of exceptions, as shown in Table 15.6.

**Table 15.6 Debug Exception Types**

| Condition | Type |
|---|---|
| Single step | Trap |
| Instruction breakpoint | Fault |
| Data breakpoint | Trap |
| Task switch | Trap* |
| Debug registers access | Fault |

*Task switch traps are generated after a task is switched into and before the first instruction in the task.*

There's a special RF flag in the EFlags register to suppress looped invocations of the debug handler. Before exit, the debug handler must set the RF flag to disable INT 1. Otherwise, INT 1 will be generated again and again at the same instruction. The processor clears the RF flag after successful execution of each instruction, so the debug handler must set this flag in the EFlags' image on the stack. The processor sets the RF bit in the copy of EFlags on the stack when invoking any fault handler. This prevents repeated invocation of the INT 1 handler after the fault handler recovers the fault.

## Single Step Trap

Now, briefly, about the single step trap. This trap occurs after each instruction if the TF flag is set. The processor clears the TF flag before invoking any exception handler or executing an INT instruction. That's why to debug an interrupt handler, your operating system must detect and emulate INT instructions.

The TF flag is not cleared when the current privilege level is changed without a task switch. If you want to protect your operating system from the intervention of a debugger, you have to intercept the single step trap and disable it according to the CPL.

# Summary

This chapter gave you the theoretical basis for further practical study of this topic. We tried to squeeze into one chapter the vast amount of information related to the features of 386+ processors and their protected mode. All those descriptors, selectors, pages, tasks, privileges, virtual machines and so on, easily deserve more than a chapter, and could easily fill a book, but now at least you can speak protected mode.

Turn the page and get ready for real programming in protected mode.

# Practical Protected Mode Programming

## Introduction

So far so good, but here we come to the trickiest chapter in the book. It's dedicated to writing your own protected mode software. The deeper you get into this book, the more aspects of system programming you see. Protected mode uses specific system registers and requires handling of many specific system structures, like descriptor tables and page tables. Just entering into protected mode takes a lot of PC hardware programming. Another problem is that, unlike with real mode, DOS and BIOS functions are not designed to work in protected mode and therefore can't be used directly. In this chapter, I'll show how you can enter protected mode and live in it, illustrating this with a working program which I'll call the protected mode kernel, or just kernel. I'm far from encouraging you to forget all your duties, retire and roll up your custom DOS extender, but looking at this task from the inside is a good way to teach yourself system programming in all x86 modes: real, protected, and virtual-86.

If you've just flipped this book open at this page and you're not familiar with protected mode and DOS/PC architecture, put the book down. If you feel like getting into the subject, please read at least two previous chapters.

# Why Program in Protected Mode?

It's not that long ago that 640Kb of memory was regarded as impressive. In those days, it seemed that any reasonable program could run freely within this 640K. As usually happens with any limited resource, the 8086's 1Mb memory limit had been rapidly outgrown

Then came the 80286, which could address 16 megabytes of memory. Then we had the 80386, meaning programmers could address up to 4 gigabytes. Unfortunately though, MS-DOS only knew how to use the first megabyte. Even if a particular application doesn't need more than 64Kb, it's actually harmful to be restricted like this. Moreover, there are advanced features to support multitasking, multi-threading, and other sophisticated techniques which require more than 1 megabyte.

DOS-based programmers can't take advantage of these tempting features because DOS is unable to run in protected mode. However, using protected mode features of the 80286+ is not so very difficult. Suppose you need to address memory above 1Mb limit. All you have to do is:

- Disable interrupts, including the Non-Maskable one (NMI).

- Prepare 2 or 3 segment descriptors in the GDT (Global Descriptor Table) to point to the desired memory locations.

- Switch to protected mode.

- Perform what you want to do (say, swap a memory block to an address below 1Mb).

- Switch back to real mode.

- Enable interrupts.

- Enjoy overcoming the 1MB-barrier.

Pretty easy, isn't it? It may not look very convenient, but it works. Moreover, if you don't want to concern yourself with protected mode, engage your XMS driver (nowadays everyone has one, say HIMEM.SYS), or, at least, INT 15h

Function 87h (Move Memory Block). If, for any reason, you don't want to use BIOS or XMS, then you can step through the BIOS code using a debugger and see how it implements its INT 15h.

You can go even further and design a whole program to operate in protected mode. However, your programs need to access disks, the keyboard, and other interrupt-driven resources, usually by DOS and BIOS calls. This isn't trivial, because DOS and the BIOS still need to run in real mode using data structures in conventional memory, whereas your program is running in protected mode using both conventional and extended memory. In addition, it would be excellent to have a memory manager, DLLs, multitasking, and all of those tempting pleasures of protected mode.

There is another way, after all: you can use a DOS extender. A DOS extender is a service provider that manages all the specific protected mode system structures and allows you to write programs in virtually the same style as for real mode. At the same time, it provides the necessary mechanism for interrupt-driven I/O and DOS and BIOS calls. However, even if you rely on a DOS extender (which would seem to be the best solution), it's still worth reading on - by understanding the inner world of protected mode system programming, you'll be able to write more efficient programs.

# Anatomy of the Kernel

The protected mode kernel needs to implement the following:

**Entry to and exit from protected mode.** When the kernel starts, it must check if it can work in the current environment (will it interfere with other installed software?), and if it can, then it must switch the processor into protected mode. The kernel is also in charge of supporting the integrity of protected mode system structures.

**The interrupt management system.** This must correctly handle hardware and software interrupts and processor exceptions and pass DOS and BIOS service interrupts to the original handlers below 1Mb.

**The memory manager.** This is responsible for the allocation of memory blocks throughout the whole of the system memory and keeping order in protected mode tables. Also, a good memory manager must support virtual memory using some disk storage.

**The task manager which performs switching between tasks.** I didn't implement multitasking in my kernel - this is a wider step towards an operating system. However, it's not mandatory for all protected mode applications. It complicates all the other subsystems (interrupt and memory managers mostly), because you need to share memory, address space, interrupts, I/O ports, and CPU time across several tasks.

**Application programming interface**. However good a kernel may be, it'll be useless unless an interface is established between it and application programs. They will ask the kernel to allocate memory, install an interrupt handler, run a task, retrieve the information about system resources and state, etc. The kernel needs a public relations agent, and this is what the API is for. There's an industry standard for interfacing with protected mode service providers called DPMI (DOS Protected Mode Interface).

In the next section, I'll discuss these components (both those that are implemented and, briefly, those that aren't), the ways to make them work, and problems that appear on the way.

# Practical Implementation

In my protected mode kernel demo, I implement a segmented memory model, paging and virtual memory, and interrupt translation via virtual-86 mode.

## The Entry and Exit

First, I enter protected mode itself. I have to prepare all tables: IDT, GDT, LDT, page directory and second-level page tables (the kernel works with paging on), and the kernel's TSS. Then I switch the processor into protected mode. There's no standard specification for scheduling the process of where and when you have to fill up, keep, and move these tables.

That isn't all. I can't assume the program environment to be virginal when the kernel starts. There will probably be a memory manager like HIMEM.SYS or/and EMM386.EXE, Smart Drive (or RAM Drive) using a bulk of memory above 1Mb, etc. The kernel must coexist with them in harmony.

Firstly, I check if the processor is 386+. If it's not, I quit, since the kernel demonstrates features of the 386+. The next check is to see if an XMS manager is present. If it's not present, I assume I can use all the memory resources (I retrieve the amount of extended memory available via INT 15h function 88h). If working under an XMS manager, I use XMS functions to allocate the largest free extended memory block.

After that, I build the protected mode system tables in a DOS memory block, and move them to extended memory by using the INT 15h or XMS function Move Memory Block (refer to Chapter 14 'Memory Above 1Mb' for a detailed description). Then I intercept critical interrupts: INT 15h (to emulate function Move Extended Memory Block, which is used by XMS driver in virtual-86 mode, so that Smart Drive can work normally), and DOS interrupts 23h: Ctrl-Break, 24h: Critical Error and 19h: Reboot. Having done all this, I switch to protected mode passing control to the 32-bit part of the kernel.

The exit routine works in the reverse direction.

Take a closer look at all the subtasks step-by-step. You can refer to the source code module SERVER16.ASM supplied on the accompanying disk.

## Grabbing XMS Memory

I retrieve the size of the largest extended memory block available. Straight away, I allocate a block of exactly that size. I remember the size and handle for the block to free it when (if) exiting back to DOS. Then I lock the block for two reasons: to prevent the XMS manager from moving it to another place, and to obtain the physical address of the block. The following essential fragment from module SERVER16.ASM demonstrates using XMS for this purpose:

```
        mov ah,8
        call XMS_farcall        ; Get size of largest extended
                                ; memory block in Kb
        shr dx,2                ; /4 (to translate to pages)
        mov Ext_free_mem,dx     ; save it in 4Kb pages

        shl dx,2                ; *4
        mov [di],dx             ; save size of block
        mov ah,9
        call XMS_farcall        ; allocate extended memory block
```

```
        dec ax                  ; error check
        jnz err_mem
        mov [di+2],dx           ; save handle
        mov ah,0ch
        call XMS_farcall        ; lock extended memory block
                                ; and get 32-bit linear address
        dec ax                  ; check error
        jnz err_mem
        mov [di+4],bx           ; DX:BX = 32-bit block address
        mov [di+6],dx
```

## Building the Tables

To prepare the tables, I allocate several DOS memory blocks. I create Page Tables, the Page Directory, and Global Descriptor Tables.

First, a word about creating the Page Directory and Page Tables.

As described in Chapter 15 'Programming in Protected Mode', a Page Table entry has three bits (9-11) reserved by Intel for operating system programming. I use these bits as flags for virtual memory management:

Bit 9, Occupied:            Set if the page is occupied.

Bit 10, On Disk:            Set if there's a copy of this page on disk (for virtual memory).

Bit 11, Not Discardable:    Set if the page can't be swapped to disk (for virtual memory).

Then I ask the CMOS how much base and extended memory (in Kb) is installed in the system, because I need access to all physical memory. Adding them and dividing by 4, I get the total number of pages. Dividing this by 1024 (the maximum number of pages in a Page Table), I get the number of Page Tables (and Page Directory Entries). Of course, every division is rounded to the next greatest integer value. For simplicity, I initialize pages so that linear addresses are equal to physical addresses. Default attributes are: User, Read/Write, Present. The flags: Occupied, Not On Disk, Not Discardable. Then I go through free blocks in memory, and mark the corresponding pages as not Occupied and Discardable. At this stage, I add some disk space as virtual pages.

Now I find the place above 1Mb for the Page Tables and Page Directory (I think it's just good style to put them above 1Mb - in the larger pool). I look for the first free pages, and mark them as Supervisor, Locked, and Occupied. I remember the addresses to move the tables in there at a later phase. Also, I create the Page Directory entries according to the tables' addresses. I don't use the reserved bits in Page Directory entries, and mark the entries as User, Read/Write, Present. If I marked an entry as a Supervisor, then all the pages in the corresponding second-level table would be inaccessible from the User level. I can regulate protection in the second-level Page Tables on a page-by-page basis. Naturally, the page containing the Page Directory is marked as a Supervisor, Read/Write, Present, Occupied, Not On Disk, and Not Discardable. I remember the address of the Page Directory to load it into the CR3 (PDBR) register before entering protected mode.

Please refer to the source code on disk for implementation details (SERVER16.ASM, the procedure fill_tables).

## Creating the Global Descriptor Table (GDT)

From the very start, I reserve a GDT for 4096 descriptors (this is not a sacred number, you can choose a different one). This should be enough, because the GDT keeps descriptors for system code, data, and other system structures. User segments will be addressed through Local Descriptor Tables. I initialize the GDT with zeroes. Note that, in this implementation, I interpret the Available bit in descriptors as Occupied (the same way as for Page Table entries). Then I begin creating the descriptors necessary for the kernel:

Descriptor 0 -     in GDT is not used and remains zeroed.

Descriptor 1 -     'flat', specifies a data segment for the whole 4Gb address space. It lets the kernel access every bit in memory.

Descriptor 2 -     'GDT alias', opens access to the GDT itself, allowing the kernel to modify descriptors.

Descriptor 3 -     'Code32', the 32-bit code segment for the kernel.

Descriptor 4 -     'Data32', the 32-bit data segment for the kernel.

Descriptor 5 -     'Stack32', the 32-bit stack segment for the kernel.

Descriptor 6 -     'Code16', the 16-bit code segment for the kernel.

Descriptor 7 -     'Data16', the 16-bit data segment for the kernel.

Descriptor 8 - 'IDT alias', opens access to the IDT, allowing the kernel to modify gate descriptors in it. This descriptor is not privileged and can be used either by the kernel or applications.

Descriptor 10 - 'Real mode buffer', specifies the pre-allocated 64Kb DOS memory block, the buffer to transfer data between protected mode applications and real mode interrupts (see section 'Interrupt Management').

Descriptor 11 - 'Kernel's TSS alias', provides the kernel with access to its own TSS.

Descriptor 12 - Kernel's TSS descriptor.

Please refer to the source code on disk for implementation details (SERVER16.ASM, the procedure FILL_GDT).

Similarly to the Page Tables and Directory, I occupy Page Table entries (thus allocating pages) for the GDT, IDT, and the kernel's TSS and stack. The kernel's data and code are left below 1Mb.

Now that all the tables are ready, I move them to the extended memory allocated for them by using INT 15h or the XMS function (if XMM present).

## Switching to Protected Mode

All the boring and perplexing tables are prepared and moved to the right places, so we are ready to switch to the heady world of protected mode.

First, I 'CLI', so that no-one interferes with your business. I also turn off the Non-Maskable Interrupt. Second, I reprogram the interrupt controller, so that hardware interrupts from IRQ0 to IRQ7 are handled via vectors 50h to 57h (I do it to distinguish between hardware interupts and processor exceptions). You can choose other reserved vectors if you prefer. Then I save the IDTR register to restore it after exiting protected mode. By the way, in real mode, it appears to be always the same: base = 0 and limit = 3FFh. I save the state of the A20 line and enable it by means of the XMS manager or by programming the keyboard controller. I load the GDTR and IDTR with the bases found before, and with the predefined limits: (256x8)-1 for IDTR, and (4096x8)-1 for GDTR. Then I load the CR3 register with the Page Directory base address. I set the Paging and

Protection Enable bits in the CR0 register, and the next instruction is executed in protected mode. This next instruction must be intersegment JMP with a selector as the operand to flush the prefetch queue. I use this obligatory jump to start the 32-bit kernel.

Now the actual code (from the module SERVER16.ASM) for switching to protected mode (the code assumes that all the tables are already prepared):

```
        sidt old_idt                  ; Save old IDTR
        mov eax,gdt_address
        mov dword ptr gdt_reg+2,eax   ; Prepare image of GDTR
        mov word ptr gdt_reg,gdt_size

        mov eax,idt_address
        mov dword ptr idt_reg+2,eax   ; Prepare image of IDTR
        mov word ptr idt_reg,idt_size

        call get_A20_state
                                      ; AL = 1 if A20 enabled
        shl ax,15
        or System_flags,ax            ; Save A20 state
        test ah,80h
        jnz A20_active                ; Already enabled

        call Enable_A20

        call get_A20_state            ; Check if enabled O.K.
        mov dx,offset mess_A20_err
        test al,1
        jz error_exit                 ; Failed to enable A20

A20_active:

        mov bx,5070h
        call SetPIC                   ; Redirect IRQ0-IRQ7 to int50-int57

        cli

        lgdt gdt_reg                  ; Load GDTR
        lidt idt_reg                  ; Load IDTR

        mov eax,cr3                   ; Get CR3
        and eax,0fffh
        or eax,page_dir_address
        mov cr3,eax                   ; Set CR3 (Page Directory Base Register)

        mov eax,cr0
        or eax,80000001h
        mov cr0,eax                   ; TURN paging and protection ON

        db 66h                        ; Intersegment jmp selector:offset
        db 0eah
        dd offset entry32
        dw code32_sel                 ; Transfer control to 32-bit Kernel
```

**611**

For readability, I have left out the procedures that control A20 and PIC. You can find them in the module SERVER16.ASM.

So that's how to get in. O.K., let's get out.

## Exiting from Protected Mode

There's one thing you must be careful of when switching back to real mode. When you get into real mode, all the segments must have limits exactly 0FFFFh, be byte granular (G bit clear), expand-up (E bit clear), writeable (W bit set), and present (P bit set). So, you have to either keep your last protected mode code segment with the 0FFFFh limit, or set its limit before you switch (this is actually the way I do it). Then I execute a JMP to this segment to update the invisible part of the CS register. With other segment registers it's easier: I simply load them with a selector for a descriptor with the limit equal to 0FFFFh.

Now I turn off the Paging and Protection Enabled bits in CR0, and jump to the real mode code segment to flush the prefetch queue. In this real mode code, I restore all the registers that had been saved before I switched to protected mode. Also, I restore the original state of the A20 line and the Interrupt Controller. Now I can enable interrupts. As I intercepted some DOS and BIOS interrupts, I restore the original vectors. I free the allocated extended memory block, and that's it. When the kernel terminates, DOS frees all DOS memory blocks it has allocated. You have the black screen, the DOS prompt, and no trace of a protected mode program ever having worked in your system.

I have described the exit from protected mode just briefly. You can find the implementation details in the module SERVER16.ASM.

# Interrupt Management

## Exceptions and Hardware Interrupts Conflict

Processor exception indexes overlap with hardware interrupt indexes: IRQ0 to IRQ7 are by default serviced through interrupts 8 to 15, while a 386+ processor generates exceptions 0 to 17. There is a problem of how to distinguish, for example, the timer interrupts from double fault exception. To separate processor exceptions from hardware interrupts, I reprogram the Interrupt Controller so that IRQs are serviced through different interrupts (I use reserved indexes 50h - 57h).

## Passing DOS and BIOS Function Calls

The kernel is not a complete operating system, because it sits on top of DOS. Naturally, it must leave DOS and BIOS services transparent to application programs. But DOS is alien to protected mode, and can't simply transfer control to real mode handlers: the protected mode addresses consisting of selectors and 32-bit offsets (instead of segment:offset as in real mode) are strange to DOS. So, when the kernel receives an interrupt that refers to a DOS or BIOS function, it has to switch to either of the 8086 modes (real or virtual).

As my kernel provides a simple monotask environment, I could use real mode for servicing DOS and BIOS calls (as a matter of fact, such DOS extenders like TNT by Phar Lap and DOS/4GW do it this way). If you think this would be easy, look at the steps it has to take in this case (Figure 16.1 will help you).

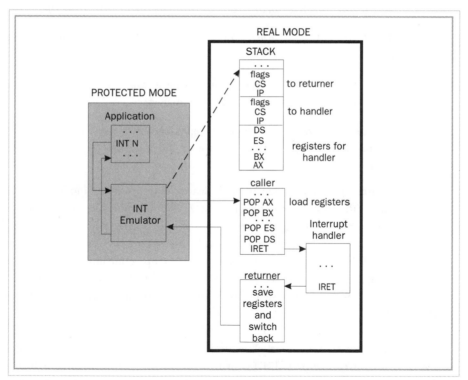

**Figure 16.1 Interrupt Emulation via Real Mode**

**1**  It has to keep the interrupt emulation frame in a real mode code segment: the caller (which passes control to the DOS interrupt handler) and the returner (which returns execution to the protected mode interrupt manager). They work with a known stack segment which transfers registers from protected to real mode.

**2**  The protected mode part of the interrupt manager sends three structures to this stack: the address of the returner, then the address of the DOS interrupt handler, and then the register contents for the DOS handler (the function parameters).

**3**  The interrupt manager exits protected mode, passing control to the caller.

**4**  The caller loads the registers from the stack, and executes the IRET instruction, which emulates an interrupt call to the DOS handler.

**5**  The DOS or BIOS handler works, and its IRET transfers control to the returner.

**6**  The returner saves the registers in a known data segment and switches back to the protected mode interrupt manager

**7**  The protected mode interrupt manager loads registers with values saved by the returner, and returns control to the interrupted program.

However, switching to real mode instantly leaves your protected mode environment with absolutely no defense: the real mode interrupt handler has access to all hardware ports, memory addresses under 1Mb, and all interrupts that occur during this real mode switch-back, bypassing your interrupt manager. That's why I will not consider the real mode interrupt emulation in this chapter. In a multitasking, fully featured, protected environment you can't put up with real mode switch-back, but have to use virtual-86 mode for interrupt translation. This is what I'll demonstrate here.

This is how I do it. My protected mode interrupt manager has an INT-emulator, and a virtual-86 counterpart, IRET-emulator. Every interrupt is routed to the INT-emulator, which switches to virtual-86 mode to the DOS interrupt handler address. The emulator is responsible for keeping the stack pointer for privilege level 0 (PL0) and virtual-86 stack pointer consistent (you can find the description of how cross-level interrupts are serviced in the Chapter 15 'Programming in Protected Mode', Section 'Interrupts and Exceptions'). I run the kernel at privilege level 0, and the user code at privilege level 3. When the user program executes the instruction INT, it causes a general protection fault, and the handler for this fault routes the execution to the INT-emulator (which reads the index of the interrupt from the user code). Now here's how the INT-emulator works, step by step:

**1** On entry, the INT-emulator pushes the segment registers on to the PL0 stack and updates the copy of the PL0 stack pointer in the current TSS (to keep this stack consistent, in case a hardware interrupt occurs during interrupt handling in virtual-86 mode).

**2** Then the INT-emulator creates a structure to switch to virtual-86 mode on the PL0 stack. This structure includes segment registers, the stack pointer for my virtual-86 mode stack, and the address of the DOS interrupt handler (read from the Interrupt Vector Table).

**3** The INT-emulator creates an interrupt return structure on the virtual-86 mode stack (equivalent to what the processor creates when servicing interrupts in real mode: Flags, CS, IP). The CS:IP in this structure points to IRET in virtual-86 mode code. This allows for intercepting returns from interrupt handlers other than by IRET (e.g. RET 2). I have an internal variable, the virtual-86 stack pointer, which I adjusted with every interrupt in virtual-86 mode.

**4** Now, the INT-emulator sets the VM flag in the copy of EFlags on the PL0 stack and executes IRET. The processor switches to virtual-86 mode, and passes control to the real mode interrupt handler (DOS or BIOS function).

When emulating an interrupt in virtual-86 mode, the interrupt manager of a protected system must retain control over all instructions that deal with interrupts: CLI, STI, PUSHF, POPF, INT, and IRET. As was described in Chapter 15 'Programming in Protected Mode', 386+ processors have hardware support for this: the above instructions at IOPL less than 0 cause a general protection fault, so the kernel can emulate them (see the code on disk in module EXC_13.INC for the implementation). The emulation of the IRET instruction allows me to return control to the interrupted procedure in protected mode. The IRET-emulator works as follows.

When the general protection fault handler recognizes the IRET instruction, it checks the copy of CS:IP on the virtual-86 mode stack to find out where this IRET wants to return control to. If it wants to go to the special IRET (see above), then switch back to protected mode. If not, then check the copy of CS:EIP on the PL0 stack: if this points to the special IRET, switch back to protected mode again. If neither of the two checks are satisfied, it means that it's a local V86 IRET (a return from a nested interrupt), and I emulate the IRET instruction to return to virtual-86 mode to the address read from the V86 stack. In all three cases, I adjust the V86 stack pointer (the way IRET in real mode would do). Before switching back to protected mode, I always adjust the copy of the stack pointer in the TSS and restore the segment registers.

Along with registers, I must transfer the Flags register, as returned by the interrupt handler, back to the protected mode program. Normally, the interrupt handler terminates with IRET, and my exception handler reads the copy of 16-bit flags from the virtual-86 stack. Then I write them to the lower word of the copy of 32-bit Eflags on the PL0 stack (to preserve the higher word and the NT and IOPL flags). This copy will be loaded into the Eflags register when control passes back to the interrupted program. So, the protected mode specific flags are preserved and the flags returned by the real mode interrupt handler get through to the program.

It can happen that a weird interrupt service routine terminates in a non-standard way, e.g. via the RET 2 instruction. In this case, the exception handler reads the lower word of the copy of EFlags on the PL0 stack, and writes it (masking the NT and IOPL flags) to the EFlags copy that pertains to the interrupted program.

The interrupt emulator is implemented in the module EXC_13.INC.

## Transferring Parameters to DOS and BIOS Calls

The interrupt manager must also transfer parameters to real mode handlers. When parameters are passed to and from the handler in registers only, the interrupt emulation as described in the above section works well with no extra hassle. But many functions transfer data in memory buffers (file reads and writes are the best example). Naturally, you can't pass protected mode addresses to DOS functions. To solve this problem, my INT-emulator calls the actual DOS functions with pointers to buffers below 1Mb. As all DOS and BIOS functions work with buffers no more than 64Kb, I pre-allocate one 64Kb buffer in DOS memory before starting the DOS extender kernel. I could use a smaller buffer, but in this case I have to call each function repeatedly. In my demo kernel I chose the simplest way.

Another problem is that 'buffered' functions vary in interface: the pointer to a buffer and the byte count is in different registers for different functions, for example, DOS function 3Fh, Read File, receives data pointed to by DS:DX and the byte count in CX, whereas BIOS interrupt 10h function 1Ch, Save Video State, writes data to the buffer pointed to by ES:BX (and you have to ask for the required buffer size with a separate call beforehand). Now you'll see the emulation of two DOS functions, Read File and Write File.

For the task of transferring data to and from DOS interrupts, I added two entities to my interrupt manager: the caller and the returner. The caller moves the data to the virtual-86 mode buffer (if so needed), prepares the registers for virtual-86 mode, and invokes the INT-emulator. The returner is called from the IRET-emulator and copies the V86 buffer to the application's buffer (if needed). Now in detail, step by step.

**DOS function Read File (INT 21h, AH = 3Fh)** When the interrupt manager detects the instruction INT 21h with 3Fh in AH, it checks its internal tables and finds out that this interrupt is buffered and receiving (the buffer is to be copied during return from the interrupt). All it has to do is translate registers and instruct the returner to copy the V86 buffer to the protected mode buffer. Then it passes control to the INT-emulator, which invokes the DOS function. The latter reads from the file into the V86 buffer, and IRETs. This turns on the IRET-emulator, which calls the returner. It finds the caller's note "Would you please copy our V86 buffer to this protected address" and obeys. Before exiting, it restores the registers for the interrupted application, and the work is finished.

**DOS function Write File (INT 21h, AH = 40h)** When the interrupt manager detects the instruction INT 21h with 40h in AH, it checks its internal tables and finds out that this interrupt is buffered and transmitting (the caller is to copy the buffer itself before invoking the interrupt). It copies the application's buffer to the V86 buffer, translates registers and instructs the returner not to copy the buffer. Then it passes control to the INT-emulator, which invokes the DOS function. The latter writes from the V86 buffer to the file, and IRETs. This turns on the IRET-emulator, which calls the returner. It finds the caller's note "Stand by, copy nothing" and copies nothing. It just restores the registers for the interrupted application, and the work is done.

Here it's worth mentioning a group of DOS and BIOS functions that don't need to be translated literally.

There are certain DOS and BIOS functions that are crucial in protected mode. These are DOS memory allocation functions 48h to 4Ah. There's no point calling the DOS handler for these functions, because DOS just can't allocate memory above 1Mb. A good idea is to ask the memory manager to allocate the required memory block somewhere in the memory that its system supports (including virtual memory).

I find it possible to omit outdated and worthless functions, like those dealing with FCBs instead of file handlers. To be quite honest, as the kernel is only a demo, I only implemented emulation of a few of the main DOS and BIOS functions which involve buffer transfers.

## Memory Management

The memory manager is one of the essential subsystems of any protected mode operating environment. Greed for the whole PC memory (and enlarged via the virtual memory concept at that) is the most compelling motive for those who venture into protected mode programming. In this section, I'll demonstrate how to organize memory management in a DOS extender. There are obviously other ways to manage memory, but this seems a good way.

In this implementation, I chose a multi-segment, not flat, memory model (see Chapter 15 for the difference between them). There are at least two reasons for this choice: first, the multi-segment model is more suitable for writing complex but stable operating environments; second, it's more convenient for the memory management I implemented (see below).

A preliminary note before I get to the practical details. I assume two levels of memory management: the low-level part that works closer to the CPU and the protected mode system tables, and the high-level part that provides a convenient and flexible application programming interface - something like a heap manager in languages like C or Pascal. A sophisticated memory manager just can't work using system tables only, because an LDT is limited by 8192 descriptors. You wouldn't want to keep each dynamically allocated string in a separate segment, would you? So, the low-level part only operates on the system tables, manipulating large page-aligned segments (let's call it the global heap manager). When an application starts, the kernel allocates separate segments for its code, stack, and data: three global heap blocks. When an application requests dynamic allocation of a memory block, the local heap manager resizes the data segment appropriately and returns the offset of the allocated local heap block in the data segment. Why do I keep the local heap in the data segment? This ensures that all the data lies in a single segment, so there's no need to reload the segment registers, and the performance of the system is the same as in the flat model.

Here, I'll only discuss the low-level management, because the tasks on the high-level are absolutely not protected mode specific; it's just straightforward programming. The duties of the memory manager fall into two separate subtasks:

- Heap management (allocation, deallocation, and resizing of segments).

- Virtual memory support.

## Heap Management

The multi-segment model and paging allow an elegant solution to memory allocation and deallocation. In our implementation, free memory always appears as an contiguous area in the linear address space, and you can allocate it as a single segment.

Allocation is simple: keep the pointer to the heap top (the index of the first free Page Table entry, actually), that gives the linear address of the segment to be created. The global heap manager finds an unused descriptor in the GDT or LDT, depending on whether the kernel or user is requesting memory, fills it up, and marks as Occupied. Then mark the requested amount of pages as Occupied and increment the heap top pointer. Here is the code for allocating a segment:

```
;WORD (PASCAL) allocate_segment (WORD pages,BYTE, Discardable_flag);
; Returns:
; if succesful CF clear,AX = selector
; if error    CF set, AX = error code
; Parameters:
req_pages     EQU word ptr [ebp+16] ; size in pages
discard_flag EQU byte ptr [ebp+12] ; discardable flag

allocate_segment proc far
    push ebp
    mov ebp,esp

    push ds
    mov eax,data32_sel            ; Switch to the kernel DS
    mov ds,eax

    mov eax,flat_sel              ; All memory is addressable via ES
    mov es,eax

    mov memerror_code,0           ; error code for debugging purposes

    movzx eax,req_pages
    cmp ax,Ext_free_mem           ; Are there enough pages available?
    ja nomorefreepages
    or eax,eax                    ; Asked for 0 pages?
    jz zero_pages_req             ; Drivel! Exit.

    movzx ebx,first_free_page     ; Heap top pointer (offset
                                  ; of the first free page
                                  ; table entry in the page
                                  ; tables array)
    mov esi,ebx

    add ebx,page_tables_address   ; EBX points to the first
                                  ; free page entry in the flat
                                  ; segment
    xor edx,edx
    mov ecx,[ebp+8]               ; check caller RPL
    and cl,3
    cmp cl,3
    jb superpage                  ; Supervisor pages
    or dl,PAGE_USER               ; User pages

superpage:

    cmp discard_flag,TRUE
    jne nondis
    or dx,PAGE_DISCARD

nondis:
```

```
        or dx,PAGE_OCCUPIED OR PAGE_WRITE

alloc_nextpag:

        test word ptr es:[ebx],PAGE_OCCUPIED  ; Is the page occupied?
        jnz bad_page_array                     ; Fatal error! Exit.
        and word ptr es:[ebx],0f199h
        or es:[ebx],edx                        ; set page attributes
        add ebx,4
        dec eax
        jnz alloc_nextpag                      ; Loop until all the pages for
                                               ; the segment are allocated

        mov first_free_page,bx                 ; Increase heap top pointer

        xor ebx,ebx
        mov ecx,items_in_LDT

        sldt dx                                ; get current LDT selector
        sub dx,8                               ; DX - alias LDT selector

        test byte ptr [ebp+8],3                ; check caller RPL
        jnz no_zero_ring
        mov edx,GDT_sel                        ; Allocate descriptor in GDT
        mov bl,8                               ; skip null descriptor
        mov ecx,items_in_GDT

no_zero_ring:

        mov es,edx

next_descr:                                    ; Find free descriptor

        test byte ptr es:[ebx+6],ALLOC_SEG     ; Is occupied?
        jz found                               ; No, use this one
        add ebx,8                              ; Next descriptor
        dec ecx
        jnz next_descr                         ; Check next
        jmp short nomorefreedescr              ; Oops!

found:

        cmp byte ptr es:[ebx+5],0ddh           ; First free descriptor?
        jne no_last_descr                      ; No
        mov byte ptr es:[ebx+8+5],0ddh         ; Mark the next one
                                               ; as the 1st free
no_last_descr:

        push ebx

        mov edx,esi                            ; ESI = previous first_free_page value
        shl edx,10                             ; page_entry_offset/4*12 = page_number
        movzx ecx,req_pages
        push ecx
```

```
        dec ecx                                ; ECX = segment limit in pages
        mov ah,RW_DATA
        mov al,[ebp+8]
        and al,3                               ; AL = caller CPL
        or ah,al                               ; DPL = caller CPL
        mov al,BIG_SEG OR ALLOC_SEG OR BIG_GRANUL
        call fill_descriptor32                 ; fill up descriptor
        pop eax

        sub Ext_free_mem,ax                    ; Decrease free extended memory counter
        pop eax
        and eax,0ffffh

        mov cl,[ebp+8]
        and cl,3
        or al,cl                               ; RPL = caller CPL
        test byte ptr [ebp+8],3                ; check caller CPL
        jz desc_in_gdt
        or al,TI

desc_in_gdt:

        clc                                    ; Clear CF, AX = selector
        pop ds
        pop ebp
        retf 8                                 ; Normal exit

; Errors
nomorefreedescr:
        inc memerror_code ; 4
nomorefreepages:
        inc memerror_code ; 3
zero_pages_req:
        inc memerror_code ; 2
bad_page_array:
        inc memerror_code ; 1

        mov eax,memerror_code
        stc                                    ; Set CF, EAX = error code
        pop ds
        pop ebp
        retf 8
allocate_segment endp
```

To make life simpler, I keep Page Tables in adjacent pages so that they appear as a single array of entries. This is not necessary, but simplifies searching and moving entries.

Moving is needed to keep the heap contiguous. Almost every time you deallocate a block, the heap becomes fragmented. To defragment the heap in the linear address space, I move all the segments above the deallocated one to the lower linear addresses. This is when the elegance of paging is clearly exhibited. You don't need to move the actual bulky segments in physical memory, but just their compact page table entries! Then I search for the descriptors of the moved segments and adjust the base addresses in them. The programs work with segment selectors and offsets, so they never even notice the change of the base linear addresses. Then I decrease the heap top pointer (see Figure 16.2). The last step is to refresh the TLB (Translation Lookaside Buffer), the processor's internal cache for page table entries; this is done by reading and writing back the contents of the CR3 register (PDBR). Before page table entries are moved, I disable interrupts, and enable them only when the TLB has been refreshed.

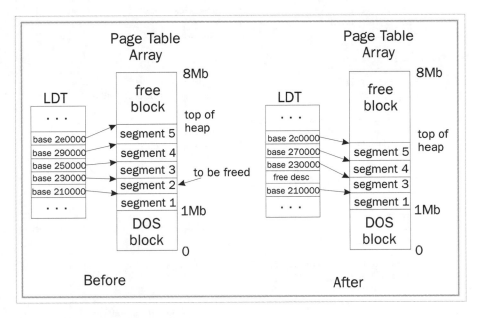

**Figure 16.2. Deallocating a Segment**

```
; WORD free_segment (WORD selector);
; Parameters:
free_selector    EQU word ptr [ebp+12] ; Selector to free
; Local variables
segment_size     EQU dword ptr [ebp-4]
segment_base     EQU dword ptr [ebp-8]
free_pages_ofs   EQU dword ptr [ebp-12]

free_segment proc far
    push ebp
```

```
        mov ebp,esp
        sub esp,12

        push ds
        cld

        mov eax,data32_sel               ; Switch to the kernel's DS
        mov ds,eax

        mov memerror_code,0

        sldt dx                          ; get current LDT selector
        sub dx,8                         ; DX - alias LDT selector

        test byte ptr [ebp+8],3          ; check caller CPL
        jnz no_zero_ring1
        mov edx,GDT_sel                  ; The descriptor is in GDT

no_zero_ring1:

        movzx ebx,free_selector
        and bl,0fch                      ; Extract descriptor index
        mov es,edx
        test byte ptr es:[ebx+6],ALLOC_SEG
        jz dealloc_error                 ; Error! The segment wasn't allocated
        and byte ptr es:[ebx+6],not ALLOC_SEG; mark descriptor
                                         ; as free

        movzx edx,byte ptr es:[ebx+6]
        and dl,0fh
        shl edx,16
        mov dx,es:[ebx]
        inc edx                          ; get segment size = Limit+1 (in pages)
        mov segment_size,edx

        movzx eax,byte ptr es:[ebx+7]
        shl eax,24
        mov edi,es:[ebx+2]
        and edi,0ffffffh
        or edi,eax                       ; get segment base address
        mov segment_base,edi

        shr edi,10
        add edi,page_tables_address      ; EDI = offset of the
                                         ; segment's first page in
                                         ; the page tables array
        mov free_pages_ofs,edi

        mov eax,flat_sel
        mov es,eax

;------ mark pages as free (set default attributes) -----

make_free_page:
```

```
        test word ptr es:[edi],PAGE_OCCUPIED  ; Is page occupied?
        jz free_free_page                     ; Error! Already free.
        and word ptr es:[edi],0f199h          ; clear D,A,U/S,R/W,
                                              ; Discardable,
                                              ; On Disk and Occupied bits

     add edi,4
     dec edx
     jnz make_free_page                    ; Next page

;------- save page entries to be freed -------------

     push edi                              ; EDI points to first allocated page
                                           ; after this segment
     mov ecx,segment_size
     mov edi,swap_buff_address
     mov esi,free_pages_ofs

     rep movs dword ptr es:[edi],es:[esi]  ; save the freed
                                           ; pages in
                                           ; swap_buffer

;------- shrink array of entries ----------------------

     pop esi                               ; EDI points to first allocated page
                                           ; after this segment

     mov edi,free_pages_ofs

     movzx ecx,first_free_page

     mov eax,segment_size
     shl eax,2
     sub first_free_page,ax                ; decrease heap top

     add ecx,page_tables_address
     sub ecx,esi
     jz free_last_block                    ; Was this the top segment?

     shr ecx,2                             ; /4 dword counter (page entries to move)
     push edi
     push esi
     push ecx

     cli                                   ; no interrupts !!!
     rep movs dword ptr es:[edi],es:[esi]  ; Pull down the page
                                           ; table entries above
                                           ; the freed segment

;-- move entries to be freed immediately above the heap top --

     mov esi,swap_buff_address
     mov ecx,segment_size

     rep movs dword ptr es:[edi],es:[esi]
```

```
;------- shrink statistics table, too ---------------------

    mov eax,page_tables_address
    mov ebx,page_use_stat_address

    pop ecx
    pop esi
    pop edi
    sub esi,eax
    sub edi,eax

    add esi,ebx
    add edi,ebx

    rep movs dword ptr es:[edi],es:[esi]

;------ adjust base addresses of descriptors ------------

free_last_block:

    mov edi,segment_base                ; EDI = base address of the
                                        ; segment being freed
    mov esi,segment_size
    shl esi,12                          ; ESI = base decrement

    mov eax,GDT_sel                     ; begin with GDT
    mov ds,eax

    mov ebx,8                           ; skip 0 descr in GDT

chk_ndesc:

    test byte ptr [ebx+6],ALLOC_SEG
    jz free_seg

    mov al,[ebx+5]
    test al,10h                         ; System bit
    jnz no_sys_descr                    ; DATA or CODE

    and al,0fh
    cmp al,2
    je LDT_descr                        ; LDT descriptor

    and al,00001101b
    cmp al,00001001b                    ; TSS descriptor ?
    jne descr_wo_base

no_sys_descr:

    call change_base                    ; change base addr of segment
    jmp short free_seg

LDT_descr:

;------------ LDT ----------------------------------------
```

```
        call change_base                ; change base addr of LDT
        push ebx
        push ds

        sub ebx,8
        mov ds,ebx                      ; load DS with LDT alias selector

        xor ebx,ebx

chk_ndesc1:

        test byte ptr [ebx+6],ALLOC_SEG
        jz free_seg1
        call change_base                ; change base addr of segment

free_seg1:

        add ebx,8
        cmp byte ptr [ebx+5],0ddh       ; if descriptor type = 0ddh
                                        ; then it's the last in table
        jnz chk_ndesc1
        pop ds
        pop ebx


;---------------------------------------------------------

free_seg:

descr_wo_base:

        add ebx,8
        cmp byte ptr [ebx+5],0ddh       ; if descriptor type = 0ddh
                                        ; then it's the last in table
        jnz chk_ndesc                   ; Check next descriptor

        mov eax,cr3
        mov cr3,eax                     ; refresh TLB

        sti
        mov eax,data32_sel
        mov ds,eax

        mov eax,segment_size
        add Ext_free_mem,ax             ; inc free extended memory counter

        clc                             ; Success, clear CF
        pop ds
        mov esp,ebp
        pop ebp
        retf 4

free_free_page:
        inc memerror_code
dealloc_error:
        inc memerror_code
```

```
    mov eax,memerror_code
    stc                             ; Set CF
    pop ds
    mov esp,ebp
    pop ebp
    retf 4
free_segment endp


; This procedure checks if the base in a descriptor is higher
; than the deallocated segment, and decreases the base
; appropriately
change_base     proc near
    movzx eax,byte ptr [ebx+7]
    shl eax,24
    mov edx,[ebx+2]
    and edx,0ffffffh
    or edx,eax                      ; get segment base address
    cmp edx,edi
    jb no_adj                       ; No adjustment required
    jne adj                         ; Adjust the base

    ; descriptor with same base as the deallocated segment
    ; must be killed, too.and byte ptr [ebx+6],not ALLOC_SEG
    ; mark descriptor as free

    ret

adj:

    sub edx,esi                     ; Decrease the base
    mov [ebx+2],dx                  ; load address back to descriptor
    shr edx,16
    mov [ebx+4],dl
    mov [ebx+7],dh
no_adj:
    ret
change_base     endp
```

Resizing an existing segment is pretty similar to deallocating it. I distinguish between two cases: expanding and shrinking. To shrink a segment, I change its limit to the new size, create a segment descriptor for the remaining part (the tail of the old segment), and deallocate this 'tail segment'. To expand a segment, I move all the segments above it to the higher linear addresses. Then I search for the descriptors of the moved segments and adjust the base addresses in them. I adjust the limit field of the descriptor for the expanded segment to match the new size. I increase the heap top pointer, and, at the last step, refresh the TLB. Of course, before page table entries are moved, I disable interrupts, and enable them only when the TLB has been refreshed.

## Local Heap Management

The kernel allocates memory by segments. Of course, an application needs smaller blocks to allocate variables like strings and relatively small objects. For this purpose, the kernel must have and manage the local heap: the application's data segment which holds all variables and objects. Now here's how it could be implemented.

When an application is loaded, the local heap manager resizes the data segment to create some space for local heap, and keeps account of local heap blocks with the help of two variables: the heap top offset in the segment and the offset of the first free block. In the beginning of every free block, the manager stores the 32-bit size of the block and the 32-bit offset of the next free block. This organization allows it to do without extra tables and lists because free blocks themselves keep information about themselves.

When the application asks to allocate a block of N bytes, the manager searches for the smallest free block that fits the requested size. Then it moves the size-offset record N bytes further into the found free block, and decreases the size field by N. If the free block is exactly N bytes long, then it's taken out from the free chain, and the offset field in the previous free block is changed to point to the next one.

When the application deallocates a block, a new free block is created and linked with the previous and/or the next free blocks. If there's a free block before or after the new free block, they are glued together to compose a single continuous block.

When the application runs out of local heap space, the manager asks the global heap manager to resize the segment. This is transparent to the application program.

As I've said above, in the code on the disk I actually implement the global heap manager, so this subsection is purely theoretical, although I hope these guidelines will allow you to implement something similar if you feel like it.

## Virtual Memory

To add some memory using disk storage, I extend the Page Table array - for example, if I want extra an 16Mb, I must add 4 extra Page Tables

16Mb / (1024 entries per table * 4Kb per page) = 4 tables

and consequently, 4 more Page Directory entries.

As was described in Chapter 15, if a Page Table entry has a clear Present bit (bit 0), then the rest of that entry is available for system programming. So, I record a clear Occupied bit (bit 9). In bits 12-31, I store the index of a record in the swap file.

The heap manager treats present and non-present pages equally. The virtual memory support proper is performed by the page fault handler. So, the heap manager will allocate pages regardless of whether they are present or not. When the processor wants to access a page A that is absent from memory, the page fault handler will find a discardable page D, which it will write to the swap file, store the record index for the page D into its Page Table entry, read the page A from the swap file to the physical address of page D, and store this address in the Page Table entry for the page A.

But do I always need to write a discardable page to the swap file? And which discardable page should I choose when I need to swap? I need criteria to form the algorithm for the page fault handler.

I use the Least Recently Used (LRU) criteria to choose which page to discard. The statistics are collected in the following way: on every 9th timer interrupt (i.e. twice a second), I check the Accessed bit in every Page Table entry. If this bit is set, I put the current_polling_time into the last_access_time (DWORD) for this page. I need an array of the same size as the total size of Page Tables, that is, say, one kilobyte for every megabyte of memory. It's less than 0.1%. It might seem to you that this timer-based approach is too performance-costly, but in fact, it costs no more than 0.1-0.4% of the CPU time, depending on the processor type and the size of virtual memory. But I think that precise statistics are important for virtual memory performance.

Then, whenever a page fault invokes the handler, I look through the statistics to find the entry with the minimum last_access_time, skipping non-discardable entries. It corresponds to the page that was least recently accessed. This one will be discarded to give room for an absent page.

Using the Dirty bit in Page Table entries is essential for optimizing the page discarding algorithm. If this bit is clear, it means the page hasn't been modified since it was last loaded from the swap file. Then I do not need to write the same copy back to disk, if of course, the copy of that page still exists on disk (it may have been overwritten by another page). There's no standard way to organize the swap file, and it's clear that a Page Table entry can't hold all the necessary information about the place in the swap file where the page was loaded from. That's why I keep a special index table, which tracks the relationship between the record index in the swap file and the physical address of the page. The index in this table corresponds to the record offset in the swap file, and the 32-bit entry holds the physical address of the page where this record was loaded to. This table has its entries initialized with -1 (0FFFFFFFFh), which is a constant meaning 'empty record'. To mark a record in the file which contains an exclusive (not present in RAM) image of a swapped page, I use another constant -2 (0FFFFFFFEh).

When the page fault handler needs to discard a page, it finds the least recently used discardable page. There can be three types of situations each of which requires separate treatment.

1   Not Dirty, On Disk. Such a page is not written to the swap file. The handler looks through the index table for the same physical address as in the discarded page's entry, and stores the system constant -2 into this index table entry.

2   Dirty, On Disk. This page is written to the old place in the file. The handler searches for the physical address of this page in the index table to find out the record index. After that, this index table entry is stored as that value minus 2.

3   Not On Disk. This page is to be written to the swap file, but the handler must find a place for it. This is the trickiest situation which deserves several paragraphs of 'logic'.

The handler first searches for an empty record (-1 in the index table). If one is found, the handler writes the page into this record and stores -2 into this entry of the index table. The page is discarded.

If there are no more empty records in the swap file (which is very probable), then the handler looks through all the Page Tables entries for a Present Dirty page, for which there is a copy On Disk (bits 0, 6, 10 set). It tries to find a Dirty page because 'clean' pages save unnecessary disk writes, and are therefore very valuable from the performance point of view. If a Dirty page is found, the handler clears the On Disk bit, finds its physical address in the index table, writes the page being discarded to the corresponding record in the swap file, and stores -2 into the index table entry.

If there are no pages with the Present, Dirty, and On Disk bits set, then the handler takes any entry from the index table, and finds a Page Table entry with corresponding physical address to clear the bit On Disk. The discarded page is then written to this record in the swap file, and -2 is stored in the index table entry.

Yes, it is tedious. The algorithm for discarding pages is the most complicated job of the virtual memory manager. Now you have it all.

This may not be the perfect virtual memory manager. There are probably other effective ways to organize the swap file to access disk (via BIOS or DMA).

# Multitasking

Multitasking is a very tempting feature of modern operating systems and environments. All of us would, no doubt, like to be able to play a game or type a letter while a huge database was being processed, a big file received through the modem, or a 3D scene rendered. We can see it in Windows, and even better in OS/2, though playing Windows card games during critical disk operations is not a good idea.

Multitasking should not be regarded as just a feature of operating systems. In fact, for some purposes it's the most natural and elegant way of programming. Take role-playing games: you engage a crew of warriors who are to fight various foes and monsters. A single-task approach forces you into perplexed solutions like a dispatching routine that schedules actions of all characters one by one. But if you can program every individual as an independent task, you simplify the development and modification of the game. Once you have a multitasking environment, you can easily add a new character with specific behavior.

In this section, I'll point out the work you have to do when writing a multitasking environment.

Multitasking systems can be divided into two categories: pre-emptive and non pre-emptive. The first is preferable: it provides smoother time-sharing between tasks and allows a high-priority task to interrupt all other activities at any time. In the non pre-emptive concept, applications give up control voluntarily when they decide to.

A pre-emptive system is harder to implement. Although true, pre-emptive multitasking, especially with time-sharing, is an excellent basis for combining independent processes: for example, in multimedia applications where you need sound and video to run smoothly side by side (by the way, it is possible in Windows 3.1, and still video files, .AVIs, are 'audio-video interleaved' and play within a single task).

Still, the non pre-emptive variant also has a right to survive. Your program is guaranteed to retain control until it gives it up or calls an API function (where the system can take over and pass control to other concurrent tasks). This allows optimal performance of critical operations which involve a lot of computing, like image processing or other mathematics.

Here's a non pre-emptive model with time-sharing among background tasks. In this concept there is one active task at any time which has full control over the CPU time, and several background tasks which are given one time slice each when the active task reports that it's inactive. Of course, interrupts are serviced as they occur. The active task can give up control either explicitly, via the API function Idle, or implicitly, via a user input request (e.g. the API function Get_Key_Or_Mouse). The task manager must have a mechanism for task switching: via a reserved keystroke that pops-up a list of tasks, or by assigning hot-keys to individual tasks, or the API function Activate_Me for pop-up tasks.

Background tasks are given time slices one after another. The initialization part of the DOS extender reprograms the system timer to tick at a higher rate (you could default the time-slice to, say, 1/36 of a second, but make it user-definable). There are two cases which determine how time slices are shared between the active task and the background ones.

The first case is when the active task becomes idle explicitly. The task manager then suspends it and resumes the first task from the background tasks queue. On every timer interrupt, it suspends the current tasks and resumes the active task. If it's still idling, the task manager passes control to a background task further down the queue. When the condition that makes the active task stop waiting is satisfied, the latter regains control with minimum delay (no more than one time slice). The idle loop can look like this:

```
while (!my_condition(bla,bla,bla) ) idle;
```

The second case is when control is taken from the active task implicitly within an API function, like Get_Key_Or_Mouse. Then the task manager itself knows which condition wakes the idling task up. It gives away time slices to the background tasks one by one, skipping the 'active' task. When the keyboard or mouse has stirred, the current time slice is taken from the current task, and control returns to the API function, which returns the event code to the active task.

You could also implement a single-task mode which suspends execution of all tasks except the active task or specified ones, so that the active task could still have all the API and user interface and at the same time gain maximum performance for real-time jobs.

That was just a raw outline of a multitasking. A mature multitasking system is much more complex to design, and there's a lot of aspects to consider.

# Dos Protected Mode Interface (DPMI)
## History

DPMI stands for DOS Protected Mode Interface. It's a software specification which allows programs to take the advantages of the 286 and higher processors and coexist in protected mode without conflict. It was originally designed by

Microsoft in 1989 for Windows 3.0 and soon became the most popular base for designing operating systems and environments, especially multitasking ones. VCPI, which had become an industrial standard, was beaten in popularity by this new, much more advanced specification.

It's clear why DPMI won. VCPI works only on 386 and higher machines and is totally based on hardware paging. It can't provide full virtualization and so is inapplicable for multi-tasking purposes. VCPI has too concise an API, and so leaves the programmer face to face with all the gory details of protected mode. It has no means of preventing an application from working at the highest possible privilege level. Protected mode under VCPI is absolutely defenseless.

DPMI provides a mighty API for mode switching, local descriptor table management, memory management (conventional and extended), controlling interrupt system, accessing CPU control registers, and cooperation with real mode applications. A DPMI host (an operating system or environment which implements DPMI services, otherwise called a server) can run, at a more privileged level than clients, applications that request those services, thus virtualizing memory and devices according to a supervisor-user protection model.

VCPI eventually surrendered to DPMI. Phar Lap joined the DPMI Committee and in May 1990 the DPMI specification version 0.9 was published. Version 1.0 came out in March 1992 armed with a set of advanced features. In this section we'll overview them both.

# Overview of DPMI Services

Before discussing DPMI function groups, here are some basic concepts.

Your program calls a DPMI function to switch to protected mode and after that it's registered as a DPMI 'client'. The DOS environment with your client application is a virtual machine. A virtual machine can contain several clients. The DPMI host keeps account of clients in a virtual machine by managing a stack (least recently created at the bottom, most recently created at the top). The top-most client is called the primary client. Some DPMI servers allow several virtual machines to run concurrently.

Each virtual machine is given its own address space, which is shared by all clients in this virtual machine. DPMI versions 0.9 and 1.0 organize this sharing differently. Under DPMI 0.9, every virtual machine has its own LDT and IDT used by all clients within it. Under 1.0, every client has its own LDT and IDT.

Some DPMI implementations can run several virtual machines at a time in pre-emptive multitasking. Each virtual machine becomes an independently dispatched task (but only one client is active within each virtual machine). A well-behaved client should never think it's the only one in the whole machine, owning all the resources. It should always give other programs a chance to work, issuing INT 2Fh function 1680h (Multiplex Interrupt function Release Time Slice) when it's idle (e.g. waiting for a keystroke). The DPMI host then passes the CPU to a client in another virtual machine. If all programs follow this rule, the performance of the whole multitasking system can be improved greatly.

DPMI implementations designed to run exclusively on 386+ computers normally use the hardware protection mechanism to protect system integrity. They use the 'supervisor/user' model, virtualizing input, output, and interrupts. You should make no assumptions about your application's privilege level, but get the level value from CS (bits 0 and 1, CPL), like this:

```
mov ax,cs
and al,3 ; AL = CPL
```

For example, allocating a memory block and putting the corresponding descriptor into LDT, you should set DPL equal to your application's own CPL. Otherwise, the block with the higher privileged descriptor will be inaccessible to the client.

Since DPMI version 1.0, even clients in different virtual machines can communicate via a DPMI shared memory block, which can contain both code and data. Within a single virtual machine there are other ways of communication: via resident service providers and DOS memory blocks.

You can use a comprehensive set of DPMI functions to allocate a memory block in memory and build a descriptor (to make the block addressable). Under 32-bit hosts, 32-bit clients can be written using either the flat or segmented memory model.

Many DPMI hosts support virtual memory, allowing clients to allocate more memory than is physically present in the system (in this case, the total amount of virtual memory is limited only by storage media space). Memory owned by a client is, by default, swappable (and pageable on demand), while DOS memory, (i.e. below 1Mb in the client's virtual machine) is, by default, locked (not able to swap). These attributes can be changed via DPMI functions. You should not unlock DOS memory, or memory occupied by interrupt handlers because a critical situation can arise when the host will not be able to load the required block from disk.

As you can see, DPMI is a powerful platform for programming in protected mode. Windows stands firmly on it. I decided to include an overview of DPMI service, with a more detailed function reference in Appendix C. If you're interested in DPMI programming and need a complete description, please refer to DPMI specification available from Intel Literature JP26, 3065 Bowers Ave., P.O. box 58065, Santa Clara, CA 95051-8065, telephone (800) 548-4725.

# Service Groups

You access DPMI services via interrupt vectors 2Fh and 31h. Most of 2Fh functions can be supported in both real and protected modes (depending on the implementation). There are only four functions in the 2Fh vector.

## DPMI Service Functions

      1680h   Release Current Virtual Machine's Time Slice
      1686h   Get CPU Mode
      1687h   Return Real-to-Protected Mode Switch Entry Point
      168Ah   Get Vendor-Specific API Entry Point

INT 31h functions are available in protected mode only. The function number is placed in AX. On return, CF is set if there was an error and the error code is in AX. All functions preserve flags and registers and are reentrant if not specified explicitly in the function description. When a 32-bit client calls a 32-bit host, DPMI assumes extended registers (i.e. ES:EDI instead of ES:DI).

Following is a list of the INT 31h functions by categories.

# Extended Memory Management Functions

## EMM Functions

The principal functions in this group are:

| | |
|---|---|
| 0501h | Allocate Block |
| 0502h | Free Block |
| 0503h | Resize Block |
| 050Ah | Get Block's Size and Base |

They allow allocation of memory above 1Mb. Only the linear address is returned, after allocation of a block, you have to call DPMI functions (as a separate step) to create and initialize a descriptor for the block (to make it addressable). In many implementations memory blocks are page-aligned.

32-bit hosts provide extra service.

## EMM Functions (32 bit hosts)

| | |
|---|---|
| 0504h | Allocate Linear Block |
| 0505h | Resize Linear Block |

These functions always allocate page-aligned blocks and allow you to request a block at a specific linear address. But if you allocate a block in the linear address space containing uncommitted pages (not corresponding to physical memory or disk space), it will cause an error. As with the principal functions, it's up to you to set up a descriptor for the newly allocated block.

| | |
|---|---|
| 0506h | Get Page Attributes |
| 0507h | Set Page Attributes |

Every page is assigned attributes: committed or uncommitted, read-only or writeable, was accessed or not, was modified or not.

## Trans-process Communications Functions

The functions for trans-process communication are:

| | |
|---|---|
| 0D00h | Allocate Shared Memory |
| 0D01h | Free Shared Memory |

| 0D02h | Serialize on Shared Memory |
| 0D03h | Free Serialization on Shared Memory |

For convenience of process-to-process communication, DPMI gives names to shared memory segments. Serialization allows a client to temporarily reserve rights of access to a shared memory block, read or write the newest data, and release the access rights to make the block accessible for other applications. Of course, as before you must build descriptors by yourself.

## Memory Information Functions

| 0500h | Get Free Memory Information |
| 050Bh | Get Memory Information |
| 050Bh | Get Page Size |

Certainly, in a multitasking environment the information received from these functions is liable to sudden changes. A concurrent client can capture a huge slice of memory resources, or the host can decide to lower your application's 'memory credit'.

# LDT Descriptor Management Functions

Because functions for extended memory allocation don't create descriptors, DPMI has a set of functions to allocate, modify, and free entries in client's LDT. These functions are as follows.

## Management Functions for LDT Descriptors

| 0000h | Allocate LDT descriptor |
| 0001h | Free LDT descriptor |
| 0002h | Map Real-Mode Segment to Descriptor |
| 0003h | Get Selector Increment Value |
| 0006h | Get Segment Base Address |
| 0007h | Set Segment Base Address |
| 0008h | Set Segment Limit |
| 0009h | Set Descriptor Access Rights |
| 000Ah | Create Alias Descriptor |
| 000Bh | Get Descriptor |
| 000Ch | Set Descriptor |

| 000Dh | Allocate Specific LDT Descriptor |
|---|---|
| 000Eh | Get Multiple Descriptor |
| 000Fh | Set Multiple Descriptor |

To work with a segment under DPMI you have to perform the following basic steps:

**1** Allocate a memory block.

**2** Allocate a descriptor in your client's LDT.

**3** Initialize the descriptor (set base address, limit, and access rights).

**4** Work with the memory block (addressing it via the selector returned at step 2).

**5** Free the LDT descriptor.

**6** Free the memory block.

## DOS Memory Management Functions

Perfectly analogous to DOS functions 48h, 49h, and 4Ah, these DPMI functions are as follows.

### Memory Management Functions for DOS

| 0100h | Allocate DOS Memory Block |
|---|---|
| 0101h | Free DOS Memory Block |
| 0102h | Resize DOS Memory Block |

Unlike extended memory allocation functions, these create and destroy descriptors as necessary.

## Page Management Functions

This function set is provided by 32-bit hosts that support page-oriented virtual memory.

## Page Management Functions

There are four functions for locking/unlocking pages.

| | |
|---|---|
| 0600h | Lock Linear Region |
| 0601h | Unlock Linear Region |
| 0602h | Mark Real-Mode Region as Pageable |
| 0603h | Relock Real-Mode Region |

All locking and unlocking calls are counted, so if you ask to lock a page four times, you have to call the unlocking functions the same four times to unlock it.

There are two additional functions to improve the performance:

| | |
|---|---|
| 0702h | Mark Page as Demand Paging Candidate |
| 0703h | Discard Page Contents |

# Interrupt Management Functions

This comprehensive set of functions allows you to organize handling of software and hardware interrupts and processor exceptions in real and protected mode.

### Interrupt Management Functions

| | |
|---|---|
| 0200h | Get Real Mode Interrupt Vector |
| 0201h | Set Real Mode Interrupt Vector |
| 0202h | Get Processor Exception Handler Vector |
| 0203h | Set Processor Exception Handler Vector |
| 0204h | Get Protected Mode Interrupt Vector |
| 0205h | Set Protected Mode Interrupt Vector |
| 0210h | Get Extended Processor Exception Handler Vector for Protected Mode |
| 0211h | Get Extended Processor Exception Handler Vector for Real Mode |
| 0212h | Set Extended Processor Exception Handler Vector for Protected Mode |
| 0213h | Set Extended Processor Exception Handler Vector for Real Mode |

These seemingly overlapping functions (e.g. Set Processor Exception Handler Vector and Set Protected Mode Interrupt Vector) allow you to handle different kinds of interrupt differently, even if they have the same vector number. You can also distinguish between real and protected mode interrupts.

## Multitasking Enviroment Interrupt Functions

To safely emulate interrupt enabling/disabling in a multitasking environment, DPMI provides the following functions:

| | |
|---|---|
| 0900h | Get and Disable Virtual Interrupt State |
| 0901h | Get and Enable Virtual Interrupt State |
| 0902h | Get Virtual Interrupt State |

When your application executes the CLI instruction (or calls function 0900h), the host sets the virtual interrupt state to 'disabled', which actually means that the host won't pass hardware interrupts to the client (the DPMI server can't allow a client to actually suppress hardware interrupts, because this could interfere with his activities or other concurrent clients). This state remains until your program executes STI (or calls function 0901h).

# Translation Functions

Your protected-mode program can use real-mode procedures by using the following functions:

## Real Mode Translation Functions

| | |
|---|---|
| 0300h | Simulate Real-Mode Interrupt |
| 0301h | Call Real-Mode Procedure with Far Return Frame |
| 0302h | Call Real-Mode Procedure with Interrupt Return Frame |

You use all three in the same fashion. Prepare a special data structure containing values for real mode registers and call the required DPMI function. The DPMI host saves the values of the protected mode registers, switches the CPU into real mode, loads real mode registers, and passes control to the specified destination. On return, it stores values of the real mode registers back into this data structure, switches back to protected mode, and resumes execution of your client.

Conversely, DPMI allows a real mode program to call protected mode procedures with implicit mode switches. This is implemented via a mechanism called real mode callback.

### Protected Mode Translation Functions

| 0303h | Allocate Real Mode Callback Address |
| 0304h | Free Real Mode Callback Address |

Rcal mode callback mechanism can be used to handle interrupts that occur in real mode by handlers working in protected mode.

In addition, this group has two functions which allow you to quickly switch between real and protected mode. By using these functions, you're responsible for saving and restoring the system state in both modes. DPMI hosts have two procedures to save and restore the system state, one for each mode. You can retrieve the entry points of Save/Restore procedures, as well as the entry points of mode-switching procedure via the following functions:

### State Saving Functions

| 0305h | Get Address of Save-Restore-State Procedures |
| 0306h | Get Address of Raw CPU Mode Switch Procedure |

# Debug Support Functions

As in a multitasking environment, debug registers may be supported individually for every client. You should use the following functions to work with them.

### Debug Functions

| 0B00h | Set Debug Watchpoint |
| 0B01h | Clear Debug Watchpoint |
| 0B02h | Get State of Debug Watchpoint |
| 0B03h | Reset Debug Watchpoint |

# Miscellaneous Functions

## Host Information Retrieval Functions

| | |
|---|---|
| 0400h | Get DPMI Version |
| 0401h | Get DPMI Capabilities |
| 0402h | Get Vendor-Specific API Entry Point |

## Protected Mode Service Providers

| | |
|---|---|
| 0C00h | Install Resident Service Provider Callback |
| 0C01h | Terminate and Stay Resident |

## Coprocessor Information Functions

The following two functions allow you to retrieve information about whether a numeric coprocessor is present, its type, and whether or not the host or the client is providing coprocessor emulation:

| | |
|---|---|
| 0E00h | Get Coprocessor Status |
| 0E01h | Set Coprocessor Emulation |

The following simple program illustrates how to enter protected mode and allocate a memory block using DPMI. The program requires a DPMI host to be installed (MS Windows 3.1 will do).

```
.model small
.stack 200h
.data
DPMI_not_inst_mess db 'DMPI host not installed',10,13,'$'
error_mess db 'Error.',10,13,'$'
ok_mess db 'DPMI works OK.',10,13,'$'

PM_door  dd 0            ; entry point to the entry procedure
block_handle dw 0,0      ; Parameters of a block which will be
linear_addr dw 0,0       ; allocated
block_selector dw 0
.code
.286
Start:
    mov ax,@data
    mov ds,ax            ; Load data segment

    mov bx,ss
    sub bx,ax
    shl bx,4
```

```
        cli
        mov ss,ax                 ; Load stack pointer
        add sp,bx
        sti

        mov bx,sp
        add bx,15                 ; Round up to next paragraph
        shr bx,4
        add ax,bx                 ; AX = SS + SP / 16 = segment address
                                  ; of the end of the program space
        mov bx,es
        sub ax,bx                 ; AX = required ammount of paragraphs
        mov bx,ax
        mov ah,4ah
        int 21h                   ; Resize block
        jnc Resize_ok
        jmp error

Resize_ok:

        mov ax,1687h
        int 2fh                   ; get address switch entry point
        or ax,ax                  ; error if AX != 0
        jz DPMIpresent
        jmp DPMI_not_inst

DPMIpresent:

                                  ; Int 2fh/1686h returns:
                                  ; BX, bit 0: clear = 16-bit host, set = 32-bit
                                  ; CL - processor type
                                  ; 2 - 286
                                  ; 3 - 386
                                  ; 4 - 486
                                  ; 5 - P5 ...
                                  ; DH - DPMI major version
                                  ; DL - DPMI minor version
                                  ; SI - number of paragraphs required for
                                  ; DPMI host private data
                                  ; ES:DI - points to protected mode switch
                                  ; entry point

        mov word ptr PM_door,di   ; Fill Up PM_door
        mov word ptr PM_door+2,es

        or si,si
        jz no_priv_data           ; No private DPMI data

        mov bx,si
        mov ah,48h
        int 21h                   ; allocate some paragraphs for DPMI
                                  ; host private data
        jnc alloc_ok
        jmp error
```

```
alloc_ok:

    mov es,ax

no_priv_data:

    mov ah,0                    ; AX: bit 0 =
                                ;0 for 16-bit application
                                ; 1 for 32-bit application
                                ; ES host private data segment

    call PM_door                ; switch to  protected mode

; ---- we are in protcted mode with:

        ; CS = selector with base real mode CS and 64K limit
        ; SS = selector with base real mode SS and 64K limit
        ; DS = selector with base real mode DS and 64K limit
        ; ES = PSP selector with 256 byte limit
        ; FS = GS = 0

    mov ax,0501h                ; DPMI function Allocate Memory Block
    xor bx,bx                   ; BX:CX = Byte count
    mov cx,40000
    int 31h                     ; allocate 40000 bytes in extended memory
    jc error

    mov block_handle,di
    mov block_handle+2,si
    mov linear_addr,bx
    mov linear_addr+2,cx

    xor ax,ax                   ; DPMI function 0 Allocate an LDT descriptor
    mov cx,1
    int 31h                     ; allocate 1 LDT descriptor, return selector
                                ; in AX
    jc error
    mov block_selector,ax

    mov ax,7                    ; DPMI function 7, Set segment base address
    mov dx,linear_addr+2
    mov cx,linear_addr
    mov bx,block_selector
    int 31h                     ; set segment base address
    jc error

    mov ax,8                    ; DPMI function 8, Set segment limit
    xor cx,cx
    mov dx,40000-1              ; limit field = 39999
    mov bx,block_selector
    int 31h                     ; set segment limit
    jc error

    mov ax,9                    ; DPMI function 9, Set access rights
    mov bx,block_selector
    mov cx,cs
    and cx,3 ; get CPL
```

```
        shl cl,5
        or cl,92h                ; Present,Data,Expand-up,Read/Write segment
        int 31h                  ; set descriptor access right
        jc error

        ; play with memory block
        ; . . .
        ; I fill the allocated block with 12h
        mov es,block_selector
        xor di,di
        mov al,12h
        mov cx,40000
        rep stosb

        mov ax,1                 ; DPMI function 1, Free descriptor in LDT
        mov bx,block_selector
        int 31h                  ; free descriptor
        jc error

        mov ax,0502h             ; DPMI function 0502h,
                                 ; Free extended memory block
        mov di,block_handle
        mov si,block_handle+2
        int 31h                  ; free extended memory block
        jc error

        mov dx,offset ok_mess    ; Report success
exit:
        mov ah,9                 ; Output string
        int 21h

        mov ax,4c00h             ; Terminate program
        int 21h

error:

        mov dx,offset error_mess
        jmp short exit

DPMI_not_inst:

        mov dx,offset DPMI_not_inst_mess
        jmp short exit
end Start
```

# Summary

In this chapter I've covered the implementation of a protected mode kernel. It's merely a demo program, the main purpose of which was to illustrate to you the inner life of the PC in protected mode and some ways to make it work. Of course, it didn't cover all the protected mode jobs you have to accomplish in professional programming, but it has covered the basic details.

# CHAPTER SEVENTEEN

# Viruses and Antiviruses

## Introduction

In this chapter we will look at one of the most important problems facing the computer industry - that of computer viruses. We will explain about safety precautions - how to minimize the possibility of infection, how to recognize a virus in your PC if it does become infected, how to delete it and how to check the programs and disks on your computer for the presence of viruses.

A special note here for anyone who may be hoping for hints on how to write a virus: don't bother to read this chapter. Note also, that a lot of countries have laws that punish those who design and produce computer viruses. Under US law you can be imprisoned for 5 years for such an offence.

This chapter covers the following topics:

- Minimizing the possiblity of infection: computer hygiene

- Analyzing computer viruses: how to recognize a virus in your system

- Deleting computer viruses: how to delete viruses in your computer

- Other (non-standard) methods of controlling viruses

The disk supplied with this book contains a working antivirus program which can delete several viruses. You can add new types of antiviruses to it yourself.

# Fundamental Knowledge

## What is a Virus?

The problem of viruses arose at the end of the punch card era, when it became possible to enter commands directly into a computer from the keyboard.

The idea of creating self-made mechanisms was thought up by John von Neuman in 1951, though it was Fred Kohen who first applied the word virus to computer programs. The term was used because, like human viruses, computer viruses are able to reproduce themselves. They can travel from one body to another at a very high speed.

How can we define a virus? In our opinion, the best definition of a virus appeared in the book 'The Computer Virus Crisis' written by P. Fites, P. Johnston and M. Kratz in 1989. It stated that 'a computer virus is a program which makes some unnecessary actions in your computer system without you being aware of it'.

## A Bit of History

One of the first examples of a really dangerous computer virus was Morris' virus. This appeared on November 2, 1988. Computer experts termed the event the greatest offensive to date on computer networks. A US university student, Robert Morris Junior, had tried to create an experimental program to test the safety system of a computer network. However, due to an error in the program, it immediately started to travel via the network and within 2 days Morris' virus had contaminated about 6000 computers. Although it could only do one thing - reproduce itself - it demanded such great resources that the network was actually paralyzed; it took many scientists who worked on infected networks to struggle to destroy the virus.

The Morris virus sent itself to all nodes accessible by the current user and repeated this action from there. It used a small table of the most useful passwords (about 800 words) and then, using a very simple algorithm, tried to find the current user's real password.

The total expenditure for deleting this virus was about 100 million dollars. The virus also managed to penetrate into the military network MilNet, but fortunately, it did not cause any serious damage here. Imagine what could have happened if it had.

Morris was brought before the court, fined 10,000 dollars and forced to do 400 hours of community service.

In Russia, a disgruntled programmer at the Gorky automobile plant created a virus which halted the whole factory. The programmer inserted some code, including the virus, into the controlling program and this destroyed the application.

One more example of a computer virus is what happened with the database of AIDS Information. This was a free-of-charge information package with a database about the symptoms of AIDS. In December 1989, about 20,000 copies of this database were sent out to different clients, including some medical organizations from the USA, England, Germany, etc. At first there were no problems - the program worked fine. However, it contained damaging code. After a few days, it began to encrypt all the information on the user's disk and the message "Pay $378 into account XXXXXXX and the disk will be restored" was printed on the screen. In February 1990, Joseph Popp, who turned out to be the distributer of this Trojan Horse, was arrested.

There are also a lot of examples of viruses interfering with bank activities. In 1986, a college professor, Rifkin, who was employed by the Security Pacific National Bank as a computer consultant, stole $10.2 million. In 1987, a bank clerk in Australia, wrote a program that robbed a bank of about 4 million dollars. These are just a couple of the many examples of bank viruses.

Viruses in local PCs will only trouble you and other users of your computer. They might cause letters to drop off the screen (the virus 'Fall letters'), make a mirror reversal of the screen ('Mirror'), sing you songs ('Yankee doodle', 'Voronezh') etc, but they can also cause more serious damage by formatting your floppy disk ('Den Zuk') or encrypting the information on your hard disk ('Disk kill').

# Virus Classification

What types of virus are there? The four most widespread types of virus program are as follows:

## Real Viruses

Like human viruses, these infect the program's body or the boot sectors of disks, and can duplicate themselves. This type includes:

**File viruses on PCs**. These viruses live inside executable files.

**Boot viruses.** These viruses are situated in boot sectors or in master boot sectors, i.e. in the special system areas which are run by BIOS before all other applications. This type of virus is very dangerous. Once the virus has been loaded, the normal boot or master sector gains control, loads itself into the memory and starts to execute.

**Root viruses.** This is quite a new type. There will only be one copy of the virus on the whole logical drive, but the infected program starts from the body of the virus. This type of virus changes the FAT table so that the first cluster of infected programs points to the virus body. These viruses are usually located in the reserved blocks of disk space between the FAT and ROOT areas. Once the virus has been loaded, the contaminated program is allowed to be loaded into the computer's memory.

These can be further separated into two subtypes:

**Non-resident viruses.** These viruses take control of the operating system when an infected program is loaded into the memory. They try to contaminate all the executable files they can find or else just one important file, for instance COMMAND.COM. Control is then passed to the normal application.

**Resident viruses.** These leave their bodies in the computer's memory. To do this, the virus cuts off part of the system memory, usually at the high addresses and writes its body into this part. It then intercepts one or more interrupts that control the operating system. For instance, if a virus controls interrupt 21h, it can control the processes of executing, opening, and creating a file. A virus that intercepts function 4Bh (program execution) can write its body into the program and then pass control to the normal processor of the DOS interrupt.

## Trojan Horses

The second type of virus program is what is known as a Trojan horse. This is not a real virus but a program that does something nasty, for example, deleting everything on a disk, deleting any applications, setting new passwords, etc. Like the real Trojan horse, these viruses live under the guise of interesting or useful applications. For example, there is a Trojan version of the popular archiver ARC, which looks like a real ARC, but deletes all the files you put into the archive. Trojan programs are the most destructive type of virus.

## Time Bombs

The third type is known as the Time bomb. This constitutes part of the code in an application. This code cannot reproduce itself, but it can cause destructive or unexpected actions. The Salami bank method is an example of this type of virus. This method starts to work after the code has been inserted into a bank type application. All bank operations bring some profit to the bank (0.1, 0.2, 1.5, etc percent interest). Salami intercepts these actions and rounds up the result of the percentage calculation. For instance, if you want to get 1.53 percent from the sum of US$1235 you will get US$1253.8955. Since you cannot share out US$0.0055 in a normal situation, the bank rounds up the result. However, Salami puts this US$0.0055 into a special account held by the people who created Salami. Each bank performs hundreds of operations per day - try and work out how much it could lose due to this virus. It will make you realise why it is so necessary to perform constant antivirus controls.

## Worms

The fourth type of virus program includes the type known as Worms. The best example of this type is Morris' virus. These viruses creep through networks like worms. The one positive thing about this type of virus is that it can detect holes in a network's defence systems.

# Virus Types

To identify viruses, we will use the following system:

**1** The primary identifier stands for the name of the virus type.

- V for viruses of the first type

- T for Trojan horses

- B for Time bombs

- W for Worms

**2** The value in the middle is the length of the virus. Most viruses have their own length, so this value will be unique. If two viruses have the same length, we will add a letter to differentiate them, for instance 1024A, 1024B etc.

**3** The third value is the index of the resident virus: R if a virus has a resident part, otherwise just space. For example, the virus Fall letters will have the index V1701R, Trojan horse ARC will have the index T103212, etc.

Some viruses have different versions. In these cases, we place the letter S before the main identifier and the number of the version after that. For instance, a mutant of the Fall letters virus will have the index S1V1701R.

If a virus encrypts its body, we will indicate this by putting the letter E prior to the primary identifier of the index. For instance, the virus Sverdlovsk encrypts its body with a very simple algorithm. This virus will be indexed as EV1021R. If necessary we will also designate viruses with their signatures (see below). However, this is inconvenient due to the large number of bytes in a signature (up to 64 bytes).

One more convenient method of classifying viruses was suggested by one of the best virusologists of the former USSR, Bezrukov. He suggested that viruses should be designated by their I-signature. An I-signature is a short way of characterizing a virus. It consists of a string of the descriptors and descriptors' attributes. Table 17.1 illustrates the set of descriptors suggested by Mr. Bezrukov.

**Table 17.1 Files Virus Descriptors (authorized by N. Bezrukov (c) 1990)**

| Descriptor | Description | Property | Function |
|---|---|---|---|
| A | Type of READ_ONLY files processing | y | Clears and restore |
| | | n | Does not infect them |
| | | r | Clears and does not restore |
| B | Processing of the critical interrupt handling (INT 24) | y | Follows it |
| | | n | Does not follow it |
| C | Infecting of the COMMAND.COM | y | Infects COMMAND.COM |
| | | n | Does not infect it |
| | | o | Infects only command processor |
| | | s | Infects it using the information from COMSPEC |
| D | Changing of the date and time of file creation | y | Changes date and time |
| | | n | Does not change date and time |
| | | s | Changes only the seconds value |
| E | Way of determining | e | Determines it by the extension file type |
| | | s | Determines by the EXE files signature (MZ) |
| F | Minimum length of the infected files | \<number\> | Length is equal to the \<number\> |

*Continued*

Table 17.1 Files Virus Descriptors (Continued)

| Descriptor | Description | Property | Function |
|---|---|---|---|
| | | n | There is no control of the minimum length |
| I | Increasing of the file length during contamination | c | Constant |
| | | p | Aligns to the paragraph margin |
| | | n | Not present |
| J | Processing of the first instruction in the infected files | n | Not processed |
| | | j | Infects only COM files with JMP as the first instruction |
| | | s | Does not infect COM files with JMP as the first instruction |
| K | Number of infections | <number> | Infects <number> times |
| | | m | Infects files many times |
| L | Virus length | <number> | <Number> is a length |
| | | i | Length is equal to the length increase |
| M | Mask effect | c | Encrypts its body |
| | | I | Masks the interrupt interception |
| | | m | Is not visible in the memory maps |
| | | t | Self-cures virus |
| | | n | No mask effects |

*Continued*

**Table 17.1 Files Virus Descriptors (Continued)**

| Descriptor | Description | Property | Function |
|---|---|---|---|
| P | Place of virus implantation | h | To the file's top |
|  |  | m | To the file's centre |
|  |  | t | To the file's bottom |
| S | Infection strategy | e | Infects the loadable modules |
|  |  | p | Infects only files pointed to in PATH |
|  |  | r | Infects files opened for reading |
|  |  | o | Infects all opening files |
|  |  | c | Infects all files from the current directory |
| T | Infected file's extensions | b | BIN |
|  |  | c | COM |
|  |  | e | EXE |
|  |  | o | OVL, OVR |
|  |  | s | SYS |
| U | Length of the infected files | n | Infects all COM files whose length (after contamination) will be more than 64K |
|  |  | y | Does not infect files pointed to above |
|  |  | e | Does not infect EXE files whose length will be more than 64K |

*Continued*

Table 17.1 Files Virus Descriptors (Continued)

| Descriptor | Description | Property | Function |
|---|---|---|---|
| X | Virus actions | b | Blocks the execution of executable files |
| | | c | Corrupts or damages data files |
| | | d | Deletes some executable files |
| | | f | Formats disks |
| | | k | Corrupts some executable files |
| | | m | Has sound or music effects |
| | | s | Destroys some disk sectors |
| | | v | Has visual effects |
| | | t | Prints text on the screen |
| | | z | Deletes information in the files or in the FAT tables etc. |
| Z | Accessory effects | a | Under AUTOEXEC.BAT execution shutdown is possible |
| | | e | Zero divide error etc. |
| | | o | Corrupts overlay programs |
| | | r | Corrupts resident programs |
| | | x | Corrupts extended EXE files |

Therefore, the virus Fall Letters (V1701R) has the descriptor:

AyByCyDnEsFnIcJxK1LiMcPtSeUyXvZar.

# Virus Effects

Now a few words about the damage that viruses can cause. Yes, they are very dangerous, but only to your software. It is not true that there are viruses that can physically destroy hard disks or the CPU. Some viruses can scorch out pieces of the luminiphorous layer on monochrome displays, but not on color ones.

### Symptoms of Contamination

There are some symptoms that can help to determine whether your computer has been infected by a virus. You should watch out for:

- An increase in the length of a infected program, especially COMMAND.COM.

- Messages such as "Write protect error" when information is read or executable files are loaded from a floppy disk.

- The breaking down of resident programs.

- A reduction in the memory size.

- The appearance of new bad clusters.

# Computer Hygiene

## How Real are the Dangers?

Two viruses are reported to be spreading at the time of writing. They are called Queeg and Pathogen, both highly polymorphic - which means that with each new PC these viruses infect, they change their appearance, making them very difficult to detect. Pathogen writes random sectors onto your hard disk every Monday evening at 5 o'clock. Queeg is a mutant of Pathogen which acts in a similar way on a Sunday.

These viruses are very destructive - they can scramble information on your hard disk, making it unusable. You may only be aware of their presence when a random quote from the UK science fiction TV series 'Red Dwarf' appears on your screen, but in the short split second before this happens, the damage will have been done...

New viruses take us by surprise - but what can we do? How can we protect our PCs from their attack? In this chapter, you will learn how to diagnose and treat some of the known viruses for yourself. Firstly we will set the scene for your treatment room, and describe the operating procedure. If you were a doctor, before any diagnosis, you would take precautions to scrub up, and make sure you had all the equipment you would need to hand. The equivalent, in PC terms, is what we would advise you to do before you take the life of your PC into your hands.

## A Clean Boot Disk

First of all, it's essential that you have a virus-free write-protected boot diskette. You will be using this diskette to boot from whenever you wish to examine your system for viruses, rather than from your hard disk, in case the latter is already infected. Making it write-protected sets a physical barrier to ensure no virus code can be written to it during the boot process.

Ideally, you should have this disk already prepared from the day you acquired your PC, and you will have, of course, updated it if you have upgraded your operating system. It will contain a copy of your DOS system software - the files IO.SYS, MSDOS.SYS (the names may vary, depending on your version of DOS), and COMMAND.COM, the command line processor. In addition, you may like to have a copy of one or more DOS utilities, for instance FORMAT (FORMAT.COM), and a low level disk recovery program such as SCANDISK which comes with MSDOS 6.2, or DISKFIX, a similar utility included with Central Point's PC TOOLS. Remember that you also need to have the associated data files - for instance, SCANDISK.INI - and it might be useful to have a copy of your favourite backup and restore software as well, if there's room.

You can copy the system files onto the disk either by formatting the disk using the /s option - for example, FORMAT A: /s, or by using the SYS command [type SYS A:] to make a copy of the system files on an existing blank, ready formatted disk. Both of these options copy all three files, IO.SYS, MSDOS.SYS and COMMAND.COM - the first two are hidden files which reside in the root directory of your boot disk, the latter is simply an executable .COM file.

After you have copied the operating system and your chosen software to your disk, make sure that you write-protect the disk. Then check, and check again, that the disk is still write-protected whenever you are going to boot from it. Finally, try booting from the disk. You don't want to find out it doesn't work when you most need it.

## Backing Up Your Data

Secondly, make sure you have an up-to-date backup of your important programs and data. As you have already learnt, some viruses can corrupt information on your hard disk, which may include your data files as well as program executables. Establishment and practice of a reliable, regular and tested backup and restore scheme means that if this happens, when you have removed the cause of the damage and unscrambled your corrupted disk, you will always be able to restore your valuable data. Ideally you should follow a weekly cycle of full backup on one chosen day, and incremental backup (backup of the files which have changed since the last backup) on the remaining 6.

*Your data itself will not be infected by a virus, but it may be damaged by the virus' effect.*

## Virus Monitoring

Thirdly, you need an independent anti-virus package to check your system regularly for virus attacks. DOS itself may come to your rescue here - version 6.x includes a virus scanner program, MSAV (or MWAV for Windows) which will detect more than 800 different viruses in program files, and remove them if it finds them. It also includes VSAFE, a memory resident program (TSR) which monitors vital functions of your computer's activity and warns you of anything unusual.

Whilst the former aids detection of known viruses, the latter procedure may be helpful for detecting the presence of new viruses. VSAFE maintains a record of checksums of each of your executable files, so it can identify if files have changed since the last time they were accessed. It keeps this record in a file named CHKLIST.MS, so do not be alarmed if you use VSAFE and copies of this new file appear in directories where you keep executable files. In addition, it monitors writes to disk and warns you of attempts to write to executable files.

You will learn more about the principles behind these procedures later on in this chapter; however, you should also be aware that some software will legitimately update .EXE files directly. VSAFE will not prevent this, but when it detects it is about to happen, it will ask you if you wish to continue the operation.

Prior to using it, make a copy of the MSAV (or MWAV) files on a clean disk, and again write-protect the disk. The command to load VSAFE may be added to your AUTOEXEC.BAT file, to ensure it is there in the background monitoring system activity.

## Alternative Antivirus Software

Various other anti-virus packages are available besides those which come with DOS 6.x. Both commercial and shareware, they will usually consist of two elements which essentially perform the same function as MSAV and VSAFE. In particular, the shareware package produced by McAfee Associates, which includes a combined SCAN and CLEAN package to detect viruses and disinfect infected files if it finds them with the memory resident program VSHIELD, is considered to be very good.

Now, whenever you buy new software, or a friend or colleague lends you a program on disk to try out, run your scan detect program on it first, before you try to execute your new software. Remember before you do so, to reboot from your clean master boot diskette, and to execute your virus scanner from its own write-protected disk.  Routine scanning on receipt of *all* new program executables is a prudent precaution, because even commercial products are not immune. Shrink-wrapping doesn't guarantee a commercial program or disk is not infected, and there have been instances of viruses found inside commercial products in the past. However, the major software companies do operate stringent security precautions, and the probability of your system becoming infected in this way is extremely low.

Also be aware that you cannot 'catch' a virus from a plain text file, a graphics file, or word processor document. The only files from which your PC is at risk are executables - those with extension .COM, .EXE or .BIN, or indeed any that contain executable code, such as the Windows Dynamic Link Libraries (.DLL) and the overlay code (.OVL) which come with many software packages. Even then your PC is only at risk if you execute the code in an infected file.

You can usually set the parameters of your SCAN software to scan selected files only, instead of all files. However, remember that executable files may be hiding within other files - for instance within shareware packages, often compressed using the PKZIP utility. You should be aware that although some virus scanners do examine executables within these files, you should not rely on this to take place. Consult your program documentation to find out whether you need to unpack these files before scanning, or whether your virus detection software will do this for you.

Exploitation of the features of these virus products will guard against nearly all the methods of virus introduction described in this chapter. However, maximum protection against specific viruses can only be gained by updating your chosen virus scanner package regularly with protection against the newer viruses.

In summary, as a routine procedure, and if at any time you suspect for any reason that your system may be infected, use the following procedure:

1    Perform a COLD reboot of the system from your clean write-protected floppy.

2    Take the disk out of the drive, insert your scan software diskette, also write-protected, and execute.

3    If the software identifies a virus, after you have followed the disinfection procedure, try to identify where it came from. In particular, be suspicious of any or all floppy disks you may have used recently, and scan them for traces. Hopefully one of them will contain the culprit which infected your system in the first place.

4    Remember the simplest forms of virus removal are the DOS commands DEL (or ERASE), SYS, FDISK and FORMAT commands. DEL deletes infected files, the FORMAT command reinitializes disks. Indeed, if all else fails, there is a very simple command you can execute from your write-protected floppy:

```
A:FORMAT C:
```

# Analyzing Viruses

## How Can You Detect Viruses in a PC?

The main aim of analyzing viruses is to find out where, i.e. in which files, the virus is, what kind of virus it is, and where it saves the information needed to restore the infected file. You have to be very careful when analyzing a virus, because it is easy to activate even more destructive protection procedures. You should try to do it on a computer that does not contain any important information.

## Software Tools for Analyzing Viruses

To analyze a virus you will need the following instruments:

- A dump maker

- An advanced full screen debugger, eg. AFD professional from AdTec Gmbh

- The Norton utilities, or similar for low level analysis of your disks

Program 17.1 contains the source text for a dump maker. This is also included on the accompanying disk.

```
/////////////////////////////////////////////////
//Program 17.1
/////////////////////////////////////////////////
/* This program produces a dump of the files pointed to in    *
 * the command string. You can point to more than one file.   *
 * To save information in a text file, the command line should *
 * have the following format: DUMP file1 file2 ... >out_file   *
 * This means that you want to redirect output from the screen *
 * to the file OUT_FILE                                       */

#include <stdio.h>
#include <string.h>
#include <stdlib.h>

void do_dump(char *f_name)
{
  FILE *f=fopen(f_name,"rb");
  long offs=0;
  unsigned char buf[20];
  char string[200];

  printf("File: %s\n\n",f_name);
```

```
   printf("Address              Hexadecimal              Characters\n\n");
   for(;;)
   {
      int i=fread(buf,1,16,f); //Try to read 16 bytes from the input file
      if(!i) break;  //if EOF - return
      char s[20];
//Point to the offset of the first byte in the string
      sprintf(string,"%08X   ",offs);
//Hexadecimal representation
      for(int j=0;j<16;j++)
      {
         if(j<i)
                 sprintf(s,"%02X ",buf[j]);
         else
                 sprintf(s,"   ");
         strcat(string,s);
      }
      strcat(string,"   ");
//Character representation
      for(j=0;j<16;j++)
      {
         if(j<i)
                 sprintf(s,"%c",(buf[j]>=0x20)?buf[j]:'.');
         else
                 sprintf(s," ");
         strcat(string,s);
      }
                 printf("%s\n",string);
                 offs+=i; //Increase offset
   }
   fclose(f);
   printf("\n\n\n");
}


void main(int argc,char *argv[])
{
 if(argc<2)
  {
                 puts("Format: DUMP file_name1 file_name2 ...");
                 exit(1);
  }
  for(int i=1;i<argc;i++)
  {
                 do_dump(argv[i]);
  }
}
```

A dump maker enables you to obtain a file dump, i.e. a table in which the contents of a file are presented in two ways: in hexadecimal and character form. The following is a simple example of a dump.

Table 17.2 File: command.com

| Address | Hexadecimal | Characters |
|---|---|---|
| 00000000 | E9 5D 14 00 78 14 00 00 B7 0E 00 00 75 0D 00 00 | é ] . . x . . . . · . . . u . . . |
| 00000010 | 85 11 00 00 00 00 00 00 00 00 00 00 00 00 00 00 | ¼ . . . . . . . . . . . . . . . |
| 00000020 | 00 00 00 00 00 00 00 00 00 00 00 00 00 00 00 00 | . . . . . . . . . . . . . . . . |
| 00000030 | 00 00 00 00 00 FB E8 64 00 1E 0E 2E FF 2E 04 01 | . . . . . û è d . . . . ÿ . . . |
| 00000040 | FB E8 59 00 1E 0E 2E FF 2E 08 01 FB E8 4E 00 1E | û è Y . . . . ÿ . . . û è N . . |
| 00000050 | 0E 2E FF 2E 0C 01 FB E8 43 00 1E 0E 2E FF 2E 10 | . . ÿ . . . û è C . . . . ÿ . . |
| 00000060 | 01 E8 39 00 1E 0E 2E FF 2E 14 01 E8 2F 00 1E 0E | . è 9 . . . . ÿ . . . è / . . . |
| 00000070 | 2E FF 2E 18 01 E8 25 00 1E 0E 2E FF 2E 1C 01 E8 | . ÿ . . . è % . . . . ÿ . . . è |
| 00000080 | 1B 00 1E 0E 2E FF 2E 20 01 E8 11 00 1E 0E 2E FF | . . . . . ÿ . . è . . . . . ÿ |
| 00000090 | 2E 24 01 E8 07 00 1E 0E 2E FF 2E 28 01 9C 2E 80 | . $ . è . . . . . ÿ . ( . œ . _ |

Dumps provide information about the exact location of any character or code strings in a file.

The Advanced Fullscreen Debugger from AdTec Gmbh is a very convenient software tool for analyzing code. It gives all the information you need about program execution. You can also step through interrupts in real mode. It is easy to set breakpoints even in a TSR - you can leave AFD in resident mode.

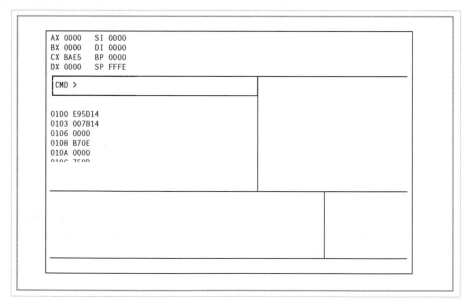

Figure 17.1 The AFD Screen

## How Can a Virus Implant its Body into a Program?

There are three possible ways of doing this.

The first way is for the virus to append its body to the end of a file. The virus will then need to change the entry point of the program because it must be loaded in memory first, before the rest of the program. This principle is illustrated in Figure 17.2:

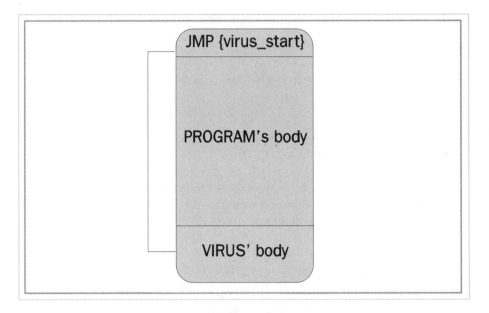

**Figure 17.2 Method One**

The second way is to write the virus body into the middle of a file. To do this, a virus can use stack space (for instance, COMMAND.COM has about 2500 bytes of free space) or it can move the rest of the file, and write its body into the free space. This method also requires the entry point of the program to be changed. Figure 17.3 illustrates this method.

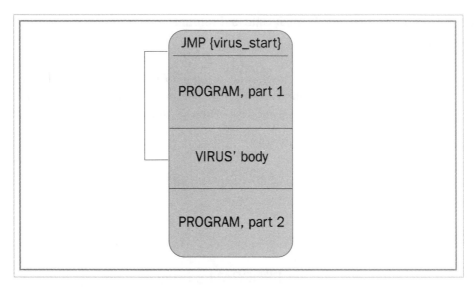

**Figure 17.3 Method Two**

The third way is to write the virus body at the beginning of a file. In this case, a virus does not need to change anything in the program, but has to move the whole file. This method is illustrated in Figure 17.4:

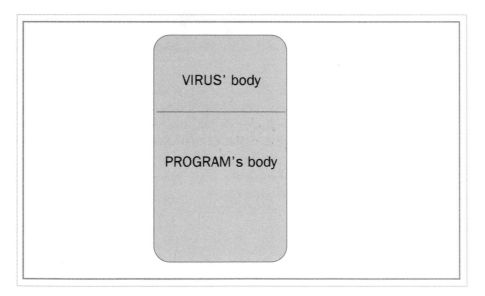

**Figure 17.4 The Third Method**

These methods are all possible both for COM and EXE files.

## DOS Executable File Formats

There are two types of executable file in DOS. The first type is the simplest COM format.

## COM Files

This kind of file is the legacy of versions of DOS before version 3.0. These systems could only operate with executable files which can fit into a 64K memory segment. DOS loads these files directly into the memory without any preparation for execution. All jumps should be short or near. If you want to use far jumps, you have to point directly to the address to which you want to go, i.e. you cannot use relative addresses which are set according to the loading segment address. If you don't know exactly which segment address DOS will load your program into, you should correct far jumps manually, according to the current segment your program is in.

COM files are not structured. They consist of executable code only, with no other special information for DOS.

## EXE Files

The second type is the more complicated and advanced EXE format. It allows programs to be more than 64K long. This type of executable file has a special structure which includes information about all related jumps and pointers which DOS has to correct, depending on the loading address.

We shall be using the word paragraph a lot. This term refers to a block of memory that is 16 bytes in size (the minimum distance between segment starts for Intel 80x86 CPUs).

There is a special structure at the beginning of EXE files called the EXE file header. Its structure looks like this:

**Table 17.3 The EXE File Header**

| Offset | Length | Content | Description |
|--------|--------|---------|-------------|
| +0 | 2 | 4Dh 5aH | 'Signature' of EXE file ('MZ') |
| +2 | 2 | PartPag | Length of last non-full page |
| +4 | 2 | PagCnt | Length of the program code in 512-byte pages |
| +6 | 2 | ReloCnt | Number of elements in relocation table |
| +8 | 2 | HdrSize | Header length in paragraphs |
| +0AH | 2 | MinMem | Minimum memory left (paragraphs) |
| +0CH | 2 | MaxMem | Maximum memory left (paragraphs) |
| +0EH | 2 | ReloSS | Segment correction for stack (SS) |
| +10H | 2 | ExeSP | Value of SP (stack pointer) |
| +12H | 2 | ChkSum | Checksum (negative sum of all words in file) |
| +14H | 2 | ExeIP | Value of IP (instruction pointer) |
| +16H | 2 | ReloCS | Segment correction for CS (command segment) |
| +18H | 2 | TablOff | Offset of the first relocation element in file |
| +1AH | 2 | Overlay | Overlay number (0 for main module) |
| | | | |
| Unformatted Section | | | |
| Relocation table consists of 4-byte elements | | | |
| + ? | 4*? | offs. segm ... offs. segm | |
| + ? | ? | Align bytes to paragraph margins | |
| + ? | ? | Code beginning | |

The two characters MZ are the EXE file signature. These letters are the initials of Mark Zbikowsky, the programmer who designed the EXE file format.

When DOS loads an EXE file, it reads the relocation table. This table consists of the addresses of the words inside the file. For all the words pointed to in this table, DOS adds the value of the loading segment address. For example, if a program is loaded to segment 2000h, then the string in the program would be as follows:

```
JMP  300h:1254h
```

This instruction would have the following representation:

```
JMP  2300h:1254h   ;2300h=300h(old value) + 2000h(seg addr)
```

This method allows program addresses to be calculated relative to the loading address and so the executable files can be more than the maximum segment address in length.

One more advantage of EXE files is that the file header contains information about the code size and DOS will load only part of the file with this size. This allows compilers to create a small loading program (3K-50K) which will load the necessary part of an EXE file to the memory. Therefore, instead of having to load the whole program, you can load just that part which is necessary for the current moment of execution.

## How DOS Loads Programs into Memory

The algorithm for loading a program into memory depends on whether a COM or an EXE is being loaded. Figure 17.5 shows a general outline of the loading process. The block marked EXE file preparation will be discussed below.

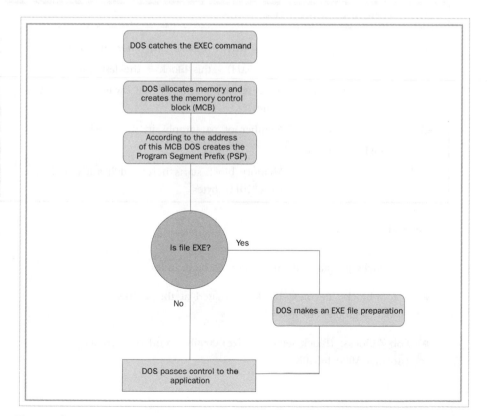

**Figure 17.5 The Loading Process**

In the case of a COM file, DOS just passes control to the address PSP:100h:

```
JMP PSP:100h
```

We'll look first at the MCB and PSP blocks. These two structures will be very important when we come to talk about viruses in the memory.

## Memory Control Blocks

A memory control block (MCB) is the DOS structure which preceeds all memory allocated blocks. This structure includes all the information about the address of the start of the block and the length of the block in paragraphs. All the blocks are bound in a chain, so DOS can travel from one block to another. The structure of an MCB is shown in Table 17.4:

**Table 17.4 Structure of a Memory Control Block**

| Off | Length | Contents | Description |
|---|---|---|---|
| +0 | 1 | Type | > 'M'(4dH) - blocks exist after this one |
| | | | > 'Z'(5aH) - this block is the last one |
| +1 | 2 | Owner | Address (paragraph) of the owner (if 0 - self-owner) |
| +3 | 2 | Size | Number of paragraphs in this block |
| +5 | 0bH | reserved | |
| +10H | ? | | Memory block starts here and has a length of (Size*10H) bytes |

You should note that:

- All blocks are aligned on paragraph boundaries

- For M-blocks: the next block is situated at the address (Block_segment+Size):0000h

- For Z-blocks: (Block_segment+Size):0000h = end of memory (normal:A000H=640K)

Therefore, all memory blocks have to be preceded by an MCB.

The following program (PROG17_2.ASM on the disk) demonstrates how you can move through MCB blocks. In this program, we have used the undocumented DOS function 52. This function returns the 'DOS list of lists' in pairs ES:BX. This list includes many different table addresses, for example, the address of the first driver in the system, the address of the first file-handle block, etc.

The word at address ES:BX-2 is the segment of the first MCB.

```
;////////////////////////////////////
;Program 17.2
;////////////////////////////////////
_TEXT   segment          para public 'CODE'
        assume           cs:_TEXT, ds:_TEXT
Start:
; Firstly we must call the DOS function #52
; This function gives you a "DOS List of lists"
        push     cs
        pop      ds
        mov      ah,52h
        int      21h
; The word with address ES:BX-2 is the address of the first MCB
        mov      ax,es:[bx-2]
        push     ax
        pop      es
; Go through all blocks in the memory
All_Blocks:
; Output segment address
        mov      ax,es
        push     es
        push     ds
        pop      es
        push     ax
        call     Out_Value
        pop      ax
        pop      es
; Check if it is last block
        cmp      byte ptr es:[0],'Z'
; If yes - break the cycle
        jz       Last_Block
; Else - get address of the next block
        add      ax,es:[3]
        inc      ax
        push     ax
        pop      es
        jmp All_Blocks
Last_Block:
        mov      ax,4c00h
        int      21h
```

```
; This procedure just outputs the number in AX
Out_Value  proc    near
           mov     di,offset String
           mov     cx,0ch
           mov     bx,0f000h
Make_Loop:
           push    ax
           and     ax,bx
           shr     ax,cl
           mov     si,30h
           cmp     al,9
           jbe     Number
           add     si,7
Number:
           add     ax,si
           cld
           stosb
           pop     ax
           or      cx,cx
           jz      Last_Digit
           sub     cx,4
           shr     bx,1
           shr     bx,1
           shr     bx,1
           shr     bx,1
           jmp     Make_Loop
Last_Digit:
           mov     dx,offset String
           mov     ah,9
           int     21h
           ret
String:            db            0,0,0,0,0dh,0ah,'$'
Out_Value     endp

_Text    ends
end Start
```

## Program Segment Prefix

The next important block is the Program Segment Prefix (PSP). This block includes all the information necessary for normal execution of a program, such as the maximum available memory size, the address of the environment and parameters string, etc. For all programs in the memory, this block is the first block after the MCB. Its structure is:

**Table 17.5 Structure of the Program Segment Prefix**

| Offset | Size | Description |
|--------|------|-------------|
| 00h | word | Machine code INT 20 instruction (CDh 20h) |
| 02h | word | Top of memory in segment (paragraph) form |
| 04h | byte | Reserved for DOS, usually 0 |
| 05h | 5 bytes | Machine code instruction long call to the DOS function dispatcher (obsolete CP/M) |
| 06h | word | .COM programs bytes available in segment (CP/M) |
| 0Ah | dword | INT 22 terminate address; DOS loader jumps to this address upon exit; the EXEC function forces a child process to return to the parent by setting this vector to code within the parent (IP,CS) |
| 0Eh | dword | INT 23 Ctrl-Break exit address; the original INT 23 vector is *not* restored from this pointer (IP,CS) |
| 12h | dword | INT 24 critical error exit address; the original INT 24 vector is *not* restored from this field (IP,CS) |
| 16h | word | Parent process segment addr. COMMAND.COM has a parent id of zero, or its own PSP. |
| 18h | 20 bytes | File handle array; if handle array element is FFh then handle is available. Network redirectors often indicate remote files by setting these to values between 80h-FEh. |
| 2Ch | word | Segment address of the environment, or zero |
| 2Eh | dword | SS:SP on entry to last INT 21 function |
| 32h | word | Handle array size |
| 34h | dword | Handle array pointer |
| 38h | dword | Pointer to previous PSP |
| 3Ch | 20 bytes | Unused in DOS before 4.01 |
| 50h | 3 bytes | DOS function dispatcher 21h |
| 53h | 9 bytes | Unused |

*Continued*

Table 17.5 Structure of the Program Segment Prefix (Continued)

| Offset | Size | Description |
|--------|------|-------------|
| 5Ch | 36 bytes | Default unopened FCB #1 (parts overlayed by FCB #2) |
| 6Ch | 20 bytes | Default unopened FCB #2 (overlays part of FCB #1) |
| 80h | byte | Count of characters in command tail; all bytes following command name; also default DTA (128 bytes) |
| 81h | 127 bytes | All characters entered after the program name followed by a CR symbol |

These two structures, the MCB and the PSP, are changed by almost every virus. We will discuss the problem of restoring information to these blocks when we talk about deleting viruses from memory. Obviously, some of the information included in these blocks is very important for the normal workings of the computer. For example, if a virus cuts off the size of an MCB block, the total memory of the computer will be less than 640K. Due to the existence of the PSP, all programs will be loaded not from offset zero, but from the top of the PSP, i.e. the loading offset will be 100h.

Now that you know a bit about the system structures which have to be initialized by DOS, we can talk in more detail about the process of loading EXE files.

## Loading EXE Files

As mentioned above, DOS has to recalculate all relative addresses in the body of an EXE file. This means that the loading segment address will be added to all segments which take part in the addressing inside the program. Suppose you want to create your own program to load EXE files. You have to perform the following steps:

1   Read 1Ch bytes of EXE file (the EXE header).

2   Determine the module size. This will be equal to:

Size=((PagCnt*512)-(HdrSize*16))-PartPag.

3   Determine the file offset of the loaded module HdrSize*16.

**4**    Choose the loading segment address START_SEG (usually PSP_segment+10H).

**5**    Read the file to the memory area which begins with the address START_SEG:0000.

**6**    Set the file pointer to the beginning of the relocation table.

**7**    For each element in this table do the following:

- Read the element as two words. These two words are the address (Offs, Seg) of the word which must be changed.

- Compute the relative segment RELO_SEG=(START_SEG+Seg).

- Add START_SEG to the word in the memory with the address RELO_SEG:Offs.

**8**    Allocate memory for the program according to MaxMem and MinMem.

The loading program should then initialize the registers:

```
ES = DS = PSP
AX = 0, if all disk letters in the command string were correct
SS = START_SEG+ReloSS, SP = ExeSP
CS = START_SEG+ReloCS, IP = ExeIP
```

## How Viruses Fasten Themselves to Executable Files

You know how DOS loads executable files. To change this process, a virus has to change the entry point to a program or insert commands at the normal entry point which will pass the control to the body of the virus.

The most common way for a resident virus to infect a program involves the following steps:

**1**    The MS-DOS version is checked.

**2**    All changed bytes in the file are restored.

**3**    Checks are made to see if memory has been contaminated. If memory has already been infected by the virus, control is passed to the infected program.

4     The body of the virus is written to memory and changes are made to the operating system blocks to reserve this part of the memory.

5     All necessary interrupts are intercepted.

6     Control is passed to the infected program.

For non-resident viruses, steps 3 to 6 are replaced by following ones:

3     The next victim(s) is located.

4     Checks are made to see if the victim has already been contaminated.

5     All necessary bytes in the victim program are changed.

6     The virus body is written into the victim program.

7     Control is passed to the infected program.

There are no problems with this in COM files. The simplest way of carrying out the process is to save the first three bytes in the virus body and include a jump command to the first virus command. All the virus has to do is to compute the length of this jump. If you look at an infected file in a debugger, you will see this jump and from it you will be able to trace the virus entry point.

Then, once a virus body has been executed, it has to restore the old information from the first three bytes and execute just one command:

```
JMP  100h
```

For EXE files, the process is more complicated. First of all the virus has to fasten its body to a file. Then it has to change the EXE file header. Next, the fields in this structure have to be changed.

- PartPag

- PagCnt

- ReloCS

- ExeIP

Before changing these fields, the virus has to save the old information from them.

Some viruses have an error - they do not change PagCnt or PartPag, or else change them in the wrong way. This means that after infection, the EXE program cannot be loaded into the memory because the size of the file which is read into memory is wrong.

There is another error that is present in some viruses. This means that the viruses determine the file type by checking the file extension. If it has a COM extension, they infect it like COM file. However, DOS recognizes the file format by the presence of the MZ signature at the top of a file, so you can rename any EXE file to a COM one and it will work in the same way. This type of error in viruses would then destroy the normal structure of the EXE file, so DOS tries to execute it as a COM file. As a result, the program may output the string 'EXE file was corrupted' or just shut down altogether, or more likely crash your PC.

## Recovering Program Information

Taking this information into account, you can see that the main problem when analyzing file viruses is to gather the information that was destroyed by the virus. How can you do this?

Let's have a look at a virus body. Below is a dump of a code fragment of a COMMAND.COM which has been infected by the virus Minsk Ghost.

**Table 17.6 File: ghost.ccc**

| Address | Hexadecimal | Characters |
|---------|-------------|------------|
| 00000000 | E8 00 00 5E 83 EE 03 50 EB 12 90 4D 49 4E 53 4B | è. .^¦î.Pë._MINSK |
| 00000010 | 20 47 48 4F 53 54 2C 31 39 39 31 20 B8 07 C8 31 | GHOST,1991 ..È1 |
| 00000020 | DB CD 21 83 FB FF 75 03 E9 1E 01 1E 5B 4B FA 8E | ÛÍ!¦ûÿu.é...[Kú_ |
| 00000030 | DB A1 03 00 BF 60 00 29 F8 A3 03 00 06 1F A1 02 | Û¡...¿`.)ø£....¡. |
| 00000040 | 00 29 F8 A3 02 00 2E 89 84 D4 01 2E C7 84 D2 01 | .)ø£...‰„Ô..ç„Ò. |

Have a look at the first string: E8 00 00 5E 83 EE 03 50, etc. After disassembling, these codes will be transformed into the following set of commands:

```
       ........
       CALL Next
  Next:
       POP    SI
       SUB    SI,3
       .......
```

This is present in almost every virus. What happens when the CPU performs these instructions? First of all the CPU performs the instruction CALL. This command pushes the address of the next instruction onto the stack and makes IP equal to the address pointed to in the command. The address of the next instruction is on the stack, but the next performing command pops this address from the stack, decreases it and puts it in the SI register. Therefore, this set of instructions helps the virus to locate its place in the memory. All the addresses of the virus' variables will now be corrected according to the value of the SI register. It was necessary to decrease the value because the initial offset required is the start of the program - the address of the CALL command, not the following instruction.

# Writing Virus Protection Programs

As we said, this code, or the alternative - a jump instruction to the first virus code - exists in almost all viruses. Once you know this, you can design a program to catch any suspicious files on your computer.

First of all though, you have to know what type of file you are going to analyze - COM or EXE. You should make two checks: one to check what will be performed, based on the file extension, and the other, in the test procedure, to check the contents of the first two bytes to see whether they are equal to the MZ signature.

## Identifying Suspicious Files

The test procedures must do the following:

- For COM files: check whether the first three bytes are the jump instruction. If they are, test the first four bytes in the code to which the JMP instruction points.

- For EXE files: use the HdrSize, ReloCS and ExeIP information from the
  header to find the entry point and test the first four bytes in the code to
  which the JMP instruction points.

```
//////////////////////////////////////////
//Program 17.3 - Detecting Suspicious Files
//////////////////////////////////////////
#include <stdio.h>
#include <stdlib.h>
#include <dos.h>
#include <string.h>
#include <conio.h>

int Susp_Count=0;         //Counter of suspicious files

void TestExe(char *);

void TestCom(char *fname)
{
    FILE *f=fopen(fname,"rb");
    unsigned char buf[10]; //buffer for reading bytes
    unsigned offs;

    if(!f) return;
    fread(buf,1,3,f);
    if((*buf=='M')&&(*(buf+1)=='Z'))
    {
    //MZ signature was found, it is EXE file
            fclose(f);
            TestExe(fname);
            return;
    }
    if(*buf!=0xe9) return; //Not jump
    //JMP was found, compute offset
    memcpy(&offs,buf+1,2);
    fseek(f,offs,SEEK_CUR);
    fread(buf,1,3,f);
    if((*buf==0xe8)&&(!*(buf+1))&&(!*(buf+2)))
    {
    //File Fname is suspicious!
            cprintf("%c - File is suspicious. Check it!\n",7);
            Susp_Count++;
    }
    fclose(f);
}

void TestExe(char *fname)
{
    FILE *f=fopen(fname,"rb");
    unsigned char buf[100]; //buffer for reading bytes
    unsigned hdr_size;
    unsigned ReloCS,ExeIP;
```

```
    if(!f) return;
    fread(buf,1,0x18,f);
    if((*buf!='M')||(*(buf+1)!='Z'))
    {
    //MZ signature was not found, it is COM file
            fclose(f);
            TestCom(fname);
            return;
    }
    //Compute header size
    memcpy(&hdr_size,buf+0x8,2);
    //Compute ReloCS and ExeIP
    memcpy(&ReloCS,buf+0x16,2);
    memcpy(&ExeIP,buf+0x14,2);
    fseek(f,(long)hdr_size*16L+(long)ReloCS*16L+(long)ExeIP,SEEK_SET);
    fread(buf,1,3,f);
    if((*buf==0xe8)&&(!*(buf+1))&&(!*(buf+2)))
    {
    //File Fname is suspicious!
            cprintf("- %cFile is suspicious. Check it!\n",7);
            Susp_Count++;
    }
    fclose(f);
}


void Find_All(char *path)
{
    struct ffblk buffer; //structure for the findfirst/findnext functions
    int res;
    char temp[81];

    strcpy(temp,path);
    strcat(temp,"*.*");
    res=findfirst(temp,&buffer,FA_DIREC);
    while(!res)
    {
            if(buffer.ff_attrib&FA_DIREC&&buffer.ff_name[0]!='.')
        {
            strcpy(temp,path);
            strcat(temp,buffer.ff_name);
            strcat(temp,"\\");
            Find_All(temp);
        }
        res=findnext(&buffer);
    }

    strcpy(temp,path);
    strcat(temp,"*.COM");
    res=findfirst(temp,&buffer,0xff);
    while(!res)
    {
         if(!(buffer.ff_attrib&FA_DIREC))
         {
                strcpy(temp,path);
```

```
                strcat(temp,buffer.ff_name);
                gotoxy(1,wherey());
                clreol();
                cprintf("%s",temp);
                TestCom(temp);
        }
        res=findnext(&buffer);
    }

    strcpy(temp,path);
    strcat(temp,"*.EXE");
    res=findfirst(temp,&buffer,0xff);
    while(!res)
    {
        if(!(buffer.ff_attrib&FA_DIREC))
        {
                strcpy(temp,path);
                strcat(temp,buffer.ff_name);
                gotoxy(1,wherey());
                clreol();
                cprintf("%s",temp);
                TestExe(temp);
        }
        res=findnext(&buffer);
    }
}


void main(int argc, char *argv[])
{
    char path[81];

    if(argc<2)
    {
            printf("Illegal format. Use: %s drive_1 drive_2 ....\n",argv[0]);
            exit(1);
    }
    for(int i=1;i<argc;i++)
    {
    //Call the procedure which finds all executable files on the disk
    //and tests them.
            sprintf(path,"%c:\\",*argv[i]);
            Find_All(path);
    }
    printf("\n\nSummary: suspicious files number: %d\n",Susp_Count);
}
```

When this program finds the suspicious string mentioned above (e.g. E9h 00 00), it will beep and write the string "File file_name is suspicious. Check it!".

*Don't panic if this program tells you that the files PRINT.COM, FORMAT.COM etc. are suspicious. These files were transformed from EXE to COM by the EXE2BIN program. This DOS program uses the same technique to determine to which address a program was loaded.*

Obviously, Program 17.3 is not a universal one. A virus can pre-determine during the process of contamination to which address it will be loaded and save this value as a constant in its body. However, the program will catch a lot of viruses which use the CALL_NEXT technique.

So, you know how to find the virus entry point. However, things now get a bit more complicated. You need to determine exactly where the virus saves the bytes you need - both the first bytes of a COM file and the information from the EXE header for EXE files.

## Locating Lost Data

There is no one algorithm for finding this data. Viruses differ from one to another and they use different techniques. However, there is one thing common to almost all viruses in COM files: you can go through a virus step by step and see when it begins to restore the data to the address SEG:100h. Therefore, you can work out the addresses where it saves the necessary information. For example, the virus Minsk Ghost saves the three bytes of a COM file in the location offset 1BBh from the start of code. The offset can be determined when we reach code similar to this:

```
22A0:026C  BF0001   MOV DI,0100h
                              ;CX - number of elements for restoring
22A0:026F  B90300   MOV CX,0003
                              ;SI - entry point offset
22A0:0272  81C6BB01 ADD SI,01BBh
                              ;SI - Saving area address
22A0:0276  FC       CLD
22A0:0277  F3A4     REP MOVSB
                              ;Prepare stack for exit
22A0:0279  0E       PUSH CS
22A0:027A  BB0001   MOV BX,0100h
22A0:027D  53       PUSH BX
22A0:027E  CB       RET Far
```

SI saves the information about the entry point address (see the earlier description of the CALL_NEXT technique) and the virus just adds the offset of the saving area to this value.

Note that this fragment of code makes a return to the normal COM file when it is restored, but it makes it via the stack, i.e. it pushes the CS and 100h values and then makes a far return. The same thing occurs when EXE files are processed.

Once you think that you have found all the information you need to restore the file, you should check the values against the non-infected files. For instance, a normal COMMAND.COM has a jump at the top. The jump goes to code to set the value for the stack pointer, and to set the process ID (INT 21h function 50h). You can look at the jump address and compare your value with the value of the pure file.

## Virus Signatures

One more method of analyzing viruses is to find some constant strings in the file body. These constant strings (for example, the virus entry procedure) are called the virus signature. The main principle of the signature method is to extract some bytes from a virus body which do not change from one virus installation to another. It can be quite hard to find a string of this kind, because there are viruses which encrypt their body so that almost no constant strings are left. Program 17.4 demonstrates an example of this method. This program can detect the existence of the virus Diana (so called because it has the text string Diana in its body) or V2000R in our classification. The program uses the fact that the virus has a constant string with a length of 10 bytes, shown below:

**Table 17.7 File: diana.com**

| Address | Hexadecimal | Characters |
|---------|-------------|------------|
| 00000000 | E8 00 00 5E 81 EE 63 00 FC 2E è | . . ^ _ î c . ü . |

The program to detect Diana follows:

```
/////////////////////////
//Program 17.4
/////////////////////////
#include <stdio.h>
#include <stdlib.h>
#include <dos.h>
#include <string.h>
#include <conio.h>

int Sign_Len=10; //Signature length
//This is the virus signature. You can change it for other virus types
unsigned char Sign[]={0xe8,0x00,0x00,0x5e,0x81,0xee,0x63,0x00,0xfc,0x2e};

void TestExe(char *);

void TestCom(char *fname)
{
```

```
    FILE *f=fopen(fname,"rb");
    unsigned char buf[15];  //buffer for reading bytes
    unsigned offs;

    if(!f) return;
    fread(buf,1,3,f);
    if((*buf=='M')&&(*(buf+1)=='Z'))
    {
    //MZ signature was found, it is EXE file
            fclose(f);
            TestExe(fname);
            return;
    }
    if(*buf!=0xe9) return; //Not jump
    //JMP was found, compute offset
    memcpy(&offs,buf+1,2);
    fseek(f,offs,SEEK_CUR);
    int i=fread(buf,1,Sign_Len,f);
    if((i==Sign_Len)&&(!memcmp(buf,Sign,Sign_Len)))
    {
    //File Fname is suspicious!
            cprintf("%c - File is probably infected by the V2000R virus. Check
    it!\n",7);
    }
    fclose(f);
}


void TestExe(char *fname)
{
    FILE *f=fopen(fname,"rb");
    unsigned char buf[100]; //buffer for reading bytes
    unsigned hdr_size;
    unsigned ReloCS,ExeIP;

    if(!f) return;
    fread(buf,1,0x18,f);
    if((*buf!='M')||(*(buf+1)!='Z'))
    {
    //MZ signature was not found, it is COM file
            fclose(f);
            TestCom(fname);
            return;
    }
    //Compute header size
    memcpy(&hdr_size,buf+0x8,2);
    //Compute ReloCS and ExeIP
    memcpy(&ReloCS,buf+0x16,2);
    memcpy(&ExeIP,buf+0x14,2);
    fseek(f,(long)hdr_size*16L+(long)ReloCS*16L+(long)ExeIP,SEEK_SET);
    int i=fread(buf,1,Sign_Len,f);
    if((i==Sign_Len)&&(!memcmp(buf,Sign,Sign_Len)))
    {
    //File Fname is suspicious!
            cprintf("%c - File is probably infected by the V2000R virus. Check
            it!\n",7);
```

```
        }
    fclose(f);
}


void Find_All(char *path)
{
    struct ffblk buffer; //structure for the findfirst/findnext functions
    int res;
    char temp[81];

    strcpy(temp,path);
    strcat(temp,"*.*");
    res=findfirst(temp,&buffer,FA_DIREC);
    while(!res)
    {
            if(buffer.ff_attrib&FA_DIREC&&buffer.ff_name[0]!='.')
            {
                    strcpy(temp,path);
                    strcat(temp,buffer.ff_name);
                    strcat(temp,"\\");
                    Find_All(temp);
            }
            res=findnext(&buffer);
    }

    strcpy(temp,path);
    strcat(temp,"*.COM");
    res=findfirst(temp,&buffer,0xff);
    while(!res)
    {
            if(!(buffer.ff_attrib&FA_DIREC))
            {
                    strcpy(temp,path);
                    strcat(temp,buffer.ff_name);
                    gotoxy(1,wherey());
                    clreol();
                    cprintf("%s",temp);
                    TestCom(temp);
            }
            res=findnext(&buffer);
    }

    strcpy(temp,path);
    strcat(temp,"*.EXE");
    res=findfirst(temp,&buffer,0xff);
    while(!res)
    {
            if(!(buffer.ff_attrib&FA_DIREC))
            {
                    strcpy(temp,path);
                    strcat(temp,buffer.ff_name);
                    gotoxy(1,wherey());
                clreol();
```

```
                    cprintf("%s",temp);
                    TestExe(temp);
        }
        res=findnext(&buffer);
    }
}


void main(int argc, char *argv[])
{
    char path[81];

    if(argc<2)
    {
            printf("Illegal format. Use: %s drive_1 drive_2 ....\n",argv[0]);
            exit(1);
    }
    for(int i=1;i<argc;i++)
    {
    //Call the procedure which finds all executable files on the disk
    //and tests them.
            sprintf(path,"%c:\\",*argv[i]);
            Find_All(path);
    }
}
```

## Virus Checking for Previous Infection

Firstly, if a virus wants to check whether it is present in a file, it can check the file body and test for its signature by comparing, for example, the file entry procedure with its own one. If the comparison operations succeed, the virus will not contaminate this file. If not, the process of infection will start. Another group of viruses leave evidence of its activity in the root directory, or directory structure. For example, they may set the value of the file creation time (in seconds) to 62. This value will not be shown by DOS, but it helps to determine if a file is infected or not.

Yet one particular virus group does not check anything at all. The virus Phoenix, for example, writes its body to any vacant space in the body of a file. After the Phoenix virus all contaminated files look like a piece of Swiss cheese!

# Boot Viruses

First of all, let's examine how the BIOS loads an operating system and why the boot sector (or master boot sector) is necessary.

A boot sector is a special sector on the disk which saves important system information such as sector size, number of tracks, etc. It is situated in the first sector and its structure is described in Table 17.8.

**Table 17.8 Boot Sector (since DOS 2.0)**

| Offset | Size | Description |
|--------|------|-------------|
| 00 | 3bytes | Jump to executable code |
| 03 | 8bytes | OEM (Original Equipment Manufacturer) name and version |
| 0B | word | Bytes per sector |
| 0D | byte | Sectors per cluster (allocation unit size) |
| 0E | word | Number of reserved sectors (starting at 0) |
| 10 | byte | Number of FAT's on disk |
| 11 | word | Number of root directory entries (directory size) |
| 13 | word | Number of total sectors (0 if partition > 32Mb) |
| 15 | byte | Media descriptor byte |
| 16 | word | Sectors per FAT |
| 18 | word | Sectors per track |
| 1A | word | Number of heads |
| 1C | word | Number of hidden sectors |
| 20 | dword | Number of sectors if offset 13 was 0 |
| 24 | byte | Physical drive number |
| 25 | byte | Reserved |
| 26 | byte | Signature byte (29h) |
| 27 | dword | Volume serial number |
| 2B | 11bytes | Volume label |
| 36 | 8bytes | Reserved |

The start code of the boot sector is situated after this table.

When the process of loading from the disk is started by the BIOS, the boot sector will be read to a fixed place in the memory. The address of this is 0000:7c00h. After the sector has been read, the BIOS passes control to this address and execution of the initializing procedure begins. This procedure just reads the system files (often IO.SYS and MSDOS.SYS) and passes control to IO.SYS.

The procedure mentioned above will be slightly different if you try to load a system from a hard disk. As well as a boot sector, all hard disks have a special structure: a master boot sector. Like a boot sector, this structure contains important information about the disk, but the information relates to the location of each logical disk (partition) on the surface of the hard disk, each of which has its own boot sector. When you load your system from a hard disk, the master boot sector indicates the logical disk on which the boot sector for the loading process is situated. When this problem has been solved, the normal boot sector starts to perform as described above.

When a boot virus tries to infect a disk, it performs the following steps:

1 It performs a test to see whether the disk has been infected by the virus.

2 It finds a place for the normal boot sector.

3 It writes the normal boot sector to the place found in the previous step and remembers this place.

4 It writes its body to the first disk sector.

If you try to load your computer from a contaminated disk, the boot virus receives control from DOS. It stores its body in the memory, usually the high memory area, and intercepts all the interrupts it needs. The virus then reads the normal boot sector from where it was previously saved, and passes control to it under DOS. If it intercepts a disk operation - for example, an INT 13h or INT 40h command - it performs all the above operations and tries to infect a new disk.

The main problem with analyzing boot viruses is that you have to find the normal boot sector for the disk. This can be hidden in a lot of places. For example, the virus Marijuana (B512R), which contains the string Legalize Marijuana, hides the normal sector in the last sector of the root directory on a disk. The virus Italian bouncing (B1024R) hides the normal boot sector in a free cluster and marks it as a bad one (i.e. it puts the mark FFFEh in the disk FAT), though this method is very inconvenient for the virus - bad sectors are visible during disk map viewing. Figure 17.6 shows the map of a floppy disk infected by the Italian bouncing (B1024R) virus. Note that the length of this virus is not one sector (512 bytes), but two sectors. This means that B1024R consists of two segments. The other one is also hidden in a bad cluster.

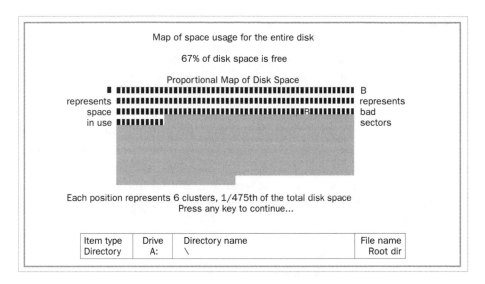

**Figure 17.6 Map of a Floppy Disk Infected by the Italian Bouncing Virus**

Some viruses hide all traces of themselves. We will discuss this in the section on stealth viruses.

Before analyzing a boot virus, try checking your disk. If there are any bad sectors, check them. You may find that the virus has hidden the normal boot sector there. To analyze the code of a boot virus, you must cut it out from the disk. You can do this using any disk editor which can save sector information to a file. Save the contents of the first logical sector - it is the boot one. Note however, that if your hard disk is one of the more modern ones, an IDE drive, there is almost certainly something seriously wrong if you find a bad sector. The logic of the onboard disk processor is such that if it identifies a physically bad area on the surface of the disk, it will allocate space from a free area to take its place - all at a low-level, so disk-checking utilities, like Norton Disk Doctor, will never show the bad sector.

You can then try to debug the virus. To load the file from the address 7c00h (you have to load it from this address, because the boot sector only works there), you should start AFD.EXE and give it the following commands:

```
L /7C00 BOOT.CCC
D 7C00
```

You should now see the first JMP virus instruction.

*Take care when debugging the boot sector. It will be making changes to the zero segment. If you don't want to make any changes in your system area, it is best not to perform these instructions.*

To find where a virus has saved the normal boot, trace it until it starts to perform INT 13 with AX=2. This is when it tries to read something from the disk. You can perform this instruction and see what information is read from disk. If it looks like a normal boot sector (i.e. if it has the name OEM, string IO.SYS, MSDOS.SYS), note where the information was saved. All parameters will be saved in these registers:

| | | |
|---|---|---|
| CH | = | cylinder number |
| CL | = | sector number |
| DH | = | drive number, 0 = Drive A, etc |
| DL | = | diskette side, or fixed disk read/write head number |

Another way is to search through the disk for the boot sector signature 55AAh. This signature is situated at the bottom of the boot sector (see Table 17.8).

Very often boot viruses use stealth features because they need to intercept all requests to the boot sector and redirect them to the normal boot.

## Viruses in Memory

Most viruses save their body in the memory, so they have resident parts. To do this, some viruses cut off an area at the top of memory, some use the driver's area, some of the older ones just save themselves as simple resident programs, and the most exotic ones write their body to the interrupt vector table or to the screen area (B000:0000h, etc.).

Before you start to delete viruses from files, you should delete them from memory. If you don't, the resident part of the virus will re-infect all the files that you have cleaned because viruses generally examine all files that will be opened or executed to find uncontaminated ones.

If the virus cannot intercept interrupts, the resident part is as good as dead.

The main sign of intercepting interrupts is to change the interrupt table (addresses 0:interrupt_no*4). The change is visible if you look at the table or at the interrupt map. All changed interrupts will point to the location of the virus in memory and you will be able to catch the virus easily.

If a virus intercepts interrupts using the standard DOS functions 35h and 25h, you can intercept this operation and destroy the procedure which precedes it. A safer method - at least from the point of view of the virus - is to change the interrupt table directly. The following fragment of code shows how INT 21 is intercepted:

```
PUSH    DS              ;Clear the AX register
XOR     AX,AX
PUSH    AX              ;Load zero to the DS register
POP     DS              ;CLI instruction is necessary to prohibit
                        ;other interrupts from taking control
CLI                     ;Load the offset of the new interrupt handler to the
                        ;address of the 21st interrupt (21h*4=84h)
MOV     [84h],offset Interrupt_Handler      ;Move the segment
MOV     [86h],CS        ;Enable interrupts
STI
POP     DS
```

Sometimes viruses use the float technique to intercept interrupts. They check the interrupt table and if a program has changed the interrupt in question, they change it back again.

If you look at the interrupt table using the AFD debugger, you can trace all the interrupts you need. For example, if INT 21h looks suspicious because it points to the address 922ah:178h, you should inspect the commands following that address.

```
D 922a:178
```

If you execute this command, the disassembling window will show you the contents of this area.

## How Viruses Reserve Memory

Old viruses, such as Fall Letters (V1701R) and Fall Letters-2 (V1702R), reserved memory using just the standard DOS function 48h. However, this method was very inconvenient. DOS itself reserved the memory block, so it was visible to other programs (see, for example, Program 17.2). This method was superceded by viruses which could simply cut off the last memory block so that DOS couldn't see the rest of memory. This meant that viruses could load their body to the free area. With this method, the loading action would be performed twice: firstly with the MCB for the current program (offset 3, in paragraphs, see Table 17.4), secondly for the PSP block (offset 2, see Table 17.5). After this DOS will be unable to see the memory block located at segment A000h. You will find a lot of viruses there.

Another method of cutting memory is frequently used by boot viruses. These viruses reduce the value of the available memory at the word which is situated at the address 40h:13h. This word is the value of the available memory in kilobytes and interrupt 12h returns this value.

## Checking Memory

Program 17.5 demonstrates how you can determine the status of your PC's memory. This program uses function 62h of INT 21h. This function returns the segment of the current process' PSP. It also examines all the critical interrupts (8h, 13h, 21h, 40h) and shows which memory areas they point to.

```
/////////////////////////
//Program 17.5
/////////////////////////
#include <stdio.h>
#include <stdlib.h>
#include <dos.h>
#include <string.h>
#include <conio.h>


void main()
{
  unsigned far *MemPtr,*MemPtr1;
  union REGS rgs;

  printf("Memory observer has been started.\n");
  MemPtr=MK_FP(0x40,0x13); //Check the memory value
  printf("Memory size reported by DOS: %d K.\n",*MemPtr);
  //Get the PSP segment address
  rgs.h.ah=0x62;
  intdos(&rgs,&rgs);
  printf("Current PSP address: %04X\n",rgs.x.bx);
  //Offset 2 - top of the memory
  MemPtr=MK_FP(rgs.x.bx,2);
```

```
printf("Memory top reported by PSP: %04X\n",*MemPtr);
if(*MemPtr<0x9fff)
{
        printf("Memory capacity was reduced!\n");
}
printf("Interrupts:\n");
//Segment 0, offset interrupt_no*4: interrupt handler address
MemPtr=MK_FP(0,8*4);
MemPtr1=MK_FP(0,8*4+2);
printf("Interrupt #8: %04X:%04X\n",*MemPtr1,*MemPtr);
MemPtr=MK_FP(0,0x13*4);
MemPtr1=MK_FP(0,0x13*4+2);
printf("Interrupt #13: %04X:%04X\n",*MemPtr1,*MemPtr);
MemPtr=MK_FP(0,0x21*4);
MemPtr1=MK_FP(0,0x21*4+2);
printf("Interrupt #21: %04X:%04X\n",*MemPtr1,*MemPtr);
MemPtr=MK_FP(0,0x40*4);
MemPtr1=MK_FP(0,0x40*4+2);
printf("Interrupt #40: %04X:%04X\n",*MemPtr1,*MemPtr);
}
```

The main aim of analyzing a virus's resident part is to extract the normal values of the interrupt handlers. In most cases this is not difficult. Just trace the infected interrupt as the virus will call something like this:

```
CALL CS:[234h]
```

or

```
JMP  CS:[234h]
```

and the value in this call will be similar to the normal interrupt handler address. You should trace this call because you have to be sure that you find the real interrupt handler.

The following part of the virus 'Minsk Ghost' (V1447R) includes this type of instruction:

```
9839:0287    80FC03        CMP      AH,03
9839:028A    740A          JZ       0296
9839:028C    80FC0B        CMP      AH,0Bh
9839:028F    7405          JZ       0296
;the next instruction is a jump to the real interrupt 21 handler
9839:0291    2EFF2E0400    JMP      Far CS:[0004]
9839:0296    1E            PUSH     DS
9839:0297    56            PUSH     SI
```

Some viruses use another interception technique. They do not change anything in the interrupt table. Instead, they change the entry point of the interrupt handler. For example, the normal handler for INT 21h may have the instructions PUSH or CMP or MOV or something similar. A virus can, for example, change this entry procedure to the following:

```
JMP 9200:0345h
```

This means the interrupt table will appear as normal, but the interrupt will be intercepted by a virus. In this case, a virus has to perform the preliminary operations which the normal handler for the interrupt would do before it can proceed.

Some viruses use interception of interrupts not only for the infection process, but also for their stealth life. This means that the virus will not be visible to DOS or to a user during simple operations with the infected file: for instance, reading it or finding its size. If a virus of this kind intercepts a request to get the size of a contaminated file, it just reduces its size by the value of the virus' length. For boot stealth viruses, this means that when you read the contaminated boot sector, you will not see anything other than the normal boot sector.

This method is very simple: a virus just intercepts all requests to read the infected area and does not allow anything to be read from there. This is another reason why the resident virus part should be deleted first.

We should add here some more information about virus signatures. These are often divided into two classes:

- Code signatures. These signatures consist of several bytes of the virus code and are unique.

- String signatures. These signatures are not present in every file, but they give the virus its name. For example, the virus V1474R contains the string 'Minsk Ghost' and is therefore called the Minsk Ghost virus.

Some viruses use text signatures to indicate that the file is infected. For example, if the signature MsDos is present in a file, it may be infected by the virus Israel.

However, the presence of a text signature in a file (especially at the end of a file) can mean that this file has been vaccinated (see below).

The method of finding a signature was demonstrated in Program 17.4, where the code signature for the Diana virus was found.

# Observing and Deleting Viruses

## The Classification of Antivirus Programs

Virus eradicators and analyzers can be divided into several classes.

The first class consists of detect programs. These programs can only test whether or not any viruses exist in the tested file. The best known example of this kind of program is the SCAN checker, which can determine the existence of more than 900 viruses. A very simple example of a detect program was given in Program 17.4.

The second class contains revisors. This type of program checks file information which was saved somewhere on the disk, for example, the file's length, checksum, etc. A new idea for revisors is that they will be able to restore files after infection.

The third class contains virus removal tools. As well as detecting viruses, these programs can delete and eradicate them from your system.

There are also other kinds of antivirus software. We will talk about these in the last section.

## Revisors

We will start our examination of antiviruses by showing how to design revisors. Our first revisor will be able to store information about files in a special database and check these files against the saved information.

Program 17.6 illustrates the technique. This program can only perform two operations: it can 'Insert' (Add) files to the database and check all files which are contained there. Program 17.6 saves the following information:

1  The name of the file to be checked. Therefore, if you delete or move
   files which were entered to the database, it will not find them.

2  The first 512 bytes of the file. This is sufficient both to restore the EXE
   file header and the starting bytes of COM files.

3  The length of the saved value (see point 2). A file may be less than 512
   bytes, so you have to control this size.

4  The normal file length. This value is necessary for viruses which change
   the file length, although they do not change the first bytes of a
   program.

```
/////////////////////////////////////////////////
//Simple Revisor program 17.6.
/////////////////////////////////////////////////
//This program checks the files in the database.
//We will get the information about the position of the database file from
//the environment variable REV_DBS=<path>
#include <stdio.h>
#include <stdlib.h>
#include <dos.h>
#include <dir.h>
#include <string.h>
#include <conio.h>

//Structure of the database file
struct DATABASE
      {
          char fname[80]; //File name
          unsigned head_len; //Length of the checked part
          unsigned char first512[512]; //Buffer for the checked part
          unsigned long length; //File length
      } database;

char dbs_name[80]; //Name of the database file for this session
FILE *dat_file;

void main(int argc, char *argv[])
{
  int i;
  ffblk buf;

  char drive[5],dir[80],name[12],ext[4];

  if(argc<2)
  {
    printf("Illegal format. Use: %s <key> [file_list]\n",argv[0]);
    printf("Where <key> is:\n");
    printf("A - add new file(s) to the database\n");
```

```
    printf("C - check files which were placed in the database\n");
    exit(1);
}
if(getenv("REV_DBS")) //Try to find the REV_DBS string in the environment
{
    strcpy(dbs_name,getenv("REV_DBS"));
    if(dbs_name[strlen(dbs_name)-1]!='\\')
        strcat(dbs_name,"\\");
}
else *dbs_name=0;
strcat(dbs_name,"REVISOR.DAT");
dat_file=fopen(dbs_name,"a+b"); //Open the database file
if(*argv[1]=='a'||*argv[1]=='A') //Add operation was pointed to
{
    for(i=2;i<argc;i++) //Do this for all files pointed to in the command line
    {
        int res=findfirst(argv[i],&buf,0xffff);
        while(!res)
        {
            fnsplit(argv[i],drive,dir,name,ext);
            if(!*dir) getcwd(dir,79);
            fnmerge(database.fname,drive,dir,buf.ff_name,"");
            FILE *f=fopen(database.fname,"rb");
            if(f) //File was opened normally
            {
                //Read the saving part
                database.head_len=fread(database.first512,1,512,f);
                fseek(f,0,SEEK_END);
                database.length=ftell(f);
                fclose(f);
                //Write the file information to the database
                fwrite(&database,1,sizeof(database),dat_file);
                printf("File %s has been written to the database.\n",
                    database.fname);
            }
            else
                printf("Cannot open file %s\n",database.fname);
            res=findnext(&buf);
        }
    }
}
else if(*argv[1]=='c'||*argv[1]=='C') //Check operation was pointed to
{
    for(;;)
    {
        //Read next structure from the database
        int res=fread(&database,1,sizeof(database),dat_file);
        //If it was the last one - exit
        if(res<sizeof(database)) break;
        printf("File %s is checking. ",database.fname);
        FILE *f1=fopen(database.fname,"rb");
        unsigned char buffer[512];
        fread(buffer,1,database.head_len,f1);
        fseek(f1,0,SEEK_END);
        //Compare the saved part and the existing one.
```

```
      //Also check the file length
      if(memcmp(buffer,database.first512,database.head_len)||
        ftell(f1)!=database.length)
      {
        printf("%cFile has been changed!\n",7);
      }
      else
        printf("\n");
      fclose(f1);
    }
  }
  fclose(dat_file);
}
```

There are two things to note about this program. Firstly, if you are going to use this program you have to be sure that your computer is clean of viruses first. If not, your revisor will save data from the infected files and all contaminated files will be interpreted as normal ones. Secondly, Program 17.6 does not check memory. However, you could insert a small piece of code which will perform a checksum on memory status, and monitor this as well. The values of the interrupt handler's addresses are usually constants (but this depends on the hardware configuration). Therefore, you can store and check these values. In this case though, you should remember that legitimate memory resident programs may be loaded after your memory checksum calculation, which may give false reporting of virus activity.

Another concept is illustrated in Program 17.7. This is also a resident program, but it has an extra feature. This revisor is able to restore the information changed by any virus.

If Program 17.7 finds any changes in a file, it will ask you if you want to restore the file status. If you say yes, it will write the stored 512 or less bytes to the top of the file and truncate the file to the normal length.

```
///////////////////////////////////////////////////////////
//Second version of the Revisor program with restoring 17.7.
///////////////////////////////////////////////////////////
//This program checks the files in the database.
//We will get the information about the position of database file from
//the environment variable REV_DBS=<path>
#include <stdio.h>
#include <stdlib.h>
#include <dos.h>
#include <dir.h>
#include <io.h>
#include <string.h>
#include <conio.h>
```

```
//Structure of the database file
struct DATABASE
        {
          char fname[80]; //File name
          unsigned head_len; //Length of the checked part
          unsigned char first512[512]; //Buffer for the checked part
          unsigned long length; //File length
        } database;

char dbs_name[80]; //Name of the database file for this session
FILE *dat_file;

void main(int argc, char *argv[])
{
  int i;
  ffblk buf;

  char drive[5],dir[80],name[12],ext[4];

  if(argc<2)
  {
    printf("Illegal format. Use: %s <key> [file_list]\n",argv[0]);
    printf("Where <key> is:\n");
    printf("A - add new file(s) to the database\n");
    printf("C - check files which were placed in the database\n");
    exit(1);
  }
  if(getenv("REV_DBS")) //Try to find the REV_DBS string in the environment
  {
    strcpy(dbs_name,getenv("REV_DBS"));
    if(dbs_name[strlen(dbs_name)-1]!='\\')
      strcat(dbs_name,"\\");
  }
  else *dbs_name=0;
  strcat(dbs_name,"REVISOR.DAT");
  dat_file=fopen(dbs_name,"a+b"); //Open the database file
  if(*argv[1]=='a'||*argv[1]=='A') //Add operation was pointed to
  {
    for(i=2;i<argc;i++) //Do this for all files pointed in the command line
    {
      int res=findfirst(argv[i],&buf,0xffff);
      while(!res)
      {
        fnsplit(argv[i],drive,dir,name,ext);
        if(!*dir) getcwd(dir,79);
        fnmerge(database.fname,drive,dir,buf.ff_name,"");
        FILE *f=fopen(database.fname,"rb");
        if(f) //File was normally opened
        {
          //Read the saving part
          database.head_len=fread(database.first512,1,512,f);
          fseek(f,0,SEEK_END);
          database.length=ftell(f);
          fclose(f);
          //Write the file information to the database
          fwrite(&database,1,sizeof(database),dat_file);
```

```
                printf("File %s has been written to the database.\n",
                    database.fname);
            }
            else
                printf("Cannot open file %s\n",database.fname);
            res=findnext(&buf);
        }
    }
}
else if(*argv[1]=='c'||*argv[1]=='C') //Check operation was pointed to
{
    for(;;)
    {
        //Read next structure from the database
        int res=fread(&database,1,sizeof(database),dat_file);
        //If it was the last one - exit
        if(res<sizeof(database)) break;
        printf("File %s is checking. ",database.fname);
        FILE *f1=fopen(database.fname,"r+b");
        unsigned char buffer[512];
        fread(buffer,1,database.head_len,f1);
        fseek(f1,0,SEEK_END);
        //Compare the saved part and the existing one.
        //Also check the file length
        if(memcmp(buffer,database.first512,database.head_len)||
            ftell(f1)!=database.length)
        {
            printf("%cFile has been changed! Restore it? ",7);
            if((getche()&0x5f)!='Y') printf("\n");
            else
            {
            //now we will try to restore information
                printf("Restoring.\n");
                fseek(f1,0,SEEK_SET);
                //Write first bytes to the file top and
                //check the restoring process
                res=fwrite(database.first512,1,database.head_len,f1);
                if(res==database.head_len)
                    printf("Restored!\n");
                else
                    printf("Not restored!\n");
                //Cut file length to the normal status
                chsize(fileno(f1),database.length);
            }
        }
        else
            printf("\n");
        fclose(f1);
    }
}
fclose(dat_file);
}
```

Of course, this revisor is not a universal one. You can improve it, for example, by saving more than 512 bytes of the file. It will help you to delete viruses which move the top of a file to the end of a file and write their body into the free part.

## Deleting Viruses from Memory and Files

In order to delete something from the memory, you have to be sure that this something is actually situated in the memory. You can solve this problem by using the signature method. You just have to test if the virus' signature is present in memory in some of the areas pointed to by the interrupt vectors. You can use the file's signatures, but it is probably more convenient to extract some new signatures, for example, signatures from the interrupt handler's entry point.

You also have one more problem to solve - where does the virus save the information about the normal addresses of the interrupt handlers? This can be solved using a similar method to the one for searching for hidden bytes in the file part of the virus.

In our discussion of virus analysis, we talked about the problem of identifying viruses that exist in executable files (see Program 17.4).

This program worked like a simple detector. We will now add a feature to Program 17.4 so that it can delete viruses. This 'addition' is very simple. However, first we have to determine where this virus ('Diana', V2000R) saves the information about all the bytes that need restoring (3 bytes for COM files, and ReloCS, ReloIP for EXE ones).

Another task is to determine the exact length of the virus. In the case of the 'Diana' virus, this is fairly simple. We just look at the infected file whose length we know (COMMAND.COM for DOS 5.0 has a length 47845 bytes) and reduce the infected file's length to the normal length. However, some viruses round up their length to the next paragraph boundary. Therefore, these files will need to be truncated to the minimum virus length. For example, the Jerusalem virus has a variable length, but its minimum length is 1805 bytes.

We are now ready to start designing the antivirus program. We will use Program 17.4 as a basis. The changes that we make to this program should mean that after the virus has been identified, the program will not only show the message "This file was probably infected by the 'Diana' virus" but will also try to delete the virus from the infected file.

The first step is to design a procedure which will delete the virus from COM files. This format is the simplest one and so we will use these files to show you how to delete a virus.

Suppose you have all the information you need to delete a virus. You then need to clean up memory and check all the COM and EXE files present. For COM files, you have to check for the existence of the virus' signature and, if it exists, read the hidden bytes from the virus' body and write them into the top of the file. You should then change the file size.

For EXE files, you have to collect all information about ReloCS, ExeIP, etc. and write it to a file. You should then change the values of the PagCnt and PartPag so that they correspond to the normal (virus free) file length.

Program 17.8 on the disk illustrates a simple example of a Virus Removal program. This program can only delete one virus. If you want to process a different one, you have to create new procedures, similar to the existing ones. You have to do this every time you want to insert a new virus profile.

## Multiple Virus Removal

There is, however, a more efficient way. The technique we are about to describe - the table driven technique - illustrates how you can create an antivirus which will delete new viruses without requiring any major changes.

This technique requires us to create two structures. Each of them will represent both the memory part and the file part of a virus. The memory part structure will be as follows:

```
struct MEM_PART
    {
        char VirName[15]; //Virus' name
        //If memory was infected
        //each intercepted interrupt
        //has a unique offset for each
        //virus. If any offset is equal to zero
```

```
          //it means that this virus does not
          //intercept this interrupt
          unsigned ofs8,ofs13,ofs9,ofs21,ofs40;
          //These variables show where the normal addresses
          //of the interrupt handlers are saved.
          signed nofs8,nofs13,nofs9,nofs21,nofs40;
          signed nseg8,nseg13,nseg9,nseg21,nseg40;
      };
```

The file part structure will be:

```
      //This structure represents the information about the file part of a virus
      struct FILE_PART
          {
          char VirName[15];       //Virus' name
          long VirSize;           //Virus' size (minimal if variable)
          unsigned SignLen;       //Length of the signature
          signed SignOfs;         //Offset of the signature
                                  //concerning to the entry point
          unsigned char Sign[32]; //Signature
          //InfExe - (boolean) if this virus is able to infect EXE files
          //InfCom - (boolean) if this virus is able to infect COM files
          //HidLen - number of bytes (for COM files) which were changed by
          //this virus
          char InfExe,InfCom,HidLen;
          //Offsets for hidden bytes and data from the EXE header
          signed Hid,IP,CS,SS,SP;
          };
```

We should now create arrays which will consist of the elements of these structures. All the procedures which analyze and delete viruses, either from the memory or from files, will use these arrays to gather information. Program 17.9 on the disk demonstrates the table driven technique.

It is sometimes necessary to decontaminate the virus body itself: if a virus encrypts its body, you have to decrypt it. To allow for this, you can insert one more field into the FILE_PART structure PrepProc. This field will be filled by NULL if it is not necessary to decode the virus body, otherwise you can point to the address of the preparation procedure. You should change the delete procedure as follows:

```
      if(file_part[i].PrepProc) PrepProc(f);
```

# Other Types of Antivirus Program

In the previous sections we have dealt with different types of antivirus program. You know about disinfection procedures, detect programs, revisors etc. We will now discuss other types of antivirus software.

## Memory Controllers

This type of antivirus software is based on the assumption that a virus will try to execute the infection process via the standard DOS functions FileOpen, FileRead, FileWrite. The memory controller intercept attempts to write to EXE files and gives a warning message. Unfortunately, this method is no longer efficient because many new viruses call DOS functions directly from DOS. They detect the DOS entry point and apply their requests directly to this entry point. The following fragment of code illustrates this method:

```
;In AX - DOS Function, Write to file
  mov AH,40H
  mov BX,CS:[FileHandle]
  mov DX,offset Buffer
  mov CX,VirusLen
;Now apply directly DOS handler
  call FAR CS:[Int21Handler]
```

If you want to intercept execution of the DOS function 40h, your strategy will fail because the virus will access it directly.

A memory controller can enhance its functions by using the virus technique described in the section about viruses in memory. It can build the JMP instructions onto its own interrupt handler. The instructions have to be built as the first commands to be executed of the normal interrupt handler. This technique will allow the memory controller to intercept all requests to the interrupt handler.

There is one more method of controlling memory that is used by the Periscope debugger with a special Periscope board. This combination of software and hardware can even intercept requests to the ports on the hardware layer. Obviously this debugger is most convenient for analyzing and controlling viruses.

## On-the-fly Controllers

The on-the-fly control method is rather exotic. This software is divided into two parts.

The first part consists of a resident program which performs CheckSum computations whenever files are accessed. Whenever you want to execute one of your EXE or COM files, this controller will calculate a fresh CheckSum of the file being loaded. For EXE files, this sum may be extracted from the EXE file header (see Table 17.3). If this control sum is not equal to the saved one, it means that this file has been changed.

Another CheckSum method is to calculate control sums for several files and save this information in a database. The most useful way is to calculate the CRC16 value for a file.

The CRC16 algorithm is based on the computation of the polynomial's coefficient. This method is described in the CCITT V.41 specification. The polynomial produces a 16-bit remainder polynomial and is expressed as:

$$X^{16} + X^{12} + X^5 + 1$$

In a theoretical 16-bit CRC calculation, the individual bits of a message are concatenated to form the coefficients of a data polynomial. The high-order bit of the first byte of the data is the coefficient of the high-order term of the data polynomial. The low-order bit of the last byte of the data is the coefficient of the term 1.

Before division, the data polynomial is multiplied by $X^{16}$. This appends 16 zero bits to the end of the original data polynomial. The data polynomial is then divided by the generator polynomial. Note that ordinary arithmetic division is not used to calculate the CRC. Instead, modulo-two (no carries or borrows) arithmetic is used. In practice, this is implemented using the XOR instruction. The 16 extra zero bits serve to flush all the message bits through the division operation. The remainder of this division is the desired CRC.

Program 17.10 illustrates the calculation of the CRC16 algorithm.

```
;////////////////////////////
;Program 17.10 CRC16 algorithm
;////////////////////////////
;    Entry:     AL    =    data byte
;               BX    =    CRC16 generator polynomial
;               DX    =    CRC accumulator (0 for initial call)
;

CRC16_BIT       PROC   near
;CX - number of bits
                    mov        CX,8
    BACK:
;XOR CRC with data byte for SF setting
                    mov        AH,DH
                    xor        AH,AL
                    clc
                    rcl        DX,1
                    jns        FORW
;XOR CRC with generator polynomial
                    xor        DX,BX
  FORW:
                    shl        AL,1
;Repeat for each bit
                    loop       BACK
                    ret
CRC16_BIT       ENDP

;
;Example:
;                   mov        AL,0F6h
;                   mov        BX,1231h
;                   xor        DX,DX        ;Move zero to DX
;                   call       CRC16_BIT
;
```

An on-the-fly checker will compute this CRC sum for all modules being loaded and compare it with the database values.

The next part of an on-the-fly controller checks for viruses that exist in the files being loaded. It works like a simple detector, but only performs this verification when a file is loaded.

This type of antivirus software is very convenient. The disadvantage is that it makes the loading process slower than under just DOS.

## Antiviruses With External Tables

Like antivirus programs (detectors and disinfectors), this type of antivirus tool uses information about viruses (signatures). It works like Programs 17.8 and 17.9 described above, but saves all signatures and eradication tables in the database on disk. Users can modify these tables with information about new viruses, which makes the External Table antiviruses very interesting and attractive to users.

More complex external table software tools can parse a real 'antivirus language'. One of the better instances of this software is the AVSP program. For example, one of the virus' patterns for the virus CUB-70 can be presented as follows:

```
call 0000/pop $1/sub $1,03h/mov $,$1
```

This string means that this virus is self-modifying (it can modify its body) and its entry procedure performs the following operations:

1    CALL next command (see CALL_NEXT technique)

2    POP any register to get the start address

3    SUB the CALL instruction length

4    Save the entry address in the memory

These patterns are given in a lot of specialist newspapers and magazines and are helpful to a lot of users.

## Some Useful Features of Computer Viruses

In this chapter we have discussed the damaging features of computer viruses. So we should also mention their useful features.

First of all, techniques used in designing viruses are very useful for the design of copy-protected programs. You just 'bind' your copy-protector part to the protected program and make it check the program installation and loading processes. Like a normal virus, this part will substitute for the entry point of the program being loaded, and it will intercept interrupts to prohibit unlicensed copying.

One more useful feature of virus techniques is that they can help you create demonstration programs. As in the above case, you just write your part of the code to the program in preparation and change the program's entry point to this part of the code. Later your 'patch' can fill the keyboard buffer with the values required to demonstrate various features of your program or to protect different points of your menus from being accessed.

# Summary

This chapter has explained what viruses are and how you can deal with them. There are many viruses in the world. Some of them damage software. They can destroy data of any kind, even your bank account. This chapter has given you some idea of how to detect the existence of a virus in your computer and how to delete it.

Unfortunately, there is no universal antivirus program. We have just tried to show you the main ways of analyzing viruses. The antivirusologist's work is a real art. There are hardly any universal instructions about how to write antivirus programs. We can only give you some generai ideas about how to deal with viruses.

## CHAPTER EIGHTEEN

# Pentium
# Programming

## Introduction

This book would not be complete without a few words on the latest and greatest microchip technology break-through by Intel - the Pentium. It's the first CISC processor with a superscalar architecture. The Pentium has 3.1 million transistors and 273 pins.

In designing the Pentium, Intel's main goal was to double the performance from the previous generation. This time they produced so many architectural improvements that programming has become a bit like solving a Chinese puzzle. Everything written for the 486 and previous still works, and works faster, but not as fast as it might.

# What's New In the Pentium And Why

For reasons of backwards compatibility with the previous generations of Intel processors, the Pentium supports all the features of the Intel 486. In addition, it has several significant enhancements. The following are most often mentioned:

- Superscalar architecture, i.e. two integer pipelines able to execute some instructions in parallel.

- Separate code and data caches, 8 Kb each, designed to allow simultaneous access for all execution units and write-back organization for the data cache.

- Dynamic branch prediction, that allows execution of branches without a pipeline stall in the case of a correct prediction.

- Pipelined FPU, which provides significantly increased performance in comparison with Intel 486.

- 64-bit data bus that allows 8 bytes of information to be transferred to/from the system memory in a single bus cycle.

The Pentium's architecture is at least twice as sophisticated as that of Intel 486, but its origin may seem unclear. Here's a short historical overview.

When it was first introduced, the IBM PC was a well balanced machine. Its processor, the Intel 8088, running at 4.77 MHz, and the available DRAM chips suited each other well. However, the market required more and more powerful computers and at last the x86 family processors reached a clock speed which DRAM memory could no longer support. Slow memory became the first bottle-neck. The following solutions were engineered to treat this problem.

## Prefetcher

It was noticed that the instructions are usually located sequentially in the system memory. So if a buffer, organized as a queue, is placed between the system memory and the execution unit, it will be able to unlock the processor from the slow memory. The prefetcher utilizes the idle bus cycles while the execution unit is busy with the current instruction. The next sequential instruction is placed into the prefetching queue. The faster the execution unit, the deeper the queue should be. The 386 processor has a prefetcher queue 16 bytes deep, and the 486 has a 32-byte queue. The Pentium has two 64 byte queues (one for each of the pipelines).

## External SRAM (L2) Cache

Another possible solution was to use another kind of memory chip - SRAM (Static Random Access Memory) which can be up to 5 times faster than DRAM. However, it was impractical to completely change to SRAM, because the chips were physically larger and more expensive. It was decided to implement a relatively small external cache using SRAMs. Special hardware, called a cache controller, handles this small intermediate memory, and keeps it synchronized with the system memory. At first, the size of the external cache was about 32 - 64Kb, now it can be as much as 512 Kb.

How did this small but fast intermediate memory speed up the memory access? When the processor requires some information (initiates a memory read cycle), the cache controller determines whether the requested information is in the cache. If so, the controller immediately transfers the information to the processor (this is called a cache hit). Otherwise, the cache controller initiates a read from the system memory. The processor gets what it needs anyway, but in the latter case, the copy of the requested information stays in the cache. Why does it help? The key idea is the same as for the prefetcher. Usually programs are local, i.e. the processor is likely to read from (nearly) the same positions in memory again and again (consider loops, for example).

Described above is the 'read policy' of caching. Now a few words about the 'write policy'. Assume the processor initiates a write cycle. It may be that the cache already contains a copy of the information which is about to be overwritten. Here arises the problem of cache consistency (validity) because cache and system memory may go 'out of sync'. In other words, the processor must change the cache element which contains the information overwritten in the main memory.

The easiest way to treat this problem is to 'write through' the cache. That means every write request is handled by the cache controller and results in immediate writing to the system memory and to the cache, if the latter is necessary. However, this leads to performance losses, because the system memory access is slow.

There is a more creative policy, called 'write back'. In this case, when the processor writes, it only updates the cache memory. The cache controller keeps track of the writes that have occurred and updates the system memory when the processor is busy with something else.

The external cache approach was limited because each memory access still required one bus cycle. The bus speed became a new bottle-neck.

## Internal On-chip (L1) Cache

The solution to the problem seems obvious. Just make the bus faster. However, there's a lot of technical obstacles to increasing the speed of the bus (slow external devices, etc.). It was found more convenient to implement an on-chip cache so the execution unit could access this internal cache through the processor's internal data bus, which is significantly faster than the external one.

The internal, Level 1, cache (called L1 to distinguish it from the external, L2) was first introduced in the 486 chip. This processor incorporates a common code and data cache. However, it was found to be inefficient, because both the execution unit and the prefetcher could request access to the cache simultaneously, and this made cache validation a problem. That's why, although it's not the only reason, the code and the data caches are separate.

With the internal cache on board, the bus speed bottle-neck was overcome (faster buses were designed, too). Next the execution unit itself became the bottle-neck.

The most straight-forward solution looks obvious again. Just increase the clock speed of the processor (make it 200 MHz or so). Unfortunately, the simplest solution was the hardest to implement. The problem required a creative break-through in microprocessor architecture. The following architecture enhancement for the 486 and the Pentium was made in order to alleviate this problem.

## Pipelined Execution Unit

This is nothing more than the application of the idea of conveyor systems to the instruction stream (the same way it was applied to assembling cars).

Assume that the execution of an instruction is broken into five stages and you have a separate piece of hardware for each stage. This means it's possible to make a conveyor system or pipeline which will have the overall performance of one instruction per cycle. In particular, this is how the integer pipeline of the 486 operates:

**1** Instruction fetch.

**2** Instruction decode.

**3** Address generation.

**4** Execution itself.

**5** Register write back.

| Clocks | Conveyor stages | | | | | |
|---|---|---|---|---|---|---|
| | 1 | 2 | 3 | 4 | 5 | 6 |
| Instruction i | Instruction Fetch | Instruction Decode | Address Generation | Execute | Write Back | |
| Instruction i+1 | | Instruction Fetch | Instruction Decode | Address Generation | Execute | Write Back |
| Instruction i+2 | | | Instruction Fetch | Instruction Decode | Address Generation | Execute |

**Figure 18.1 How an Instruction Passes Through i486 Pipeline**

Pipelined execution is beneficial, but only if most of the instructions are one-cycle, i.e. if they can pass the pipeline without a stall. One-cycle pipelined execution is the key to the high performance of RISC processors. Anyway, within the framework of a CISC architecture, it was quite a job to make the most of the 486 instruction set execute in one cycle.

## Superscalar Architecture

Continuing our analogy of the processor and a car assembly line, we can immediately borrow another performance enhancement idea. Imagine two (or more) conveyors working in parallel. If there are enough parts fetched, such an innovation should, theoretically, provide double capacity.

A similar concept was introduced in processor architecture. Two pipelines working in parallel could hardly be considered a vector processor yet, so the architecture was called superscalar. Once again it was first implemented in RISC processors. Unfortunately, it is rather difficult to execute two adjacent instructions in parallel. There is the problem of dependency. If an instruction uses the result of the previous one, it's impossible to execute them at the same time. Below, in the section on 'Pentium-Aware Optimization', the rules of the Pentium's superscalar execution are explained.

## Branch Prediction

As soon as the execution unit was pipelined, it became obvious that the prefetcher treated branches ineffectively. Assume your instruction stream contains a branch that is about to be taken. When the branch instruction reaches the execution stage, the next two (for the 486 pipeline) instructions are already in the pipe. So if the branch is taken, the processor has to stall and flush the conveyor. For a superscalar architecture the problem is even more severe, because the number of instructions in the pipe is doubled.

This performance bottleneck was solved by the Pentium designers by implementing branch prediction logic. It's implemented as a small set-associative cache with 256 entries, which is referred to as the Branch Target Buffer or BTB. Each entry keeps track of a branch instruction's history, i.e. how often this branch has been taken (and certainly the address to fetch instructions from). A simple algorithm predicts whether the branch is about to be taken or not, using the BTB statistics. Prediction is, in most cases, correct, at least for loops.

# Pentium Architecture

## Structural Scheme of the Chip

It's now time to look at the structural scheme of the Pentium (see Figure 18.2). It contains slightly less blocks than in the Intel documentation, but the most significant ones are present.

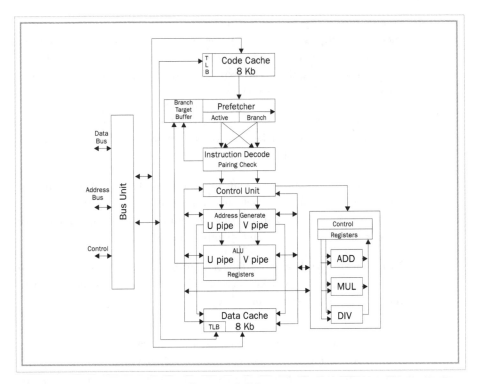

**Figure 18.2 Pentium Processor Structural Scheme**

Below is a brief description of the Pentium architecture and technical details with an emphasis on topics of interest to programmers.

## Code and Data Caches

As mentioned above, the Pentium incorporates separate code and data caches of 8KB each. Each of the caches is a 2-way set-associative and contains 128 sets. Each set contains 2 lines of 32 bytes. The storage array of the data cache is four bytes interleaved that allows access to each 4-byte data bank independently.

Replacement in both caches is performed in a single burst cycle (four 8 byte transfers) and is governed by a LRU (Least Recently Used) algorithm that requires one bit per cache set. The data cache of the Pentium supports a write back feature, using the MESI (Modified/Exclusive/Shared/Invalid) protocol. The code cache is write protected and supports the SI subset of MESI. It takes two state bits for the data cache and one state bit for the code cache. Every line of the Pentium's data cache can be in one of the four MESI states:

M: M-state means that the line is modified, i.e. it differs from the system memory (write back needed). If the whole system contains several copies of a particular memory location, then only one M-state copy of the information stored there can exist. The M-state line can be accessed (read/write) without a bus cycle.

E: E-state means that this line is only present in this particular cache, but not yet modified. It can be read or written without a bus cycle, but write access changes its state to M (modified).

S: S-state means this line is potentially shared by other caches in the system. A read from an S-state line can be performed without a bus cycle. A write access to such a line generates a write-through bus cycle causing invalidation of copies in other caches.

I: I-state means this line is no longer available in the cache (invalid). Read access to I-state line will be a cache miss and makes the Pentium fetch the line from the system memory.

The states of the lines of every cache in a system can be changed due to the activity of any bus master, so for instance, the Pentium Cache Consistency Protocol significantly simplifies design of multiprocessor systems. Examples are already commercially available.

Both the data and code caches of the Pentium can be accessed simultaneously. Moreover, the data cache can be accessed simultaneously by both pipes (except when they both address the same cache bank).

The caches are accessed via physical addresses and each of them has a pair of Translation Lookaside Buffers (TLBs) in order to translate linear addresses into physical ones. One TLB supports 4Kb paging and another 4Mb paging. If you are an application programmer, you'll hardly ever deal with TLB's. However, if you're used to changing page tables yourself, you should invalidate the TLB's by loading the CR3 register, explicitly:

```
mov cr3,eax
```

or implicitly, by task switching. Also, there's an instruction INVLPG which can invalidate an individual TLB entry.

Cache operating mode is controlled by two bits, CD (Cache Disable) and NW (Not Write Back) in CR0. To get the highest performance, both bits should be clear. If, for some reason, you need your Pentium to work a little slower, just set both bits and you'll immediately achieve the realistic performance of a 20MHz 386.

# U and V Pipelines. Superscalar Architecture

As you saw in Figure 18.2, the Pentium has two independent pipelines, U and V. They allow the chip to execute two instructions at a time, but only if a set of pairing conditions are satisfied. The Pentium also has a branch prediction mechanism implemented that allows the processor to treat branching more effectively (not flush the pipeline if a branch is taken). However branch prediction, as well as pairing, requires some checks at the early stages of execution.

This is why, during stage D1 (instruction decoding), two instructions entering the two pipelines are checked for the following:

- If either of them is a branch instruction, the prediction is made as to whether the branch will actually be taken or not. If the branch is predicted to be taken, the branch prediction logic tells the prefetcher to switch to its other queue (see Figure 18.2) and start fetching from the branch target address. Branch prediction is described in more detail below.

- The instructions are checked to see if they meet the pairing criteria. If they are not pairable, the second instruction in the pair is excluded from the V pipe, moved to the U pipe and placed exactly after the first one (i.e. it enters stage D1 when the first proceeds to D2). There are quite a lot of pairing rules, as well as exceptions, which are covered in the section on 'Pentium-aware Optimization'. However, the key idea of pairing is pretty simple. Adjacent instructions shouldn't depend on (use the result of) each other.

When paired, instructions in both pipelines must pass through conveyor stages in unison. This is easy to achieve if both instructions are one-cycle. (The latter term means that each stage of conveyor execution takes exactly one clock.)

There are, however, multi-cycle instructions. If the instruction in one pipeline stalls at some stage, the partner instruction in the other pipeline waits until the stalling stage of the other is over.

In Figure 18.2, both U and V pipelines look the same, but they do differ. The U pipe is the more capable of the two. It can execute any instruction from the Pentium instruction set, while the V pipe can only execute a rather limited subset of simple, RISC-like instructions (see the section on 'Pentium-aware Optimization').

# Prefetchers and Branch Prediction

In Figure 18.2 you probably noticed that the Pentium has two prefetcher buffers (a 486 has just one). Initially, the reason seems to be two pipelines. After all, each pipeline has its own fetching queue. Unfortunately, that's not it. The Pentium needs two fetching queues just to make its branch prediction logic work. Let's find out how it operates.

The Pentium has two prefetching queues, each able to hold two 32 byte lines, or 64 bytes. Only one of the queues is active at any one time. The prefetcher continues to fetch the code from the code cache to the active queue sequentially, until the branch instruction enters D1 stage and the prediction logic predicts the branch to be taken. If this happens, the BTB supplies the predicted branch target address to the prefetcher. The prefetcher switches to the other queue and begins to fetch from the branch target memory address. The newly active queue then supplies instructions to the two instruction pipelines immediately behind the jump instruction predicted to cause a branch.

So, if the result of a branch operation is correctly predicted, no pipeline stall occurs. However, when a branch is predicted incorrectly, a 3-cycle penalty in the U pipe, or a 4-cycle penalty, in the V pipe is incurred.

As mentioned above, the prediction mechanism is implemented using a small set-associative cache with 256 entries: the Branch Target Buffer, BTB. Each entry of the BTB contains the following information:

● Validation bit that indicates whether the entry is valid.

- History bits that keep track of the branching results statistics.

- Source memory address of the branch instruction.

- Target memory address to branch to.

Here's how it works. The first time a branch instruction enters either pipeline's instruction decoding stage, its source memory address is used to perform a lookup in the BTB. Since the instruction has not been processed before, the lookup results in a BTB miss, i.e. the branch prediction logic has no history on this instruction. However, the branch will be predicted as not taken. The fact is that even unconditional jumps are predicted to be not taken for the first time.

When the instruction reaches the execution stage, the branch can either be taken or not taken. If it isn't taken (as predicted), then nothing happens. The prefetcher goes on feeding instructions from the active queue. So, there aren't any changes in the BTB until the branch is taken for the first time. When the branch is taken, the execution unit provides feedback to the prefetcher's branch prediction logic. A BTB entry is created, and the branch's target address is recorded into it. History bits of this new entry are set to indicate that the branch was previously taken.

The history bits of a BTB entry can indicate one of the four possible states.

++  Strongly taken. This state is set when the entry is first created or if a branch marked weakly taken is taken again. Prediction: taken.

+-  Weakly taken. If a branch of this state is taken again, it is upgraded to a strongly taken, otherwise it is downgraded to a weakly not taken state. Prediction: taken.

-+  Weakly not taken. If a branch marked so is taken again, it is upgraded to the weakly taken state, otherwise it is downgraded to the strongly not taken state. Prediction: not taken.

−   Strongly not taken. If a branch marked strongly not taken is taken, it is upgraded to the weakly not taken state, otherwise, nothing happens. Prediction: not taken.

On a lookup check during the D1 stage, a hit on a strongly or weakly taken entry (++ or +-) will result in a branch to be predicted as taken. Otherwise, a hit on the strongly or weakly not taken state (-+ or --) will lead to a not taken prediction.

The state of history bits of a BTB entry is upgraded (from -- to ++) or downgraded (from ++ to --) depending on whether the prediction proves correct. As you can see, two "weak" states are intermediate and are changed (up- or downgraded) on every BTB hit, while two strong states are changed only when mispredicted.

# Pipelined FPU

The floating-point unit in the Pentium has been greatly improved compared with the 486DX. Like the integer execution unit, it's pipelined and can accept one floating-point instruction every cycle (or even two, if one of them is FXCH). Of course, to squeeze top performance, you have to optimize ('Pentualize'). We'll discuss this in detail in the section on 'Pentium-aware Optimization'.

Execution is divided into the 8 following stages. Note that the first 5 stages are shared with the integer unit.

1    Instruction fetch.

2    Instruction decode.

3    Address generation.

4    Memory and register read or memory write, if required by the instruction (with conversion of internal format to external memory format).

5    Execution stage 1: conversion of external memory format to internal format and write data to the FP registers.

6    Execution stage 2: execution of the operation itself.

7    Rounding and writing the result into the registers.

8    Error report, status word updating.

# Pentium-aware Optimization

## Testing

The testing methodology is crucial whenever the performance ratio and optimization are concerned. This is especially important for the Pentium. Fortunately, Intel foresaw the problem and provided the necessary facilities for performance monitoring, though these are not publicly documented by Intel and are available only under a non-disclosure agreement.

The Pentium has a handful of Model Specific Registers (MSR) (see the section on 'Undocumented Innovations'). One of these, 10h, is called the Time-Stamp Counter (TSC). This is a 64-bit register which is set to zero by reset and is incremented with each processor clock cycle. So if you have a 90 Mhz Pentium, each second will add 90,000,000 to this counter. (A 64-bit counter is large enough for more than 6,000 years of continuous operation without overflow.)

This register allows you to measure the performance of your instruction sequence with one cycle accuracy. This is important when you want to achieve maximum optimization (say for some deep nested loops).

There are two possible ways to read the TSC:

- Using the instruction RDTSC (Read Time Stamp Counter), which has opcode 0Fh 31h (you won't find many assemblers supporting this instruction). RDTSC puts the TSC value into EDX:EAX.

- Using the instruction RDMSR (Read Model Specific Register), which has opcode 0Fh 32h. This instruction puts the value of an MSR specified in ECX into EDX:EAX. As mentioned above, TSC has the index 10h. Look at the following example:

```
mov ecx,10h      ; specify MSR 10h
db 0fh,32h       ; read the value of TSC
```

*RDMSR is only allowed in real mode (but not in virtual 86!) and protected mode at privilege level 0. RDTSC is allowed in all modes, but in protected mode it can be prohibited by bit 2 of CR4.*

Consider the following fragment. You can use it as a template for monitoring performance of your own code:

```
        ...
        db 0fh,31h                     ; RDTSC instruction
        mov old_time,eax               ; save TSC value
        mov old_time[4],edx

        mov cx,10000                   ; number of repetitions
mm1:
        ...                            ; place here your instruction
        ...                            ; sequence to be tested
        dec cx
        jnz mm1

        db 0fh,31h                     ; RDTSC instruction
        sub eax,old_time
        sbb edx,old_time[4]            ; get the difference
        call PutDecDWord               ; output the elapsed time in clocks
        ...
```

As a rule, you have to optimize the deepest-level loop which is critical for performance. We put the instruction sequence of such a loop into the template. The number of repetitions was taken large (10000 or so) to eliminate the influence of all side effects.

The program "TEST\PIPETEST.ASM", used to exercise the U and V pipes, is supplied on the accompanying disk.

## Integer Optimization

Here, we will look at the Pentium-specific optimization rules. Powerful architecture innovations such as branch prediction, separated write-back code and data caches, pipelined FPU, etc, allow the Pentium to work much faster than a 486 chip at the same clock rate. The beauty is that you don't have to do anything yourself to make these things work for you.

However, the most unique and powerful feature of the Pentium - superscalar execution of more than one instruction per cycle - is tricky. As stated above, the Pentium has two integer pipelines, called the U and V pipes, which can execute two separate instructions simultaneously, but only under certain conditions. This section demonstrates the conditions of superscalar execution and recommends some ways to satisfy these conditions.

As you know, the U and V pipes are not equivalent. The U pipe is the more capable of the two. It can execute any instruction from the Pentium instruction set, while the V pipe can only execute a limited set of simple instructions. So the key idea to Pentium superscalar optimization is that you should have enough V pipe suitable commands in your instruction stream and eliminate, as far as possible, instruction combinations that take the V pipe out of action.

Although the list of V pipe suitable instructions is not too long, and the list of U pipe pairable instructions is short, they are most often used in programs. So, some pairing takes place even in normal Pentium-unaware code.

## Pairing Rules

Basically, instructions can only be paired if they comply to the Pairing Rules. Making two instructions execute in parallel can be tricky, not only because the subset of V pipe executable instructions is rather limited, but also because they can only be paired with certain U pipe instructions.

Here we should separate specific instruction subsets according to their pairability. Following Intel, we'll distinguish:

- **UV** - instructions, which are pairable in both U and V pipes. These are as follows:

  add, and, or, sub, xor
  mov
  cmp
  inc, dec
  lea
  nop
  pop reg
  push reg/imm
  test reg, reg
  test accum, imm

- **PU** - instructions executable only in the U pipe and pairable with suitable instructions in the V pipe: UV or PV. These are as follows:

  adc, sbb,

  all forms of shift (rcl, rcr, rol, ror, sar, sal, shl, shr) with operands reg/mem, imm

- **PV** - instructions executable in both U or V pipes and pairable with UV or PU instructions when being executed in the V pipe. There are only three PV instructions:

  jmp near (in the same segment)

  call near (in the same segment)

  jcc

The rest of instructions are NP (not pairable at all).

## How Pairing Works

Suppose the processor is executing an instruction sequence. Assume the current instruction (or a pair of them) has completed and the i-th instruction is loaded in the U pipe. The processor checks the next instruction, i+1, for being V pipe executable (UV or PV), and to see if all the pairing rules are satisfied. If so, the instructions are executed as a pair. Otherwise, the instruction i+1 waits until the U pipe is free and then executes in it. The instruction i+2, in its turn, is tested for the V pipe. In other words, UV or PU instructions should be executed in the U pipe with simultaneous UV or PV instructions handled by the V pipe. For example, the following code abstract:

```
next_w:
        mov eax,[esi*4]
        mov edx,[edi*4]
        shl eax,2
        inc esi
        add eax,edx
        inc edi
        mov [ebx*4],eax
        inc ebx
        dec ecx
        jnz next_w
```

will be paired this way:

```
U pipe                      V pipe
mov eax,[esi*4]             mov edx,[edi*4]
shl eax,2                   inc esi
add eax,edx                 inc edi
mov [ebx*4],eax             inc ebx
dec ecx                     jnz next_w
```

Actually this is not too difficult. The problem to keep in mind (and avoid) is the long list of prohibition rules - that is the conditions that prohibit pairing. The cases of unpairability are described here in detail.

## Unpairability Due to Register Contention

Register contention occurs when two instructions attempt to change the same register during their parallel execution. There are two types of register contention:

- **Read-after-write** contention - this occurs when an instruction tries to read from a register which was changed by the previous instruction.

```
mov edx,[ebx]
add eax,edx             ; edx was changed
```

- **Write-after-write** contention - this occurs when an instruction tries to write to a register which was changed by the previous instruction.

```
mov eax,[ebx]
mov eax, edx            ; eax was changed
```

Note that you can freely use, a **write-after-read** sequence, such as:

```
mov eax,edx             ; U - pipe
add edx,8               ; V - pipe
```

Two adjacent instructions that access portions of the same 32-bit register are unpairable, e.g.:

```
mov al,0
mov ah,7                ; no pairing
```

## Exceptions

There are two exceptions to the rule of register contention. These involve implicit writes to condition codes and implicit access to the ESP register:

- Compare followed by branch operations.

```
cmp eax,edx          ; U pipe
jne label1           ; V pipe

; add/and/or/sub/xor/inc/dec followed by branch operations

sub eax,4            ; U pipe
jnz loop1            ; V pipe
```

- Stack pointer reference. The following instruction sequences are pairable:

```
push reg/imm followed by push reg/imm
pop reg/imm followed by pop reg/imm
push reg/imm followed by call
```

## Stalling Due to the Address Generation Interlock (AGI)

AGI occurs if a register, changed during the immediately preceding cycle, is used as the base or index component in address calculation. It's nearly impossible to use this register to address the memory during the current and next cycle in any of the pipes. Consider the following example:

```
                    U                    V
mov edi,ebx        ; mov edi,ebx        Idle
mov al,[edi]       ; Idle (AGI)         Idle
add ebx,300        ; mov al,[edi]       add ebx,300
add edx,eax        ; add edx,eax        dec ecx
dec ecx
```

Such instruction sequences occur quite often and there is no way to avoid an AGI in them. What you can do is to schedule your instruction stream so that up to 3 simple instructions are placed between AGI-causing instructions. For instance, our previous example may be scheduled this way:

|  | U | V |
|---|---|---|
| mov edi,ebx | ; mov edi,ebx | mov al,[esi] |
| mov al,[esi] | ; inc esi | add ecx,eax |
| inc esi | ; mov al,[edi] | add ebx,300 |
| add ecx,eax | ; add edx,eax | dec ecx |
| mov al,[edi] | | |
| add ebx,300 | | |
| add edx,eax | | |
| dec ecx | | |

*No AGI occurs if an instruction implicitly changes the ESP register (push/pop). However, if the instruction which explicitly changes ESP is followed by an instruction addressing explicitly or implicitly through ESP, then an AGI will occur.*

For example:

```
    sub esp,20      ; explicitly addresses ESP
    push eax        ; AGI, one clock penalty
```

but:

```
    pop eax         ; implicitly addresses ESP
    mov edx,[esp+8] ; no AGI
```

## Unpairability During Prefix Opcodes Decoding

All prefix opcodes (lock, address size, operand size, segment override, and second opcode map), with the exception of NEAR JCC (near conditional jump), require one additional clock to decode. Only the U pipe is able to decode prefix opcodes. During this decoding, the V pipe is idle. Look at the following example:

|  | U | V |
|---|---|---|
| mov ax,fs:[edx*4] | ; decode fs: | Idle |
| mov ebx,2 | ; decode opsize | Idle |
|  | ; mov ax,fs:[edx*4] | mov ebx,2 |

Avoid prefixes if at all possible.

## Unpairability Due to Immediate-Displacement Combination

Instructions that contain immediate-displacement combinations are not pairable. Here is a couple of examples of such instructions:

```
mov var1,3
mov dword ptr [ebx+1234],5678
```

By the way, you can break this instruction into two pairable ones by loading the constant (5678) into a register. It'll be especially useful if you plan to use it regularly.

```
mov eax,5678
;...
mov [ebx+1234],eax
mov [ebx+1238],eax
;...
```

## Cache Related Conditions

No pairing occurs if neither instruction is in the code cache, except if the first is a one-byte instruction. If the instructions to be executed have not been executed at least once (i.e. they were not loaded into the internal code cache), they can only pair if the first (U pipe) instruction is exactly one byte long (dec reg, inc reg, push reg and so on).

No pairing occurs if both instructions use the data from the same data cache bank (i.e. bits 2-4 of both physical addresses are the same). The internal data cache of the Pentium was designed to satisfy both pipes' memory access without any delay. The cache banks are independent of one another, so if the data is in the cache and the U and V pipes don't try to read from the same bank in the same cycle, there's no problem. Otherwise the cache bank collision stalls the V pipe for one cycle (see Figure 18.3).

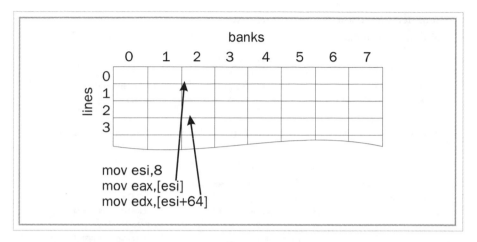

**Figure 18.3 An Attempt to Access the Same Data Cache Bank**

## Misalignment of Data

Appropriate data alignment is extremely important for Pentium (and 486) optimization. If your data falls across the cache bank boundary it costs you 2 extra clocks in both pipes to access the memory. Misaligned data access should be avoided at all cost. The rules are:

- WORD must be at physical addresses 0, 2, 4...

- DWORD must be at 0, 4, 8...

- QWORD must be at 0, 8, 16...

## Multicycle Instructions

Multicycle instructions should be considered only partly pairable. When two instructions pair, both execution units are engaged until both instructions are done (i.e. the Pentium can't execute, say, two 1-cycle instructions in the V pipe, while a 2-cycle instruction is executed in the U pipe). It means that both pipes are busy for at least the number of cycles required by the longer instruction, plus possibly some extra cycles for pairable instructions which can't fully overlap.

Consider the following. Two 2-cycle ADD instructions (instructions with register destination operands) can be executed in 2 cycles (fully overlapped):

```
                        clock        U                    V
add eax,mem1            ;1       read from mem1       read from mem2
add ebx,mem2            ;2       add                  add
```

However, 3-cycle ADD instructions (with memory destination) behave differently:

```
                        clock        U                    V
add mem1,eax            ;1       read from mem1       Idle
add mem2,ebx            ;2       add                  Idle
                        3        write to mem1        read from mem2
                        4        Idle                 add
                        5        Idle                 write to mem2
```

The Pentium executes such instruction pairs with only one cycle overlap.

That's all about the rules of pairing. If all the mentioned conditions are satisfied, you have good a chance of getting maximum benefit from the Pentium's superscalar architecture. Below is a summary of pairing conditions.

Two instructions can be executed simultaneously only if the following conditions are satisfied:

- Both instructions are pairable, i.e. UV or PU instruction in U pipe and UV or PV instruction in V pipe.

- There's no read-after-write or write-after-write register contention.

- If the instructions cause an AGI, then they should be scheduled so that up to 3 simple AGI-free instructions are between them.

- None of the instructions contain an immediate-displacement combination.

- None of the instructions contain prefix opcodes (other than 0F in JCC instructions).

- Both instructions are in the code cache, or the U pipe instruction is one byte long.

- There's no cache bank collision (i.e. the instructions don't require data from the same data cache bank).

## Using the LEA instruction

Using LEA (one clock and UV pairable) is beneficial because it can replace rather long sequences of instructions. For example:

```
lea ecx,[eax+ebx*4+5678h]
```

can replace:

```
mov ecx,ebx
shl ecx,2
add ecx,eax
add ecx,5678h
```

However remember that using LEA increases the risk of AGI.

## Using the TEST instruction

It's better to use TEST when comparing data in a register with 0. TEST doesn't change the value in the register (compared with the more traditional way: OR AX, AX), so it lowers the risk of AGI or register conflict. TEST is a one cycle and pairable instruction if the form is:

```
test eax,imm or test reg,reg
```

otherwise it takes two cycles and doesn't pair.

## 'RISCification'

It seems this term was introduced by M. Abrash in his article 'Pentium Rules' in PC Techniques April/May 1994. The author states that the best policy for Pentium optimization is to replace complex instructions with the equivalent sequences of simple (read 'pairable') instructions. This approach not only lets you get more of the V pipe, but also gives you more freedom for the appropriate scheduling of your code (just to avoid register contention and AGI's).

As a rule, precise ('hand-made') RISC-like optimization is only necessary for the deepest level loop, so don't worry about the code growing larger. Anyway, RISCification for Pentium-aware optimization is certainly within the capabilities of compilers.

Almost everything can be performed by some combination of pairable instructions. Consider the following simple examples:

Normal:

```
        push dword ptr [esi]        ; 2 clocks
```

RISCified:

```
        mov eax,[esi]               ; Can be interleaved and paired
        ...                         ; to take 1 clock
        push eax
```

Normal:

```
        add mem1,eax                ; These two instructions
        sub mem2,edx                ; take 5 clocks
```

RISCified:

```
        mov ecx,mem1                ; 3 clocks for the bunch
        mov ebx,mem2
        add eax,ecx
        sub ebx,edx
        mov mem1,eax
        mov mem2,ebx
```

Normal:

```
        inc mem (dec mem)           ; 3 clocks
```

RISCified:

```
        mov eax,mem                 ; If scheduled takes 1.5 clocks
        ; ...
        inc eax
        ; ...
        mov mem,eax
```

Normal:

```
        movzx eax,byte ptr [edi]    ; 4 clocks
```

RISCified:

```
        xor eax                     ; If scheduled takes 1 clock
        ;...
        mov al,[edi]
```

# Floating-Point Optimization

It's the FPU of the Pentium that provides the major break-through in performance. As mentioned above, the Pentium is the first chip in the x86 family that has a pipelined FPU. This allows it to perform some floating point instructions (including the most necessary ones: FADD, FSUB, FMUL) in 'one' clock cycle. More than that, the FPU pipe is just another pipeline that can work in parallel with the integer pipes. Intel allows pairing of some floating point instructions and pairing them with the integer instructions as well. In this section, some rules of scheduling and pairing of floating-point instructions are demonstrated.

## Floating-Point Instruction Pairing

The only floating-point instruction that can be paired with another FPU instruction is FXCH. Furthermore, pairing can only occur if the other instruction is simple in nature. All the following forms of floating-point instructions are pairable with FXCH.

    fadd, fsub, fmul, fdiv

    fld, ftst

    fcom, fucom

    fchs

    fabs

It's clear why this particular instruction, FXCH, was selected as the focus of enhancement. The operands of floating-point instructions must be on the top of the FPU register stack. That's why you usually need quite a lot of FXCH instructions in floating-point code, just to move the current operand to the top of the stack. One-clock and pairable FXCH instructions let you work with the Pentium FPU register stack almost as freely as if they were general purpose registers. Compared with 4-clock FXCH's of the 486, the Pentium version looks great.

The fact that several integer instructions can be executed simultaneously with a single floating-point one is not that surprising. After all, the FPU is just a separate piece of hardware. Anyway, look at the following code fragment:

```
fld dword ptr [esi]
fdiv dword ptr [edi]        ; 39 clocks
fstp dword ptr [ebx]
```

and:

```
fld dword ptr [esi]
fdiv dword ptr [edi]
mov eax,edx                          ; 1st pair
mov ecx,[ebp+8]
add esi,4                            ; 2d pair
add edi,4

; ...                                ; 36 more pairs

mov [ebp+16],eax                     ; 39th pair
mov ecx,edx
fstp dword ptr [ebx]
```

As you can see, up to 39 pairs of 1-cycle integer instructions can be executed while the FPU is deep inside the FDIV instruction. This is exactly the number of clocks Intel gives for FDIV execution. This code illustrates the Pentium's pairing abilities. All three execution units work in parallel.

Not every floating-point instruction is as flexible as FDIV. There are 'transcendental' floating-point instructions (see Table 18.1) that use all the resources of the Pentium and so can't be paired. By the way, Intel states that its hardware implementations of the transcendental instructions are much faster than, and therefore preferable to, any kind of software emulation.

**Table 18.1 The List Of Transcendental Floating-point Instructions**

| Mnemonic | Clocks | Operation |
|----------|--------|-----------|
| FSIN | 16-126 | Sine |
| FCOS | 18-124 | Cosine |
| FSINCOS | 17-137 | Sine and Cosine |
| FPTAN | 17-173 | Tangent |
| FPATAN | 17-173 | Arctangent of $ST(1)/ST$ |
| F2XM1 | 13-57 | $2^x - 1$; x is in ST |
| FYL2X | 22-111 | $Y * \log_2 X$; Y is in ST(1), X is in ST |
| FYL2XP1 | 22-103 | $Y * \log_2(X+1)$; Y is in ST(1), X is in ST |

## Scheduling Of The Floating-Point Instructions

To finish this section on Pentium-aware optimization, we'll give a couple of "real life" examples to illustrate the scheduling of floating-point instructions. First, though, some important tips.

The Pentium's FPU is pipelined and it is able to execute, say, FADD or FMUL in 'one clock cycle'. However, you should understand that you can only use the result of each particular addition or multiplication three cycles later. That's why, if each floating-point instruction of your instruction stream uses the result of the previous one, you'll never enjoy this 'one cycle' floating-point performance.

This leads us to the following conclusion. There are algorithms that are suitable for Pentium optimization and those that are not. What makes the difference is the possibility of scheduling. You simply need something that can be scheduled between floating-point instructions. This can be an FPU instruction as well, but working with independent data.

Now the examples. It's become a good tradition to use matrix multiplication as a test for floating-point optimization. We've chosen 4x4 fixed size matrices because they can be useful for projecting in 3-D graphics applications. Strictly speaking, the crucial routine in projecting is multiplication of a 4x4 matrix (transformation) by a 4x1 vector (coordinates) and multiplying matrix by matrix. If you need it for work, you can modify the code yourself. The following simple C fragment reminds you of the rules of matrix multiplication:

```
void mult_matr(matrix &matr1,matrix &matr2,matrix &res_matr) {
int i,j,k;
long double t;
for(i=0;i<4;i++)
 for(j=0;j<4;j++) {
t=0;
for(k=0;k<4;k++) t+=matr1[i][k] * matr2[k][j];
res_matr[i][j]=t;
   }
}
```

Now this routine using assembly language:

```
        les di,M1                   ; ES:DI points to the matrix M1
        lds si,M2                   ; DS:SI points to the matrix M2
        lgs bx,Mres                 ; GS:BX points to the resulting matrix Mres
        mov al,4                    ; AL = row counter
next_row:
        mov si,OffsetM2             ; DS:SI points to M2
        mov ah,4                    ; AH = column counter

next_item:                          ; M1.col[j] * M2.row[i]
        fld dword ptr es:[di]
        fmul dword ptr [si]
        fld dword ptr es:[di+4]
        fmul dword ptr [si+4*4]
        fld dword ptr es:[di+2*4]
        fmul dword ptr [si+8*4]
        fld dword ptr es:[di+3*4]
        fmul dword ptr [si+12*4]
        faddp st(1),st
; addition takes 3 clocks because the result is used in the next
; instruction
        faddp st(1),st              ; the same 3 clocks
        faddp st(1),st              ; the same 3 clocks

        fstp dword ptr gs:[bx]      ; resulting matrix [i,j]

        add si,4                    ; M2, next column
        add bx,4                    ; Mres, next item
        dec ah
        jnz next_item               ; loop

        add di,16                   ; M1, next row
        dec al
        jnz next_row                ; loop
```

This is the most straight-forward way to multiply matrices. In the following version, as many pipeline stalls as possible are eliminated:

```
        les di,M1                   ; ES:DI points to the matrix M1
        lds si,M2                   ; DS:SI points to the matrix M2
        lgs bx,Mres                 ; GS:BX points to the resulting matrix Mres
        mov al,4                    ; AL = row counter
next_row1:
        mov si,OffsetM2             ; DS:SI points to M2
        mov ah,4                    ; AH = column counter
```

```
next_item1:                             ; M1.col[j] * M2.row[i]
        fld dword ptr es:[di]
        fmul dword ptr [si]
        fld dword ptr es:[di+4]
        fmul dword ptr [si+4*4]
        fld dword ptr es:[di+2*4]
        fmul dword ptr [si+8*4]
        fxch st(2)
; while the previous multiplication is in progress, start addition
        faddp st(1),st
        fld dword ptr es:[di+3*4]
        fmul dword ptr [si+12*4]
        fxch st(2)
; while the previous FMUL is in progress, start addition
        faddp st(1),st

; The following two additions are executed simultaneously with
; the previous FADDP
        add si,4                        ; M2, next column
        add bx,4                        ; Mres, next item
        faddp st(1),st
        fstp dword ptr gs:[bx-4]        ; resulting matrix [i,j]

        dec ah
        jnz next_item1                  ; loop
        add di,16                       ; M1, next row
        dec al
        jnz next_row1                   ; loop
```

*This procedure accepts three far pointers to the matrices, because they can be in different segments. If your application program allows to keep them in a single segment (e.g. in the data segment), then you can get rid of the segment prefixes when addressing matrices' elements. It will give you a clock per prefix performance benefit.*

You can make it even faster if you unroll the loop, and schedule multiplication of every following row with the two last FADD instructions. The code works about 30% faster than the first unoptimized version, but is almost four times longer. You can find all three versions of this routine on the disk in the program MATRIX\MUL_MATR.ASM. Table 18.2 shows the results of performance tests (the program MATRIX\TEST.C) for different versions of MULT_MATRIX - execution time in seconds for 1 million multiplications on the Pentium and Intel486 DX2/66.

**Table 18.2 Performance Test**

|                        | 486DX2 (66) | Pentium (60) |
|------------------------|-------------|--------------|
| No Pentium optimization | 26.2        | 9.0          |
| Scheduled              | 27.5        | 7.5          |
| Scheduled Unrolled     | 27.6        | 6.0          |

You can also find two examples of computationally costly graphics applications optimized for the Pentium on the disk with full source code. They are:

- Mandelbrot and Julia sets explorer to produce great fractal pictures (EXPLORER\FASTMAND.ASM contains the low-level routines, EXPLORER\EXPLORER.CPP is the main module).

- The utility FILTER\FASTFILT.EXE for digital image enhancement (FILTER\FILTER.ASM contains the low-level routines, FILTER\FILT.CPP is the main module).

(You will find more detailed information in 'The Revolutionary Guide To Bitmapped Graphics'). Consider the assembly implementations of the most internal loops, they give you two more examples of Pentium-aware optimization.

Now some technical notes related to scheduling floating-point instructions:

- The operations MUL and IMUL (integer multiplication) are executed by the FPU, so they can't be paired.

- The FXCH causes a 1-clock delay if followed by an integer instruction.

- The FST instruction after a floating-point instruction causes a one cycle delay.

```
fld dword ptr [edi]                ; 1 clock
                                   ; 1 clock penalty
fstp dword ptr [esi]               ; 2 clocks

fmul dword ptr [edi]               ; 3 clocks
                                   ; 1 clock penalty
fstp dword ptr [esi]               ; 2 clocks
```

● The FSTSW instruction that is usually used after floating-point comparison (FCOM) causes a 3-cycle delay, which, however, can hide simple instructions.

    a.

```
fcomp dword ptr [ebx]              ; 3 clocks
fnstsw ax                          ; Waits until FCOMP is over
sahf
```

    b.

```
    fcomp dword ptr [ebx]
; Now hide a flock  of 1-clock integer instructions under FCOMP
    mov edx,eax
    mov esi,[edi]
    add eax,50
    add edi,8
    shr edx,2
    add esi,eax
    fnstsw ax                      ; Zero delay!
    sahf
```

● Floating-point multiplication FMUL is delayed for 1-cycle if the previous instruction was the same FMUL or a FMUL/FXCH pair.

● Avoid direct integer arithmetic in the FPU (FIADD, FISUB, etc.). They take 4 clocks and don't pair. A faster way is to split them into loading and operation steps, as follows:

    a.

```
    fiadd word ptr [ebx]           ; 4 clocks
```

b.

```
        fild word ptr [ebx]
; Now hide a flock 1-clock integer instruction under FILD
        mov eax,[esi]
        add ebx,8
        add eax,edx
        inc ecx
        faddp st(1),st
```

Finally, proper data alignment is as important for floating-point performance as for integers. It's perhaps even more crucial, because floating-point data is usually longer, so there's more risk of misalignment.

# Undocumented Innovations

This section concerns the new features of the Pentium. Unfortunately, the official documentation published by Intel provides little information: most of these features are just vaguely mentioned (with references to Appendix H, which is harder to find than the Holy Grail), or simply undocumented. Apparently, the Pentium is still a subject of exploration.

The following instructions were added in the Pentium:

- CPUID

- CMPXCHG8B

- RDTSC

- RDMSR

- WRMSR

- RSM

In detail:

## CPUID

Opcode 0Fh A2h. This instruction reports processor-specific information, which identifies the CPU type, vendor and other details.

The instruction has at least 2 subfunctions: 0 (Vendor Information) and 1 (Model Information). The subfunction is selected in the EAX register.

Subfunction 0 returns:

- EAX: the highest subfunction number recognized by the processor (always 1 for the Pentium)

- EBX, EDX, ECX: contain the vendor identification string, in the following format:

      EBX + EDX + ECX.

The original Intel Pentium returns "GenuineIntel" so

      EBX = "Genu"
      EDX = "ineI"
      ECX = "ntel"

Subfunction 1 returns Stepping ID, Model, and Family in EAX, as shown in Figure 18.4, and feature flags in EDX. EBX and ECX are reserved and zeroed.

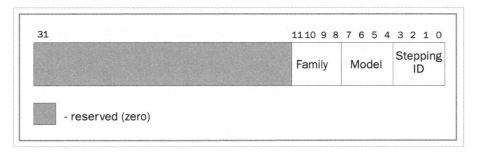

**Figure 18.4 EAX After CPUID, Subfunction 1**

Family is 5 for the Pentium, 4 for the 486.

EDX reflects the features supported by the processor. A set bit corresponds to a supported feature.

Bit 0 means 'FPU on chip'.
Bits 1 to 6 are explained in the Intel Appendix H.
Bit 7 means 'Machine Check Exception Generated'.
Bit 8 means 'CMPXCHG8B Supported'.
The higher bits, 9 - 31, are reserved (0).

## CMPXCHG8B (Compare and Exchange 8 Bytes)

Opcode 0Fh C7h <m64>. Compares a 64-bit value in EDX:EAX with a 64-bit value at the destination address in memory. If they are equal, the 64-bit value from ECX:EBX is loaded into the destination and the ZF flag is set. If they are different, the destination is loaded into EDX:EAX and the ZF flag is cleared. It is for use in multi-processor operating systems, i.e. SMP (symetric multi-processor).

## RDTSC (Read Time-stamp Counter)

Opcode 0Fh 31h. Undocumented. It reads the time-stamp counter (a 64-bit integer) into EDX:EAX. Allowed only in real mode and in protected mode at privilege level 0. See section on 'Model Specific Registers' for details about the time-stamp.

## RDMSR (Read Model Specific Register)

Opcode 0Fh 32h. Reads the specified Model Specific Register (a 64-bit value) into EDX:EAX. The register to read is selected in ECX. Allowed only in real mode, and in protected mode at privilege level 0. See section on 'Model Specific Registers' for details.

## WRMSR (Write Model Specific Register)

Opcode 0Fh 30h. Loads the specified Model Specific Register with a 64-bit value in EDX:EAX. The register to load is selected in ECX. Allowed only in real mode, and in protected mode at privilege level 0. See section on 'Model Specific Registers' for details.

## RSM (Resume from System Management Mode)

Opcode 0Fh 0AAh. Exits System Management Mode (SMM): restores the processor state and returns control to the interrupted program. Only executes in SMM - an attempt to execute it in any other modes generates an invalid opcode exception.

SMM is another mode among real, protected, and virtual-86 modes. It's not intended for application or system programming, but rather for firmware (security or power management systems). It can't be entered by software means, only by the SMI pin of the processor. If you're intrigued, see published Intel documentation for details.

## The CR4 Register

The new register, CR4, shown in Figure 18.5, enables and disables the new features of the Pentium.

**Figure 18.5 The CR4 Register**

Here is an outline of these features with references to the sections where they will be described in detail.

- Virtual Mode Extensions (VME bit). When set, enables virtual-86 mode extensions (see section on 'Virtual-86 Mode').

- Protected Mode Virtual Interrupts (PVI bit). When set, enables virtual interrupt processing.

- Time-Stamp Disable (TSD bit). Doesn't actually disable time-stamp count when set. Try clearing and setting this bit - the time-stamp counter just won't stop! In fact, setting this bit makes RDTSC a privileged instruction.

- Debug Extensions (DE bit). When set, enables Debug Extensions (see section on 'Debugging').

- Page Size Extensions (PSE bit). When set, enables Page Size Extensions (see section on 'Paging Gets Big').

- Machine Check Enable (MCE bit). When set, enables the Machine Check exception (see section on 'Exceptions').

## Debugging

Debug extensions, controlled by the DE bit in the CR4 register, don't seem to extend debugging by a great amount. However, a noticeable feature has been added: I/O breakpoint. As stated in Chapter 15, 386+ processors specify four separate breakpoint conditions in pairs of bits RW0 to RW3. The code in RWx determines the event triggering the debug exception INT 1. The code reserved in 486 processors, 10b, means I/O breakpoint in the Pentium. An attempt to address a hardware I/O port specified in a DR0..DR3 register will generate the debug exception INT 1.

Another noticeable extension: with a set DE bit the Pentium doesn't alias the reserved debug registers DR4 and DR5 as DR6 and DR7, as 486s do. Neither does the Pentium use these registers: an attempt to address DR4 or DR5 will be interpreted as an invalid opcode.

## Paging Gets Big

The Pentium supports two page sizes: 4Kb and 4Mb. When the PSE bit in the CR4 register is set, enabling paging extensions, you can create pages of both sizes. To support this feature, a special bit has been added to the format of page directory entry. Bit 7, called PS bit, indicates the page size. If the PS bit is clear,

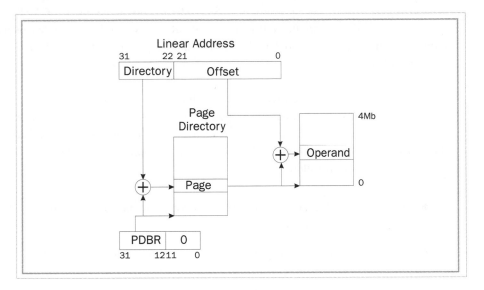

**Figure 18.6 Address Translation with 4Mb Pages**

The alternative address translation works this way:

● The processor reads the page directory entry specified by the highest ten bits of the linear address.

● If the PS bit in the page directory entry is clear, then the page is small and the standard translation is used (see Chapter 15).

● Else, if the PS bit is set, the processor interprets bits 22-31 in the page directory entry as the base address of the big page.

● Bits 0-21 of the linear address specify the offset in the big page.

# Flags

Three new flags were added to the EFlags register. The ID flag (bit 21) reports that the CPUID instruction is available. The VIP and VIF will be discussed in the section 'Virtual-86 Mode'.

# Model Specific Registers

The Pentium has several 64-bit registers to support its specific features. They are referred to as model specific registers (MSR). There's no mnemonics for MSR, they are accessed through the instructions RDMSR and WRMSR. The index of a model specific register is stored in ECX, then the MSR is read to or written from EDX:EAX.

There are ten indexes recognized by the Pentium: 0 to 2, 4 to 9, 0Bh, 0Ch, 0Eh, 10h to 13h. Most of them are undocumented and hold information about the processor's internal affairs. You can read them, but it's not safe to write to them. However, there are four model specific registers with quite definite purposes These are as follows:

- Registers 0 and 1 are machine check registers, to be discussed in the section on 'Exceptions'.

- Register 2, called Test Register 12 (TR12), is shown in Figure 18.7.

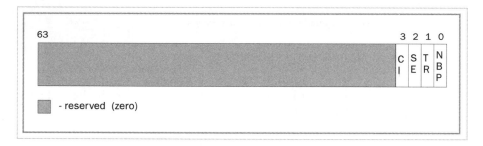

**Figure 18.7 Test Register 12**

NBP and SE bits are still unknown.
Tracing Enable (TR bit). When set, enables branch report in a special bus cycle.
Cache Inhibit (CI bit). Heard to inhibit the internal processor cache (allegedly!).

- Register 10h, Time-Stamp Counter. This register holds a 64-bit integer that counts clocks since the last reset.

## Exceptions

The Pentium generates a general protection fault, INT 13, on any attempt to set a reserved bit in any of the special registers.

Also, when the processor finds a set bit in a reserved position in a page table entry, page directory entry, or CR3, Page Directory Base Register, it generates a page fault, INT 14.

A new exception has been added in the Pentium: Machine Check Exception, INT 18, enabled by the MCE bit in the CR4 register. It's generated on a parity error during a read bus cycle, or an unsuccessful bus cycle.

Machine Check is an abort - an exception triggered by a bus cycle, not an instruction, possibly in the middle of a command, so the image of EIP on the stack can be invalid. This exception doesn't push the error code onto the stack.

The error type and address appear in read-only model specific 64-bit registers MCT (Machine Check Type) and MCA (Machine Check Address). MCA holds the physical address for the cycle that caused the error. The bitmap of the MCT is shown in Figure 18.8.

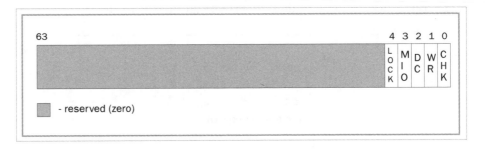

**Figure 18.8 The Machine Check Type Register (MCT)**

Check (CHK bit).    Is set by the processor when exception 18 occurs and the Machine Check Registers are latched with valid information. The CHK bit is cleared after the MCT is read (via the RDMSR instruction), so you have to read the MCA before the MCT. When the CHK bit is clear, the contents of the Machine Check Registers are undefined.

Write/Read (RW bit).  0 = error during a write cycle;
1 = error during a read cycle;

Data/Code (DC bit).  0 = error during a data cycle;
1 = error during a code fetch cycle;

Memory/IO (MIO bit).  0 = error during an I/O cycle;
1 = error during a memory cycle;

The LOCK bit  Reflects the state of the LOCK# hardware line for the cycle.

# Virtual-86 Mode

The Pentium has new features that simplify programming in virtual-86 mode. This is the most provocative and mysterious area in the undocumented Pentium.

One feature is interrupt redirection. On 486s you had to process interrupts occurring in a V86 task and redirect interrupt calls to DOS functions. The Pentium does it for you (if the VME bit in CR4 is set). When an interrupt occurs in virtual-86 mode, the processor checks the Interrupt Redirection Bitmap, a new structure in the Task State Segment (see Figure 18.9).

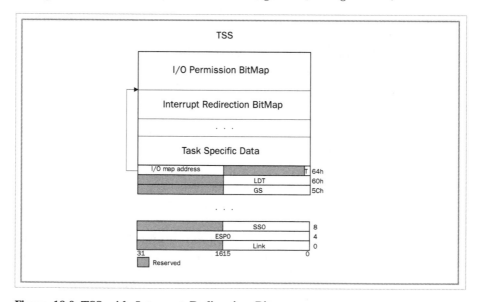

Figure 18.9 TSS with Interrupt Redirection Bitmap

The Interrupt Redirection Bitmap is a 256-bit array, a bit for every interrupt vector. If the bit corresponding to the interrupt number is set, the processor redirects this interrupt to the vector in the virtual machine's interrupt table.

Another feature has something to do with disabling and enabling of interrupts. A multitasking operating system can't allow a V86 task to disable interrupts. So 386+ processors generate a general protection fault on an attempt to change the state of the IF flag, and the operating system has to emulate disabling interrupts for this task. The flag was not actually changed, and the virtual mode manager has to keep a variable to reflect the state of the virtual IF for this task. The Pentium has this flag inside: the VIF flag. Instructions that try to modify the IF actually cause the processor to modify the VIF.

# Summary

In this chapter we described the Pentium processor architecture, its new features, instructions, registers, and how its internals work. We covered the topic of Pentium-aware optimization using the two pipelines, and aspects of floating-point optimization. You can estimate yourself whether the Pentium is worth its price by running different versions of the same routine (included on the disk).

# Assembly Language Libraries

## Introduction

The idea of this chapter is to present the concepts of assembly language libraries, their purpose, qualities and the mechanics of using them. Also, a number of routines will be developed and placed into a library. These routines will be part of a larger library supplied on the accompanying disk (see CH19\LIBRARY).

# Qualities of a Good Library

There are three basic concepts in building a library that we will cover in this chapter:

- Using the library maintenance utility program.

- How to organize the routines for inclusion in a library.

- How to write the actual library code.

We'll start by discussing the organization of the library modules. To really be useful, a library should have certain properties beyond just debugged routines. When a programmer uses a simple routine it should be a simple process, such as a routine to convert a string to lowercase. In addition, there should not be any significant side effects. For example, the size of the resulting executable file should not grow unexpectedly large.

## Granularity

The term 'granularity' refers to the capability of linking to a routine in a library and having the resultant .EXE (or .COM) file contain only those routines that your program uses. The linker can only link complete object modules. Object modules can be contained in object files (.OBJ) or library files (.LIB). An object file can only contain one object module. Library files may contain one or more object modules. When the linker does not resolve all the external references within the set of object files that are being linked, then the library files (if any) are searched. When the linker resolves an external symbol reference by matching it to a public symbol in a library file, it links in the entire object module containing the symbol. Because of this, the best library design dictates that each object module should contain the minimum amount of code or data required to perform its purpose.

For example, the C language has a powerful and versatile printf function. However, its design is not granular. When you use it to print a simple string you get about the same amount of code as when you use it to print several different data types. This is because the data conversions are specified in a string that can vary at run-time. The language designers decided that this capability of the printf function was more important than granularity and code size. You must make the same design choices when designing your own libraries. There is no universal design criteria to guide you. You should just be aware of the choices that you are making.

## Passing Parameters

In assembly language, it is common to pass parameters to subroutines via the CPU registers. However, it is possible to pass parameters using other methods. Most high-level languages (HLL) do not have a choice because parameters are usually passed on the system stack. In assembly language, it is normal to use registers for parameters (as we will be doing later). Registers have a number of advantages:

- Speed

- Compact code

- Simple to use

- They allow for re-entrant code

Using the system stack for passing parameters has the following advantages:

- It handles any number of parameters

- It is independent of machine architecture for HLL

- It allows for re-entrant code

We'll show how this is done in an example later.

Other methods exist for passing parameters, such as using a global memory area for each routine where the parameters are placed before the call (i.e. a parameter block.). We'll also use a form of this method later.

## Common Register Usage

In assembly language it is important to carefully choose the registers used for passing parameters to subroutines. High-level languages do not have this problem, because parameters are passed on the system stack and are passed using the names of the variables. The idea of using the 'right' registers is based on the fact that it makes the subroutines smaller and easier to write. For example, the CX register is frequently used as a counter register. If a subroutine is going to use a loop, then it is convenient to have the CX register pre-loaded with the loop count.

If there appears to be no particular reason to use one register or another to return a value from a function, the 80x86 convention is to use the AX register. If a 32-bit value must be returned, use DX:AX for 16-bit code and EAX for 32-bit code. The examples in this chapter are all 16-bit code.

High-level languages, such as C and Pascal, have specific conventions for returning parameters. When writing assembly language routines to be called by a HLL, you must follow these conventions for proper operation.

## Data Structures

When a complex set of parameters must be passed to a subroutine, it is usually most efficient to pass only a pointer to a data structure. In general, this could prevent the code from being re-entrant, although measures can be taken to allow re-entrancy. Declaring data structures is done as follows:

```
date        STRUC
            day         db      ?       ; first field
            month       db      ?       ; second field
            year        db      ?       ; third field
date        ENDS

example use:

...
lea         si, date1
call        day_of_week
...

date1       struc   date    <2,12,95>
```

An entire structure is passed to a subroutine by passing a pointer to the structure. In this example the structure is only 3 bytes long. We'll use this technique for passing a number of parameters to a subroutine.

## Naming Conventions

Naming conventions do nothing to improve performance or reduce code size. However, the use of a good naming convention tends to make the routines in a library easier to understand, maintain and use. For the routines in the library we'll be using, I've chosen a convention where the first three letters identify the family of routines, as follows:

| | |
|------|----------|
| CUR | cursor |
| KEY | keyboard |
| NUM | numeric |
| SCR | screen |
| WIN | window |

## Simple Setup Routines

Another library feature that we'll use is setup routines. When a complex data structure is required for a routine, it can be tedious to initialize every detail of the structure every time it is used. A better way is to provide a set of intelligent default values based on various conditions.

These setup routines are similar in nature to the concept of 'constructors' in object-oriented languages. It may also be useful, in some situations, to build the corresponding 'destructor' routines. The destructor routines would perform any cleanup activities, such as deallocating memory.

# How to Use the LIB Utility

Now that we've discussed the various properties and qualities that we would like to have in a library, we need to know the mechanics of using the library maintenance utilities.

The Microsoft Library Manager is named LIB. The Borland Library Manager is named TLIB. In all the examples, we'll show the use of the LIB commands. The use of TLIB is the same except that the semicolon is not used.

The LIB and TLIB utilities are tools that allow you to create and maintain libraries of object modules. Object files (.OBJ) are created using an assembler and/or compiler. Object files can have a full path name, such as C:\PROJECT1\POPUP.OBJ. Object modules only have a name such as POPUP.

# Basic Operations

The LIB utility works by creating a new library if the specified library name does not exist, or by modifying the specified library as required. In the following section I'll show some simple library operations - see the documentation that comes with your library utility for a complete description of all operations. In the following examples, we'll be using the following names:

```
library name        newlib
object module #1    proc1
object module #2    proc2
```

## Creating a Library

To create the library, run the library utility with the name of the new library as the only parameter, as follows:

```
LIB     newlib;
```

*The semi-colon (;) terminates the LIB command. Borland's TLIB does not require a semi-colon.*

## Add Module to Library

Libraries can be created and modules added at the same time. Object modules are added to the library using the add command. The add command is the plus sign (+) and is used as follows:

```
LIB     newlib    +proc1;
LIB     newlib    +proc2;
```

The above commands add the PROC1.OBJ and PROC2.OBJ object files to the library NEWLIB.LIB. The PROC1.OBJ and PROC2.OBJ object files could contain one or more procedures and/or data items, just as any object file could.

Alternatively, both object modules could be added in the same command, as follows:

```
LIB     newlib    +proc1   +proc2;
```

## Delete

If a module is not needed in a library file, it can be deleted by using the delete command. The minus sign (-) is used to delete, as follows:

```
LIB     newlib    -proc1;
```

## Replace

After the library has been created and contains various object modules, it is often necessary to perform updates as the code is modified. The command to perform a replacement looks suspiciously like a delete and then an add. However, the replace command is more efficient because it performs these operations in just one step. The replace command is the minus sign followed by the plus sign (-+), as follows:

```
LIB     newlib    -+proc1   -+proc2;
```

## Extract (Copy)

To extract or copy an object module from the library to a standard object file you can use the extract command. This might be done to place a copy of a module into another library or to directly link an object file without using the library file. The asterisk (*) is used for the extract command, as follows:

```
LIB     newlib    *proc1;
```

Because the asterisk is also used for specifying wildcards in file names, its use could be confusing. The Microsoft library utility does not allow wildcards for any file names. If you attempt to use wildcards in a file name, you may get an error message relative to the extract command.

## Listing

To obtain a listing of the contents of a library file, you must place a comma after the list of operations to be performed, if any, followed by the name of a listing file. For example:

```
LIB     newlib,newlib.lst;
```

The file NEWLIB.LST will then contain a list of the object modules in the library. Other information, such as the size of the modules, is also listed. The Microsoft Library utility listing looks like this:

```
PROC1........proc1                  PROC2............proc2

proc1        Offset: 00000010H  Code and data size: 6H
   PROC1

proc2        Offset: 000000a0H  Code and data size: 6H
   PROC2
```

The first portion is an alphabetical listing of the object modules and their public symbols. The second section is a listing of public symbols, their starting point in the library and their size.

The Borland Library utility listing looks like this:

```
Publics by module

PROC1     size = 6

PROC2     size = 6
```

# Example Library

Now that we know the basics of using a library maintenance utility and the good qualities we should strive for in a library, we'll start building a library of routines. We'll use these routines in examples in the next two chapters. You'll also find these routines to be useful in your everyday programming.

We'll begin with a few common string and keyboard routines. Next, we'll add some routines to write strings to the screen. And then, building upon these, we'll write routines to pop-up and remove windows on the screen. In this book, we'll discuss in detail some major routines and categories of routines. The library included on the disk contains all these and more.

Although the library routines we'll develop will be relatively small due to space constraints, it is important to understand the overall architecture and organization of the library. We'll discuss it more after we've developed the routines.

All of the library routines are written for the small memory model. All the routines have the same basic directives for declaring the memory model, code segment and data segment, as follows:

```
.model small

.data           ; (if required)

  ... (supporting data, if needed)

.code

  ... (procedure of interest here)

  end
```

The order of the code and data segments does not matter. In your code, you can put them in any order or even alternate them, as required.

## String Operations

Strings are defined in various ways for different languages. For example, in BASIC, a string consists of a block called a string descriptor which contains a pointer to the actual string data and an integer length. In Pascal, strings are arrays of characters with a maximum length of 255. The length of a Pascal string is stored at the very first offset in the array, which is why the length is limited to fit in a one byte field (255). In C, strings are arrays of ASCII characters, followed by a single byte of zero (also called a null). These strings are commonly called ASCIIZ, the Z standing for zero. Assembly language programs usually use ASCIIZ strings, though it is not uncommon to write assembly language routines to access BASIC, C or Pascal strings. Caution should be used when accessing BASIC strings. In general, BASIC strings can only be read or modified without changing the string length. To change the length requires calling BASIC run-time routines which can be troublesome.

## String Length

The first routine for the library will be a routine to calculate the length of an ASCIIZ string. This procedure works by using the REPNE SCASB instruction to search for the terminating null byte. Before the search starts, the CX register is initialized with -1 (0FFFFh), the maximum length of a string in a 64K segment. When the REPNE SCASB instruction finishes, the CX register has been decremented for each byte scanned, including the null. Subtract CX from -2 (1 less than the initial -1, to account for the null byte) to determine the length.

```
str_len proc
;─────────────────
; Length of string
;
; inputs:  ES:DI  ptr to ASCIIZ string
;
; outputs: AX  length of string
;─────────────────

push   cx
push   di
pushf                   ; save caller's flags

mov    cx, -1           ; maximum string length
xor    al, al           ; clear AL
cld                     ; ensure correct string direction

repne  scasb            ; repeat while ES:[DI] <> 0
mov    ax, -2
sub    ax, cx           ; get string length

popf                    ; restore caller's flags
pop    di
pop    cx
ret

str_len endp
```

If the string does not contain a null, then this routine will return a length of 0FFFEh (-2). Also, a valid string length of 0FFFFh cannot be detected by this routine. Because of the way the SCASB instruction works, if the offset reaches the end of a segment, scanning will continue at the beginning of the segment (i.e. it will wrap around).

## String Copy

Next we'll write a routine to copy a string. Each byte is loaded into the AL register, copied to the destination, then checked to see if it is a null byte. If the byte is a null, then the procedure finishes, else copying continues. When finished, the length of the string copied is calculated.

```
str_copy proc
;─────────────────────
;  Copy an ASCIIZ string
;
; inputs: DS:SI ptr to source
;         ES:DI ptr to destination
;
; outputs: destination string
;          SI, DI advanced
;          AX length of source string
;─────────────────────

    push   bx
    mov    bx, di
sc_1:
    lodsb                   ; read a byte
    stosb                   ; store the byte
    or     al, al           ; check for the final null
    jnz    sc_1             ; loop back if not a null

    mov    ax, di           ; calculate length copied
    sub    ax, bx
    dec    ax

    pop    bx
    ret

str_copy  endp
```

# Keyboard Functions

Most programs require some type of keyboard input at one time or another. The Keyboard routines use the BIOS functions to check the status of the keyboard, read the keyboard buffer, and read and edit a string from the keyboard.

Writing programs to properly handle the various keyboards is somewhat more complicated than it might appear at first glance. Most advanced programs bypass the DOS functions and use the BIOS functions for keyboard input. There are several reasons for this. The primary advantage is that the BIOS gives simple, direct control of the keyboard. And although the DOS functions add some functionality to the very primitive BIOS functions, they do not add enough to make them very useful. Therefore, it is the usual practice to build more useful keyboard functions, starting with the BIOS functions.

As an example, the disk contains a library procedure named KEY_LINE_EDIT. This procedure allows full editing of an input string in a scrolling window on the screen. The editing of the input string can be controlled with the left and right cursor keys, home and end keys, and the backspace and delete keys. This is far beyond the basic functionality of the most advanced DOS function, interrupt 21h, function 0Ah. It is also not possible to build upon the DOS function to just add what it doesn't have.

It is also easiest to bypass DOS for even the simplest case of reading a single keystroke. The DOS interrupt 21h, function 1 (direct console input) requires that a second function call be made when the keystroke does not have an ASCII value (i.e. a cursor key or function key like F1).

There is one major disadvantage in using the BIOS functions. To write programs that are portable to all members of the IBM PC family, it is necessary to work with all the various keyboard types. The following routine detects whether the BIOS supports the advanced keyboard functions and whether an advanced keyboard is installed. The advanced keyboard was introduced by IBM after the IBM PC/AT began shipping. These are the 101-key keyboards (with the F11 and F12 keys).

When the new keyboard was announced there was a (valid) fear that the new machines might crash when run with older software. The reason is that these older programs did not know (and could not have known) about these new keys. The programs would probably crash and may have caused data loss when a key such as the F11 key was pressed. Because of this, the BIOS was modified in such a way as to maintain compatibility with the older software.

The original BIOS functions to read keys from the keyboard buffer were modified to intentionally ignore these new keys. But the old BIOS functions would translate the duplicated keys (the separate cursor pad, for example) so that they appeared to have the exact same scan codes as the original keys.

New BIOS functions were added that have the exact same interface as the older functions, but the new functions have full support for all the new keys. The obvious thing to do is to write every program to use the new BIOS functions for keyboard input. But, not so fast! What if the program is run on a machine that does not have the new BIOS routines? In this case, the program will just hang, waiting endlessly for a keystroke. (From about 1986 to 1989 the transition took place. Some hardware and BIOS makers were fully compatible sooner than others. Most machines shipped in 1988 and later support the new BIOS functions.)

The solution to this minor problem is to check for the BIOS support and type of keyboard installed before your program does any keyboard input. The following routines do this.

```
.model small

.code

  public key_auto_setup
  key_auto_setup proc
  ;───────────────────────
  ; Automatically determines keyboard type
  ;
  ; inputs: none
  ;
  ; outputs: key_bios_type internal variable
  ;             AL  1  newer AT support (101-key)
  ;                 2  only older PC support (83-key)
  ;───────────────────────

  mov    al, 1
  call   key_test_enhanced
  jz        ka_1
  inc       al
ka_1:
  mov       key_bios_type, al
  ret
```

```
key_auto_setup endp

  public key_test_enhanced
  key_test_enhanced proc
  ;————————————
  ; Test for a BIOS that supports the enhanced (101-key) keyboard
  ; (this routine flushes the keyboard buffer first)
  ;
  ; inputs: none
  ;
  ; outputs: ZF set if enhanced keyboard BIOS supported
  ;————————————

  push    ax
  push    cx

; flush keyboard buffer
kt_1:
  mov     ah, 1
  int     16h
  jz      kt_2
  mov     ah, 0
  int     16h
  jmp     kt_1

; load dummy char/scan code into keyboard buffer
kt_2:
  mov     cx, -1
  mov     ax, 502h
  int     16h
  or      al, al
  jnz     kt_ret

; test for the dummy char showing up
; (older keyboard BIOS routines do not pass -1 through)

  mov     ah, 10h                 ; read the char, check for the dummy one
  int     16h
  cmp     ax, -1
kt_ret:
  pop     cx
  pop     ax
  ret

key_test_enhanced endp

.data
        EXTRN key_bios_type : byte
end
```

## Check for a Key

The KEY_GET_STATUS procedure is a simple way to check the keyboard buffer to see if a key has been entered.

```
.model small

.code

    public key_get_status
    key_get_status proc
    ;────────────────────
    ; Get keyboard status (checks for enhanced keyboard)
    ;
    ; inputs: none
    ;
    ; outputs: ZF set if no key
    ;           else AL ASCII char
    ;                AH scan code
    ;────────────────────

    push    bp                  ; (preserve BP due to bug in some BIOS versions)

    mov     ah, 11h             ; (assume enhanced)
    cmp     key_bios_type, 1
    je          kgs_1
    mov         ah, 1           ; else use old routine
    kgs_1:
    int     16H
    pop     bp
    ret

    key_get_status endp

.data

    EXTRN key_bios_type : byte

    end
```

## Read a Key

The following routine reads a keystroke from the keyboard buffer.

```
.model small

.code
```

```
    public key_read_char
    key_read_char proc
    ;——————————————
    ; Read character from keyboard
    ;
    ; inputs: none
    ;
    ; outputs: AL  ASCII char
    ;          AH  scan code
    ;——————————————

    push   bp                        ; (preserve BP due to bug in some BIOS versions)

    mov    ah, 10h                   ; (assume enhanced)
    cmp    key_bios_type, 1
    je             krc_1
    mov    ah, 0                     ; else use old routine
    krc_1:
    int    16H
    pop    bp
    ret

    key_read_char endp

.data
    public key_bios_type
    key_bios_type db 0              ; 0 = unknown, 1=use new, 2=use old
end
```

## Screen Functions

The primary purpose of the screen functions is to display characters and their video attributes to the screen. These routines provide a fast, device-independent method for reading and writing text and attributes.

The secondary purpose of the screen functions is to control the operation of the mouse, if any. When the mouse cursor is displayed on the screen in one of the text modes, it is displayed in reverse video attributes. If text is written to the screen at the position of the mouse cursor and then the mouse is moved, a mouse dropping is left behind. A mouse dropping is the term used to describe the incorrect video attribute left at the previous location of the mouse cursor. To prevent this from occurring, all the screen routines turn off the mouse before performing any screen activity and then turn the mouse back on when finished. These routines are provided as macros so that the library may be easily re-assembled without the mouse functions.

```
;————————————
; Screen library Mouse macros
;————————————


mouse_off MACRO
;————————————
; hide the mouse
; (called before a screen update)
;————————————
ifndef no_mouse_code
        call scr_mouse_hide
endif

ENDM


mouse_on MACRO
;————————————
; "un"-hide the mouse
; (called after a screen update)
;————————————
ifndef no_mouse_code
        call scr_mouse_unhide
endif

ENDM


mouse_externals MACRO
;————————————
; Declare external mouse procedures.
; This macro should be placed next
; to other EXTRN directives
;————————————
ifndef no_mouse_code
        EXTRN scr_mouse_hide   : proc
        EXTRN scr_mouse_unhide : proc
endif

ENDM
```

These 3 mouse macros are in the LIBMAC.INC include file. They should be used as follows:

MOUSE_EXTERNALS:      Place the MOUSE_EXTERNALS macro after including the LIBMAC.INC include and before the ".CODE" directive. This could also be placed after the .CODE for the small memory model.

MOUSE_OFF:      The MOUSE_OFF macro is used to hide the mouse before making changes to the screen.

MOUSE_ON:      The MOUSE_ON macro is used to unhide the mouse after making changes to the screen. Be sure to properly match uses of MOUSE_OFF and MOUSE_ON. The mouse is not necessarily displayed when MOUSE_ON is used. A counter is kept by the mouse driver to determine whether to display the mouse cursor.

## Controlling Video Attributes

One of the reasons for writing our own library of functions to control the video screen is because the low-level BIOS routines do not provide a lot of useful options and are also somewhat slower. One characteristic that we'd like to have is better control over the video attributes. Three different attribute types to be used when writing to the screen are defined in this library:

- 0 - Default attributes

- 1 - Attributes provided

- 2 - Existing attributes

The attribute type and attribute byte (optionally) are provided as parameters for each routine that writes to the screen. For an attribute type of 0, a default attribute byte is used. The default attribute can be set to any value with another function call. For an attribute type of 1, the attributes must be provided by another parameter. For an attribute type of 2, there are no attributes, only the characters are written to the screen. All the details of the attribute types are taken care of by low-level routines, so the application programs are relieved of the effort of handling video attributes.

A more complex commercial version of this library (Quantasm Power Lib) has additional attribute types that allow strings to contain embedded attribute codes.

## Screen System Initialization

Before any of the screen or window routines can be used, the system must be initialized by a call to the SCR_INIT routine. This is necessary because the system must detect the type of video card installed and various parameters, such as the number of rows and columns for the current video mode.

For brevity, all these routines are not shown in the book, but are contained on the disk with all the other routines shown here. When using this library in a TSR (terminate and stay resident) program, it is necessary to call the SCR_INIT routine each time the TSR is invoked. This is because the system may be in a different configuration each time.

The next section contains an example of using SCR_INIT.

## Writing a String to the Screen

One of the most basic operations that a program would like to have for screen output is the ability to display a string at any location with any attributes. This is the purpose of SCR_DISPLAY_STRING. This routine can use ASCIIZ strings or a pointer to the first character in the string to be displayed and the length to be displayed.

The code for SCR_DISPLAY_STRING is shown below. The code is designed to be granular, as described previously. Some of the code may appear to be over granular. All these routines may be used elsewhere internal to the library or are provided for application programmers use. In addition, some routines may seem simplistic because they only perform one simple task, such as retrieving a variable stored in memory. This design methodology allows memory models to be changed with very little effort on the part of the programmer using the library.

```
.model small

    EXTRN scr_get_strlen          : proc
    EXTRN scr_set_attributes      : proc
    EXTRN scr_offset              : proc
    EXTRN scr_display_line_text   : proc

.data

    EXTRN scr_video_seg : word

.code

    public scr_display_string
    scr_display_string proc
    ;————————————————
    ; Display string with constant attributes
    ;
    ; inputs: DS:SI  string for screen
    ;         CX     len of string (if 0, then ASCIIZ)
    ;         AL     attribute type
    ;                0  default attributes
    ;                1  use attributes in AH
    ;                2  use existing attributes
    ;         AH     attributes
    ;         BH     row
    ;         BL     col
    ;————————————————

    push    ax
    push    bx
    push    cx
    push    dx
    push    di
    push    si
    push    ds
    push    es

    call    scr_get_strlen            ; get len if CX = 0
    jz      dstr_ret                  ; return if zero len string
    call    scr_set_attributes

    push    ax
    call    scr_offset
    mov     di, ax
    pop     ax
    mov     es, scr_video_seg         ; (expects DS=@DATA)
    call    scr_display_line_text

dstr_ret:
```

```
    pop     es
    pop     ds
    pop     si
    pop     di
    pop     dx
    pop     cx
    pop     bx
    pop     ax
    ret

    scr_display_string endp
end
```

```
.model small

    include libmac.inc
    mouse_externals

.code

    public scr_display_line_text
    scr_display_line_text proc near
    ;————————————
    ; Display a line
    ;
    ; inputs: ES:DI   dest on screen
    ;         DS:SI   string
    ;         CX      len
    ;         AL      0,1 use attributes in AH
    ;                 2   use existing attribute
    ;         AH      attributes (if AL = 0,1)
    ;
    ; outputs: DI, SI, AX    undefined
    ;————————————

    pushf
    mouse_off
    push    cx
    cld
    cmp     al, 2                   ; branch on attr type
    je      dlet2

; text and attr
dlet1:
    lodsb
    stosw
    loop    dlet1
    jmp     dlet_ret

; text only (use existing attributes)
dlet2:
    lodsb
    stosb
```

```
    inc     di
    loop    dlet2

dlet_ret:
  pop     cx
  mouse_on
  popf
  ret

  scr_display_line_text endp
end


.model small

.data

  public scr_default_attr
  scr_default_attr  db 07h

.code


  public scr_set_attributes
  scr_set_attributes proc
  ;————————————————
  ; Set attributes (used internally to setup attr)
  ;
  ; inputs: AL attribute type
  ;             0   default attributes
  ;             1   use attributes in AH
  ;             2   use existing attr
  ;         AH  attributes
  ;         DS  @data
  ;
  ; outputs: AH attributes
  ;————————————————

  or      al, al
  jnz     sa_ret
  mov     ah, scr_default_attr

sa_ret:
  ret

  scr_set_attributes endp
end
```

```
.model small

  EXTRN scr_get_max_col : proc

.code
```

```
      public  scr_offset
      scr_offset proc
      ;———————————
      ; Calculate screen offset from row, col
      ;
      ; inputs: BH      row
      ;         BL      col
      ;
      ; outputs: AX     screen offset
      ;———————————

      push    bx
      push    dx

      call    scr_get_max_col
      xchg    ax, dx                  ; DL = max col

      mov     al, bh
      xor     bh, bh
      mul     dl                      ; mult row by 80 (or max col)
      add     ax, bx                  ; add column offset
      add     ax, ax                  ; mult by 2

      pop     dx
      pop     bx
      ret

      scr_offset endp
end
```

```
.model small

.data

  EXTRN scr_max_row : word
  EXTRN scr_max_col : word

.code

  public  scr_get_max_col
  scr_get_max_col proc
  ;———————————
  ; Get the maximum number of screen columns
  ;
  ; inputs: none
  ;
  ; output: AL max col
  ;         (AH always 0)
  ;———————————

  push    ds

  mov     ax, @data
  mov     ds, ax
```

```
        mov     ax, scr_max_col
        cmp     ax, 40
        jae     sg_1
        mov     ax, 80                  ; defaults to 80 if < 40

sg_1:
        pop     ds
        ret

        scr_get_max_col endp

        public scr_get_max_row
        scr_get_max_row proc
        ;────────────────
        ; Get the maximum number of screen rows
        ;
        ; inputs: none
        ;
        ; output: AL max row
        ;          (AH always 0)
        ;────────────────

        push    ds

        mov     ax, @data
        mov     ds, ax

        mov     ax, scr_max_row
        or      ax, ax
        jnz     mr_1
        mov     al, 25                  ; defaults to 25 if = 0

mr_1:
        pop     ds
        ret

        scr_get_max_row endp
end
```

```
.model small

    EXTRN str_len : proc

.code

    public scr_get_strlen
    scr_get_strlen proc near
    ;────────────────
```

```
        ; Get strlen of string
        ; (used internally to get len when CX = 0)
        ;
        ; inputs: DS:SI string
        ;         CX len or 0
        ;
        ; outputs: CX len
        ;          ZF set if CX = 0
        ;─────────────────────

        push    ax
        or      cx, cx
        jnz     gsl_1
        call    scr_str_len
        mov     cx, ax
        or      cx, cx

gsl_1:
        pop     ax
        ret

        scr_get_strlen endp

        public scr_str_len
        scr_str_len proc
        ;─────────────────
        ; Len of string at DS:SI
        ;─────────────────

        push    di
        push    es

        push    ds
        pop     es
        mov     di, si

        call    str_len

        pop     es
        pop     di
        ret

        scr_str_len  endp

end
```

The SCR_DISPLAY_STRING function may appear to be complicated from looking at the source code, but the opposite is true when observing its use. Here is an example program that uses the SCR_DISPLAY_STRING function - see LST19-1.ASM on the disk:

```
;///////////////////////////////
;Hello World example using scr_display_string
;///////////////////////////////
  .model small

    .stack

  .code

    EXTRN scr_init          : proc
    EXTRN scr_display_string : proc

    main proc

    mov    ax, @data
    mov    ds, ax
    mov    es, ax

    call   scr_init

    lea    si, message              ; ptr to string
    mov    cx, 0                     ; indicate string is ASCIIZ
    mov    al, 0                     ; use default attributes
    mov    bl, 34                    ; column
    mov    bh, 10                    ; row

    call   scr_display_string

    mov    ax, 4c00h                 ; successful completion
    int    21h

    main endp

  .data

    message db 'Hello World',0

end main
```

## Fill and Blank Screen

The next routines fill the screen (or a portion of it) with a specified character and attribute. The SCR_BLANK_SCREEN routine uses the BIOS function to erase the screen. The SCR_FILL_SCREEN routine allows a portion of the screen to be filled. The count (CX) is considered a continuous stream, wrapping from the end of one row to the start of the next row down.

We'll start with SCR_FILL_SCREEN. Notice that the structure of this routine is similar to that of the previous ones. Once the basic internal routines are built, it becomes easier to construct new routines to perform other similar low-level functions.

```
.model small

  include libmac.inc

  EXTRN scr_offset          : proc
  EXTRN scr_set_attributes  : proc
  mouse_externals

.data

  EXTRN scr_video_seg : word

.code

  public scr_fill_screen
  scr_fill_screen proc
  ;————————————
  ; Fill screen area with constant character
  ;    and attributes
  ;
  ; inputs: DL    char
  ;         CX    count of characters to fill
  ;         AL    attribute type
  ;               0  default attributes
  ;               1  attributes in AH
  ;               2  existing attr
  ;         AH    attributes (for type = 1)
  ;         BH    starting row
  ;         BL    starting column
  ;
  ;————————————
  pushf
  push    ax
  push    bx
  push    cx
  push    dx
  push    di
  push    si
  push    es

  jcxz    sf_exit

  call    scr_set_attributes

  push    ax
  call    scr_offset
  mov     di, ax
  pop     ax
  mov     es, scr_video_seg
```

```
    mouse_off

    xchg    al, dl
    cld
    cmp     dl, 2                    ; check for existing attr
    je      sf_3
    rep     stosw

sf_ret:
    mouse_on
sf_exit:
    pop     es
    pop     si
    pop     di
    pop     dx
    pop     cx
    pop     bx
    pop     ax
    popf
    ret

sf_3:
    stosb                           ; use existing attr
    inc     di
    loop    sf_3
    jmp     sf_ret

    scr_fill_screen endp

end
```

```
.model small

    include libmac.inc

    EXTRN scr_get_max_col : proc
    EXTRN scr_get_max_row : proc
    mouse_externals

.code

    public scr_blank_screen
    scr_blank_screen proc
    ;————————————
    ; Blank the screen (uses BIOS scroll)
    ;
    ; inputs: AL attributes
    ;
    ;————————————

    push    ax
    push    bx
    push    cx
    push    dx
```

```
    push    bp

    mov     bh, al              ; attributes for blanked area
    xor     cx, cx              ; upper left row & column
    call    scr_get_max_row
    mov     dh, al              ; lower row
    call    scr_get_max_col
    mov     dl, al              ; right column
    dec     dl                  ; adjust to zero relative
    dec     dh
    mov     ax, 0600h           ; BIOS scroll function

    mouse_off
    int     10h                 ; call BIOS
    mouse_on

    pop     bp
    pop     dx
    pop     cx
    pop     bx
    pop     ax
    ret

    scr_blank_screen endp

end
```

The following example uses the SCR_BLANK_SCREEN and SCR_FILL_SCREEN functions - see LST19-2.ASM on the disk.

```
;////////////////////////////////
;Example using QWL Library
;and scr_blank_screen and scr_fill_screen
;////////////////////////////////
  .model small

  .stack

  .code

  EXTRN scr_init          : proc
  EXTRN scr_fill_screen   : proc
  EXTRN scr_blank_screen  : proc
  EXTRN scr_display_string : proc
  EXTRN key_read_char     : proc

  main proc

  mov     ax, @data
  mov     ds, ax
  mov     es, ax

  call    scr_init
```

```
        mov     al, 7                   ; attributes
        call    scr_blank_screen

        mov     dl, 176                 ; fill portion of screen
        mov     cx, 10*80               ; with dot pattern
        mov     al, 0
        mov     bl, 0
        mov     bh, 5
        call    scr_fill_screen

        lea     si, message
        mov     cx, 0                   ; indicate ASCIIZ string
        mov     al, 0                   ; use default attributes
        mov     bl, 34                  ; column
        mov     bh, 10                  ; row
        call    scr_display_string

        call    key_read_char           ; wait for keystroke

        mov     ax,4c00h                ; successful completion
        int     21h

    main endp

.data

    message db 'Hello World',0

end main
```

# Window Functions

The Window routines perform direct reads and writes to (or from) video memory to display and manipulate rectangular, overlapping windows. Any number of windows may be displayed (nested and overlapped), based on available memory. A window is displayed by calling WIN_POPUP and removed by calling WIN_REMOVE.

The concept for the library window system in this book is that when a routine writes the data to the screen, it must first save the underlying screen data. When the window is removed, it must restore the data to the screen. When the WIN_POPUP routine is called, one of the parameters is a pointer to a buffer to store the screen data being overwritten. In contrast, GUI's (graphical user interfaces), such as Microsoft Windows, usually require the program responsible for a window to redraw the data in a window when it becomes visible again.

To use this system effectively in a complex program, you would need to keep a list of these pointers and allocate/deallocate memory as required. (The Quantasm Power Lib has three windowing systems, two of which provide a built-in memory management feature.)

The following is the declaration of the window data structure (from LIBSTRUC.INC):

```
window_struc struc
  win_col        db ?         ; column of upper left corner (zero based)
  win_row        db ?         ; row of upper left corner (zero based)
  win_height     db ?         ; height
  win_width      db ?         ; width
  win_attr       dw ?         ; ptr to attribute byte
  win_left_ind   db ?         ; left indent for text
  win_top_ind    db ?         ; top indent for text
  win_str_ptr    dw ?         ; ptr to ASCIIZ array
window_struc ends
```

## Save Window

The first routine we'll study will save a window from the screen to a buffer. This is a straight-forward routine that we'll need to use internal to the WIN_POPUP routine later.

```
.model small

  include libstruc.inc
  include libmac.inc
  mouse_externals

  EXTRN scr_col_setup      : proc
  EXTRN win_setup_screen_loc : proc

.data

  EXTRN scr_video_seg : word

.code

  public win_save_window
  win_save_window proc
  ;────────────────────
  ; Saves window area from screen (char/attr)
  ;
  ; inputs: DS:DI ptr to buffer for screen data
  ;         BL    left column
```

```
;               BH      top row
;               DL      width
;               DH      height
;
; outputs:
;               AX      undefined
;————————————————

        push    bx
        push    cx
        push    dx
        push    di
        push    si
        push    ds
        push    bp
        push    es

        push    ds
        pop     es

        call    scr_col_setup
        mov     ds, scr_video_seg
        call    win_setup_screen_loc
        mov     si, ax                  ; save screen offset

        or      dx, dx                  ; exit if zero width
        jz      wsw_ret
        mov     bx, cx                  ; line count
        or      bx, bx                  ; exit if zero lines
        jz      wsw_ret
        mouse_off

wsw_1:
        push    si
        mov     cx, dx                  ; words to copy
        rep     movsw                   ; copy char/attr for line
        pop     si
        add     si, bp                  ; point to next video line
        dec     bx
        jnz     wsw_1                    ; repeat for next line
        mouse_on

wsw_ret:
        pop     es
        pop     bp
        pop     ds
        pop     si
        pop     di
        pop     dx
        pop     cx
        pop     bx
        ret
```

```
    win_save_window endp

end
```

```
.model small

.data

    EXTRN scr_max_col : byte

.code

    public win_setup_screen_loc
    win_setup_screen_loc proc
    ;─────────────────────
    ; Setup window parameters from corners
    ;
    ; inputs: BL  left column
    ;         BH  top row
    ;         DL  width
    ;         DH  height
    ;
    ; outputs: AX screen offset
    ;          CX number of lines
    ;          DX characters per line
    ;─────────────────────

    push    bx
    push    ds

    mov     ax, @data
    mov     ds, ax

    mov     al, bh
    mov     cl, byte ptr scr_max_col
    shl     cl, 1
    mul     cl
    xchg    ax, bx
    xor     ah, ah
    add     ax, ax
    add     ax, bx

    xor     cx, cx
    mov     cl, dh
    xor     dh, dh

    pop     ds
    pop     bx
    ret

    win_setup_screen_loc endp

end
```

```
.model small

  EXTRN scr_get_max_col : proc

.code

  public scr_col_setup
  scr_col_setup proc
  ;───────────────
  ; Return bytes per line
  ;
  ; outputs: BP  scr_max_col * 2
  ;───────────────

  xchg    ax, bp                      ; save ax
  call    scr_get_max_col
  add     ax, ax
  xchg    ax, bp                      ; restore ax
  ret

  scr_col_setup endp

end
```

## Popup Window

The win_popup routine pops up a window on the screen, preserving the screen data being overwritten in a supplied buffer. The routine is very simple to use - there are two parameters, a pointer to the window data structure and a pointer to the buffer for the screen data being preserved.

The operation of the routine itself is also relatively simple. Some initializations are performed, the screen data is preserved and then the specified text is displayed. The details of all the operations are performed in lower level routines.

Of particular interest are the WIN_DISPLAY_WINDOW and WIN_XFER_BUFFER routines. These routines are used to format the text in a temporary buffer and then display the text. Strings that are too long are clipped to fit into the window area.

```
.model small

  EXTRN scr_init              : proc
  EXTRN scr_mouse_init        : proc
  EXTRN win_get_coordinates   : proc
  EXTRN win_push_window       : proc
  EXTRN win_display_area      : proc
```

```
.data

   EXTRN scr_video_seg : word

.code

   public win_popup
   win_popup proc
   ;─────────────────
   ; Display a popup window
   ;
   ; inputs: DS:SI  window structure
   ;         ES:DI  buffer for screen data
   ;
   ; outputs: CF set if error
   ;          AL error code
   ;             1 window off screen
   ;             2 not enough buffer space
   ;             3 too many windows
   ;
   ;─────────────────

   push    bx
   push    cx
   push    dx
   push    di
   push    si
   push    bp
   push    ds
   push    es

; auto setup if scr_video_seg not set

   cmp     scr_video_seg, 0
   jnz     wp_1
   call    scr_init
   call    scr_mouse_init

wp_1:
   call    win_get_coordinates

; save screen window area

   call    win_push_window
   jc      wp_ret                       ; returns with error code

; display the window data and/or blank out the area

   xor     cx, cx                       ; set 0 indent
   call    win_display_area
   clc                                  ; successful

wp_ret:
   pop     es
   pop     ds
```

```
    pop     bp
    pop     si
    pop     di
    pop     dx
    pop     cx
    pop     bx
    ret

    win_popup endp

end
```

```
.model small

    include libstruc.inc

.code

    public win_get_coordinates
    win_get_coordinates proc
    ;————————————
    ; Get the window column/row and width/height
    ;
    ; inputs: DS:SI  window structure
    ;
    ; outputs: BL     col
    ;          BH     row
    ;          DL     width
    ;          DH     height
    ;————————————

    mov     bl, [si].win_col
    mov     bh, [si].win_row
    mov     dl, [si].win_width
    mov     dh, [si].win_height
    ret

    win_get_coordinates endp

end
```

```
.model small

    include libstruc.inc

    EXTRN win_check_coordinates  : proc
    EXTRN win_save_window        : proc
    EXTRN cur_get_pos_type       : proc

.code

    public win_push_window
    win_push_window proc
```

```
;────────────────
; Save window parameters and data in specified buffer
;
; inputs: BL column
;         BH row
;         DL width
;         DH height
;         DS @data
;         ES:DI save buffer
;
; outputs: CF set if error
;          AL = 1 window off screen
;
;────────────────

        push    bx
        push    cx
        push    dx
        push    di
        push    si
        push    ds

        call    win_check_coordinates
        mov     al, 1
        jc      pw_ret

        push    es
        pop     ds

; save items in buffer

        mov     si, di
        mov     [si].scr_row, bh
        mov     [si].scr_col, bl
        mov     [si].scr_width, dl
        mov     [si].scr_height, dh
        lea     di, [si].scr_cur_type+2        ; end of struct+1
        mov     [si].scr_buffer, di
        push    dx
        call    cur_get_pos_type
        mov     [si].scr_cur_pos, dx
        mov     [si].scr_cur_type, cx
        pop     dx

; save the screen data

        call    win_save_window
        clc                                    ; successful

pw_ret:
        pop     ds
        pop     si
        pop     di
        pop     dx
        pop     cx
```

```
    pop     bx
    ret

    win_push_window endp

end
```

```
.model small

    include libstruc.inc

    EXTRN win_determine_attr: proc
    EXTRN win_fill_window   : proc
    EXTRN win_display_window: proc

.code

    public win_display_area
    win_display_area proc
    ;————————————
    ; Display window area data
    ;
    ; inputs: DS:SI window structure
    ;         BL    column
    ;         BH    row

    ;         CL    indent amount
    ;         DL    width
    ;         DH    height
    ;
    ; outputs: AX   undefined
    ;          BX   undefined
    ;          DX   undefined
    ;
    ;————————————

    push    si

    call    win_determine_attr

    mov     al, ' '
    call    win_fill_window

; adjust starting row, height

    add     bh, [si].win_top_ind
    sub     dh, [si].win_top_ind

; set left indent, width

    add     bl, [si].win_left_ind
    sub     dl, [si].win_left_ind

; setup string source
```

```
    mov    si, [si].win_str_ptr
    or     si, si
    jz     dwa_ret

; display

    call   win_display_window

dwa_ret:
    pop        si
    ret

    win_display_area endp

end
```

```
.model small

.data

    EXTRN scr_max_row : byte
    EXTRN scr_max_col : byte

.code

    public win_check_coordinates
    win_check_coordinates proc
    ;————————————————
    ; Check to insure that coordinates are OK
    ;
    ; inputs: BL  column
    ;         BH  row
    ;         DL  width
    ;         DH  height
    ;         DS  @data
    ;
    ; outputs: CF set if error
    ;————————————————

    push       bx

    add        bx, dx                          ; bl = column + width
                                               ; bh = row + height

    cmp        bh, byte ptr scr_max_row
    ja         wcc_err

    cmp        bl, byte ptr scr_max_col
    ja         wcc_err
    clc

cc_ret:
    pop        bx
    ret
```

```
wcc_err:
  stc
  jmp      cc_ret

  win_check_coordinates endp

end
```

```
.model small

  include libstruc.inc
  include libmac.inc

.data

  EXTRN scr_default_attr : byte

.code

  public win_determine_attr
  win_determine_attr proc
  ;————————————
  ; Determine attributes required for window
  ;
  ; inputs: DS:SI  window structure
  ;
  ; outputs: AH attributes
  ;————————————

  push     di
  mov      di, [si].win_attr
  or       di, di                              ; if ptr is zero, use default
  jz       wda_2
  mov      ah, [di]

wda_ret:
  pop      di
  ret

wda_2:
  mov      ah, scr_default_attr
  jmp      wda_ret

  win_determine_attr endp

end
```

```
.model small

  include libmac.inc
  mouse_externals
```

```
   EXTRN win_setup_screen_loc : proc
   EXTRN scr_col_setup        : proc

.data

   EXTRN scr_video_seg : word

.code

   public win_fill_window
   win_fill_window proc
   ;————————————
   ; Fill window with constant char/attr
   ;
   ; inputs: AL  ASCII value
   ;         AH  attribute
   ;         BL  left column
   ;         BH  top row
   ;         DL  width
   ;         DH  height
   ;         DS  @data
   ;
   ;————————————

   push    bx
   push    cx
   push    dx
   push    di
   push    si
   push    bp
   push    es

   push    ax
   mov     es, scr_video_seg
   call    win_setup_screen_loc
   mov     di, ax
   pop     ax
   call    scr_col_setup

   or      dx, dx                          ; exit if zero width
   jz      fw_ret
   or      cx, cx                          ; exit if zero lines
   jz      fw_ret

   mov     bx, cx
   mouse_off

fw_1:
   push    di
   mov     cx, dx
   rep     stosw
   pop     di
   add     di, bp
   dec     bx
   jnz     fw_1
```

```
    mouse_on

fw_ret:
    pop     es
    pop     bp
    pop     si
    pop     di
    pop     dx
    pop     cx
    pop     bx
    ret

    win_fill_window endp

end
```

```
.model small

    include libequ.inc

    EXTRN win_xfer_buf       : proc
    EXTRN win_restore_window : proc

.data

    EXTRN scr_default_attr : byte

win_tmp_len     dw max_win_size
win_tmp_ptr     dd win_buf
win_buf         db max_win_size dup(0)

.code

    public win_display_window
    win_display_window proc
    ;————————————————
    ; Display window from ASCIIZ strings
    ; (clips excess data)
    ;
    ; inputs: DS:SI buffer of ASCIIZ strings
    ;              (followed by an additional null)
    ;         AL    default ASCII char (normally 0 or 20h)
    ;         AH    attributes (0 = use default)
    ;         CL    indent amount
    ;         BL    left col
    ;         BH    top row
    ;         DL    width
    ;         DH    height
    ;
    ; outputs: AX   undefined
    ;————————————————

    pushf
```

```
        push    bx
        push    cx
        push    dx
        push    di
        push    si
        push    bp
        push    ds
        push    es

        cmp     cl, dl                          ; insure indent not too much
        jl      dw0
        xor     cl, cl

dw0:
        add     bl, cl                          ; move col over
        sub     dl, cl                          ; reduce width

        mov     bp, bx                          ; save row/col

        cmp     al, 0                           ; default char
        jne     dw1
        mov     al, ' '

dw1:
        cmp     ah, 0                           ; attributes
        jne     dw2
        mov     ah, scr_default_attr

dw2:

; fill buffer with default char and attributes

        push    cx
        push    es
        mov     cx, win_tmp_len
        shr     cx, 1
        les     di, win_tmp_ptr

        cld
        rep     stosw
        pop     es
        pop     cx

        mov     cl, dh                          ; height
        mov     bh, dl                          ; width

; fill buffer with text

        push    dx
        xor     dx, dx                          ; no left margin
        push    es
        les     di, win_tmp_ptr
        call    win_xfer_buf
        pop     es
        pop     dx
```

```
; copy tmp buffer to the screen

  mov       bx, bp                              ; restore row/col
  lds       si, win_tmp_ptr
  call      win_restore_window

dw_ret:
  pop       es
  pop       ds
  pop       bp
  pop       si
  pop       di
  pop       dx
  pop       cx
  pop       bx

  popf
  ret

  win_display_window endp

end
```

```
.model small

.code

  public win_xfer_buf
  win_xfer_buf proc
  ;————————————————
  ; Transfer strings to window buffer
  ;
  ; inputs:  AH    attributes
  ;          ES:DI destination ptr
  ;          DS:SI source ASCIIZ strings
  ;          BH    window width
  ;          CL    window height
  ;          DX    string left margin
  ;
  ; outputs: AX, BX, CX, DI, SI   undefined
  ;————————————————

  push      bp
  xor       ch, ch

fwb1:
  mov       bl, bh                              ; reset width
  or        dx, dx
  jz        fwb3

  mov       bp, dx

; scan by non-displayed portion of string
```

```
fwb2:
    lodsb                                       ; read a char
    or      al, al
    jz      fwb6                                ; done with line if a null
    dec     bp
    jnz     fwb2

fwb3:
    lodsb                                       ; read a char
    or      al, al
    jz      fwb6                                ; done with line if a null
    stosb                                       ; store a char
    inc     di
    dec     bl                                  ; check for too many char
    jnz     fwb3

fwb4:
    lodsb                                       ; scan to null (clipping line)
    or      al, al
    jnz     fwb4

fwb6:
    push    dx
    xor     dx, dx                              ; skip DI to next window line
    mov     dl, bl
    shl     dx, 1
    add     di, dx
    pop     dx
    cmp     byte ptr [si], 0                    ; check for end of window text
    je      fwb7
    loop    fwb1                                ; loop for next line

fwb7:
    pop     bp
    ret

    win_xfer_buf endp

end
```

## Remove Window

The final routine needed for a windowing system is to be able to remove a window by restoring the previous contents of the screen. This is done by the WIN_REMOVE function. In addition, this routine restores the cursor type and location that were saved in the WIN_PUSH_WINDOW routine. You can think of the operation of these routines like a stack, pushing and popping windows.

```
.model small

    include libstruc.inc
```

```
        EXTRN win_restore_window: proc
        EXTRN cur_set_pos       : proc
        EXTRN cur_set_scan      : proc

    .code

        public win_remove
        win_remove proc
        ;————————————————
        ; Remove window from the screen, restore screen data
        ;
        ; inputs: ES:DI ptr to buffer of screen data
        ;           DS    @data
        ;————————————————

        push    ax
        push    bx
        push    cx
        push    dx
        push    di
        push    si
        push    ds

        push    es
        pop     ds

    ; restore the screen

        mov     si, [di].scr_buffer
        mov     bh, [di].scr_row
        mov     bl, [di].scr_col
        mov     dl, [di].scr_width
        mov     dh, [di].scr_height
        call    win_restore_window

    ; restore the cursor

        mov     ax, [di].scr_cur_pos
        call    cur_set_pos
        mov     ax, [di].scr_cur_type
        call    cur_set_scan

        pop     ds
        pop     si
        pop     di
        pop     dx
        pop     cx
        pop     bx
        pop     ax
        ret

        win_remove endp

    end
```

```
.model small

  include libmac.inc
  mouse_externals

  EXTRN scr_col_setup      : proc
  EXTRN win_setup_screen_loc : proc

.data

  EXTRN scr_video_seg : word

.code

  public win_restore_window
  win_restore_window proc
  ;─────────────────────
  ; inputs: DS:SI buffer with screen char and attr
  ;         BL    left column
  ;         BH    top row
  ;         DL    width
  ;         DH    height
  ;
  ; outputs: AX   undefined
  ;─────────────────

  push    bx
  push    cx
  push    dx
  push    di
  push    si
  push    bp
  push    es

  call    scr_col_setup
  mov     es, scr_video_seg
  call    win_setup_screen_loc
  mov     di, ax
  or      dx, dx
  jz      rw_ret

  mouse_off

rw_1:
  push    cx
  push    di
  mov     cx, dx
  rep     movsw
  pop     di
  pop     cx
  add     di, bp
  loop rw_1
  mouse_on

rw_ret:
```

```
        pop      es
        pop      bp
        pop      si
        pop      di
        pop      dx
        pop      cx
        pop      bx
        ret

        win_restore_window endp

end
```

# Summary

Now that we've seen all the basic functions in the library, it is time to pull them all together in an example program. The example does this by using the WIN_POPUP routine to popup a message on the screen after the screen has been erased. In addition, a new function, the SCR_SETUP_ATTR_TBL routine will be introduced.

SCR_SETUP_ATTR_TBL is another important feature of the library that easily allows application programmers to control the video attributes in a program. This example only uses two video attributes, but it could just as easily use any number. The window structure requires a pointer to a video attribute byte. The use of a table allows any number of mono and color video attributes to be defined for any purpose internal to the program. The table is arranged in records of mono and color attribute bytes. Because they are all contained in one table, they can easily be configured by some type of user controllable option. The SCR_SETUP_ATTR_TBL routine then copies the color attributes on top of the mono attributes if the video display is color. (Switching between monitors on a dual-monitor system is not automatically supported and would require an additional routine to refresh the attributes after popping up in a TSR.) Below is LST19-3.ASM from the disk.

```
;////////////////////////////
;Example using win_popup
;////////////////////////////
  .model small

    include libstruc.inc

  .stack

  .code

    EXTRN scr_init            : proc
    EXTRN win_popup           : proc
    EXTRN win_remove          : proc
    EXTRN key_read_char       : proc
    EXTRN scr_blank_screen    : proc
    EXTRN scr_setup_attr_tbl  : proc

    main proc

    mov     ax, @data
    mov     ds, ax
    mov     es, ax

; initialize library for screen

    call    scr_init

    lea     si, attr_tbl
    mov     cx, attr_tbl_len
    call    scr_setup_attr_tbl

; erase screen

    mov     al, attr1
    call    scr_blank_screen

; popup window

    lea     si, win1
    lea     di, buf1
    call    win_popup
    jc      exit                              ; exit on error

; wait for key
```

```
    call    key_read_char                       ; wait for keystroke

; remove window

    call    win_remove
    xor     al,al                               ; successful completion
exit:
    mov     ah, 4ch
    int     21h


    main endp

.data

    h1      equ 4
    w1      equ 20
    win1 window_struc <30, 10,  h1, w1,  attr2, 7, 1, str1>
                ; col, row, ht, wid, attr,  l, t, strings

    attr_tbl label byte
    attr1   db 7h,  7h
    attr2   db 70h, 17h
    attr_tbl_len equ ($ - attr_tbl)/2

    str1    db ' Hello',0
            db ' World',0
            db 0

    buf1    db (size screen_struc) + ( h1 * w1 * 2) dup (0)

    end main
```

# Advanced Assembly Language Techniques

## Introduction

In this chapter we'll work on some example programs using more advanced techniques. These techniques will make it easier for you to program larger projects in assembly and usually make the code smaller and/or faster as well. Some of the examples are too large for describing in a book, but we will be making good use of the library routines developed in Chapter 19.

# Using Tables

Using tables in the right situations can make programs that might otherwise be fairly complex seem rather simple. That is, they seem to be simple once you've discovered how to make the data drive the program rather than the other way around. One of the most powerful reasons for using assembly language is the ability to define and declare complex data structures with relative ease.

In the next examples, we'll use the screen functions in the library to display data of various types on the screen. We'll see how easy it is to write code that uses the data to determine what to do.

In the first example, we'll use a table for each item to be displayed. The table will look like this:

```
dw ptr
db col, row
```

where:          ptr is a near pointer to an ASCIIZ string
                col is the screen column
                row is the screen row

The program will step through each record in the table, load the required parameters and call the SCR_DISPLAY_STRING routine. The table is terminated with a record that begins with a word containing a value of -1. The program below is LST20-1.ASM on the disk.

```
;/////////////////////////////////
;Table driven screen display using QWL
;/////////////////////////////////
      .model small

      .stack

      .code

            includelib qwl

            extrn scr_init            : proc
            extrn scr_display_string  : proc
            extrn scr_blank_screen    : proc
            extrn mem_shrink          : proc
```

```
        main proc

        mov     ax, @data
        mov     ds, ax

        call    mem_shrink              ; discard extra memory

        push    ds
        pop     es

; initialize library for screen

        call    scr_init

; erase the screen

        mov     al, 7                   ; attr to erase with
        call    scr_blank_screen

; display the text

        call    display_info

; terminate program

        mov     ax, 4ch                 ; successful completion
        int     21h

        main endp

        display_info proc
        ;———————————————
        ; Display table of data
        ;———————————————

        lea     di, disp_tbl

dsp_1:
        mov     si, [di]
        cmp     si, -1                  ; check for end of table
        je      dsp_ret

; load parameters for display

        mov     bl, [di+2]              ; column
        mov     bh, [di+3]              ; row
        mov     al, 1                   ; provide attribute
        mov     ah, 7                   ; attributes
        xor     cx, cx                  ; indicate ASCIIZ string
        call    scr_display_string

        add     di, 4
        jmp     dsp_1

dsp_ret:
```

```
        ret

        display_info endp

.data

        disp_tbl label byte

        dw str1                           ; ptr to string
         db 1,3                           ; column, row
        dw str2
         db 1,4
        dw str3
         db 1,5
        dw str4
         db 40,3
        dw str5
         db 40,4
        dw str6
         db 40,5


        dw -1                             ; end of table

        str1 db 'First Name:',0
        str2 db 'Last Name:',0
        str3 db 'Course:',0
        str4 db 'Date:',0
        str5 db 'Grade:',0
        str6 db 'Credits:',0

    end main
```

## Tables with Numeric Data

In this next example, we'll make some modifications to allow the display data to be string or numeric data. Here is what a data record will look like in this example:

```
dw ptr
db col, row
db flag
```

where:    ptr is a near pointer to a ASCIIZ string
col is the screen column
row is the screen row
flag is 0 for string, 1 for number

If you're worried about optimum performance, you may be inclined to pad this structure with an extra byte, so that word-size memory accesses are always on even byte boundaries. In this case, you would be wasting memory because the few cycles saved would not be noticed in the thousands of cycles required to display data on the screen. In other situations, you may want to take data alignment into account when constructing data structures.

The basic DISPLAY_INFO procedure only needs a small modification and then we need to add the code to convert integers to strings. We'll also add some additional data. See LST20-2.ASM on the disk.

```
;//////////////////////////////////////
;Table driven screen display with numeric data
;//////////////////////////////////////
      .model small

      .stack

      .code

            includelib qwl

            extrn scr_init            : proc
            extrn scr_display_string  : proc
            extrn scr_blank_screen    : proc
            extrn mem_shrink          : proc
            extrn num_int_to_ascii    : proc


            main proc

            mov     ax, @data
            mov     ds, ax

            call    mem_shrink                    ; discard extra memory

            push    ds
            pop     es

      ; initialize library for screen

            call    scr_init

      ; erase the screen

            mov     al, 7                         ; attr to erase with
            call    scr_blank_screen

      ; display the text
            call    display_info
```

```
        ; terminate program

                mov     ax, 4ch                         ; successful completion
                int     21h

                main endp

                display_info proc
                ;──────────────────
                ; Display table of data
                ;──────────────────

                lea     di, disp_tbl

        dsp_1:
                mov     si, [di]
                cmp     si, -1
                je      dsp_ret

        ; check for numerical data

                cmp     byte ptr [di+4], 0
                je      dsp_3

                push    di
                mov     ax, [si]                        ; get value
                lea     di, temp_num
                call    num_int_to_ascii
                mov     si, di
                pop     di

; load parameters for display

        dsp_3:
                mov     bl, [di+2]                      ; column
                mov     bh, [di+3]                      ; row
                mov     al, 1                           ; provide attributes
                mov     ah, 7                           ; attributes
                xor     cx, cx                          ; indicate ASCIIZ string

                call    scr_display_string

                add     di, 5
                jmp     dsp_1

        dsp_ret:
                ret

                display_info endp

        .data

                disp_tbl label byte

                dw str1                                 ; ptr to string
```

```
          db 1,3                                ; column, row
          db 0                                  ; string type
       dw str2
          db 1,4
          db 0
       dw str3
          db 1,5
          db 0
       dw str4
          db 40,3
          db 0
       dw str5
          db 40,4
          db 0
       dw str6
          db 40,5
          db 0

       dw str1a
          db 13,3
          db 0
       dw str2a
          db 13,4
          db 0
       dw str3a
          db 13,5
          db 0
       dw str4a
          db 50,3
          db 0
       dw num5a
          db 50,4
          db 1
       dw num6a
          db 50,5
          db 1

       dw -1                                    ; end of table

str1   db 'First Name:',0
str2   db 'Last Name:',0
str3   db 'Course:',0
str4   db 'Date:',0
str5   db 'Grade:',0
str6   db 'Credits:',0

str1a db 'John',0
str2a db 'Smith',0
str3a db 'CS101',0
str4a db '01/01/95',0
num5a dw 90
num6a dw 3

temp_num db 7 dup(0)                            ; reserve space for signed integer

end main
```

## Tables with Conversion Types

The next step will be to completely generalize the DISPLAY_INFO procedure so that any new data type can be added without any further code, except to generate the string to be displayed. To do this we'll simply allow the flag byte in the data record to have any value. This value will correspond to an index into a table of procedures. Each of these procedures will have the same inputs and outputs. The only input will be a near pointer (SI) to the data (which could have any format and be different for each type). The outputs will be a pointer to the string to be displayed (SI) and the length of the string (CX). If the string is an ASCIIZ string, then the length will be set to 0. A new data type has also been added for the grade. The conversion for this type takes a numeric value and converts it to a string. For example, a value of 90 converts to an 'A'. See LST20-3.ASM on the disk.

```
;////////////////////////////////////////
;Table driven screen display with conversion types
;////////////////////////////////////////
    .model small

    .stack

    .code

        includelib qwl

        extrn scr_init           : proc
        extrn scr_display_string : proc
        extrn scr_blank_screen   : proc
        extrn mem_shrink         : proc
        extrn num_int_to_ascii   : proc


        main proc

        mov    ax, @data
        mov    ds, ax

        call   mem_shrink                    ; discard extra memory

        push   ds
        pop    es

; initialize library for screen

        call   scr_init

; erase the screen
```

```
        mov     al, 7                           ; attr to erase with
        call    scr_blank_screen

; display the text

        call    display_info

; terminate program

        mov     ax, 4ch                         ; successful completion
        int     21h

        main endp

        display_info proc
;────────────────────
; Display table of data
;────────────────────

        lea     di, disp_tbl

dsp_1:
        mov     si, [di]
        cmp     si, -1
        je      dsp_ret                         ; check for end of table
        xor     bx, bx
        mov     bl, [di+4]                      ; get conversion type
        add     bx, bx
        call    CS:convert[bx]                  ; call conversion routine

; load parameters for display

    dsp_3:
        mov     bl, [di+2]                      ; column
        mov     bh, [di+3]                      ; row
        mov     al, 1                           ; provide attributes
        mov     ah, 7                           ; attributes
        call    scr_display_string

        add     di, 5
        jmp     dsp_1

    dsp_ret:
        ret
        convert label word
        dw conv_string
        dw conv_num
        dw conv_grade

        display_info endp

        conv_string proc

        xor     cx, cx
        ret
```

```
                conv_string endp

                conv_num proc

        push    di
        mov     ax, [si]                        ; get value
        lea     di, temp_num                    ; ptr to dest
        call    num_int_to_ascii
        mov     si, di                          ; return ptr to string
        xor     cx, cx
        pop     di
        ret

                conv_num endp

                conv_grade proc
        ;————————————————
        ; Convert numerical grade to letter
        ;————————————————

        mov     al, [si]                        ; get value
        lea     si, num_to_grade

cg_1:
        cmp     al, [si]
        jae     cg_2
        add     si, 3
        jmp     cg_1

cg_2:
        inc     si                              ; return pointer to string
        mov     cx, 2                           ; length of string

        ret

                conv_grade endp


        .data

        disp_tbl label byte

        dw str1                                 ; ptr to string
         db 1,3                                 ; column, row
         db 0                                   ; string type
        dw str2
         db 1,4
         db 0
        dw str3
         db 1,5
         db 0
        dw str4
         db 40,3
```

```
            db 0
            dw str5
            db 40,4
            db 0
            dw str6
            db 40,5
            db 0

            dw str1a
            db 13,3
            db 0
            dw str2a
            db 13,4
            db 0
            dw str3a
            db 13,5
            db 0
            dw str4a
            db 50,3
            db 0
            dw num5a
            db 50,4
            db 2
            dw num6a
            db 50,5
            db 1

            dw -1                          ; end of table

    str1  db 'First Name:',0
    str2  db 'Last Name:',0
    str3  db 'Course:',0
    str4  db 'Date:',0
    str5  db 'Grade:',0
    str6  db 'Credits:',0

    str1a db 'John',0
    str2a db 'Smith',0
    str3a db 'CS101',0
    str4a db '01/01/95',0
    num5a dw 90
    num6a dw 3

    temp_num db 6 dup(0)                  ; reserve space for signed integer

    num_to_grade label byte
    db 100, 'A+'
    db  90, 'A '
    db  80, 'B '
    db  70, 'C '
    db  60, 'D '
    db   0, 'F '

end main
```

*The jump table code (after label dsp_1) does not check for the entries to be in a valid range. When debugging or when using data that has not been specifically tested, it is a good idea to check for valid index values to prevent a jump or call to a random memory location.*

## Tables with Conversion Procedures

A similar way to accomplish the same level of abstraction in the code is to use pointers to the conversion procedures in the data records. In this case, a data record would look like this:

```
dw ptr
db col, row
dw proc
```

where:       ptr is a near pointer to a ASCIIZ string

col is the screen column

row is the screen row

proc is a ptr to the conversion procedure

The following listing shows only the changes to the previous listing that must be made to implement this change. The full program is LST20-4.ASM.

```
;////////////////////////////////////
;Table driven screen display with procedures
;////////////////////////////////////
            display_info proc
            ;————————————
            ; Display table of data
            ;————————————

            lea     di, disp_tbl

    dsp_1:
            cmp     word ptr [di], -1
            je      dsp_ret
            call    [di+4]                      ; call conversion routine

; load parameters for display

    dsp_3:
            mov     bl, [di+2]                  ; column
            mov     bh, [di+3]                  ; row
            mov     al, 1                       ; provide attributes
            mov     ah, 7                       ; attributes
            call    scr_display_string
```

```
        add    di, 6
        jmp    dsp_1

dsp_ret:
        ret

        display_info endp

        disp_tbl label byte

        dw str1                         ; ptr to string
         db 1,3                         ; column, row
         dw conv_string
        dw str2
         db 1,4
         dw conv_string
        dw str3
         db 1,5
         dw conv_string
        dw str4
         db 40,3
         dw conv_string
        dw str5
         db 40,4
         dw conv_string
        dw str6
         db 40,5
         dw conv_string

        dw str1a
         db 13,3
         dw conv_string
        dw str2a
         db 13,4
         dw conv_string
        dw str3a
         db 13,5
         dw conv_string
        dw str4a
         db 50,3
         dw conv_string
        dw num5a
         db 50,4
         dw conv_grade
        dw num6a
         db 50,5
         dw conv_num
        dw -1                           ; end of table
```

# Using Macros and Structures to Declare Data

The final step for this example will be to use macros and structures to make the code and data more readable and easier to maintain. As a general rule, any table with more than 2 fields per record, or more than one data type per record, should be declared as a structure.

Structures and macros make it easy to declare and use data. For example, you can define a structure, such as:

```
dsp_struc struc
dsp_ptr  dw ?
dsp_col  db ?
dsp_row  db ?
dsp_type db ?
dsp_struc ends
```

> *This STRUC uses the structure from the example that uses a byte data type variable, not the function pointer.*

You can then use this structure name as a data type (just like DB, DW, etc). This helps prevent errors and makes the code more readable, as follows:

```
item1  dsp_struc     <str1, 1, 3, 0>
```

The following example program (LST20-5.ASM) uses a slightly different method for declaring the data — macros. Macros are slightly more difficult to use, because you must declare the macro. However, they are easy to understand and can be a much more powerful way to apply default values and to avoid errors.

```
;/////////////////////////////
;Table driven screen display with macros
;/////////////////////////////

  .model small

  .stack

    .code

        includelib qwl
        include    libstruc.inc

        extrn scr_init          : proc
```

```
        extrn scr_display_string : proc
        extrn scr_blank_screen   : proc
        extrn scr_setup_attr_tbl : proc
        extrn win_popup          : proc
        extrn win_remove         : proc
        extrn key_read_char      : proc
        extrn mem_shrink         : proc
        extrn num_int_to_ascii   : proc

        dsp MACRO dptr, col, row, typ
         dw dptr
        ifb <typ>
         db col, row, 0
        else
         db col, row, typ
        endif
        ENDM

        dsp_struc struc
          dsp_ptr  dw ?
          dsp_col  db ?
          dsp_row  db ?
          dsp_type db ?
        dsp_struc ends


        main proc

        mov           ax, @data
        mov           ds, ax

        call          mem_shrink            ; discard extra memory

        push          ds
        pop           es

; initialize library for screen

        call    scr_init

; erase the screen

        mov    al, 7                        ; attr to erase with
        call   scr_blank_screen

; display the text

        call    display_info

; terminate program

        mov    ax, 4ch                      ; successful completion
        int    21h

        main endp
```

```
            display_info proc
            ;————————————
            ; Display table of data
            ;————————————

            lea     di, disp_tbl

dsp_1:
            mov     si, [di].dsp_ptr
            cmp     si, -1
            je      dsp_ret

            xor     bx, bx
            mov     bl, [di].dsp_type          ; get conversion type
            add     bx, bx
            call    CS:convert[bx]             ; call conversion routine

; load parameters for display

    dsp_3:
            mov     bl, [di].dsp_col           ; column
            mov     bh, [di].dsp_row           ; row
            mov     al, 1                      ; provide attributes
            mov     ah, 7                      ; attributes
            call    scr_display_string

            add     di, size dsp_struc
            jmp     dsp_1

    dsp_ret:
            ret

            convert label word
            dw conv_string
            dw conv_num
            dw conv_grade

            display_info endp

            conv_string proc

            xor     cx, cx                     ; no conversion required
            ret

conv_string endp

conv_num proc

            push    di
            mov     ax, [si]                   ; get value
            lea     di, temp_num
            call    num_int_to_ascii
            mov     si, di                     ; return ptr to string
            xor     cx, cx
            pop     di
```

```
            ret

conv_num endp

conv_grade proc
;───────────────
; Convert numerical grade to letter
;───────────────

            mov     al, [si]                    ; get value
            cmp     al, 90                      ; check for good grade
            jb      cg_0
            push    ax                          ; popup congratulatory msg
            push    di
            lea     si, win1
            lea     di, buf1
            call    win_popup
            call    key_read_char
            call    win_remove
            pop     di
            pop     ax

    cg_0:
            lea     si, num_to_grade

    cg_1:
            cmp     al, [si]
            jae     cg_2
            add     si, 3
            jmp     cg_1


    cg_2:
            inc     si                          ; return pointer to string
            mov     cx, 2                       ; length of string
            ret

            conv_grade endp

    .data

            disp_tbl label byte

            dsp str1,   1, 3                    ; ptr, column, row, type
            dsp str2,   1, 4
            dsp str3,   1, 5
            dsp str4,  40, 3
            dsp str5,  40, 4
            dsp str6,  40, 5
            dsp str1a, 13, 3
            dsp str2a, 13, 4
            dsp str3a, 13, 5
            dsp str4a, 50, 3
            dsp num5a, 50, 4, 2
            dsp num6a, 50, 5, 1
```

```
               dw -1    ; end of table

        str1  db 'First Name:',0
        str2  db 'Last Name:',0
        str3  db 'Course:',0
        str4  db 'Date:',0
        str5  db 'Grade:',0
        str6  db 'Credits:',0

        str1a db 'John',0
        str2a db 'Smith',0
        str3a db 'CS101',0
        str4a db '01/01/95',0
        num5a dw 90
        num6a dw 3

        temp_num db 6 dup(0)                 ; reserve space for signed integer

        num_to_grade label byte
        db 100, 'A+'
        db  90, 'A '
        db  80, 'B '
        db  70, 'C '
        db  60, 'D '
        db   0, 'F '

        h1        equ 4
        w1        equ 30
        win1 window_struc <25,  8, h1, w1, attr2, 2, 1, msg1>

        attr_tbl label byte
        attr1 db 70h, 17h                    ; mono then color attr
        attr2 db 07h, 47h
        attr_tbl_len equ ($ - attr_tbl)/2

        msg1 db '    Congratulations!',0
             db " An 'A' in this class.",0
             db 0

        buf1 db (size screen_struc) + ( h1 * w1 * 2) dup (0)

    end main
```

# Advanced Macro Techniques and Conditional Assembly

The macro in the previous example program introduced a new assembler feature - conditional assembly directives. In the macro declaration, the IFB directive (IF Blank) allows checking a macro parameter to see if it is blank. If it is blank, then a default value can be supplied or an error can be generated.

```
dsp MACRO dptr, col, row, typ
dw dptr
ifb <typ>
db col, row, 0
else
db col, row, typ
endif
ENDM
```

Other useful conditional assembly directives are:

```
IF                              if expression true  (not zero)
IFE                             if expression false (zero)
IFDEF   IFNDEF                   if defined, if not defined
```

These conditional assembly directives can be used in macros for testing arguments (or parameters) passed to the macro:

```
IFB     IFNB                    if blank, if not blank
IFIDN                           if arguments identical
IFIDNI                          if arguments identical, ignore case
IFDIF                           if arguments different
IFDIFI                          if arguments different, ignore case
```

All conditional assembly directives may be used with an ELSE directive (also ELSEIFxxx). Directives must be properly nested, ending with an ENDIF.

Data records can be tested by declaring the data with macros, as follows:

```
dsp MACRO dptr, col, row, typ
dw dptr
ifb <typ>
db col, row, 0
else
if (typ GT 2)
.err
%out type error
endif
db col, row, typ
endif
ENDM
```

More complicated tests can also be done. Here is an example with a structure and a macro that allows date data to be declared:

```
             date struc
              day    db ?
              month db ?
              year   db ?
             date ends

             datem macro lbl, mday, mmonth, myear

             ifidn <mmonth>, <2>
              if mday gt 29
                .err
                %out leap year error
              endif
             endif

             if mday gt 31
                .err
                %out days too large
             endif

             if mmonth gt 12
                .err
                %out month too large
             endif

             lbl date <mday,mmonth,myear>

             endm

             .data

             datem d1,1,1,95
             datem d2,30,2,95
```

## Conditional Assembly for Different Memory Models

Another handy use for conditional assembly is to allow the same code to be used for different memory models. This is especially useful when writing general purpose library routines and/or for code that will be called from a high-level language.

There are two predefined equates that make this a simple technique - @datasize and @codesize. They are defined in Table 20.1:

**Table 20.1 @datasize and @codesize**

| Memory Model | @datasize | @codesize |
| --- | --- | --- |
| Tiny | 0 | 0 |
| Small | 0 | 0 |
| Compact | 1 | 0 |
| Medium | 0 | 1 |
| Large | 1 | 1 |
| Huge | 2 | 1 |

When writing procedures to be called from a high-level language, such as C, it would appear that the changes from one memory model to another would be automatic. For example, an assembly program that is passed two pointers from C might have the following two statements:

```
.model small, C
...
strcopy PROC USES di si, string1:ptr, string2:ptr
```

It would appear that the .MODEL and PROC directives would take care of all the details. But, of course, this is not true because the pointers must be handled differently when they are far pointers as opposed to when they are near pointers.

```
.model small, C                        ; change "small" to any model

.code

        strcopy PROC USES di si, string1:ptr, string2:ptr

        if @datasize

; save segment registers and load far pointers

            push  ds
            push  es
            les   di, string1
            lds   si, string2

        else
```

```
; load near pointers

    mov   di, string1
    mov   si, string2
    endif

; copy the string

sc_1:
    lodsb
    stosb
    test   al, al
    jnz    sc_1

    if @datasize

; restore segment registers

    pop    es
    pop    ds
  endif

    ret

strcopy endp
```

# Advanced Integer Math

When programming a CPU with a specific register size (i.e. 16 bits on the 8088 and 80286, and 16 or 32 bits on the 386 and above), it takes special code to perform arithmetic on data that contains more bits than the register size. In this section, we'll write routines to handle data that is at least twice the normal size.

## Multi-byte/word Addition

Adding two integers in memory that are 16 bits in length is fairly easy, as follows:

```
    mov    ax, [si]
    add    [di], ax
```

In this example, SI points to one 16-bit integer and DI points to the other. The result is stored in the word pointed to by the DI register. However, if these pointers are now pointing to 32-bit integers, we'll need to perform a few more instructions, as follows:

```
mov     ax, [si]
add     [di], ax
mov     ax, [si+2]
adc     [di+2], ax
```

The first ADD instruction sets the carry flag if an arithmetic carry occurred, and the ADC (add with carry) instruction brings the carry forward into the second word of the integers. The same type of operations can be used with 32-bit code to handle 64-bit integers, as follows:

```
mov     eax, [esi]
add     [edi], eax
mov     eax, [esi+4]
adc     [edi+4], eax
```

A loop to handle an integer of any byte length can be constructed as follows:

```
        clc
        mov     cx, 8                   ; number of bytes to process

loop1:
        mov     al, [si]
        adc     [di], al
        inc     si
        inc     di
        loop    loop1
```

In this example, the carry flag is cleared before the loop starts, so that the ADC instruction can be used for every addition.

Most of the time you will use integers that are an even number of bytes in length, so it is more efficient to add words instead of bytes:

```
        clc
        mov     cx, 4                   ; number of words to process

loop2:
        mov     ax, [si]
        adc     [di], ax
        inc     si
        inc     si
        inc     di
        inc     di
        loop    loop2
```

In this case, the pointers are still advanced with the INC instruction. The INC instruction does not affect the state of the carry flag, so this allows the carry state from one addition to be properly carried into the next addition. The code can be made more efficient by using the LEA instruction to advance the pointers:

```
        clc
        mov     cx, 4                       ; number of words to process

loop2:
        mov     ax, [si]
        adc     [di], ax
        lea     si, [si+2]
        lea     di, [di+2]
        loop    loop2
```

Also note that the LOOP instruction can be replaced with the combination of DEC CX and JNZ loop2 because the DEC instruction does not modify the carry flag.

```
        clc
        mov     cx, 4                       ; number of words to process

loop2:
        mov     ax, [si]
        adc     [di], ax
        lea     si, [si+2]
        lea     di, [di+2]
        dec     cx
        jnz     loop2
```

## Multi-byte/word Subtraction

Multi-byte and multi-word precision subtraction can be performed in the same manner as addition. The subtract with borrow (SBB) instruction uses the carry flag as an arithmetic borrow. The following code subtracts two 32-bit integers:

```
        mov     ax, [si]
        sub     [di], ax
        mov     ax, [si+2]
        sbb     [di+2], ax
```

The following 32-bit code subtracts two 128-bit integers:

```
        clc
        mov     ecx, 4                      ; dwords to process

loop3:
        mov     eax, [esi]
        sbb     [edi], eax
        lea     esi, [esi+4]
        lea     edi, [edi+4]
        dec     ecx
        jnz     loop3
```

## Multi-byte/word Multiplication

As we've now seen, extended precision addition and subtraction are relatively easy and straight-forward to program. Multiplication is somewhat more difficult. First, let's take a look at the 16-bit unsigned multiply instruction (MUL) to recall how it works:

```
        mov     ax, [si]
        mul     [di]
```

To multiply two 16-bit integers, one must be in the AX register. However, the result when multiplying two 16-bit integers can be as large as 32 bits. The result is placed into DX:AX, with DX holding the high word and AX holding the low word.

When using 32-bit registers, 32-bit results are placed into EAX and 64-bit results are placed into EDX:EAX, with EDX holding the high dword and EAX holding the low dword.

A problem arises when we want to go beyond these limits for 16-bit or 32-bit code. There is no multiply with carry instruction - it does not make any sense. Instead, we need to remember how we first learned to multiply. For example, to multiply two base 10 numbers, the process is as follows:

```
                    12
                    23
                   ────
                     6        (3 x 2)
                    30        (3 x 10)
                    40        (20 x 2)
                   200        (20 x 10)
                   ────
                   276        (sum the partial results)
```

To multiply two 32-bit integers (using 16-bit registers) requires that we use a process like this:

```
operand 1:    AAAABBBB     (letters are symbols, not values)
operand 2:    CCCCDDDD     (i.e. AAAA is a 16-bit hex number)
```

```
                        AAAABBBB
                        CCCCDDDD
                        ──────────────
                        DBDBDBDB        (DDDD x BBBB)
                        DADADADA        (DDDD x AAAA)
                        CBCBCBCB        (CCCC x BBBB)
                        CACACACA        (CCCC x AAAA)
                        ──────────────
                        CACAABCDABCDDBDB
```

The following listing shows how to implement the above process as a procedure. On entry, DS:DI is a pointer to the first operand and DS:SI is a pointer to the second operand. DS:DI is also a pointer to the 8-byte destination buffer. (Note that the input is 4 bytes in length and the output is 8 bytes.)

```
        push    ax
        push    bx
        push    cx
        push    dx

        mov     cx, [di+2]              ; load high word #1
        mov     ax, [di]                ; load low word #1
        mov     bx, ax                  ; save low word #1
        mov     word ptr [di+6], 0      ; init high word to 0
```

```
; low x low

        mul     word ptr [si]
        mov     [di], ax
        mov     [di+2], dx

; high #2 x low #1

        mov     ax, bx
        mul     word ptr [si+2]
        mov     [di+4], dx
        add     [di+2], ax
        adc     word ptr [di+4], 0

; low #2 x high #1

        mov     ax, cx
        mul     word ptr [si]
        add     [di+2], ax
        adc     [di+4], dx
        adc     word ptr [di+6], 0

; high x high

        mov     ax, cx
        mul     word ptr [si+2]
        add     [di+4], ax
        adc     [di+6], dx

        pop     dx
        pop     cx
        pop     bx
        pop     ax

        ret
```

This same process can be used for multiplying two 64-bit values in 32-bit code with a 128-bit result, as follows:

```
        push    eax
        push    ebx
        push    ecx
        push    edx

        mov     ecx, [edi+4]                ; load high dword #1
        mov     eax, [edi]                  ; load low dword #1
        mov     ebx, eax                    ; save low dword #1
        mov     dword ptr [edi+12], 0       ; init high dword to 0
```

```
; low x low

        mul     dword ptr [esi]
        mov     [edi], eax
        mov     [edi+4], edx

; high #2 x low #1

        mov     eax, ebx
        mul     dword ptr [esi+4]
        mov     [edi+8], edx
        add     [edi+4], eax
        adc     dword ptr [edi+8], 0

; low #2 x high #1

        mov     eax, ecx
        mul     dword ptr [esi]
        add     [edi+4], eax
        adc     [edi+8], edx
        adc     dword ptr [edi+12], 0

; high x high

        mov     eax, ecx
        mul     dword ptr [esi+4]
        add     [edi+8], eax
        adc     [edi+12], edx

        pop     edx
        pop     ecx
        pop     ebx
        pop     eax

        ret
```

The same method of summing partial results could be used to multiply values with more bits, but due to the small number of registers on the 80x86 CPUs, all values would need to be kept in memory. Three operands would be needed, 2 source pointers and a pointer to the destination buffer.

## Multi-byte/word Division

The details of the extended precision multiplication are much more complicated than those for addition and subtraction, but the basic concept is not too difficult. However, division is another story. What we'd like to be able to do here is to divide a 64-bit value by a 32-bit value using 16-bit registers (and to be able to divide a 128-bit value by a 64-bit value using 32-bit registers). First, let's review the basic unsigned DIV instruction:

```
mov     ax, [si]
mov     dx, [si+2]
div     [di]
```

In this code, DX:AX is divided by the value at DS:DI. Upon completion, the quotient is in the AX register and the remainder is in the DX register. There are two things that can go wrong during a division. First, an attempt to divide by zero is an undefined operation and will cause a divide-by-zero interrupt (interrupt 0). Second, the result may be too large to fit in the implied destination register. This is a divide overflow and it generates the same divide-by-zero interrupt. Recall that the value to be divided can be as large as $2^{32}-1$, but the divisor can be as small as 2. The following code checks for both error conditions:

```
        mov     ax, [si]                    ; load operands
        mov     dx, [si+2]
        mov     bx, [di]
        cmp     bx, 0                       ; check for divide by zero
        je      div_err
        cmp     dx, bx                      ; check for overflow
        jae     div_err
        div     bx
        ...
div_err:
```

Checking for a possible overflow is done as shown, by comparing the divisor with the high word of the dividend. The divisor must be smaller than the high word or the result cannot be represented in just a single word. Failing to make this check is a common error in many programs.

There is no obvious algorithm for dividing numbers larger than is provided by the hardware. That is except for one way: repetitive subtraction. However, we can easily determine that this method is of no practical use. We already know that we can divide numbers up to 64 bits in length by a number up to 32 bits in length. Just performing this division could take 10 to 100 cycles per loop and up to 4 billion loops. Even at 100Mhz, this could take as long as 4000 seconds. Also recall that we want to be able to handle values as large as 128 bits. So we're now talking about measurements in lifetimes, not seconds.

The simplest method for performing division of values larger than provided for by the hardware is to use long division, but in binary. Here is a long division example, in decimal:

Units

```
  12 ⌐3457
      2400            200
      ————
      1057
       960             80
      ————
        97
        96              8
      ————           ————
         1            288
```

remainder:    1
result:         288

When writing this long division algorithm in binary, it is actually a little bit simpler, in that there is no need to perform any multiplications before the subtractions. In binary, each value that divides only needs to be multiplied by one before subtraction. This is how to write this algorithm in binary:

```
num_long_div proc
;————————————————
; Unsigned division
;    64-bit operand by a 32-bit operand
;
; inputs: DX:AX  operand 1 (32-bit)
;         DS:SI  ptr to operand 2 (64-bit)
;                (operand 2 changed to 32-bit quotient)
;
; outputs: BX:CX longword  quotient
;          DX:AX longword remainder
;          CF    set if divide by zero
;————————————————


push    bp

mov     bp, 64                    ; number of bits to divide
cmp     ax, 0                     ; check for div by zero
```

```
        jne     nld_0
        cmp     dx, 0
        je      nld_err

nld_0:
        mov     cx, ax                          ; low word of divisor
        mov     bx, dx                          ; high word

        xor     ax, ax
        xor     dx, dx

nld_1:
        clc
        rcl     word ptr [si], 1                ; shift result and source
        rcl     word ptr [si+2], 1
        rcl     word ptr [si+4], 1
        rcl     word ptr [si+6], 1
        rcl     ax, 1
        rcl     dx, 1

        cmp     dx, bx                          ; check high words
        jb      nld_3                           ; if below, go to next bit
        ja      nld_2                           ; if above, do subtract
        cmp     ax, cx                          ; check low words when
        jb      nld_3                           ;   high words equal

nld_2:
        sub     ax, cx                          ; sub when divisor is smaller
        sbb     dx, bx
        inc     word ptr [si]                   ; inc result

nld_3:
        dec     bp                              ; next bit
        jnz     nld_1

        mov     cx, [si]                        ; low word of result
        mov     bx, [si+2]                      ; high word of result
        clc                                     ; successful

nld_ret:
        pop     bp

        ret

nld_err:
        stc                                     ; error if divide by zero
        jmp     nld_ret

        num_long_div endp
```

# Random Number Generator

There are chapters of books, and even entire books, devoted to the theory of pseudo-random number generation. We will not attempt to fully discuss the theory of random numbers in this book. Primarily, we'll show how to write a procedure that generates pseudo-random numbers based on the well-known linear congruential method. But first, we'll discuss some of the terminology of random numbers.

When people speak of a random number they usually mean an arbitrary number. When asking for an arbitrary number, you don't really care what number you get. By contrast, a random number is a precisely defined mathematical concept. When selecting a random number, every number (within a specified range) should be equally likely to occur. A random number is an arbitrary number, but an arbitrary number is not a random number.

When random numbers are needed in a program, it is usually the case that an entire sequence of numbers is required, not just a single number. It should be noted that a program cannot generate a sequence of truly random numbers because once the algorithm is written, knowing one number in the sequence makes the next number known. In a sequence of true random numbers, every number in the range is equally likely to occur. The best that we can do is to write an algorithm that exhibits the properties of a truly random sequence. This is why we call these computerized sequences pseudo-random number generators.

This brings us to the question of "What are the properties of random numbers that must be taken into account when writing a pseudo-random number generator?" This is where the mathematicians take over and you need to trust the developed algorithms. Needless to say, this is the subject of many sophisticated tests. For example, it's easy to see that one property should be that each number is equally likely to occur. However, given the range of 1 to 10, the sequence [1,2,3,4,5,6,7,8,9,10] satisfies this property but is not a useful approximation of a random sequence.

The linear congruential is the most well-known method for generating pseudo-random numbers. It was introduced by D. Lehmer in 1951. The algorithm works like this:

$$R2 = ((R1 * X) + 1) \bmod Y$$

where:

R1 is the seed value or previous R2

R2 is the next number in the sequence

X is a constant

Y is a constant

Although the expression appears relatively simple (and it is), much detailed analysis has been done on this formula. Primarily, this helps us in choosing the constants X and Y. The value for Y can be the word size of the CPU, so a value of $2^{16}$ or $2^{32}$ can be used. This makes the algorithm very simple because the modulus function is automatically performed as a result of just ignoring arithmetic overflow. Thus, it is advantageous to choose Y = 65536 and the MOD operation can be eliminated.

The selection of the value for X is somewhat more complex. By experimenting, you can see that there are some good values and some not-so-good values. Through his analysis, Donald Knuth has proposed rules for the value X as follows:

● Not too small and not too large, compared to Y.

● One less digit (decimal) than Y is a good choice.

● Should be a constant with no particular pattern except it should end with ...n21, where n is even.

The following is an assembly language procedure that implements the linear congruential method and uses the values of X = 9421 and Y = 65536.

```
.model small

.code

        num_random_word proc
        ;─────────────────────────
        ; Generate the next random number
        ;
        ; inputs: none
```

```
        ;
        ; outputs: AX  generated random number
        ;—————————————

        push    dx
        push    ds

        mov     ax, @data
        mov     ds, ax

        mov     ax, num_rnd_val
        mul     num_rnd_mult
        inc     ax
        mov     num_rnd_val, ax

        pop     ds
        pop     dx

        ret

        num_random_word endp
.data

        num_rnd_val  dw 12345            ; arbitrary seed value
        num_rnd_mult dw 9421             ; multiplier (X)
```

It is often necessary to use the same sequence of random numbers two or more times. This could be for testing, to provide a repeatable condition for debugging or for other purposes such as simulations or cryptography. In cryptography, the goal would be to encrypt a message using a sequence of pseudo-random numbers, then have the recipient of the message use the same sequence to decode it. To use the same sequence, the random number generator must be started, or seeded, with the same initial value.

Other times it may be required to start a sequence with an arbitrary value. Such situations might be in a game when a supposedly random starting point is chosen. A good choice for choosing this number would be to look at the internal hardware timer (clock ticks) when the program starts.

The following routine allows the seed value of the random number generator to be set to a specific value (when repeatability is needed) or to an arbitrary value.

```
num_random_word_init proc
;————————————
;
; Set the random number generator initial value
;
; inputs: AX init value (if 0 use clock tick)
;
; outputs: initial value stored
;————————————

        push    ds
        or      ax, ax
        jnz     nr_1

        mov     ax, 40h
        mov     ds, ax
        mov     ax, DS:[6ch]              ; get low timer tick word
        add     ax, DS:[6eh]              ; add high timer tick word

nr_1:
        push    ax
        mov     ax, @data
        mov     ds, ax
        pop     ax
        mov     num_rnd_val, ax

        pop     ds
        ret

        num_random_word_init endp
```

# Summary

In this chapter we've seen how to use the library presented in Chapter 19. These examples show how the basic building blocks of the library can be used in various ways in applications. We've also seen the details of some more advanced arithmetic library routines. The idea of these routines, just like any other routine you may write, is to make the interface to the routine simple, no matter how complex its internal workings. Using these concepts and library functions or your own library functions should enable you to master more complex programs.

**CHAPTER TWENTY ONE**

# Assembly Language Optimizations

# Introduction

In this chapter we'll look at a number of code optimizations, both simple and advanced. We'll look at both general techniques, such as the choice of algorithms and the skills required to analyze individual instructions. Optimizations tend to fall into one of four categories; algorithm selection,
code/data alignment, instruction ordering and instruction selection.

We'll discuss each of these topics, starting with the most important, algorithms.

# Algorithms

Most of the time, the best way to optimize a program, in any language, is to choose the best algorithm. Only in some rare cases can other factors have more effect on the overall performance than that of the algorithm selection. For example, Table 21.1 contains the times for several common sorting algorithms. Each algorithm was tested on the same table of random integers on an 80486 (33 Mhz):

**Table 21.1 Integer Sorting Times (486-33) (times in secs)**

| Algorithm | Size of Array being Sorted (Words) | | | | | |
|-----------|------|------|------|------|-------|-------|
|           | 1000 | 2000 | 4000 | 8000 | 16000 | 32000 |
| Bubble    | .22  | .88  | 3.57 | 15.3 | 62.0  | 249   |
| Selection | .16  | .61  | 2.42 | 10.3 | 41.9  | 168   |
| Insertion | .06  | .38  | 1.43 | 6.04 | 26.2  | 107   |
| Quicksort | .006 | .01  | 0.03 | 0.06 | 0.14  | 0.29  |

Each of these algorithms was written in assembly language. All are (relatively) small in size (see Table 21.2). As can be seen from the table, it would be senseless to put much effort in optimizing the bubble sort routine. The bubble sort would need to be optimised by almost 1000 times just to be comparable to the quicksort. The non-linear time increments for the given number of entries to be sorted is a known factor that is inherent to the algorithm.

**Table 21.2 Sort Algorithm Code Size (bytes)**

| Algorithm | Bytes |
|-----------|-------|
| Bubble    | 166   |
| Selection | 163   |
| Insertion | 164   |
| Quicksort | 292   |

So there is no doubt, you must know the characteristics of your algorithms. There is no substitute for the proper algorithm, especially when it comes to known techniques, such as sorting. But you must also know your data. Every algorithm must be matched with the appropriate data. (A complete description of the quicksort algorithm is beyond the scope of this book, but there are some details that you should know. A good book that does describe quicksort is 'Algorithms' by Robert Sedgewick.) Quicksort works by breaking the array to be sorted into parts and then recursively calling itself to sort these smaller parts. It is possible to write a non-recursive implementation, but it would still use an additional array or stack space to keep track of each partition that still needs to be sorted. Even assuming that the arrays to be sorted are less than 65,536 elements, this means at least 6 to 8 bytes of data that needs to be stored per pair of partitions. The worst-case arrangement of the data can cause a quicksort to easily overflow the stack. The bottom line is that you must know your algorithms and your data and how they work together.

In the case of choosing a sorting algorithm, you should time a representative sample of your data. Be sure to perform the timing on a machine that has the same performance as the users of your program. For an example of how the machine can affect your code, see Table 21.3:

**Table 21.3 Sort Times for 32000 Integers by CPU**

| Algorithm | CPU Type and Speed | | | |
| | Pent-90 | 486DX-33 | 386DX-25 | 386SX-16 |
| --- | --- | --- | --- | --- |
| Insertion | 17 seconds | 1.8 minutes | 6 minutes | 13 minutes |
| Quicksort | 0.1 seconds | 0.3 seconds | 1 second | 2 seconds |

As can be seen from the table, if you need to sort anywhere near 32000 records on a 386 machine, you'll have a long wait without the use of quicksort; you may even be convinced that you have a bug in your code and your machine has crashed. You should be aware that the 386DX-25 (and above) machines may have external processor caches, while the 486DX-33 and Pentium machines also have internal ones. This substantially increases the performance, especially when sorting simple arrays of integers. Sorting long records or records with long keys will significantly decrease performance from the numbers shown above. An important consideration in choosing algorithms is the interaction of the cache(s) and the amount of data being processed.

# Execution Timing

It is possible that what is thought to be the 'best' algorithm (in terms of speed), isn't actually the fastest. As shown above with the sorting algorithms, it is extremely important to check your assumptions by timing your code.

Many programs don't require any special timing tools. You can usually time 1000 repetitions using a watch or even a wall clock. Clearly most assembly code is too fast to time using such a medium with only one repetition. However, you must be cautious when doing this on machines with caches, because the second and subsequent executions of the code may be substantially faster.

There are a number of products available that use the PC timer chip to perform fairly accurate timing tests. If required, you should use one of these. However, the most important consideration when comparing two or more procedures or blocks of code is to be sure that you are comparing apples to apples. In other words, are you really performing a fair test? For example, let's say you test two procedures and get the results shown Table 21.4.

**Table 21.4 Testing Times**

| Program | Time (min) | Code Size (bytes) |
|---------|-----------|-------------------|
| PROG1   | 1.2       | 3000              |
| PROG2   | 1.0       | 7000              |

Because speed is your main concern you conclude that PROG2 is the best, even though the code is larger. However, this might not be the case, as we'll see later.

If PROG1 took several times as long then you could be reasonably assured that this initial test is all you needed to do. (Of course all this assumes that the difference in 4000 bytes of code size and the time to analyze the results is warranted.)

There are many things that can add up to cause a speed difference of 20% between two programs. Here are some of them:

- Data Alignment

- Code Alignment

- Instruction Ordering

- Instruction Selection

- Address Generation Interlocks (AGI's)

- Cache Effects

And that's the focus of the rest of this chapter - the details that can make your code run faster or slower. You must be sure that you know what you are observing: a better algorithm or a difference in some other aspect of program execution that you were previously unaware of.

# Data Alignment

Aligning data is more difficult than it may seem at first, as we shall see. It is simple to align data on word boundaries because all segments are always automatically aligned on an even word boundary. To ensure word alignment of a data element, you place the EVEN directive before the start of the item, as follows:

```
even            ; even byte alignment
dw 100 dup(0)   ; 100 words on even word boundary
```

Aligning dwords is not as simple. The ALIGN directive can be used to align to any location that is a power of two. The following code would appear to align an array of dwords on a dword boundary:

```
align 4         ; dword alignment
dd 100 dup(0)   ; 100 dwords on even dword boundary
```

However, there are other factors that affect how the alignment will work. For the dword alignment to work, the segment must be declared with an alignment type of dword or above. The default alignment type is PARA (paragraph) or 16 bytes when using the SEGMENT directive. When using the simplified segmentation directives, the alignment type is WORD for code segments and data segments.

When using the simplified segmentation directives, MASM 5.1 will allow you to specify an alignment that is greater than the segment alignment (which is a word). This will only work for single module programs or when the ALIGN directive is in the first module to be linked. Otherwise, it is hit or miss. TASM and MASM 6.0 and above will generate an error when you attempt to use an ALIGN value that cannot be guaranteed.

It is possible to use a mix of simplified segmentation directives and the full SEGMENT declaration directives to ensure proper alignment. However, it would not be wise to rely on this method if you intend to upgrade assemblers. Declare a paragraph aligned data segment as follows:

```
_data             segment public para 'data'

data1             dw 0     ; sample data

align 16
data2 dd 100 dup(0)        ; sample data para aligned

_data ends
```

Once the segments are properly declared, there are several techniques that can be used for aligning data:

- Declare global data with proper alignment.

- Use structures with proper alignment.

- Align string operations by address alignment in code (discussed later).

## Local Stack Variables

Allocating stack space for local variables that must be aligned can be difficult. In real mode and 16-bit protected mode, you can assume that the stack pointer (SP) is aligned to an even word boundary. It is possible to manipulate the BP register to force 32-bit alignment as follows:

```
push  bp
mov   bp, sp
sub   sp, local_space + 4

; (push required registers)
```

```
; (access passed parameters, if required)
; align BP for local variables

push   bp
mov    ax, bp
and    ax, 3
sub    bp, ax             ; align BP to dword boundary

...

pop    bp

; pop saved registers

mov    sp, bp
pop    bp
ret
```

When programming in 32-bit, every PUSH and POP uses four bytes of stack space. This is true even when pushing and popping segment registers. When pushing a segment register, the high word is pushed as a zero keeping pure 32-bit code from misaligning ESP from a dword boundary. However, it is still possible to push word values by using an operand-size prefix. This could occur in any 32-bit program. Align EBP to a dword boundary in a 32-bit procedure as follows:

```
push   ebp
mov    ebp, esp
sub    esp, local_space + 4

; (push required registers)
; (access passed parameters, if required)
; align EBP for local variables

push   ebp
mov    eax, ebp
and    eax, 3
sub    ebp, eax           ; align EBP to dword boundary

...

pop    ebp

; pop saved registers

mov    esp, ebp
pop    ebp
ret
```

# Measuring and Correcting the Data Misalignment Penalty

Now that we've seen how to align data you may be wondering, is it really worth it? It is easy enough to test. Table 21.5 shows the misalignment penalty for the REP MOVSW instruction:

**Table 21.5 Data Misalignment Penalty for REP MOVSW**

| Processor | SI alignment | DI aligned | DI misaligned |
|---|---|---|---|
| Pentium | SI aligned | 0% | 50% |
| (cache hit) | SI misaligned | 0% | 50% |
| Pentium | SI aligned | 0% | 45% |
| (cache miss) | SI misaligned | 0% | 45% |
| 486 cache hit | SI aligned | 0% | 26% |
| | SI misaligned | 36% | 67% |
| 486 cache miss | SI aligned | 0% | 20% |
| | SI misaligned | 40% | 50% |
| 386 cache hit | SI aligned | 0% | 8% |
| | SI misaligned | 36% | 70% |
| 386 cache miss | SI aligned | 0% | 13% |
| | SI misaligned | 46% | 57% |
| 386SX no cache | SI aligned | 0% | 73% |
| | SI misaligned | 73% | 123% |

Delays are calculated as a percentage increase in execution time from the case where SI and DI are aligned.

From Table 21.5 we can see the penalty for misalignment can be quite large. The largest penalty is when both the source and the destination are misaligned. It is a simple matter to correct this case. It is always most advantageous to read from aligned data and write to misaligned data (except on the 386SX where there is no difference). This is because the CPU must wait for a read operation to complete, but may buffer write operations to be completed later.

The exact numerical results of Table 21.5 apply to the REP MOVSW instruction. The following code listing shows how to align SI for the REP MOVSW:

```
                        ; Listing
        test    si, 1    ; check for odd address (0->CF)
        jz      ok
        movsb            ; move one byte at odd SI
        dec     cx       ; reduce word count
        jz      mv       ; branch down if only 1 word to move
        stc              ; CF set for odd start

ok:
        rep     movsw    ; move words
        jnc     done

mv:
        movsb            ; move final remaining odd byte
done:
```

The same tests can be performed on the REP MOVSD instruction, as shown in the following Table 21.6:

**Table 21.6 Data Misalignment Penalty for REP MOVSD**

| Processor | SI alignment | DI aligned | DI+1 | DI+2 | DI+3 |
|---|---|---|---|---|---|
| Pentium | SI aligned | 0% | 100% | 100% | 100% |
| (cache hit) | SI +1 | 0% | 100% | 100% | 100% |
| | SI +2 | 0% | 100% | 100% | 100% |
| | SI +3 | 0% | 100% | 100% | 100% |
| Pentium | SI aligned | 0% | 80% | 80% | 80% |
| (cache miss) | SI +1 | 0% | 80% | 80% | 80% |
| | SI +2 | 0% | 80% | 80% | 80% |

*Continued*

Table 21.6 Data Misalignment Penalty for REP MOVSD (Continued)

| Processor | SI alignment | DI aligned | DI+1 | DI+2 | DI+3 |
|---|---|---|---|---|---|
| | SI +3 | 0% | 80% | 80% | 80% |
| 486 cache hit | SI aligned | 0% | 36% | 36% | 27% |
| | SI +1 | 55% | 96% | 96% | 96% |
| | SI +2 | 55% | 96% | 96% | 96% |
| | SI +3 | 60% | 96% | 96% | 96% |
| 486 cache miss | SI aligned | 0% | 18% | 18% | 18% |
| | SI +1 | 36% | 60% | 60% | 60% |
| | SI +2 | 36% | 60% | 60% | 60% |
| | SI +3 | 36% | 60% | 60% | 60% |
| 386 cache hit | SI aligned | 0% | 33% | 33% | 33% |
| | SI +1 | 66% | 116% | 116% | 116% |
| | SI +2 | 66% | 116% | 116% | 116% |
| | SI +3 | 66% | 116% | 116% | 116% |
| 386 cache miss | SI aligned | 0% | 18% | 18% | 18% |
| | SI +1 | 50% | 66% | 66% | 66% |
| | SI +2 | 50% | 66% | 66% | 66% |
| | SI +3 | 50% | 66% | 66% | 66% |
| 386SX no cache | SI aligned | 0% | 25% | 0% | 25% |
| | SI +1 | 25% | 50% | 40% | 66% |
| | SI +2 | 0% | 40% | 33% | 58% |
| | SI +3 | 25% | 66% | 58% | 66% |

Again, the timing results shown in Table 21.6 show that aligning the source register (SI or ESI) can minimize the misalignment penalty. The string instructions tend to show the greatest data misalignment penalty because the instructions are optimized to utilize the memory bus near its maximum capacity. Most other operations would not be using as much bus bandwidth. However, it is interesting to note that on the Pentium, it is always best to align DI, whereas on the previous processors it was always best to align SI.

The code to align SI for the REP MOVSD is more complicated than for aligning for REP MOVSW. Here is one way to do this:

```
                    ; Listing
        xor    dx, dx
        test   si, 3      ; check for odd address
        jz     ok

        movsb             ; move one byte at odd SI
        mov    dx, 3
        dec    cx         ; reduce dword count
        jz     mv         ; branch down only if 1 dword

        test   si, 3      ; check for odd address
        jz     ok
        movsb
        dec    dx

        test   si, 3      ; check for odd address
        jz     ok
        movsb
        dec    dx

ok:
        rep    movsd      ; move dwords
        test   dx, dx
        jz     done

mv:
        mov    cx, dx
        rep    movsb      ; move final bytes
done:
```

Table 21.7 shows the misalignment penalty for independent data read and writes:

**Table 21.7 Read and Write Misalignment Penalty**

| Processor | 16-bit read | 16-bit write |
| --- | --- | --- |
| Pentium cache hit | 70% | 50% |
| Pentium cache miss | 40% | 50% |
| 486 cache hit | 20% | 25% |
| 486 cache miss | 22% | 25% |

*Continued*

**Table 21.7 Read and Write Misalignment Penalty (Continued)**

| Processor | 16-bit read | 16-bit write |
|-----------|-------------|--------------|
| 386 cache hit | 12% | 23% |
| 386 cache miss | 15% | 23% |
| 386SX no cache | 17% | 14% |

# Code Alignment

We've seen how misalignment of data can degrade performance and why it occurs. Now we'll take a look at code alignment. Procedures and loops can be aligned on even word, dword or paragraph boundaries and improve performance. Each 80x86 CPU fetches instructions on certain boundaries. Aligning a frequently fetched instruction will improve performance. The prefetch units on the various 80x86 CPUs fetch instructions on differing boundaries, as follows:

**Table 21.8 Prefetch Boundaries**

| Processor | Boundary |
|-----------|----------|
| 8088/188 | byte |
| 8086/186 | word |
| 80286 | word |
| 80386SX | word |
| 80386DX | dword |
| 80486 | paragraph (cache-line boundary) |
| Pentium | 32-byte (cache-line boundary) |

When the first instruction to be executed after a change in the IP (or EIP) register (CALL, JMP, etc.) is an instruction that straddles a prefetch boundary, the CPU must perform twice the number of bus accesses before execution may resume. If the first instruction is wholly contained at the end of the prefetch boundary, there may be a delay before the second instruction can execute, especially if the first instruction executes in a single cycle.

Because of the branch prediction on the Pentium, there is little need to perform code alignment for the Pentium. The only times that performance should matter is in a loop or a frequently called procedure. These cases should normally be handled automatically by the branch prediction logic. The only situation that might need any alignment tuning is the case of a conditional jump inside a loop that is predicted correctly a small percentage of the time. The branch target destination is predicted based on the destination of 2 of the last 3 executions of the branch instruction. Therefore a branch that is taken randomly may only be predicted correctly 50% of the time. A branch that has a pattern of 2 taken, 2 not taken, 2 taken, 2 not taken and so on will be mispredicted every time.

Aligning for the 486 is the worst case that should be taken into account. Branch prediction eliminates the need for code alignment on the Pentium because the only time that alignment is a real concern is when a section of code is repeatedly the target of a branch. The branch prediction will detect this and begin prefetching in the second prefetch queue in advance.

On the 486 the performance penalty can be as high as 50%, as shown in the following listing:

```
        mov     cx, 1000

        align   16              ; align to paragraph
        rept    15              ; insert 15 NOP's to get the SUB
        nop                     ; to straddle the prefetch boundary
        endm

loop1:
        sub     cx, 1
        jnz     loop1

        mov     cx, 1000
        align   16              ; align to paragraph
loop2:
        sub     cx, 1
        jnz     loop2
```

The first loop (misaligned) in the listing takes up to 50% longer than the second loop on the 486. The performance degradation is so great because this is the worst-case code alignment problem for the 486. The loop is small (only two instructions consisting of five bytes) and the first instruction in the loop, the SUB instruction, is three bytes in length straddling the prefetch boundary in this case. Twice as many prefetch bus cycles must be executed before any code can be executed.

On the 386DX instructions are prefetched four bytes at a time on dword boundaries. The first loop in the above listing takes only 7% longer than the second loop on the 386DX. Although the same conditions exist as on the 486, the penalty is still the same - twice as many prefetch cycles before execution of the SUB instruction may start. However, on the 386DX there are fewer bytes to prefetch (8 vs. 32) and the execution time of the instructions in the loop is much greater (10 vs. 4).

The following listing contains loops that are longer and more representative of a loop you might have in your own code. Loops are shown with the worst-case code alignment and aligned on a paragraph boundary.

```
        mov     cx, 1000

        align   16              ; align to paragraph
        rept 15                 ; insert 15 NOP's to get the ADD
        nop                     ; to straddle the prefetch boundary
        endm

loop1:
        add     ax, [si]
        add     si, 2
        dec     cx
        jnz     loop1

        mov     cx, 1000
        align   16

loop2:
        add     ax, [si]
        add     si, 2
        dec     cx
        jnz     loop2
```

In this example, the 486 takes as much as 25% longer on the first loop than the second loop. The 386 takes only 3% longer for this loop. The change in percentages is based primarily on the fact that the penalty stayed the same, but the total time to execute the other instructions in the loop is greater.

That's the bad news about code alignment on the 486. The good news is that it is usually not necessary to paragraph align procedures and loops. Near optimum performance can be attained by positioning the first instruction to be contained within a paragraph (or prefetch) boundary. Here is an example:

```
        mov     cx, 1000

        align   16                      ; align to paragraph
        rept    14                      ; insert 14 NOP's to get the SUB
        nop                             ; in one prefetch boundary and the
        endm                            ; JNZ in another

loop3:
        sub     cx, 1
        jnz     loop3
```

The difference between this loop and the previous case where the loop was paragraph aligned is negligible. In other words, because of the high-speed internal cache on the 486, the second prefetch can occur during the execution of even a simple, one-cycle instruction such as the SUB.

The bottom line on 486 code alignment seems to be that you must ensure that critical loops are aligned so that the first instruction does not straddle a prefetch boundary. This can usually be done with the EVEN directive (for 2-byte instructions) or ALIGN 4 (for 3- or 4-byte instructions).

Recall the two hypothetical programs, PROG1 and PROG2, presented earlier. Knowing what you now know about 486 code alignment, would you blindly accept those timings?

Of course, running the code on a Pentium tends to eliminate the entire problem of code alignment altogether. Again, this is because of the branch prediction logic that allows the second prefetch buffer to get a head start compared to the execution on a 486. So once your code has been code aligned for the 486, you'll probably never need to be concerned with it again.

The assembler pads the code with NOP's (90h). Of course, the size of your code will be much larger if you align every loop and procedure, so only use code alignment when appropriate. Usually, this means frequently used nested loops, frequently called procedures and the entry points for interrupt handlers.

## Alignment of Delay Loops

Here is another code alignment mystery that you may have encountered. It is common for code written to interface with various hardware devices to include a small software delay loop. The purpose of such loops is usually to provide a delay between IN or OUT instructions, as required by the bus or the device. Most devices don't currently require this, but in the past they may have. The typical loop looks like this:

```
        mov   cx, 100
delay:
        loop  delay
```

The actual length of the delay can vary quite a bit based on whether or not the LOOP instruction straddles a prefetch boundary. The delay varies by as much as 8% on the 386 and 30% on the 486. Using the EVEN directive eliminates the variance.

```
        mov   cx, 100
        even
delay:
        loop  delay
```

## Address Generation Interlocks - AGIs

Address generation interlocks, or AGIs, are delays inserted into the instruction pipeline by the CPU. AGIs can occur on the 486 and the Pentium. An AGI is generated when a register is used as a component of an effective address and is also the destination register of an instruction in the previous cycle. For example:

```
lea     bx, table
mov     ax, [bx]
```

Although both of these instructions are each documented as taking only one cycle on the 486, they take three instructions when combined together. Because the BX register is the destination of the first instruction and it is also a component of the memory address used in the second instruction, the CPU must insert a one-cycle delay to allow the first instruction to complete before it can determine the address to be used in the second instruction.

If you've never heard of AGIs before, it is because they are a new programming consideration, beginning with the 486. The reason for AGIs is that the CPU executes instructions one stage per cycle. So, even though an instruction is documented as taking a single cycle, it really takes 5 cycles to get through the pipeline. But, another single-cycle instruction can finish in the very next cycle. Here are the pipeline stages for the 486 and Pentium (which has two pipelines, both the same):

**1**  PF Prefetch

**2**  D1 Decode

**3**  D2 Address Generation

**4**  EX Execute (read data and store register results)

**5**  WB Write Back (store in memory)

As can be seen from the pipeline stages, it would not be possible to calculate a memory address that relies on the result of an instruction that has not yet completed stage 4. This is why the CPU detects this condition and generates the AGI. AGIs get even more difficult to contend with on the Pentium. This is because the Pentium can pair two instructions, effectively bringing instructions closer together in relative clock cycles. The following code can cause an AGI delay on the Pentium, but not on the 486:

```
lea    bx, table
mov    cx, 2
mov    dx, 3
mov    ax, [bx]
```

# Instruction Selection and Ordering

Tremendous optimizations can be made by the proper selection and ordering of instructions. When we think of optimizing code, it is usually of making a trade-off between code size and speed. But this is not always the case, as we'll see. The proper ordering of instructions is also important. We'll see how important this is for the 486 and the Pentium in the section dealing with AGIs. And finally, the ultimate optimization exercise is proper instruction ordering on the Pentium. These optimizations are covered in Chapter 18 which is devoted to a general discussion of the Pentium chip.

# Code Size vs Speed

Many code selection optimizations boil down to a trade-off between code size and speed. Many widely known optimizations have both a code size and speed advantage. Two of the most widely known and used optimizations are setting a register to zero and multiplying by two:

```
mov    ax, 0          ; 3 ways to zero a register
xor    ax, ax
sub    ax, ax

mov    eax, 0         ; (32-bit methods)
xor    eax, eax
sub    eax, eax
```

There are at least three ways to multiply a 16-bit register by two:

```
mov    bx, 2
mul    bx             ; multiply AX by 2

shl    ax, 1          ; also multiplies AX by 2

add    ax, ax         ; also multiplies AX by 2
```

Here are four ways to multiply a 32-bit register by two:

```
mov    ebx, 2
mul    ebx

shl    eax, 1

add    eax, eax

lea    eax, [eax+eax]
```

## Comparing Similar Instructions

Let's look at the details of the various ways to set a 32-bit register to zero. See Table 21.9.

**Table 21.9 Zeroing a Register**

| Instruction | Code Size | Flags Affected | Cycles | | |
|---|---|---|---|---|---|
| | | | Pentium | 486 | 386 |
| mov | 5 | none | 1 | 1 | 2 |
| xor | 2 | all arith | 1 | 1 | 2 |
| sub | 2 | all arith | 1 | 1 | 2 |

It is rare that there are two ways to do exactly the same thing. XOR and SUB are a rare case. The cycle counts are the same for all three instructions. The only differences are the affect on the flags and the code size.

Here's the details of the different ways to multiply a 32-bit register by two.

**Table 21.10 Multiplying by 2**

| Instruction | Code Size | Flags Affected | Cycles | | |
|---|---|---|---|---|---|
| | | | Pentium | 486 | 386 |
| mov/mul | 5+2 | CF OF | 1/10 | 1/13 | 2/9 |
| shl | 2 | all arith | 1 | 1 | 2 |
| add | 2 | all arith | 1 | 1 | 2 |
| lea | 3 | none | 1 | 1 | 2 |

The following steps can be used to sort through various instruction sequences:

- Compare the effects of alternatives for your situation.

- Determine the code size bytes.

- Count the cycles for each target CPU for baseline info.

- Time the sequences on each target CPU.

- Time the sequences in your code for each target CPU.

These steps tell you several things. First, you can identify whether two code sequences produce the same results. Second, it tells you the code size of each choice of instructions.

Another more complicated example is multiplying by two with identical data results. MUL and SHL leave the flags in a different state. But more important, they don't produce the same data. MUL accepts operands of 8- 16- or 32-bits and returns a 16-, 32- or 64-bit result. SHL accepts operands of the same size and returns results of the same size. The carry flag must be shifted into a zeroed register to get the same result for large initial values. If we needed SHL to allow for large values, we would need to use one of these examples:

```
mov    ah, 0                      ; 8->9 bits
shl    ax, 1

xor    dx, dx                     ; 16->17 bits
shl    ax, 1
rcl    dx, 1
```

Of course, it really pays to know your data so you can eliminate most of this complication when it is not required. Multiplying by 4 or 8 is even more complicated. Again, in this next example, there are several methods to choose from. Here are three ways of advancing a pointer by two:

```
inc    si                        ; inc method
inc    si

add    si, 2                     ; add method

lea    si, [si+2]                ; lea method
```

**Table 21.11 Advancing a Pointer by 2**

| Instruction | Code Size | Flags Affected | Pentium | Cycles 486 | 386 |
|---|---|---|---|---|---|
| inc | 2 | all but CF | 2 | 2 | 4 |
| add | 3 | all arith | 1 | 1 | 2 |
| lea | 3 | none | 1 | 1 | 2 |

The INC method is smaller only when advancing a pointer by one or two. LEA has the advantage of not affecting the flags, when this is required. However, the LEA instruction is much more powerful and versatile as we'll see in the next section.

## LEA

The official purpose of the LEA instruction is to load an effective address. However, due to the possible complexities of address generation, you can take advantage of the special internal hardware allocated for this instruction. Specifically, the LEA instruction can add three operands at once, placing the result in another register, and in 32-bit addressing modes it is even more powerful. This leads to a number of interesting optimizations, such as:

- Pointer addition without changing the flags.

- Fast multiplications.

- Two, three and four operand addition.

There is a hidden disadvantage to the LEA instruction on the 486 and the Pentium. Because it uses the address generation unit, it is possible to have an LEA instruction delayed due to an AGI when an ADD or some other instruction would not have the same delay. This is because the execution of the LEA occurs in a different pipeline stage than the ADD. Normally, this will not be of any concern since it would rarely be an issue.

In 32-bit mode, the LEA instruction can add any two registers and an immediate value. One of the two registers can also be multiplied by 2, 4 or 8. This makes LEA especially useful in 32-bit mode code. Here are some sample uses:

Using LEA to multiply:

```
lea  eax, [eax+eax]        ; mult by 2
lea  eax, [ebx+ebx*2]      ; mult by 3
lea  eax, [ecx*4]          ; mult by 4
lea  eax, [edx+edx*4]      ; mult by 5
lea  eax, [esi*8]          ; mult by 8
lea  eax, [edi+edi*8]      ; mult by 9
```

```
        add  eax, eax
        lea  eax, [eax+eax*2]          ; mult by 6

        add  ebx, ebx
        lea  ebx, [ebx+ebx*4]          ; mult by 10

        add  ecx, ecx
        lea  ecx, [ecx+ecx*8]          ; mult by 18

        mov  ebx, eax
        lea  ebx, [ebx+ebx*8]
        lea  eax, [eax+ebx*2]          ; mult by 19

        mov  ebx, eax
        lea  ebx, [ebx+ebx*8]
        lea  eax, [eax+ebx*4]          ; mult by 37

        mov  ebx, eax
        lea  ebx, [ebx+ebx*8]
        lea  eax, [eax+ebx*8]          ; mult by 73
```

Using LEA to add:

```
        lea  eax, [eax+ebx]           ; two operands

        lea  eax, [ebx+ecx]           ; three operands
                                      ; replaces MOV and ADD

        lea  eax, [ebx+ecx+4]         ; four operands
                                      ; replaces MOV & 2 ADDs

        lea  eax, [eax+1]             ; replaces INC
        lea  eax, [eax+4]             ; pointer addition

        lea  eax, [eax-1]             ; replaces DEC
        lea  eax, [eax-4]             ; pointer subtraction
```

## Code Size Optimizations for 32-bit Instructions

Because of the way that 32-bit operands work, there are some interesting quirks in the instruction set. When using these optimizations, you must keep in mind that they apply only to code written for 32-bit segments (i.e. declared with USE32). When used in a 16-bit segment, you must take into account that the assembler will automatically insert an operand-size prefix and/or address-size prefix.

The 32-bit immediate move always takes 4 bytes for the data and 2 bytes for the MOV opcode in a 16-bit segment. For example, to move a 1 into a register:

```
mov eax, 1
```

This instruction takes 6 bytes of code. The combination of instructions to zero a register (XOR or SUB) and then increment is slightly shorter:

```
sub eax, eax
inc eax
```

These instructions take 2 bytes and 1 byte, respectively (for 32-bit code). This is only half the length of the more straight-forward MOV shown previously. Because of the prefix bytes, in 16-bit code the MOV would be 7 bytes and the SUB/INC would be 4, as follows:

```
sub eax, eax      ; 3 bytes
inc al            ; 1 byte
```

The ALU (arithmetic logic unit) instructions have several different forms that are automatically chosen by the assembler. Instructions that use the accumulator (AL, AX or EAX) can have one opcode byte or two. The assembler will normally generate the shorter form. In addition, the 16-bit and 32-bit register-immediate and memory-immediate forms of these instructions have a built-in sign extension capability. When an immediate value is in the range of -128 to +127 for a 16-bit or 32-bit ALU instruction, then the assembler can use the sign-extension instruction format.

The sign-extension instruction format is not available for the single opcode accumulator forms of the instructions. Therefore, in the original 8088/86 CPUs, the BX, CX, DX, BP, SI, DI and word ptr to memory forms of the instruction saved a single byte. However, when using 32-bit code, the sign-extension format saves 3 bytes. Table 21.12 shows the code size for the various forms:

**Table 21.12 Code Size for ALU Instructions**

| Destination | Immediate data size | | |
|-------------|------|------|-------|
| Operand | byte | word | dword |
| AL | 2 | - | - |
| AX | 3 | 3 | - |
| EAX | 3 | 5 | 5 |
| reg8 | 3 | - | - |
| reg16 | 3 | 4 | - |
| reg32 | 3 | 6 | 6 |
| mem8 | 3 | - | - |
| mem16 | 3 | 4 | - |
| mem32 | 3 | 6 | 6 |

*The table assumes no prefix bytes and no address displacement.*

You must keep in mind that when mixing 16-bit and 32-bit code, there is an additional one-byte or two-byte prefix that is automatically inserted by the assembler. These prefix bytes override the default operand size and/or address size of the instruction based on the D-bit for the current segment. When set to 1, the D-bit defines the segment as containing 32-bit code. When set to 0, the D-bit defines the segment as containing 16-bit code. The D-bit is located in the LDT (local descriptor table) or GDT (global descriptor table) for the selector of the current CS.

Here are some 32-bit examples of code that take advantage of the sign-extension and accumulator instruction formats:

```
mov     eax, 2          ; 5 bytes

sub     eax, eax        ; 2 bytes
add     al, 2           ; 2 bytes


mov     eax, -1         ; 5 bytes

or      eax, -1         ; 3 bytes
```

```
mov     eax, -2          ; 5 bytes

xor     eax, eax         ; 2 bytes
dec     eax              ; 1 byte
dec     eax              ; 1 byte


add     ebx, 128         ; 6 bytes

add     ebx, 127         ; 3 bytes
inc     ebx              ; 1 byte
```

# Instruction Set Quirks

On a 486, shifts and rotates with immediate values of greater than 1 are faster than with 1. This quirk occurred because Intel optimized the shifts and rotates that use an additional immediate byte, but not the single byte shift and rotate instructions. The immediate byte of a shift or rotate can accept a value of 1. However, the assembler does not generate this.

```
shl     eax, 1           ; 3 cycles, 2 bytes
shl     eax, 2           ; 2 cycles, 3 bytes
```

To get the faster form on the 486 you can do the following:

```
db 0c1h, 0e0h, 1         ; same as shl eax, 1
```

This quirk applies to all the shifts and rotates; SHL, SHR, SAL, SAR, ROL and ROR.

## Mixing 16-bit and 32-bit Code

Mixing 16-bit and 32-bit code can provide tremendous optimization opportunities. But first, let's look at the various categories of mixing 16-bit and 32-bit code:

- Adding 32-bit operands to 16-bit code.

- Using 16-bit operands in 32-bit code.

- Writing code with both 16-bit and 32-bit segments.

# Adding 32-bit Operands to 16-bit Code

MS-DOS runs programs that are 16-bit. If you know your program is running on a 386 or above, you can put 32-bit instructions into your code. You could require a 386+ to run your program and check this on startup, or you could just call a different set of routines when a 386+ is detected. A good example would be the use of the larger registers for performing division.

In Chapter 20, we developed a set of extended precision multiplication and division routines. These routines can take 500 to 1000 times as long as the single MUL and DIV instructions on the 386 and above. You could write your code to take advantage of the 32-bit multiply as follows:

```
        lea     si, operand1
        lea     di, operand2
        cmp     flag386, 1
        je      fast
        call    num_long_mult
        jmp     fin
  fast:
        call    num_long_mult386
  fin:
```

Another method for doing the same thing would be to store the address of the procedure in a variable in memory. This variable would be initialized to the standard routine, but modified if a 386+ was detected, as follows:

```
        lea     si, operand1
        lea     di, operand2
        call    word ptr long_mult
        ...
  long_mult    dw      num_long_mult
```

Somewhere in your initialization, you would have a section of code that initializes the pointer to the optional 32-bit version of the multiply routine. For example:

```
        cmp     flag386, 1
        jne     done
        lea     ax, num_long_mult386
        mov     long_mult, ax
```

Keep in mind that what we have just done is to add 32-bit operands to 16-bit code. This code will still be run from a 16-bit environment, such as MS-DOS, and will still have the same basic restrictions as any other MS-DOS program.

## Using 16-bit Operands in 32-bit Code

Just as we used 32-bit operands in a program that is running in a 16-bit segment, we can do the reverse. We can use 16-bit operands in a program running in a 32-bit segment. You may be wondering, 'Why would you want to do this?'. There are two reasons:

- Re-use of old working code.

- Optimized use of data types.

Re-use of old working code is a valid reason for mixing 16-bit and 32-bit code. If you have some working code, changing it may introduce bugs. However, there are several precautions that must be taken. You cannot use old libraries and object files without re-assembling them. As a minimum, the code must be edited to declare each applicable segment as a USE32 code segment. When using the simplified segmentations directives, this requires the .386 directive (or .486/.586 directives) before the .model directive. A strange quirk of the assembler then sets the default segment type to USE32, instead of USE16.

The optimized use of data types has more to do with the size of data elements and structures declared in memory than the speed of execution. The execution speed of reading or writing words rather than dwords may actually be slower when running 32-bit code. This is because the additional prefix bytes will cause the code to be larger and take additional machine cycles on some CPUs. The following is an example of mixing 16-bit and 32-bit code:

```
.386
.model small

.code

        checksum proc near
        ;-----------------------------------
        ; 16-bit checksum procedure
        ;
        ; inputs: DS:EDX ptr to block to checksum
        ; (ends with a word of FFFFh
        ;
        ; outputs: AX 16-bit checksum
        ;-----------------------------------
```

```
            push    ebx
            push    edx

            xor     eax, eax

    c1:
            mov     bx, [edx]          ; operand-size prefix
            cmp     bx, -1             ; operand-size prefix
            je      c2
            add     ax, bx             ; operand-size prefix
            add     edx, 2
            jmp     c1
    c2:

            pop     edx
            pop     ebx

            ret

            checksum endp
```

The above example contains 3 instructions with operand-size prefixes. The code for each of these instructions is prefixed by the operand-size prefix (66h). If the speed of the code is important, it is sometimes easy to eliminate some of the prefix bytes. In this case it would be possible to make some changes so that the inner loop has fewer prefix bytes, as follows:

```
    .386
    .model small

    .code

            checksum proc near
            ;------------------------------------
            ; 16-bit checksum procedure
            ;
            ; inputs: DS:EDX ptr to block to checksum
            ; (ends with a word of FFFFh
            ;
            ; outputs: AX 16-bit checksum
            ;------------------------------------

            push    ebx
            push    edx

            xor     eax, eax
            xor     ebx, ebx
```

```
c1:
        mov     bx, [edx]                   ; operand-size prefix
        cmp     ebx, 0000FFFFh              ; no operand-size prefix
        je      c2
        add     eax, ebx                    ; no operand-size prefix
        add     edx, 2
        jmp     c1
c2:

        pop     edx
        pop     ebx

        ret

        checksum endp
```

## Mixing 16-bit and 32-bit Segments

There are probably very few cases when you would write code that has both 16-bit and 32-bit segments. The primary use for this is in writing operating systems, memory managers and other such utilities. But, there are two other important cases: when using a DOS extender or using a DPMI host as a DOS extender.

In the following example, a DPMI host such as the one included in the 386MAX memory manager is used to allow the execution of true 32-bit code, when run from the DOS prompt. The DPMI host in Windows can also be used from a DOS window in enhanced mode. However, because Windows will periodically interrupt the DOS session (for multi-tasking), you cannot perform meaningful time measurements and performance is degraded compared to running without Windows. Explanations for each block of code are included at the end of the listing. There is a stand alone version of this program on the disk in LST21-1.ASM:

```
.model small

    ;------------------------------------------------
    ; General template for mixing 16-bit and 32-bit
    ; protected mode code with DPMI
    ;------------------------------------------------

    .stack
    .386

    .data
```

```
    ; message strings

msg1    db 'Mixed 16- and 32-bit code example.',13,10,0
msg32   db 'In protected mode, 32-bit segment.',13,10,0
emsg1   db 'DPMI host not detected.',13,10,0
emsg2   db 'Could not allocate memory.',13,10,0
emsg3   db 'Could not switch to protected mode.',13,10,0


code32_sel dw 0
main32_addr df main32                      ; (see note 11)

; data returned from INT 2Fh function 1687h

DPMI_mem        dw 0
DPMI_entry      dd 0

cs_descriptor label dword
cs_limit            dw 0                    ; descriptor limit
cs_low_addr         db 0,0,0               ; low order 3 bytes of address
cs_access           dw 0                    ; descriptor access bytes
cs_high_addr   db 0                         ; high order byte of address

.code

main proc

        mov     ax, @data
        mov     ds, ax

; (1) re-size memory allocated

        mov     bx, ss                     ; start of stack segment
        mov     ax, es                     ; start of PSP
        sub     bx, ax                     ; para for code & data
        mov     ax, sp                     ; get stack size
        shr     ax, 4                      ; divide by 16 to get para
        add     bx, ax
        inc     bx                         ; BX = total para needed
        mov     ah, 4ah                    ; modify memory allocation
        int     21h

; (2) check to see if DPMI is available

        call    DPMI_check                 ; check for a DPMI server
        jc      error1                     ; exit if none
```

```
        ; (3) Print intro message

                lea     si, msg1        ; intro message
                call    print_string

        ; (4) Allocate memory for DPMI server

                mov     ax, 0                      ; use 0 if no memory needed
                mov     bx, DPMI_mem               ; get para cnt for DPMI
                test    bx, bx
                jz      main_2                     ; skip down if none required
                mov     ah, 48h                    ; allocate memory
                int     21h
                jc      error2                     ; check for allocate error

        ; (5) switch to protected mode
        main_2:
                mov     es, ax
                mov     ax, 1                      ; indicate 32-bit application
                call    dword ptr DPMI_entry
                jc      error3                     ; if CF set, error in switch

        ; <<< 16-bit Protected Mode code here >>>

        ;=====================================
        ; setup to switch to 32-bit mode
        ;=====================================

        ; (6) allocate a descriptor for use32 segment

                mov     ax, 0                      ; allocate LDT descriptor
                mov     cx, 1                      ; 1 descriptor
                int     31h                        ; call DPMI host
                mov     code32_sel,ax              ; selector to use32 segment
                mov     word ptr main32_addr[2], ax ; store selector

        ; (7) get copy of LDT entry

                mov     bx, cs                     ; get current CS descriptor
                lea     di, cs_descriptor          ; point to result buffer
                movzx   edi, di                    ; (convert to 32 bits)
                push    ds                         ; ES:EDI => buffer
                pop     es
                mov     ax, 000bh                  ; get descriptor request
                int     31h                        ; call DPMI host
```

```
        ; (8) set segment base address

                mov     ax, seg code32              ; linear address of code32
                movzx   eax, ax ;
                shl     eax, 4                      ; segment value times 16
                mov     dx, ax                      ; move to cx:dx
                mov     ecx, eax
                shr     ecx, 16
                mov     bx, code32_sel              ; identify selector
                mov     ax, 7                       ; set segment base address
                int     31h                         ; call DPMI host

        ; (9) set segment limit

                mov     cx, 0000h                   ; set segment limit to 64K
                mov     dx, 0ffffh
                mov     bx, code32_sel              ; identify selector
                mov     ax, 8h                      ; set segment limit request
                int     31h                         ; call DPMI host

        ; (10) switch to 32-bit mode by changing the D bit

                mov     cx, cs_access               ; start with current cs access
                or      ch, 40h                     ; change to 32 bit default
                mov     bx, code32_sel              ; identify selector
                mov     ax, 0009h                   ; set access rights request
                int     31h                         ; call DPMI host

        ; (11) Execute a 16:16 far call to 32-bit code

                call    dword ptr main32_addr

        ; When we return we are still in 16-bit PM.

        main_exit:
                mov     ax, 4c00h                   ; DOS exit
                int     21h

        ; error messages

        error1:
                lea     si, emsg1                   ; DPMI host not found
                jmp     err0

        error2:
                lea     si, emsg2                   ; could not allocate memory
                jmp     err0

        error3:
                lea     si, emsg3                   ; could not switch to PM
```

```
err0:
        call    print_string
        jmp     main_exit

main endp


        DPMI_check proc near
        ;----------------------------------------
        ; Check for existence of a DPMI server
        ;
        ; outputs: CF set if no DPMI server found
        ;----------------------------------------

        push    ax
        push    bx
        push    cx
        push    dx
        push    di
        push    si
        push    es

        mov     ax, 1687h                   ; request DPMI host address
        int     2fh                         ; via multiplex int 2Fh
        test    ax, ax                      ; AX = 0 if success
        jnz     not_found                   ; exit with error if not found

        and     bl, 00000001b               ; check bit 0 to see if 32-bit
        setne   al                          ; code supported (Not used in this
                                            ; example)

        mov     DPMI_mem, si
        mov     word ptr DPMI_entry[0], di
        mov     word ptr DPMI_entry[2], es
        clc

dc_ret:
        pop     es
        pop     si
        pop     di
        pop     dx
        pop     cx
        pop     bx
        pop     ax
        ret

not_found:
        stc                                 ; CF set if not found
        jmp     dc_ret
```

```
DPMI_check endp

public print_string
print_string proc near
;---------------------------------------
; Print ASCIIZ string
;
; inputs: DS:SI ptr to string
;---------------------------------------

        push    ax
        push    bx
        push    cx
        push    dx

        call    str_len
        mov     cx, ax
        mov     dx, si
        mov     bx, 1                   ; stdout
        mov     ah, 40h                 ; DOS write handle
        int     21h

        pop     dx
        pop     cx
        pop     bx
        pop     ax
        ret

print_string endp

public str_len
str_len proc near
;---------------------------------------
; Get length of string
;
; inputs: DS:SI ptr to string
;
; outputs: AX length
;---------------------------------------

        push    cx
        push    di
        push    es

        push    ds
        pop     es
        mov     di, si

        mov     cx, -1                  ; max str len
        xor     al, al                  ; char to look for
```

```
        cld

        repne   scasb                           ; repeat while ES:[DI] <> 0
        mov     ax, -2
        sub     ax, cx                          ; len

        pop     es
        pop     di
        pop     cx
        ret

str_len endp

code32  segment public para use32 'code'
assume cs:code32

public main32
main32 proc far
;-------------------------------------
; 32-bit code main entry point
;
; DS = @data from 16-bit code
;-------------------------------------

        pusha

; (12) display message that we're in 32-bit mode

        mov     esi, offset msg32
        call    print_string32

; (13) call any 32-bit code from here

        call    your_32_bit_code

; restore registers

        popa

; (14) return to the 16-bit code segment we came from

        db      66h                     ; operand size prefix (see note below)
        ret

;----------------------------------------------------------
; Note: If a RET is used without the operand-size prefix
; the assembler would generate a normal RETF for 32-bit
; code (16:32). We need this return to match the CALL
; that got us here (16:16).
;----------------------------------------------------------
```

```
main32 endp

your_32_bit_code proc

        ret

your_32_bit_code endp

public print_string32
print_string32 proc near
;--------------------------------------
; 32-bit Print ASCIIZ string
;
; inputs: DS:ESI ptr to string
;--------------------------------------

        push    eax
        push    ebx
        push    ecx
        push    edx

        call    str_len32
        mov     ecx, eax
        mov     edx, esi
        mov     ebx, 1                  ; stdout
        mov     ah, 40h                 ; DOS write handle
        int     21h

        pop     edx
        pop     ecx
        pop     ebx
        pop     eax
        ret

print_string32 endp

public str_len32
str_len32 proc near
;--------------------------------------
; 32-bit Get length of string
;
; inputs: DS:ESI ptr to string
;
; outputs: EAX length
;--------------------------------------

        push    ecx
        push    edi
        push    es
```

```
        push    ds
        pop     es
        mov     edi, esi

        mov     ecx, -1                    ; max str len
        xor     al, al                     ; char to look for
        cld

        repne   scasb                      ; repeat while ES:[DI] <> 0
        mov     eax, -2
        sub     eax, ecx                   ; len

        pop     es
        pop     edi
        pop     ecx
        ret

str_len32 endp

code32  ends

end main
```

Here is an explanation of the code in the above listing. Comments in the code correspond to the numbers:

(1) The program starts by resizing memory to the amount actually used by the program. If you change the segment configuration, be sure to change this calculation. It is based on the stack being at the end of the memory image.

Alternatively, this code can be removed and the LINK option CP:1 can be used to change the number of paragraphs of memory to be allocated to the minimum required.

(2) The code checks for the presence of a DPMI server. If none, then the program exits with an error message. The program has been tested with 386MAX version 6.0 and 7.0.

(3) An initialization message is output to the screen.

(4) DOS memory is allocated, if required, for the DPMI server. When the check is made for the presence of a DPMI server, the number of paragraphs of memory is returned. It may be zero.

(5) Switch into protected mode. When the check is made for the presence of a DPMI server, the far address for the procedure used to enter protected mode is returned. This entry point is used only for the first switch into protected mode by an application.

When the switch to protected mode is complete the application gains control with the following segment register settings:

| | | |
|---|---|---|
| CS | = | selector matching CS on entry with size of 64K |
| DS | = | selector matching DS on entry with size of 64K |
| SS | = | selector matching SS on entry with size of 64K |
| ES | = | selector for PSP with a size of 100h |
| FS | = | 0 |
| GS | = | 0 |

If SS and DS are the same on entry there will be only one descriptor allocated and SS and DS will be the same on return. The environment pointer (at PSP:2Ch) in the PSP is automatically converted to a valid selector if it is not 0 on entry.

(6) Allocate a descriptor for USE32 segment. Although our 32-bit code is in memory, the DPMI host does not know about it. We must allocate a descriptor for this segment.

(7) After the descriptor is allocated we must get a copy of the LDT (local descriptor table) entry so that we may make modifications to it.

(8) Set the segment base address. The first modification is to specify the starting address of our 32-bit code segment.

(9) Set the segment limit. The second modification is to specify the size of our 32-bit code segment. Because this code was loaded by DOS in low memory, the code size is limited to less than 640K, just like DOS programs. To run a larger program memory must be allocated beyond 1MB and then an EXE loader program must load the large program into the allocated memory.

(10) The final modification is to identify our 32-bit code segment as such by changing the D bit in the access rights/type bytes. When the DPMI server allocates a descriptor, the default value for the D bit is zero which is for 16-bit code segments.

(11) The next step is to execute a call to our 32-bit code. This call is a protected-mode 16:16 far call. This means we have an address in memory that is a 16-bit offset followed by a 16-bit selector. This address is stored in the data segment in a variable named main32_addr. The data type of main32_addr always needs to be a dword (DD), even if you change memory models. Various versions of assemblers may generate errors and require a DF declaration. This is not a problem because main32_addr is declared as a pointer to main32, but the second word is always overwritten with the actual selector obtained during program execution, always providing a correct dword ptr for 16-bit code.

(12) A message is displayed upon entry to the 32-bit code. It is important to note that the utility routines used in the 32-bit code must be separate from those used in the 16-bit code.

(13) Call your own 32-bit code here.

(14) This is the return to the 16-bit code segment where we came from. This return may seem odd, but is very important. The return must match the call. A near return for a USE32 segment is a 32-bit offset. A far return for a USE32 segment is a 6-byte far pointer (32-bit offset and 16-bit selector). The call to the main32 procedure is a 16-bit far call (16-bit offset and 16-bit selector). To execute the proper RET instruction requires using an operand size prefix byte (66h). In most cases, MASM and TASM can automatically generate prefix bytes when required. In this case, there is no way for the assembler to know the proper type of RET to be generated, therefore the operand-size prefix byte must be manually inserted.

This operand-size-prefixed return instruction is only required if you need to return to the original 16-bit protected mode code. If not, you can just issue an INT 21h, function 4Ch and exit back to DOS. The DPMI server automatically intercepts this interrupt call and performs all required steps to return to DOS.

The DPMI functions used are documented in the DPMI Specification version 1.0 (see Appendix B). The Microsoft Developer Network CD-ROM contains version 0.9 of the DPMI specification.

# Summary

When optimizing code you should always start with a good design and a good algorithm, regardless of the language you are using. After this you should consider alignment of code and data and the other various techniques presented above. You should always test your optimizations by timing your code with representative data. Finally, be sure that you know what it is that you are measuring - a difference due to the changes you made or a side effect.

APPENDIX A

# Microsoft Real-time Compression Interface (MRCI)

There are a lot of different compression utilities in the PC world. Some are fast but provide a low compression ratio, others are slow but will pack to an unbelievably small size; others again are weak in both techniques. However, as usual, Microsoft stepped in, and decided to help the community establish law and order, and came up with its own standard. It provides a kind of internal compression utility, the MRCI server, that systems and applications can both use.

They've engaged a simple variant of the Lempel-Ziv compression technique for the MRCI. Although there are compression programs around which work better and faster, we think we should give a description of the MRCI interface as well as some recipes on how to make it work for you. After all, you may already have this engine installed (in the body of DOS 6.x) so why shouldn't you use it?

# Detecting the MRCI Server Presence

You can use interrupt 2Fh Function 4A12h to check whether an MRCI server is present in memory, or interrupt 1Ah Function 0B001h to determine whether a ROM BIOS MRCI server is present. Both functions return the address of an MRCINFO structure, if a server is present.

Example:

```
            OLD_CX  EQU     'MR'
            OLD_DX  EQU     'CI'
            NEW_CX  EQU     'IC'
            NEW_DX  EQU     'RM'

            MRCI_Info   dd          0

            mov         cx,OLD_CX       ; Great innovation of Microsoft
            mov         dx,OLD_DX       ; just to determine MRCI presence

            mov         ax,4A12h        ; Function 4Ah Subfunction 12h
            int         2Fh             ; Multiplex interrupt

            cmp         cx,NEW_CX       ; Check signature
            jne         not_present
            cmp         dx,NEW_DX
            jne         not_present

            mov         word ptr MRCI_Info,di        ; es:di contains the
            mov         word ptr MRCI_Info+2,es      ; MRCINFO address

            . . .

    not_present:

            . . .
```

You can use this same code fragment to determine if the ROM BIOS MRCI server is present except for the number of the interrupt and the function call. They must be changed to 1Ah and 0B001h respectively.

## Acquiring the Windows Disk-critical Section

When working in Windows 386 enhanced mode, you must acquire the Windows disk-critical section before the actual call to the MRCI. It will prevent the MRCI server from being re-entered. When you finish with MRCI you should release the critical section.

Example of acquiring the critical section:

```
push    ax
mov     ax,8001h
int     2Ah
pop     ax
```

Example of releasing the critical section:

```
push    ax
mov     ax,8101h
int     2Ah
pop     ax
```

## Data Compressing

You can simply call the MRCI server to compress your data for you. Before the actual call, you should create a MRCREQUEST structure (see below, MRCI Data Structures, for what this structure should contain) to specify the source data and target buffer - where to place the result of the compression.

Fragment of MRCI function call.

```
mrcr    MRCREQUEST <>
MRCI_Info       dd      0               ; Address of MRCI server
buffer1         db      4096 dup(?)     ; Uncompressed data
buffer2         db      4096 dup(?)     ; Compressed data

lea             si,mrcr
mov             ax,ds

;       Initialize the input buffer
mov             word ptr ds:[si].mrcr_bSrc,offset buffer1
mov             word ptr ds:[si].[mrcr_bSrc+2],ax
mov             word ptr ds:[si].mrcr_cSrc,4096

;       Initialize the output buffer
```

```
mov             word ptr ds:[si].mrcr_bDst,offset buffer2
mov             word ptr ds:[si].[mrcr_bDst+2],ax
mov             word ptr ds:[si].mrcr_cDst,4096

;       Initialize the minimum required savings in bytes.
mov             word ptr ds:[si].mrcr_cChunk,1

mov             ax,1                    ; Set type of operation
xor                       cx,cx         ; Set type of client

    les                       bx,MRCI_Info
;       Call compression routine
    call                      dword ptr es:[bx].mi_pfnOperate
    or                        ax,ax          ; Check for errors
    jnz                       error
```

You can read the field  mrcr_cDst from MRCREQUEST structure to obtain the size of the compressed data.

## Data Decompressing

You can decompress already compressed data like this.

```
mrcr    MRCREQUEST <>
MRCI_Info       dd      0               ; Address of MRCI server
buffer1         db      4096 dup(?)     ; Compressed data
buffer2         db      4096 dup(?)     ; Decompressed data

lea             si,mrcr
mov             ax,ds

;       Initialize the input buffer
mov             word ptr ds:[si].mrcr_bSrc,offset buffer1
mov             word ptr ds:[si].[mrcr_bSrc+2],ax
mov             word ptr ds:[si].mrcr_cSrc,4096

;       Initialize the output buffer
mov             word ptr ds:[si].mrcr_bDst,offset buffer2
mov             word ptr ds:[si].[mrcr_bDst+2],ax
mov             word ptr ds:[si].mrcr_cDst,4096

mov             ax,2                    ; Set type of operation
xor                       cx,cx         ; Set type of client

les                       bx,MRCI_Info
;       Call decompression routine
call                      dword ptr es:[bx].mi_pfnOperate
or                        ax,ax          ; Check for errors
jnz                       error
```

# MRCI Data Structures

## MRCINFO

```
MRCINFO            STRUC
mi_lVendor         dd      ?
mi_wVendorVersion  dw      ?
mi_wMRCIVersion    dw      ?
mi_pfnOperate      dd      ?
mi_fCapability     dw      ?
mi_fHWAssist       dw      ?
mi_cMax            dw      ?
MRCINFO            ENDS
```

This structure contains the following information about MRCI server:

- mi_lVendor — Contains the vendor identifier. For Microsoft this field contains "MSFT".

- mi_wVendorVersion — Contains the version number of the MRCI server. For instance 5.17 will be stored as 0511h.

- mi_wMRCIVersion — Contains the MRCI version number.

- mi_pfnOperate — Contains the 32-bit address of the MRCI operation function (see below).

- mi_fCapability — Specifies the capability of the server (see Table A.1).

**Table A.1 Server Capability**

| Value | | Meaning |
|-------|---|---------|
| 0h | (micapNONE) | No capabilities |
| 1h | (micapSTANDARD) | Standard compression |
| 2h | (micapDECOMPRESS) | Standard decompression |
| 20h | (micapINCDECOMP) | Incremental decompression |
| 8000h | (micapREADONLY) | MRCINFO structure is read-only |
| 0FFFFh | (micapDEINSTALL) | De-install service |

- mi_fHWAssist     This field is analagous to the field mi_fCapability and specifies the hardware-assisted server capabilities.

- mi_cMax     Contains maximum number of the bytes which server can compress or decompress. All MRCI servers support at least 8192-byte blocks.

## MRCREQUEST

| MRCREQUEST | STRUC | |
| mrcr_bSrc | dd | ? |
| mrcr_cSrc | dw | ? |
| mrcr_Reserv | dw | ? |
| mrcr_bDst | dd | ? |
| mrcr_cDst | dw | ? |
| mrcr_Chunk | dw | ? |
| mrcr_IncDecomp | dd | ? |
| MRCREQUEST | END | |

The information from this structure is used by the server to compress or decompress data. The fields are as follows:

- mrcr_bSrc     Contains the 32-bit input buffer address. Its meaning depends on the type of the operation (see Table A.2)

**Table A.2 Operation Type and Contents**

| Type | Contents |
| --- | --- |
| 1 (micapSTANDARD) | Buffer contains uncompressed data |
| 2 (micapDECOMPRESS) | Buffer contains compressed data |

*Continued*

**Table A.2 Operation Type and Contents (Continued)**

| Type | Contents |
|------|----------|
| 20h (micapINCDECOMP) | Buffer contains the next section of compressed data to be decompressed. After each decompress operation server updates the value in field mrcr_bSrc so you should not modify it between operations on the same block. |

- mrcr_cSrc field is     Specifies the size of the input buffer in bytes. This ignored for decompression.

- mrcr_Reserv     Reserved

- mrcr_bDst     Contains the 32-bit output buffer address. Its meaning depends on the type of the operation (see Table A.3)

**Table A.3 Operation Type and Contents**

| Type | Contents |
|------|----------|
| 1 (micapSTANDARD) | Buffer receives compressed data |
| 2 (micapDECOMPRESS) | Buffer receives uncompressed data |
| 20h (micapINCDECOMP) | Buffer contains the address of the next section of uncompressed data to be stored in the destination buffer. After each incremental decompress operation the server updates the value in this field so you should not modify it between operations on the same block. |

- mrcr_cDst     Specifies the size of the destination buffer in bytes. This value has the meanings shown in Table A.4.

Table A.4 Operation Type and Meaning

| Type | | Meaning |
|---|---|---|
| 1h | (micapSTANDARD) | If compressed data would overflow this length, the operation fails. |
| 2 | (micapDECOMPRESS) | MRCI server uses this value to determine when to stop decompressing. |
| 20h | (micapINCDECOMP) | A single compressed block can be decompressed in steps by making an incremental decompression operation for a smaller block. The server updates this field with the size of the resulting data. |
| mrcr_cChunk | | This value specifies the minimum required savings, in bytes. If the length of the source data is less than this minimum, the server will (de)compress the data. |
| mrcr_IncDecomp | | The server updates this field with new state information after each incremental decompression operation, for use with the next incremental decompression operation. You should not modify this field between subsequent incremental decompression operations on the same compressed block. Initially, this field must be set to zero. |

To call the MRCI operation function (mi_pfnOperate) you should prepare the following:

Input:

| | |
|---|---|
| AX: | Operation |
| CX: | ClientType |
| DS:SI: | Address of the filled MRCREQUEST structure |

The Operation field specifies the type of the operation. This field may contain the following values:

| | |
|---|---|
| 1 | (micapSTANDARD), |
| 2 | (micapDECOMPRESS), |
| 20h | (micapINCDECOMP). |

The ClientType field specifies the type of the MRCI client. The possible values are as follows:

| | |
|---|---|
| 0 | (mcAPPLICATION), |
| 1 | (mcSYSTEM). |

For more information see MRCINFO field mi_fCapability.

| | |
|---|---|
| Call: | CALL dword ptr [mi_pfnOperate] |
| Output: | AX:Returns 0 if successful |
| | If error, returns the values shown in Table A.5 |

**Table A.5 Error Values and Meanings**

| Value | Meaning |
|---|---|
| 1 | Unsupported operation |
| 2 | Server is busy |
| 3 | The receive buffer is too small |
| 4 | Data could not be compressed |
| 5 | Compress data format is invalid |

APPENDIX B

# Graphics File Formats

It is an important point to understand that despite the prior existence of numerous widely accepted formats, developers can't resist the tempation to invent 'new and improved' formats. Understandably, without an supreme governing council, this leads to a proliferation of standards.

With this in mind, during this appendix, we will look at the leading contenders in the standards debate.

# BMP/DIB

| | |
|---|---|
| Name: | Microsoft Windows Device Independent Bitmap. |
| | (`.BMP`, `.DIB`) |
| Owner/Creator: | Microsoft. |
| Compression: | RLE or none. |
| Video Range: | Whole, from 1 to 24 bits per pixel. |
| Occupation: | Image display and interchange under MS Windows. |

**Table B.1 DIB File Header**

| Offset bytes | Size | Description (bytes) |
|---|---|---|
| **FILE HEADER** | | |
| 0 | 2 | ASCII string 'BM' |
| 2 | 4 | Size of the file in bytes |
| 6 | 2 | Reserved - 0 |
| 8 | 2 | Reserved - 0 |
| 10 | 4 | Image offset, counting in from the beginning of the file |
| **IMAGE HEADER** | | |
| 14 | 4 | Size of the image header (always 40 bytes) |
| 18 | 4 | Image width in pixels |
| 22 | 4 | Image height in pixels |
| 26 | 2 | Number of planes, always 1 |
| 28 | 2 | Bits per pixel (1,4,8,24 possible) |
| 30 | 4 | Compression type (0 = uncompressed, other = RLE) |
| 34 | 4 | Compressed image size, in bytes |
| 38 | 4 | Horizontal resolution, in pixels per meter |
| 42 | 4 | Vertical resolution, in pixels per meter |

*Continued*

**Table B.1 DIB File Header (Continued)**

| Offset bytes | Size | Description (bytes) |
|---|---|---|
| 46 | 4 | Number of colors (palette entries) used |
| 50 | 4 | Number of the most important colors (first in the palette) |
| 54 | 4*N | Color map (palette) |

*Normally N may be 2, 16 or 256 for 1, 4 or 8 bits per pixel (24 bits per pixel stands for the direct colors). The palette entry is 4 bytes long and contains RGB components, but in reverse order, i.e. B,G,R. The fourth byte is reserved, perhaps for the alpha channel.*

# Format Details

DIB is an excellent format across the Windows world, sometimes even supported abroad, for example, 3D Studio 3.0. You'll certainly find it convenient, except for its compression algorithm. You just need to remember that, in order to be able to display it properly, an image is written from the bottom to the top.

# Format Traps

There is a strange trap with the image row length in DIB. The size is accurately specified in the header - OK, no problem. However, each line is padded to a 4 byte boundary. Some applications pad by adding bytes while others prefer to truncate lines. If you rely on just adding, you risk getting your image 'sheared'. The only reliable approach we know works in this way:

```
Line length(in bytes) = (File size(in bytes)-Image offset) / Image height.
```

# Compression Details

The MS Windows DIB format is meant to support four and 8-bit RLE compression. However, we find this version of RLE decompression too sophisticated to implement. Most MS Windows applications have their own, usually unique, interpretation of DIB's RLE. Some of them don't even read the compressed DIBs that they themselves write.

# PCX

| | |
|---|---|
| Name: | PCX (`.PCX`) |
| Owner/Creator: | ZSoft. |
| Compression: | RLE or none. |
| Video Range: | Whole, from 1 to 24 bits per pixel (except for 15 and 16 bits per pixel HighColor). |
| Occupation: | Image display and interchange across the PC world. |

PCX is one of the oldest formats still extensively in use on the PC. Originally created by ZSoft for their paint software, the PCX format can at present be read and written by almost any PC graphics software. A new version of the PCX format even supports 24 bits per pixel. A PCX file starts with a header of 128 bytes.

**Table B.2 PCX File Header**

| Offset bytes (bytes) | Size | Description |
|---|---|---|
| 0 | 1 | Zsoft Flag (0Ah) |
| 1 | 1 | Version (always 5 so far) |
| 2 | 1 | Always 1 (means RLE encoded) |
| 3 | 1 | Number of bits per pixel for each plane |
| 4 | 2 | X Left |
| 6 | 2 | Y Upper |
| 8 | 2 | X Right |
| 10 | 2 | Y Lower |
| 12 | 2 | Horizontal resolution (dots per inch) |
| 14 | 2 | Vertical resolution (dots per inch) |
| 16 | 48 | Palette (see below) |
| 64 | 1 | Reserved, always 0 |
| 65 | 1 | Number of planes |

*Continued*

**Table B.2 PCX File Header (Continued)**

| Offset bytes (bytes) | Size | Description |
|---|---|---|
| 66 | 2 | Bytes per each plane line |
| 68 | 2 | Header palette interpretation, rarely used 1 |
| 70 | 2 | Screen size X (seems used only by PaintBrush 4) |
| 72 | 2 | Screen size Y |
| 74 | 54 | Zeros down to the end of the header. |

# Palette and Image Practice

The PCX format covers the widest range of video modes amongst the formats we are reviewing in this chapter, which is surely an advantage. However, the PCX file format provides next to nothing when you are considering the image type. To help you out, first find out which particular image type you are going to operate upon, and then look at the table given below:

**Table B.3 PCX Image Type Interpretation**

| Bits/pixel per plane | Number of planes | Description |
|---|---|---|
| 1 | 1 | Monochrome |
| 1 | 2 | 4 colors (is it still used?) |
| 2 | 1 | 4 colors |
| 1 | 4 | 16 colors 4 planes, standard mode, |
| 4 | 1 | 16 colors 2 pixels in each byte, |
| 8 | 1 | 256 colors, palette in the end of file |
| 8 | 3 | 16.7M-colors no palette, TrueColor |

*Note that the 4 plane, 1 bit per plane, 16-color mode is the best for PCX. It's main advantage is that separate planes are more easily compressed by the RLE algorithm. That's why we consider choosing 1 plane, 4 bits per pixel (two pixels in each byte), 16-color images type a mistake. In our opinion, it's the worst way to store a 16-color image. However, there are painting programs that prefer this way of storing images.*

The PCX format provides two ways of storing the image palette. The first is the EGA/VGA standard palette which resides in the header - 48 bytes starting from 16 and going up to 63. It's arranged in triads, 1 byte per RGB component. For VGA modes you have to divide the value of components by 4, and by 64 for EGA, if you want to obtain the levels of intensity.

For 256-color images, the whole palette must have 256 3-byte entries. There isn't enough space in the header, and therefore the palette lies at the end of file. It starts 768 bytes before the end of the file with the marker 0Ch. Again, the value of each byte should be divided by 4.

## Format Traps

Some applications pad each line of each plane to a word (two-byte) boundary. Again, the only reliable way involves some simple calculations:

```
Line length (in bytes) = ((XRight-XLeft+1) * Bits per pixel+ 7) / 8
```

Then you can compare the obtained value with the bytes-per-line field. If they are the same then OK, but if not, then during the decompression, you should skip the last byte of each plane line.

*Never believe anyone who says that the image scan lines, or plane scan lines, in PCX are always separated. Sometimes they are, but be prepared to face a PCX dialect which separates only image scan lines or even writes the continuous byte stream.*

In general, the PCX format suffers from its great age. Since it was first introduced in the early 80s, too many graphics standards have been established and too many versions of the format implemented. So the plain and short decompressing code introduced by ZSoft at present looks like a Chinese puzzle. (See the PCX reader on the accompanying disk.) We can't be sure that it covers all dialects, but at least it shows any PCX file we've ever seen. By the way, the compression ratio (if any) is poor for 8- and 24-bit images.

# TARGA

| | |
|---|---|
| Name: | TARGA (**.TGA**) |
| Owner/Creator: | Truevision, Inc. |
| Compression: | RLE or none. |
| Video Range: | Highend, 8, 15, 16, 24, and 32 (Alpha channel) bits per pixel. |
| Occupation: | Image storage and interchange, used by high-end graphics software and some scanners. |

TARGA files may contain:

- A fixed size (18 bytes long) header

- An optional ID string of variable size up to 255 bytes

- An optional color map

- An image section

- An optional footer

**Table B.4 TARGA File Header**

| Offset bytes | Size in bytes | Description |
|---|---|---|
| 0 | 1 | ID filed length |
| 1 | 1 | Color map flag (1 = paletted image, 0 = TrueColor) |
| 2 | 1 | Image type (see table overleaf) |
| **COLOR MAP SECTION** | | |
| 3 | 2 | First color map entry |
| 5 | 2 | Color map size |
| 7 | 1 | Color map entry size |

*Continued*

**Table B.4 TARGA File Header (Continued)**

| Offset bytes | Size in bytes | Description |
|---|---|---|
| IMAGE DATA SECTION | | |
| 8 | 2 | X Left |
| 10 | 2 | Y Upper |
| 12 | 2 | Image width in pixels |
| 14 | 2 | Image height in pixels |
| 16 | 1 | Number of bits per pixel |
| 17 | 1 | Image descriptor byte. (See below) |

The image type field specifies the type of image and the compression method employed, which is always RLE, but maybe... one day... See the following table for details:

**Table B.5 Codes Used In The Image Type Field**

| Code | Description |
|---|---|
| 0 | No image |
| 1 | Color mapped (palette), uncompressed |
| 2 | TrueColor (no palette), uncompressed |
| 3 | Black and white, uncompressed |
| 9 | Color mapped (palette), RLE coded |
| 10 | TrueColor (no palette), RLE coded |
| 11 | Black and white, RLE coded |

**Table B.6 The Bit Codes Of The Image Descriptor Byte**

| Bits | Meaning | Values |
|------|---------|--------|
| 0-3 | Number of attributes bits per pixel (Alpha chan.) | |
| 4-5 | The order in which the pixels are stored | 00 - left to right, bottom to top |
| | | 01 - right to left, bottom to top |
| | | 10 - left to right, top to bottom |
| | | 11 - right to left, top to bottom |
| 6-7 | Scan line interleave | 00 - no interleave |
| | | 01 - two way interleave |
| | | 10 - four way interleave |

## Palette and Image Practice

If the color map flag is set to 1, the image has the color map, if it's set to 0, there is no palette and the image contains actual color, and if so, all bytes of the color map section must be zeros. At present TARGA files are hardly ever paletted. If, however, you face a TARGA file with the color map flag set, then:

- First color map entry - the smallest pixel value in the file

- Color map size - specifies the range of pixel values

- Color map entry size - may be 15, 16, 24 or 32 (bits)

For 15- and 16-bit color map entry sizes, the two byte entry looks like this: **ARRRRRGG  GGGBBBBB** - 5 bits per RGB component. The **A** attribute is optional and may be set to 0 (as you can guess, **A** is for Alpha). A 24-bit entry contains 3 bytes: **B**, **G**, **R** in this order. A 32-bit entry is similar to 24-bit plus one byte for the alpha channel: **B**, **G**, **R**, **A**.

## The Image Itself

Color mapped images are usually a byte per pixel. You have to read the corresponding palette entry to get the actual color.

Pixels of TrueColor images contain from 15(16) to 32 bits each and have a structure similar to a palette entry:

**Tablle B.7 TrueColor Image Pixel Structure**

| Bit (Byte) to color map | Image type |
| --- | --- |
| **ARRRRRGG GGGBBBBB** | for 15, 16 bits per pixel |
| **B**, **G**, **R** | for 24 bits |
| **B**, **G**, **R**, **A** | for 32 bits per pixel |

Some applications, and therefore manufacturers, prefer the reverse order of **R**, **G**, **B**, **A** or **A**, **R**, **G**, **B**, just to make things confusing. We don't know any reliable method of detecting the RGB component order.

## Format Details

TARGA files of the version 2.0 format allow a footer containing additional data, such as aspect ratio, gamma and color correction information, and even a 'postage stamp' version of the image, which is not larger than 64x64 pixels. However, only a few programs at present can read, write and use the footer information correctly.

## Compression Details

TARGA format provides probably the best implementation of RLE compression. It is so good, we used it to illustrate RLE in the 'Common Encoding and Compression Techniques' section earlier. This is quite ironic because the TrueColor images TARGA usually deals with are almost incompressible by RLE.

## Format Traps

However, even TARGA is not blemish-free and the trap is typical of RLE implementations. Yes, you've guessed it, line termination. Never believe that each row is compressed separately.

# GIF

| | |
|---|---|
| Name: | Graphic Interchange Format, (**.GIF**) |
| Owner/Creator: | CompuServe |
| Compression: | LZW |
| Video Range: | Low end, from 1 to 8 bits per pixel. |
| Occupation: | Image display and interchange under MS Windows. |

GIF files were originally developed by CompuServe as a machine independent image file format. GIF files are the most popular way of storing 8-bit, scanned or digitized images. Moreover, the compression ratio provided by GIF's LZW algorithm is usually better than any other for 8-bit formats.

We can't, shouldn't, and won't provide the full GIF specification, including plain text, graphics control and application extensions. Anyone who really feels they are deprived without this information can contact CompuServe for details. Unfortunately, we have never met any **.GIF** file with these parts included. In this section, we'll just give you the information necessary to show images.

GIF appears to be a more sophisticated format than the previous ones. Its organization is strictly sequential; understandable, as it was designed for transmitting rather than for storage. GIF has 5 sections, each consisting of one or more blocks. All 5 sections are usually present:

- The header

- The logical screen descriptor

- The global color table (optional)

- The data section (image descriptor, local palette, image data)

- The trailer (terminating code)

# GIF File Header

The 6-byte-long header identifies the Data Stream as GIF, the first 3 bytes always contain the ASCII string 'GIF'. The last 3 are used to specify the format version, which is ASCII '87a' or ASCII '89a' for the latest version.

# The Logical Screen Descriptor

This section, and only this section must be in the file. It contains the parameters for the image display. The details are in the following table:

**Table B.8 GIF, The Structure Of The Logical Screen Descriptor**

| Offset bytes | Size in bytes | Description |
|---|---|---|
| 0 | 2 | Logical screen width (in pixels) |
| 2 | 2 | Logical screen height (in pixels) |
| 4 | 1 | Packed fields byte (see below) |
| 5 | 1 | Background color index |
| 6 | 1 | Pixel aspect ratio. Actual aspect ratio is calculated as: (Pixel Aspect Ratio +15)/64 (if the field isn't zero, of course) |

**Table B.9 The Bit Codes Of The Packed Fields Byte**

| Bits | Meaning | Values |
|---|---|---|
| 0-2 | size of global palette, $3*2^{(\text{field value} + 1)}$ bytes | |
| 3 | sort flag | 0 = not sorted<br>1 = sorted palette |
| 4-6 | bits per primary color -1 | |
| 7 | global palette flag | 0 = not present<br>1 = global palette present |

## Global Color Table (Palette)

If the global palette flag is set, then the global palette is present and it immediately follows the logical screen descriptor. It's arranged in exactly the same way as all palettes are, one byte for each primary (RGB) color. The number of global palette entries (for instance RGB triads) is defined by the size of global palette field as shown in the table below, and so GIF files can only store palette size as the nearest power of 2.

## Data Section

### Image Descriptor

The image descriptor contains the set of parameters necessary to handle the image. There must be exactly one descriptor per image in a **.GIF** file. The details are included in the table below.

**Table B.10  The Structure of The Image Descriptor**

| Offset bytes | Size in bytes | Description |
|---|---|---|
| 0 | 1 | Image separator (always 2Ch) |
| 1 | 2 | Image left position (in pixels) |
| 3 | 2 | Image top position (in pixels) |
| 5 | 2 | Image width (in pixels) |
| 7 | 2 | Image height (in pixels) |
| 8 | 1 | Packed fields byte (see below) |

**Table B.11  The Bit Codes Of The Image Descriptor Packed Fields Byte**

| Bits | Meaning | Values |
|---|---|---|
| 0-2 | size of local palette, - $3*2^{(\text{field value} + 1)}$ bytes | |
| 3-4 | reserved | |

*Continued*

Table B.11 The Bit Codes Of The Image Descriptor Packed Fields Byte

| Bits | Meaning | Values |
|------|---------|--------|
| 5 | sorted flag | 0 = not sorted |
|  |  | 1 = sorted palette |
| 6 | interlaced flag | 0 = not interlaced |
|  |  | 1 = the image is interlaced |
| 7 | local palette flag | 0 = not present |
|  |  | 1 = global palette present |

## Local Color Table (Palette)

If the local palette flag is set, then the local palette is present and it immediately follows the image descriptor. It's organized in exactly the same way as the global palette, and affects only the image that follows it.

## Image Data

The image data section begins with a 1-byte field which holds the LZW Minimum Code Size, the details of which we have already covered. Then comes the data sub-blocks, each starting with a 1-byte field which specifies the size of the sub-block, which must not be larger than 256 bytes. The data blocks contain LZW encoded pixel values with indices in the global or the local palette. The pixels are organized from left to right, top to bottom. There is a problem in the way GIF packs LZW variable length codes into bytes. The codes within each byte are packed from right to left. Look at the following example, where 5-bit code is assumed:

11111 is the first code, 22222 is the second:

```
Byte 1          Byte2       ...
22211111        43333322    ...
```

## The Trailer

This single-byte block merely terminates GIF Data Stream. It always has the value 3Bh.

## Format Details

The GIF format has two versions, referred to in the header as 87a and 89a. The newer, 89a version provides a set of additional facilities; unfortunately, they are almost never used. Although the syntax of the header, logical screen descriptor, and image descriptor remains the same, there are many programs that fail to read GIFed images of the 89a version. So maybe you'd better use the older one.

## Compression Details

The LZW algorithm, used by GIF, appears to provide the best way of compressing a byte per pixel image. It competently handles the patterns which stall the RLE compression algorithm.

# JPEG

| | |
|---|---|
| Name: | JPEG (**.JPG**) |
| Owner/Creator: | Joint Photographic Experts Group (JPEG). |
| Compression: | Sophisticated, four-step coding routine. |
| Video Range: | High-end, usually 24 bits per pixel or gray scale. |
| Occupation: | Storage and interchange of the photorealistic images. |

JPEG is a new type of image file format that uses a lossy compression technique to achieve high compression ratios. It's used mostly for photographic images.

In this section we will venture to give an overview of the JPEG compression method, the representation being mostly based on the JPEG group shareware source code and it's description.

The JPEG compression method is a kind of multi-pass routine including a series of reasonably complex mathematical transformations of the initial image:

- Color space conversion

- Discrete cosine transforms

- Quantization

- Entropy (usually Huffman) coding

# Color Space Conversion

The image is converted to a YCbCr color space with separate luminance (Y) and chrominance (CbCr) components. The YCbCr color system differs from the YIQ system that we discussed in Chapter 4. The formulas for RGB to YCbCr transformation look like this:

```
Y  = 0.299 * R + 0.587 * G + 0.114 * B;
Cb = 0.169 * R - 0.331 * G + 0.5 * B;
Cr = 0.5 * R - 0.419 * G - 0.081 * B;
```

The third digit is surely for decorative purposes only, and sometimes they even give four.

Generally speaking, this transformation isn't lossy yet, since you still have all the information in the YCbCr triads that you had in RGB. However, in the RGB color system, the components, or primary colors, are almost all of the same importance, while in YCbCr one Y 'color' holds the main part of the video information. This is based on the idea that the human eye is more sensitive to variations of brightness than variations of color. Therefore, we can use significantly less Cb and Cr samples, scarcely affecting the resulting image.

The reduction of the number of samples for a color component is called **downsampling**. It's the first real lossy step of the JPEG compression. It's usually performed in the following way. For each 2x1 (2x2, or even 4x4) rectangular block of pixels, only one Cb and one Cr sample are used. This step gives the compression ratio 2/3, 1/2 for 2x2 downsampling.

# Discrete Cosine Transforms

This step usually looks like the most complicated in the JPEG algorithm, but the key idea is pretty simple. Photorealistic images consist mostly of areas with smooth variations of brightness and/or color, and it is this structure that JPEG takes advantage of. The luminance and chrominance information is separately transformed to the frequency domain using a two dimensional discrete cosine transformation (DCT) operating on 8x8 pixel blocks. After DCT, we get a 8x8 matrix of 'intensities' of different spatial frequencies. Because of the smoothness of realistic images, in most transformed blocks only the upper-left corner significantly differs from zero. The upper-left corner of the transformed block indicates the lower spatial frequencies. The following figure shows two sample pixel blocks and their frequency representation.

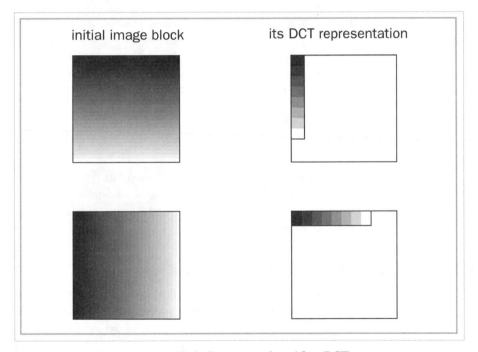

**Figure B.1 Pixel Blocks and Their Representation After DCT**

## Quantization

The transformed data is then quantized, so adding one more lossy step. The 'higher frequencies' are quantized using fewer levels than lower frequencies, and it is here that you can control the quality and compression ratio by scaling a set of quantization levels. JPEG uses the linear quantization which means that each DCT co-efficient is divided by the value of the quantization level and rounded to an integer. JPEG operates using an 8x8 table of quantization levels, one number for each spatial frequency. As a matter of fact, there are usually two tables, one for Y and another one for Cb and Cr. The tables are stored in the JPEG file to be used during decompression.

A typical quantization table looks like this:

| 3 | 5 | 7 | 9 | 11 | 13 | 15 | 17 |
|---|---|---|---|----|----|----|----|
| 5 | 7 | 9 | 11 | 13 | 15 | 17 | 19 |
| 7 | 9 | 11 | 13 | 15 | 17 | 19 | 21 |
| 9 | 11 | 13 | 15 | 17 | 19 | 21 | 23 |
| 11 | 13 | 15 | 17 | 19 | 21 | 23 | 25 |
| 13 | 15 | 17 | 19 | 21 | 23 | 25 | 27 |
| 15 | 17 | 19 | 21 | 23 | 25 | 27 | 29 |
| 17 | 19 | 21 | 23 | 25 | 27 | 29 | 31 |

It can be seen that the values increase away from the top left. So dividing by these higher values means that there are more zeroes as you move down or right. And because of this, the 'higher frequencies', which are normally weak, are cut down even more by quantization.

## Entropy (Usually Huffman) Coding

Next the quantized data is compressed using an entropy coder. Normally Huffman coding is used, even though arithmetic coding would be significantly better. But before coding, the DCT co-efficients are reordered to the specific 'zigzag' order.

*Unfortunately, arithmetic coding can't be used because of patent limitations.*

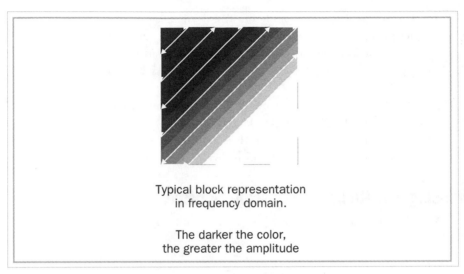

Typical block representation
in frequency domain.

The darker the color,
the greater the amplitude

**Figure B.2 Reordering DCT Co-efficients before Entropy Coding**

The reason for such a mysterious operation becomes obvious if you look at figures B.1 and B.2. The 'tail end' of the reordered table usually contains only zeros.

Huffman coding of the reordered co-efficients can be performed using either a predefined coding table or an image-specific one. A custom table produces a slightly better compression, but it does require a two-pass operation.

## Some Format Tips

Since JPEG compression was designed for continuous tone photographic images, don't be surprised by poor results when compressing line drawings or the like.

Due to JPEG compression working on 8×8 pixel blocks it may produce a parquetry effect, especially for higher compression ratios. The boundaries of the blocks are visible, but smoothing can attempt to reduce this phenomenon.

When you decompress a JPEG image, you get an image that is not quite the same as the original; this is because JPEG compression is lossy. However, the loss is generally very small and, as a matter of fact, almost every image conversion operation is lossy to some degree.

JPEG is designed to work mostly on TrueColor images, or at least it hasn't been adapted to operate on paletted ones. If you engage the usual JPEG compressor to work on a 256-color paletted image, it first converts it to actual colors, making it 3 times larger, and then tries to compress it.

And finally, one last comment on JPEG. Because the user can select the compression level, JPEG can shrink 200Kb files down to as little as 2Kb. The smaller the file, the more 'pixellated' it appears, by which we mean that it appears to look as if it is made up of lots of small squares.

## Choosing the Right Compression Scheme

You should always try to select the scheme most appropriate to your particular task:

- PCX is the best for 16-color, 4-plane images, its RLE implementation treats each plane separately and therefore it usually compresses 16 colors well.

- GIF is certainly the best for 256-color paletted images, its LZW technique manages them really well.

- JPEG is for photos - no doubt about that.

- DIB is for MS Windows (but beware of its compressed version; even now some Windows applications fail to read the compressed DIB files they have written themselves).

- Lastly, what about the TARGA format? We like it simply for convenience. But it's a personal opinion with which you may or may not agree.

# DOS Protected Mode Interface (DPMI) Function Reference

This appendix is reproduced from part of the Intel reference document #240977-001, and is reprinted by permission of Intel Corporation, copyright/Intel Corporation 1991. Developers should refer to the complete DPMI specification version 1.0 for detailed reference.

The following is provided as a guide to the functions relating to the DOS Protected Mode Interface. Each function is listed with a description of what it does, how to call it, and what it will return.

This reference covers INT 2Fh and INT 31h.

## INT 2Fh Function 1680h: Release Current Virtual Machine's Time Slice

Called by a client program to indicate that the program is idle (for example, waiting for keyboard input). This allows the DPMI host to pass the CPU to other clients, or take power-conserving Measures on laptop and notebook computers.

Call with:

AX = 1680h

Returns:

if function supported by host
AL = 0

if function not supported by host
AL = unchanged (80h)

## INT 2Fh Function 1686h: Get CPU Mode

Returns information about the current CPU mode. Programs which only execute in protected mode do not need to call this function.

Call with:

AX = 1686h

Returns:

if executing in protected mode
AX = 0

if executing in real mode or Virtual 86 mode
AX = non-zero

# INT 2Fh Function 1687h: Obtain Real-To-Protected Mode Switch Entry Point

This function can be called in real mode only to test for the presence of a DPMI host, and to obtain an address of a mode switch routine that can be called to begin execution in protected mode.

Call with:

AX = 1687h

Returns:

if function successful

AX = 0

BX = flags

| Bit | Significance |
|-----|--------------|
| 0 | 0 = 32-bit programs are not supported |
| | 1 = 32-bit programs are supported |
| 1-15 | not used |

CL = processor type

02h = 80286

03h = 80386

04h = 80486

05h-FFh   Reserved for future Intel processors

DH = DPMI major version as a decimal number (represented in binary)

DL = DPMI minor version as a decimal number (represented in binary)

SI = number of paragraphs required for DPMI host private data maybe 0)

ES:DI = Segment:offset of procedure to call to enter protected mode

if function unsuccessful (no DPMI host present)

AX = non-zero

## INT 2Fh Function 168Ah: Get Vendor-Specific API Entry Point

Reruns an address which can be called to use host-specific extensions to the standard set of DPMI functions. This function is available only in protected mode.

Call with:

> AX = 168Ah
> DS:(E)SI = selector:offset of ASCIIZ (null-terminated) string
> identifying the DPMI host vendor

Returns:

> if function successful
> AL = 0
> ES:(E)DI = extended API entry point
>
> and DS, FS, GS, EBX, ECX, EDX, ESI and EBP are preserved.
>
> if function unsuccessful
> AL = unchanged (8Ah)

## INT 31h Function 0000h: Allocate LDT Descriptors

Allocates one or more descriptors in the task's Local Descriptor Table (LDT). The descriptor(s) allocated must be initialized by the application with other function calls.

Call with:

> AX = 0000h
> CX = number of descriptors to allocate

Returns:

> if function successful
> Carry flag = clear
> AX = base selector

if function unsuccessful

Carry flag = set

AX = error code

8011h  descriptor unavailable

## INT 31h Function 0001h: Free LDT Descriptor

Frees an LDT descriptor.

Call with:

AX = 0001h

BX = selector for the descriptor to free

Returns:

if function successful

Carry flag = clear

if function unsuccessful

Carry flag = set

AX = error code

8022h  invalid selector

## INT 31h Function 0002h: Segment To Descriptor

Maps a real mode segment (paragraph) address onto an LDT descriptor that can be used by a protected mode program to access the same memory.

Call with:

AX = 0002h

BX = real mode segment address

Returns:

if function successful

Carry flag = clear

AX = selector for real mode segment

if function unsuccessful
Carry flag = set
AX = error code
      8011h   descriptor unavailable

## INT 31h Function 0003h: Get Selector Increment Value

The DPMI functions Allocate LDT Descriptors (INT 31h Function 0000h) and
Allocate DOS Memory Block (INT 31h Function 0100h) can allocate an array of
contiguous descriptors, but only return a selector for the first descriptor. The
value returned for this function can be used to calculate the selectors for
subsequent descriptors in the array.

Call with:

    AX = 0003h

Returns:

    Carry flag = clear (this function always succeeds)
    AX = selector increment value

## INT 31h Function 0006h: Get Segment Base Address

Returns the 32-bit linear base address from the LDT descriptor for the specified
segment.

Call with:

    AX = 0006h
    BX = selector

Returns:

    if function successful
    Carry flag = clear
    CX:DX = 32-bit linear base address of segment

if function unsuccessful
Carry flag = set
AX = error code
    8022h  invalid selector

## INT 31h Function 0007h: Set Segment Base Address

Sets the 32-bit linear base address field in the LDT descriptor for the specified segment.

Call with:

AX = 0007h
BX = selector
CX:DX = 32-bit linear base address of segment

Returns:

if function successful
Carry flag = clear

if function unsuccessful
Carry flag = set
AX = error code
    8022h  invalid selector
    8025h  invalid linear address (changing the base would cause the
           descriptor to reference a linear address range
           outside that allowed for DPMI clients)

## INT 31h Function 0008h: Get Segment Limit

Sets the limit field in the LDT descriptor for the specified segment.

Call with:

AX = 0008h
BX = selector
CX = 32-bit segment limit

Returns:

if function successful
Carry flag = clear

if function unsuccessful
Carry flag = set
AX = error code
  8021h  invalid value (CX <> 0 on a 16-bit DPMI host; or the
         limit is greater than 1MB, but the low twelve bits are
         not set)
  8022h  invalid selector
  8025h  invalid linear address (changing the limit would cause
         the descriptor to reference a linear address range
         outside that allowed for DPMI clients.)

# INT 31h Function 0009h: Set Descriptor Access Rights

Modifies the access rights and type fields in the LDT descriptor for the specified
segment.

Call with:

AX = 0009h
BX = selector
CL = access rights/type byte
CH = 80386 extended access rights/type byte

Returns:

if function successful
Carry flag = clear

if function unsuccessful
Carry flag = set
AX = error code
  8021h  invalid value (access rights/type bytes invalid)
  8022h  invalid selector

8025h  invalid linear address (changing the access rights/type
bytes would cause the descriptor to reference a
linear address range outside that allowed for DPMI
clients).

# INT 31h Function 000Ah: Create Alias Descriptor

Creates a new LDT data descriptor that has the same base and limit as the
specified descriptor.

Call with:

AX = 000Ah
BX = selector

Returns:

if function successful
Carry flag = clear
AX = data selector (alias)

if function unsuccessful
Carry flag = set
AX = error code
8011h  descriptor unavailable
8022h  invalid selector

# INT 31h Function 000Bh: Get Descriptor

Copies the local descriptor table (LDT) entry for the specified selector into an
8-byte buffer.

Call with:

AX = 000Bh
BX = selector
ES:(E)DI = selector:offset of 8-byte buffer

Returns:

>
> if function successful
> Carry flag = clear
>
> and buffer pointed to by ES:(E)DI contains descriptor
>
> if function unsuccessful
> Carry flag = set
> AX = error code
>     8022h   invalid selector

# INT 31h Function 000Ch: Set Descriptor

Copies the contents of an 8-byte buffer into the LDT descriptor for the specified selector.

Call with:

>
> AX = 000Ch
> BX = selector
> ES:(E)DI  = selector:offset of 8-byte buffer containing descriptor

Returns:

>
> if function successful
> Carry flag = clear
>
> if function unsuccessful
> Carry flag = set
> AX = error code
>     8021h   invalid value (access rights/type byte invalid)
>     8022h   invalid selector
>     8025h   invalid linear address (descriptor references a linear
>             address range outside that allowed for DPMI
>             clients)

## INT 31h Function 000Dh: Allocate Specific LDT Descriptor

Allocates a specific LDT descriptor.

Call with:

> AX = 000Dh
> BX = selector

Returns:

> if function successful
> Carry flag = clear
>
> and descriptor has been allocated
>
> if function unsuccessful
> Carry flag = set
> AX = error code
> > 8011h   descriptor unavailable (descriptor is in use)
> > 8022h   invalid selector (references GDT or beyond the LDT
> > limit)

## INT 31h Function 000Eh: Get Multiple Descriptors

Copies one or more local descriptor table (LDT) entries into a client buffer.

Call with:

> AX = 000Eh
> CX = number of descriptors to copy
> ES:(E)DI = selector:offset of a buffer in the following format:

| Offset | Length | Contents |
|--------|--------|----------|
| 00h | 2 | Selector #1 (set by client) |
| 02h | 8 | Descriptor #1 (returned by host) |
| 0Ah | 2 | Selector #2 (set by client) |
| 0Ch | 8 | Descriptor #2 (returned by host) |
| . | . | . |
| . | . | . |
| . | . | . |

Returns:

if function successful
Carry flag = clear

and buffer contains copies of the descriptors for the specified selectors

if function unsuccessful
Carry flag = set
AX = error code
    8022h   invalid selector
CX = number of descriptors successfully copied

# INT 31h Function 000Fh: Set Multiple Descriptors

Copies one or more descriptors from a client buffer into the local descriptor table (LDT).

Call with:

AX = 000Fh
CX = number of descriptors to copy
ES:(E)DI = selector:offset of a buffer in the following format:

| Offset | Length | Contents |
|--------|--------|----------|
| 00h | 2 | Selector #1 |
| 02h | 8 | Descriptor #1 |
| 0Ah | 2 | Selector #2 |
| 0Ch | 8 | Descriptor #2 |
| . | . | . |
| . | . | . |
| . | . | . |

Returns:

if function successful
Carry flag = clear

if function unsuccessful

Carry flag = set

AX = error code

    8021h   invalid value (access rights/type bytes invalid)

    8022h   invalid selector

    8025h   invalid linear address (descriptor references a linear address range outside that allowed for DPMI clients)

CX = number of descriptors successfully copied

# INT 31h Function 0100h: Allocate DOS Memory Block

Allocates a block of memory from the DOS memory pool, i.e. memory below the 1 MB boundary that is controlled by DOS. Such memory blocks are typically used to exchange data with real mode programs, TSRs, or device drivers. The function returns both the real mode segment base address of the block and one or more descriptors that can be used by protected mode applications to access the block.

Call with:

    AX = 0100h

    BX = number of (16-byte) paragraphs desired

Returns:

    if functional successful

    Carry flag = clear

    AX = real mode segment base address of allocated block

    DX = selector for allocated block

    if function unsuccessful

    Carry flag = set

    AX = error code

        0007h   memory control blocks damaged (also returned by DPMI 0.9 hosts)

        0008h   insufficient memory (also returned by DPMI 0.9 hosts)

        8011h   descriptor unavailable

    BX – size of largest available block in paragraphs

## INT 31h Function 0101h: Free DOS Memory Block

Frees a memory block that was previously allocated with the Allocate DOS Memory Block function (INT 31h Function 0100h).

Call with:

>> AX = 0101h
>> DX = selector of blocked to be freed

Returns:

>> if function successful
>> Carry flag = clear

>> if function unsuccessful
>> Carry flag = set
>> AX = error code
>>> 0007h  memory control blocks damaged (also returned by DPMI 0.9 hosts)
>>> 0009h  incorrect memory segment specified (also returned by DPMI 0.9 hosts)
>>> 8022h  invalid selector

## INT 31h Function 0102h: Resize DOS Memory Block

Changes the size of a memory block the was previously allocated with the Allocate DOS Memory Block function (INT 31h Function 0100h).

Call with:

>> AX = 0102h
>> BX = new block size in (16-byte) paragraphs
>> DX = selector of block to modify

Returns:

>> if function successful
>> Carry flag = clear

if function unsuccessful

Carry flag = set

AX = error code

    0007h   memory control blocks damaged (also returned by DPMI 0.9 hosts)

    0008h   insufficient memory (also returned by DPMI 0.9 hosts)

    0009h   incorrect memory segment specified (also returned by DPMI 0.9 hosts)

    8011h   descriptor unavailable

    8022h   invalid selector

BX = maximum possible block size (paragraphs)

# INT 31h Function 0200h: Get Real Mode Interrupt Vector

Returns the contents of the current virtual machine's real mode interrupt vector for the specified interrupt.

Call with:

    AX = 0200h

    BL = interrupt number

Returns:

    Carry flag = clear (this function always succeeds)

    CX:DX = segment:offset of real mode interrupt handler

# INT 31h Function 0201h: Set Real Mode Interrupt Vector

Sets the current virtual machine's real mode interrupt for the specified interrupt.

Call with:

    AX = 0201h

    BL = interrupt number

    CX:DX = segment:offset of real mode interrupt handler

Returns:

    Carry flag = clear (this function always succeeds)

# INT 31h Function 0204h: Get Protected Mode Interrupt Vector

Returns the address of the current protected mode interrupt handler for the specified interrupt.

Call with:

> AX = 0204h
> BL = interrupt number

Returns:

> Carry flag = clear (this function always succeeds)
> CX:(E)DX= selector:offset of exception handler

# INT 31h Function 0205h: Set Protected Mode Interrupt Vector

Sets the address of protected mode handler for the specified interrupt into the interrupt vector.

Call with:

> AX = 0205h
> BL = interrupt number
> CX:(E)DX = selector:offset of exception handler

Returns:

> if function successful
> Carry flag = clear
>
> if function unsuccessful
> Carry flag = set
> AX = error code
> > 8022h    invalid selector

## INT 31h Function 0210h: Get Extended Processor Exception Handler Vector (Protected Mode)

Returns the address of the client's protected mode handler for the specified protected mode exception. DPMI 1.0 clients should use this function in preference to INT 31h Function 0202h.

Call with:

>>      AX = 0210h
>>      BL = exception number (00h-1Fh)

Returns:

>>>     if function successful
>>>     Carry flag = clear

>>>     if function unsuccessful
>>>     Carry flag = set
>>>     AX = error code
>>>>         8021h   invalid value (BL not in the range 00h-1Fh)

## INT 31h Function 0211h: Get Extended Processor Exception Handler Vector (Real Mode)

Returns the address of the client's protected mode handler for the specified real mode exception.

Call with:

>>      AX = 0211h
>>      BL = exception number (00h-1Fh)

Returns:

>>>     if function successful
>>>     Carry flag = clear
>>>     CX:(E)DX = selector:offset of exception handler

if function unsuccessful

Carry flag = set

AX = error code

8021h invalid value (BL not in range 00h-1Fh)

# INT 31h Function 0212h: Set Extended Processor Exception Handler Vector (Protected Mode)

Sets the address of the client's protected mode handler for the specified protected mode exception. DPMI 1.0 clients should use this function in preference to INT 31h Function 0203h.

Call with:

AX = 0212h

BL = exception/fault number (00h-1Fh)

CX:(E)DX= selector:offset of exception handler

Returns:

if function successful

Carry flag = clear

if function unsuccessful

Carry flag = set

AX = error code

8021h invalid value (BL not in the range 00h-1Fh)

8022h invalid selector

# INT 31h Function 0213h: Set Extended Processor Exception Handler Vector (Real Mode)

Sets the address of the client's protected mode handler for the specified real mode exception.

Call with:

AX = 0213h
BL = exception/fault number (00h-1Fh)
CX:(E)DX= selector:offset of exception handler

Returns:

if function successful
Carry flag = clear

if function unsuccessful
Carry flag = set
AX = error code
    8021h   invalid value (BL not in range 00h-1Fh)
    8022h   invalid selector

# INT 31h Function 0300h: Simulate Real Mode Interrupt

Simulates an interrupt in real mode. The function transfers control to the address specified by the real mode interrupt vector. The real mode handler must return by executing an IRET.

Call with:

AX = 0300h
BL = interrupt number
BH = flags

| Bit | Significance |
|-----|--------------|
| 0 | reserved for historical reason, must be zero |
| 1-7 | reserved, must be zero |

CX = number of words to copy from protected mode to real
    mode stack
ES:(E)DI = selector:offset of real mode register data structure in the
           following format:

| Offset | Length | Contents |
|--------|--------|----------|
| 00h | 4 | DI or EDI |
| 04h | 4 | SI or ESI |
| 08h | 4 | BP or EBP |
| 0Ch | 4 | reserved, should be zero |
| 10h | 4 | BX or EBX |
| 14h | 4 | DX or EDX |
| 18h | 4 | CX or ECX |
| 1Ch | 4 | AX or EAX |
| 20h | 2 | CPU status flags |
| 22h | 2 | ES |
| 24h | 2 | DS |
| 26h | 2 | FS |
| 28h | 2 | GS |
| 2Ah | 2 | IP (reserved, ignored) |
| 2Ch | 2 | CS (reserved, ignored) |
| 2Eh | 2 | SP |
| 30h | 2 | SS |

Returns:

if function successful

Carry flag = clear

ES:(E)DI = selector:offset of modified real mode register
data structure

if function unsuccessful

Carry flag = set

AX = error code

8012h   linear memory unavailable (stack)

8013h   physical memory unavailable (stack)

8014h   backing store unavailable (stack)

8021h   invalid value (CX too large)

# INT 31h Function 0302h: Call Real Mode Procedure With IRET Frame

Simulates a FAR CALL with flags pushed on the stack to a real mode procedure. The real mode routine must return by executing an IRET instruction.

Call with:

AX = 0302h

BH = flags

| Bit | Significance |
|-----|--------------|
| 0 | reserved for historical reason, must be zero |
| 1-7 | reserved, must be zero |

CX = number of words to copy from protected mode to real mode stack

ES:(E)DI = selector:offset of real mode register data structure in the following format:

| Offset | Length | Contents |
|--------|--------|----------|
| 00h | 4 | DI or EDI |
| 04h | 4 | SI or ESI |
| 08h | 4 | BP or EBP |
| 0Ch | 4 | reserved, ignored |
| 10h | 4 | BX or EBX |
| 14h | 4 | DX or EDX |
| 18h | 4 | CX or ECX |
| 1Ch | 4 | AX or EAX |
| 20h | 2 | CPU status flags |
| 22h | 2 | ES |
| 24h | 2 | DS |
| 26h | 2 | FS |
| 28h | 2 | GS |
| 2Ah | 2 | IP |
| 2Ch | 2 | CS |
| 2Eh | 2 | SP |
| 30h | 2 | SS |

Returns:

> if function successful
> Carry flag = clear
> ES:(E)DI = selector:offset of modified real mode register
> data structure

> if function unsuccessful
> Carry flag = set
> AX = error code
> 8012h   linear memory unavailable (stack)
> 8013h   physical memory unavailable (stack)
> 8014h   backing store unavailable (stack)
> 8021h   invalid value (CX too large)

# INT 31h Function 0303h: Allocate Real Mode Callback Address

Returns a unique real mode segment:offset, known as a "real mode callback", that will transfer control from real mode to a protected mode procedure. Callback addresses obtained with this function can be passed by a protected mode program to a real mode application, interrupt handler, device driver, or TSR, so that the real mode program can call procedures within the protected mode program or notify the protected mode program of an event.

Call with:

> AX = 0303h
> DS:(E)SI = selector:offset of protected mode procedure to call
> ES:(E)DI = selector:offset of a 32h-byte buffer for real mode register
> data structure to be used when calling callback
> routine.

Returns:

> if function successful
> Carry flag = clear
> CX:DX = segment:offset of real mode callback

if function unsuccessful

Carry flag = set

AX = error code

    8015h   callback unavailable

## INT 31h Function 0304h: Free Real Mode Callback Address

Releases a real mode callback address that was previously allocated with the Allocate Real Mode Callback Address function (INT 31h Function 0303h).

Call with:

    AX = 0304h

    CX:DX = real mode callback address to be freed

Returns:

    if function successful

    Carry flag = clear

    if function unsuccessful

    Carry flag = set

    AX = error code

        8024h   invalid callback address

## INT 31h Function 0305h: Get State Save/Restore Addresses

Returns the addresses of two procedures used to save and restore the state of the current task's registers in the mode which is not currently executing.

Call with:

    AX = 0305h

Returns:

    Carry flag = clear (this function always succeeds)

    AX = size of buffer in bytes required to save state

BX:CX = real mode address of routine used to
　　　　save/restore state

SI:(E)DI = protected mode address of routine used to
　　　　save/restore state

# INT 31h Function 0306h: Get Raw Mode Switch Addresses

Returns addresses that can be called for low-level mode switching.

Call with:

AX = 0306h

Returns:

Carry flag = clear (this function always succeeds)
BX:CX = real-to-protected mode switch address
SI:(E)DI = protected-to-real mode switch address

# INT 31h Function 0400h: Get Version

Returns the version number of the DPMI Specification implemented by the DPMI host. Clients can use this information to determine which function calls are supported in the current environment.

Call with:

AX = 0400h

Returns:

Carry flag = clear (this function always succeeds)
AH = DPMI major version as a binary number
AL = DPMI minor version as a binary number
AL = flags

| Bits | Significance |
|------|--------------|
| 0 | 0 = host is 16-bit (80286) DPMI implementation |
| | 1 = host is 32-bit (80386+) DPMI implementation |
| 1 | 0 = CPU returned to Virtual 86 mode for reflected interrupts |
| | 1 = CPU returned to real mode for reflected interrupts |
| 2 | 0 = virtual memory not supported |
| | 1 = virtual memory supported |
| 3 | reserved, for historical reasons |
| 4-15 | reserved for later use |

CL = processor type

    02h = 80286

    03h = 80386

    04h = 80486

    05h-FFh  reserved for future Intel processors

DH = current value of virtual master PIC base interrupt

DL = current value of slave PIC base interrupt

# INT 31h Function 0401h: Get DPMI Capabilities

Returns information about the capabilities of the DPMI host, including its support or lack of support for the optional features in the DPMI Specification. Clients can use this information to optimize their use of system resources in the current environment.

Call with:

    AX = 0401h

    ES:(E)DI = selector:offset of 128-byte buffer

Returns:

    if function successful

    Carry flag = clear (this function always succeeds in DPMI 1.0)

    AX = capabilities flags

| Bits | Significance |
|------|--------------|
| 0 | 0 = PAGED ACCESSED/DIRTY capability not supported |
|   | 1 = PAGED ACCESSED/DIRTY capability supported |
| 1 | 0 = EXCEPTIONS RESTARTABILITY capability not supported |
|   | 1 = EXCEPTIONS RESTARTABILITY capability supported |
| 2 | 0 = DEVICE MAPPING capability not supported |
|   | 1 = DEVICE MAPPING capability supported |
| 3 | 0 = CONVENTIONAL MEMORY MAPPING capability not supported |
|   | 1 = CONVENTIONAL MEMORY MAPPING capability supported |
| 4 | 0 = DEMAND ZERO-FILL capability not supported |
|   | 1 = DEMAND ZERO-FILL capability supported |
| 5 | 0 = WRITE-PROTECT CLIENT capability not supported |
|   | 1 = WRITE-PROTECT CLIENT capability supported |
| 6 | 0 = WRITE-PROTECT HOST capability not supported |
|   | 1 = WRITE-PROTECT HOST capability supported |
| 7-15 | reserved |

CX = reserved, must be 0

DX = reserved, must be 0

ES:(E)DI = selector:offset of 128-byte buffer filled in by host with information as follows:

| Offset | Length | Contents |
|--------|--------|----------|
| 0 | 1 | Host major version number as a decimal number |
| 1 | 1 | Host minor version number as a decimal number |
| 2 | 1-126 | ASCIIZ (null-terminated) string identifying the DPMI host vendor |

if function unsuccessful

Carry flag = set (this function always fails in DPMI 0.9)

## INT 31h Function 0500h: Get Free Memory Information

Returns information about the amount of available physical memory, linear address space, and disk space for page swapping. Since DPMI clients will often run in multitasking environments, the information returned by this function should only be considered as advisory. DPMI 1.0 clients should avoid use of this function.

Call with:

> ΛX = 0500h
> ES:(E)DI = selector:offset of 48-byte buffer

Returns:

> Carry flag = clear (this function always succeeds)

and the buffer is filled in with the following information

| Offset | Length | Contents |
| --- | --- | --- |
| 00h | 4 | Largest available free block in bytes |
| 04h | 4 | Maximum unlocked page allocation in pages |
| 08h | 4 | Maximum locked page allocation in pages |
| 0Ch | 4 | Linear address space size in pages |
| 10h | 4 | Total number of unlocked pages |
| 14h | 4 | Total number of free pages |
| 18h | 4 | Total number of physical pages |
| 1Ch | 4 | Free linear address space in pages |
| 20h | 4 | Size of paging file/partition in pages |
| 24h | 0Ch | Reserved, all bytes set to 0FFh |

# INT 31h Function 0501h: Allocate Memory Block

Allocates and commits a block of linear memory.

Call with:

      AX = 0501h
      BX:CX = size of block (bytes, must be non-zero)

Returns:

      if function successful
      Carry flag = clear
      BX:CX = linear address of allocated memory block
      SI:DI = memory block handle (used to resize and free
            block)

      if function unsuccessful
      Carry flag = set
      AX = error code
         8012h   linear memory unavailable
         8013h   physical memory unavailable
         8014h   backing store unavailable
         8016h   handle unavailable
         8021h   Invalid value (BX:CX = 0)

# INT 31h Function 0502h: Free Memory Block

Frees a memory block that was previously allocated with either the Allocate Memory Block function (INT 31h Function 0501h) or the Allocate Linear Memory Block function (INT 31h Function 0504h).

Call with:

      AX = 0502h
      SI:DI = memory block handle

Returns:

if function successful
Carry flag = clear

if function unsuccessful
Carry flag = set
AX = error code
8023h   invalid handle

# INT 31h Function 0503h: Resize Memory Block

Changes the size of a memory block that was previously allocated with either the Allocate Memory Block function (INT 31h Function 0501h) or the Allocate Linear Memory Block function (INT 31h Function 0504h).

Call with:

AX = 0503h
BX:CX = new size of block (bytes, must be non-zero)
SI:DI = memory block handle

Returns:

if function successful
Carry flag = clear
BX:CX = new linear address of memory block
SI:DI = new handle for memory block

if function unsuccessful
Carry flag = set
AX = error code
8012h   linear memory unavailable
8013h   physical memory unavailable
8014h   backing store unavailable
8016h   handle unavailable
8021h   invalid value (BX:CX = 0)
8023h   invalid handle (in SI:DI)

# INT 31h Function 0504h: Allocate Linear Memory Block

Allocates a block of page-aligned linear address space. The base address of the block may be specified by the client, and pages within the block may be committed or uncommitted.

Call with:

AX = 0504h
EBX = desired page-aligned linear address of memory block
      or zero if linear address unspecified
ECX = size of block (bytes, must be non-zero)
EDX = flags

| Bit | Significance |
|-----|--------------|
| 0 | 0 = create uncommitted pages |
| | 1 = create committed pages |
| 1-31 | reserved, should be zero |

Returns:

if function successful
Carry flag = clear
EBX = linear address of memory block
ESI = handle of memory block

if function unsuccessful
Carry flag = set
AX = error code

| | |
|------|------|
| 8001h | unsupported function (16-bit host) |
| 8012h | linear memory unavailable |
| 8013h | physical memory unavailable |
| 8014h | backing store unavailable |
| 8016h | handle unavailable |
| 8021h | invalid value (ECX = 0) |
| 8025h | invalid linear address (EBX not page aligned) |

## INT 31h Function 0505h: Resize Linear Memory Block

Changes the size of a memory block that was previously allocated with the Allocate Linear Memory Block function (INT 31h Function 0504h).

Call with:

AX = 0505h

ESI = memory block handle

ECX = new block size (bytes, must be non-zero)

EDX = flags

| Bit | Significance |
|-----|--------------|
| 0 | 0 = create uncommitted pages |
| | 1 = create committed pages |
| 1 | 0 = do not update segment descriptors |
| | 1 = segment descriptor update required |
| 2-31 | reserved, must be zero |

and, if bit 1 of EDX is set (1):

ES:EBX = selector:offset of a buffer containing an array of selectors, 1 word (16 bits) per selector

EDI = count of selectors in array

Returns:

if function successful

Carry flag = clear

EBX = new linear base address of memory block

ESI = new handle for memory block

if function unsuccessful

Carry flag = set

AX = error code

    8001h   unsupported function

    8012h   linear memory unavailable

    8013h   physical memory unavailable

    8014h   backing store unavailable

    8016h   handle unavailable

    8021h   invalid value (ECX = 0)

    8023h   invalid handle (in ESI)

# INT 31h Function 0506h: Get Page Attributes

Returns the attributes of one or more pages within a linear memory block previously allocated with INT 31h Function 0504h.

Call with:

    AX = 0506h

    ESI = memory block handle

    EBX = base offset in memory block of page (or of first page, if requesting attributes for multiple pages)

    ECX = number of pages

    ES:EDX = selector:offset of a buffer to receive page attributes, 1 word (16-bits) per page

Returns:

    if function successful

    Carry flag = clear

    and buffer at ES:EDX filled in with page attributes

    if function unsuccessful

    Carry flag = set

    AX = error code

        8001h   unsupported function (16-bit host)

        8023h   invalid handle (in ESI)

        8025h   invalid linear address (Specified range is not within specified block)

# INT 31h Function 0507h: Set Page Attributes

Sets the attributes of one or more pages within a linear memory block previously allocated with INT 31h Function 0504h. This function can be used to change a committed page or a mapped page to an uncommitted page, change an uncommitted page to a committed page, or modify the read/write bit and optionally the accessed and dirty bits on a committed or mapped page.

Call with;

>       AX = 0507h
>       ESI = memory block handle
>       EBX = offset within memory block of page (s) whose attributes
>               are to be modified
>       ECX = number of pages
>       ES:EDX = selector:offset of a buffer containing page attributes, 1
>                   word (16-bits) per page

Returns:

>       if function successful
>       Carry flag = clear
>
>       if function unsuccessful
>       Carry flag = set
>       AX = error code
>           8001h   unsupported function (16-bit host)
>           8002h   invalid state (page in wrong state for request)
>           8013h   physical memory unavailable
>           8014h   backing store unavailable
>           8021h   invalid value (illegal request in bits 0-2 of one or
>                       more page attribute words)
>           8023h   invalid handle (in ESI)
>           8025h   invalid linear address (specified range is not within
>                       specified block)
>       ECX = number of pages that have been set

# INT 31h Function 0508h: Map Device In Memory Block

Maps the physical addresses assigned to a device onto the linear addresses of a memory block previously allocated with INT 31h Function 0504h.

Call with:

> AX = 0508h
> ESI = memory block handle
> EBX = offset within memory block of page(s) to be mapped
>      (must be page-aligned)
> ECX = number of pages to map
> EDX = physical address of device (must be page-aligned)

Returns:

> if function successful
> Carry flag = clear
>
> if function unsuccessful
> Carry flag = set
> AX = error code
> > 8001h   unsupported function (Device Mapping Capability not supported)
> > 8003h   system integrity (invalid device address)
> > 8023h   invalid handle (in ESI)
> > 8025h   invalid linear address (specified range is not within specified block or EBX/EDX is not page-aligned)

# INT 31h Function 0509h: Map Conventional Memory In Memory Block

Aliases linear addresses below the 1 MB boundary onto the linear addresses of a memory block previously allocated with INT 31h Function 0504h.

Call with:

> AX = 0509h
> ESI = memory block handle
> EBX = offset within memory block of page(s) to be mapped
>       (must be page-aligned)
> ECX = number of pages to map
> EDX = linear address of conventional memory (must be page-
>       aligned)

Returns:

> if function successful
> Carry flag = clear
>
> if function unsuccessful
> Carry flag = set
> AX = error code
> > 8001h   unsupported function (Conventional Memory Mapping
> >       Capability not supported)
> > 8003h   system integrity (invalid conventional memory address)
> > 8023h   invalid handle (in ESI)
> > 8025h   invalid linear address (specified range is not within
> >       specified block, or EBX/EDX is not page aligned)

## INT 31h Function 050Ah: Get Memory Block Size And Base

Returns the size of a memory block that was previously allocated with INT 31H Function 0501h or 0504h.

Call with:

AX = 050Ah
SI:DI = memory block handle

Returns:

if function successful
Carry flag = clear
SI:DI = size of memory block (bytes)
BX:CX = base address of memory block

if function unsuccessful
Carry flag = set
AX = error code
    8023h   invalid handle

## INT 31H Function 050BH: Get Memory Information

Returns information about available physical and virtual memory. Since DPMI clients will often run in multitasking environments, some of information related to shared resources returned by this function should only be considered as advisory.

Call with:

AX = 050Bh
ES:(E)DI = selector:offset of 128-byte buffer

Returns:

if function successful
Carry flag = clear (this function always succeeds in DPMI 1.0)

and the buffer pointed to by ES:(E)DI is filled in with the following information:

| Offset | Length | Contents |
|--------|--------|----------|
| 00h | 4 | Total allocated bytes of physical memory controlled by DPMI host |
| 04h | 4 | Total allocated bytes of virtual memory controlled by DPMI host |
| 08h | 4 | Total available bytes of virtual memory controlled by DPMI host |
| 0Ch | 4 | Total allocated bytes of virtual memory for this virtual machine |
| 10h | 4 | Total available bytes of virtual memory for this virtual machine |
| 14h | 4 | Total allocated bytes of virtual memory for this client |
| 18h | 4 | Total available bytes of virtual memory for this client |
| 1Ch | 4 | Total locked bytes of memory for this client |
| 20h | 4 | Maximum locked bytes of memory for this client |
| 24h | 4 | Highest linear address available to this client |
| 28h | 4 | Size in bytes of largest available free memory block |
| 2Ch | 4 | Size of minimum allocation unit in bytes |
| 30h | 4 | Size of the allocation alignment unit in bytes |
| 34h | 4Ch | Reserved, currently zero |

if function unsuccessful
Carry flag = set (this function always fails in DPMI 0.9)

## INT 31h Function 0600h: Lock Linear Region

Locks the specified linear address range.

Call with:

> AX = 0600h
> BX:CX = starting linear address of memory block
> SI:DI = size of region to lock (bytes)

Returns:

> if function successful
> Carry flag = clear
>
> if function unsuccessful
> Carry flag = set
> AX = error code
> > 8013h   physical memory unavailable
> > 8017h   lock count exceeded
> > 8025h   invalid linear address (unallocated pages)

## INT 31h Function 0601h: Unlock Linear Region

Unlocks a linear address range that was previously locked using the Lock Linear Region function (INT 31h Function 0600h).

Call with:

> AX = 0601h
> BX:CX = starting linear address of memory to unlock
> SI:DI = size of region to unlock (bytes)

Returns:

if function successful
Carry flag = clear

if function unsuccessful
Carry flag = set
AX = error code
    8002h  invalid state (page not locked)
    8025h  invalid linear address (unallocated pages)

# INT 31h Function 0602h: Mark Real Mode Region As Pageable

Advises the DPMI host that the specified memory below the 1 MB boundary may be paged to disk.

Call with:

AX = 0602h
BX:CX = starting linear address of memory to mark as pageable
SI:DI = size of region to be marked (bytes)

Returns:

if function successful
Carry flag = clear

if function unsuccessful
Carry flag = set
AX = error code
    8002h  invalid state (region already marked as pageable)
    8025h  invalid linear address (region is above 1MB boundary)

# INT 31h Function 0603h: Relock Real Mode Region

Relocks a memory region that was previously declared as pageable with the Mark Real Mode Region as Pageable function (INT 31h Function 0602h).

Call with:

AX = 0603h
BX:CX = starting linear address of memory to relock
SI:DI = size of region to relock (bytes)

Returns:

if function successful
Carry flag = clear

if function unsuccessful
Carry flag = set
AX = error code
    8002h   invalid state (region not marked as pageable)
    8013h   physical memory unavailable
    8025h   invalid linear address (region is above 1 MB boundary)

# INT 31h Function 0604h: Get Page Size

Returns the size of a single memory page in bytes.

Call with:

AX = 0604h

Returns:

if function successful
Carry flag = clear
BX:CX = page size in bytes

if function unsuccessful
Carry flag = set
AX = error code
  8001h   unsupported function (16-bit host)

## INT 31h Function 0702h: Mark Page As Demand Paging Candidate

Notifies the DPMI host that a range of pages may be placed at the head of the page-out candidate list, forcing these pages to be replaced ahead of other pages even if the memory has been accessed recently. The contents of the pages will be preserved.

Call with:

AX = 0702h
BX:CX = starting linear address of pages to mark as paging candidates
SI:DI = size of region to mark (bytes)

Returns:

if function successful
Carry flag = clear

if function unsuccessful
Carry flag = set
AX = error code
   8025h   invalid linear address (range unallocated)

## INT 31h Function 0703h: Discard Page Contents

Discards the entire contents of a given linear memory range. This function is used when a memory object (such as a data structure) that occupies a given area of memory is no longer needed, so that the area will not be paged to disk unnecessarily. The contents of the discarded region will be undefined.

Call with:

AX = 0703h
BX:CX = starting linear address of pages to discard
SI:DI = size of region to discard (bytes)

Returns:

> if function successful
> Carry flag = clear
>
> if function unsuccessful
> Carry flag = set
> AX = error code
>> 8025h   invalid linear address (range unallocated)

# INT 31h Function 0800h: Physical Address Mapping

Converts a physical address into a linear address. This function allows device drivers running under DPMI hosts which use paging to reach physical memory that is associated with their devices above the 1MB boundary. Examples of such devices are the Weitek numeric co-processor (usually mapped at 3GB), buffers that hod scanner bit maps, and high-end displays that can be configured to make display memory appear in extended memory.

Call with:

> AX = 0800h
> BX:CX = physical address of memory
> SI:DI = size region to map (bytes)

Returns:

> if function successful
> Carry flag = clear
> BX:CX = linear address that can be used to access the
>> physical memory
>
> if function unsuccessful
> Carry flag = set
> AX = error code
>> 8003h   system integrity (DPMI host memory region)
>> 8021h   invalid value (address is below 1 MB boundary)

## INT 31h Function 0801h: Free Physical Address Mapping

Releases a mapping of physical to linear addresses that was previously obtained with the Physical Address Mapping function (INT 31h Function 0800h).

Call with:

AX = 0801h
BX:CX = linear address returned by physical address mapping call

Returns:

if function successful
Carry flag = clear

if unsuccessful
Carry flag = set
AX = error code
8025h   invalid linear address

## INT 31h Function 0900h: Get And Disable Virtual Interrupt State

Disables the virtual interrupt flag and returns the previous state of the virtual interrupt flag.

Call with:

AX = 0900h

Returns:

Virtual interrupts disabled
Carry flag = clear (this function always succeeds)
AL = 0 if virtual interrupts were previously disabled
   = 1 if virtual interrupts were previously enabled

## INT 31h Function 0901h: Get And Enable Virtual Interrupt State

Enables the virtual interrupt flag and returns the previous state of the virtual interrupt flag.

Call with:

AX = 0901h

Returns:

Virtual interrupts enabled
Carry flag = clear (this function always succeeds)
AL = 0 if virtual interrupts were previously disabled
= 1 if virtual interrupts were previously enabled

## INT 31h Function 0902h: Get Virtual Interrupt State

Returns the current state of the virtual interrupt flag.

Call with:

AX = 0902h

Returns:

Carry flag = clear (this function always succeeds)
AL = 0 if virtual interrupts were disabled
= 1 if virtual interrupts were enabled

## INT 31h Function 0B00h: Set Debug Watchpoint

Sets a debug watchpoint at the specific linear address.

Call with:

AX = 0B00h
BX:CX = linear address of watchpoint
DL = size of watchpoint (1, 2, or 4 bytes)

DH = type of watchpoint
    0 = execute
    1 = write
    2 = read/write

Returns:

if function successful
Carry flag = clear
BX = watchpoint handle

if function unsuccessful
Carry flag = set
AX = error code
    8016h   too many breakpoints
    8021h   invalid value (in DL or DH)
    8025h   invalid linear address (linear address not mapped or alignment error)

# INT 31h Function 0B10h: Clear Debug Watchpoint

Clears a debug watchpoint that was previously set using the Set Debug Watchpoint (INT 31h Function 0B00h), and releases the watchpoint handle.

Call with:

AX = 0B01h
BX = watchpoint handle

Returns:

if function successful
Carry flag = clear

if function unsuccessful
Carry flag = set
AX = error code
    8023h   invalid handle

## INT 31h Function 0B02h: Get State Of Debug Watchpoint

Returns the state of a debug watchpoint that was previously set using the Set Debug Watchpoint function (INT 31h Function 0B00h).

Call with:

AX = 0B02h
BX = watchpoint handle

Returns:

if function successful
Carry flag = clear
AX = watchpoint status

| Bit | Significance |
|-----|--------------|
| 0 | 0 = watchpoint has not been encountered |
|   | 1 = watchpoint has been encountered |
| 1-15 | reserved |

if function unsuccessful
Carry flag = set
AX = error code
    8023h   invalid handle

## INT 31h Function 0B03h: Reset Debug Watchpoint

Resets the state of a previously defined debug watchpoint; i.e. a subsequent call to INT 31h Function 0B02h will indicate that the debug watchpoint has not been encountered.

Call with:

AX = 0B03h
BX = watchpoint handle

Returns:

if function successful
Carry flag = clear

if function unsuccessful
Carry flag = set
AX = error code
8023h   invalid handle

# INT 31h Function 0C00h: Install Resident Service Provider Callback

Protected mode resident service providers (protected mode TSRs) can provide services to 16-bit DPMI programs, 32-bit DPMI programs, or both. A resident service provider uses this function to request notification from the host whenever another DPMI program in the same virtual machine is loaded or terminated.

Call with:

AX = 0C00h
ES:(E)DI  = selector:offset of 40-byte buffer with the following
                structure:

| Offset | Length | Contents |
|--------|--------|----------|
| 00h | 8 | Descriptor for 16-bit data segment |
| 08h | 8 | Descriptor for 16-bit code segment |
| 10h | 2 | Offset of 16-bit callback procedure |
| 12h | 2 | Reserved |
| 14h | 8 | Descriptor for 32-bit data segment |
| 1Ch | 8 | Descriptor for 32-bit code segment |
| 24h | 4 | Offset of 32-bit callback procedure |

Returns:

if function successful
Carry flag = clear

if function unsuccessful
Carry flag = set
AX = error code
    8021h  invalid value (access rights/type bytes invalid, or offset
           outside segment limits)
    8025h  invalid linear address (descriptor references a linear
           address range outside that allowed for DPMI
           clients)
    8015h  callback unavailable (host unable to allocate resources
           for resident handler initialization callback)

## INT 31h Function 0C01h: Terminate And Stay Resident

A resident service provider uses this function after its initialization to terminate
execution while leaving its protected mode memory (and optionally some real
mode memory) allocated.

Call with:

AX = 0C01h
BL = return code
DX = number of paragraphs (16-byte blocks) of DOS memory
     to reserve

Returns:

Nothing (this call never returns)

# INT 31h Function 0D00h: Allocate Shared Memory

Allocates a memory block that may be shared by DPMI clients.

Call with:

AX = 0D00h
ES:(E)DI = selector:offset of shared memory allocation request
structure in the following format:

| Offset | Length | Contents |
|--------|--------|----------|
| 00h | 4 | Requested length of shared memory block (set by client, mat be zero) |
| 04h | 4 | Length actually allocated (set by host) |
| 08h | 4 | Shared memory handle (set by host) |
| 0Ch | 4 | Linear address of shared memory block (set by host) |
| 10h | 6 | selector:offset32 of ASCIIZ (null-terminated ASCII) name of block |
| 16h | 2 | Reserved |
| 18h | 4 | Reserved, must be zero |

Returns:

if function successful
Carry flag = clear

if function unsuccessful
Carry flag = set
AX = error code
    8012h   linear memory unavailable
    8013h   physical memory unavailable
    8014h   backing store unavailable
    8016h   handle unavailable
    8021h   invalid value (name for the memory block is too long)

and the request structure fields at offsets 04h, 08h and 0Ch
unmodified by host

## INT 31h Function 0D01h: Free Shared Memory

Deallocates a shared memory block.

Call with:

>AX = 0D01h
>SI:DI = handle of shared memory block to free

Returns:

>if function successful
>Carry flag = clear
>
>if function unsuccessful
>Carry flag = set
>AX = error code
>>8023h   invalid handle

## INT 31h Function 0D02h: Serialize On Shared Memory

Requests serialization of a shared memory block. Successful serialization symbolizes ownership or right of access to a block, and can be used by DPMI clients to synchronize the inspection or modification of a memory block.

Call with:

>AX = 0D02h
>SI:DI = shared memory block handle
>DX = option flags

| Bit | Significance |
|-----|--------------|
| 0 | 0 = suspend client until serialization available |
| | 1 = return immediately with error if serialization not available |
| 1 | 0 = exclusive serialization requested |
| | 1 = shared serialization requested |
| 2-15 | reserved, must be zero |

Returns:

if function successful
Carry flag = clear

if function unsuccessful
Carry flag = set
AX = error code
    8004h   deadlock (host detected a deadlock situation)
    8005h   request canceled with INT 31h Function 0D03h
    8017h   lock count exceeded
    8018h   exclusive serialization already owned by another client
    8019h   shared serialization already owned by another client
    8023h   invalid handle

# INT 31h Function 0D03h: Free Serialization On Shared Memory

Releases a shared memory block serialization that was previously obtained with INT 31h Function 0D02h.

Call with:

AX         = 0D03h
SI:DI     = shared memory block handle
DX         = option flags

| Bit | Significance |
|---|---|
| 0 | 0 = release exclusive serialization |
| | 1 = release shared serialization |
| 1 | 0 = don't free pending serialization |
| | 1 = free pending serialization |
| 2-15 | reserved, must be zero |

Returns:

if function successful
Carry flag = clear

if function unsuccessful

Carry flag = set

AX = error code

    8002h   invalid state (client does not own a successful serialization

                of the specified type)

    8023h   invalid handle

# INT 31h Function 0E00h: Get Co-processor Status

Returns information about whether or not a numeric co-processor exists, the type of co-processor available (if any), and whether or not the host or client is providing co-processor emulation.

Call with:

    AX = 0E00h

Returns:

if function successful

Carry flag = clear (this function always succeeds in DPMI 1.0)

AX = co-processor status

| Bit | Significance |
|-----|-------------|
| 0 | MPv (MP bit in the virtual MSW/CR0) |
| | 0 = numeric co-processor is disabled for this client |
| | 1 = numeric co-processor is enabled for this client |
| 1 | EMv (EM bit in the virtual MSW/CR0) |
| | 0 = client is not emulating co-processor instructions |
| | 1 = client is emulating co-processsor instructions |
| 2 | MPr (MP bit from the actual MSW/CR0) |
| | 0 = numeric co-processor is not present |
| | 1 = numeric co-processor is present |
| 3 | EMr (EM bit from the actual MSW/CR0) |
| | 0 = host is not emulating co-processor instructions |
| | 1 = host is emulating co-processor instructions |
| 4-7 | co-processor type |
| | 00h = no co-processor |
| | 02h = 80287 |

03h = 80387

04h = 80486 with numeric co-processor

05h-0Fh reserved for future numeric processors

8-15    not applicable

if function unsuccessful

Carry flag = set (this function always fails in DPMI 0.9)

# INT 31h Function 0E01h: Set Co-processor Emulation

Enables or disables the numeric co-processor for this virtual machine and the reflection of co-processor exceptions to the client.

Call with:

AX = 0E01h

BX = co-processor bits

| Bit | Significance |
|-----|--------------|
| 0 | new value of MPv bit for client's virtual CR0 |
| | 0 = disable numeric co-processor for this client |
| | 1 = enable numeric co-processor for this client |
| 1 | new value of EMv bit for client's virtual CR0 |
| | 0 = client will not supply co-processor emulation |
| | 1 = client will supply co-processor emulation |
| 2-15 | not applicable |

Returns:

if function successful

Carry flag = clear

if function unsuccessful

Carry flag = set

AX = error code

8026h   invalid request (client requested disabling co-processor on a processor which does not support this)

# APPENDIX D

# Sound File Formats

## VOC File Format

Creative Labs' VOC file consists of a header, followed by series of data blocks of various types. The last block must be a terminator.

## VOC File Header Layout

| Offset | Size | Contents |
|--------|------|----------|
| 00h | 13h | ASCII text "Creative Voice File" |
| 13h | 01h | 1Ah (End-of-File marker) |
| 14h | 02h | Offset of first data block in the file (normally 1Ah) |
| 16h | 02h | Version number (minor, major) (010Ah for 1.10) |
| 18h | 02h | Twos complement of version number + 1234h |
| | | (1129h for version 1.10) |
| Total | 1Ah | |

The first byte in each data block is the Block Type. It indicates the type of data contained in the block. The following table lists all possible types of data for VOC files in versions up to 1.10.

# VOC File Data Block Types

| Value | Type |
| --- | --- |
| 00 | Terminator |
| 01 | Sound |
| 02 | Sound continue |
| 03 | Silence |
| 04 | Marker |
| 05 | ASCII |
| 06 | Repeat |
| 07 | End repeat |
| 08 | Override sound parameters |
| 09 | New style sound block |

The next three bytes contain the Block Length in the form of a 24-bit integer. This is the number of bytes in the data block, excluding the Block Type and Block Length fields, so it's actually the size in bytes of the Info field, which immediately follows the Block Length, and is the last entry in a Data Block. Only a Terminator block has neither Block Length, nor Info field.

Depending on the Block Type, the Info field may contain voice attributes (such as sampling rate and packing), voice data, or other information (e.g. Marker and ASCII text).

Of course, your program may not bother to interpret all types of blocks (if any). In most applications, your program can simply pass the address of a Data Block to the CT-VOICE driver, which will interpret it and play accordingly. You could just skip blocks like markers or ASCII text, if your program doesn't make use of them.

For the most conscientious (or hackerish) readers, here are head-cracking descriptions of some types of data blocks.

## Sound Block

| Offset | Size | Contents |
|--------|------|----------|
| 0 | 1 | 1 (Sound block tag) |
| 1 | 3 | 2 + sample length |
| 4 | 1 | Time constant = 256 - (1000000/sampling rate) |
| 5 | 1 | Compression method: |
| | | 0: 8-bit |
| | | 1: 4-bit |
| | | 2: 3-bit |
| | | 3: 2-bit |
| 6 | ? | Sample data |

Why Creative Labs didn't reserve a word to record explicitly the sampling rate, will forever remain a mystery. Fortunately, the new style (type 9) includes this information.

## Sound Continue Block

This block serves as a continuation of the last sound block.

| Offset | Size | Contents |
|--------|------|----------|
| 0 | 1 | 2 (Sound Continue tag) |
| 1 | 3 | Sample length |
| 4 | ? | Sample data |

## Silence Block

Defines a pause in voice output.

| Offset | Size | Contents |
|--------|------|----------|
| 0 | 1 | 3 (Silence tag) |
| 1 | 3 | 3 |
| 4 | 2 | Length of silence - 1 (in sampling periods) |
| 5 | 1 | 256 - (1000000/sampling rate) |

## Marker Block

| Offset | Size | Contents |
|--------|------|----------|
| 0 | 1 | 4 (Marker tag) |
| 1 | 3 | 2 |
| 4 | 2 | Marker number |

## ASCII Block

| Offset | Size | Contents |
|--------|------|----------|
| 0 | 1 | 5 (ASCII tag) |
| 1 | 3 | Length of string |
| 4 | ? | null terminated (ASCIIZ) string |

## Repeat Block

Repeats all subsequent blocks up to the next End-Repeat block a given number of times (or endlessly).

| Offset | Size | Contents |
|--------|------|----------|
| 0 | 1 | 6 (Repeat tag) |
| 1 | 3 | 2 |
| 4 | 2 | Repeat count + 1 (0FFFFh means "endless") |

## End-Repeat Block

Marks the end of a series of blocks that are to be repeated. Used in conjunction with the Repeat Block (type 6).

| Offset | Size | Contents |
|--------|------|----------|
| 0 | 1 | 7 (End Repeat tag) |
| 1 | 3 | 0 |

## Override Block

This block is a prefix to a Sound Block, which must follow immediately after the Override Block. Blocks of this type have no digitized voice data themselves, but serve only to specify parameters of the following Sound Block. The parameters given in the Sound Block itself are in this case ignored. The Override block is used for stereo or high-frequency sound.

| Offset | Size | Contents |
|--------|------|----------|
| 0 | 1 | 8 (Override block tag) |
| 1 | 3 | 4 |
| 4 | 2 | Time constant = 65536 - 256000000/(sampling rate*Number of channels) |
| 6 | 1 | Compression method (as for Sound block) |
| 7 | 1 | 0 for mono, 1 for stereo sample |

Note that for 22,050Hz stereo and 44,100Hz mono samples, the time constant is the same:

(i.e. 65536 - 256000000/(22050*2) = 65536 - 256000000/(44100*1) = 59732 [0E95h])

## New Style Sound Block

Since VOC file version 1.20, Creative Labs has adopted a more reasonable format for the sound block, which eliminates block types 1 and 8

| Offset | Size | Contents |
|--------|------|----------|
| 0 | 1 | 9 (tag) |
| 1 | 3 | 12 + sample length |
| 4 | 4 | Sampling rate (explicit!) |
| 8 | 1 | Bits per sample |
| 9 | 1 | Channels: 1 for mono, 2 for stereo |
| 10 | 2 | Compression: |
| | | 0000h : 8-bit unsigned |
| | | 0001h : 8 to 4-bit |
| | | 0002h : 8 to 3-bit |
| | | 0003h : 8 to 2-bit |
| | | 0004h : 16-bit signed |
| | | 0006h : CCCIT a-Law |
| | | 0007h : CCCIT_m-Law |
| | | 0200h : 16 to 4-bit |
| 12 | 4 | 000000h (reserved) |
| 16 | ? | Sound data |

The value at offset 4 is the real sampling rate, regardless of whether mono or stereo sound is recorded. Bits per sample is the resulting number of bits after compression (if any): e.g., 4 for both compression types 0001h and 0200h, 16 for 8-bit stereo and 16-bit mono.

# WAV File Format

Microsoft RIFF format is used to store various multimedia items, including sound, pictures, animation, and video. A RIFF file consists of a header and a data chunk, which determines the type and parameters of stored information. A WAVE chunk contains digital sound.

The RIFF file header is simply the ASCII text 'RIFF' and a double-word value that specifies the size of the data chunk. The structure of a WAVE chunk is shown below.

| Offset | Size | Contents |
|--------|------|----------|
| 00 | 8 | ASCII 'WAVEfmt ' |
| 08 | 4 | 010h |
| 10 | 2 | 01h |
| 12 | 2 | Channels (0001 - mono, 0002 - stereo) |
| 14 | 4 | Samples per second (11000, 22050 or 44100) |
| 18 | 4 | Bytes per second |
| 22 | 2 | Bytes per sample |
| 24 | 2 | Bits per channel (8 - 8-bit, 16 - 16-bit) |
| 26 | 4 | ASCII 'data' |
| 30 | 4 | Length of data in bytes |
| 34 | ? | Sound data |

# INDEX

## The Revolutionary Guide to Visual C++

Building on your knowledge of C, this book is a complete guide to writing C++ applications for Windows using Microsoft's Visual C++ compiler. We focus on the Microsoft Foundation Class (MFC) and show you how it can be used to produce professional looking programs. A truly comprehensive guide to all the Visual C++ tools.

Ben Ezzell   ISBN 1-874416-22-2
$39.95 / C$55.95 / £37.49

## The Revolutionary Guide to OOP using C++

Benefit from the authors' years of experience using C and C++ in some of the most complex and demanding programming environments around today. This book aims to ease the difficulties in making the transition from C to C++, and will show you the power of object-oriented C++.

V. Olshevsky and A. Ponomarev   ISBN 1-874416-18-4
$39.95 / C$55.95 / £37.49

## The Revolutionary Guide to Bitmapped Graphics

This guide gives programmers using a combination of C++ and assembler all of the techniques and tools needed to write programs using bitmapped graphics. This book covers all of the major file formats in use today, as well as fractals, morphing, image manipulation and everything you will ever need to know about 3D images. Includes CD.

Control-Zed   ISBN 1-874416-31-1
$44.95 / C$62.95 / £41.99

## The Revolutionary Guide to Assembly Language

Take the Challenge. Learn how to design, develop and debug powerful assembly language routines. Take control of your system and increase the power of your high level programs. Why learn unnecessary information when you can accomplish the task with expert assistance.

"At £35.00, it's worth every penny!" (Syd Anderson, The Association of C and C++ Users).

Vitaly Maljugin et al.   ISBN 1-874416-12-5
$39.95 / C$55.95 / £34.95

## Instant C++ Programming

If you want a swift route to proficiency in C++, this no-nonsense, fast-paced tutorial teaches you all you need to know in an instant and gets you writing programs from day one. The book is ideal for the programmer moving to a new language. Lots of example code and self-check exercises enable you to quickly become proficient in C++ and then move to object-oriented programming.

Ian Wilks   ISBN 1-874416-29-X
$19.95 / C$27.95 / £18.49

## The Beginner's Guide to OOP using C++

This Beginner's Guide teaches OOP to programmers from the procedural world, assuming a small amount of programming knowledge. You will learn all you need to know about the C++ language - not only the tools, but also the methodology to use them.

L. Romanovskaya et al   ISBN 1-874416-27-3
$29.95 / C$41.95 / £27.99

## The Beginner's Guide to Visual Basic 3

If you're a beginner to programming, this book is the place to start. We'll show you how easy, fun and powerful Visual Basic can be. If you're familiar with another language, you'll learn how Visual Basic does things in terms you'll understand. Along the way, you'll get all the background information you need on Windows Programming to help you develop really professional applications.

Peter Wright   ISBN 1-874416-19-2
$29.95 / C$41.95 / £27.99

## The Beginner's Guide to C++

The ideal start for the newcomer to the world of programming languages, this Beginner's Guide contains comprehensive coverage of the language syntax. You'll master procedural programming in easy stages, and then learn object-oriented programming - the essential programming methodology of the future.

O. Yaroshenko   ISBN 1-874416-26-5
$24.95 / C$34.95 / £22.99

# Notes

# Notes

# Notes

# Notes

## WIN FREE BOOKS

### TELL US WHAT YOU THINK!

Complete and return the bounce back card and you will:

- Help us create the books you want.
- Receive an update on all Wrox titles.
- Enter the draw for 5 Wrox titles of your choice.

---

**FILL THIS OUT to enter the draw for free Wrox titles**

Name _____

Address _____

_____

_____

_____ Postcode/Zip _____

Occupation _____

How did you hear about this book ?
- ☐ Book review (name) _____
- ☐ Advertisement (name) _____
- ☐ Recommendation
- ☐ Catalog
- ☐ Other _____

Where did you buy this book ?
- ☐ Bookstore (name) _____
- ☐ Computer Store (name) _____
- ☐ Mail Order
- ☐ Other _____

What influenced you in the purchase of this book ?
- ☐ Cover Design
- ☐ Contents
- ☐ Use of Color
- ☐ Other (please specify)

How did you rate the overall contents of this book ?
- ☐ Excellent
- ☐ Good
- ☐ Average
- ☐ Poor

What did you find most useful about this book ?
_____

What did you find least useful about this book ?
_____

Please add any additional comments. _____
_____

What other subjects will you buy a computer book on soon ?
_____

What is the best computer book you have used this year ? _____

**Please do not put me on your mailing list** ☐

*WROX PRESS INC.*

Wrox writes books for you. Any suggestions, or ideas about how you want information given in your ideal book will be studied by our team. Your comments are always valued at WROX.

Free phone from USA 1 800 814 3461
Fax (312) 465 4063

Compuserve 100063,2152.
UK Tel. (4421) 706 6826  Fax  (4421) 706 2967

——— *Computer Book Publishers* ———

**NB.** If you post the bounce back card below in the UK, please send it to:
Wrox Press Ltd. Unit 16 Sapcote Industrial Estate, 20 James Road,
Tyseley, Birmingham B11 2BA